THE JUDICIAL SYSTEM AND REFORM IN POST-MAO CHINA

The Rule of Law in China and Comparative Perspectives

Series Editors:
Yuwen Li, Erasmus University Rotterdam, The Netherlands
Fu Hualing, University of Hong Kong, Hong Kong

There is no doctrine more effective than the rule of law in portraying the complex transformation of Chinese society from the rule of men towards the rule of law – a process inaugurated in post-Mao China which is continuing to advance legal reforms to the present day. In other parts of the world, striving for the rule of law is also evident: countries in transition face a similar mission, while the developed democratic countries are forced to tackle new challenges in retaining the high benchmark of the rule of law that has been established.

Research on the legal system in China and in comparison with other countries in the framework of the rule of law covers broad topics of public and private law, substantive law and procedural law, citizens' rights and law enforcement by courts. Based on this broad understanding of the rule of law, the series presents international scholarly work on modern Chinese law including: comparative perspectives, interdisciplinary, and empirical studies.

Other titles in this series

Administrative Litigation Systems in Greater China and Europe
Edited by Yuwen Li
978-1-4724-3608-5

The Judicial System and Reform in Post-Mao China

Stumbling Towards Justice

YUWEN LI

Erasmus University Rotterdam, The Netherlands

Routledge
Taylor & Francis Group
LONDON AND NEW YORK

First published 2014 by Ashgate Publishing

Published 2016 by Routledge
2 Park Square, Milton Park, Abingdon, Oxfordshire OX14 4RN
711 Third Avenue, New York, NY 10017, USA

First issued in paperback 2016

Routledge is an imprint of the Taylor and Francis Group, an informa business

British Library Cataloguing in Publication Data
A catalogue record for this book is available from the British Library

Library of Congress Cataloging-in-Publication Data
Li, Yuwen, 1962– author.
The judicial system and reform in post-Mao China : stumbling towards justice / By Yuwen Li.
p. cm. -- (The rule of law in China and comparative perspectives)
Includes bibliographical references and index.
ISBN 978-1-4724-3605-4 (hardback) -- ISBN 978-1-4724-3606-1 (ebook) -- ISBN 978-1-4724-3607-8 (epub) 1. Justice, Administration of--China. 2. Law reform--China. I. Title.
KNQ470.L5 2014
347.51'01--dc23

2014011765

ISBN 13: 978-1-138-63762-7 (pbk)
ISBN 13: 978-1-4724-3605-4 (hbk)

Contents

List of Figures

List of Tables

List of Abbreviations

ACLA	All China Lawyers Association
ALL	Administrative Litigation Law
BPCs	Basic People's Courts
CASS	Chinese Academy of Social Sciences
CiPL	Civil Procedure Law
CPC	Communist Party of China
CPLC	Central Political and Legal Committee
CrPL	Criminal Procedure Law
HPCs	Higher People's Courts
HPP	Higher People's Procuratorate
ICCPR	International Covenant on Civil and Political Rights
IPCs	Intermediate People's Courts
LGJSR	Leading Group for the Judicial System Reform
MOJ	Ministry of Justice
MPS	Ministry of Public Security
MSS	Ministry of State Security
NBE	National Bar Examination
NGOs	Non-governmental organisations
NJC	National Judges College
NPC	National People's Congress
NPCSC	National People's Congress Standing Committee
NUJE	National Unified Judicial Examination
OLPC	Organic Law of the People's Courts
PCSC	People's Congress Standing Committee
PLA	People's Liberation Army
PLC	Political and Legal Committee
PRC	People's Republic of China
RTL	Re-education Through Labour
SOE	State-owned enterprise
SPC	Supreme People's Court (of the PRC)
SPP	Supreme People's Procuratorate (of the PRC)

Preface and Acknowledgements

This book is the result of my decade-long effort to understand and assess the development of the judicial system over the past 30 years of post-Mao China. I was an intern at the Intermediate People's Court in Beijing in 1983 when the first 'Strike Hard' anti-crime campaign was launched in China, and this brief yet unforgettable experience of working at the Court had a long-lasting impact on my academic interest in the Chinese judicial system. Since 1985, I have studied and worked outside China; however, my curiosity and passion concerning the court, as a place where justice can be fairly applied, has always lived with me simply because, as a legal academic, one has to constantly face the issue of law enforcement by the courts. Since 1999, I have grasped any opportunity possible to visit courts in different parts of China, despite the strict entrance controls applying to people without a Chinese ID card. Moreover, since 2001, I have co-directed training courses for Chinese judges, prosecutors and lawyers in China under a number of projects sponsored by the Netherlands Embassy in China. This has provided me with ample opportunities to learn about, and witness, the way in which the Chinese judicial system has transited towards a sophisticated and contentious operating mechanism. Nowadays, Chinese courts bear the onerous task of resolving disputes that often involve legal, economic, social and political interests which are frequently contradictory. Having published my first article on the judicial system in China in 2002, I decided to write my monograph in 2007. My thoughts on the matter have always been there, despite the demands that other work priorities inevitably placed on me. It has taken an unexpectedly long journey to complete this book, however, I must admit that the passage of time has enabled me to rethink time and again the many complex and entangled issues present in a judicial practice undergoing transition.

No doubt over the past years I have learned from, and been inspired by, a large number of colleagues and friends in China. I am deeply grateful to those judges, lawyers, legal scholars and prosecutors who generously shared their experiences and opinions with me at the various stages of my writing this book. For reasons of confidentiality, I cannot mention their names here, but I must acknowledge that without their insightful and up-to-date information, I could never have attained the sufficient knowledge and confidence required to produce this book.

Moreover, I owe a great debt of gratitude to a number of Dutch colleagues who have encouraged me or created a working environment to enable me to concentrate on and to complete this research. I would like to mention in particular Professor Fried van Hoof, Professor Cees Flinterman, Professor Maarten Kroeze, Professor Ellen Hey, and Professor Suzan Stoter for their trust and support over the years. My thanks also goes to Marianne Breijer who has recently taken on some managerial tasks at the Erasmus China Law Centre, which has freed up some of my time to allow me to complete the writing of this book. My heartfelt gratitude also goes to Ma Yun, one of my PhD candidates, who has patiently assisted me in the final phase of writing this book by collecting updated materials and checking footnotes and so on. Of course, any errors are my own.

I am also grateful to Zhu Sanzhu at the School of Oriental and African Studies in London and Edwin Bleichrodt at the Erasmus School of Law for their comments on some chapters of the book. Furthermore, Alison Kirk at Ashgate, as always, has shown her critical as well as enthusiastic and efficient support in producing this book.

Nevertheless, it goes without saying that my deepest appreciation goes to my family – my husband Nico Schrijver, daughter Lineke and son Kees. Your love, humour and encouragement lighten my mind and always help me to realise the worthiness of my writing. I also would like to thank my mother, brothers and sisters in China who have provided me with unparalleled support whenever it was needed.

I consider myself to have been privileged to have both studied and worked in China, which has enabled me to gain an insightful understanding of the complexity and enormity of the challenges faced by the Chinese judiciary. At the same time, being an 'outsider' allows me to take an independent academic stand in examining many of the problems which are deeply-rooted in the country's political system and within traditions which inevitably need to be reformed and altered if China wishes to strive for, and ultimately succeed in cultivating, a fair, independent and efficient judicial system.

Yuwen Li

Introduction

A Synopsis of the History of China's Judicial System

During China's long history of feudalism, the judicial system was a mere limb of the administration. No judges and courts specifically carried out a judicial function; instead, such a function was fulfilled by administrators, and the punishment of crimes was the main focus of the system. In the final years of the Qing dynasty at the end of the nineteenth century, along with the introduction of Western law in China, the Western court system was gradually instituted. In 1907, the 'Trial Guideline for Courts at All Levels' was issued, which separated criminal cases from civil cases for the first time.[1] In 1908, the 'Regulations for the Organisation of the Courts' set up courts at four levels: a Supreme Court (*Daliyuan*), superior courts, local courts and courts of first instance. The Regulations also provided instructions for separating judicial power from administrative power, and a system for selecting judges from those who graduated from the new 'schools of law and government'.[2] This initial court system was developed by the Nanjing Temporary Government of the Republic of China and the Kuo Mindang until 1949, when the People's Republic of China was founded by the Communist Party of China (hereafter the CPC).

During the mid-1930s through to the 1940s, while the Kuo Mindang controlled large parts of China, the CPC undertook the Long March and established 'revolutionary base areas' in the north-west of China. In these areas, a judicial system was established to serve the needs of the revolutionaries. There was no clear distinction between Party cadres and judicial officers. The dispute settlement system involved judicial officers visiting the site where a dispute took place, collecting evidence and meeting the parties concerned, and eventually settling the dispute through mediation. This is recorded as the 'Ma Xiwu' model.[3]

After the People's Republic of China (hereafter the PRC) was established in 1949, a structure of government, court and legislature was introduced. In 1951, the Supreme People's Court (hereafter the SPC) and 2,547 local courts were established all over China. Most of the courts had criminal and civil divisions, with administrative and secretarial offices. Approximately 25,000 judges were recruited.[4] Judicial work at that time mainly served the CPC policy to punish opponents and serve the people. Judges were selected on the basis of political standards rather than legal background. Criminal trials were the main work of the courts; civil disputes were infrequent and limited to such matters as divorce, family disputes or small debt. In 1954, the first Constitution and the Organic Law of the People's Courts declared that judicial power belonged to the courts, and that no

---

1 Philip C.C. Huang, *Code, Custom, and Legal Practice in China: The Qing and the Republic Compared* (Stanford, CA: Stanford University Press, 2001), pp. 35–36.

2 *Ibid.*, pp. 37–38.

3 Zhang Weiping, 'The Evolution and Reform of Civil Procedure in Mainland China and the Revisions of Its Civil Procedure Law', in Dennis T.C. Tang and Peng-Hsiang Wang (eds), *Cross-Strait, Four-Regions: Law Development in Taiwan, China, Hong Kong and Macau*, vol. 2: *Civil Procedure and Criminal Procedure* (Taipei: Institutum Iurisprudentiae/Academia Sinica, 2007), p. 174. Ma Xiwu was a judge at a court in the 'revolutionary base area'. He succeeded in handling numerous cases by meeting clients in places where disputes took place and patiently mediating between the parties. In the 1950s he became one of the Vice-Presidents of the Supreme People's Court.

4 Xin Chunying, *Chinese Courts: History and Transition* (Beijing: Law Press, 2004), pp. 13–14.

other organisations, groups or individuals could exercise such power. The courts were required to conduct trials independently, according to law and free from any interference. The systems of open trial, collegiate panel, defence and withdrawal were also established to protect litigant's rights.[5] However, this system and the new principles could not be fully exercised in practice.

In 1957, a wide-scale Anti-Rightist political campaign took place, during which a large number of judges were criticised as 'rightists' who wanted to use the people's courts against the people. During the Cultural Revolution, which lasted from 1967 to 1977, the court system that had been instituted in the early 1950s was completely destroyed. In many regions, the public security organs, procuratorates and courts were merged into a single organisation under the control of the revolutionary committee, and most of the judicial personnel were sent to the countryside to do labour. Special case groups (*zhuan'an xiao zu*) were set up arbitrarily and empowered to try and sentence individuals. Legal procedure was entirely abandoned.[6] In 1976, the death of Chairman Mao marked the start of a new era. Some high-level political leaders who suffered gravely from the lawless political struggle during which they were physically assaulted by 'Red Guiders', expelled to the countryside or sent to prison, realised how important it was to construct a legal system that included functioning courts.

The third session of the Eleventh Communist Party's Congress in 1978 marked a turning point in modern Chinese history. At that moment, it was formally declared that there would be a shift in the priority of the Party away from class struggles and towards a new focus on the economic development of the country. This had a decisive impact on the judicial system, which since then has been undergoing a process of reconstruction and reform, and indeed the progress achieved so far demonstrates the increasing significance of the courts in China's transition from a rigid socialist country to a more open and diversified society. The evolution of the judicial system in this post-Mao period is the focus of this book.

The Structure of the Book

For those who have followed the development of the judicial system in China over the past three decades, it is indisputable that profound changes have taken place. Within this relatively short period, the judicial system has been strengthened and the courts now play an increasingly important and irreplaceable role in society. Nowadays, with approximately 200,000 judges working at 3,559 courts, they handle about 11 million cases annually. For years, the judicial reform has followed an evolutionary path, with reform measures touching upon a variety of needs and issues emerging out of the country's rapid path of economic and social modernisation. However, the reality is that public concern for, and criticism of, the judicial system is also increasing. The judiciary has not been able to establish authority in the eyes of the public. Clearly, there are some inherent problems with the Chinese judicial system, including *inter alia* the low professional quality of judges, a lack of judicial independence, a lack of transparency in decision-making, a weak capacity to enforce civil judgments and a serious degree of judicial corruption. Moreover, external factors determine, to a large extent, the current situation as well as the degree of judicial reform. Furthermore, the judicial system is not only part of the wider political system but also controlled by politics. Even though political changes in recent years have allowed some space for judicial reform, it is becoming increasingly clear that the slow process of political reform is proving to be an obstacle for fundamental and substantial changes in the judicial system. The lack of judicial independence

5 *Ibid.*, p. 22.

6 *Ibid.*, pp. 44–69.

from the Party and the government constitutes an institutional barrier to building judicial authority, and the lack of such authority results in a low institutional guarantee of justice. Thus, it is no exaggeration that in China any substantive judicial reforms depend on concurrent political reforms.

This book examines the most fundamental, as well as the most controversial, subjects concerning the operation of the courts. It includes an evaluation of the professional quality of judges; the interrelationship between higher and lower courts, and the courts' relationships with other state organs; the three litigation systems in the courts' handling of criminal, civil and administrative cases; and the position of lawyers in the judicial process. Reflecting on the complex progress that China has made, and continues to make, towards the modernisation of its judicial system, the book intends to offer a better and updated understanding on how the judicial system has transformed and what challenges lay ahead for further enhancement.

The book comprises four parts, the first of which contains Chapters 1 and 2. It starts with a concise introduction on the jurisdiction of the courts in general. It then examines the vertical relationship between the higher and lower courts to illustrate the dependence of lower courts on higher courts in judgment-making concerning major and difficult cases. Such a relationship will often render the well-designed appeal system meaningless in these circumstances, given that a lower court often uses instructions from a higher court in its judgment. Chapter 1 also discusses the people's assessor system and the functions of the adjudication committee in each court, which are both quite particular to the Chinese court system. Chapter 2 examines the horizontal relationships between the courts and other state power organs; the latter include the legislature, the executive organs, the procuratorate and the Communist Party. This institutional backdrop illustrates the complex political and legal context in which the Chinese courts operate, which is very different to the way in which courts function in many Western countries.

The second part of the book confronts the professionalisation of the judiciary. The judiciary as a professional group is a relatively new phenomena. Courts were abolished *de facto* during the Cultural Revolution and most of the judges who were recruited in the 1980s and early 1990s had no legal education. With the expansion of legal education at universities, increasingly more law graduates have entered into China's courts. In 1995, the first Law on Judges (amended in 2001) was promulgated, which established the basic qualifications for judges. In 2002, a National Unified Judicial Examination system was introduced, which further raised the benchmark of academic standards for judges. However, as a whole, the Chinese judiciary is infantile, insufficiently competent and, moreover, judicial corruption is found at all levels and has severely tarnished judicial authority, and indeed continues to do so.

The third part of the book comprises Chapters 4–6. It discusses the court procedures, which encompasses the criminal trial system as well as civil and administrative litigation. The court reforms, initiated in the mid-1980s by local courts, began with the overhauling of the civil trial procedure to meet the challenge of the burgeoning caseload resulting from the country's economic and social transformation. In the 1990s, the Civil Procedure Law and the Criminal Procedure Law were amended and the first Administrative Litigation Law became effective; together these pieces of legislation established more detailed procedural rules for adjudication in courts. However, the implementation of the laws has proved to be more problematic. These chapters not only examine the most controversial legal issues in law, but also discuss how they have been applied in judicial practice and their consequential impact on public assertions of social justice, judicial credibility and judicial authority.

The fourth part of the book provides an in-depth discussion on the legal profession. As is commonly known, the legal profession never bourgeoned in Chinese history and its role in the contemporary court system remains largely neglected. This is particularly true with regard to criminal defence lawyers. A vast gulf exists between the rights of lawyers in the litigation process as provided by law and the actual application and protection of those rights in practice. The difficulties and dilemmas which Chinese lawyers face illustrate, from another perspective, the deeply-rooted institutional problems of, and the competence lacking in the Chinese judiciary.

The methodology applied in this book combines traditional modes of legal analysis, case studies and empirical research. The legal analysis includes examining and interpreting various legal sources, such as laws, judicial opinions and case materials, as well as comparing scholarly ideas and critically reviewing positive and negative aspects of the judicial reform in the context of political, economic and social transformation. Case studies are particularly prominent in Chapter 4, when looking at the criminal justice system. A selection of cases of injustice, first exposed at the end of the 1990s, reflects the chilling reality that the victims of these injustices were horrifically treated in today's China, which is truly paradoxical given the country's endeavours to build a fair and efficient judicial system.

The empirical elements of the research consist of qualitative interviews with judges, prosecutors, lawyers, legal scholars, and the observation of case hearings in courtrooms. In April, May and July of 2007, 2008, 2010, 2012 and 2013 I conducted interviews with judges, lawyers, prosecutors and leading scholars in Beijing, Wuhan, Shanghai, Kunming, Tianjing, Dalian, Enshi, Shenzhen and Nanning. The interviews helped clarify research issues that were difficult to find answers to in academic publications or when there was a need to double-check the information provided in such publications. I also obtained insightful information from those who had been directly involved in the reform of trial proceedings in local courts, including information on how the local experiments had been recognised and legitimised by the SPC. These interviews helped me understand the reform as a complicated and slow experimental process: when some old issues were resolved, new problems surfaced, and conventional judicial practice would linger over time. Publications and Party documents referred to by the interviewees also helped me discover new written materials.

In addition, I observed 14 public hearings in the courtrooms of 11 courts: three civil trial hearings in the Basic People's Court in Hai Dian district, Beijing; two civil trials in the Basic People's Court in Xi Cheng district, Beijing; one criminal trial in the No. 2 Intermediate People's Court in Beijing; two civil trials in two People's Tribunals in Wuhan; one criminal trial in the Basic People's Court in Hongshan district, Wuhan; one trial of an economic case in the Higher People's Court in Wuhan, Hubei province; one criminal trial in the Basic People's Court in Chang Ning district, Shanghai; one criminal case in the Intermediate People's Court in Kunming, Yunnan province; one trial of an economic case in the Higher People's Court in Urumqi, Xinjiang Uighur Autonomous Region; and one criminal trial in the Intermediate People's Court in Shenzhen.

Not holding a Chinese ID card has made access to court hearings in China very difficult for me. My observations in court sessions in Beijing, Wuhan, Shanghai and Shenzhen were made possible through contacts in these localities. In Kunming I was able to visit the court while I was there organising a training course for public prosecutors. A visit to the Higher People's Court in Xinjiang materialised when I was on a trip to the area. In Chapter 4 I discuss my observations of the criminal trial sessions in the Basic People's Court in Hongshan district, Wuhan; the No. 2 Intermediate People's Court in Beijing; and the Intermediate People's Court in Kunming.

After three decades of reconstruction and reform, the Chinese judicial system has a new standing and is facing new tests. As the country's transition towards a market economy deepens and people's consciousness toward civil and political rights is raised, more and more new and challenging cases are brought to the courts. Public expectancy to see courts as impartial arbitrators delivering fair judgments is high, whilst the courts' aptitude to meet such demand is restrained by both internal and external factors. It seems, therefore, that Chinese courts must continue with the process of judicial reform in order to respond to new challenges. A fair, independent and effective judicial system constitutes an intrinsic part of the rule of law, which can be expected to guarantee economic prosperity and social stability in China in the long run. In 2013, with the transition in the country's leadership to Xi Jinping, the newly issued Decisions on Several Major Issues Concerning Comprehensively Deepening Reforms of the Central Committee of the Communist Party of China contain some emphasis on the further pursuit of judicial reform.[7] This offers a positive, inspiring signal as to future judicial reform; nonetheless, how this will be implemented remains to be observed in the years to come.

7 The full text in Chinese is available at http://news.xinhuanet.com/politics/2013-11/15/c_118164235.htm; for an English translation, see http://chinacopyrightandmedia.wordpress.com/2013/11/15/ccp-central-committee-resolution-concerning-some-major-issues-in-comprehensively-deepening-reform/. Both were last visited in January 2014.

Chapter 1
Jurisdiction, Hierarchy and Actors

Introduction

Courts in China consist of the Supreme People's Court (SPC) at the central level, local people's courts at three levels, and special people's courts. Local courts are established on the basis of administrative divisions; they include 32 higher people's courts (HPCs) which can be found in the capitals of provinces and autonomous regions, and four municipalities directly under the central government (Beijing, Shanghai, Tianjin and Chongqing); 409 intermediate people's courts (IPCs) in prefectures and cities; and 3,117 basic people's courts (BPCs) at the county level, including districts within cities.[1] Special courts include maritime, railway transportation and military courts. Maritime courts adjudicate all forms of maritime cases. They are established at the intermediate level and handle only cases of first instance; appeal cases are handled by the higher people's courts. Rail transportation courts are erected along the main railway lines and function at both the basic and intermediate levels. Military courts comprise three levels and handle both criminal and civil matters concerning military personnel.[2] The SPC serves as the highest instance court for military cases. The structure of the court system is illustrated in Figure 1.1.

Conventionally, Chinese courts operate a two-tier appellate system. A party may appeal a judgment or the decision of a local court to the corresponding court at the next level; judgments or decisions given at this elevated level are final. However, special trial supervision procedures are in place which have the potential to re-try a case, despite an effective judgment having been given. In addition, for cases involving the death penalty, upon the judgment of a second instance court, a subsequent procedure of review by the SPC exists.

---

1 'Renmin Fayuan Jianjie' (A Brief Introduction to People's Courts). Available at http://www.court.gov.cn/jgsz/rmfyjj/. Last visited September 2013.

2 See Xinhuanet, 'Judicial System in China'. Available at http://news.xinhuanet.com/ziliao/2003-08/21/content_1038323.htm. Last visited September 2013. According to Article 20 of the Explanations concerning Several Issues in the Implementation of the Criminal Procedure Law issued by the SPC in 1998 (*Fashi* No. 23 [1998]), if a crime is jointly-committed by an active army man and non-army man, the case would be separately tried by a military court and an ordinary court unless the case is related to state military secrets, whereby the jurisdiction of the case would belong entirely to the military court. In June 2001, the SPC issued a Reply on Tentative Trial of Civil Cases within the Armed Forces by Military Courts which states that military courts handle civil cases in which both of the parties concerned are active servicemen, retired cadres under the management of the army, permanent workers and staff of the armed forces, or legal persons within the armed forces. With regard to a case involving an application for declaring a serviceman as missing or dead, where the applicant files an application with a military court, the court may accept the case. See *Fahan* No. 33 [2001], available at http://www.law-lib.com/law/law_view.asp?id=40732. Last visited September 2013.

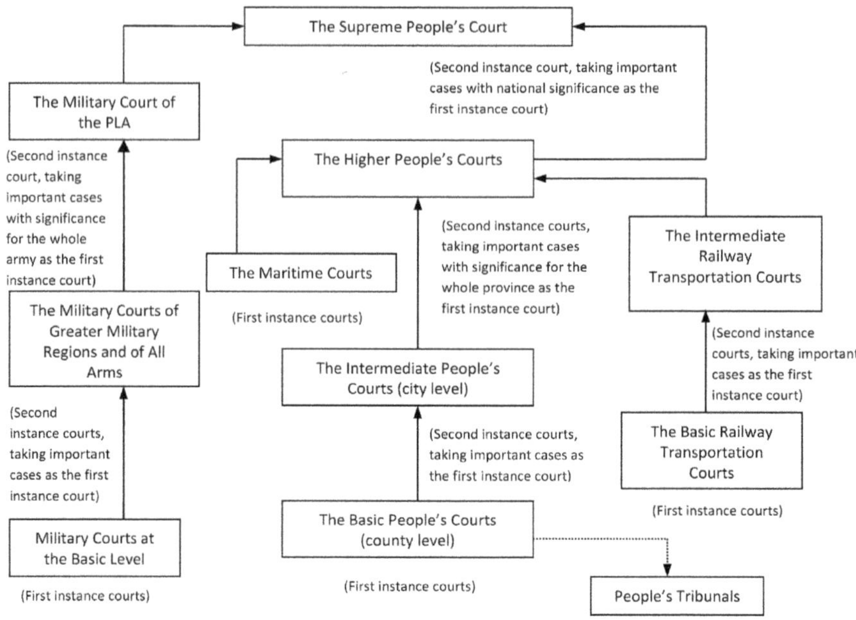

Figure 1.1 Structure of the Chinese courts

Each court has several trial chambers and administrative divisions. Trial chambers are divided into criminal, civil and administrative chambers;[3] other substantive divisions cover case filing,[4] enforcement of judgments, trial supervision and research. The administrative division includes a general administrative affairs office, a personnel office and a judicial administrative apparatus office (*sifa xingzheng zhuangbeichu*), which presides over the management of permanent assets, vehicles, police facilities of the courts and so on. A distinctive feature of the organisational aspect of the Chinese courts is the presence at each court of a Communist Party organ to ensure that the Party's policies are followed by both the courts and the judges.

In administering justice, Chinese courts apply the collegiate panel system. All first instance cases are brought before a collegiate panel of judges or a combination of judges and people's assessors. However, with simple civil cases, minor criminal cases and cases otherwise provided for by the law, these may be tried by a single judge. In practice, at BPCs any minor criminal or simple

3 There is no special administrative court in China; administrative cases are handled by administrative chambers at each court. There is also no constitutional court; courts under the Chinese Constitution do not have the power to review the Constitution. Interpretation of the Constitution can only be made by the National People's Congress and its Standing Committee.

4 In 1997, the SPC issued the Provisional Regulations Concerning Filing Cases by People's Courts. The Regulations provide for the principle that case filing and adjudication should be separated and a special division established to be responsible for case filing. All complaints brought to a court are accepted and registered by this division; it then distributes the cases to the relevant trial chambers according to the nature of the case. The case-filing division also deals with people's complaints by 'letters or visits'. Nowadays more than 90 per cent of Chinese courts have erected a lobby to take in people's complaints by letters or visits. See the SPCs Work Report to the NPC in March 2012. Available at http://www.court.gov.cn/xwzx/rdzt/2012qglh/wjbg/201203/t20120319_175177.html. Last visited September 2013.

civil case will be handled by a single judge, whereas courts at the intermediate level and courts at a higher tier will use the collegiate panel system.

This chapter examines some of the basic features of the court system in China. It begins with a description of the jurisdiction of courts at the various levels and locations, as well as the special jurisdiction afforded to the handling of cases with foreign elements. It then explores the vertical relationship between the higher and lower-level courts, and the varying supervisory role that exists between them. Such supervision tends to be seen in the systems of remand for re-trial (*fahui chongshen*), the re-opening of a trial (*zaishen*) and requests for instruction by a lower-level court to a higher-level court (*qingshi baogao zhidu*). With regard to the trial system as a whole, the functions of people's assessors and the adjudication committee in the trial process reflect particular Chinese characteristics, and thus are also examined in this chapter. Though the people's assessors system was largely overlooked during the course of the 1990s, its resurgence in the 2000s and its promotion by the SPC as part of the judicial democratisation movement continues to generate much debate in present-day China. The adjudication committee system reflects the collective leadership within a court on adjudicating cases; its functions, procedure of working, and its positive and negative effects in realising a fair trial and judicial independence are discussed.

Jurisdiction of the Courts

The jurisdictions of the various courts are set out in the Organic Law of People's Courts (OLPC),[5] the Criminal Procedure Law (CrPL), the Civil Procedure Law (CiPL), the Administrative Litigation Law (ALL) and a number of the SPC's judicial interpretations.[6] They can be classified into jurisdiction by levels (*jibie guanxia*), territorial jurisdiction (*diyu guanxia*), transferred and designated jurisdiction (*yisong* and *zhiding guanxia*), and jurisdiction over foreign-related cases.

---

5 The OLPC provides the general principles of the operation of courts, the structure and functions of courts, as well as the basic qualification and appointment of judges. The first OLPC was issued in 1979, and was subsequently amended in 1983, 1986 and 2006. The articles cited in this chapter are from the 2006 amended OLPC unless otherwise specified.

6 For example, Specific Provisions of the Supreme People's Court on the Jurisdiction of Foreign-related Maritime Actions (31 January 1986), available at http://www.law-lib.com/law/law_view.asp?id=3521; Provisions of the Supreme People's Court on Certain Issues Concerning Jurisdiction over Civil and Commercial Cases Involving Foreign Elements (*Fashi* No. 5 [2002]), available at http://www.law-lib.com/law/law_view.asp?id=17055; Notice on Strengthening the Jurisdiction over Foreign-related Commercial Cases (*Fashi* No. 265 [2004]), available at http://www.law-lib.com/law/law_view.asp?id=106265; Provisions on Issues Concerning the Jurisdiction over Administrative Cases (*Fashi* No. 1 [2008]), available at http://www.law-lib.com/law/law_view.asp?id=243717; Provisions of the Supreme People's Court on Several Issues Concerning the Trials of Cases on Objection to Hierarchy-based Jurisdiction over Civil Actions (*Fashi* No. 17 [2009]), available at http://www.law-lib.com/law/law_view.asp?id=302097; Notice of the Supreme People's Court on the Issue of Jurisdiction over Civil Dispute Cases Involving the Determination of Well-Known Trademarks (*Fashi* No. 3 [2009]), available at http://www.law-lib.com/law/law_view.asp?id=278791. All last visited September 2013.

Jurisdiction According to Level

This is also commonly referred to as tier jurisdiction or hierarchical jurisdiction, which alludes to the division of the work-load and authority between the four levels of the courts.[7] The basic principle of jurisdiction in this regard is that most cases are handled by the BPCs; yet, cases concerning large amounts of money, with a more profound societal impact, or concerning special subjects such as foreign citizens or legal persons, large state-owned enterprises or higher-level governmental organs and officials, are dealt with by either IPCs or HPCs. In principle, the SPC does not handle cases of the first instance.

The BPCs are the lowest-level courts. They may establish people's tribunals according to the conditions of the locality, population and cases. A people's tribunal handles ordinary civil cases, directs the work of people's mediation committees, organises legal propaganda and receives people's letters and visits. Such a tribunal is a part of the basic people's court structure and any judgments or orders given have the same legal effect as those made by a BPC.[8] The overwhelming majority of lawsuits begin and end in BPCs. Generally speaking, the judges at BPCs are the most experienced adjudicators. However, many judges at this level do not retain the expected standard of university education in the legal field, which in turn affects the quality of justice attained.[9] A commonly cited depiction of BPCs centres on the notion of 'three 80 per cent' statistics: they handle approximately 80 per cent of first instance cases; approximately 80 per cent of the judicial personnel across the whole country work at this level; and roughly 80 per cent of judicial corruption cases occur at the BPC level.[10]

IPCs, as the second-lowest people's courts, are established in prefectures of a province or autonomous region, in municipalities directly under the central government, in municipalities directly under the jurisdiction of a province or autonomous region and in autonomous prefectures. They handle cases of first instance assigned by law; cases of first instance transferred from the basic people's courts; cases of appeal and of protests lodged against judgments of the basic people's courts by the people's procuratorates; and cases of protest raised by the people's procuratorates in accordance with the trial supervision procedure.[11]

The criminal, civil and administrative procedural laws all contain certain provisions which categorise the cases to be specifically handled by the IPCs as the first instance court.[12] According to the Criminal Procedure Law, these cases include those involving threatening national security or terrorist activities and criminal cases which may involve life imprisonment or the death penalty. Under the Administrative Litigation Law, IPCs are authorised to hear cases concerning

7 Arts. 17 to 20 of the 2012 amended CiPL; Arts. 19 to 22 of the 2012 CrPL; Arts. 13 to 16 of the ALL.

8 Art. 19 of the OLPC.

9 The academic background of judges at BPCs in large cities, such as Beijing and Shanghai, is quite different to that of judges in remote areas. For more information, see Chapter 3 of this book.

10 President of the SPC, Xiao Yang stated this in the 2001 Work Report of the Supreme People's Court to the National People's Congress, available at http://www.court.gov.cn/qwfb/gzbg/201003/t20100310_2631.htm. Last visited September 2013. Further investigation is needed to ascertain whether the current reality remains the same or similar. The recently exposed horrendous judicial corruption in the Higher People's Court in Shanghai causes doubt about identical, if not even more shameful, corruption among judges at higher levels. See 'Shanghai 4 Ming Zhaopiao Faguan Zhiwu Ji Piaochang Jingguo Gongbu' (The Posts of the Four Judges in Shanghai Who Solicit Prostitutes and the Process of their Prostitution is Released), available at http://news.xinhuanet.com/legal/2013-08/07/c_125127317.htm. Last visited September 2013.

11 Arts. 22 to 24 of the OLPC.

12 Art. 20 of the 2012 amended CrPL; Art.19 of the 2012 amended CiPL; Art. 14 of the ALL.

the verification of patent rights; customs-handling; suits against administrative actions taken by State Council departments or governments at the provincial level; and other significant and complex cases. According to the Civil Procedure Law, IPCs have the authority to preside over cases involving foreign elements; cases which have major ramifications; any disputes regarding their jurisdiction; and cases brought by order of the SPC.

HPCs handle cases of first instance which have been assigned by the law; cases of first instance which have been transferred from the people's courts at lower levels; cases of appeal and of protest lodged against judgments of lower people's courts; and cases of protest lodged by people's procuratorates in accordance with the trial supervision procedure.[13] HPCs review cases of first instance in which the death penalty is imposed by an IPC and the accused renounces the right to appeal. If a HPC raises no objection to the death penalty sentence, it then submits the case to the SPC for their final approval; if the latter disagrees with the death penalty sentence, it can either re-examine the case or remand the case back to the original IPC for re-trial.[14] Regarding civil cases, HPCs are courts of first instance for cases that are deemed to have a potentially significant impact at the provincial level. Typically, the amount of money under dispute in a case determines which tier of the court structure will have jurisdiction to adjudicate.

The SPC is the highest judicial organ of the state. It has jurisdiction as the court of first instance over cases which are likely to have a major bearing on the country as a whole. Cases which the SPC has jurisdiction over, as the court of final instance, include cases of appeal, cases of protests lodged against judgments of HPCs and special people's courts, and cases of protest lodged by the Supreme People's Procuratorate in accordance with the trial supervision procedure.[15] However, in practice, the SPC has rarely handled any cases of first instance; the exception being the 1978 trial of the 'Gang of Four'.[16]

While the jurisdiction of the various courts, according to a tier structure, is generally provided for in the three aforementioned procedural laws, the SPC has issued a number of judicial opinions to clarify and reset a number of rules on court jurisdiction at the different levels. This is typically reflected in the handling of three types of civil and commercial cases: cases involving large sums of money, intellectual property cases, and cases with foreign elements.

As cases involving large sums of money have increased, the caseload of the HPCs has also multiplied. If an HPC acts as the first instance court, parties appeal to the SPC, and this consequently increases the SPC caseload. To tackle this problem, in 2008 the SPC issued the Notice on the Adjustments of Jurisdiction Standards of Higher People's Courts and Intermediate People's Courts over Civil and Commercial Cases of First Instance,[17] to raise the threshold criteria for determining when a case is to be handled by IPCs and HPCs. For instance, for a case to be accepted by a HPC in Beijing, Shanghai, Guangdong, Jiangsu or Zhejiang provinces, the disputed amount cannot be

13 Arts. 25 to 27 of the OLPC.

14 Art. 236 of the 2012 amended CrPL.

15 Arts. 29 to 32 of the OLPC.

16 This is the trial of the 'Lin Biao and Jiang Qing Counter-revolutionary Clique' in 1980–1981, during which a special trial chamber was formulated at the SPC and government-appointed lawyers were assigned to represent the accused. See The Editorial Board of the Series of Contemporary China, *Dangdai Zhongguo De Shenpan Gongzuo* (Trial Work in Modern China) (Beijing: Dangdai Zhongguo Chubanshe, 1993), pp. 459–484. The accused were convicted of such crimes as 'counterrevolutionary homicide or injury', 'extorting a confession by torture' and 'unlawful detention'. See Zhou Hong (ed.), *Guoshi Tongjian* (History of the People's Republic of China), vol. 4 (Beijing: Hongqi Chubanshe, 1993).

17 *Fafa* No. 10 [2008], promulgated and became effective on 3 February 2008, available at http://www.law-lib.com/law/law_view.asp?id=269951. Last visited September 2013.

less than RMB 200 million; for a case to be accepted by a HPC in Tianjin, Chongqing, Shandong, Fujian, Hubei and others, the disputed amount cannot be less than RMB 100 million; for a case to be accepted by a HPC in Gansu, Guizhou, Xinjiang, Inner Mongolia and Yunnan, the disputed amount cannot be less than RMB 50 million. In order for a case to be accepted by an IPC in Beijing, Shanghai, the capital cities of Guangdong, Jiangsu and Zhejiang provinces, and other economically-developed cities, the disputed amount has to be above RMB 50 million.

With regard to intellectual property cases, the Opinions on Several Issues concerning the Implementation of the Civil Procedure Law issued by the SPC in 1992[18] provides that patent disputes are to be heard by those IPCs to be decided by the SPC. In January 2010, the SPC issued the Notice on Adjusting the Standard for Jurisdiction of Local People's Courts at All Levels over First Instance Civil Cases Involving Intellectual Property Rights[19] which stated: (1) for cases with disputed amounts over RMB 200 million, or over RMB 100 million where one party concerned is not domiciled within the area of jurisdiction or where the case involves foreign characteristics or matters relating to Hong Kong, Macao or Taiwan, the first instance jurisdiction will be conferred upon the HPCs; (2) for cases below the aforesaid amount, except for especially-designated local people's courts, the first instance jurisdiction will be conferred upon the IPCs; (3) some BPCs designated by the SPC are capable of trying cases involving intellectual property rights at the first instance where the disputed amount is less than RMB 5 million, or between RMB 5 million and RMB 10 million where the domiciles of both parties are within the area of jurisdiction of the HPC or IPC to which the basic court belongs.

In January 2010, the SPC also issued the Notice on the Standards for Some Basic People's Courts' Jurisdiction over Civil Cases of First Instance Involving Disputes over Intellectual Property Rights.[20] These two Notices comprehensively adjusted and unified the standard for the jurisdiction of courts at all levels over civil cases involving intellectual property rights. In general, the scope of jurisdiction of basic courts over general civil cases involving intellectual property rights has been notably broadened; furthermore, centralised jurisdiction across different regions of intermediate and basic courts is encouraged.

At the end of 2011, the number of IPCs with jurisdiction over cases relating to patents stood at 82, new varieties of plants at around 45, integrated circuit layout designs at 46, and the recognition of well-known trademarks at 41. The number of the BPCs with jurisdiction over general civil cases involving intellectual property rights amounted to 119, three of which have been approved for the trial of certain civil cases involving disputes over utility models or design patents.[21]

In addition, the SPC has led reforms in some local courts in order to allocate the Chamber of Intellectual Property Rights the authority to uniformly hear civil, administrative and criminal cases involving disputes over intellectual property rights (that is, a combination of three trials in one). In July 2010, a forum on this pilot work was held by the SPC in Kunshan city, Jiangsu province. The IPC of Fuzhou city; the IPC of Xiamen city; the BPCs and the IPC of Shenzhen city, Foshan city and Zhongshan city; the BPC of the Gulou district of Fuzhou city; and the BPC of

18 Article 1(2) of the Opinions (*Fashi* No. 22 [1992]), available at http://www.law-lib.com/law/law_view.asp?id=54915. Last visited September 2013.

19 *Fafa* No. 5 [2010], available at http://www.court.gov.cn/qwfb/sfwj/tz/201002/t20100222_1511.htm. Last visited September 2013.

20 *Fafa* No. 6 [2010], available at http://www.court.gov.cn/qwfb/sfwj/tz/201002/t20100222_1512.htm. Last visited September 2013.

21 The Supreme People's Court, *Renmin Fayuan Gongzuo Niandu Baogao (2011)* (Annual Report of Work of the People's Court (2011)) (Beijing: Renmin Fayuan Chubanshe, 2012), p. 21.

the Siming district of Xiamen city, were approved to conduct such combined trials. At the end of December 2010, five HPCs, 49 IPCs and 42 BPCs had conducted such related pilot trials.[22]

Territorial Jurisdiction

This way of determining which case should be attributed to which court is decided according to geographical location. The 1991 Civil Procedure Law, the 1992 SPC Opinions on Several Issues Concerning the Implementation of the Civil Procedure Law and the 2008 Notice of the Supreme People's Court on Adjustments of Jurisdiction Standards of High People's Courts and Intermediate People's Courts over Civil and Commercial Cases of First Instance contain detailed provisions on territorial jurisdiction over civil lawsuits. Based on the judicial practice and the SPC judicial interpretations, the 2012 amended CiPL made some changes to the courts' territorial jurisdiction. Generally speaking, territorial jurisdiction under the 2012 amendments can be understood from six perspectives.[23]

The first, general territorial jurisdiction, refers to the court where the defendant is domiciled or habitually resides; however, when the case relates to the personal status of persons not residing within the territory of China, the personal status of persons whose whereabouts are unknown or those declared missing, those brought against persons who are undergoing rehabilitation through labour or those brought against persons who are imprisoned, jurisdiction will be conferred upon the court within the domicile of the plaintiff (CiPL: Arts. 21 and 22).

The second, special territorial jurisdiction, allows for jurisdiction according to special legal relationships or the place relevant to the object or subject matter of the dispute. For instance, a contract dispute will come under the jurisdiction of the court in the place where the defendant is domiciled or where the contract is in fact performed. Such jurisdiction also applies to insurance contract disputes; bill disputes; disputes caused by the establishment or confirmation of shareholders' qualifications; profit distribution or dissolution of a company; disputes over a railway, road, waterway or air transportation contract; torts; claims for damages caused by transportation; disputes relating to expenses of maritime salvage (CiPL: Arts. 23–32).

The third alludes to exclusive territorial jurisdiction. In cases involving disputes over real estate, harbour operations and succession, jurisdiction will be exclusively conferred upon the court where the estate or the harbour is located, where the deceased resided prior to death, or where the principal part of their estate is located (CiPL: Art. 33).

The fourth, jurisdiction by agreement, allows parties to a contract or other property dispute to choose by written agreement the jurisdiction of a court in the location of the defendant's or the plaintiff's domicile; in the location where the contract is performed or signed; in the location of the subject matter; or in other locations which have connections with the dispute, provided such jurisdiction is not in contravention of territorial jurisdiction or exclusive jurisdiction (CiPL: Art. 34). In the 1991 CiPL, jurisdiction by agreement was provided separately in Article 25 which applied to domestic disputes and Article 244 under the special provisions on disputes involving foreign elements: the subject, the scope of the dispute and the court of choice were all different. The 2012 amended CiPL removed Article 244, and made Article 34 apply to both domestic civil

22 *Ibid.*

23 The order of the six types of territorial jurisdiction here follows the order of the articles in the 2012 amended CiPL. However, in practice when deciding the jurisdiction of a concrete case, different orders will be used. For instance, in dealing with a contract dispute the order can be exclusive jurisdiction, jurisdiction by agreement, special territorial jurisdiction, general territorial jurisdiction. In terms of tortious dispute the special territorial jurisdiction can be directly used.

cases and cases involving foreign elements.[24] Under Article 34, parties to a contract or other property disputes, in using jurisdiction by agreement, should choose a court which has 'actual connections with the dispute'. This means that the principle of 'genuine link' applies to jurisdiction by agreement. How this principle will be applied by courts and interpreted by the SPC remains to be observed. The lack of consistency in the SPC's interpretations on a number of foreign-related cases in the past signals a restrictive approach in applying this principle.[25]

The fifth relates to shared jurisdiction. When two or more courts have jurisdiction over the same lawsuit, the plaintiff may decide which court to bring the lawsuit to; if the plaintiff brings the lawsuit to two or more courts, the court in which the case was first filed should have jurisdiction over the case (CiPL: Art. 35).

The sixth concerns consent jurisdiction. Under Article 127 of the 2012 amended CiPL, in cases where a civil case is brought to a court and a party responds to the action without challenging the jurisdiction, the court accepting the case should be deemed to have the jurisdiction on the condition that doing so is not in contravention of jurisdiction according to level or exclusive jurisdiction. Such consent jurisdiction was only applicable to foreign-related cases under the 1991 CiPL. The 2012 CiPL makes it applicable to both domestic and foreign-related cases.

For criminal cases, the general principle stands that the court in the location where the criminal offence was committed has jurisdiction to preside over the case. If it is more appropriate for the case to be tried by the court in the location of the residency of the accused then that court may have jurisdiction over the case. If two or more courts at the same level have jurisdiction over a case, the case should be tried by the court that was the first to accept it. When necessary, a case can be transferred for trial to the court in the principal place where the crime was committed (CrPL 2012: Arts. 24 and 25).

As for administrative cases, the general principle is that the court in the location where the administrative organs initially undertake concrete administrative actions has jurisdiction. For cases that have been reconsidered and the original administrative actions have been changed following reconsideration, the court where the reconsideration organ is located may also have jurisdiction (ALL: Art. 17). There are also several specific rules for jurisdiction over administrative cases. These include the rule that any lawsuit against compulsory administrative measures which restrict the freedom of the person come under the jurisdiction of the court which corresponds to where the defendant or the plaintiff is located, and the rule that any real estate cases come exclusively under the jurisdiction of the court where the real estate is located (ALL: Arts. 18, 19). Similar to the civil procedure, the plaintiff may have the right to choose between various courts which may all have jurisdiction. If a plaintiff has brought a suit to two or more courts, the one that first received the bill of complaint has jurisdiction (ALL: Art. 20).

The overlapping of courts' jurisdiction can occur in judicial practice. A phenomenon in China is that sometimes courts compete for jurisdiction when economic interests are at stake; courts are especially eager to preside over commercial cases where litigation fees can be beneficial for the courts.[26] Numerous media reports have showcased such lawsuits in practice. In 2010, a case arose concerning a construction contract dispute between two companies, which was brought before the BPC of Dongyang city in Zhejiang province and the IPC of Weihai city in Shandong

24 Art. 259 of the 2012 CiPL states that when special provisions for civil procedure of cases involving foreign elements are not provided, other relevant provisions of the CiPL should apply.

25 See *infra* note 41.

26 Cai Dingjian, 'Development of the Chinese Legal System since 1979 and Its Current Crisis and Transformation', 11(2) (1999) *Cultural Dynamics*, pp. 146–154. It should be noted that the situation has been improved in some courts resulting from the separation of revenues from expenditures.

province simultaneously. Though it had been agreed in the contract that the court in Weihai should have jurisdiction over any disputes arising from the implementation of the contract, the courts in Dongyang argued that the cause of action relating to the case was tortious rather than contractual in nature, and thus the agreement of jurisdiction in the contract should not be applied.[27] In another case which was lodged in 2008, the two parties respectively brought lawsuits to two courts in Jiangsu and Shandong provinces with similar claims, including the termination of the contracts which had been concluded and their requests that the other party bear the liability for breaching the contracts. Though both parties had raised their objections to the jurisdiction of the court to which the other party had brought the lawsuit, after a careful examination of those objections, both courts ruled that they had jurisdiction, both claiming that the legal relationships and targets of the contracts came under their jurisdiction. Finally in 2010, the two courts gave opposing judgments toward the dispute, each supporting the claims of the company located in its own province.[28] These cases highlight the local judicial protectionism and competition for interests that influence jurisdiction decisions.

Transferred and Designated Jurisdiction

In practice courts can have different opinions on a case's jurisdiction and on when it is inappropriate for a court with jurisdiction to preside over the case. Thus, the Civil Procedure Law, the Administrative Litigation Law and the Criminal Procedure Law, all contain provisions on transferred and designated jurisdiction.

Under the 2012 amended CiPL such jurisdiction applies to three different situations. Firstly, the provision deals with the transfer of a case from a non-competent to a competent court. Article 36 provides for the rectification of situations where a court discovers that a case it has accepted does not fall under its jurisdiction, the court could then transfer the case to the court which does have jurisdiction. The court to which a case has been transferred should in turn accept the case; however, if it considers that the transferred case does not come under its jurisdiction, it is required to report to a superior court for the designation of jurisdiction and cannot transfer the case to another court without prior authorisation. Secondly, Article 37 provides that if for some special reasons a court with jurisdiction is unable to exercise jurisdiction, a superior court must designate another court to exercise jurisdiction on its behalf. Further, any dispute over jurisdiction arising amongst the courts is to be be resolved by the disputing parties through consultation; if consultation fails, the disputing courts are required to ask their corresponding superior court to designate jurisdiction. Thirdly, under Article 39, higher-level courts have the authority to try civil cases over which courts at lower levels have jurisdiction as the courts of first instance; they may also transfer civil cases, over which they themselves have jurisdiction as courts of first instance, to courts at lower levels for adjudication.

Articles 21 to 23 of the Administrative Litigation Law contain provisions similar to those of the CiPL concerning the transferral and designation of jurisdiction.

Under the 2012 amended CrPL, Article 23 provides that when necessary, courts at the higher levels are able to preside over criminal cases, which technically come within the jurisdiction of

27 For the details of this case, see 'Shandong Zhejiang Liangdi Fayuan Zheng Guanxiaquan Tongshen Yijian Anjian (Courts in Shandong and Zhejiang Compete for the Jurisdiction over the Same Case)', available at http://news.sina.com.cn/c/p/2010-09-27/174721180951.shtml. Last visited September 2013.

28 For the details of this case, see 'Jiangsu Shandong Liangdi Zheng Guanxiaquan, Fayuan Panjue Jieguo Jing Xiangfan (Courts in Jiangsu and Shandong Province Compete for Jurisdiction with Opposite Judgments)', available at http://news.sohu.com/20110311/n279777600.shtml. Last visited September 2013.

lower-level courts as first instance courts. Thus, if a court at a lower-level considers a criminal trial case in the first instance as too significant or complex and in need of adjudication at a higher level, it may request that the case be transferred to a higher-level court for trial. Article 26 states that a court at a higher level may instruct a court at a lower level to try a case, where the issue of jurisdiction is unclear. Similarly, higher-level courts have the power to transfer cases between lower-level courts.

Jurisdiction over Foreign-related Cases

With regard to cases concerning foreign subject matter, two issues arise which must be solved in turn when considering jurisdiction: whether courts in a country have jurisdiction over a case and, if this is settled, which court in that particular country has the jurisdiction. This section deals with only the latter situation, though it is important to note the former.

Foreign-related cases can take the form of civil, criminal or administrative matters. However, in practice foreign-related administrative cases are extremely rare.[29] The 1989 Administrative Litigation Law does not contain special provisions on courts' jurisdiction over foreign-related cases. In 2008, the SPC issued the Provisions on Issues Concerning the Jurisdiction over Administrative Cases, which clarified that IPCs are the courts of first instance in adjudicating significant cases involving elements pertaining to foreign countries and the Special Administrative Regions of Hong Kong, Macao or Taiwan.[30]

Foreign-related criminal cases generally involve foreigners who have committed crimes in China or Chinese citizens who have committed criminal offences against foreigners.[31] There are no publically-available statistics on the numbers of such cases, nor is it ever specifically mentioned in the SPC's work reports to the National People's Congress (NPC), although the number of foreign-related commercial cases is at times mentioned. In recent years, in parallel with the increase in the number of foreigners entering China, including those within the categories known as the 'three illegals' (people illegally entering China, illegally living in China and illegally working in China), the number of criminal cases in which foreigners are the offenders has also increased. For instance, research conducted at the No. 2 Intermediate People's Procuratorate (IPP) in Beijing

29 For discussion of foreign-related administrative cases, see John Wagner Givens, 'On Their Best Behaviour: Foreign Plaintiffs in Chinese Administrative Litigation', Research Center for Chinese Politics and Business Working Paper No.17, January 2012. Available at http://www.indiana.edu/~rccpb/Working_Paper/Givens%20RCCPB%2017%20Litigation.pdf. Last visited September 2013. He concluded that only a handful of foreign litigants directly challenged the Chinese state in court. Any challenges were mainly made in the instances of patent or trademark litigation brought by multinational companies. In practice, most of the foreign-related administrative disputes were settled *ad hoc*, such as through direct meetings between state officials and foreign companies.

30 *Fashi* No. 1 [2008], available at http://www.chinacourt.org/law/detail/2008/01/id/123190.shtml. Last visited September 2013.

31 Zhang Xiaowei, 'Shewai Fanzui Yu Kuaguo Fanzui, Guoji Fanzui De Bijiao Yanjiu' (Comparative Studies among Foreign-related Crime, Transnational Crime and International Crime), 1 (2006) *Huadong Zhengfa Daxue Xuebao* (East China University of Political Science and Law Journal), p. 80. Available at http://article.chinalawinfo.com/Article_Detail.asp?ArticleID=63261#4. Last visited September 2013. Under Article 291 of the 1998 Explanations concerning Several Issues in the Implementation of the Criminal Procedure Law issued by the SPC, foreign-related criminal cases include two types: one is in China's territory where foreigners committed crimes or Chinese citizens committed criminal offences against foreigners; the other is outside China's territory where Chinese citizens committed crimes or foreigners committed crimes against Chinese citizens or the state. This section deals only with the former.

shows that, in 2003 they dealt with eight cases involving 13 foreign offenders, which accounted for 5 per cent of the total cases handled; in 2004 they dealt with 32 cases involving 52 foreign offenders, amounting to 9 per cent of the total cases; in 2005 they dealt with 38 cases with 70 foreign offenders, again accounting for 9 per cent of the total cases.[32] It has been reported that the Public Security Bureau in Guangzhou city of Guangdong province handled four cases involving five foreign offenders in 2002, while in 2003 the number of cases increased to 14 involving 21 foreign offenders. In early 2004, the number of cases reached 12 and involved 16 such offenders, which was three times more than for the same period in 2003.[33] It was reported that between 2007 and 2008, the IPC of Kunming city in Yunnan province[34] tried 50 foreign-related criminal cases, which accounted for 1.52 per cent of the total number of criminal cases that had been tried over that same period. Within the 50 aforementioned criminal cases, 47 related to drug-trafficking.[35] According to the survey completed by the No. 2 People's Procuratorate in Beijing, most of the criminal cases involving foreigners were property-related cases, such as stealing, fraud, smuggling and so on.[36] Though not in many in number, some criminal cases of a serious nature have roused international attention and criticism in recent years. An example of such is the case against Akmal Shaikh, a British citizen, who was convicted of smuggling drugs and consequently executed in December 2009.[37] Furthermore, with regard to commercial bribery, in March 2010, four Rio Tinto executives were found guilty of bribery and the theft of commercial secrets and were punished by the court with lengthy jail sentences.[38]

In the 2012 Revision of the CrPL, the original Article 20(3), which provided that IPCs were the court of first instance in adjudicating foreign-related criminal cases, was omitted. Consequently, from 1 January 2013, basic courts also have jurisdiction over foreign-related criminal cases. This shift reflects the growing number of foreign-related criminal cases coming before the courts.

Most cases with foreign elements are civil and commercial cases. Foreign-related civil cases refer to those in which one party or both parties are foreigners, stateless persons, foreign enterprises

32 Zhang Xuming and Yu Hao, 'Jin Sannian Zaijing Waiguoren Fanzui Qingkuang Guankui' (A Restricted View on Foreigners Committing Crimes in Beijing over the Last Three Years), 7 (2006) *Renmin Jiancha* (People's Procuratorate), p. 41.

33 Zhang Ruiqing, Su Zhijie and Zhang Weirong, 'Waiguoren Xingshifanzui De Tedian Ji Dafang Duice' (Characteristics and Counter-measures Relating to Criminal Cases Committed by Foreigners), 10 (2004) *Gong'an Yanjiu* (Policing Studies), pp. 56–58.

34 Kunming City is located in east-central Yunnan Province and is the closest major city to the Golden Triangle in Southeast Asia. Hence, it has a crucial role as a major conduit point in international drug trafficking, which is why criminal cases relating to drug trafficking have accounted for a large proportion of cases tried by the court in Kunming.

35 'Kunming Zhongyuan Fenxi Jinnianlai Shouli Shewai Xingshi Anjian Tedian Ji Zuofa' (IPC of Kunming City Analyses the Characteristics and Practices of Trying Foreign-related Criminal Cases in Recent Years), available at http://www.gy.yn.gov.cn/Article/xwgj/xwgc/200905/14344.html. Last visited September 2013.

36 Zhang Xuming and Yu Hao, *supra* note 32, p. 41.

37 'Akmal Shaikh Execution Draws Scathing Criticism from Amnesty', available at http://www.guardian.co.uk/world/2009/dec/29/amnesty-akmal-shaikh-execution-reaction. Last visited September 2013.

38 In the judgment Australian Stern Hu was punished with a 10-year sentence. Wang Yong was given 14 years, Liu Caikui seven years and Ge Minqiang eight years. The court proceeding was not open to the public. Australian diplomats were also refused attendance at parts of the hearing dealing with commercial espionage charges. This has resulted in complaints by many foreign businessmen. See 'Rio Tinto Executives Handed Lengthy Jail Terms', available at http://news.bbc.co.uk/2/hi/business/8592226.stm. Last visited September 2013.

or foreign organisations; or where the legal fact of establishment, modification or termination of the civil legal relationship between the parties occurred in a foreign country; or in which the object or subject matter of the action is located in a foreign country.[39] Over the last two decades, the number of foreign-related civil cases has increased dramatically and this trend will inevitably continue.[40]

The 1982 Civil Procedure Law (for Trial Implementation) contained seven general principles on foreign-related civil litigation in China. The 1991 CiPL, for the first time, introduced a new chapter on Special Provisions Governing Procedures for Civil Cases Involving Foreign Interests, comprising 10 articles. Four articles related to the courts' jurisdiction, which included territorial jurisdiction, jurisdiction by agreement, consent jurisdiction and exclusive jurisdiction. The 2012 amended CiPL integrated jurisdiction by agreement and consent jurisdiction for both domestic and foreign-related civil cases. Consequently, under the 2012 revised CiPL, only two articles concerning territorial jurisdiction and exclusive jurisdiction especially provide for foreign-related cases.

Territorial jurisdiction applies in cases concerning a contractual dispute or other disputes relating to property rights and interests, brought against a defendant who is not a resident in the territory of China, if the contract is signed or performed on Chinese terrain; if the object of the action is located within China and its territories; if the defendant has distrainable property or if the defendant has its representative office within the territory of China. Jurisdiction goes to the court of the place where the contract is signed or performed, where the object of the action is located, where the defendant's distrainable property is located, where the torts are committed, or where the defendant's representative office is located (CiPL 2012: Art. 265).

Exclusive jurisdiction appears in Article 266 of the 2012 amended CiPL. It stipulates that Chinese courts have jurisdiction over disputes arising from the performance of a contract for Chinese-foreign equity joint ventures, Chinese-foreign cooperative joint ventures, or Chinese-foreign cooperative exploration and the development of natural resources in China. This special exclusive jurisdiction is based on the Sino-Foreign Equity Joint Venture Law, which provides that such a joint venture has a status of Chinese legal person to be protected by and under the jurisdiction of Chinese law. A Sino-foreign cooperative joint venture is a cooperative formulated in China, with the place of signing the contract, performance of the contract and main business of the parties usually all undertaken in China, which confirms such an application of territorial jurisdiction. With contractual disputes concerning Sino-foreign cooperative exploration and the development of natural resources concerning resources inside China, territorial jurisdiction is based on the principle of state sovereignty over natural resources.

It should be mentioned that Article 244 of the 1991 CiPL (Art. 242 of the 2007 revised CiPL) allowed parties to a dispute over a contract concluded with a foreign element, or over property rights and interests involving a foreign element, to reach a written agreement to choose a court located in a place that has an actual connection with the dispute, as the court to adjudicate the dispute. This can be viewed as a limited jurisdiction by agreement. The 2012 revised CiPL removed this article; subsequently the limited jurisdiction by agreement in Article 34 applies to both domestic and foreign-related cases. In previous practice, Chinese courts have displayed incoherence in recognising the validity of such agreements. Chinese research articulates that in the 1990s, the SPC supported such

39 See Art. 304 of the Opinions on Issues concerning the Implementation of the PRC Civil Procedure Law, issued by the Supreme People's Court (*Fafa* No. 22 [1992]).

40 The statistics on foreign-related civil cases handled by courts in China are not systematically published. The numbers given in the work reports of the SPC to the NPC can be used as a reference, however, the criteria of calculating the numbers were not always the same. According to the work report of the SPC the number of foreign-related cases concluded from 1998 to 2002 was 26,399; from 2003 to 2007 the number was 64,558; in 2011 alone the number was 22,000.

agreements by accepting the parties' agreed choice of a neutral court as a legal action which gave that court outside China 'actual connection with the dispute'. However, in a few cases brought to the SPC in the 2000s, the SPC took a negative stand and did not accept that the choice of court made in the agreement had created an actual connection with the dispute.[41] From this, a tendency of Chinese courts to exercise thoroughly their jurisdiction over foreign-related cases may be observed.

The capacity of Chinese courts to handle foreign-related commercial cases has often led to widespread concern.[42] In judicial practice, in order to improve the quality of the handling of foreign-related commercial cases and ensure a unified application of the law, the SPC has initiated reform measures to formulate a model of centralised jurisdiction over foreign-related civil and commercial cases by entrusting some courts with special jurisdiction, setting up specific trial chambers in such courts, and reserving specific trial judges to handle such cases.[43] In 2002, the SPC issued the Provisions Concerning Court's Jurisdiction over Civil and Commercial Cases Involving Foreign Elements (hereafter referred to as the Provisions).[44] The Provisions centralised jurisdiction over foreign-related civil and commercial cases – which in the past had been dispersed amongst various basic and intermediate courts – to a few intermediate and basic courts with a greater degree of experience in, and more capable of, dealing with such cases. The Provisions contain seven articles. Article 1 provides the following courts with first instance jurisdiction over civil and commercial cases involving foreign elements:[45]

41 Cheng Bing, 'Foreign-Related Jurisdiction by Agreement and the Principle of Genuine Link', 6 (2012) *China Law*, pp. 40–43. He discussed the case between Sinochem Jiangsu Lianyungang Import and Export Corporation (Chinese company) and the Middle East Starfish Omnibus Trade Corporation (UAE companies), in which the parties agreed that the contract was to be governed by the law in force in Switzerland and that a dispute should be submitted to the Zurich court. The SPC took the position that 'both parties of this case chose application of Swiss law in the contract, which makes Swiss law the governing law applicable to the case in order to deal with contractual relations. The fact is enough to show that Switzerland has a "genuine link" with the dispute of this case.' However, in the dispute between Delixi Energy Private Limited and Dongming Zhongyou fuel Petrochemical Co., Ltd., though the parties agreed that the contract was to be subject to English law and accepted the jurisdiction of the London High Court, the SPC took the view that the parties failed to demonstrate that Britain had a genuine link with the case. In the dispute between Tianheng Shipping Co., Ltd. and Grand International (Hong Kong) Co., Ltd., the SPC recognised the Chinese court's jurisdiction by repudiating that the British High Court had a genuine link with the case. A similar argument was used by the SPC in the dispute between Shanghai Yanliu International Transport of Goods Agency Ltd. and the Evergreen Marine Corporation.

42 For general analysis on this issue see Mo Zhang, 'International Civil Litigation in China: A Practical Analysis of the Chinese Judicial System', 25 (2002) *Boston College International and Comparative Law Review*, pp. 59–97; Susan Finder, 'Inside the People's Courts: China's Litigation System and the Resolution of Commercial Disputes', 10 (1996) *China Law & Practice*, pp. 16–21.

43 See Notice of the Supreme People's Court on Conscientious Studying and Implementing Provisions on Jurisdiction over Civil and Commercial Cases Involving Foreign Elements (*Fa* No. 22 [2002]). This Notice requires that intermediate people's courts having jurisdiction over civil and commercial cases involving foreign elements should establish a special division or chamber to deal with such cases. Those in areas where the number of foreign-related cases is small should set up special collegial panels to deal with such cases.

44 *Fashi* No. 5 [2002], issued on 25 February 2002, effective as of 1 March 2002. For explanations on the meanings of, and reasons for, the Provisions from the perspective of the SPC, see Zhang Jinxian, 'Guanyu Shewai Minshangshi Anjian Susong Guanxia Ruogan Wenti De Guiding De Lijie He Shiyong' (Understanding and Implementing the Provisions Concerning Court's Jurisdiction over Civil and Commercial Cases Involving Foreign Elements), 4 (2002) *Renmin Sifa*, pp. 4–5.

45 Since the 2002 Provisions were issued, the SPC has publicised a number of replies and approvals to authorise some basic people's courts and intermediate people's courts with the jurisdiction of handling first instance civil and commercial cases involving foreign elements. A list of the replies and approvals from 2002

1. BPCs in the economic and technological development zones approved by the State Council;
2. IPCs in the capital cities of provinces and autonomous regions as well as municipalities directly under the central government;
3. IPCs in special economic regions and especially designated cities in the state plan;
4. Other IPCs as designated by the SPC;
5. HPCs.

Article 2 states that, in the event of any dissatisfaction with the ruling or decision of the first instance rendered by a BPC, established in an economic and technological development zone upon the approval of the State Council, the case in the second instance should be subject to the jurisdiction of an IPC in the area concerned.

The scope of centralised jurisdiction encompasses five categories: contractual and tortious cases involving foreign elements; disputes over letters of credit; applications for the cancellation, recognition or enforcement of international arbitration awards; review of the legal effect of civil or commercial arbitration clauses involving foreign elements; applications for the recognition and compulsory enforcement of civil and commercial judgments and decisions made by foreign courts (Art. 3). The Provisions do not apply to cases involving border trade disputes occurring in border provinces adjoining foreign countries, real estate cases or copyright cases involving foreign elements (Art. 4).

Article 5 of the Provisions provides that issues relating to the jurisdiction over civil and commercial cases involving parties from Hong Kong, Macau or Taiwan should be handled through reference to these Provisions. According to Article 6, HPCs should supervise the allocation of jurisdiction of civil and commercial cases involving foreign elements. If any court accepts a civil and commercial case involving a foreign element by exceeding its statutory power, the relevant HPC should notify the court or make a ruling to transfer the case to the relevant people's court with the appropriate jurisdiction (Art. 7).

The number of foreign-related cases has largely increased due to the increasing frequency of transnational trade between China and other countries. To deal with this, the SPC has, in recent years, endowed certain IPCs and BPCs with jurisdiction over foreign-related cases in the form of individual approval. In December 2004, the SPC issued the Notice on Strengthening the Jurisdiction over Foreign-related Commercial Cases,[46] which required HPCs to apply for and obtain approval from the SPC concerning which IPC under their jurisdiction can be assigned to handle first instance commercial disputes with foreign elements. Moreover, Article 2 of the 2004 Notice states that the HPCs of Guangdong province and the four municipalities directly under the central government are authorised, in light of actual needs, to designate BPCs to exercise jurisdiction over foreign-related commercial cases within their respective jurisdictional area. Such HPCs are required to clarify the case jurisdiction division between BPCs and IPCs and to report the information to the SPC to keep on record. Consequently, jurisdiction over the trial of commercial cases involving foreign elements at the first instance has been expanded to include designated courts at the basic level.

The system of centralised jurisdiction has resulted in major adjustments to the Civil Procedure Law over the jurisdiction of foreign-related commercial cases. Aside from the HPCs, only a few BPCs and specific IPCs have such jurisdiction. This exclusive, centralised jurisdiction system has thus excluded most basic and intermediate courts from the jurisdiction of handling certain first

to 2012 is available at http://clink.chinalawinfo.com/pkulaw/slc/slfc.aspx?Gid=39353&Tiao=0&km=chl&subkm=4&db=chl. Last visited September 2013.

46 *Fa* No. 265 [2004], available at http://www.law-lib.com/law/law_view.asp?id=106265. Last visited September 2013.

instance foreign-related commercial cases.[47] The new system has upgraded the first instance of foreign-related commercial cases to selected IPCs; the majority of such cases are tried in the second instance by HPCs. Another consequence of this reform measure is the increase in the number of foreign-related commercial cases tried by the SPC.[48] To avoid more cases being brought to the HPCs and the SPC, the SPC has adjusted its policy to improve the centralised jurisdiction model, at the same time giving more IPCs and BPCs jurisdiction over foreign-related commercial cases. According to an official source at the SPC, in 2010, 167 IPCs and 67 BPCs were authorised by the SPC to handle foreign-related civil and commercial cases, with around 3,000 highly-qualified judges specialised in presiding over such cases.[49] However, some BPCs and IPCs are motivated by economic interest and do not want to give up their jurisdiction on foreign-related civil and commercial cases. Thus, if a party brings such a lawsuit to court, the court will accept and handle the case. The superior courts usually will not interfere with this.[50]

According to statistics released by the Fourth Civil Chamber of the SPC, in terms the foreign-related civil and commercial cases tried by Chinese courts in 2010, the top five countries whose citizens were related to the cases included the United States, Japan, South Korea, Germany and the United Kingdom. These cases accounted for 40 per cent of the total number of cases tried by courts.[51]

The Relationship between Higher and Lower Courts

The court structure in China is like a pyramid, with the SPC as the highest judicial authority supervising the administration of justice by courts at all local levels as well as special courts, along with the higher courts, who in turn supervise the trial work of the lower courts.[52] Under

47 Under Article 18 of the 1991 and 2007 CiPL (which is Art. 17 of the 2012 amended CiPL), basic people's courts have jurisdiction as courts of first instance over civil cases, unless otherwise provided in the CiPL. This means that the jurisdiction over civil cases at first instance, whether foreign-related or not, should generally be conferred upon basic people's courts, unless otherwise provided in the law. Article 19 of the 1991 and 2007 CiPL (which is Art. 18 of the 2012 amended CiPL) states that intermediate people's courts have jurisdiction as courts of first instance over 'major cases involving foreign elements'. According to Article 1 of the Opinions on Issues concerning the Implementation of the PRC Civil Procedure Law, which was issued by the SPC in 1992, the 'major cases involving foreign elements' refer to the cases involving foreign elements in which the sum of the disputed amount is large, the case is complex, or the number of parties concerned residing abroad is large. Thus, except for the 'major cases involving foreign elements', which is defined by the SPCs judicial interpretation, the jurisdiction over ordinary civil cases involving foreign elements should be reserved to basic people's courts.

48 Du Huanfang, 'Shiping Zuigao Renmin Fayuan Guanyu Shewai Minshangshi Anjian Susong Guanxia Ruogan Wenti De Guiding' (Commentary on the Provisions of the Supreme People's Court on Court's Jurisdiction over Civil and Commercial Cases Involving a Foreign Element), available at http://vip.chinalawinfo.com/newlaw2002/SLC/slc.asp?gid=335567750&db=art. Last visited February 2013.

49 Wang Doudou, 'Zuigaofa Tiaozheng Shewai Minshangshi Anjian Jizhong Guanxia Geju' (The SPC Adjusted the Structure of Centralised Jurisdiction on Foreign-related Civil and Commercial Cases) (1 November, 2011), *Fazhi Ribao* (Legal Daily). Available at http://news.xinhuanet.com/legal/2011-01/11/c_12966647.htm. Last visited September 2013.

50 *Ibid.*

51 *Ibid.*

52 See Article 127 of the 2004 Constitution. At the very beginning of the establishment of the PRC, the Provisional Organic Regulations of Courts, issued by the central government on 3 September 1951, provided that the adjudicative work of lower level courts should be led and supervised by higher-level courts. However,

the Constitution, the relationship between higher and lower courts is one of 'trial supervision', which is different to the 'leadership' relationship between higher and lower prosecution services. However, in practice the way in which higher courts supervise lower courts goes further than mere supervision. This is typically reflected in the re-trial systems, which include: remand for re-trial (*fahui chongshen*), re-opening a case (*zaishen*) and placing a request for further instruction (*qingshi baogao zhidu*).

The Remand for Re-trial System (Fahui Chongshen)

According to the CrPL, the CiPL and the ALL, an appellate court can remand a case to the first instance court for re-trial if the facts in the original judgment are unclear, the evidence insufficient, or if the original court has violated procedural rules prescribed for in the law. This system is commonly referred to as the *fahui chongshen* (re-trial) system.[53] The system is considered a supplementary remedy for the litigation rights of parties. The first instance court is situated near the litigants and retains most of the information concerning the case, which is convenient for litigants as well as conducive to ensuring that litigation is efficiently carried out.[54]

However, the application of this re-trial system has resulted in various problems. In judicial practice, numerous 'hidden rules' on re-trial have developed, one of which relates to judges at appellate courts often using the re-trial system in order to decrease their own caseload. Chinese research has shown that the percentage of cases remanded back to first instance courts for re-trial during the latter half of a year is for some reason higher than that in the first half. This can be attributed to the fact that some judges link the decision to remand cases back to the original courts to the number of cases they conclude annually. The number of cases which a judge is capable of concluding is used as an important indicator in evaluating the work of both trial chambers and judges within a court. Thus, both individual judges and courts take their statistics very seriously. Under such a system, judges often remand those cases which they deem too difficult to conclude within the year back to the first instance court for re-trial, thus improving their statistics. Consequently, some cases which should be adjudicated by the court of appeal are returned to the first instance court.[55]

Another hidden rule sees judges use the re-trial system to send back complicated and sensitive cases so as to avoid the risks associated with taking responsibility for the case. Between 1995

---

such a leadership relationship is not provided for in any law later on. Article 127 of the 1982 Constitution provides that the Supreme People's Court supervises the adjudicative work of local people's courts at all levels as well as special people's courts, and higher-level people's courts, which in turn supervise the adjudicative work of lower-level courts. Based on the Constitution, the OLPC, the CrPL, the CiPL and the ALL, all provide for the means and procedure of supervision. Such supervision is over individual cases and takes place after a case has been handled by a lower-level court. Consequently, according to the Constitution, the OLPC and the procedural laws, the relationship between higher- and lower-level courts is one of supervision rather than leadership.

53 This system is provided in Art. 153(3)(4) of the 1991 CiPL; Art. 61 of the ALL; and Art. 191 of the 1996 CrPL. None of these laws mentioned how many times an appellate court can send back a case for re-trial. The 2012 revised CrPL (Art. 225) and CiPL (Art. 170) made clear that remanding a case for re-trial can only take place once.

54 Zhang Yanli and Li Desheng, 'Dui Woguo Fahui Chongshen Zhidu De Sikao' (Reflections on the Remand for Re-trial System in China), 7(4) (2005) *Beijing Ligong Daxue Xuebao (Shehui Kexue Ban)* (Journal of the Beijing Institute of Technology, Social Science Edition), pp. 22–25.

55 Wang Fuhua and Rong Tianming, 'Minshi Susong Fahui Chongshen Zhidu Zhi Jiantao' (Examination of the Remand for Re-trial System in Civil Litigation), 1 (2007) *Faxue Yanjiu* (CASS Journal of Law), p. 7.

and 1998, some provincial higher courts issued regulations on judges' responsibility in ensuring that cases are handled correctly. Statistics show that during this period, the percentage of cases remanded for re-trial was also higher, since when judges were unsure of their judgment and were in jeopardy of being punished for handling cases incorrectly, remanding a case back for re-trial was deemed a safer option.[56]

In addition, when a case is sent back, the court of appeal usually sends an internal document indicating which pieces of evidence are needed, which facts require clarification, which laws should be applied and ultimately what the judgment should be. Although this can aid the lower court in deciding the case, it also imposes the opinions of the higher court on the lower court; consequently the latter can no longer make an independent decision.[57] Such a situation makes the appeal procedure meaningless, since the judgment of the original court merely mirrors the opinion of the court of appeal.

In connection with this, a common misunderstanding arises in the appeal procedure: if the court of second instance changes the original judgment, this is often seen as an indication that the case was incorrectly handled by the court of first instance. Thus, it appears as if the re-trial system aims to maintain a positive relationship between the higher and lower courts by trying not to undermine the original judgment or portray it as incorrect.[58] However, in practice the re-trial system causes conflict, not only between the lower and higher courts, but also between the parties concerned and the courts. Most of the cases that come before the appeal procedure are complicated cases which are difficult to handle and may involve external interference. As a result, some judges at the courts of appeal hope to avoid taking responsibility for such cases, and to do so send the cases back to the original courts for re-trial. Within the lower courts, the re-trial of a case also generates tension between judges. After a case is sent back, a new collegial panel will be formed and the re-trial may lead to a different judgment. A system whereby judges within one court change each other's judgments places judges under the supervision of one another. All these factors are capable of influencing a party's confidence in the lower courts.[59]

Re-opening a Trial (Zaishen)

If a higher-level court finds a definite error in a legally-effective judgment of a lower level court, it has the power to direct a lower court to conduct a re-trial (*zaishen*). It should be noted that those capable of invoking *zaishen* are not limited to the higher courts: a president of a court can also decide for *zaishen* in a case in which a legally effective judgment has been given by judges of the same court; the SPC and the SPP have the power to invoke *zaishen* in any legally effective judgments made by any lower-level courts; and a party to a case can also lodge a petition against a legally effective judgment for the purposes of a re-trial.[60]

---

56 *Ibid.*, p. 7.

57 Chen Weidong and Li Fengfei, 'Xingshi Ershen "Fahui Chongshen" Zhidu Zhi Chonggou' (Redesigning the System of "Remand for Re-trial" in the Second Instance Criminal Procedure), 1 (2004) *Faxue Yanjiu* (CASS Journal of Law), p. 124.

58 Cai Hui, 'Shishi Buqing Fahui Chongshen: Yige Yu Renshilun He Zhengju Guize Maodun De Zhidu' (Remand for New Trial on the Basis of Unclear Facts: A System Contradictory to Epistemology and Rules of Evidence), 9 (2006) *Falu Yingyong* (Journal of Law Application), p. 49.

59 *Ibid.*

60 See Article 13 of the OLPC; Arts. 203 to 207 of the 1996 CrPL; Arts. 241 to 243 of the 2012 amended CrPL; Arts. 177 to 179 of the 1996 CiPL; Arts. 198 to 213 of the 2012 amended CiPL; Arts. 62 to 64 of the 1989 ALL.

Zaishen is a trial supervision procedure provided for in the criminal, civil and administrative procedural laws. According to a survey conducted by distinguished Chinese legal scholars with the support of the SPC, the SPP and the NPC, although the trial supervision procedure can be applied to criminal, civil and administrative cases, civil cases account for a large proportion of all re-trial cases (for instance in one HPC in the centre of China, the figure stood at 90 per cent), and the rate of changes to the original judgment is also the highest for civil cases (in one HPC in the north of China, it was 85 per cent). In contrast, the rate of re-trial and the alteration of original judgments in criminal cases was around 20 per cent. Most of the cases concerned 'errors' of fact recognised by courts, as parties and courts usually have different opinions on what constitutes key evidence for the purposes of the court's decision. Some cases were re-tried on numerous occasions, each time resulting in different judgments; sometimes after multiple re-trials, the final judgment reverts back to the original judgment. Too often courts are forced to impose compulsory mediation on parties, since the evidence is incapable of producing a result that meets the expectations of the parties or the supervisory institutions. According to statistics, in a mere 10 per cent of cases investigated, both parties were satisfied with the result of the re-trial. The decisive factor that leads parties to bring an end to a lawsuit is that both parties had exhausted their remedy resources. The main motivator behind initiating a re-trial surrounds economic interests, which is also why debt cases have the highest rate of re-trial, as well as of revision of the original judgment. In most of these cases, parties find support from governmental officials. Some lawyers have expressed the view that the re-trial procedure had become a remedy specially designed for either those with power or rascals. Some judges estimated that the rate of success stood at around 5 per cent for parties that convinced the courts to trigger the re-trial supervision procedure solely on the basis of errors in the judgments and without using links to governmental officials. Around 50 per cent of re-trial cases that were concluded by mediation ended with the violation of the rights and interests of the creditors, and some cases were even concluded contrary to the law, but in keeping with the expectations of the supervisory institutions.[61]

The theoretical principle behind the *zaishen* system is that 'wrong judgments must be corrected'. Some Chinese scholars have argued that

> … seeking truth was the ideological belief of the Party and should also guide courts in handling cases. If an effective judgment was wrong by error of either identification of facts or application of law, the judgment should be corrected according to the principle that wrong judgments must be corrected. It was unrealistic to expect that all judgments would be correct due to the complexity of cases and limitations of judges. Some wrong judgments are unavoidable. If a case was wrongly judged, one must face the reality and correct it. In doing so, one could be called a good judge.[62]

Some also rationalise the situation by stating that the Chinese judicial system remains at a preliminary stage and the professional quality of judges is not as high as it should be, which inevitably results sometimes in wrongly-handled cases. The re-trial procedure is conducive to the exercising of the parties' right to petition, as well as the prosecution office's power of supervision.[63]

61 Fu Yulin, *Minshi Sifa Zhidu De Gongneng Yu Jiegou* (The Function and Structure of the Civil Judicial System) (Beijing: Beijing Daxue Chubanshe, 2006), pp. 87–89.

62 Chai Fabang (ed.), *Tizhi Gaige Yu Wanshan Susong Zhidu* (Institutional Reform and Perfecting the Litigation System) (Beijing: Zhongguo Renmin Gong'an Daxue Chubanshe, 1991), p. 273.

63 This was summarised by Chen Ruihua, 'Xingshi Zaishen Chengxu Yanjiu' (Research on the Re-trial System in Criminal Procedure), 6 (2000) *Zhengfa Luntan* (Tribune of Political Science and Law), pp. 105, 110.

However, growing criticism of the *zaishen* system from Chinese scholars and judges has indicated that the procedure creates tension between judges at lower and higherlevel courts, is usually too time-consuming with the parties involved suffering indefinitely, and often results in the finality of the effective judgment being fundamentally undermined.[64] Moreover, the power of the prosecution office to trigger the re-trial procedure in criminal and civil cases undermines the court's authority as the final judicial decision-maker. Consequently scholars have proposed the system of protest through the prosecution office against effective judgments be abolished.[65] On the other hand, voices from the prosecution office contend that the Constitution has empowered them with the function of supervising the courts' work, and a request for re-trial is one of the legitimate ways of realising this function.[66] Obviously, abolishing the procuratorate's power to invoke the re-trial of a case would involve modifying the supervisory power of the procuratorate within the Constitution, which could only be achieved if the Constitution is amended; at present there is no such sign that the Communist Party and the central government are willing to undertake such an action.

In response to the challenges put forward by critics and in order to improve the re-trial system, the 2007 amended CiPL produced some major changes. Firstly, an application for re-trial can only be submitted to a court at the next higher level. Thus, the court of first instance will no longer be put in the disagreeable position of being required to recognise its own mistakes or errors. Secondly, the legal arguments for a party initiating a re-trial were expanded from five in the 1991 CiPL to 13 under the 2007 CiPL, with specific emphasis on procedural errors.[67] Thirdly, the procedure for submitting a petition for re-trial, the time period in which the court must reply to the petition, as well as the time limit on informing the other party involved in the case, were outlined anew. Fourthly, courts are required to make a decision on whether to accept or reject a petition for re-trial within three months of receiving it; if an extension of the term is necessary in special circumstances, it must be approved by the president of the court. Fifthly, the time limit for a party to submit such an application for re-trial is within two years of the legally-binding judgment being passed.

The System of Request for Instruction (Qingshi Baogao Zhidu)

This refers to the system whereby a lower-level court requests a higher-level court to give its opinions on difficult or complicated cases; these opinions are in turn taken as instructions and reflected in the lower court's judgments. Different from the systems of remanding a case for re-trial

64 Jiang Baozhong, 'Xingshi Fahui Chongshen Zhidu De Wenti Yu Guifan' (Remand for the Re-trial System in Criminal Trials: Problems and Regulation), 11 (2010) *Fazhi Yanjiu* (Research on Rule of Law), pp. 76–80.

65 He Bing and Pan Jianfeng, 'Sifa Zhi Genben: Zuihou De Shenpan Yihuo Zuihao De Shenpan? – Dui Woguo Zaishen Zhidu De Shenshi' (The Foundation of the Administration of Justice: The Last Trial or the Best Trial? – A Re-Examination of the Re-trial System in China), 4 (2000) *Bijiaofa Yanjiu* (Journal of Comparative Law), p. 423. See also Zhou Shiqing, 'Shenpan Jiandu Zhidu De Gaige Yu Wanshan' (Reforming and Perfecting the Adjudicative Supervision Procedure), in Liang Baojian (ed.), *Renming Fayuan Gaige Lilun Yu Shijian* (Theory and Practice of the Reform of People's Courts) (Beijing: Renmin Fayuan Chubanshe, 1999), p. 326.

66 Qu Weidong and Zhang Yu, 'Xingshi Ershen Kangsu Zhidu Zhi Wanshan: Yi Bijiaofa Wei Shijiao De Zhankai' (Improvement of the System of Protection by Procuratorates in Second Instance Criminal Trials: From the Perspective of Comparative Law), 6 (2010) *Heilongjiang Shehui Kexue* (Heilongjiang Social Sciences), pp. 141–144.

67 See Article 179 of the 2007 CiPL.

and re-opening the trial of a case, the system of request for instruction is not provided for in any law; instead it has developed as an informally-improvised judicial practice. Liu Jiachen, former Vice-President of the SPC, once wrote:

> In most cases, when lower courts have difficult cases in hand, they request higher courts' opinions. The higher courts, if they have found that a case to be dealt with by the lower courts may have great impact, could take the initiative to give their instructions; this is conducive to correcting the application of law and reducing the number of wrongly handled cases at the preliminary stage. This could reduce the litigation costs as a whole and facilitate litigation efficiency … . if a higher court does not give timely instructions to a lower court, resulting in the occurrence of wrongly handled cases and causing harm to parties, this is considered as negligence of duty of the higher court.[68]

The practice of lower courts requesting instructions from higher courts already existed in the 1950s. Since the 1980s, the SPC has issued numerous documents intending to standardise the request procedure and the scope for requesting instruction. For instance, the SPC issued the Notice on Several Issues concerning Request for Instruction on Civil Cases in 1985;[69] the Notice on Issues to be Cautious of When Making Requests for Instruction in 1986;[70] the Notice on the Scope and Issues to be Cautious of When Making Requests for Instruction on Criminal Cases in 1995;[71] and the Notice on Strictly Implementing the System of Request for Instruction in Administrative Litigation in 2000.[72] Generally these notices require that the lower courts make requests for instruction to the next-level higher court; the request should be in written form and the case concerned should have been discussed by the adjudication committee of the court who made the request. The tendency of the SPC has been to gradually limit the scope of the cases and issues that can fall within the remit of the system of request for instruction: such cases are now required to have a major societal impact and provoke considerable legal controversy.[73]

Chinese scholars point out that the reasons underlying the existence of the system of request for instruction are multiple.[74] Firstly, the higher court has direct control over the lower courts' judicial decision-making. Such control includes the review by a higher court of any judgment made by a lower court, using a so-called evaluative system. The number of appeals, the number of cases in which a higher court rescinds the original judgment and remands the case back for re-trial, or makes a judgment contrary to the original one, are all elements for consideration in determining the success or failure of the work carried out by lower courts. Such evaluative results

---

68 Cited by He Weifang, 'Zhongguo Sifa Guanli Zhidu De Liangge Wenti' (Two Problems in China's Judicial Administration), 6 (1997) *Zhongguo Shehui Kexue* (China Social Sciences), p. 128; Liu Jiachun, *Susong Jiqi Jiazhilun* (Litigation and Its Value) (Beijing: Beijing Shifan Daxue Chubanshe, 1993), pp. 46–47.

69 *Faminzi* No. 5 [1985]. Available at http://vip.chinalawinfo.com/NewLaw2002/Slc/slc.asp?db=chl&gid=2346. Last visited September 2013.

70 *Fa (xingyi) han* No. 20 [1986]. Available at http://law.chinalawinfo.com/NewLaw2002/SLC/slc.asp?db=chl&gid=2737. Last visited September 2013.

71 *Fa* No. 151 [1995]. Available at http://law.chinalawinfo.com/newlaw2002/SLC/slc.asp?db=chl&gid=13504. Last visited September 2013.

72 *Faxing* No. 44 [2000]. Available at http://www.lawyee.com/Act/Act_Display.asp?RID=189160. Last visited September 2013.

73 Zhu Jingwen, *Zhongguo Falu Fazhan Baogao: Shujuku He Zhibiao Tixi* (Report on China Law Development: Database and Indicators) (Beijing: Zhongguo Renmin Daxue Chubanshe, 2007), pp. 182–183.

74 Chen Ruihua, 'Wei Zhongguo Anjian Qingshi Bamai' (A Diagnosis of the Practice of 'Request for Instruction on the Handling of Individual Cases' in China), 5 (2009) *Falu Zixun* (Legal Information), pp. 54–55.

have a direct impact in determining whether a court is qualified as a positive model of a court. Unsurprisingly, these factors compel lower courts to seek higher courts' opinions before they make their own judgments so as to prevent judgments from being rescinded and cases sent back for re-trial. Secondly, a president of a lower court regards his relationship with a higher court as significant, not only for his own future career opportunities and promotions, but also in terms of the court's overall operation. Within a court, the president has decisive influence over the outcome of a case. Thus, while handling difficult or complicated cases, a president of a lower court often takes the initiative to report the case to a higher court. Thirdly, the local Communist Party organisation, local government and local people's congress all have a degree of control over the local court's budget and personnel. Some local courts use the request for instruction to higher courts as a means to avoid conflict with local authorities. Under such circumstances, the opinion of the higher court can be used by the lower court to deliver a judgment without any outside interference from local institutions.

Although the system of request for further instruction may be justified by existing practical needs, the harm caused to the judicial independence of the lower courts is both evident and dramatic. Such requests are exercised as internal working methods; parties involved in a case are completely excluded from the procedure. Trial procedure becomes a mere formality as the decision has been made behind closed doors. In addition, a judgment of the lower court has actually been asserted by a higher court, and as such the original judgment represents both courts. Consequently, changing the judgment through the appeal procedure becomes an impossibility.[75]

Recognising the deficiencies of the system, the SPC recently urged courts to follow the procedure of the transfer of jurisdiction in dealing with cases in which the application of law would have a broad influence on similar cases.[76] In December 2010, the SPC issued the Opinions on Regulating the Trial Work Relations between the People's Courts at Different Levels,[77] which transformed the system of request for instruction into a system of the transfer of jurisdiction to the next higher-level court (*tiji*). Article 3 of the Opinions provides that when necessary, basic or intermediate people's courts may, according to the relevant legal provisions, submit a written application to the court at the next higher level asking the latter to try any of the following cases of the first instance which it has accepted: (1) major, difficult and complicated cases; (2) new-type cases; (3) cases bearing general significance in the application of law; and (4) cases for which it is improper for the people's court to have the jurisdiction to exercise judicial power. Article 4 states that the higher-level courts should promptly decide whether or not to try a case and issue a written decision approving or disapproving the trial transfer submitted by the lower-level courts.

However, it is likely that the abolition of the system of request for instruction cannot be simply achieved by the transfer of jurisdiction to a higher court; other systems, such as using the rate of appeal and the rate of re-trial cases to evaluate the work of lower courts, and the system of the responsibility of courts for wrongly-handled cases, need to be changed in order to guarantee that lower courts are capable of exercising their adjudicative power independently and without fear.

75 *Ibid.*, pp. 55–56.

76 Transfer of jurisdiction is provided in Arts. 20 and 24 of the Organic Law of the People's Courts, which allows basic and intermediate courts to request to transfer a case to a higher–level court if they consider the case to be significant and should be handled by a higher–level court. One could argue that it is actually contradictory to the OLPC if a court does not transfer a case, but instead asks for instruction from a higher court.

77 *Fafa* No. 61 [2010], available at http://www.court.gov.cn/qwfb/sfwj/yj/201104/t20110427_19930.htm. Last visited September 2013.

People's Assessors

The people's assessor system allows ordinary citizens, selected by courts, to participate in court hearings. People's assessors under the law enjoy the same powers as judges: they are responsible both for establishing the facts and for the application of the law.

The origins of the system can be traced back to the 1930s and 1940s in the Communist-controlled revolutionary base areas in the northwest of China, where the Communist Party invited masses of people to participate in dispute settlement in accordance with the policy of mass line.[78] Since the founding of the PRC in 1949, the people's assessor system has prevailed. Article 75 of the 1954 Constitution clearly stipulated that people's courts adjudicate cases by implementing the people's assessor system according to the law, thus rendering the people's assessor system a constitutional system. During the Cultural Revolution, this system vanished alongside the whole court system, but in the late 1970s the system was restored.

Article 41 of the 1978 Constitution provided that 'people's courts, in handling cases, implement the people's assessor system according to law'. However, the 1982 Constitution did not mention the people's assessor system, thus making it no longer a constitutional principle. In 1983, the NPC Standing Committee (NPCSC) issued the Decisions on the Amendment of the Organic Law of People's Courts, which stated that the collegiate panel of the first instance court might also consist of only judges. Since then, the people's assessor system has become merely optional for courts. This is reflected in the 1989 ALL (Art. 46), the 1991 CiPL (Art. 40), the 1996 CrPL (Art. 147) and the 2012 amended CiPL (Art. 39) and CrPL (Art. 178).

In the 1980s and 1990s, the people's assessor system as an optional device was used differently in the various courts. The system did not vanish; however, it also did not gain any serious attention.[79] As far as selection of assessors is concerned, some courts appointed certain individuals to act as people's assessors only when the need arose.[80] Some basic courts selected people's assessors from those laid-off from state-owned enterprises; these individuals acted as people's assessors for years.[81] Other courts preferred to select people's assessors from among the heads of residents' committees[82] and administrative officers, with the intention of controlling them more easily. Further, some courts tended to invite deputies of the local people's congress, members of the local committee of the Chinese People's Political Consultative Conference, and officials of basic-level administrative

78 Wang Liming, *Sifa Gaige Yanjiu* (Research on Judicial Reform) (Beijing: Falu Chubanshe, 2000), p. 384.

79 Wang Mingyuan, 'Zhongguo Peishen Zhidu Jiqi Wanshan' (China's Assessor System and Its Improvement), 21(4) (1999) *Faxue Yanjiu* (CASS Journal of Law), pp. 29–31.

80 Song Bing, 'Lun Renmin Peishenyuan De Zige' (Discussion on the System of Qualification of People's Assessors', in Liang Baojian (ed.), *supra* note 65, p. 279.

81 Lu Min, 'Guannian Bian Ge Yu Zhidu Chuangxin' (Change in Conception and Innovation of the System), in Liang Baojian (ed.), *supra* note 65, p. 288.

82 According to the Organic Law of the Urban Residents Committees of the People's Republic of China, an urban residents' committee is a mass organisation for self-government at the grassroots level, in which the residents manage their own affairs, educate themselves, and serve their own needs. Their main tasks include: publicising the Constitution, laws, regulations and state policies; handling the public affairs and public welfare services of the residents in the local residential area; mediating disputes among the residents; assisting in the maintenance of public security; assisting the local government or its agency in its work related to the interests of the residents; and conveying the residents' opinions and demands and making suggestions to the local government or its agency.

organs to act as people's assessors. Such choices were motivated by the fact that local courts needed the support and cooperation of the institutions that these individuals represented.[83]

Remuneration for these assessors was also problematic. The Organic Law of the People's Courts requires courts to give a reasonable allowance to people's assessors. However, many basic courts themselves suffer from limited financial resources and consequently are reluctant to incur further expenses by retaining assessors. Furthermore, economic reforms have contributed to a shift in perceptions, and individuals' sense of their value and role in society has changed. Individuals pay increased attention to their own interests and this has diluted their enthusiasm for participating in trials as a political activity.[84]

Moreover, even when people's assessors participated in the adjudication of cases, their role was often neglected, and their opinions were rebutted. Their appearance in court was merely a show (*pei er bu shen*).[85] Thus, unsurprisingly, many courts have long since ceased to invite people's assessors to participate in trials. In the 1990s, some scholars proposed the abolition of the people's assessor system in its entirety.[86]

However, following the early years of the 2000s, with the democratisation of the judicial system, the people's assessor system has been revitalised. In September 2000, the SPC submitted the Draft Decision on Perfecting the People's Assessor System to the National People's Congress Standing Committee.[87]After careful deliberation, in 2004 the NPCSC passed the Decisions on the Perfection of the People's Assessor System.[88] This was the first time that a law on people's assessors was issued by the NPCSC.

The Decisions require that when a people's court tries the following first instance cases, the people's assessors and judges should form a collegiate panel, except in cases for which the summary procedure is applicable or the law specifies otherwise: (1) criminal, civil and administrative cases with a substantial impact upon society; and (2) cases in which a criminal defendant, a civil plaintiff or defendant, or a plaintiff of an administrative case, files an application requesting the people's assessors to participate in a trial by the collegiate panel (Art. 2).[89]

---

83 Wang Mingyuan, *supra* note 79, pp. 44–46.

84 Yuwen Li, 'Court Reform in China: Problems, Progress and Prospects', in Jianfu Chen et al. (eds), *Implementation of Law in the People's Republic of China* (The Hague: Kluwer Law International, 2002), pp. 66–67.

85 Zhang Yunfeng, 'Lun Woguo Peishenyuan Zhidu' (Discussion of Our Country's Assessor System), in Liang Baojian (ed.), *supra* note 65, p. 266.

86 See Wang Liming, *supra* note 78, p. 388.

87 'Zuigaoyuan Dawen Guanyu Wanshan Renmin Peishenyuan Zhidu De Jueding' (The SPC Explanation on the Decisions of the National People's Congress Standing Committee on Improvement of the People's Assessor System), available at http://www.china.com.cn/chinese/law/649985.htm. Last visited September 2013.

88 Quanguo Renmin Daibiao Dahui Changwuweiyuanhui Guanyu Wanshan Renmin Peishenyuan Zhidu De Jueding (Decisions of the National People's Congress Standing Committee Regarding the Perfection of the System of People's Assessors), issued on 28 August 2004, effective on 1 May 2005. The document is available at http://www.china.com.cn/chinese/PI-c/648665.htm. Last visited September 2013.

89 In November 2009 the SPC issued the Provisions on Several Issues relating to the Participation of People's Assessors in Adjudication Activities, which concretise cases that 'have a substantial impact on society' into the following four categories: (1) cases involving the interests of a group; (2) cases involving public interests; (3) cases causing widespread concern among the general public; (4) cases with other major social impacts. *Fashi* No. 2 [2010], available at http://www.court.gov.cn/qwfb/sfjs/201002/t20100223_1736.htm. Last visited September 2013.

Citizens are qualified as people's assessor if they uphold the PRC Constitution; have reached the age of 23; are of good moral character and good health; and generally possess at least a junior college degree. Qualified citizens may be recommended to a basic court by their work unit or the local residents' committee where they are registered. A qualified citizen may also apply on their own initiative to a basic court. The basic court and the judicial administrative organ of the government at the same level will jointly examine the qualification of candidates, and a list of people's assessors will then be submitted by the president of the basic court to the people's congress standing committee for formal appointment. Citizens who are members of a people's congress standing committee, or who work in courts, the procuratorate, public security, state security, judicial administrative organs, or who are practising lawyers, cannot be people's assessors. Moreover, one is not qualified to be a people's assessor if one has been convicted of any crime or been dismissed from public office (Arts. 4, 5, 6 and 8).

The Decisions also state that the number of people's assessors is determined by the basic courts, according to their need, and approved by the people's congress standing committee at the same level. Once assigned by a people's congress standing committee, people's assessors serve a term of five years. When people's assessors are needed by a basic court to participate in hearing a case, they are selected randomly by computer from a list of people's assessors. When an intermediate people's court or a higher people's court needs people's assessors to join a collegiate panel, it must select them from a list of people's assessors of the basic people's court of its city.

Courts are required to provide people's assessors with subsidies for travel and food expenses incurred in their participation in trials and adjudicative activities. The employers of people's assessors, if any, should not openly, or in any disguised form, make deductions from assessors' wages, bonuses or other material benefits during the period of their participation in these activities. Courts should provide people's assessors, who have no fixed income, with subsidies on the basis of actual working days, by referring to the average level of local employee wages in the previous year. The subsidies to which people's assessors are entitled for their participation, and the expenses necessarily incurred in implementing the system of people's assessors by a court and judicial administrative organ, are to be included in the operational expenditure of the court and the judicial administrative organ, and should be guaranteed by the governmental treasury at the same level (Arts. 7, 9, 14, 18 and 19).

In 2010, the SPC issued the Provisions on Several Issues Relating to the Participation of People's Assessors in Adjudication Activities,[90] and the Certain Opinions Regarding Further Reinforcement and Advancement of the Work of People's Assessors.[91] These two documents further confirm the merits of the people's assessor system and improve the implementation of this system. The Certain Opinions emphasise that the people's assessor system contributes to the construction of a socialist judicial system and the realisation of judicial democracy, guaranteeing the fairness and honesty of the judiciary and strengthening judicial authority. It also specifies the scope and procedures for selection of assessors, the mechanism of random selection, the training of people's assessors and the funds they should be guaranteed.

The recent revival of the people's assessor system has been supported by numerous Chinese scholars, who argue that the system is necessary, because in the last 20 years the number of judges has not correlated to the increased number of cases; this has resulted in the expansion of the application of the summary procedure in both civil and criminal cases. Summary procedures are handled by a single judge; the combination of this with the low-level professionalism of judges has increased the

---

90 *Fashi* No. 2 [2010], available at http://www.court.gov.cn/qwfb/sfjs/201002/t20100223_1736.htm. Last visited September 2013.

91 *Fafa* No. 24 [2010], available at http://www.court.gov.cn/qwfb/sfwj/yj/201010/t20101027_10444.htm. Last visited September 2013.

risk of judges' authoritarianism. The participation of people's assessors in adjudicating cases can reduce the workload of judges as well as provide a deterrent for judges.[92] He Bing went as far as suggesting that the crux of the people's assessor system is to let the people be judged by ordinary people, rather than by judicial power laying completely with bureaucrats. He takes the view that the main problem facing the Chinese judicial system is judicial bureaucracy and the bureaucratic judgment style. Assessors derive from the masses and do not represent any bureaucratic apparatus, which could prevent them from becoming bureaucrats. Moreover, assessors represent the interests of society and have the potential to resist the tyranny of powerful organs.[93] He further argues that the people's assessor system could eventually contribute to juridical independence in China, since people's assessors are appointed by people's congresses, which implies that the decision of selection is made democratically. In this process, although it is impossible to prevent officials entirely from controlling the selection process, the increased number of people's assessors makes this control difficult. Since people's assessors do not have close links with governmental institutions, government control over them will also be weak, which contributes to the independence of people's assessors, and eventually to judicial independence.[94] This line of academic thinking places an ideal expectation on the people's assessor system. However, whether in practice the system is capable of developing in this way needs further observation.

At present there seems to be no comprehensive data on the actual number of people's assessors participating in the adjudication of cases. In the 2010 Work Report of the SPC to the NPC, it was stated that the number of people's assessors throughout the country had increased from 57,000 to 77,000, and that they had participated in the trials of 632,000 cases (25.1 per cent more than the previous year).[95] The Work Report of the SPC to the NPC in 2012 indicated that the total number of people's assessors had expanded to 83,000, and that the scope of participation in cases had also expanded to 1.116 million cases, which accounted for around 46.5 per cent of the total cases tried according to ordinary first instance procedures.[96]

A new phenomenon relevant to the people's assessor system is the emerging court initiative referred to as the people's jury experiment. In March 2010, An Dong, President of the Higher People's Court of Shaanxi province, who was also a deputy of the National People's Congress, submitted a draft bill to the NPC on establishing a jury system with Chinese characteristics. After this, the Higher People's Court of Shaanxi province selected three intermediate people's courts and 11 basic people's courts to conduct an experiment using a jury system in the trial of criminal cases. It was reported that courts in Shaanxi province have established a database of a jury pool consisting of deputies of the people's congress, members of local committees of the Chinese People's Political Consultative Conference, teachers from schools and universities, social workers and ordinary citizens who are enthusiastic about public interest work and have a good moral character – these individuals must have at least a high school education and social experience (a systematic legal education is not required), and must not have a criminal record. Jurors were then selected from the database by a computer, and a jury was consequently formed, consisting

92 He Bing, 'Sifa Zhiyehua Yu Mingzhuhua' (Professionalisation and Democratisation of the Judicial Work), 4 (2005) *Faxue Yanjiu* (CASS Journal of Law), p. 110.

93 *Ibid.*, p. 109.

94 *Ibid.*, p. 111.

95 Renmin Fayuan Gongzu Niandu Baogao (2010) (The Annual Work of the People's Court in 2010), available at http://www.court.gov.cn/qwfb/gzbg/201007/t20100716_7756.htm. Last visited September 2013.

96 Renmin Fayuan Gongzu Niandu Baogao (2012) (The Annual Work of the People's Court in 2012), available at http://www.court.gov.cn/qwfb/gzbg/201204/t20120413_175925.htm. Last visited September 2013.

of nine or 13 jurors. A chairman was selected by the jury to organise the members to attend court hearings, preside over jury discussions, and summarise the juries' opinions. According to the vice-president of the Higher People's Court of Shaanxi province, six or seven cases were tried with the participation of a people's jury in 2010 in Shaanxi province. The jury experiment should be considered a supplement to the people's assessor system, a working mechanism but not yet a fully-fledged system. At the core of such an experiment is judicial democracy and judicial openness, which aims at incorporating public opinion into judicial decision-making. The outcome of the jury's deliberations is used by the collegiate panel as an important reference; however, it is not necessarily used as the basis for the judgment given by the panel. Similar experiments have been carried out in courts in Henan province.[97]

Since such experiments are new and innovative no convincing studies have yet been undertaken to outline their pros and cons. Theoretically speaking though, the use of people's juries is conducive to expanding public participation in adjudication, reducing the number of petition cases which is now a priority of courts under political pressure, and strengthening public trust in judicial authorities. However, Chinese legal scholars are questioning the composition, functions and usefulness of the opinions of the jury. One scholarly comment observed that the experiment on jury trials is based more on political than legal considerations; more idealistic than rationalistic. This typically reflects the current feature of judicial reform in which the political preference determines the direction of the judicial reform.[98]

Adjudication Committees

According to the Organic Law of People's Courts, each court is required to set up an adjudication committee, generally comprising the president, vice-presidents, heads of the trial divisions and senior judges. The committee sums up judicial experience, and discusses important or difficult cases and other issues relating to judicial work. The president of a court presides over the meetings of the adjudication committee.[99] In essence, the adjudication committee is a permanent organ with adjudicative, political and administrative powers in court.

The most controversial issue relating to the adjudication committee is its function in discussing important and difficult cases. Neither the OLPC nor the 1991 CiPL and the 1989 ALL specify how this function is to be exercised. Only Article 149 of the 1996 CrPL provides that, in dealing with a difficult, complicated or major case on which the collegiate panel considers it difficult to make a decision, the collegiate panel should refer the case to the president of the court in order to decide whether to submit the case to the adjudication committee for discussion and decision; the collegiate panel should execute the decision of the adjudication committee. The substance of this Article is retained by Article 180 of the 2012 amended CrPL; however, which cases fall within the category of 'difficult, complicated and major cases' is not defined. The 1998 SPC judicial interpretation on Explanations on Several Issues concerning the Implementation of the Criminal Procedure Law (for Trial Implementation), provides that difficult, complicated and major cases include: (1) cases which may result in the imposition of the death penalty; (2) cases in which the members of the collegiate panel have seriously differing opinions; (3) cases challenged by the procuratorate; (4)

97 Xu Xin et al., *Zhongguo Sifa Gaige Niandu Baogao 2010* (Annual Report on China's Judicial Reform [2010]), p. 20. The Report is available at http://blog.sina.com.cn/s/blog_656952ec0101pogd.html. Last visited January 2014.

98 *Ibid.*

99 See Article 10 of the Organic Law of the People's Court.

cases which have had a significant societal influence; (5) other cases which need to be determined by the collegiate panel.[100]

There is no comprehensive survey on how often adjudication committees in various courts hold meetings to discuss difficult and complicated cases. Yet, some sporadic sources may offer an insight into general practice. According to the statistics of a higher people's court in 1998, the adjudication committee held a total of 138 meetings within that year and discussed and approved 1,011 cases, which accounted for approximately one third of the total number of cases concluded in that year. In order to guarantee that most cases could be discussed and approved on time, the court ruled that the adjudicative committee should organise two meetings a week to discuss cases. Since members of the adjudication committee consist of the president, vice-presidents and heads of various trial divisions, not all members could attend the scheduled meetings. Sometimes the committee had to decide on cases with half of its members absent.[101] It was said that the adjudication committee in the Higher People's Court of Hubei province held meetings once a week to discuss cases (mainly criminal cases with a possible death penalty sentence). The Adjudication Committee of the SPC holds one regular meeting per week. Nowadays this committee is divided into two groups: one specialising in criminal matters and the other specialising in civil and administrative affairs.[102]

A judge at an intermediate people's court described how the adjudication committee discussed cases at his court:

> a specific responsible judge (*chengban faguan*) reports a case orally, and even though the reported contents may not reflect the true facts of a case, one can hardly discover or correct them; some responsible judges take a long time to report all the details without a clear order, and members of the adjudication committee ask questions repeatedly, which results in protracted meetings; the oral report, and the fact that members of the adjudication committee comment immediately without time to study the case and the relevant laws, means that the quality of the decision cannot be guaranteed. Sometimes a decision of the adjudication committee is changed later by the same committee.[103]

Since the 1990s, the system of adjudication committees has been one of the central issues of debate in Chinese legal circles. Those who support the system have argued that it offers the possibility of using the collective wisdom of a court and of avoiding the limitations of a judge or a collegiate panel. They emphasise that most members of adjudication committees are senior judges, who have greater judicial and social experience; in contrast, Chinese judges are generally relatively young and lacking in such experience. Consequently, the adjudication committee system can be used as

---

100 See Article 115 of the Explanations. Since the fifth point is open-ended, in practice the range of cases discussed and decided by the adjudication committee is rather wide. For instance, such committees also determine cases in which an accused may be found innocent, or a case in which the victim has a special position, such as a member of the people's congress, a well-known person, a foreigner, a citizen from Hong Kong, Macao or Taiwan. See Chen Ruihua, 'Zhengyi De Wuqu: Ping Fayuan Shenpan Weiyuanhui' (A Misunderstood Area in the Administration of Justice: A Commentary on the Adjudication Committee System), 2 (1998) *Beida Falu Pinglun* (Peking University Law Review), p. 385. In 2010, the SPC produced Implementing Opinions on Reforming and Perfecting the Adjudication Committee System of People's Courts, which lists the functions and scope of the adjudication committee of the SPC and local courts on adjudicating cases, supervision, administration and guiding adjudicating work. *Fafa* No. 3 [2010], available at http://www.court.gov.cn/qwfb/sfwj/yj/201003/t20100331_3604.htm. Last visited September 2013.

101 Liang Baojian (ed.), *supra* note 65, pp. 233–234.

102 Interview with a judge at the Supreme People's Court in July 2012.

103 *Supra* note 101, p. 236.

a device to reduce the incidence of misjudged cases. They also contend that since courts can find themselves in a situation in which extra-judicial interference in a court's work is not uncommon and there is a lack of protection for individual judges against such interference, the adjudication committee may use its collective power to deter external interference.[104] In an empirical study of adjudication committees in basic people's courts, Su Li concluded that the existence of such a committee was conducive to precluding judicial corruption, since it was easier to corrupt one single judge or three judges in a collegiate panel than to do so with members of an adjudication committee. He also pointed out that the committee could ensure unified law enforcement within its jurisdiction.[105]

However, it could be argued that the fundamental shortcomings of the adjudication committee system lay in the separation of the trial from the decision-making processes. Even though the OLPC merely provides the adjudication committee with the power to 'discuss' cases, in reality, committees 'decide' cases. Judges who are involved in the trial do not deliver the final judgment and members of the adjudication committee (who do not hear the case) make the final decision for the judges. This can be equated to 'handling a case in camera' or a 'black box operation' (*anxiang caozuo*). Adjudication committee members do not usually attend the hearings, nor do they have time to read the case files. Furthermore, adjudication committee meetings are conducted in closed sessions; this is contrary to the system of open trial, and the rights of the defence are thus rendered useless. Consequently, some Chinese lawyers have complained that while they make their defence in court, the judges do not listen to them (*nibian nide, wopan wode*). The system of the adjudication committee emphasises the hierarchical relationship between the president, other leaders and the judges; this is a typical example of how the administrative management of adjudication within Chinese courts undermines the internal independence of judges. The adjudication committee system may also be abused by committee members, who can interfere with the function of the collegiate panel, and offer favours to one of the parties involved in the litigation.[106] Concurrently, judges may use the adjudication committee system to shirk the responsibilities and risks in handling cases.[107]

Unsurprisingly, an increasing number of scholars have criticised the deficiencies of the adjudication committee system, in particular its negative impact on open trials and judicial independence. They advocate the abolition of the system, and argue that judges and the collegiate

---

104 Chen Guangzhong and Daniel Prefontaine (eds), *Lianheguo Xingshi Sifa Zhunze Yu Zhongguo Xingshi Fazhi* (The United Nations Standards and China's Legal System of Criminal Justice) (Beijing: Falu Chubanshe, 1998), p. 93. See also Su Li, *Songfa Xia Xiang* (Bring the Law to the Countryside) (Beijing: Zhongguo Zhengfa Daxue Chubanshe, 2000).

105 Su Li, 'Jiceng Fayun Shenpan Weiyuanhui Zhidu De Kaocha Ji Sikao' (Investigation and Thought on Adjudicative Committees at Basic People's Courts), 2 (1998) *Beida Falu Pinglun* (Peking University Law Review), pp. 320–364. Available at http://article.chinalawinfo.com/Article_Detail.asp?ArticleId=3655. He Weifang challenged Su Li's finding with more convincing arguments – that the adjudication committee system is in contravention of the basic components of a fair trial; has no role in restricting judicial corruption; and cannot resolve, but only worsen, public trust in judicial authority. See He Weifang, 'Guanyu Shenpan Weiyuanhui De Jidian Pinglun' (A Few Comments on the Adjudication Committees), 2 (1998) *Beida Falu Pinglun* (Peking University Law Review), pp.365-373. Available at http://article.chinalawinfo.com/Article_Detail.asp?ArticleId=3663. Both last visited September 2013.

106 Wang Chenguang, 'Introduction: An Emerging Legal System', in Wang Chenguang and Zhang Xianchu (eds), *Introduction to Chinese Law* (Hong Kong: Sweet & Maxwell Asia, 1997), p. 25.

107 Su Li, *supra* note 105, p. 14.

panel should be entrusted with unrestrained, substantive independence, thus giving the parties involved in a case the opportunity to have their case heard openly and without prejudice.[108]

Recognising some shortfalls, the SPC has taken measures to improve the system. The First Five-Year Reform Programme of People's Courts, issued by the SPC in October 1999 outlines a proposal to reduce the number of cases to be handled by adjudication committees. Item 20 of the Programme stated that, except for the difficult, complicated and major cases which were referred to the president of the court by the collegiate panel and were to be discussed by the adjudication committee, all cases should be heard and judged by the collegiate panel; the president and heads of trial divisions should not individually change the decision made by the collegiate panel. Item 22 pointed out that the responsibilities of adjudication committees should be standardised: the adjudication committee should, on a gradual basis, only discuss the issues surrounding the application of law on a limited number of difficult, complicated and major cases.[109]

The Second Five-Year Reform Programme of People's Courts re-emphasised the further reform of the adjudication committee system by strengthening the professional quality of the committees. It set up the goal that the SPC would establish specialised criminal and civil/administrative adjudication committees; the HPCs and IPCs could establish criminal committees and civil/administrative committees according to their need. It also made clear that the composition of adjudication committees should be reformed to ensure that experienced and qualified judges could partake in the committees. Furthermore, it was established that the working method of adjudication committees should be reformed from a system of meetings to hearings, and that members of adjudication committees could form the collegiate panel by themselves or with other judges to hear difficult, complicated or major cases, or those involving common questions of the application of law.[110]

In the Third Five-Year Reform Programme of People's Courts, issued by the SPC in 2009, no concrete objectives were set out to deepen the reform further. Instead, the Programme called for the implementation of a system in which the chief procurators and vice-chief procurators have the right to attend, without voting rights, the meetings of the adjudication committees of the people's courts at the corresponding level.[111] In January 2010, the SPC and SPP co-issued Implementing Opinions on the Attendance of the Chief Procurators of the People's Procuratorates at the Meetings of the Adjudication Committees of the People's Courts.[112] Under the Opinions, chief procurators are entitled to attend meetings of adjudication committees on public prosecution cases in which the defendant may be ruled not guilty; cases in which the defendant may be sentenced to death; cases

---

108 Cai Dingjian argued that the adjudication committee 'should be abolished. The responsibility for the proper handling of cases should rest with the presiding judge. This will reduce the need for multiple judges, lower the number of procedural steps, and shorten the time of litigation, thereby lowering procedural costs and increasing procedural efficiency.' Cai Dingjian, *supra* note 26, p. 154. He Weifang, *Sifa De Linian Yu Zhidu* (Judicial Theory and System) (Beijing: Zhongguo Zhengfa Daxue Chubanshe, 1998), pp. 139–151. Xia Jingwen and Zhang Hua, 'Dangdai Zhongguo Sifa Yunzuo Xianzhuang De Shizheng Kaocha Ji Lixing Sikao' (The Current Situation of the Administration of Justice in China: Empirical Research and Rational Reflection), 5 (2000) *Faxue Yanjiu* (CASS Journal of Law), p. 55.

109 *Fafa* No. 28 [1999]. The text of the first Five-Year Reform Programme of People's Courts is available at http://law.chinalawinfo.com/newlaw2002/SLC/slc.asp?db=chl&gid=23701. Last visited September 2013.

110 *Fafa* No. 18 [2005]. The text of the Second Five-Year Reform Programme of People's Courts is available at http://www.law-lib.com/law/law_view.asp?id=120832. Last visited September 2013.

111 *Fafa* No. 14 [2009]. The text of the Third Five-Year Reform Programme of People's Courts is available at http://old.chinacourt.org/public/detail.php?id=350101. Last visited September 2013.

112 *Fafa* No. 4 [2010]. Available at http://www.court.gov.cn/qwfb/sfwj/yj/201003/t20100331_3606.htm. Last visited September 2013.

with a court judgment against which the people's procuratorate protests; or when the adjudication committee discuss other topics relating to procuratorial work.

All of the participants, with or without voting rights, are required to maintain secrecy regarding the content of discussion during the meeting. The SPC and the SPP made it clear that the implementation and improvement of the provision on the attendance of the meetings of the adjudication committees of the people's courts by the chief procurators or vice-chief procurators who were entrusted by the chief procurators was one of the tasks prescribed by the document (*Zhongban* No. 28 [2008]) issued by the Central Committee of the CPC.[113] Procurators' participation at the meetings of adjudication committees can be viewed as a judicial retreat.

Conclusion

Over the past years court jurisdiction has become increasingly complicated and has not only been provided for in the Organic Law of the People's Courts, the CiPL, the CrPL and the ALL but also concretised and modified by the judicial documents of the SPC. There are mainly four types of jurisdiction: jurisdiction by levels, territorial jurisdiction, transferred and designated jurisdiction, and jurisdiction over foreign-related cases. While it may not be difficult for a public procuratorate to decide in which court to prosecute a case, it is not that easy for private parties to decide to which court they should bring their civil or administrative disputes. For administrative cases conventional experience dictates that a plaintiff should seek to bring his case to a court at as high a level as possible. This is mainly to prevent an administrative case being handled by a BPC where local governmental intervention is most likely to occur. The rate of losing cases by administrative agencies is used in some courts as a benchmark in evaluation of the performance of the courts, which consequently affects the decision of courts on whether or not to accept administrative cases. The difficulty of getting an administrative case accepted by a court (*li an nan*) is the first hurdle for plaintiffs. For civil cases, with regard to territorial jurisdiction, parties are inclined, for convenience, to choose the court of the place where he or she is domiciled. When it comes to contract disputes, the most controversial question in practice is how to identify the place where the contract is performed. This is frequently disputed between plaintiffs and defendants who prefer to choose the jurisdiction most favourable to themselves. The uncertainty in law and lack of judicial interpretation intensify the dispute and allow parties to engage in 'forum shopping'. In addition, China has set up a special jurisdiction for foreign-related cases which is an outcome of the government policy that dictates 'any foreign-related matters are not small matters' (*waishi wu xiaoshi*). Chinese courts are more cautious in dealing with foreign-related cases. As a result of the centralised jurisdiction over foreign-related commercial cases introduced by the SPC since 2002, most of such cases are handled by competent judges at IPCs in Beijing, Shanghai, Guangzhou and a few economically developed cities.

The relationship between the higher- and lower-level courts is not simply a matter of different levels to ensure that any case can be appealed to a court at a higher level. In China, a higher court can influence the judgment-making of a lower court in various ways. The higher courts are often treated as 'leaders' of the lower courts. Such a relationship, together with the system of adjudication committees within each court, reflects the administrative character of the adjudicative system. Apart from this, the administrative means of appointment, promotion and management of

113 *Ibid.*

judges, and the frequent governmental intervention into judicial work, has forced Chinese courts to operate in a way similar to that of administrative organs.

With regard to the system of people's assessors, people's assessors are supposed to enjoy the same rights as judges. They are in charge not only of the establishment of the facts, but also of the application of law. Given that most assessors do not have sufficient legal knowledge, it is almost impossible for them to fulfil both functions. In practice, most assessors indicate that they hold the same views as the judges. Even in cases where they do have different opinions, they tend not to express them; furthermore, even when they do decide to speak out, it is by no means certain that their contribution will have any impact on a judge's decision.[114] The recent resurgence of the people's assessor system is largely the result of political motives, and has an *ad hoc* nature. The new experiment that sees a jury's participation in public hearings can be assessed as a supplement to the people's assessor system.

---

114 Lu Min, *supra* note 81, p. 288. See also Stanley Lubman, *Bird in a Cage: Legal Reform in China after Mao* (Stanford, CA: Stanford University Press, 1999).

Chapter 2
Courts' Relationships with Extra-Judicial Bodies

Introduction

China does not separate legislative, executive and judicial powers in the Western style, but has its own system for fulfilling state functions: each of the three functions are carried out by the people's congresses (parliament), government and courts respectively. The operation of these organs is based on the principles of separation of functions, mutual coordination and mutual restriction. This structure forces the courts to have close links with, and indeed remain under the supervision of, the legislative and executive powers. Furthermore, as in the Soviet model of the procuratorate system, Chinese procuracy is entrusted by the Constitution and procedural laws with the unique power of the supervision of the courts' work. Perhaps most importantly, the Communist Party of China (CPC) holds a superior position above all state powers. This renders the Party's policies and decisions being carried out by all state organs, the courts being no exception.

The horizontal relationships between the court and the legislature, the CPC, government organs and the procuratorate significantly shape the current Chinese court system. This chapter discusses the most controversial issues between courts and other organs, especially on matters that are significant to the courts' independent adjudication of cases. Generally speaking, one can assume that nowadays courts decide most cases according to law.[1] However, the legitimacy provided by law concerning the supervision of the courts' work by extra-judicial organs creates practical uncertainty and unpredictability: interference in a court's work by the Party, government, the people's congresses and procuracy may occur in any case, at any time and in any place. Compared to other state powers, especially executive power, judicial power remains weak. Nevertheless, the relationship between the courts and other functions of the state has undergone, and is still undergoing, quiet changes. As a consequence of the economic reform and social transition, the role of courts in society has significantly strengthened. Citizens and companies are increasingly using courts to settle their disputes, which raises the social legitimacy of courts. At the same time, the courts' handling of large cases strengthens the courts' 'political legitimacy' in dealing with other state powers.

Courts and the People's Congress

People's congresses are the legislative organ in China. At the central level the National People's Congress (NPC) is the highest legislature.[2] There are three local-level people's congresses at provincial, city and county levels. The NPC has about 3,000 deputies; they are not full-time legislators but have jobs as workers, farmers, civil servants, business people or academics. The NPC holds one plenary session of approximately two weeks each year. Its daily operation is in

1 Randall Peerenboom, 'Judicial Independence and Judicial Accountability: An Empirical Study of Individual Case Supervision', 55 (2006) *The China Journal*, p. 67.

2 The NPC is the highest organ of state power. See Art. 57 of the 2004 Constitution.

the hands of the NPC Standing Committee (NPCSC), which has approximately 175 members and holds bimonthly meetings.[3] The NPC and its Standing Committee have the power to enact, revise and abolish law, and provincial people's congresses have the power to make local regulations.

The relationship between people's congresses and courts manifests in two ways: people's congresses appoint and dismiss presidents and judges of courts at the corresponding level,[4] and they supervise the implementation of law by the courts. The routine supervisory work takes place in various forms, such as the review and approval of the court's work reports, reviewing whether judicial interpretation is in compliance with the law, investigating and making proposals to courts on issues of serious public concern, and handling petitions and complaints regarding alleged unlawful conduct by judicial officers.[5] The most controversial issues surrounding the court's relationship with people's congresses are whether such supervision could extend to interfere with individual cases handled by courts, and the approval of the annual report of the court's work by the people's congresses.

The Supervision of Individual Cases (Ge An Jiandu) by People's Congresses

The most controversial issue in relation to the courts and people's congresses is the supervision of individual cases by the latter. This phenomenon emerged in the late 1980s at some local people's congress standing committees when they handled people's visits and letters regarding complaints of judicial corruption, resulting from cases wrongly or unfairly decided by the courts. In 1990, Jiang Zemin, President of China at the time, pointed out at a conference:

> At present, the phenomena that courts do not follow law or enforce law strictly are very serious, the public are very critical about these. If we allow such phenomena to exist, they will harm the seriousness and the authority of law and threaten the stability of the state and the society. The people's congresses and their standing committees should play their role of legal supervision justly and forcefully.[6]

---

3 The number of members of the NPCSC has changed over time. At the 1st and 2nd NPCSC there were 79 members, increasing to 155 during the 6th to 9th NPCSC; since the 10th NPCSC the number has remained at 174. See Zhu Jingwen (ed.), *Zhongguo Falu Fazhan Baogao Shujuku He Zhibiao Tixi* (Report on China Law Development: Database and Indicators) (Beijing: Zhongguo Renmin Daxue Chubanshe, 2007), p. 79.

4 According to Articles 62 and 67 of the 2004 amended Constitution and Art. 34 of the 2006 amended Organic Law of the People's Court, the President of the SPC is elected and removed by the NPC; deputy presidents and judges of the SPC are nominated by the President of the SPC and appointed and dismissed by the NPCSC. At the local level, presidents of local courts are elected and dismissed by the corresponding level people's congresses; deputy presidents and judges are nominated by the president and appointed and dismissed by the people's congress standing committees of the corresponding level. However, this is the procedure provided by the laws which can only be viewed merely as a formality since candidates have been first examined and approved by the relevant Party and government organs. China follows a system of 'Party controls the cadres'. Presidents of courts and judges are different rankings of cadre. The general rule is that the higher the position, the more of a political appointment it will be.

5 People's congresses not only scrutinise judicial work, they oversee the government as well. For the growing strength of local people's congresses in governmental oversight, see Young Nam Cho, 'From "Rubber Stamps" to "Iron Stamps": The Emergence of Chinese Local People's Congresses as Supervisory Powerhouses', 171 (2002) *China Quarterly*, pp. 724–740.

6 Cited in Zuo Weimin and Feng Jun, 'Xunqiu Guifan Yu Jishu De Helixing: Zuigao Fayuan Yu Quanguo Renda De Guangxi Yanjiu' (Research on the Relationship between the SPC and the NPC), in Zuo Weimin et al. (eds), *Zuigao Fayuan Yanjiu* (Research on Supreme Courts) (Beijing: Falu Chubanshe, 2004), p. 238.

By the end of the 1990s, the supervision of individual cases by people's congresses reached its height. A number of local people's congresses issued regulations and rules to guide such supervision.[7] This supervisory role had a wide scope, including cases of effective judgments which were suspected of incorrect fact-finding and application of law; pending cases which might involve the violation of procedural law, such as excessive detention beyond the period provided for in the law, illegal detention, torture, illegal sealing or confiscation of property; cases where judicial officers had accepted illegal gains and other matters involving corruption; cases in which files were refused by courts; cases where the judgment given could not be enforced; and cases which had a wide social impact and regarding which the mass media showed great concern. However, a field study has shown that in reality supervision has even extended beyond the scope established in the regulations, touching upon all kinds of civil, criminal, administrative and enforcement cases relating to the application of law, procedural issues and judicial corruption.[8]

There were also cases where courts found themselves in a difficult position due to various interventions and thus took the initiative to ask the people's congress to engage in supervision.[9] The supervisory procedure was also varied; some people's congresses sent supervision letters to courts, some just made phone calls, some exchanged their opinions with the courts and some just directly gave their own opinions. Some supervisory acts took place while a case was pending while other interventions were triggered after a judgment had become effective. Some people's congresses initiated supervision through their legal committees, or through internal and judicial committees, while some set up specific investigation committees.[10] Obviously, supervision by some local people's congresses was lacking in procedure and without limits in its scope. Consequently, such supervision, which was intended to ensure that courts handle cases fairly and correctly, has become a problem in itself.

Some Chinese commentators have challenged the supervision by people's congresses in individual cases by arguing that the legal basis for such supervision was lacking; that it was not conducive to fostering judicial independence and could easily be abused to effect more illegal intervention in a court's adjudicative work; that the adjudication of cases demands professional judges, and people's congresses do not have such professional quality; and that the lack of procedural rules resulted in some deputies interfering in cases on their own initiative, meaning that supervision by people's congresses became supervision by a deputy. Moreover, judicial unfairness and corruption are mainly caused by institutional shortcomings and the low quality of judges,

---

7 For instance, in 1997 the People's Congress Standing Committee of Guangdong Province issued the Rules of All People's Congress Standing Committee in Guangdong Province in Implementing Supervision of Individual Cases; in 1999 the People's Congress Standing Committee of Weifang City in Shandong Province issued the Provisional Methods of the People's Congress Standing Committee of Weifang City on Exercising Supervision of Individual Cases Handled by Judicial Organs and Administrative Law Enforcement Organs within the City; in 2005 the People's Congress Standing Committee of Tanyin County in Henan Province issued the Provisional Methods on Implementing Supervision on Individual Cases. See Zhu Jingwen, *supra* note 3, p. 177.

8 Cai Dingjian (ed.), *Jiandu Yu Sifa Gongzheng: Yanjiu Yu Anli Baogao* (Supervision and Judicial Fairness: Research and Case Report) (Beijing: Falu Chubanshe, 2005), p. 49.

9 Chen Sixi, 'Tanxun Ge'an Jiandu Yu Sifa Gongzheng De Qihe' (Discussion on Supervision of Individual Cases and Judicial Fairness), in Cai Dingjian (ed.), *ibid.*, p. 77.

10 Wang Chenguang and Zhang Huning, 'Renda Jiandu Yu Sifa Duli He Sifa Gongzheng' (Supervision by People's Congress and Judicial Independence and Judicial Fairness), in Cai Dingjian (ed.), *supra* note 8, p. 105.

which can only be resolved by further reforms to increase judicial independence and impartiality, and to improve judicial professionalism as a whole, and not by external supervision.[11]

Arguments supporting such supervision held that as people's congresses had the power to supervise law enforcement, which included supervising individual cases; that such supervision could help resolve some cases of injustice; that such supervision reflected public demand, people's congresses, as organisations representing people, should respond to such needs.[12]

Strictly speaking there is no sound legal basis for a people's congress to supervise a court's handling of individual cases, since the Constitution only provides in general terms that people's congresses supervise courts' work and ensure laws are respected and enforced. However, popular support for the supervision of individual cases came about due to widespread judicial corruption, common complaints of low-quality judges and an increase in the number of cases wrongly handled by the courts.

In practice both positive and negative instances of such supervision have been reported. Positive effects include ensuring that justice is upheld and that courts feel compelled to correct their mistakes. For example, a judge in a basic court had beaten one of the parties involved in the case – this individual petitioned to various organs but to no avail. Only with the assistance of the local people's congress could the judge be punished for his behaviour. In another case, a judge at a basic court cooperated with a party to fabricate evidence in order to get money from another party, but with the supervision of the people's congress the perpetrators were found guilty.[13] In a criminal case in Hefei city of Anhui province, Wang Luncai was accused of intentional injury to Wang Liping based on forensic identification issued by the public security bureau of Hefei city. Proceedings began in 1996, with the case going to the basic people's court of Feidong county on three occasions, following three protests by the procuratorate at the same level. The intermediate court of Hefei city finally handed down a guilty verdict in December 1999. The people's congress standing committee of Hefei city established an *ad hoc* investigatory committee in 2000 and finally ruled that the evidence brought forward in the case was insufficient, and Wang Luncai should not be found guilty.[14] In 2003, the people's congress standing committee of Xingcheng city of Liaoning province established an *ad hoc* investigatory committee to investigate the action of the people's court of Xingcheng city during the enforcement of a case which it concluded in 1997. It was discovered that, in the enforcement, the grain, houses and land which was seized by Xingcheng people's court was valued at a price which was obviously

---

11 Wang Liming, *Sifa Gaige Yanjiu* (Research on Judicial Reform) (Beijing: Falu Chubanshe, 2000), pp. 463–465. Cai Dingjian, 'Renmin Daibiao Dahui Ge'an Jiandu De Xianzhuang Jiqi Gaige' (Current Situation and Reform of Supervision of Individual Cases by the People's Congress), in Cai Dingjian (ed.), *supra* note 8, p. 69; Long Zongzhi, *Lun Renda Dui Fayuan De Ge'an Jiandu* (Research on Supervision of Individual Cases by the People's Congress) (Beijing: Falu Chubanshe, 2003); Shen Qingzhong, 'Dui Renda Xingshi Jianduquan De Sikao' (Thoughts on the People's Congress's Exercise of Power to Supervise Individual Cases), 6 (2000) *Falu Shiyong* (Journal of Law Application).

12 Wang Fan, 'Qianyi Difang Renda De Ge'an Jiandu' (Research on the Supervision of Individual Cases by Local People's Congress), 1 (1998) *Xiandai Faxue* (Modern Law Science); Chen Sixi, 'Chongtu Yu Pingheng: Renda Jiandu Yu Sifa Duli' (Conflict and Balance: Supervision by the People's Congress and Judicial Independence), 6 (2002) *Renmin Sifa* (People's Judicature).

13 For a collection of 165 supervision cases by the NPC and local people's congress, procuratorates and courts, see Cai Dingjiang, 'Renda Jiandu Fayuan Anli' (Cases on People's Congresses Supervised Courts), in Cai Dingjiang (ed.), *supra* note 8, pp. 461–766.

14 For detail of this case, see 'Hefei Shouci Yunyong Teding Wenti Diaocha Weiyuanhui Jiandu Sifa Anjian' (Hefei Supervises Judicial Cases by Using an *ad hoc* Investigation Committee for the First Time). Available at: http://www.people.com.cn/GB/channel1/11/20001018/276290.html. Last visited September 2013.

lower than the actual value. The investigatory committee finally ruled that the court should revoke its former award of enforcement and re-try the case.[15]

Yet, there have also been instances where people's congress deputies have interfered improperly with a court's decision-making, resulting in the unnecessary suffering of the parties concerned and undermining judicial authority. A well-known case was reported as 'three levels of courts, four judgments, eight years' litigation, one piece of useless paper'.[16] The case was an ordinary economic contract dispute that had been tried by two local courts in Henan province. The SPC had intervened by giving its opinion twice, but this could not be followed by the local court. This was because some deputies of the local people's congress jointly made a statement to support the party who lost the case. One deputy was the legal representative of the losing party and he was extremely active in lobbying against the SPC decision. The local people's congress brought the case to the provincial people's congress on numerous occasions, and their opinion was transferred by the provincial people's congress to the National People's Congress, and the NPC passed it eventually to the SPC. It took three years to re-try the case. Despite the final outcome reflecting the SPC's opinion, the judgment reduced the fine for breaking the contract by half, due to the external intervention in the case.

The most renowned case in recent years regarding the wrongful supervision of courts by the local people's congress is the so-called 'seed case' in Henan province. This was again an ordinary case of contract dispute, this time between two companies and handled by the intermediate people's court in Luoyang city in 2003. The plaintiff insisted that compensation should be decided according to the Seed Law of the People's Republic of China, whereas the defendant held that the legal source should be the local Regulation on Seed issued by the People's Congress in Henan province. The trial judge, Li Huijuan, decided that the judgment should be based on the national law, and moreover she wrote in the judgment: 'After the national Seed Law became effective, the price of maize was to be regulated by the market. The Regulation on Seed issued by the People's Congress in Henan province as a local regulation which has a lower status than the national law, and which is contradictory to the Seed Law, is invalid … .'[17] The People's Congress Standing Committee in Luoyang city reported the judgment to the People's Congress Standing Committee in Henan province and the latter issued a document indicating that the local Regulation on Seed did not contradict the national Seed Law; the judgment of the court, which declared the local regulation invalid, was an illegal review of the local regulation, violated the people's congress system and infringed the power of the people's congress, and thus was a serious illegal act. It requested the People's Congress in Luoyang city 'to exercise its supervision power according to law, correct the illegal act of the intermediate people's court in Luoyang city, and punish the person

15 For detail of this case, see 'Liaoning Difang Renda Shouci Chushi "Hongpai" Chexiao Fayuan Panjue' (Local People's Congress in Liaoning Province Shows 'Red Card' for the First Time and Revokes the Court's Judgment). Available at: http://review.jcrb.com/zyw/n618/ca377376.htm. Last visited September 2013.

16 Shou Beibei, 'San Ji Fayuan Si Ge Panjue Ba Nian Guansi Yi Zhang Baizhi' (Three Levels of Courts, Four Judgments, Eight Years' Litigation, One Piece of Useless Paper), *Nanfang Zhoumo* (Southern Weekend), 5 June 1998. See also Wang Chenguang, 'Lun Fayuan Yifa Duli Shenpan He Renda Dui Fayuan Ge'an Jiandu Quan De Chongtu Ji Qi Tiaozheng Jizhi' (Analysis on the Conflicts Between and the Adjustment Mechanism Over Courts' Right to Independent Trial and the Supervision Over Individual Cases by People's Congress), 1 (1999) *Fa Xue* (Law Review), p. 18.

17 Liu Haibo, 'Cong Liangge Shijian Kan Woguo Zhongyang Yu Difang Guanxi Tizhi' (From Two Events to Examine the System between Central and Local Relationship), in Li Lin et al. (eds), *Yifa Zhiguo: Shinian Huigu Yu Zhanwang* (Ruling the Country in Accordance with Law: A Decade of Retrospect and Prospect) (Beijing: Zhongguo Fazhi Chubanshe, 2007), pp. 415–418.

involved in handling the case in the Court'.[18] Judge Li Huijuan was at first punished by the local court; however, due to media pressure and support from the Supreme People's Court, she was later cleared.[19] In its Reply to the Request concerning the Contract Dispute Case of the Seed Company in Ruyang county and the Seed Company in Yichuang county in Henan province, the SPC rightly stated that a judge has the right to choose which law should be applied in deciding a case.[20]

In 1999, the Internal and Judicial Committee of the NPC submitted a bill to the National People's Congress Standing Committee on Decisions on the Supervision of Cases that Violated Law by Court and Procuratorate. The bill was discussed twice by the NPC Standing Committee without approval due to fervent protest by legal scholars and judicial officers.[21] In 2006 the Law on the Supervision of People's Congresses Standing Committees at Various Levels was promulgated by the National People's Congress, in which it did not legalise the power of the people's congress standing committee to supervise courts in individual cases. Thus, from the legislative point of view, the supervision by people's congresses of individual cases handled by courts was more or less wiped out. Instead the Law provides an inquiry system, which is a kind of interference but follows certain procedures, and it applies to courts, as well as the government, governmental agencies and the procuratorate.

Under the Law, 10 or more members of the National People's Congress Standing Committee, five or more members of the people's congress standing committees at the provincial level, or three or more members of the people's congress standing committee at the county level, may jointly submit a written proposal to the standing committee for addressing queries to the people's government, including its departments, and to the people's court or people's procuratorate at the corresponding level (Art. 35). In instances where a proposal is submitted to the organ for addressing queries and more than half of the members of the standing committee are dissatisfied with their reply, they may demand a further response. (Art. 37).

Most scholars and commenters award high praise to this inquiry system stipulated in the Supervision Law, stating that it 'activates' the supervisory function of the people's congresses and endows it with new connotations;[22] it guarantees the right to information of the people's congresses and provides solutions to social problems.[23]

In several cases inquiries were made by deputies of the people's congress to courts before the Supervision Law was enacted. For example, in 1989, four members of the PCSC of Xunke county of Heilongjiang province made inquiries to the basic people's court on the issue of the discipline of judges; in 1994, 11 deputies of the people's congress from Funing county in Yunnan province addressed an inquiry to the intermediate court on an administrative tort case; in 1996, 13 members of the PCSC of Heyuan city in Guangdong province made inquiries to the intermediate court on the issue of personnel adjustments made in the court without approval by the PCSC; in 1999, six members of the PCSC of Jianli county in Hubei province made inquiries to the basic people's court, forestry administration and health administration of Jianli county on the issue of

---

18 *Ibid.*

19 *Ibid.* See also Stephanie Balme, 'Ordinary Justice and Popular Constitutionalism in China', in S. Balme and M. Dowdle (eds), *Building Constitutionalism in China* (New York: Palgrave Macmillan, 2009), p. 180.

20 The Reply was issued by the SPC on 30 March 2004.

21 Cai Dingjian, *supra* note 8, p. 39.

22 Chen Kouxi, 'Xunwen,Zhixun De Qidong: Renda Jiandu De Xin Neihan' (Initiation of Inquiry and Questioning: New Connotations of Supervision by People's Congress), 12 (2011) *Renda Yanjiu* (People's Congress Studying).

23 Lu Yifeng, 'Xi Jiandufa Kuangjia Xiade Zhixun Zhidu Sheji Ji Wanshan' (Analysis on the Design and Perfection of the Inquiry System under the Framework of Supervision Law), 5 (2009) *Renda Yanjiu* (People's Congress Studying).

the court's improper use of funds;[24] in 2002, 22 deputies of the people's congress of Shenyang city in Liaoning province made inquiries to the court, procuratorate and public security bureau of the city on an individual case; in 2003, several deputies of the People's Congress in Beijing made inquiries to the Higher People's Court of Beijing on its delayed response to the deputies' opinions; in May 2005, 33 deputies of the People's Congress of Mayang Autonomous county in Hunan province jointly submitted a proposal to the People's Congress of Mayang Autonomous county to address inquiries to the Basic People's Court of Mayang on one civil case in which the court auctioned a house which should have belonged to the complainant.[25]

Since the Supervision Law became effective in 2007, the inquiry system has rarely been initiated by the PCSC against courts. Despite the cool-down in the supervision of individual cases by the people's congresses, in order to get the support of people's congresses and indeed to avoid petitions and complaints, courts at all levels have taken some measures to involve the people's congresses in handling cases, such as inviting deputies of the people's congresses to be people's assessors to participate in trial cases, and appointing deputies of the people's congresses to be supervisors of the courts' work. In October 2009, the SPC issued the Regulation on the Work of *Ad Hoc* Supervisors of the Supreme People's Court (Trial) which states that *ad hoc* supervisors of the SPC are to be appointed by the SPC to supervise the trial and enforcement work of the SPC; they are to be selected from representatives of the NPC, members of the National People's Political Consultative Conference, members of democratic parties, members of associations of industry and commerce, persons without party affiliation, scholars and common citizens.[26] On 22 January 2010, the first batch of 60 *ad hoc* supervisors were appointed by the SPC.[27] At the local level, more than 100 representatives of the local people's congress and political consultative conference have been appointed to act as judicial supervisors of the Intermediate People's Court of Shenzhen city.[28]

Courts' Reports on Their Work to People's Congresses

Article 16 of the 2006 amended Organic Law of People's Courts provides that the SPC is responsible to, and reports on its work to, the NPC and NPCSC. Furthermore, the local people's courts are responsible to, and report on their work to, the local people's congresses at the corresponding levels. This is the legal basis of the system in which courts report to the people's congresses.

The most common report system requires that courts submit annual work reports to the people's congresses during the general session of the people's congresses. This system began when the SPC submitted annual work reports to the NPC in 1950. The Constitutions of 1954, 1975 and 1978 all clearly endorsed the request for reports. However, the 1982 Constitution provides only that the SPC

24 *Ibid.*

25 Sun Ying, 'Lun Renda Zhixun De Qidong Yaojian' (Analysis on the Initiating Conditions of Inquiry by the People's Congress), (6) (2010) *Renda Yanjiu* (People's Congress Studying), p. 10.

26 Article 1 of the Regulation on the Work of *ad hoc* Supervisors of the Supreme People's Court (Trial) (*Fafa* No. 51 [2009]). The text of the Regulation is available at http://www.court.gov.cn/qwfb/sfwj/jd/201003/t20100331_3585.htm. Last visited September 2013.

27 'Zuigao Fayuan Nuli Tigao Jianduyuan Jiandu Shixiao' (SPC Strives for Enhancing the Effectiveness of *ad hoc* Supervisors), available at http://news.xinhuanet.com/legal/2012-01/24/c_111459296.htm. Last visited September 2013.

28 See Qiu Mei, 'Daibiao Xingshi Jianduquan Geng Bianjie Geng Shunchang' (It Has Become More Convenient and Smooth for the Representatives of People's Congress to Exercise Their Supervision Right), *Newspaper of People's Court*, 12 February 2012. Available at http://www.rmfyb.com.cn/paper/html/2012-02/21/content_40487.htm. Last visited September 2013.

should be responsible to the NPC and the NPCSC, without mentioning reporting on their work to the latter. But, the 1983 amended Organic Law of People's Courts did not adopt the change of the 1982 Constitution, and instead stated that the SPC should be responsible to the NPC and the NPCSC and report to it. Thus, even though the report system has no constitutional basis, it has been maintained.[29]

At the national level, in March each year the President of the SPC presents its work report to the National People's Congress when the latter holds its annual session in Beijing. The report is reviewed by deputies, and a consequent decision is then made: a report is passed with the consent of 50 per cent of congress deputies. Although, until now, not one of the SPC's reports has been disapproved, criticism and concerns over judicial work by the deputies has certainly imposed pressure on the SPC. Table 2.1 shows the rate of voting in the NPC on the annual work report of the SPC.[30]

Comparing the reports of the Supreme People's Procuratorate (SPP), the State Council and the NPCSC, the SPC received the least votes in favour.[31] The low rate of approval received by the SPC's work reports is a reflection of the deputies' dissatisfaction with the court's work. It has also pressed the SPC to take measures to be more active in communicating with deputies. Usually vice-presidents of the SPC take judges with them to visit deputies to hear their critical opinions when the NPC is in session; the SPC has also set up an office of contact with NPC deputies. Recently, in preparing the work report the SPC has consulted legal experts to hear their opinions.[32]

---

29 Zuo Wemin and Feng Jun, *supra* note 6, pp. 219–220. See also Qian Ningfeng, 'Xianfa Wenben Shang De "Baogao Gongzuo" Wenti Lunxi: Jianping Fayuan Gongzuo Baogao Tongbuguo Shijian' (Analysis on the Issue of the 'Work Report' Based on the Constitutional Text: Comments on the Incidents of Disapproval of the Court's Report by People's Congress), 3(2009) *Gansu Zhengfa Xueyuan Xuebao* (Journal of Gansu Institute of Political Science and Law), pp. 35–40.

30 Such information is not always provided officially. The figures below are mostly cited from media reports or sporadic academic articles. The 1996, 1997 and 2004 figures are cited from Zuo Weimin and Feng Jun, 'Yi Jianduquan Wei Shijiao: Zuigao Fayuan Yu Quanguo Renda Guanxi De Ruogan Sikao' (From the Perspective of Supervision Power: Several Thoughts on the Relationship between the SPC and the NPC), 4 (2005) *Shehui Kexue Yanjiu* (Research on Social Science), p. 85; the 2000 figure is cited from 'Shinian "Lianghui": Biaojueqi Shang De Minyi' (The Conferences of the NPC and the Chinese Political Consultative Conference over Ten Years: Popular Will of the Voters), 27 February 2010, available at http://news.china.com.cn/txt/2010-02/27/content_19486012.htm; the 2003 figure is cited from Sun Chuanwei, 'Renda Huiyi Dipiao Tongguo Lianggao Gongzuo Baogao' (The Reports of the SPC and the SPP are Approved by the NPC with Low Rate), 19 March 2003, available at http://www.politicalchina.org/printnews.asp?newsid=21474; the 2006 figure is cited from 'Huiyi Biaojue Tongguo Guanyu Zuigao Renmin Fayuan Gongzuo Baogao de Jueyi' (Decision of the NPC to Approve the SPC Report), 14 March 2006, available at http://news.xinhuanet.com/video/2006-03/14/content_4301106.htm; the 2008 figure is cited from 'Shuzi: Zhengfu Gongzuo Baogao Jueyi Cao'an Fandui Piao Zuishao, Zuigao Renmin Fayuan Gongzuo Baogao Jueyi Cao'an Fandui Piao Zuiduo' (Figure: The Votes Opposed Are the Least with Regard to the Work Report of the State Council, and the Most with Regard to the Work Report of SPC), 18 March 2008, available at http://gb.cri.cn/18824/2008/03/18/107@1981791.htm; the 2009, 2010, 2011, 2012 and 2013 figures are cited from 'Sifa Shuju Di 46 Qi: Linian Zuigaofa Gongzuo Baogao De Weitongguo Lv You Duogao?' (Judicial Figures, Volume 46: How High Is the Rate of Opposing Votes with Regard to the Work Reports of the SPC to the NPC?), available at http://kan.weibo.com/con/3529395160263477. All last visited September 2013.

31 'Dahui Biaojue Tongguo Guanyu Zuigao Renmin Fayuan Gongzuo Baogao De Jueyi' (Decisions of the National People's Congress on Approval of the Work Report of the Supreme People's Court), available at http://news.sohu.com/20090313/n262773646.shtml. Last visited September 2013.

32 Zuo Wemin and Feng Jun, *supra* note 6, p. 223–224. The authors take the view that the SPC submitting the work report to the NPC is a product of the traditional negligence of the court's independence. The SPC, as the highest judicial organ, exercises its adjudication power independently. Judicial process is judged based on evidence and law to make decisions on individual cases, which is hardly relevant to the NPC's work. See, p. 241.

Table 2.1 The rate of voting in the NPC on the SPC work report (1996–2013)

Year	Votes in favour	Votes opposed	Votes abstained	Percentage of votes in favour
1996	2,168	243	271	80.84
1997	1,839	515	366	67.61
1998				
1999				
2000	1,953	530	306	70.03
2001				
2002				
2003	2,312	398	203	79.40
2004	2,082	585	228	71.92
2005				
2006	2,257	479	146	78.31
2007				
2008	2,287	521	120	78.11
2009	2,172	519	192	80.71
2010	2,289	479	128	79.04
2011	2,242	475	155	78.06
2012	2,311	429	115	80.95
2013	2,218	605	120	75.37

A similar report system is conducted by local courts report to the local people's congress at the corresponding level. Some local people's congresses have shown their dissatisfaction with local court work by disapproving of the work report. For instance, in February 2001 the work report of the Shenyang city Intermediate People's Court received less than 50 per cent approval; this marked the first time that a court's work report was failed by a people's congress.[33] In January 2007 the work report of the Intermediate People's Court in Hengyang city of Hunan province was similarly rejected by the people's congress. These are exceptional incidents mainly due to serious corruption in the courts that has become known to the deputies of the congresses; however, it also reflects the growing strength of the local people's congresses in exercising their supervisory power.[34]

33 'Cong Foujue Dao Gaopiao Zancheng-Shenyang Renda Liangshen Fayuan Baogao Shimo' (The Story on the Journey from Veto to Approval of the Work Report of the People's Court by the People's Congress in Shenyang), available at http://news.sohu.com/15/48/news146184815.shtml. Last visited September 2013. The main reason that the report in Shenyang was not passed was corruption at the court. Following the event, the president, and two deputy presidents of the court at the time were found guilty of corruption. In August 2001 the revised report was accepted by the People's Congress.

34 'Hunan Hengyangshi Zhongji Renmin Fayuan Gongzuo Baogao Jueyi Weihuo Tongguo' (The Work Report of the Intermediate People's Court in Hengyang City was Disapproved by Deputies), available at http://news.sohu.com/20070126/n247861707.shtml. Last visited September 2013.

Courts and the Communist Party

The CPC is very different to political parties in most other countries. As the only ruling party in China for over the last six decades, the Party has penetrated deeply into the fabric of Chinese society. Primary Party organisations are formed in enterprises, rural areas, government departments, schools, scientific research institutes, communities, mass organisations and even private law firms. Currently, there are approximately 85 million Party members. This constitutes about 6.3 per cent of the total population of China.[35]

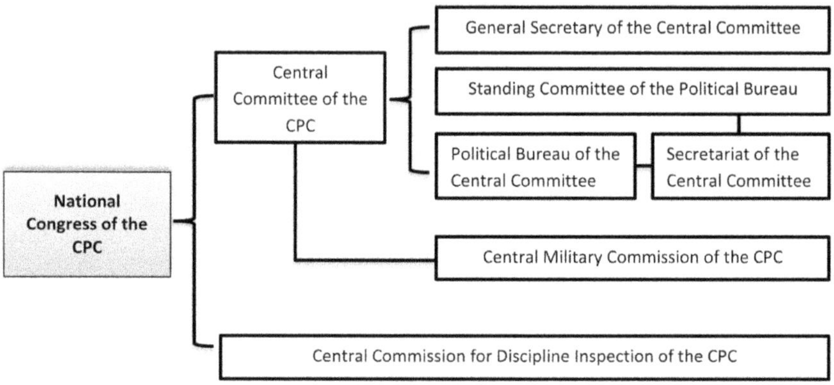

Figure 2.1 Organisational chart of the central leadership

Party organs are established from the central level to three local levels. At the central level, the highest leading body of the Party is the National Party Congress and the Central Committee (CC) elected by it. The National Party Congress is held once every five years; when it is not in session, the CC leads the entire work of the Party. Under the CC are the Political Bureau (25 members), the Standing Committee of the Political Bureau (nine or seven members), the Secretariat which is the working body of the Political Bureau and its Standing Committee, and the Military Commission which is the central leading military body of the CPC. The General Secretary of the CC is the highest leading position within the CPC Central Committee. It is elected from members of the Standing Committee of the Political Bureau and responsible for convening the meetings of the Political Bureau of the CPC Central Committee and its Standing Committee, and directs the work of the Secretariat of the Central Committee. The Secretariat is an administrative body of the Political Bureau and its Standing Committee. Its members are nominated by the Standing Committee of the Political Bureau and approved by the Plenary Session of the CPC Central Committee.

At the local level, the leading bodies of local Party organisations are the Party congresses at their respective levels and the Party committees elected by them. Party committees are responsible to, and report their work to, the Party congresses at their respective levels. Party congresses are

35 'Zhonggong Dangyuan Zongshu Tupo 8500 Wan Ming, Dangyuan Suzhi Jinyibu Tigao' (The Total Number of CCP Members Exceeds 85 Million; Competencies of Party Members are Further Improved), Jinghua Shibao (Jinghua News), 1 July 2013. Available at http://news.xinhuanet.com/politics/2013-07/01/c_124933588.htm. Data on the Chinese population is available from the National Bureau of Statistics of China. See 'China's Population Clock' at http://data.stats.gov.cn/index. Up to January 2014, it showed that China's population exceeded 1.36 billion. Both were last visited January 2014.

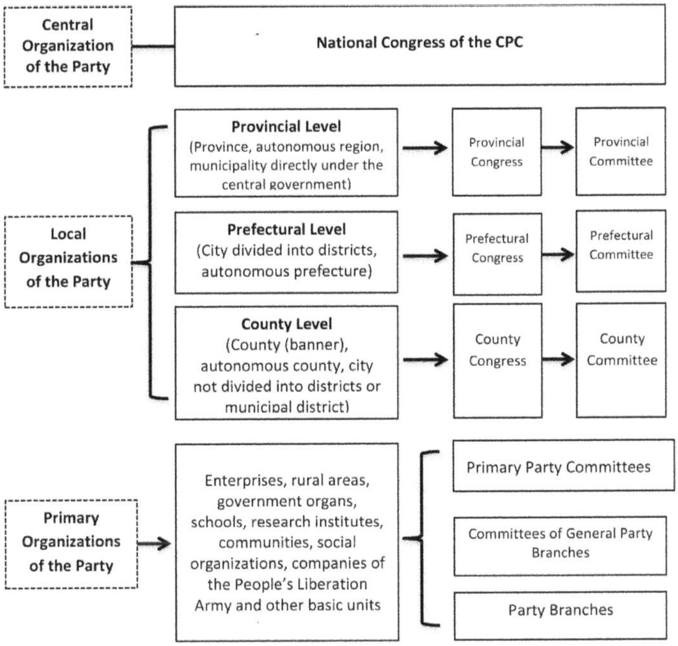

Figure 2.2 Organisational chart of the CPC

to be found at a provincial level, prefectural level and county level. Under each level of the Party congress is a Party committee, secretariat, and the committee for discipline inspection which comes under the dual leadership of the higher level committee for discipline inspection as well as the same level Party committee.

At both the central and local levels are various functional organs of the Party. For example at the central level, the Propaganda Department (*xuanchuan bu*) is in charge of ideology-related work, as well as its propaganda system; the Organisation Department (*zuzhi bu*) controls staffing positions within the CPC; the United Front Work Department (*tongzhan bu*) is in charge of managing relations with the non-Communist Party elite, including individuals and organisations holding social, commercial or academic influence, or who represent important interest groups.[36] Such organs are established at each local level to be responsible for affairs within their respective jurisdiction. The Communist Party's leadership on judicial work is mainly carried out by the Central Political and Legal Committee (CPLC) at the national level and its branches at three local levels, which are province, prefecture and county. At the township level there is no Political and Legal Committee (PLC).

Starting in 1958, the CPC set up special committees at central and local levels in charge of political and legal affairs. The first Central Leading Group of Political and Legal Affairs was established in 1958. However, the Leading Group was abolished during the Cultural Revolution. In order to recover the legal order which had been destroyed during the Cultural Revolution and to strengthen the Party's leadership on legal affairs, the CPLC was re-established in 1980 and became a working department of the Central Committee of the CPC in 1982.

36 For details of these organs, see http://cpc.people.com.cn/GB/64114/index.html. Last visited September 2013.

In the 1980s, some local PLCs were also set up. Some heads of the PLCs became heads of local courts, procuratorates or public security organs (police). The arbitrary exercise of power by local PLCs was severely criticised, especially by democratic parties.[37] Along with the political reform of the CPC and the institutional reform of the State Council, came reform of the PLC. The 13th Party Congress in 1987 made the decision to rationalise the relationship between Party organs and the people's congress, government and judicial organs in order to ensure that they carry out their respective functions toward gradual institutionalisation. In 1988, during the reform of separating the Party and government organs, the CPLC was abolished, though most local PLCs were not. The Central Leading Group of Political and Legal Affairs was established to replace the CPLC. However, one year after the abolition of the CPLC, the Tian'anmen Protest broke out. It was felt that the leadership of the CPC in handling the political and legal affairs needed to be further strengthened in order to avoid similar disturbances.[38] In 1990, the CPC decided to revive the CPLC and positioned it as the 'adviser' and 'assistant' of the Party Committee, with the function to macro-guide and coordinate political and judicial affairs; in the meantime local PLCs were strengthened. In 1999, PLCs were further positioned as 'the functional department of Party committees at various levels to lead and manage political and legal work'.[39]

The main judicial work of the CPLC takes five forms: (1) to unify thinking and actions of all political and legal departments (including the judiciary) according to the Party's policy and decisions; (2) to supervise and lead the investigation of significant cases, coordinate police, procuracy and courts in solving significant cases; (3) to organise and put forward research and judicial reform; (4) to examine and manage high-ranking leaders in the central and local political and judicial departments; (5) to assist the discipline inspection department and the Party's supervision department to investigate violations of Party discipline and law by officials in the political and judicial departments.[40]

Concretely speaking, apart from the decisive role played by the Party in appointing and dismissing high-ranking judicial officers, the Party's leadership position on judicial work is also reflected in ideological and political leadership and they are also actively involved in making decisions in complex and significant cases. The latter is mainly carried out by the PLCs. which coordinate the court, procuratorate and the police in handling complex and/or politically sensitive cases. At a local level, the members of PLCs consist of the heads of the court, procuratorate, police and department of judicial affairs (local branch of the Ministry of Justice), and often the head of PLCs is the head of the police. Where the court, procuratorate and police disagree, the committee gives its opinion, and all will then follow.

---

37 Zhou Yongkun, 'Lun Dangwei Zhengfa Weiyuanhui Zhi Gaige' (Discussion on Reforming the Political and Legal Committees of the Communist Party), 5 (2012) *Faxue* (Legal Jurisprudence), available at http://www.pkulaw.cn/fulltext_form.aspx?Db=qikan&Gid=1510111744&keyword=%e6%94%bf%e6%b3%95%e5%a7%94%e5%91%98%e4%bc%9a&EncodingName=&Search_Mode=accurate. Last visited September 2013.

38 *Ibid.*

39 Shen Xinwang and Shen Haijiao, 'Zhengfawei Shuji Jianren Gong'an Juzhang Baoshou Zhengyi Huo Zhi "Tie'an"' (Secretary of Political and Legal Committee, Concurrently Head of Police, Causes Debate or Results in 'Unchangeable Cases'), available at http://news.sohu.com/20100325/n271093854.shtml. Last visited September 2013.

40 'Zhonggong Zhongyang Zhengfa Weiyuanhui' (Central Political and Legal Committee), available at http://www.chinapeace.org.cn/2006-07/26/content_1377.htm. Last visited September 2013.

The phenomenon that the secretary of the PLC holds a concurrent post as the head of police has caused some debate among legal scholars in China.[41] In March 2010 at the NPC, deputy Wu Xiaoling proposed that the secretary of the PLC should not hold a concurrent post as head of police.[42] It is reported that, in April 2011, the Organisation Department of the CPC Central Committee issued a notice requiring that the head of the PLC at the provincial level should not hold the post of the head of the public security department concurrently.[43] When the notice was issued, a total of 14 heads of provincial PLCs concurrently held posts as heads of public security departments. Up to August 2013, out of 31 provinces, autonomous regions and municipalities directly under the central government, 27 heads of provincial PLCs do not concurrently hold posts as heads of public security departments; the four who do are in the provinces of Hebei, Hunan, Gansu and Ningxia.[44]

The Party's Leadership in Ideology, Judicial Policy and Judicial Reform

The leadership of the Party is reflected in its ideological influence on judges. As the overwhelming majority of judges in China are members of CPC,[45] they study Party policies at meetings organised regularly by the Party committee within each court. The Party also provides regular training for judges at the Party's training institutes. As a member of the Party, judges are requested to adhere to the Party line on all Party-concerned issues.

Major judicial policy is often formulated by the Central Committee of the CPC. This is revealed most noticeably in the 'striking hard' (*yanda*) anti-crime campaigns, which were first launched by the Party in 1983 to crack down on growing crime. In August 1983 the CPC issued the Decision on Striking Hard against Severe Criminal Offences. In September of the same year the NPCSC issued the Decision on Strictly Punishing Criminals who Severely Threaten Social Safety and Order. Based on these two Decisions, police, procuratorates and courts all over China initiated a 'strike hard' campaign which lasted for three years. Since then nation-wide strike hard anti-crime campaigns have been led by the Party periodically.[46]

---

41 Hou Meng, 'Sifa Gaige Beijing Xia De Zhengfa Zhili Fangshi: Jiceng Zhengfa Weiyuanhui Zhidu Ge'an Yanjiu' (Governance of Political and Legal Affairs in the Background of Judicial Reform: Research on the Case of Local Political-Legal Committee), 99 (2003) *Huadong Zhengfa Xueyuan Xuebao* (Journal of East China University of Political Science and Law); Chen Youxi, 'Sifa Duli Shenpan Ying Cong Youhua Zhengfawei Jiegou Rushou' (Modifying the Structure of the Political-Legal Committee Should Be a Starting Point of Judicial Independence), *Nanfang Zhoumo* (Southern Weekend), 24 November 2011.

42 Shen Xinwang and Shen HaiJiao, *supra* note 39.

43 'Zhengfawei Shuji Yu Gong'an Juzhang De Hehe Fenfen' (Evolution of the Posts between Head of Political and Legal Committee and Head of Public Security), *Nanfang Zhoumo* (Southern Weekend), 3 November 2011. Available at http://www.infzm.com/content/64506. Last visited September 2013.

44 'Zhengfawei Shuji Jian Gong'an Ting (Ju) Zhang 31 Shengfen Zhong Jinsheng 4 Ren' (Only 4 Left in Terms of the Number of Heads of PLC Who Concurrently Hold the Posts of Heads of Public Security Department in 31 Provinces), available at http://hunan.sina.com.cn/news/b/2013-08-20/075066646_2.html. Last visited September 2013.

45 There is no publicly available statistic on the exact number of judges who are Party members. Based on some limited empirical work of Chinese scholars more than 70 per cent, and in some courts even 97 per cent, of judges are Party members. See Si Weijiang, 'Zhongguo Sifa De Qianshi Jinsheng' (History and Present of Judiciary in China), available at http://www.21ccom.net/articles/zgyj/fzyj/article_2012051559738.html. Last visited September 2013.

46 For a comprehensive understanding of such campaigns see Susan Trevaskes, 'Severe and Swift Justice in China', 47 (2007) *British Journal of Criminology*, pp. 23–41.

The Party's influence on judicial policy is not limited to criminal offences, but covers all key aspects of judicial work. This has become evident from the end of the last century. In the 1997 report to the 15th National Congress of the CPC, the CPC Central Committee unprecedentedly proposed to 'promote the judicial reform, provide an institutional guarantee for judicial organs independently exercising their respective adjudication and prosecutorial powers, and develop a system of investigating and fixing the legal liabilities for unjustly and wrongly judged cases'.[47]

In 2002, the 16th National Congress of the CPC set up the task of promoting reform of the judicial system through seven routes: (1) improving the structure, functions and management systems of judicial organs; (2) ensuring institutionally that the judicial organs can exercise adjudicative powers independently and impartially according to law; (3) improving judicial procedures and protecting the legitimate rights and interests of citizens and legal persons; (4) solving the problem of enforcement of judgments; (5) reforming the working mechanisms of judicial organs and the management of their human, financial and material resources, and gradually separating the judicial adjudication from the administrative affairs; (6) tightening supervision over the judicial work and punishing judicial corruption; (7) building up a politically and professionally competent judicial force.[48]

Immediately following this, in May 2003 the CPC Central Committee set up the Leading Group for the Judicial System Reform (LGJSR). The LGJSR was headed by Luo Gan, who was then Secretary of the Central Political and Legal Committee. The LGJSR consists of presidents of the SPC, the SPP, the Ministers of Public Security, Justice, and other relevant high-ranking officials. At the end of 2004 the LGJSR issued the Initial Opinions of the LGJSR on the Reform of the Judicial System and its Work Mechanism (hereafter Initial Opinions)[49] which set up 35 tasks for the judicial reform.

In 2007, the 17th Party Congress demonstrated the decision of the Party in leading the judicial reform. Hu Jintao, in his report to the National Party Congress, pointed out:

> We need to deepen the reform of the judicial system, optimise the distribution of judicial functions and powers, standardise judicial practices, and build a fair, efficient and authoritative socialist judiciary system to ensure that courts and procuratorates exercise their respective powers independently and impartially in accordance with the law. We need to improve the overall quality of judicial, procuratorial and public security personnel to ensure that law enforcement is strict, impartial and civilised.[50]

47 Database of National Congress of the CPC: Report Made by Jiang Zemin in 15th National Congress of the CPC (12 September 1997). Available at http://cpc.people.com.cn/GB/64162/64168/64568/65445/4526289.html. Last visited September 2013.

48 Full text of Jiang Zemin's report at the 16th Party congress on 8 November 2002. See http://www.china-un.ch/eng/zgbd/zgbdxw/t85779.htm. Last visited September 2013.

49 This document is not publicly available. The main contents of this Initial Opinions are discussed in 'Reform of China's Judicial System Promotes Protection of Human Rights: An Interview with Wang Shengjun, Secretary-General of the Politico-Legal Committee of the CPC Central Committee', available at http://lib.cqvip.com/qk/88415X/200603/21891664.html. Last visited September 2013.

50 Hu Jintao, 'Hold High the Great Banner of Socialism with Chinese Characteristics and Strive for New Victories in Building a Moderately Prosperous Society in All Respects: Report to the 17th National Congress of the Communist Party of China on October 15, 2007', available at http://english.cpc.people.com.cn/66102/6290205.html. Last visited September 2013.

On 28 November 2008 the Politburo approved the CPLC's Opinions on Several Issues concerning Deepening the Reform of the Judicial System and its Work Mechanism. This is the first time in the past 60 years that the Politburo of the CPC reviewed and approved affairs of judicial reform. The Opinions indicated that the judicial reform should concentrate on four aspects: prioritising the distribution of judicial powers; perfecting the criminal policy of combining leniency with rigidity; strengthening the force of political and legal personnel; and reforming the judicial guarantee system.[51]

Some Chinese legal scholars are cautious about the CPC-led judicial reform. They have pointed out that the starting point of the judicial reform led by the CPC, to a certain degree, is not based on the nature of the judicial system, but based on the need of the political situation and social stability. The reform prioritised resolving the most common public complaints of the judicial system, which overlooked the controversy between the professional nature of the judicial system and public opinions. Moreover, the CPC-led judicial reform deviated from addressing the key issue of judicial reform in re-designing the relationship between judicial power and other state powers.[52]

The Party's Role in Handling Individual Cases

From 1949 to 1979, the Party's control over the judiciary was absolute both in terms of policy and through a system of examination and approval of judgments by Party committees within the courts.[53] The official position was:

> [s]ince the court is a state organ, the Party as a matter of course leads the court. As shown by the facts, only the Party's intervention in adjudication has made it possible to correct illegalities and to apply the law correctly. Party leadership is carried out through the Party organisation within the court. All important judicial matters should be decided by the Party organisation, including not only problems of political ideology or policy, but also concrete cases. By correctly handling individual cases, the Party can demonstrate how to carry out its policies and guidelines effectively. If the Party limits itself to passing on policies and guidelines, its leadership will become abstract and useless.[54]

In 1957 the Central Committee of the CPC approved the Report on the Judicial Work Conference and the Situation on the Anti-Rightist Struggle of the SPC submitted by the Party Committees of

51 The document is *Zhongfa* No. 19 [2008]. Full text is not publicly available. For a media report on the main intent of this document, see 'Sifa Gaige Jiang Zai Qidong, Jiceng Fayuan Jingfei Huo Naru Zhongyang Yusuan' (Judicial Reform Will Be Re-Launched; Budget of Basic Courts May Be Included in Central Budget System), available at http://www.21ccom.net/articles/zgyj/fzyj/article_2012051559738.html. Last visited September 2013.

52 Xiong Qiuhong, 'Zhongguo Sifa Gaige Sanshi Nian' (Thirty Years Judicial Reform in China), in The Institute of Law of the Chinese Academy of Social Sciences (ed.), *Zhongguo Fazhi Sanshi Nian 1978–2008* (Thirty Years of the Rule of Law in China 1978–2008) (Beijing: Social Sciences Academic Press, 2008), pp. 211–215.

53 Koguchi observed, "Despite its absolute leadership during this period, the Party did not intervene uniformly in all judicial matters, but rather limited its intervention to cases with far-reaching implications and to criminal cases involving a sentence of three or more years of imprisonment. This intervention in judicial decision-making was accomplished through a system of examination and approval by a Party committee.' Hikota Koguchi, 'Some Observations about "Judicial Independence" in Post-Mao China', 12 (1987) *Boston College Third World Law Journal*, p. 197.

54 Feng Ruoquan, 'Refute Jian Qian's Anti-Party Nonsense about "Independent Adjudication"', 1 (1958) *Zhengfa Yanjiu*, p. 20. Quoted in Hikota Koguchi, *ibid.*, pp. 196–197.

the SPC and the Ministry of Justice, in which it was proposed that all adjudicative work should come under the control and supervision of the Party Committee; the Party Committee thus has the power to intervene in all cases. Any judicial independence and ideas refusing the Party Committee's approval of concrete cases were wrong and had to be corrected.

Since 1979, the Party's role in the judiciary has undergone a gradual change. The Instruction of the Central Committee of the Communist Party of China concerning the Implementation of the Criminal Law and the Law of Criminal Procedure issued in 1979 formally abolished the case examination and approval system. It stated:

> … [t]he Party committees and the judicial organs must each carry out their own special functions. One must neither replace nor become confused with the other. For this reason, the Central Committee of the Party has decided to abolish the system of examination and approval by the Party committees at all levels … [e]xcept for the very few cases committed by cadres of county-level … and well-known personages, which would then require instruction from higher (courts) because of specific and important considerations … The Party leadership over the judiciary is limited to that of guidance and policy.[55]

Finder observed that reducing the Party's control over the judiciary by abolishing the examination and approval system did not entail any structural changes. Actually, it was due to the changes in the nature of the courts' work that 'Officials of the Central Committee are neither interested in nor have the background to involve themselves in issues of civil procedure or contract law, and the Party has become less involved in the technical legal issues regarding criminal and criminal procedure law'.[56] Consequently, the direct involvement of Party organs in handling individual cases has been considerably reduced. However, it has never come to an end altogether.

Before the mid-1980s, Party committees directly examining and approving cases was quite common; since this period Party organs' interference in individual cases has focused on significant or politically-sensitive cases.[57] Party organs can be Party committees, political-legal committees, disciplinary committees or organisational departments.

The controversial role of the Party in relation to intervention in individual cases is a matter of concern; however, it has only been discussed on a limited scale and less in-depth in academic circles due to the political sensitivity involved. As early as 1979, Professor Li Buyun wrote that the system in which the Party committees examined and approved cases had nine shortcomings and should be changed.[58] His article was published in the *People's Daily* and received the attention of central Party officials; in September of the same year the CPC issued the Instruction on Firmly

55 Cited in Hikota Koguchi, *supra* note 53, pp. 199–200. In August 1979, Jiang Hua, President of the SPC pointed out that 'under the current situation there is no need to continue with the system of examination and approval cases by party committees, it should be abolished … To strengthen the leadership the Party Committee on political and legal work should focus on strengthening the leadership on policy and strategy, and not on concrete cases'. He Yongjun, in Zuo Weimin et al. (eds), *supra* note 53, p. 255.

56 Susan Finder, 'The Supreme People's Court of the People's Republic of China', 7 (1993) *Journal of Chinese Law*, p. 151.

57 Cai Dingjian, *Lishi Yu Biange: Xin Zhongguo Fazhi Jianshe De Licheng* (History and Reform: Development of the Legal System in New China) (Beijing: Zhongguo Zhengfa Daxue Chubanshe, 1999), p. 292.

58 Li Buyun, 'Dangwei Shenpi Anjian De Zhidu Xuyao Gaibian' (The System of Examination and Approval of Cases by Party Committee Should be Changed), in Li Buyun, *Zouxiang Fazhi* (Toward the Rule of Law) (Changsha: Hunan Renmin Chubanshe, 1998), pp. 326–328.

Ensuring the Implementation of the Criminal Law and the Criminal Procedure Law, which formally abolished the system of examination and approval by Party committee.[59] Professor Xin Chunying once wrote that, in reality, the leadership of the Communist Party is one of the major characteristics of China's political system and Chinese courts are inevitably guided by the CPC. However, it 'does not mean that they accept Party's guide on day to day bases when dealing with concrete cases, they must strictly adhere to laws and regulations because it is a strategy of the CCP to run the country by law'.[60] Such a line of thinking involves abolishing the Party's interference in individual cases, which includes giving instructions, coordinating police, procuratorate and courts, and merely supervising the courts' handling of concrete cases.[61]

Another line of thinking represented by Zhu Suli argued,

> sometimes the CPC's 'interference' seeks to represent and promote a local population's particular understandings of what justice and fairness demand in the handling of a particular case. Such interference certainly does not respect the model of 'separation of powers', and as such, it is often criticised by many legal scholars whose appreciation for Western practice leads them to think that the CPC should 'keep quiet' with regard to cases waiting for trial. Yet, this kind of 'interference' might actually be beneficial for a majority of Chinese people, who do not care about foreign experience but simply seek justice and social solidarity.

He further claimed:

> from a Western constitutional perspective, such interference seems to be improper. But from a political perspective, it is hard to see why a purely 'legal' control over a case is always and necessarily more morally just and reasonable than a more 'political' control. Why should a technocratic and juridicalised determination always be superior to a political one? In a sense, this kind of 'interference' can conceivably constitute a legitimate and beneficial exercise of the CPC's core political function of social integration and representation.[62]

Despite his bold defence of the highly notorious system, one can hardly concur with the logic of his argument.

Under the current situation in China, the Party has the capacity to have both a positive and a negative impact on individual cases. Such intervention may help to settle some cases, and

---

59 *Ibid.*, p. 329.

60 Xin Chunying, *Chinese Courts History and Transition* (Beijing: Falu Chubanshe, 2003), p. 109.

61 Ran Jingfu, 'Jiaqiang He Gaishan Dang Dui Sifa Gongzuo De Lingdao Fangshi' (Strengthening and Improving the Leadership of the Party on Judicial Work), in Li Lin and Wang Jiafu, *Yifa Zhiguo: Shinian Huigu Yu Zhanwang* (Ruling the Country in Accordance with Law: A Decade of Retrospect and Prospect) (Beijing: Zhongguo Fazhi Chubanshe, 2007), pp. 357–358.

62 Zhu Suli, '"Judicial Politics" as State-Building', in Stephanie Balme and Michael W. Dowdle (eds), *Building Constitutionalism in China* (New York: Palgrave Macmillan, 2009), p. 28. It should be noted that open discussion, especially critical examination of the role of the Party in its relationship to the judiciary, is a high risk endeavour in China. A lively case is that of Zhang Yinghong who worked at the department of Party Organisation in Hunan province and was dismissed from the post due to his publication on a Chinese website in 2003 with an article entitled 'Political-Legal Committee Hampers Judicial Independence'. Zhou Yongkang, then the Vice-Secretary of the Central Political and Legal Committee and Ministry of Public Security condemned Zhang Yinghong for projecting a bad image abroad. See Zou Keyuan, *China's Legal Reform Towards the Rule of Law* (Leiden and Boston, MA: Martinus Nijhoff, 2006), p. 95.

even to correct instances of injustice. However, it may also turn out to be a source of injustice.[63] Moreover, such Party intervention inevitably undermines judicial authority and is harmful to judicial independence. With the improvement of judicial professionalism, courts and judges are becoming capable and should be allowed to carry out their judicial functions independently, and Party intervention in individual cases can be expected to be gradually abolished.

Courts and Government Organisations

In the earliest years of the PRC, the court was called the 'people's government's people's court'. In September 1951, the Provisional Regulations on Organisations of the People's Courts of the PRC was issued which changed the court's name to the people's court.[64] The Provisional Organic Regulations of Courts in the People's Republic of China issued by the central government on 3 September 1951 provided that the adjudicative work of the lower-level courts was to be led and supervised by higher-level courts, and that courts at all levels were part of the people's government at the same level and were to be led and supervised by the same level government. Thus, local courts came under the dual leadership of higher-level courts and the same level of the government. However, the 1954 Constitution modified the dual system by providing that the people's court was no longer affiliated to the same level of government.

The Constitution established the system of '*Yi Fu Liang Yuan*', which means that the State Council, the Supreme People's Court and the Supreme People's Procuratorate are produced by and accountable to the National People's Congress. Constitutionally speaking, the SPC and the State Council have the same legal status, both exercising the powers delegated to them by the NPC. The Constitution also provides that courts are not subject to intervention by administrative organs. However, in reality 'the intrinsic defects incarnated in the system caused the divergence between the provisions of the Constitution, laws, and the reality'.[65]

Chinese courts are not independent from government organisations, on the contrary they are dependent on government in various ways. The most obvious institutional setting is that court financing is determined by the government. The SPC's budget is determined by the Ministry of Finance, and funding for local people's courts comes from the financial departments of the corresponding level of government. The budget determines the number of staff and their salaries, the court buildings and facilities, administrative expenses, as well as judges' welfare – for instance, many courts also provide housing for the judges and their families. Thus, the government in effect controls courts' personnel, budgets and material resources (*ren, cai, wu*). This 'has put courts indirectly in a subordinate situation. They have to "look up the faces" of the administration'.[66]

Local governments funding local courts has resulted in a serious discrepancy in courts' budgets, based on regional financial resources. In economically richer regions such as the east coast, governments allocate more funds, which have resulted in courts having better working facilities, and higher income and benefits (such as housing) for judges. In contrast, courts in economically poorer regions such as the north-west receive modest funds, and are often unable to cover the

63 Numerous criminal cases have been exposed by the media which clearly demonstrate that injustice cases have come about due to harsh decisions made by local political and legal committees. See Chapter 4 of this book.

64 'Henansheng Fayuan Zuzhi Jigou' (Organisation and Structure of Courts in Henan Province), available at http://hnfy.chinacourt.org/article/detail/2003/01/id/672653.shtml. Last visited September 2013.

65 Xin Chunying, *supra* note 60, p. 104.

66 *Ibid.*

court's actual costs; the monthly salary of some basic court judges cannot be guaranteed. This can cause a shortage of judges in remote areas as law graduates do not want to work there due to low and uncertain wages.

The awkward financial dilemma of a basic court was once vividly described by a vice-president of the Higher People's Court in Hubei province. She once made an unannounced visit to a people's tribunal in a remote area. Having lost their way they had to call the tribunal; they tried all the numbers they had, but even though it was the middle of the afternoon nobody answered the phone. The vice-president was shocked and wondered why nobody was at the court during normal working hours. Finally they reached the tribunal and she saw people were working in every office and there were also two trials going on. Since the tribunal was located far from the city, judges did not go home every day. They grew their own vegetables and ate together – each judge cooked in rotation. At the dinner table the vice-president asked why nobody answered the phones in the afternoon. Looking very embarrassed the head of the tribunal replied that because the tribunal was unable to pay the cost of the phones, the local telephone bureau had over a month ago cut off their lines. Although he had implored the telephone bureau to keep one phone connected in his office, that afternoon he had been at a meeting out of the office, and thus nobody answered the calls. The vice-president was quite shocked. She was informed that the tribunal had experienced similar situations with their water and electricity supply also being cut-off, since the amount of money they received could not cover these expenses. Perhaps the worst aspect was the fact that for four months of that year the judges had not received their salaries. At the dinner table they also discussed a case in which a local judge, because his wife was ill and could not work, and because they had a child studying at university, had to operate a pedicab in the evening to earn some extra income and consequently was criticised by the court for tarnishing the image of judges. The vice-president expressed that she felt dreadful that evening because she could not connect the dignity and authority of judges and courts with the absence of salary, the blocking of telephone lines and operating a pedicab. She wrote:

> When asking myself whether all of these phenomena are just a matter of 'money', I am forced to answer no. The problem is not merely a shortage of money which can be rectified by an increase in payments to the court or a judge. Indeed, a unified legal system can only operate effectively if other unified systems, including the judicial system, financial system and personnel systems provide such guarantees.[67]

Obviously, courts' financial dilemmas cannot simply be left to local governments. It is not uncommon therefore that presidents of courts complain about financial quandaries and how much effort they have to put into raising funds for courts.[68]

Courts are required to submit all their litigation fees to the corresponding government, and receive money for their expenditure from that same government, this is the so-called the system of 'separation of revenue and expenditure'. In practice, a local government often takes into account the income generated by a court in deciding how much they will give to the court. Some local governments choose to give back an amount of money similar to that submitted by the courts; some

67 Lu Zhongmei, *Fayan Guanting: Chuanxing Yu Jiaoshou He Faguan Zhijian* (Using Legal Eyes to Observe the Court Session: Experience as a Professor and a Judge) (Beijing: Beijing Daxue Chubanshe, 2006), pp. 8–10.

68 This statement is based on my interviews with 10 presidents of the courts at different levels during the period from 2007 to 2010. I could not forget some of their concerned faces and hesitant words – they were unsure whether their actions could one day be used against them.

governments give less; it is rare that a local government gives back more than a court generates.[69] Unsurprisingly courts find various ways to seek 'financial benefit'. The vice-president of the SPC once pointed out that: 'on the one hand due to financial shortage some courts could not maintain their normal operation without generating extra income; on the other hand the task of adjudicative work serving economic interests distract courts to apply law strictly and affect the fair image of courts'.[70]

Since 2000, the central government has allocated specific designated funds to help local courts, especially basic courts in remote areas, to mitigate their financial shortcomings. Nowadays local courts are funded by both local and central government. Local government includes both provincial government and lower-level government. Despite the central government's policy to safeguard local courts' finances, the criteria in determining a court's budget and dividing the central and local proportion need to be further defined, and a complete separation of revenue and expenditure needs to be effectively carried out.[71] Consequently, local courts' dependence on local government, which undermines the courts' independence, has not been substantively improved.

Another major setback in terms of court and government relationships is the lack of judicial independence in handling administrative cases, where government agencies are defendants. First, the common problem of having administrative cases accepted by courts is partially accounted for by the fact that governmental organs are unwilling to have disputes settled by courts.[72] Secondly, even with cases which are filed by courts, the representatives of the government agencies rarely appear in courts. According to a research survey, of the 364 administrative cases, only nine explicitly indicated that the legal representatives of the defendants were present at the trial (2.5 per cent) and 172 explicitly indicated that the legal representatives were absent (47.3 per cent). In the remaining cases, there is no clear indication, from the texts of the judgments, of the attendance or not of the legal representatives of the defendants.[73] Thirdly, it is not uncommon that governmental organs send messages to pressurise courts into demanding that plaintiffs withdraw.[74]

---

69 According to the Notice on Implementation of the Measures on the Management of Court Fees of the People's Courts issued by the Higher People's Court and the Bureau of Finance of Guangdong province in 2000, 'all court fees shall be directly paid to the special account opened by the provincial financial bureau. Afterwards, 15 per cent of the money is to be allocated by the provincial government for expenditures on improving the court system of the whole province, and the remaining 85 per cent will be returned to the courts in the form of subsidiary operation fees, which is to be used by the courts to cover every sort of expenditure, including fringe benefits for judges and other employees.' See Nanping Liu and Michelle Xiao Liu, 'Trick or Treat: Legal Reasoning in the Shadow of Corruption in the People's Republic of China', 34 (2008–2009) *North Carolina Journal of International Law and Commercial Regulation*, p. 248.

70 Shen Deyong, 'Ying Jianli Yu Shichang Jingji Xiang Shiying De Fayuan Tizhi' (Establishing a Judicial System That Suits the Market Economy), *Renmin Fayuan Bao* (People's Court Daily), 6 June 1994.

71 Tang Humei, Guo Feng and Li Jun, 'Quanguo Fayuan Jingfei Baozhang Tizhi Gaige Qingkuang Diaoyan Baogao' (Investigation Report on Reforming Financial Guarantee Systems among All Courts in China), 17 (2011) *Renmin Sifa*, pp. 75–79.

72 See Chapter 6 of this book.

73 Lin Lihong, Shen Xiaoping and Huang Qihui, 'Hubei Xingzheng Shenpan Xianzhuang Diaocha Baogao' (An Investigation Report on the *Status Quo* of Administrative Trial in Hubei Province), 10 (2009) *Hubei Shehui Kexue* (Hubei Social Science), p. 170.

74 See Chapter 6 of this book.

Courts and Public Prosecution

The structure of the prosecution service corresponds to the courts. According to the China Law Yearbook (2010), there are 3,658 procuratorates in China at four levels. The top is the Supreme People's Procuratorate; below that are 33 procuratorates at the provincial level including one Military Procuratorate of the People's Liberation Army and the Procuratorate of Xinjiang Production and Construction Corps; there are 403 procuratorates at the city level,[75] 3,005 at the county level[76] and 216 procuratorate branches (*paichu jianchayuan*). The relationship between the higher and lower procuratorate is that the higher procuratorates exercise leadership over lower procuratorates.

The main functions of procuracy are: investigation, approval of arrest, prosecution and legal supervision. With regard to investigation, according to the 2012 amended Criminal Procedure Law (CrPL), in most criminal cases it is conducted by the organs of public security. The procuratorate exercises direct investigation only in the following cases: (1) Crimes of embezzlement, bribery and dereliction of duty committed by state functionaries, and crimes involving the violation of the personal rights of citizens, such as illegal detention, extraction of confessions by torture, retaliation, framing, illegal searches, and crimes involving the infringement of a citizen's democratic rights. In addition, in cases involving other grave crimes committed by state functionaries in taking advantage of their functions and powers, if it needs to be handled directly by the procuratorate, upon approval by higher people's procuratorate and the SPP, the procuratorate can investigate such cases directly (Art. 18). (2) If in examining a case the procuratorate decides that a supplementary investigation is needed, it may request that an investigation is carried out by an organ of public security, or alternatively it may conduct the investigation itself (Art. 171).

As to the function of verifying and approving arrest warrants, Article 78 of the 2012 amended CrPL provides that the arrest of a suspect must be approved by procuratorate or by decision of a court, and be executed by a public security authority.

Public prosecution is the main function of the procuratorate.[77] After examination of a case transferred by an investigative organ, a procuratorate has the power to decide whether or not to bring the case to a court. While in most cases a procuratorate will initiate a public prosecution, Article 173 of the CrPL provides that procuratorates have the power to decide on non-prosecution in the following situations: (1) when an act is very clearly minor, causing no serious harm, and is therefore not deemed a crime; (2) if the limitation period for criminal prosecution has expired; (3) where there is an exemption from criminal punishment arising from the granting of a special amnesty decree; (4) if the crime is to be handled only upon complaint according to the Criminal Law, but where there is no complaint or the complaint has been withdrawn; (5) if the criminal suspect or defendant is deceased; (6) if other laws provide an exemption from investigation of criminal responsibility. In addition, under Article 171 of the CrPL, with respect to a case for which supplementary investigation

75 At the city level there are 374 normal procuratorates, 12 branches (*jianchayuan fenyuan*) of military procuratorates and 17 branches of railway transport procuratorates.

76 At the country level there are 2,893 normal procuratorates, 53 military procuratorates and 59 railway transport procuratorates.

77 Prosecution powers include public prosecution and private prosecution. Under Article 204 of the CrPL, private prosecution can only apply to a limited number of exceptional cases: (i) cases to be handled only upon complaint; (ii) minor criminal cases; (iii) cases where victims have evidence proving that the defendants should be investigated for criminal responsibility, as their acts infringed on their personal or property rights, whereas, the public security organs or the people's procuratorate do not investigate the criminal responsibility of the accused. For all other criminal cases, the procuratorate should decide whether to initiate public prosecution and then present court proceedings in support of public prosecution.

has been conducted, if the people's procuratorate still believes that the evidence is insufficient and the case does not meet the conditions for initiation of a prosecution, the procuratorate may decide not to initiate one. This is called non-prosecution for doubtful cases. Chinese criminal procedure combines the principle of legality and the principle of discretion, giving priority to the principle of legality. Statistics have shown that among the cases examined for prosecution by procuratorates throughout China, only about 3 per cent of the cases where the procuratorates decided not to initiate prosecutions were decided according to the principle of discretion.[78]

The most controversial issues concerning the power of procuratorates relate to their supervision of the implementation of law. One is the status of the procuratorate under the Constitution. The other is the role of the procuratorate in the supervision of the court's handling of criminal, civil and administrative cases.

The Procuratorate as the State Organ of Legal Supervision

The establishment of the prosecution service in the PRC was substantially influenced by the Soviet model, which emphasised that the procuratorates should be the state organs of legal supervision in order to guarantee the unified application of law. Article 129 of the 1982 Constitution states that the people's procuratorates are state organs for legal supervision. A narrow interpretation deems that this 'refers to the supervision of the legality of the activities of the enforcement organs of criminal justice such as the public and state security organs, courts and prisons, as well as the power of public prosecution and legal investigation along with legal supervision'.[79] A broad interpretation states:

> the legal supervision by the Procuratorate consists in extensive supervision in the interest of ensuring a unified and correct implementation of the Constitution and the law. For example, some people hold that since the Constitution has only a general provision for the legal supervision power of the procuratorates, without specific limitation of its supervisory power, the procuratorates should have the power of general supervision over the implementation of all laws promulgated in the country. Therefore the procuratorates may exercise supervision over any state organ, enterprise, social organisation or citizen on account of violation or incorrect implementation of the law.[80]

However, they concluded that the prevailing view

> is that the Constitutional legal provision for the procuratorates in its original purpose of legislation may be understood in its broadest sense. But the legal supervision by the procuratorates is not supervision in the general sense, i.e. legal supervision with its specific objects, scope and content. The concrete content of the legal supervision coincided with the functions of the procuratorates vested by the law.[81]

Since the 1990s, within the broader context of judicial reform, some scholars have challenged the nature of the procuratorates as state organs of legal supervision. In their view, the feature

78 Chen Guangzhong, 'Principle and Basic Theory of Chinese Non-Prosecution System', in Hans-Jorg Albrecht and Chen Guangzhong (eds), *Non-Prosecution Policies: A Sino-German Comparison* (Freiburg i. Br.: Iuscrim, 2002), p. 102.

79 Jiang Wei and Qian Fang, 'The Position, Functions and Organisational Structure of Chinese Procuratorates', in Hans-Jorg Albrecht and Chen Guangzhong, *supra* note 78, p. 58.

80 *Ibid.*, p. 59.

81 *Ibid.*, p. 59.

of the modern prosecution system originated from public litigation, which requires that both the defendants and prosecutors stand on an equal footing. Legal supervision by the procuratorate is contrary to the nature of public litigation. The prosecutor should be under supervision, and not itself be the organ of supervision. They also argue that in modern society, supervisory powers have been diversified, and it is impossible to entrust a sole state organ with this function. Some also consider that effective legal supervision requires a neutral supervisory body; if the prosecutor simultaneously supervises a court trial, and also acts as a party within the court trial, this dual function may undermine its impartiality.[82] In connection with this, some argue that this prosecution power is an administrative, and not judicial, power. Judicial power is passive, whereas prosecution is active, investigating and prosecuting criminal offences. Judicial power is neutral, whereas the procuratorate represents the state and is not therefore neutral. Judicial power has finality, whereas procuratorate decisions must eventually be justified by the court. Based on procuratorate power as an administrative power, where the procuratorate is part of the government, the procuratorate should be subject to judicial review. Consequently, it is argued the status of procuratorate power under the current legal framework is a misallocation of state power.[83]

The opposing view is that even though the procuratorate has dual functions, the power of the procuratorate should be defined as judicial power in order to guarantee the independent exercise of its prosecutorial powers. It is argued that the power of public prosecution has a judicial nature, as the prosecutor has to examine the evidence and decide whether to prosecute a case. These powers are similar to the discretionary powers of judges in applying law. In addition, the procuratorates are relatively independent while handling a case. Procuratorate power is aimed at law application, and also at ensuring the public interest. Both prosecutors and judges are guarantors of law. The exercise of prosecutorial power is the significant step in the initiation of the judicial process. Prosecutors and judges enjoy similar professional status.[84]

Supervision of the Courts' Adjudication

The Criminal Procedure Law, the Civil Procedure Law and the Administrative Litigation Law all provide respectively for legal supervision by procuratorates over criminal, civil and administrative trials.

The supervision of criminal cases has two aspects. One is the power of the procuratorate to give their opinions on corrections (*jiu zheng yi jian*), should a procuratorate discover that a court violated litigation procedures while handling a case (Art. 203 of the 2012 amended CrPL). The other is the power to launch a protest case. The Criminal Procedure Law provides two kinds of 'protest'. The first is Art. 217, which provides that if a local procuratorate deems that there is a definite error in a judgment or order made by a people's court at the first instance, it can present a protest to the people's court at a higher level. This right of protest by the prosecution can be understood simply as a process of appeal, where the prosecutors can launch an appeal to the higher-level court. Article 218 stipulates that the procuratorate should decide whether to present a protest within five days of receiving a request by the victim or his or her legal representatives.

The second type of protest comes within the trial supervision procedure. Article 243 provides that if the SPP finds a definite error in a legally effective judgment or order of a court at any level,

82 Liu Lixian and Zhang Zhihui, 'Jiancha Jiguan Zhiquan Yanjiu' (Research on the Functions of Procuratorates), in Sun Qian and Liu Lixian (eds), *Jiancha Luncong Di Er Juan* (Prosecution Review vol. 2) (Beijing: Falu Chubanshe, 2001), p. 85.

83 *Ibid.*, p. 86.

84 *Ibid.*, pp. 101–102.

or if a procuratorate at a higher level finds some definite error in a legally effective judgment or order of a court at a lower level, the procuratorate has the power to present a protest to the same level of court.

With regard to supervision of civil cases, the Civil Procedure Law provides the SPP and higher-level people's procuratorates with the power to protest against a legally effective judgment or order of a lower court, if involving the following circumstances: insufficient evidence, a definite error in the application of law, violations of legal procedures, judicial corruption involving embezzlement, bribery and favouritism, perverting the course of justice during the trial, mediation agreement harmful to state interests or social public interests. When a protest is lodged, a court must re-try the case and request that the people's procuratorate send a representative to be present at the proceedings (Articles 208 to 213 of the 2012 amended CiPL).

As to supervision of administrative cases, the Administrative Litigation Law provides that the procuratorates have the right to exercise legal supervision over administrative proceedings (Art. 10). If a procuratorate finds violations of legal provisions and regulations in a legally effective judgment or order of a court, it has the right to lodge a protest according to the procedure of trial supervision (Art. 64).

Some legal experts consider that this protest by the procuratorate in civil and administrative cases is unnecessary, as the autonomy of the parties should be fully respected in civil litigation. If a party for various reasons gives up its right for re-trial, and the prosecutor takes up this re-trial, this can be seen as infringing on the right of disposition of the party. In judicial practice, protest cases are rarely initiated by the procuratorate alone, without a prior request from the party.[85] Some scholars argue that the re-trial procedures in civil and administrative cases initiated by the procuratorate violate the principle of equality between litigants. Namely, when the procuratorate accepts a request from one party to launch a protest, this creates a trial situation where the prosecutor and one party stand against the other party that has no such support.[86]

Conversely, some scholars deem the legal supervision of civil cases by the procuratorate necessary due to the practical existence of local protectionism and unfairness within the judiciary, which results in many case being wrongly handled by courts. Although after a wrong judgment becomes effective a party has the right to request re-trial under the supervision procedure, in practice, exercising this right is difficult. It is up to the court to decide whether it accepts a request for re-trial from individual parties. However, if a protest is lodged by the procuratorate, a court must accept the case. In addition, supervision by the procuratorate is external, which reflects the checks and balances between the procuratorial power and the judicial power. Supervision by the procuratorate is also conducive to urging judges to strictly adhere to procedure, to reduce corruption, and to decrease the number of petitions to various government organs.[87]

In recent years the SPP has escalated its support to strengthen the supervisory function of the people's procuratorate on courts, with particular emphasis of the procuratorate's involvement in large civil and economic cases. For instance, researchers of the SPP argue that the existing legal framework that limits supervision to a review of legally effective judgments and orders is insufficient, and that supervision should be extended to the entire trial process. For example, in terms of the supervision of administrative cases, the procuratorate should not only have the right to protest but should also participate in the litigation by bringing cases concerning the interests of the

---

85 Jing Hanchao and Lu Zijuan, 'Lun Minshi Shenpan Jiandu Chengxu zhi Chonggou' (Analysis on the Reconstruction of the Legal Supervision Procedures in Civil Cases), 1 (1999), *Faxue Yanjiu*, p. 35.

86 Xia Keqin, 'Tuijin Woguo Sifa Gaige De Jidian Sikao' (Some Thoughts on Promoting China's Judicial Reform), 2 (1998) *Faxue* (Law), p. 57.

87 Wang Liming, *supra* note 11, pp. 493–494.

state, society and citizens as a whole, such as environmental pollution and consumer rights.[88] Some scholars have argued that civil trials protect the autonomy of the parties, as well as public interests. In a case of infringement of state assets and resources, which could damage the public interest, the procuratorate should be empowered to represent the state to sue.[89]

The 2012 revised CiPL indeed strengthened the supervisory function of procuratorates on civil litigation in terms of supervisory scope, methods and measures. Wang Shenming, representing the NPCSC, explained that such strengthening is based on three factors. First, judicial unfairness is a problem in judicial practice and judicial authority is not high. Secondly, when the draft bill was deliberated, various sources supported the idea to strengthen such supervision. Thirdly, the SPC and the SPP had similar opinions on its necessity and how to strengthen such a supervisory function.[90]

Conclusion

The Chinese Constitution provides in a general manner that courts should exercise adjudicative power independently according to law, and should not be subject to interference by administrative organs, public organisations or individuals (Art. 126). However, the Constitution also entrusts people's congresses and procuratorates with certain functions in supervising a court's work. Moreover, in the Preamble of the Constitution the position of the Communist Party is declared as leading in all state affairs, including judicial affairs. This Constitutional setting has a profound influence on the relationships between courts and other state organs. Due to historical reasons and the political system in present day China, courts are the weakest organs compared to other state powers.

The most fundamental and serious problem is that the people's congress, the Party organ, the government and the procuratorate at all levels, all have the *de facto* power to 'supervise' courts in handling individual cases. Furthermore, when and how they use such power is highly uncertain. The necessity for such supervision is viewed by Chinese commentators in light of the wide existence of judicial unfairness and judicial corruption, which has given rise to growing public petitions to higher government authorities; the external supervision of courts handling cases could in some instances thus result in fairness and justice. However, China has overemphasised on supervision by state organs which is actually a sort of 'supervision within the institutions', and such supervision has its limits and causes new problems. Meanwhile, 'supervision outside the institutions', such as media supervision, remains largely curbed. Moreover, supervision in the form of courts applying procedural law strictly has yet to be elevated as the most significant and effective form of supervision. If open trial, due process, lawyer's rights in judicial process, public access to all judgments and so on can be firmly followed by courts and judges, judicial corruption can be, to a large extent, mitigated.

Moreover, the negative influence of external supervision on the fundamental principles of judicial independence cannot be overlooked. The Chinese central authority has taken a controversial attitude toward judicial independence. It is correctly observed that

88 Liu Lixian and Zhang Zhihui, *supra* note 82, p. 120, p. 123, and Zhang Xuedan, 'Guanyu Jiancha Jiguan Zhiquan De Zhengyi Ji Sikao' (Debate and Thoughts on the Functions of Procuratorates), in Sun Qian and Liu Lixian (eds), *supra* note 82, p. 201.

89 Wang Liming, *supra* note 11, p. 499; Zhou Qihua, *Zhongguo Jiancha Xue* (China's Procuratorial Theory) (Beijing: Zhongguo Fazhi Chubanshe, 1998), p. 119.

90 Wang Shengming, 'Jiaqiang Falv Jiandu Shi Xiugai Minshi Susongfa Zhongyao Neirong' (Strengthening Legal Supervision Is an Important Component of Amendment to the Civil Procedure Law), available at http://www.china.com.cn/news/2012-08/31/content_26390845.htm. Last visited September 2013.

> [F]rom the Party's perspective, a stronger legal system with a more independent judiciary has both advantages and disadvantages. While the Party has for years acknowledged that local protectionism is undermining the independence of the judiciary, it has refused to address the institutional causes of the problem, presumably because it fears that an authoritative and independent judiciary able to decide commercial and administrative cases on their merits would also be able to decide politically sensitive cases on their merits. Thus the dilemma facing the Party is how to strengthen the judiciary without allowing it to become too strong.[91]

It seems there is no ready solution to such a dilemma.

91 Randall Peerenboom, 'A Government of Laws: Democracy, Rule of Law and Administrative Law Reform in the PRC', 12(34) (2003) *Journal of Contemporary China*, p. 61.

Chapter 3
The Professionalisation of the Judiciary

Introduction

Given that legal education was discontinued for more than 10 years during the Cultural Revolution, and was only resumed again in 1977 at a limited number of universities, it was inevitable that many judicial officers would not have undertaken legal studies prior to being assigned the duty of adjudicating cases. Due to a lack of adequate legal education, the Chinese judiciary has thus been handicapped since its rebirth; it is clear that a fair and effective judicial system cannot be established without a foundation of qualified professional judges.

That being said, the Chinese judicial force has been developing in parallel with the enhancement of the judicial system in the post-Mao era. Legal education has expanded quickly over the past 30 years. In 1979, only six universities in China had law faculties. By 2005, that number had mushroomed to 559. A concomitant increase in law students, from 3,315 in 1979 to 449,295 in 2005, accompanied the increase in the availability of programmes.[1] Although not all law graduates join the judiciary, the percentage of judges with university law degrees increased from 6.9 per cent in 1995, to 51.6 per cent in 2005. A statistic in 2008 showed that the percentage of judges with a junior college (*dazhuan*) degree or above has reached nearly 100 per cent.[2]

Moreover, the Supreme People's Court (SPC) has for more than a decade considered the training of judges as one of its central concerns. In 1996, the SPC issued the 1996–2000 Training Plan for Court Cadres All over China.[3] In 1997, the National Judges College (NJC) was established to provide training for presidents, vice-presidents and senior judges of higher and intermediate courts as well as judge candidates.[4] The NJC and local judges' colleges have provided and strengthened training for judges on judicial ethics and adjudicative skills, and fostered judicial consciousness on judicial fairness and efficiency. China now has an impressively large judicial force of around 200,000 judges.[5] The overall professional quality of judges as a whole is, however, difficult to define. According to the report on the implementation of the Law on Judges published

1 Huo Xiandan, *Zhongguo Faxue Jiaoyu Fansi* (The Rethinking of Legal Education in China) (Beijing: Zhongguo Renmin Daxue Chubanshe, 2007), p. 59.

2 The 1995 and 2005 figures are cited from Zhu Jingwen (ed.), *Zhongguo Falu Fazhan Baogao, Shujuku He Zhibiao Tixi* (Report on China Law Development, Database and Indicators) (Beijing: Zhongguo Renmin Daxue Chubanshe, 2007), p. 34. The 2008 figure is cited from 'Shidai Guanjianci Jianzheng Faguan Duiwu 30 Nian Bianqian' (Keywords in the Era Witness Evolution of the Group of Judges within the Past 30 Years), available at http://news.xinhuanet.com/legal/2008-12/07/content_10467991.htm. Last visited September 2013.

3 '1996–2000 Nian Quanguo Fayuan Ganbu Jiaoyu Peixun Guihua' (Plan for the Education and Training of Cadres of the Court System Throughout the Country: 1996–2000), issued on 16 September 1996, the official document is numbered *Fafa* No. 29 [1996].

4 The official website of the National Judge College, see http://njc.chinacourt.org/. Last visited September 2013.

5 See 'Woguo Faguan Renshu Yijin 20 Wan Ren' (The Number of Judges in China is Nearly 200,000), 26 July 2013. Available at http://www.chinadaily.com.cn/hqpl/zggc/2013-07-26/content_9684977.html. Last visited September 2013.

by the National People's Congress Standing Committee (NPCSC) in 2007, the professionalism of some of the judges proved to be low. Their lack of capacity arose in judging facts, applying law, presiding over trials and mediating disputes, handling cases strictly according to law, following the standards and doing so in a civilised manner. This has resulted in 'human feelings cases' (*renqing an*), 'relationship cases' (*guanxi an*) and 'money cases' (*jinqian an*), which have in turn weakened the judicial authority and image of the judicial force.[6] A research report by a higher court in China has also pointed out that the quality of the judicial force as a whole remains low, and considerable differences exist amongst courts at different levels, and between economically well developed and less developed areas.[7]

The steady development of the judiciary over the past three decades reflects both on legislative endeavours, such as the promulgation of the first PRC Judges Law by the NPCSC in 1995, its amendment in 2001, and the introduction of new systems, such as the implementation of the National Unified Judicial Examination in 2002. In further steps, the SPC has taken a series of measures aimed at improving the professionalism of the judiciary, such as issuing the Code of Conduct for the Judiciary in 2001.[8]

This chapter first discusses the main and somewhat controversial issues of the qualification and appointment of judges, and protection of judges' personal rights in the context of the Judges Law promulgated by the NPCSC in 1995 and amended in 2001. Secondly, the issue of judicial corruption is examined in political and social contexts. Nowadays, studies of the Chinese judiciary cannot avoid assessing judicial corruption. This is not only because such corruption is a serious and widespread problem, but also because combating corruption is closely linked to all other judicial

6 Gu Xiulian, 'Quanguo Renda Changweihui Zhifa Jianchazu Guanyu Genzong Jiancha "Zhonghua Renmin Gongheguo FaguanFa", "Zhonghua Renmin Gongheguo Jianchaguan Fa" Shishi Qingkuang De Baogao' (Report on the Implementation of the Judges Law of the People's Republic of China and the Prosecutors Law of the People's Republic of China, submitted by the Inspection Team on Law Implementation of the National People's Congress Standing Committee). This Report was presented by Gu Xiulian, Deputy Chairman of the NPCSC, at a meeting of the NPCSC on 29 August 2007. It was published in 6 (2007) *Gazette of the NPCSC*, p. 655.

7 Jiangsu Gaoji Renmin Fayuan Ketizu (Research Team of the Higher People's Court in Jiangsu Province), 'Jiufen De Youxiao Jiejue: Renmin Fayuan Sifa Nengli Jianshe De Diaoyan Baogao' (Effectively Settling Disputes: Research Report on the Capacity Building of People's Courts), in Zuigao Renmin Fayuan Yanjiushi (Research Office of the Supreme People's Court) (ed.), *Shenpan Qianyan Wenti Yanjiu: Zuigao Renmin Fayuan Zhongdian Yanjiu Keti Baogao Ji* (Research on Hot Topics in Adjudication: Collection of Key Research Topics of the Supreme People's Court), vol. 1 (Beijing: Renmin Fayuan Chubanshe, 2007), p. 100.

8 On 18 October 2001, the Supreme People's Court issued the Code of Conduct for Judges in the PRC, which makes China one of the few countries in the world with a specific code of conduct for the judiciary. Following the amendment of the Judges Law in June 2001, the introduction of the Code represented an important effort by the SPC to improve professionalism among judges. The Code contains 50 articles, divided under the headings of six essential principles: judicial impartiality, judicial efficiency, integrity of judges, judicial decorum, self-improvement of judges and the restriction of extra-judicial activities. These general principles are similar to those provided in the US Code. However, the detailed rules under each principle also reflect Chinese characteristics. For a timely examination of the Code, see Yuwen Li, 'Professional Ethics of Chinese Judges: A Rising Issue in the Landscape of Judicial Practice', 47 (2003) *China Perspectives*, pp. 28–39. This Code was modified in 2010. Unsurprisingly, resulting from the shift in direction of the judicial reform under the then president of the SPC, Wang Shenjun, the new Code included some more politically oriented principles, such as the principle that judges should have firm faith in the conception of the socialist rule of law, be loyal to the Communist Party, to the State, to the people and to law; the judiciary should serve the people, concern people's feeling and uphold their legitimate rights and interests. For the full text of the 2010 Code of Conduct, see http://www.court.gov.cn/qwfb/sfwj/jd/201102/t20110223_14086.htm. Last visited September 2013.

reform measures. Judicial corruption undermines judicial procedures, hinders judicial justice, and damages public trust in the judicial system. In this chapter a number of sources are used to illustrate the notion that judicial corruption is rife at all levels, and a special feature of judicial corruption in modern-day China is that it exists both amongst judges as individuals and in and between courts as collective bodies. However, as the root causes of judicial corruption are complex, political, economic and social contexts cannot be overlooked in confronting the issue.

The Judges Law and Practice

In 1995, the NPCSC issued the first Judges Law, then in 2001 revised it.[9] The Law originally consisted of 45 articles but was extended to 53 when amended. It covers general provisions, judges' functions, judges' rights and duties, qualification, appointment, withdrawal, judges' grades,[10] appraisal, training, awards and punishments, salaries and other benefits, resignation and dismissal, complaint and petition, retirement, commission for examination and assessment of judges, and supplementary provisions.[11] For the purpose of this book, discussion focuses on the qualification and appointment of judges, as well as judges' rights.

The Qualification and Appointment of Judges

Article 2 of the Judges Law defines judges as the adjudicative officers who exercise the judicial authority of the state according to law, including presidents, vice-presidents, members of adjudication committees, heads of trial chambers, deputy heads of trial chambers, and judges and associate judges of courts at every level.

The law sets out two pairings of qualifications for judges: functional and political; and academic and professional (Art. 9). The functional and political requirements include: holding Chinese nationality, being at least 23 years of age, endorsing of the Chinese Constitution, having sound political and professional qualities and moral standing, and being in good health. The academic and professional criteria are: work experience of at least two years for graduates with a bachelor's degree from a university law faculty or for other graduates who have a bachelor's degree in a field other than law but who nonetheless possess professional knowledge of law – though for a position as a judge at a higher court or the SPC, at least three years' work experience for graduates with a bachelor's degree; work experience of at least one year for graduates with a master's or doctorate degree in law or for graduates with a master's or doctorate degree in a field other than law but who nonetheless possess professional knowledge of law.[12]

---

9 The English text of the Law can be found at http://www.accci.com.au/judges-law.htm. Last visited September 2013.

10 According to Articles 16 to 18, judges are divided into 12 grades. The President of the Supreme People's Court is the Chief Justice. Judges from the second grade to the twelfth grade are composed of justices, senior judges and judges. Grades of judges are to be determined on the basis of their posts, their actual working ability and political integrity, their professional competence, their achievements in judicial work and their seniority.

11 For a brief discussion on the Judges Law, see Ronald Brown, *Understanding Chinese Courts and Legal Process: Law with Chinese Characteristics* (The Hague: Kluwer Law International, 1997), pp. 101–107.

12 The 2001 amended Judges Law requires higher academic education for newly appointed judges. Under Article 9 of the 1995 Judges Law, a graduate with a law degree lower than Bachelor level, such as *dazhuan*, could also qualify to be a new judge.

When the Judges Law was amended in 2001, the requirement that newly appointed judges should hold a National Unified Judicial Examination (NUJE) certificate was added. Article 12 states that potential judges should be selected through strict examination and appraisal from among those who passed the NUJE and are best qualified for the post in accordance with the standards of political integrity and technical capability. Article 10 provides that the following persons may not hold the post of a judge: (1) persons who have been subjected to criminal punishment for committing a crime; or (2) persons who have been discharged from public employment. It should be noted that apart from passing the NUJE, a potential judge is also required to pass a National Civil Service Examination.

As far as the appointment and removal of judges is concerned, Article 11 restates the Constitutional provisions that the President of the Supreme People's Court is appointed and removed by the National People's Congress. The SPC's vice-presidents, members of the adjudication committee, chief judges and associate chief judges of divisions, and judges are appointed and removed by the NPCSC upon the recommendation of the President of the SPC. At the local level, the appointment and removal of presidents, vice-presidents and judges is conducted by the corresponding people's congresses and their standing committees. Assistant judges are appointed and removed by the presidents of the courts in which they work. It should be noted that presidents and vice-presidents of courts are political posts. They are appointed by Party organs, in consultation with relevant governmental institutions and higher-level courts. The general rule in this respect is that the higher the position of authority, the more political the appointment will be.

The Judges Law does not specify the tenure of judges although China does indeed practice a tenure system. The term for the president of a court is the same as that for the people's congress, namely five years, whilst vice-presidents, heads of divisions and judges do not need to be reappointed when people's congresses change their deputies. Judges retire at the age of 60. Ordinarily, once appointed a judge can retain his or her position for however long he or she chooses, unless any violation of the law or disciplinary or dismissal proceedings bring the appointment to an end.

In the 1980s, most judges did not have law degrees due to the historical fact that legal education was discontinued for more than 10 years up to the end of 1977. In the early years of the resumption of university-level legal studies, graduates could find jobs in various governmental and academic institutions, and consequently working in courts was not deemed to be the most popular of choices.[13] The expansion of the judicial force was instead brought about through the demobilisation of military officers, who took positions in the courts. Such practices drew criticism both inside and outside China. A distinguished Chinese professor, He Weifang, writing an article in *Nanfang Zhoumo* (Southern Weekend), entitled 'Installing Army Veterans in Courts', challenged the government policy of casting extra military officers into the judicial profession, for which a high level of specialist training is required.[14] Fortunately, as the number of legally-trained graduates has increased rapidly in the past three decades, there has been a considerable decline in the number of army veterans recruited into the judiciary.[15]

---

13 The author graduated from the Law School of Peking University in 1984 and recalled that, at that time, it was not even a preferred choice to work at the SPC in Beijing. In that year, there was not one graduate from the Law School of Peking University who was assigned to the HPC, IPC or BPC in Beijing. However, it is nowadays extremely difficult for law graduates from Peking University to get a job even in a basic court in Beijing.

14 He Weifang, *Sifa De Linian Yu Zhidu* (Concept and System of the Judiciary) (Beijing: Zhongguo Zhengfa Daxue Chubanshe, 1998), pp. 237–240. Lubman points out: 'The shortage of legally trained judges makes judicial ignorance of the law a real danger, particularly because of legislative incoherence' in China. Stanley Lubman, *Bird in a Cage: Legal Reform in China after Mao* (Stanford, CA: Stanford University Press, 1999), p. 254.

15 According to an empirical study conducted by Sida Liu in a basic court in Hebei Province, during the period 1978 to 1985, army veterans accounted for 60 per cent of the court's personnel, 40 per cent were

Whilst the 2001 amended Judges Law has raised the standard of legal education for potential judges, in practice the qualifications and appointment of judges in different courts and in different locations can still vary considerably. For instance, in Beijing courts, regardless of the level, competition for jobs is fierce and may sometimes result in unfair play. If someone wants to apply for a vacancy, that individual must: have a law degree, have passed the NUJE, and have passed the court's own written examination. Moreover, each court holds its own interview procedure. Since such interviews lack a visible standard and the decision is made behind closed doors, space is left to use '*guanxi*' (relations) to influence the final outcome. Sometimes, PhD students who score well on written examinations advance no further in the application process, while those lower on the list are employed, with no reasonable explanation given for the discrepancy.[16]

In contrast, in some remote areas, local courts have difficulty finding candidates with a legal background and so continue to hire people largely assigned by local governments. According to a survey conducted by the HPC in Sichuan province in 2005 and 2006, less than a quarter of the judges investigated had law backgrounds (including those with a diploma below the bachelor degree level); the overwhelming majority came from the ranks of demobilised military officers and those recruited from basic level cadres. The shortage of judges has been an on-going dilemma, especially with regard to courts in sparsely populated, remote areas. Understandably, young judges with a legal education leave the courts to work in the cities, those who can pass the NUJE do not want to work in such courts and the more experienced, elderly judges inevitably retire.[17] Consequently courts in remote areas continue to employ demobilised military officers, who usually follow an intensive course before being sent to work in such posts. In 2008, Zhou Yongkang, the then head of the Central Political and Legal Committee, pointed out that in order to 'guard the entrance' and truly solve the problem of the shortage of judges and prosecutors in mid-western China, the government would select certain universities of politics and law to enrol ex-servicemen from the army and armed police force who have senior high school diplomas as well as graduates from ordinary institutes of higher learning. Following graduation, they would be sent to mid-western regions to work in basic level procuratorial, judicial and public security organisations.[18]

Over and above this practical need, the Communist Party continues to exercise its policy of controlling judicial cadres through judicial appointment. According to a report from a higher people's court, a large percentage of judges, following policy arrangements, are appointed from other administrative departments without taking any examinations to work in courts. The lack of legal knowledge perpetuates a low degree of professionalism, and in the long-term leads to

---

transferred officials, and there were no college graduates. However during the period 1996 to 2000 the percentage of college graduates increased to 57 per cent, transferred officials constituted 43 per cent, and no army veterans were recruited. See Sida Liu, 'Beyond Global Convergence: Conflicts of Legitimacy in a Chinese Lower Court', 31 (2006) *Law & Social Inquiry*, p. 83.

16 My interviews with six young judges at the SPC and the Basic People's Court in Haidian District in Beijing, July 2008.

17 Sichuansheng Gaoji Renmin Fayuan Ketizu (Research Team of the Higher People's Court in Sichuan Province), 'Guanyu Sifa Gongxinli Jianshe De Diaoya Baogao' (Investigation Report on Public Confidence in the Judiciary), in Zuigao Renmin Fayuan Yanjiushi (Research Office of the Supreme People's Court) (ed.), *supra* note 7, p. 512.

18 Zhou Yongkang, 'Shenru Guanche Luoshi Kexue Fazhanguan, Cujin Jingji Pingwen Jiaokuai Fazhan, Baozheng Shehui Gongping Zhengyi, Weihu Shehui Hexie Wending' (Deepening the Implementation of the Outline on Scientific Development, Facilitating Steady and Speedy Economic Development, Guaranteeing Social Fairness and Justice, and Upholding Social Harmony and Stability), see http://www.customs.gov.cn/tabid/399/ctl/InfoDetail/InfoID/210709/mid/60432/Default.aspx?ContainerSrc=[G]Containers%2f_default%2fNo+Container. Last visited September 2013.

inefficiency. Furthermore, the pressure of caseloads compels the courts to employ increasing numbers, and while this means greater employment opportunities, the quality of individuals has not necessarily increased accordingly. In some cases those with a high standard of legal knowledge may not get an opportunity to be employed by courts, even when well-educated candidates are hired, they may depart for a higher-salaried post elsewhere shortly thereafter. This situation has created a vicious circle: the higher the number of judges needed, the more difficult it is to raise the overall quality; the lower the overall quality, the more difficult it becomes to attract individuals of a high calibre, which in turn leads to a lower quality in adjudicative work and, ultimately, inefficiency. Furthermore, due to judges' lack of pride in their profession, misconduct and corruption have spread, which has led to public distrust of the judiciary. The government, moreover, sees no need to upgrade judges' salaries as an incentive to attract more qualified people to the profession.[19]

On the whole, judges at the SPC, HPCs and IPCs have better qualifications and at least some amount of legal education. In addition, the first Five-Year Reform Programme of People's Courts (1999–2003) proposed gradually reforming the channels for recruiting judges, by establishing a system whereby judges at higher-level courts are selected from among prominent judges at lower-level courts, lawyers and high-level legal experts. Law graduates from universities, who are selected by public examination, are first to be appointed to intermediate courts and basic courts. It was stated that, within five years, the trial divisions at the SPC and the higher people's courts at the provincial level would have judges selected from lower-level courts and highly qualified legal experts. Personnel who are not qualified as judges are to be transferred to positions that support adjudication or other administrative posts.[20] There is no reliable information on whether these objectives have been met, either in full or partially. However, in 2007, when the SPC resumed the procedure for its final approval of death penalty cases, it recruited approximately 300 judges from higher and intermediate courts to establish three new criminal trial divisions. The result was that a large proportion of judges at the SPC now originate from lower courts. However, these judges are only 'borrowed' from lower courts, and they continue to receive their salaries from their original courts, albeit with some additional compensation from the SPC.[21]

The Rights of Judges

Article 8 of the Judges Law lists eight judges' rights:

1. to have the power and working conditions, which are essential to the performance of the functions and duties of judges;
2. to brook no interference from administrative organs, social organisations, and individuals in handling cases according to law;
3. to not be removed, demoted or dismissed from a post, or given a sanction, without a statutory basis and without going through statutory procedures;
4. to be remunerated for work and to enjoy insurance and welfare benefits;

---

19 Yunnansheng Gaoji Renmin Fayuan Ketizu (Research Team of the Higher People's Court of Yunnan Province), 'Guanyu Wanshan Faguan Baozhang Zhidu De Diaoyan Baogao' (Investigation Report on Improving the System for the Safeguarding of Judges' Rights), in Zuigao Renmin Fayuan Yanjiushi (Research Office of the Supreme People's Court) (ed.), *supra* note 7, p. 1063.

20 See paragraph 32 of the 'Renmin Fayuan Wunian Gaige Gangyao (1999–2003)' (Five-Year Reform Programme of People's Courts (1999–2003)), *Fafa* No. 28 [1999]. Available at http://china.findlaw.cn/info/guojiafa/xffl/124828.html. Last visited September 2013.

21 Interview with a senior judge at the SPC in July 2010.

5. to enjoy safety of the person, property and residence as ensured by law;
6. to receive training;
7. to lodge petitions or complaints;
8. to resign from their posts.

According to a comprehensive investigative report written by the Higher People's Court in Yunnan province published in 2007,[22] the realisation of these rights encounters various problems. The following focuses on some of the most serious infringements of judges' rights.

Firstly, the right 'to have the power and working conditions, which are essential to the performance of the functions and duties of judges'. While in most courts working conditions improved remarkably in the 1990s and 2000s, the disparity between courts in economically developed and those in less developed areas has often proven appalling. According to the survey report of the Higher People's Court in Yunnan province, some courts had insufficient courtrooms, basic facilities were lacking, and there was no safety control equipment. Most BPCs did not reach the required security standard, and judges' working conditions remained very poor and did not correspond to the improved economic situation in general. Moreover, judges were often required to pay for poverty relief, and to make donations for natural disasters, education and government projects. These relief payments could easily add up to the equivalent of a judge's salary. Furthermore, the standard for determining subsidies for work-related travel was calculated more than 10 years ago and thus could not cover the costs of food and accommodation at today's prices. To cut costs on work trips, some judges stayed in budget hotels. The extent of overwork among judges was also surprising. In the criminal division of the Higher People's Court in Yunnan province, each judge handled approximately 80 significant cases on average each year, with some having handled more than 100 cases. Many judges could not take any holidays and had been overworked for so long that they were mentally and physically tired.[23] Furthermore, a judge's power is sometimes severely undermined by the improper application of the system of responsibility when cases are handled wrongly. For instance, Judge Mo Zhaojun once handled a debt dispute case in a court in Guangdong province. Following the court hearing, a judgment was made in accordance with the law; as a result the losing party committed suicide in the court. Later, the police conducted an investigation and discovered that the winning party had fabricated evidence that led to an erroneous judgment. The procuratorate subsequently arrested the judge on suspicion of negligent behaviour regarding his duties as a judge. Although both the first instance and the second instance courts declared Judge Mo innocent, the accusation tormented judge Mo considerably and caused widespread concern amongst other judges. Given an absence of unified criteria to decide what constitutes a wrongly-handled case, judges find themselves in a vulnerable position since any external complaint could lead to the judge becoming the target of an investigation by the disciplinary and supervisory committee.[24]

Secondly, with regard to the right of judges to reject external interferences in handling cases according to law, it is widely recognised that Chinese judges lack independence in deciding cases due both to legalised systems (for example the systems provided by law or by SPC orders) and to hidden rules (that is, bad practice). From the few known cases, a chilling impression can be formed of how much a judge can suffer as a result of refusing to respond to external interference. In 2002, the Chinese newspaper *Nanfang Zhoumo* (Southern Weekend) reported that a judge, Jia Tingrun, who was then President of Lulong County Court in Hebei province, suffered unfair treatment

22 'Yunnansheng Gaoji Renmin Fayuan Ketizu' (Research Team of the Higher People's Court of Yunnan Province), *supra* note 19, pp. 1052–1078.

23 *Ibid.*, pp. 1068–1069.

24 *Ibid.*, p. 1068.

because he refused to try a case according to the local government's instructions. In March 1994, he dealt with a 'tough case' concerning a private business manager who faced accusations of 'embezzlement and misappropriation of cooperative funds' by the local government. Judge Jia discovered that the manager was merely a farmer and therefore, under the law, could not be charged with such a crime. Judge Jia's view was, however, rejected by the local government. The Qinhuangdao Municipal Intermediate Court (which is a level higher than the County Court) instructed Judge Jia merely to follow the local government's instructions. Local Communist Party officials also pressured Judge Jia to resolve the case as rapidly as possible. However, Judge Jia did not submit to these pressures. In August 1994, the local government announced a decision by the Qinhuangdao Party Committee to remove Judge Jia from the office of President of the County Court. A few days later he was dismissed from the court and was transferred to the county judicial bureau as an ordinary civil servant. His salary was cut from RMB 620 to 350 and his administrative ranking decreased by two levels. Moreover, the Qinhuangdao Party Committee and the Lulong County Party Committee organised several groups to investigate potential financial issues concerning Judge Jia, though nothing was discovered. Following Judge Jia's removal, the manager was sentenced to seven years' imprisonment as the local government had intended. This wrongful judgment was only corrected in 2001 after years of effort on the part of numerous lawyers. Consequently, Judge Jia's bitter experience was acknowledged.[25] This case highlights the vulnerable position in which a judge or president of a local court can find him or herself when facing the powerful and often manipulative influence of the government and the Party.

Thirdly, regarding the right that a judge should not be punished without legal basis and without following legal procedures, the overwhelming majority of judges do not experience such matters, though some reported cases demonstrate that the violation of such a right, no matter how exceptional it may be, can cause serious concerns. In December 2002, Judge Wang, who was also deputy head of the Civil Chamber of the Panshi City Court in Jilin province at that time, handled a civil case. One party to the case suspected that Judge Wang had accepted a dinner invitation from the other party and willingly delayed the case. The disgruntled party complained to the court on the basis of a lack of trust. The court immediately started an impeachment procedure to investigate Judge Wang and reached the subsequent conclusion that there was some evidence suggesting that Judge Wang might have accepted the dinner invitation and illegally handled the case. Thus, the court invited 18 people, including deputies of the people's congress, members of the people's political consultative conferences, civil servants, and both the head of and masses from the village, as well as eight judicial officers from the Court, to form an impeachment committee. The committee decided that Judge Wang had handled the case unfairly, thus he was dismissed as a judge and placed on the waiting list for another post. Such an approach and the process of impeachment has no legal basis.[26]

Another example involved Judge Hu, who, in a court in Yunnan province, brought a lawsuit against the local government when his house (bought with a bank loan) was compulsorily demolished by the government. He subsequently came under pressure from various government departments. Although he had already passed the examinations qualifying him to handle cases, suddenly in 2003, he was disqualified, sent to work in a remote area and his request to handle cases was met with no reply.[27]

---

25 See Guo Guosong, 'Keshou Faguan de Liangzhi You Duonan?' (How Difficult Is It to Scrupulously Abide by a Judge's Conscience?), *Nanfang Zhoumo* (Southern Weekend), 5 December 2002. Full text is available at http://www.southcn.com/weekend/commend/200212050016.htm. Last visited September 2013.

26 'Yunnansheng Gaoji Renmin Fayuan Ketizu' (Research Team of the Higher People's Court of Yunnan Province), *supra* note 19, p. 1067.

27 *Ibid.*, p. 1068.

Fourthly, the protection of a judge's personal safety deserves special mention as very little academic attention has been afforded to this topic. Furthermore, courts and judges usually do not want to make this a public affair. However, when I interviewed judges, most of them expressed a certain fear of being attacked by litigants and some spoke of horrifying experiences. For instance, a collegiate panel at a basic court in Wuhan once handled a divorce case in which the man did not want to be divorced and threatened that he would kill the judges and his wife if the court accepted the wife's divorce claim. Following a long period of mediation, which eventually failed to reach any agreement, the court tried the case and delivered a judgment that allowed the divorce. The man left the courtroom, but later in the afternoon attacked one of the judges as she left the court building, severely injuring her.[28] In 2005, a legal newspaper published a special focus article on judges suffering attacks and intimidation, in which it unveiled that, in Jiangsu province in the first half of 2005, there were 80 reported cases of attacks on judges resulting in personal injury; in 16 cases, people stormed and vandalised the court and the offices of the judges.[29]

Various violent and non-violent tactics are used against judges. The less serious tactics include emotional outbursts and swearing by the disgruntled parties, but also instances of judges being physically pushed by individuals. More serious tactics include threats made either by telephone or by written communication. Violent attacks against judges causing personal injury are also occasionally reported. Most reported incidents of violence occurred when judges were enforcing civil judgments, particularly where the courts undertook coercive methods, such as seizing property. Several cases were reported in the newspaper *Fazhi Zaobao*.[30] One noteworthy case occurred in August 2005 in the Yulin City IPC in Shaanxi province. In that incident, more than 100 people from a local factory, who were upset with the judgment in their case, stormed the office of the vice-president of the court. Blaming the court for the outcome of their case, they beat and humiliated the vice-president in his office. Another case of assault on a judge occurred in October 2000 in Wenling city in Zhejiang province. Dissatisfied with the judgment in a traffic dispute, a couple stormed into the judge's office and beat her. The couple also went to the judge's home, threatening to kill her. In 2005, two judges from Henan province were attacked as they travelled to Shanxi province to enforce a civil judgment in a factory. They were pulled from their car and beaten, and then followed until the police came to their rescue. A similar case occurred in July of the same year in Henan province, where two judges from a basic court were pulled from their judicial vehicle and beaten. In Hubei province, nine enforcement judges and judicial police were attacked by a family of farmers and their relatives who refused to accept the judgment in their case.

Violent attacks have also resulted in the serious injury and even death of judges. In a basic court in Jiangsu province, a man dissatisfied with the outcome of his divorce case went to the court and asked to meet with the judge. While he was in the judge's office, he took out a knife from his bag and threatened to kill her, slashing her 11 times in the end. The judge was severely injured. In September 2003, three judges from a People's Tribunal in Yunnan province travelled to a village to enforce a civil judgment of alimony, whereby a man was requested to provide financial

---

28 Interview with three judges at a basic court in Wuhan city, Hubei Province, April 2007. I once met a female judge at the training course I co-directed with the National Judge's College in Beijing in 2003 who lost her little finger. She told me that this was caused by being bitten in the courtroom by a female party in a divorce case.

29 Du Fuhai and Yao Hui, 'Faguan Anquan: Guoji Nanti Jinru Zhongguo' (Personal Safety of Judges: An International Problem That Has also Emerged in China, *Fazhi Zaobao* (Legal Morning Post), 22 August 2005.

30 *Ibid.*; the newspaper contains an extensive report on the Conference on the Protection of Judges' Rights, jointly organised by the journal *Renmin Sifa* (People's Justice) and the Intermediate People's Court of Wuxi City, Jiangsu Province.

support for his parents. The man refused to pay, and stabbed and killed one of the judges. He also injured another judge as well as his own mother. In a compensation case for personal injury in October 2001 in Liuhe County Basic People's Court in Jilin province, the losing party broke into the judge's home and stabbed the judge to death.[31] In June 2010, several judges from the Court of Changzhou district, Wuzhou city, Guangxi province went to a residential building in the district to enforce a judgment on a dispute over payment for goods. As they stood in front of the building, the persons against whom the judgment was being enforced, Ms and Mrs Liao, suddenly launched an attack on them from above the building with a large quantity of sulphuric acid. Six judges were injured by the acid, two of them suffered third degree burns on, respectively, 50 per cent and 15 per cent of their bodies.[32]

China's economic and social transition have triggered numerous new problems and conflicts. As the main remedy to solve these emerging conflicts, courts are now irreplaceable. This has, however, put courts and judges squarely in the middle of conflicts. Judges should be treated as independent, fair and neutral arbitrators between conflicting parties. However, in practice, they are sometimes mistreated by parties who make judges their targets for venting their anger and distress. Obviously, courts have to strengthen their protective capacity in order to prevent judges from being physically injured.

The author once observed a trial session at a people's tribunal in Wuhan, Hubei province. The case concerned five families that had to leave their long-term rented accommodation as the location was soon to be demolished under the local government's city expansion project. The hearing took place in a courtroom of approximately 15 square metres. A female judge and a female secretary sat beside the judge. Five plaintiffs and eight defendants sat crowded next to one another, and the observers' bench was also crowded with witnesses and observers. The room was so small that the judge's face was easily within reach of the plaintiff and the defendant sitting closest to the judge. Indeed, both the plaintiff and the defendant, who could hardly control their emotions, gesticulated animatedly in front of the judge as they loudly spoke. I recall being surprised at the judge's calm attitude in presiding over the hearing in a situation which could quickly have turned dangerous and regarding which little could have been done. This became increasingly unnerving as I noticed that at least three of the men were decidedly drunk.

After the hearing, I asked the judge whether she was afraid the parties might have lost control and started a fight. She looked at me with a gloomy smile and said: 'I am used to this.' When I discussed the situation with a deputy president of the BPC who was then in charge of this tribunal's work, she told me that the tribunal had no court police, and that, if a violent situation erupted, they would have to call the local police station located about 10 minutes from the tribunal.[33] Similarly, when I observed a civil trial hearing in the Basic People's Court in the Xicheng district of Beijing, although the small courtroom was new and clean, the parties could easily have accessed the judge's bench. No court police were present and the angry parties shouted at the presiding judge, arguing loudly in their own defence.[34]

31 *Ibid.*

32 Liang Hong and Liang Qi, 'Jiancha Jiguan Jieru Guangxi Faguan Beipo Liusuan Shijian' (Procuratorial Organisation Investigates the Sulphuric Acid Attack against Judges), available at http://news.jcrb.com/jxsw/201006/t20100608_366630.html. Last visited September 2013.

33 My observation and interview of judges in Wuhan in April 2008.

34 I observed this trial in Beijing in May 2008.

Judicial Corruption

In the absence of a legal definition on judicial corruption, Chinese legal scholars try to define the term in a broad sense by including: (1) making judgments contradictory to law, such as neglecting or even distorting facts, ignoring or misinterpreting the law in order to treat parties in a biased manner, delaying the delivery of a judgment, or making unfair judgments; (2) abusing judicial power and rent-seeking, such as using power for private profit, power and money bargaining, seeking and taking bribes, dining and taking goods, and brutally exhibiting power over people; (3) applying local judicial protectionism, such as protecting local economic interests by various means, using judicial assistance under the pretence of helping parties whilst actually worsening their situation.[35]

Henderson lists a concrete variety of acts of judicial corruption in China:

- Fabricating rulings in exchange for money;
- Blackmailing litigants into paying for, or excluding, evidence;
- Making decisions based on instructions from local government, party, or senior judicial officials, rather than the law or facts;
- Assigning, dismissing, delaying or refusing to accept cases, or refusing to properly enforce court decisions;
- Extorting kickbacks from intermediaries for passing cases to certain judges;
- Trading law enforcement services for personal gain;
- Taking bribes from the plaintiff and defendant (or their lawyers), or both;
- Manufacturing court cases;
- Embezzling court funding;
- Bowing to the demands of local officials, criminal networks, local clans, social networks or economic interests;
- Abusing the power of judges to order suspension of business operations, the confiscation of property, the eviction of tenants, or fair compensation and labour rights.[36]

The popular expression of judicial corruption in China covers wide-ranging abuses of judicial power by judicial officers for private gains. The term 'judicial officers' generally refers to judges, prosecutors and police, simply because they are the main enforcement officers in the judicial process. For the purposes of this chapter, discussion of judicial corruption is limited to judges and administrative officers working in courts. As to the latter, though their function is not in adjudicating cases, in Chinese courts, especially at local levels, they are involved in or are capable of interfering with the handling of cases by judges. Consequently, the abuse of power by administrative judicial officers can be treated as part of judicial corruption.

Due to the hidden and sensitive nature of judicial corruption, it is impossible to obtain accurate data on its frequency and scale in China. We can only refer to officially published figures, high-profile cases reported by the media, sporadic reports, findings of empirical studies and other academic works to obtain a general impression of the severity of judicial corruption. The annual work reports of the SPC usually contain the number of judicial officers who have been punished for

35 Xu Xianming and Qi Yanping, 'Lun Sifa Fubai De Zhiduxing Fangzhi' (Systemic Prevention of Judicial Corruption), in Liu Hainian et al. (eds), *Yifa Zhiguo Yu Lianzheng Jianshe* (Ruling the Country by Law and Building an Incorruptible Government) (Beijing: Shehui Kexue Wenxian Chubanshe, 2008), p. 318.

36 Keith Henderson, 'The Rule of Law and Judicial Corruption in China: Halfway over the Great Wall', in *Global Corruption Report 2007* (New York: Cambridge University Press, 2007), p. 155, citing Fan Ren, 'Calling for an Independent Judiciary', 23 (2004) *Beijing Review*, pp. 32–33.

violations of law and Party discipline. Although these figures are a consequence of anti-corruption measures, and therefore cannot accurately represent the full spectrum of judicial corruption, they can illustrate indirectly the number of judges involved in serious corruption. It seems that the actual level of judicial corruption is more serious than the SPC's reports suggest. According to a recently published empirical study on judicial corruption in China, local figures released by a few provinces on court personnel investigated were higher than the total national figures released by the SPC. For instance, for 2006 the figures released by eight provinces totalled 697, while the total figure released by the SPC was 292.[37]

Table 3.1 Judicial officials' violations of law and discipline (1988–2011)[38]

Year	Total number of judicial officials punished	Number of judicial officials subjected to criminal investigation	High-profile cases and special notes
1988	401	18	383 received disciplinary punishments (164 were judges); 18 investigated for criminal responsibilities (6 were judges)
1989	690	31	11 judges were found criminally liable
1990	887	25	326 judges were punished by Party discipline and administrative discipline, 7 faced criminal charges
1991		29	15 judges were found criminally liable
1992			
1993	850	53	35 judges were charged with crimes
1994	1,094	47	34 judges were criminally liable
1995	962	72	61 judges were convicted of crimes. Ping Yijie, President of the Higher People's Court was dismissed for violations of discipline
1996	1,051	59	50 judges were convicted of crimes
1997			
1998	2,512	221	1,654 received administrative punishment, 637 received Party disciplinary punishment, 221 were convicted of crimes. 28 presidents and vice-presidents were punished by discipline, among them, 1 was the vice-president of a HPC, 7 were from IPCs, and 20 were from BPCs. Pan Yile, vice-president of the HPC in the Guangxi Zhuang Autonomous Region was convicted of the crime of accepting bribes and sentenced to 15 years in prison.

37 Ling Li, 'Corruption on China's Courts', in Randall Peerenboom (ed.), *Judicial Independence in China: Lessons for Global Rule of Law Promotion* (New York: Cambridge University Press, 2010), pp. 201–202.

38 The figures are taken from the work reports of the SPC to the NPC from 1989 to 2012. No concrete numbers were given in the SPC work reports of 1992, 1997 and 2002.

Year	Total number of judicial officials punished	Number of judicial officials subjected to criminal investigation	High-profile cases and special notes
1999	1,450	73	32 senior judicial officers were punished. 1,377 received Party disciplinary punishment. Sun Xiaohong, president of the HPC in Yunnan province was removed due to serious violations of discipline; Yao Xiaohong, vice-president of the BPC in Jiang County in Shanxi province was sentenced to life imprisonment.
2000	1,292	46	
2001	995	85	Jia Yongxiang, president of HPC in Shenyang City was sentenced to life imprisonment on charges of fraud, corruption and using public funds.
2002			The total number of violations of discipline and law reduced from 6.7% in 1998 to 2%.
2003	794	52	Mai Chongkai, president of HPC in Guangdong province, was sentenced to 15 years in prison on a charge of corruption.
2004	461	118	
2005	378	66	
2006	292	109	
2007	218		
2008	712	105	
2009	795	137	
2010	783	113	In January 2010, Huang Songyou, the Vice President of the Supreme People's Court, was sentenced to life imprisonment for the crimes of accepting bribery and embezzlement.
2011	519	77	

The figures in Table 3.1, as well as the work of Chinese scholars and research by Western scholars, indicate that judicial corruption is a serious problem.[39] The main characteristic of judicial corruption is that it appears both as individual corruption and as collective corruption. With regard to individual corruption, a few exposed cases can be used to illustrate how rampant it can be. For example, Bai Jiang, a judge at the Yuquan BPC in Hohhot city, personally collected RMB 1.89 million over a three-year period, from court fees paid by the parties. Mr Bai actively solicited court cases to increase the amount of fees he could then collect. In one instance, in June 2002, Mr Bai

39 Nanping Liu and Michelle Xiao Liu, 'Trick or Treat: Legal Reasoning in the Shadow of Corruption in the People's Republic of China', 34 (2008–2009) *North Carolina Journal of International Law & Commercial Regulation*, pp. 179–262; Zou Keyuan, 'Judicial Reform Versus Judicial Corruption: Recent Development in China', 11 (2000) *Criminal Law Reform*, pp. 323–351; Ting Gong, 'Dependent Judiciary and Unaccountable Judges: Judicial Corruption in Contemporary China', 4(2) (2004) *The China Review*, pp. 33–54. For a general discussion of corruption issues in China, see Andrew Wedeman, 'Great Disorder under Heaven: Endemic Corruption and Rapid Growth in Contemporary China', 4(2) (2004) *The China Review*, pp. 1–31; Hilton Root, 'Corruption in China: Has It Become Systemic?', 34(8) (1996) *Asian Survey*, pp. 741–757; Ting Gong, *The Politics of Corruption in Contemporary China: An Analysis of Policy Outcomes* (Westport, CT: Praeger Publishers,1994).

heard that a commercial bank required legal documents from the court, and took the initiative to get the case. After receiving RMB 860,000 in litigation fees from the bank, he gave a RMB 320,000 bribe to people working at the bank, and kept RMB 250,000 for himself.[40]

As a consequence of the reform of the civil trial system, parties must present evidence to the court to support their claims, and risk losing the case if they do not meet the burden of proof. Civil judges know the rule that 'who claims, bears the burden of proof' better than anyone. Wang Muqing, a judge at the Xishui County BPC in Hubei province, while handling a civil case, removed a crucial document provided by one of the parties from the case file. He then attempted to 'sell' it back to the party for RMB 15,000.[41]

The aforementioned cases relate to ordinary individual judges. Other more serious examples of corruption involve the presidents and vice-presidents of courts. For instance, in 1998, Mr Pan Yile, the former vice-president of the HPC in Guangxi Zhuang Autonomous Region, was found guilty of accepting bribes. He had become acquainted with a businessman through one of his court cases, who later started a gold mining company. Mr Pan was given 10 per cent of the shares in this company, without payment. In an attempt to hide this illegal transaction, Mr Pan forged a financial document, which detailed that he had taken a loan to purchase the shares, and then re-paid the loan. Mr Pan was sentenced to 15 years in prison.[42]

The shocking corruption case of Yao Xiaohong, former vice-president of the Basic People's Court in Jiang county of Shanxi province, not only involved the mishandling of the court's financial affairs but also serves to illustrate the seriousness of malfeasance and brutality.[43] He was known throughout China as the 'Illiterate, Law-ignorant and Rogue Court President' (*san mang yuan zhang*), referring to his lack of education, his lack of legal knowledge and unwillingness to study law, and his rampant abuse of power. Originally a worker, he was first employed by the Jiang County BPC as a driver. He was later promoted to be Director of the General Office, and in 1995 became the vice-president. In his position as vice-president, Mr Yao used the judicial police as his personal mafia. While in his post, more than 1,000 people were beaten up, and more than 300 were illegally detained. One instance in May 1996 involved the beating of a judge from the IPC. For no apparent reason, Mr Yao ordered a dozen of his judicial police to beat the judge, who was at the court to handle an injury case. The judge was severely injured in the attack. Following on from this, Mr Yao used his network of connections, and paid off another judge to cover up the case. On another occasion, a newly-appointed director of the Jiang County government came to inspect the work of the BPC. Displeased with some of his comments, Mr Yao threw the director's documents and papers on the floor, and slapped him across the face. Local government officials dared not

40 Li Zebing and Bai Bing, 'Huhehaote Yi Faguan Qintun Zhixingkuan Susongfei Beipan Wuqituxing' (A Judge in Hohhot Sentenced to Life Imprisonment for Embezzling Executed Funds and Court Costs), available at http://www.people.com.cn/GB/shehui/1061/3091981.html. Last visited September 2013.

41 Lu Chengjian, 'Liyu Xunxin: Faguan Tanzang Maizheng Diyi'an' (Blinded by Greed: The First Case of Selling Evidence by a Judge), 3 (2002) *Minzhu Yu Fazhi* (Democracy and Legal System), pp. 12–14.

42 Wang Jinfu and Su Ning, 'Rang Falu De Tiankong Geng Chunjing: Guangxi Zhuangzu Zizhiqu Yuan Fuyuanzhang Pan Yile Luowangji' (Purifying the Air in the Sky of Law: The Downfall of Pan Yile, the Former Vice–President of the Higher People's Court of Guangxi Autonomous Region), *People's Daily*, 16 June 1998, available at http://www.people.com.cn/9807/16/current/newfiles/c1010.html. Last visited September 2013.

43 'Zongshu: "Sanmang Yuanzhang" An Zhenjing Zhongnanhai' (The Case of 'Illiterate, Law-ignorant and Rogue Court President' Shocked the Central Government), available at http://news.sina.com.cn/society/1999-12-24/45546.html. Last visited September 2013; 'Fayuan Qineng Chengwei Yanwangdian' (Court Should not Become a Palace of Hell), *China Youth Daily*, 15 July 1999, available at http://web.peopledaily.com.cn/zdxw/11/19990715/199907151111.html. Last visited April 2011.

intervene in the case, and the director resigned in protest. In contrast to his treatment of officials, if criticised by his superiors, Mr Yao would genuflect to show repentance.

However, Mr Yao's brutality was even more severe when dealing with the ordinary people of Jiang County. Fear of the 'living king of hell' was so widespread that parents often silenced their naughty children with the threat that 'Yao Xiaohong will come' if they misbehave. Mr Yao's brutality is illustrated by his treatment of Mr Sun, a young farmer who had taken out a loan from a local bank. Before repayment was due, Mr Yao sent his judicial police to Mr Sun's house to collect the loan. Mr Sun was brought to the court and detained for 15 days. During this time, Mr Sun was severely beaten, and died soon after his release from the injuries he had sustained. Seeking redress, Mr Sun's wife, his parents and approximately 20 other relatives went to the court. Mr Yao handcuffed them, hung them from trees, and had them beaten. They were only released when they signed a document thanking the court for 'educating them'. This was a frequent practice: local people reported to journalists that it was common to see people handcuffed and hanging from trees and from staircases around the court. Protesting the tyranny of Mr Yao, local people placed a sign in front of the court, proclaiming that the court was ruled by beasts.

As vice-president, Mr Yao was also in charge of the Court's Second Economic Chamber. An investigation into the work of this chamber revealed that over 100 people had been illegally detained, the longest for three and a half months. Mr Yao had personally approved most of the detentions. Since its establishment in 1995, the chamber had never followed the proper legal procedures in accepting and trying cases, and no records were kept on how many cases were handled. Instead, investigations displayed serious violations of litigation procedures, the handling of cases beyond the court's jurisdiction, and the unlawful collection of litigation fees and fines. The chamber's income was similarly not recorded, and money was kept in a private safe. While Yao was in charge of the financial affairs of the court as a whole, no proper records were kept of the court's fixed assets. The court had a debt of nearly RMB 1 million. Mr Yao was also accused of issuing false invoices and other false financial documents.

Despite the number of complaints against Mr Yao, the local government was powerless to take action against him, given his extensive connections. In 1999, and only with the intervention of the President of China, the President of the Supreme People's Court, the Secretary of the Central Political and Legal Committee, and the Secretary of the Shanxi Provincial Communist Party, was Mr Yao finally arrested, and eventually sentenced by the court to life imprisonment.

With regard to collective judicial corruption, a number of recently exposed *wo'an* (group cases in which president, vice-president, and a number of judges of the same courts were found to have committed economic crimes as a group) reveal the severity of judicial corruption.

The Case of the Urumqi Intermediate Railway Transport Court[44]

In 2006, the People's Procuratorate in Changjie city in Xinjiang Autonomous Region brought the Intermediate Railway Transport Court (hereafter the Railway Court) in Urumqi before the Changjie IPC, on suspicion of accepting bribes. The Railway Court's President, the Director of the Enforcement Division, and the accountant appeared as defendants before the court. The prosecutors accused the president of giving one auction company a monopoly on the auction of

44 'Shouli Fayuan Shexian Fanzui An Jiemi: Fayuan Yu Danwei Xieyi Fencheng' (Revealing the Secret of the First Suspected Case of a Court as Criminal Defendant: Court and Unit Reached Agreement on Sharing Profits), available at http://bbs1.people.com.cn/postDetail.do?boardId=9&treeView=1&view=2&id=95327293; 'Jingti Faguan Fubai Xianxiang' (Watch out for Judges' Corruption Phenomenon), available at http://news.sina.com.cn/c/2007-03-31/143412662131.shtml. Both last visited September 2013.

goods seized by the court, in return for 30 per cent of the sale profits. The President of the Railway Court arranged for the vice-president to use the name of the Association of Judges of the Railway Court to sign an agreement with the auction company. The Director of the Enforcement Division was in charge of overseeing the agreement. Between 2001 and 2005, the Railway Court received RMB 940,000 from the auction company. The prosecutor also stated that, in the second half of 2000, the President held a meeting with the head of an property assessment firm, and the heads of other intermediate companies. The President proposed that all the case-related goods be assessed, and that the assessment fee be split 40 per cent to the court and 60 per cent to the assessor firm. After the assessor firm agreed to this proposal, the Director of the Enforcement Division was put in charge of handling the deal. Within five years, the Railway Court received RMB 2.84 million. Furthermore, the Railway Court once received RMB 720,000 from an investment consulting company while handling an enforcement case.

The procuratorate considered the Railway Court to have illegally obtained approximately RMB 4.5 million, constituting the crime of bribery, and that it should be held criminally liable. This is the first case in which an entire court was suspected of accepting bribes (*danwei shouhui zui*). However, after the first session of open trial the procuratorate changed the bill of prosecution to focus on accusing only Yang Zhiming, the Court President at that time, Cai Hongjun, the former Director of the Enforcement Division and Wang Qingmei, the accountant of the court, of the crime of bribery. The three were eventually sentenced to 15 years', two years' and six years' imprisonment respectively.

The Case of the IPC in Wuhan[45]

In 2004, 13 judges, including Ke Changxin and He Changyou, former Wuhan Intermediate People's Court vice-presidents, were convicted of corruption and given prison sentences. Ten judges under their supervision were sent to jail, with another judge awaiting a verdict. This 13-member group had taken a total of RMB 4 million in bribes. In addition, the investigation implicated more than a hundred other judges and court officials at various levels, who received administrative discipline or were reassigned to other courts.

The Case of the IPC in Fuyang[46]

In May 2005, two vice-presidents, deputy chiefs of the Enforcement Division, the chief of the First Economic Division, the chief and the deputy chief of the Second Economic Division, and the deputy chief of the Second Criminal Division at Fuyang IPC, were suspects in a number of cases. In order to receive lenient treatment, they confessed to three charges of corruption at Fuyang IPC. The first concerned bribes for promotion, the second, bribery for interference in individual cases, and the last, construction of the court building.

There are several hidden rules for dividing spoils amongst judges. A characteristic typical of the corruption at Fuyang IPC was that the judges formed coalitions to share profits. When one judge was caught, however, several colleagues were also discovered. This system of profit-sharing is

---

45 'The Wuhan Court Bribery Case', available at http://hrichina.org/public/PDFs/CRF.1.2005/1.2005TheWuhanCourt.pdf. Last visited September 2013.

46 Qi Zhaowei, 'Anhui Fuyang Zhongyuan Lianxu Sanren Yuanzhang Yin Fubaian Xiama Zhenjing Quanguo' (Three Consecutive Presidents of Fuyang Intermediate People's Court Arrested One after Another for Corruption, the Cases Shocked the Country), available at http://www.hngf.gov.cn/NEWS/news_detail.asp?newsid=2006-9-25-9-14-22. Last visited September 2013.

typical of collective corruption. When a case is handled by a collegiate panel, irrespective of who is the presiding judge, the people involved, from the judge to the chief of the division, all share in the profits. For example, Judge Liu Juping accepted bribes on 23 occasions. On 12 of these occasions she shared the bribes with the vice-president, three deputy chiefs of division and two judges. On seven, she shared the bribes with the chief of her own division. Some presiding judges also distribute bribes to other judges, the vice-president and chiefs of divisions. Some deputy chiefs of divisions distribute their bribes to judges who handle the cases.

The aforementioned corruption cases and the explosion of the corruption case concerning Wang Shaoyao, who was then Deputy Secretary of the Party Committee of Anhui province, triggered the corruption cases of Shan Jun, Liu Jiayi and Zhang Zimin, three successive presidents of the Fuyang IPC. One by one they were found guilty of corruption. The fact that many judges join together is a typical reflection of the ongoing judicial corruption.

The Case of the IPC in Shenzhen[47]

In 2006, five senior judges from the Shenzhen IPC were arrested on corruption charges. Among them was Pei Hongquan, then vice-president of the IPC, who was in charge of bankruptcy cases at the court. In 2008, he was charged with the crimes of accepting bribes and of possessing a vast amount of property from unidentified sources, and was jailed for life. When Mr Pei was the president of a basic court, he introduced a number reform measures to improve judicial efficiency. Consequently he won numerous honours, including the 'Good Judge that People are Most Satisfied With' award at the national court level. However, attracted by money he took several bribes, purchased houses at discount prices, and allowed his relatives to use his connections to make numerous profits.

Judicial corruption, especially the corruption of judges with administrative titles, such as president, vice-president or chief of trial division, should be looked at in the broader context of the overall corruption of governmental officials. 'One can hardly expect judges to be honest when government and Party officials from top to bottom are busily filling their pockets.'[48] It is no exaggeration that, unfortunately, in today's China, corruption has spread widely within governmental organisations, business circles and into many aspects of social life. Public officials, including staff of the government, legislature, judiciary, state-owned enterprises and other public organisations 'have been the main perpetrators of corruption in China for the past 20 years'.[49] In 2006, the central government launched a tough anti-corruption campaign, as a result of which, both high-ranking government officials, described as tigers, and low-ranking civil servants, described as flies, who abused their power and rode roughshod over ordinary people (mostly disadvantaged groups), were punished for violating law and Party discipline. It was reported that, in Taiyuan city

47 'Shenzhen Zhongyuan Yuan Fu Yuanzhang Duoluo Guiji: Taishang Fanfu, Taixia Shouqian' (The Corruption Path of the Former Vice-President of the Intermediate People's Court in Shenzhen: Speaking about Anti-Corruption on Stage while Illegally Collecting Money Backstage), available at http://news.sina.com.cn/c/2008-01-15/104014746949.shtml; Kong Bo and Xiao Wenfeng, 'Shenzhen Zhongyuan Yuan Fu Yuanzhang Pei Hongquan Beipan Wuqi' (The Former Vice-President of the Intermediate People's Court of Shenzhen City Sentenced to Life Imprisonment), available at http://news.sina.com.cn/c/l/2008-01-04/224614669617.shtml. Both last visited September 2013.

48 Randall Peerenboom, *China's Long March toward Rule of Law* (Cambridge: Cambridge University Press, 2002), p. 322.

49 Yong Guo, 'Corruption in Transitional China: An Empirical Analysis', 194 (2008) *The China Quarterly*, p. 350.

of Shanxi province, during a three-month period of the campaign, of 452 officials suspected of being involved in violations of Party discipline and rules, 444 were punished.[50] In Beijing, during the period January 2008 to May 2009, it was reported that 404 cases of corruption and bribery were filed by the procuratorates, with 472 persons involved; 72 of those accused held positions at the bureau-general level (*chu ji*) and 29 at the director-general level (*ju ji*).[51]

As for high-ranking officials, Hu Changqing, former deputy-governor of Jiangxi province, was sentenced to death by the local court on charges of accepting RMB 5.44 million worth of bribes, possessing RMB 61 million worth of property from unidentified sources, and giving RMB 80,000 in bribes to others to further his career. He was executed on 8 March 2000.[52] Chen Kejie, former vice-chairman of the National People's Congress Standing Committee was found guilty, in collaboration with his mistress Li Ping, of having taken RMB 41 million in bribes when he served as Deputy Secretary of the Party Committee of Guangxi Zhuang Autonomous Region and Chairman of the People's Government of Guangxi. He was sentenced to death on 31 July 2000 and executed on 14 September the same year.[53] Chen Liangyu, the former Communist Party Secretary of Shanghai, was accused of accepting bribes of more than RMB 2.39 million from organisations and individuals, self-enrichment, and the unlawful enrichment of friends and relatives through shady financial and real estate deals beginning as early as 1988. In April 2008 he was sentenced to 18 years in prison for taking bribes and abusing power.[54] Other high-profile cases include those of: Liu Zhihua, former deputy mayor of Beijing; Li Baojin, former chief prosecutor-general at the Higher People's Procuratorate in Tianjin; He Shuxun, former deputy governor of Anhui province; Wang Wulong, former deputy director of the People's Congress Standing Committee in Jiansu province.[55] The most recent case concerns proceedings against the Party Chief of the Chongqing municipality and former Minister of Commerce, Bo Xilai, who was charged with receiving bribery, embezzlement and abuse of power, and sentenced to life imprisonment in September 2013.[56]

Judicial corruption has numerous root causes. First, the lack of judicial independence leaves room for judicial corruption. In practice, when a case is brought to court or assigned to a judge, court officials or the responsible judge are often contacted by various people – the most influential ones are those with government positions. As government institutions and, to a large extent, individual officials have a decisive influence on the financing of courts and the promotion of court

50 See 'Zhongyang Fanfu Juwang Huo Chengxiao: Taiyuan Baitian Chachu 444 Ming Ganbu' (Central Government's Anti-corruption Has Achieved Great Success: 444 Government Officials Were Punished within One Hundred Days in Taiyuan), available at http://news.sohu.com/20070108/n247485956.shtml. Last visited September 2013.

51 'Beijing Jiancha Jiguan Qunian Yilai Li'an Zhencha Tanfu Da'an 42 Jian' (The Procuratorial Organs in Beijing Have Filed and Investigated 42 Major Cases of Corruption and Bribery since Last Year), 22 June 2009. Available at http://news.xinhuanet.com/legal/2009-06/22/content_11580952.htm. Last visited September 2013.

52 'People's Daily Commentary on Hu Changqing Case', see http://english.peopledaily.com.cn/200003/09/eng20000309O101.html. Last visited September 2013.

53 'Cheng Kejie Sentenced to Death for Bribery', see http://english.people.com.cn/english/200007/31/eng20000731_46885.html. Last visited September 2013.

54 'Former Shanghai Party Chief Gets 18-year Term for Bribery', see http://news.xinhuanet.com/english/2008-04/11/content_7959627.htm. Last visited September 2013.

55 Andrew Wedeman, 'China's War on Corruption', in Ting Gong and Stephen K. Ma (eds), *Preventing Corruption in Asia: Institutional Design and Policy Capacity* (London: Routledge, 2009), pp. 15–16.

56 Xinhuanet, 'Bo Xilai Bei Pan Wuqi Tuxing, Boduo Zhengzhi Quanli Zhongshen' (Bo Xilai is Sentenced with Life Imprisonment and Deprivation of Political Rights for Life), 22 September 2013. Available at http://news.xinhuanet.com/legal/2013-09/22/c_117449756.htm. Last visited September 2013.

personnel, courts and judges too often have no other choice but to bend to officials' influence by ignoring the law or applying it in a biased way. In addition, the lack of recognition of the nature of the judiciary to enforce law fairly and efficiently also results in a puzzling perception of courts and judges. Courts are called upon to serve 'the central work' of the Party and 'to guard economic construction'. As a result, courts and judges have established various links with the business community, even the mafia.[57] Judicial officials 'serve' these interests, as well as benefit from them, by accepting donations and favours. Although they possess judicial power, the courts' and judges' relationships with the government, which has its own power, and economic entities, which have money, place them in a vulnerable position. Compared to administrative power, judicial power is vastly inferior.

Secondly, judicial corruption cannot be isolated from its social context.

> In the social conditions that prevail throughout China's diverse cities and villages, judges must fully integrate into the legal culture of the general public if they want to sustain their careers. They find themselves under pressure from influential groups, like government, businesses, and criminal networks. Judges may also fear repercussions from informal networks of extended family, friends, and neighbours.[58]

It is unrealistic to expect judges to operate completely outside the social environment, especially in the absence of a workable system to reduce the incidence of judicial corruption. Susan Finder points out: 'the relative social acceptability of supplemental financial payments means that bribery of judges is a widespread phenomenon'.[59] An experienced Chinese lawyer described the reality:

> when a client first approaches a lawyer to handle a litigation matter, the client's primary concern is over whether the lawyer has a personal relationship with the judge. Such a relationship ensures a fair trial at a minimum and a favourable trial at best … While this does not suggest that every Chinese judge is corrupt, it shows that the opportunity for corruption is prevalent in the judicial system. Any type of case, ranging from small, insignificant matters to important matters of national interest, can be compromised by corruption.[60]

Thirdly, certain shortcomings of the court system leave the door open for corruption. For instance, the flexible use of the re-trial system leads to the easy re-opening of cases if influential

---

57 In January 2011, Zhang Tao, the former Vice Chairman of the Higher People's Court of Chongqing Municipality, was tried at the Intermediate People's Court of Zunyi City, Guizhou Province on charges of accepting bribery and shielding mafia-style organisations. He was convicted of both crimes and sentenced to death with a two-year reprieve. Since 2005, Zhang Tao had been frequenting the 'White House' night club run by Yue Ning (the ringleader of a mafia-style organisation in Chongqing City) and became a shareholder of the club, knowing very well that Yue and his club had been engaging in criminal activities. He also practised usury through Yue Ning and connived in the various criminal activities of his mafia-style organisation. See 'Chongqing Shi Gaoji Fayuan Yuan Fuyuanzhang Zhang Tao Yidi Shoushen, Beipan Sihuan' (Zhang Tao, the Former Vice-President of the Higher Court of Chongqing Municipality, Was Sentenced to Death with a Two-Year Reprieve), available at http://news.sohu.com/20110126/n279100607.shtml. Last visited September 2013.

58 Nanping Liu and Michelle Xiao Liu, *supra* note 39, p. 244.

59 Susan Finder, 'Inside the People's Courts: China's Litigation System and the Resolution of Commercial Disputes'. cited in Stanley Lubman, *Bird in a Cage: Legal Reform in China After Mao* (Stanford: Stanford University Press, 1999), p. 279.

60 Nanping Liu and Michelle Xiao Liu, *supra* note 39, p. 185.

people wish to interfere in the case. This not only diminishes the finality of a case but also creates opportunities for using personal networking to change a court's judgment. Furthermore, the relatively low judicial salary makes judges an easy target for corruption. Judges are paid on a similar scale to civil servants. When the Judges Law was drafted, the Supreme People's Court proposed that judges should be paid higher salaries as a way of reducing corruption. This proposal was not, however, adopted by the National People's Congress.[61] A recent survey in a rural court in Shanxi revealed that 'between 2005 and 2008, local judges' salaries ranged between RMB 900 and 1,300 per month, with additional compensation for housing and family expenses that amounted to an additional RMB 250 per month. By comparison, in 2005, the average salary of a state-owned enterprise worker was RMB 1,268 per month.'[62] In modern-day China, a profession's income is too often linked to the profession's social status. Judges' low salaries are not conducive to building self-respect amongst the profession and, moreover, they constitute a major ground for fostering judicial corruption.

Fourthly, regardless of the external realities, individual judges' low ethical and moral standards make them easy targets for corruption. Examining the cases of judicial corruption reveals that the ranks of corrupted judges include both those with university legal backgrounds and those without. Academic study can be viewed as a conditional professional requirement for a qualified judge, but a clean and responsible judge needs to have professional moral standards in order to decline corruptive opportunities. Despite widespread corruption,[63] the public justifiably expect a clean, uncorrupted judiciary simply because the judicial system is the last resort that people can turn to for fair and effective handling of their disputes.

In order to foster a professional, respective judicial force, Article 32 of the 1995 Judges Law contains a list of 13 unacceptable actions for judges. Under this list, the following five actions, which relate to judicial corruption, are prohibited: embezzling money or accepting bribes, manipulating the law for personal gain, taking advantage of the functions and powers of the judiciary for personal gain or the enrichment of others, engaging in profitmaking activities, and meeting the parties or their agents without authorisation and attending dinners or accepting presents given by the parties or their agents.[64]

Similarly, in January 2009, the Supreme People's Court publicised the Rule of Five Strict Prohibitions for judges, which comprised: (1) accepting gifts or hospitality from parties to cases; (2) having improper associations with lawyers in violation of provisions; (3) interfering with

61 Pan Jianfeng, 'Gao Xinzhi: Shenpan Gongzheng, Lianjie He Faguan Gaosuzhi De Jiben Baozhang' (The System of a High Salary for Judges: A Basic Guarantee of a Fair Trial, Honesty, Cleanness and High Quality of Judges), 6 (2001) *Zhengfa Luntan* (Tribune of Political Science and Law), pp. 15–21.

62 Stephanie Balme, 'Ordinary Justice and Popular Constitutionalism in China', in Stephanie Balme and Michael W. Dowdle (eds), *Building Constitutionalism in China* (New York: Palgrave Macmillan, 2009), p. 193.

63 A saying in China has it that 'if the Party wants to crack down on corruption the Party will break up; if the Party is incapable of cracking down on corruption the country will break up'. This illustrates the seriousness of the corruption problem in the public's eyes.

64 Article 32 of the Judges Law. The other eight 'No's are: no spreading statements damaging the prestige of the state; no joining illegal organisations, or taking part in such activities as an assembly, procession and demonstration against the state, and participating in strikes; no extorting confessions by torture, concealing or falsifying evidence; no divulging state secrets or secrets of judicial work, abusing functions and powers, infringing upon the legitimate rights and interests of natural persons, legal persons or other organisations; no neglecting his or her duty so as to wrongly judge a case or to cause heavy losses to the party concerned; no delaying the handling of a case so as to affect the work adversely; and no committing of other acts in violation of law or discipline.

cases being handled by other people; (4) participating in bribery and fraud during assessments and related activities; (5) leaking secret information about trial work.[65] By October 2009, 640 officials from courts at various levels in the country had been investigated for violations of the Rule of Five Strict Prohibitions. Among them, 308 were found innocent after investigation, 96 were still under investigation, and 236 were punished for violation of the rules. Of these 236 persons, 102 were turned over to judicial organs for investigation of criminal responsibility; 86 were given disciplinary punishment by the Party; 101 were transferred from their posts or were given other punishments; eight were officials of the Supreme People's Court.[66] Although these Five Strict Prohibitions also appeared in previous SPC rules, their re-emphasis shows the seriousness of the problems. In order to facilitate the public oversight of judges the SPC set up telephone hotlines to enable people to report judges' wrongdoing. Local courts have also been urged to provide 24 hour telephone services to the public.[67]

Despite the significance of the SPC's efforts, anti-judicial corruption measures cannot be effective merely through the court's own endeavours. Given that judicial power is controlled by a network of other powers, and given the fact that judicial corruption is only part of the overall deep-seated administrative corruption, judicial corruption must be addressed within a broader political, economic and social context.

Conclusion

In 1999, Xiao Yang, then President of the SPC, stated that 'the overall professional quality of Chinese judges has not been high'.[68] In March 2009, when Wang Shengjun, the President of the SPC reported to the NPC on judicial work, he mentioned five major problems. Four of them concerned the competence of judges. First, some judges lack competence in adapting themselves to new situations and in solving new problems, which results in some cases being mishandled through improper procedure or incorrect application of the law. Secondly, some judges are too bureaucratic, irresponsible, or they delay handling cases. Thirdly, the professional ethics of some judges are low, unfair or unclean, and a few of them are even corrupt. Fourthly, some judges lack an understanding of the conceptions of a judicial system with a socialist character, which results in a lack of consciousness towards serving the country's overall development.[69] Although the

65 Zuigao Renmin Fayuan Yinfa 'Guanyu "Wuge Yanjin" De Guiding' He 'Guanyu Weifan "Wuge Yanjin" Guiding De Chuli Banfa' De Tongzhi (Circular of the Supreme People's Court on Printing and Distributing 'Measures Concerning the "Five Strict Prohibitions"' and 'Measures Concerning Violations of the "Five Strict Prohibitions"'), *Fafa* No. 2 [2009]. Available at http://www.law-lib.com/cpd/law_detail.asp?id=276955. Last visited September 2013.

66 'Zuigao Fayuan Siba Lijian Zhizhi Sifa Fubai, 102 Ren Bei Yisong Sifa' (The Supreme Court Takes Four Strong Measures against Judicial Corruption, 102 Corrupt Officials Turned Over to Judicial Departments for Prosecution), available at http://news.sohu.com/20091015/n267367404.shtml. Last visited September 2013.

67 Chen Yonghui, 'Zuigao Renmin Fayuan Gongbu "Wuge Yanjin" Guiding' (The Supreme People's Court Promulgates the Rule of Five Strict Prohibitions), see http://old.chinacourt.org/public/detail.php?id=339384. Last visited September 2013.

68 Xiao Yang, 'Program Designed to Promote the Reform of the System of the People's Court', 1 (2000) *China Law*, p. 55.

69 'Zuigao Fayuan Yuanzhang Wang Shengjun: Fayuan Gongzuo Reng Cunzai Wuda Wenti' (The President of the SPC Said That There Are Five Major Problems with Judicial Work in China), see http://news.sohu.com/20090310/n262718095.shtml. Last visited September 2013.

fourth problem is a political one, which cannot be viewed as a criteria by which to assess judges' professional competence, these critical remarks demonstrate the worrisome quality of the judicial branch, and yet also show the willingness of the SPC to improve the judiciary.

However, the professional quality of Chinese judges is not only determined by their legal knowledge, moral standards and judicial experience, but is also affected by the external environment in which they function. Since the judicial system in post-Mao China remains a young system with a range of problems, judges, as a product of the system, are also subject to these problems. The SPC has implemented a wide range of reform measures aimed at improving the quality of the judiciary, including issuing the Code of Conduct to encourage judges to be independent, impartial and responsible. However, the courts' problems are not only limited to internal shortcomings, but closely linked with the country's political system, financial system, personnel system, social environment and the like. Thus, the overall improvement of judicial quality cannot be isolated from changes in other related fields. Obviously, introducing and establishing these structural and institutional changes may be a drawn-out process.

In the short term, however, improving the ethical standards of Chinese judges is among the most critical of ongoing efforts towards judicial reform. Without substantially upgrading the strength of judicial ethics, the Chinese judiciary will not be able to strengthen its authority, which is needed for the balance of powers. A weak, and to a certain extent distrusted, judiciary cannot bear the function of the independent administration of justice.

It is generally accepted that the construction of a new Chinese judicial system is being impaired mostly by judicial corruption, which has shaken the public's confidence in, and respect for, the judicial system. As Chinese scholars have pointed out, 'Ordinary citizens' perceptions of corruption in the judicial system narrowly range from total loss of faith in the nation's judges to believing that a significant portion of judicial officers are highly corrupt'.[70] The Party, the SPC and the SPP have intensified supervision and punishment, but, so far, the result is far from promising. China has not yet established a formal system to prevent and eliminate judicial corruption.

70 Nanping Liu and Michelle Xiao Liu, *supra* note 39, p. 182.

Chapter 4
The Criminal Trial Process

Introduction

The Criminal Procedure Law (hereafter CrPL) is the basic law of the criminal justice system. From 1949 to 1979 there was no such law in the People's Republic of China. In the aftermath of the lawless period of turmoil that played out during the Cultural Revolution, the first CrPL was enacted on 1 July 1979 and subsequently became effective on 1 January 1980. The Law was drafted within seven months and consisted of 164 articles. The criminal process was divided into four stages: investigation, prosecution, adjudication and execution, which were to be carried out by the police, procuratorate, courts and prisons, respectively. A defendant's rights were generally afforded minimum protection, whilst police and judicial power were strongly imbalanced. Police were allowed to detain persons for investigation without time restraints. Lawyers were allowed to defend an accused, though they would only receive the case file seven days before a trial. Thus, during the investigation and prosecution stages, lawyers could not be involved. Furthermore, during the various anti-crime campaigns of the 1980s, the NPC Standing Committee (NPCSC) issued several decisions which undermined and weakened the 1979 CrPL. Not surprisingly, the deficiencies in the legislation, coupled with the public security forces, procuratorates and courts' lack of capacity or motivation to enforce the law, resulted in widespread violations of defendants' rights in the criminal process, generating vigorous criticism both in China and from the international community.[1]

In the 1990s, under the general policy of the Communist Party to support the reform of the criminal justice system, Chinese legal scholars, legislators, the Supreme People's Court (SPC), the Supreme People's Procuratorate (SPP), the Ministry of Justice and the Ministry of Public Security made joint efforts to initiate measures to reshape the criminal justice system. This resulted in a comprehensive amendment of the CrPL in 1996, which entered into force on 1 January 1997.[2] On

---

1 To understand the 1979 CrPL and its practice in English, see Timothy A. Gellat, 'The People's Republic of China and the Presumption of Innocence', 73 (1982) *The Journal of Criminal Law and Criminology*; Lawyers Committee for Human Rights, *Criminal Justice with Chinese Characteristics: China's Criminal Process and Violations of Human Rights* (New York: Lawyers Committee for Human Rights, 1993); Shao-chuan Leng and Hungdah Chiu, *Criminal Justice in Post-Mao China: Analysis and Documents* (Albany, NY: State University of New York Press, 1985). Some Western countries have issued reports criticising the Chinese criminal justice system. For example, *US Department of State Country Reports on Human Rights Practices for 1994* (Washington, DC, 1995), p. 555; *Report of the Australian Human Rights Delegation to China, 14–26 July 1991* (Canberra: Department of Foreign Affairs and Trade, 1991). Carlos W.H. Lo, *China's Legal Awakening: Legal Theory and Criminal Justice in Deng's Era* (Hong Kong: Hong Kong University Press, 1995).

2 For the legislative history, the major changes of the 1996 CrPL compared to the 1979 CrPL, and enforcement problems, *see* Wei Luo, *The Amended Criminal Procedure Law and the Criminal Court Rules of the People's Republic of China: with English Translation, Introduction, and Annotation* (Buffalo, NY: William S. Hein & Co., 2000). Fu Hualing, 'Chapter 5 Criminal Procedure Law', in Wang Chenguang and Zhang Xianchu (eds), *Introduction to Chinese Law* (Hong Kong and Singapore: Sweet & Maxwell Asia, 1997), pp. 129–167. The 1996 PRC Criminal Procedure Law, see http://www.npc.gov.cn/englishnpc/Law/2007-12/13/content_1384067.htm. Last visited September 2013.

the surface, the amended law adopted a number of internationally-recognised principles relating to fair trials, though not without restrictions. The most profound change was that it shifted from an extreme inquisitorial system to a model which combined inquisitorial and adversarial trial procedures. Nowadays, it is widely recognised that the traditional distinction between inquisitorial and adversarial criminal procedure has been corroded. The two systems have been integrated in such a way that countries with a traditionally inquisitorial system have adopted some adversarial features in order to ensure a higher standard of fair trials. Likewise, countries with an originally adversarial system have borrowed inquisitorial elements to improve their efficiency in handling cases. This has become particularly evident in Western Europe, where it has been stated that 'although there are unquestionably two different traditions, the borrowings between the two have been so extensive that it is no longer possible to classify any of the criminal justice systems in Western Europe as wholly accusatorial or wholly inquisitorial'.[3]

The development of the Chinese CrPL reflects this trend. However, the 1996 CrPL was either too general or lacking on a number of important procedural rules. As a result, a large number of judicial interpretations and ministerial rules were issued from the SPC, SPP, the Ministry of Public Security and the Ministry of Justice.[4] While these interpretations have supplemented some details to guide judicial organs in enforcing the CrPL, they also reflect to varying extents departmental interests. That is, some interpretations are made to favour the operations of their respective institutions, while restricting the power of other organs. One Chinese scholar has summarised that, of the approximately 1,440 articles on the interpretation of the 1996 CrPL, many contradict each other or conflict with the 1996 CrPL.[5] From 2003, the National People's Congress (NPC) emphasised in its legislative agenda the need to revise the CrPL; this resulted in the amended CrPL which was passed on 14 March 2012 and became effective from 1 January 2013.[6]

3 J.R. Spencer, 'Introduction', in Mireille Delmas-Marty and J.R. Spencer (eds), *European Criminal Procedures* (Cambridge: Cambridge University Press, 2002), p. 5.

4 The major rules implementing the 1996 CrPL include: (i) Provisions concerning Several Issues in the Implementation of the Criminal Procedure Law, which was jointly promulgated by the SPC, the SPP, the Ministry of Public Security, the Ministry of State Security, the Ministry of Justice and the Legal System Working Committee of the NPCSC on 19 January 1998 and is referred to in Chinese as 'liubuwei guiding' (Six Ministries and Committee's Provisions); (ii) Explanations concerning Several Issues in the Implementation of the Criminal Procedure Law, which was issued by the SPC on 2 September 1998, which contain a total of 367 articles; and (iii) Rules on the Criminal Process for People's Procuratorates, which was issued by the SPP on 18 January 1999. These three implementing rules can be found at http://www.cecc.gov/pages/selectLaws/criminalJustice/index.php. Last visited September 2013.

5 Liu Sida, 'Lifa, Shijian Yu Zhengzhi Guocheng: Tan "Yuan'an" Yu Lushi Xingshi Bianhunan De Chengyin' (Legislation, Practice, and Political Process: Analysis of the Reasons Causing Miscarriages of Justice and the Difficulties of Criminal Defence Lawyers), in Gao Hongjun and Zhang Jianwei (eds), 10 (2008) *Qinghua Fazhi Lunheng* (Tsinghua Forum on the Rule of Law), p. 81.

6 The Law in English is available at http://www.lawinfochina.com/display.aspx?lib=law&id=9247&CGid=. Last visited September 2013. For the implementation of the new CrPL the SPC and the SPP issued implementation rules separately. See Zuigao Renmin Fayuan Guanyu Shiyong Zhonghua Renmin Gongheguo Xingshi Susongfa De Jieshi (Interpretations on the Implementation of the Criminal Procedure Law) issued by the SPC on 20 December 2012. *Fashi* No. 21 [2012]. Available at http://www.court.gov.cn/qwfb/sfjs/201212/t20121228_181551.htm. Renmin Jianchayuan Xingshi Susong Guize (Shixing) (Regulations on Criminal Procedure of People's Procuratorates [Provisional Implementation]), issued by the SPP on 22 November 2012. Available at http://news.jcrb.com/jxsw/201211/t20121123_993092.html. 2. Zuigao Renmin Fayuan, Zuigao Renmin Jianchayuan, Gong'anbu, Guojia Anquanbu, Sifabu Guanyu Shishi Xingshi Susongfa Ruogan Wenti De Guiding (SPC, SPP, MPS, MSS and MOJ's Regulations on Several Issues concerning the Implementation

In judicial practice, implementation of the 1996 CrPL has demonstrated that a simple introduction of new legal provisions may not necessarily lead to the expected practical change if the capacities of institutions and judicial officials are deficient. Many habitual practices neglect the strict enforcement of the law and the illegal acts of judicial organs that violate procedural rules, essentially hindering the effective implementation of the CrPL. At the same time, the strengthening of criminal defence and an ever-increasing consciousness of human rights protection in the criminal process has in many cases challenged the judicial organs. Consequently, the Chinese criminal justice system is in flux, transforming from a state-power-dominated process towards a balancing act of punishing crimes and protecting human rights.

This chapter primarily focuses on examining the most fundamental and controversial subjects which have arisen in the wake of the 1996 CrPL and the 2012 amendment in both progressing and limiting the system. This includes the principle issues of the presumption of innocence, the right to remain silent, the procedural issues of courts examining case materials before trials, the expanded use of summary procedure to promote judicial efficiency, witnesses' appearance in courtrooms and their protection, the exclusion of illegally-obtained evidence, the issues of the court hearing model being either judge-centric or prosecutor-centric, and the rights of defendants and defence lawyers.

Secondly, the issue of the death penalty is discussed. Whilst recognising the significance of the resumption of approval of the death penalty by the Supreme People's Court in 2007, which contributes to the unified application of law in this regard, the lack of open trial and lawyer participation in the review procedure conducted by the SPC is evaluated.

Thirdly, the chapter examines a few ordinary and yet horrific cases of injustice, which have been widely reported and discussed in China in recent years, especially on the internet. This will fill an important gap in English academic study. The intention is to illustrate the major problems China is confronting and draw some conclusions on why and how the criminal justice system must be improved. The explosive impact of such cases reflects a gradual shift toward the media exercising its freedom. This has enabled the public at large to have access to judicial information, which in itself is progress when juxtaposed with China's record of keeping such information absolutely secret. Speaking optimistically, reflecting on such injustices could prove to be a stimulus, helping to improve future judicial practice.

The Criminal Procedure Law and Practice

The Principle of the Presumption of Innocence

Presumption of innocence is a principle which can be traced back to the advent of Roman law. This principle requires the acquittal of a defendant if there is reasonable doubt that the accused did not commit the crime. Some early commentators[7] applied this principle solely to serious punishments such as death, however, Blackstone's Commentaries expounded on this revolutionary school of thought by stating that 'it is better that ten guilty persons escape … than that one innocent suffer'.[8] This principle has been honoured in numerous legal systems throughout history. It underscores

of the Criminal Procedure Law), issued on 26 December 2012, validated on 1 January 2013. Available at http://vip.chinalawinfo.com/NewLaw2002/Slc/SLC.asp?Db=chl&Gid=191815. All last visited in September 2013.

7 Sir Matthew Hale, *The History of the Pleas of the Crown* (London: Nutt and Gosling, 1736), p. 289.

8 Sir William Blackstone, *Commentaries on the Laws of England*, vol. 4, Chapter 27 (London: Cadell and Davies, 1809), p. 352. Available at http://avalon.law.yale.edu/subject_menus/blackstone.asp. Last visited September 2013.

the establishment of legal, as opposed to actual, innocence. Moreover, by creating this legal innocence in criminal procedures, the burden of proof can never shift from the prosecution to the defendant.[9] Therefore, in the context of these legal systems, the accused is presumed innocent until a guilty verdict is rendered and thus should be provided with protections equal to those afforded an innocent person.

Various Chinese scholars have described the presumption of guilt as a principle of feudal tradition, which has a long-standing history in China.[10] In the 1950s, scholars debated whether the principle of presumption innocence should be introduced into criminal procedure. Neither supporters nor objectors could acquiesce. During the Anti-Rightist Movement, this principle was criticised as bourgeois as were those who supported it. Academic discussion of the principle became taboo.[11] When the first CrPL was drafted in the late 1970s, some suggested introducing into law the principle of the presumption of innocence; however, such propositions were rejected. When the 1979 CrPL was being revised, again a consensus could not be reached between those who supported and those who rejected the presumption of innocence. This resulted in a compromise in the 1996 CrPL, which embodies the spirit of the presumption of innocence rather than the actual principle. Article 12 of the 1996 CrPL stipulates that 'no person should be determined guilty without a judgment rendered by a People's Court according to law'. However, this could be understood as a mere proclamation of the functional responsibility of the courts, not the presumption of innocence.

Chinese judicial officers are divided on their understanding and interpretation of Article 12. One view is that Article 12, by implying that a defendant should not be considered guilty prior to a final judgment, confirms the principle of the presumption of innocence.[12] The opposite view is that Article 12 does not imply this presumption of innocence, but merely indicates that only courts are competent to decide the guilt of an accused. Their argument is based on the official explanation when the 1996 CrPL was drafted that:

> We are firmly against the presumption of guilt, but we also do not want the presumption of innocence as in the Western countries, we believe in objective facts … [The Criminal Procedure Law] does not provide that one is presumed innocent prior to a judgment of a court because, if so, why should the investigative organ conduct an investigation? Why could coercive measures be imposed? If there is a presumption of innocence, why should the public prosecutor institute a prosecution? Why should a court conduct an open trial? We uphold the principle of using facts as a base, before the court makes a judgment on the guilt. From the facts, we cannot say that a person is a criminal, but we also cannot say that he/she is not a criminal suspect. Therefore, in the quest for

---

9 Joseph L. Lester, 'Presumed Innocent, Feared Dangerous: The Eighth Amendment's Right to Bail', 32(1) (2005) *Northern Kentucky Law Review*, pp. 8–9.

10 Huang Jingfu, '"Wuzui Tuiding" Yu Woguo Xingshi Susong' (Presumption of Innocence and Criminal Procedure in China). Available at http://www.law-lib.com/lw/lw_view.asp?no=2615. Last visited September 2013.

11 Bian Jianlin, 'Wuzui Tuiding' (Presumption of Innocence), in Chen Guangzhong et al. (eds), *Lianheguo Xingshi Sifa Zhunze Yu Zhongguo Xingshi Fazhi* (The United Nations Standards and China's Legal System of Criminal Justice) (Beijing: Falu Chubanshe, 1998), p. 112.

12 Chinese judges and prosecutors with whom I have contact often cite this article as proof of the presumption of innocence in the CrPL. Even international commentators may mistakenly perceive this to be true. Lu and Miethe state: 'The defence attorney no longer has the burden of proof as the new law adopts the principle of presumed innocence, which allows them to concentrate on challenging the prosecution's case'. Lu Hong and Terance D. Miethe, 'Legal Representation and Criminal Processing in China' 42(2) (2002) *British Journal of Criminology*, p. 270.

truth, various pieces of evidence must be collected and the guilt or innocence will be determined by the court according to the facts.'[13]

In studying the 1996 CrPL as a whole, it can be ascertained that Article 12 and some other provisions reflect elements of the principle of the presumption of innocence. Firstly, Article 12 clarifies that in following the legal procedure provided in the law, it is the court's exclusive authority to determine a person's guilt or innocence. Secondly, the responsibility to prove one's guilt lies with the public prosecutor. Article 89 gives responsibility to public security organs to carry out investigations and collect and obtain the evidence necessary to prove a criminal suspect's guilt or innocence. Article 129 requires a public security organ to transfer the case file and evidence to the public procuratorate after it has concluded its investigation of a case. Article 137(1) provides that, in examining a case, a procuratorate must ascertain whether the facts and circumstance of the crime are clear, the evidence is reliable and sufficient, and the charge and the nature of the crime have been correctly determined. Article 140 provides that, if a procuratorate believes that the evidence is insufficient and the case does not meet the condition for initiation of prosecution, then the procuratorate may decide not to put the suspect on trial (*zhengju buzu bu qisu*).

Thirdly, Article 162 states that, if the evidence in a case is insufficient, the defendant cannot be found guilty and should accordingly be pronounced innocent on account of the fact that the evidence is insufficient and the accusation untenable. This implies that the burden of proving guilt lies with the prosecution rather than the defendant having to prove innocence. This also implies that if there is doubt as to the guilt of the defendant, he should be acquitted. This is the principle referred to in Chinese as *Yizui Congwu* (a doubtable crime should be treated as a 'not guilty' scenario). In order to establish guilt or innocence, Article 156 allows for the cross-examination of witnesses and expert witnesses by prosecutors, judges and defence lawyers during court sessions.

However, the 1996 CrPL also contains provisions that are contradictory to the principle of the presumption of innocence. For instance, Article 93 requires that 'a criminal suspect should answer investigators' questions truthfully'.[14] Article 35 places the responsibility on the defence lawyer to present materials and opinions, based on facts and law, that prove the innocence of the criminal suspect or defendant, highlight the pettiness of his crime, and the need for a mitigated punishment or exemption from criminal responsibility.

The lack of clarity in the 1996 CrPL certainly results in an ambiguous understanding of the principle in judicial practice. One Chinese judge wrote:

---

13 See 'Explanatory Material on Enacting and Amending the Criminal Procedure Law and Major Contents' by the Legal Working Committee of the National People's Congress Standing Committee in March 1996, cited in Chen Ruihua, *Xingshi Susong de Qianyan Wenti* (Hot Issues in Criminal Procedure) (Beijing: Zhongguo Renmin Daxue Chubanshe, 1999), p. 206.

14 An eminent Chinese criminal law scholar pointed out that in judicial practice at the investigation stage the rate of suspects voluntarily confessing or confessing after some education by investigators is about 70 per cent. He predicted that deleting the phrase 'a criminal suspect should answer investigators' questions truthfully' would not result in the refusal to reply to investigators' questions and refusal to confess by most criminal suspects. The really harmful effect of the provision 'a criminal suspect should answer investigators truthfully' is that it stimulates investigators to obtain confession by various means, even by torture, meanwhile neglecting other evidence. Consequently, erasing such a clause could compel investigators to improve investigations by focusing on collecting other evidence, which could raise the overall rate of successful investigation. See Gu Yongzhong, 'Dui Xiuzheng'an Cao'an De Youguan Jianyi' (Some Suggestions to the Draft Bill), (9–10) 2011 *Falu Xinxi* (Legal Information), p. 76.

> the presumption of innocence only applies to use by the judiciary in the courtroom. Therefore the police may use the presumption of guilt as the starting point of investigation. Similarly, for the public prosecutor, the presumption of guilt is immediately borne out of their profession to prosecute. To a certain extent, the public prosecutor is not even legally obliged to present in front of the court a defendant's exculpatory evidence.[15]

It should be noted that, in recent years, the prevailing thought amongst Chinese legal scholars is that the principle of the presumption of innocence should be explicitly provided for in the CrPL in order to make it comply with Article 14(2) of the International Covenant on Civil and Political Rights (ICCPR), which clearly states: 'Everyone charged with a criminal offence shall have the right to be presumed innocent until proven guilty according to law.' Unfortunately, the 2012 amended CrPL does not achieve this necessary clarity concerning the presumption of innocence. Moreover, Article 118, which is the former Article 93, even adds: 'When interrogating a criminal suspect, an investigator should inform the suspect of the legal provisions on leniency if a criminal suspect confesses truthfully.'

Recognising the significance of the principle of presumption of innocence in the CrPL, one Chinese legal scholar points out that the success or failure of the 2012 amended CrPL depends on how the principle of the presumption of innocence will be provided for in the Law. If the Law confirms the principle then clearly the amendment is successful; but if the Law continues with ambiguous, notorious provisions then the amendment is a failure, and inevitably will rouse further demand for amendment.[16]

The Right to Remain Silent

A principle that follows on from the presumption of innocence is that a suspect and an accused have the right to remain silent in criminal proceedings. The Chinese CrPL does not, however, accommodate this right. On the contrary, Article 93 of the 1996 CrPL, which is now Article 118 of the 2012 revision, states that a criminal suspect must 'answer investigators' questions truthfully', and is only entitled to refuse to answer questions that are 'irrelevant to the case'. Since interrogation is carried out either by the police or the prosecutor, only they can ascertain whether a suspect has answered questions truthfully. Which questions are 'irrelevant to the case' is also subject to the arbitrary discretion of the investigator. Chinese experts have pointed out that this rule not only virtually deprives suspects of their right to defend themselves but also results in turning the defendant into a *de facto* 'witness for the prosecution' through self-incrimination.[17]

In 1996, when the CrPL was amended, the right to remain silent was beyond consideration. The legislature elucidated:

---

15 Dong Xiaoming, 'Lun Wuzui Tuiding Cunzai De Fanwei' (The Scope of the Presumption of Innocence), available at www.chinacourt.org/public/detail.php?id=216074. Last visited September 2013. The author is a judge at a basic people's court.

16 Yi Yanyou, 'Lun Wuzuituiding De Hanyi Yu Xingshi Susongfa De Wanshan' (Discussion on the Implications of Presumption of Innocence and Perfecting the Criminal Procedure Law), 30(1) (2012) *Zhengfa Luntan* (Tribune of Political Science and Law), p. 20.

17 Chen Ruihua, 'Zhongguo De Xingshi Zhengju Guize' (China's Criminal Evidence Rules), in Zhonghua Renmin Gongheguo Sifabu Sifa Xiezhu Waishisi (Bureau of Foreign Affairs of Judicial Cooperation of the Ministry of Justice of the People's Republic of China) *et al.* (eds), *A Collection of Papers from the Chinese-British Symposium on Criminal Proceedings* (in Chinese and English) (Beijing: Falu Chubanshe, 2000), p. 186.

> We firmly forbid torture, but a criminal suspect should honestly answer the questions raised by the police investigator because guilt is guilt and innocence is innocence ... Whether one admits to guilt is a ruler used to measure whether one is repentant and, therefore, a plea of guilt will lead to lenient punishment.[18]

Since the 1990s some Chinese scholars have advocated the adoption of the right to remain silent in the CrPL. They believe this is a requirement of signatories to the ICCPR, which obliges the Chinese state to recognise that no one should 'be compelled to testify against himself or to confess guilt'.[19] Moreover, this right could be conducive to preventing the widespread use of torture by police and also to strengthening the defensive rights of criminal suspects and the accused.[20] In the absence of the right to remain silent, police often coerce a suspect to confess, which too often leads to false statements. Overall, this practice prevents the investigation from collecting accurate evidence, often leading to wrongful convictions.

On the other hand, many judicial officials and some scholars argue that the right to remain silent is not compatible with Chinese reality. In their view, the exercise of this right in Western countries is conditioned by institutional and social systems that 'incite' or 'force' the defendant to divulge information in the criminal process voluntarily. This reduces the difficulty in handing down a guilty verdict in the absence of a confession. They emphasise that the Chinese legal system and social environment are starkly different from those in Western countries. Exercising the right to remain silent could hinder criminal investigations tremendously, eventually resulting in many guilty persons escaping criminal punishment.[21] In opposition to this line of thought it has been suggested that the value of the right to remain silent reflects a civilising force in human history. That is, even if it might lead to reducing judicial efficiency, it is an inevitable price that human society has to pay in the pursuit of civilisation and justice.[22]

In reality, resistance to the right to remain silent reflects the deep-rooted tradition of over-emphasising confessions in the Chinese judicial process. A confession is treated as 'the king of evidence'; without one, the police consider an investigation incomplete, the procuratorate will be reluctant to institute a prosecution, and judges will lack the confidence to deliver a guilty verdict. The attitude towards the accused is judged according to whether he or she confessed. This is subsequently a factor used to determine the leniency or severity of the sentence passed. Thus, some Chinese scholars have concluded that if a 'suspect remains silent during the investigation, and refuses to answer the investigator's questions, but is convicted in the end, he will receive harsher

18 Cited in Chen Ruihua, *supra* note 13, p. 207.

19 Article 14(3)(g) of the International Covenant on Civil and Political Rights, G.A. Res. 2200A, 21 U.N. GAOR, 21st Sess., Supp. No. 16, at 49, A/6316 (1966) (entered into force on 3 January 1976).

20 Chen Ruihua, *Wenti Yu Zhuyi Zhijian: Xingshi Susong Jiben Wenti Yanjiu* (Between Problems and Doctrines: Research on Fundamental Issues in Criminal Procedure) (Beijing: Zhongguo Renmin Daxue Chubanshe, 2003), p. 392. Chen Weidong and Chen Fei, 'Zailun Chenmoquan Yu Tanbai Congkuan Wenti' (Rediscussion on the Right to Silence and Confession to Lenient Treatment), in Chen Xingliang et al. (eds), *Runwu Wusheng: Xingshi Yitihua Yu Xingshi Zhengce* (Criminal Law and Criminal Policy) (Beijing: Falu Chubanshe, 2005), p. 553.

21 Cited in Chen Ruihua, *supra* note 20. See also a summary of Chinese views by Xiong Qiuhong, 'Xingshi Susong Faxue Yanjiu Redian' (Hot Topics of Research on Criminal Procedure Law), in Xia Yong et al. (eds), *Zhongguo Fazhi Fazhan Baogao* (2) (2004) (The Development Report on Rule of Law in China: (2) 2004), (Beijing: Shehui Kexue Wenxian Chubanshe, 2005), pp. 373–374.

22 Wang Jiancheng, 'Biansu Jiaoyi, Chenmoquan Yu "Tanbai Congkuan, Kangju Congyan" De Xingshi Zhengce' (Plea Bargaining, the Right to Remain Silent and the Criminal Policy of Confession with Lenient Punishment and Resistance with Severe Punishment), in Chen Xingliang et al. (eds), *supra* note 20, p. 505.

punishment following the idea of "leniency with those who confess and severity with those who resist"' (*Tanbai Congkuan, Kangju Congyan*).[23]

The right to remain silent, coupled with the presumption of innocence, ensures that the burden of proof rests exclusively in the hands of the prosecution. The prosecution is obliged to produce the evidence that implicates the accused in the crime which, therefore, limits the likelihood of false convictions. However, the right to remain silent may not be an absolute right.[24] An example often cited by the Chinese is the 1994 Criminal Justice and Public Order Act enacted by the British Parliament, which allows judges and juries to draw adverse inferences from the defendant's silence.[25] Michael Howard, who introduced this bill to the House of Commons as Home Secretary, stated that 'it is reasonable to expect an accused person to offer an explanation of circumstances that appear to be incriminating and ... if he does not do so there is no reason why a court or jury should be prevented from taking account of his silence when considering the strength of the case against him'.[26] However, this English Act restricts the application of this right to four circumstances rather than permitting general application, while in China, 'leniency with those who confess and severity with those who resist' is a fundamental, general criminal policy. Nonetheless, the Human Rights Committee, which is the treaty body of the ICCPR empowered to monitor states parties' observance of treaty obligations, reviewed the English Act and found that it violates various provisions of Article 14 of the ICCPR.[27] It is thus unwise to use the UK example as justification to refuse the right to silence.

Substantial Examination and Procedural Examination

Under the 1979 CrPL, procuratorates were required to transfer the entire dossier to the court once they had decided to proceed with a prosecution. The court could then decide to try a case if it found 'clear facts of a crime and sufficient evidence' contained in the dossier. This procedure was referred to as the substantial pre-trial examination by the court. The flaws of such a system were evident when a judge was able to study the dossier beforehand and potentially develop a guilty perception of the accused on the basis of an accusatorial dossier. Instead, it should have been the role of the trial procedure to prove the truth in such allegations.

In order to prevent judges from arriving at conclusions prior to the judicial hearing – as system referred to as, 'decision first, trial later' (*xian ding hou shen*) – the 1996 CrPL abolished the dossier transfer system. Article 150 provides that a court should decide to try a case after it examines the

---

23 Xu Jingcun and Sun Changyong, 'Fundamental Rights of a Criminal Suspect in China', in Zhonghua Renmin Gongheguo Sifabu Sifa Xiezhu Waishisi (Bureau of Foreign Affairs for Judicial Cooperation of the Ministry of Justice of the People's Republic of China) *et al.* (eds), *supra* note 17, p. 303.

24 At the international level, different views exist: one considers 'the right as absolute and necessary to ensure a fair trial. The other views this right as subject to qualification in certain circumstances'. See Eileen Skinnider and Frances Gordon, 'The Right to Silence: International Norms and Domestic Realities', in *Breaking New Ground: A Collection of Papers in the International Centre's Canada-China Cooperation Programme*, published by The International Centre for Criminal Law Reform and Criminal Justice Policy (March 2002), p. 164, at http://www.icclr.law.ubc.ca/Publications/Reports/Breaking%20New%20Ground%20-%20May%209-02.pdf. Last visited September 2013.

25 Criminal Justice and Public Order Act, 1994 Part III, ss. 27–33.

26 'Effect of Accused's Failure to Mention Facts When Questioned or Charged', *HC Deb 13 April 1994, vol. 241, para. 279.* Available at http://hansard.millbanksystems.com/commons/1994/apr/13/effect-of-accuseds-failure-to-mention. Last visited September 2013.

27 Eileen Skinnider and Frances Gordon, *supra* note 24, p. 166.

bill of prosecution, which contains 'clear facts of the alleged crime, a list of evidence, a list of witnesses, and copies or photos of key evidence'. This Article is considered a shift from substantial pre-trial examination by judges towards procedural examination. However, it is difficult to define what 'key evidence' is. The judicial interpretations issued by the SPP alone, or in collaboration with the SPC and other organs, actually endow the public prosecutor with large discretionary powers in making this decision.[28] Although the CrPL requires the procuratorate to collect both inculpatory and exculpatory evidence, all too often the procuratorate only presents the court with evidence that is disadvantageous to the accused. Thus, Chinese scholars have criticised the introduction of Article 150 and its interpretations, for 'legally allowing public prosecutors to withhold exculpatory evidence'.[29]

Article 150 was intended to prevent judges from reviewing dossiers prior to trials and instead encouraged judges to prudently follow the questioning and debate led by the prosecutor and defence counsel in the courtroom in order to reach judgments. However, this objective is difficult to attain. As a result of judicial habits, lack of capacity amongst judges, and other facts that affect an effective hearing, such as the infrequent appearance of witnesses in courts, it is inevitable that many judges do not base their judgments merely on the information presented before them at the trial. The reality is that after the public hearing prosecutors still give the dossier to the judge in charge of the trial. The judge studies the dossier, combines it with the record of the public hearing, and then writes the judgment. This practice has merely shifted the situation from 'examination of the dossier before the trial' to 'examination of the dossier after the trial'. Furthermore, a survey has shown that some prosecutors make a few copies of only the key evidence and send that together with the dossier file to the court. Some courts also 'borrowed' dossier files from the procuratorate in order to obtain a better understanding of the case.[30]

Furthermore, the 1996 CrPL lacks the 'disclosure of evidence' requirement, which is featured in the American system. This principle requires the parties to disclose, during the pre-trial stage, all evidence that may be used at trial, including evidence that is exculpatory for the defendant. Instead, Chinese defence lawyers receive the file that the procuratorate gives to the court, which contains only limited information on the case, such as a list of major evidence and technical documentation. This ultimately hinders a lawyer's capacity to defend in the courtroom. Lawyers only have access to the dossier after the end of the trial of first instance. In view of the detrimental effect of the 1996 CrPL in this regard, combined with its limiting effect in preventing judges from examining a case before the hearing, some Chinese scholars have argued whether it would be better if the law were to revert to the previous system of dossier transfer before the trial.[31] This view has since been adopted in the 2012 amendment.

The 2012 revised CrPL Article 172 (originally Article 141 of the 1996 CrPL) requires the prosecutor to transfer the case dossier and evidence to the court when proceeding with a prosecution. Meanwhile, the original Article 150 is replaced by Article 181, requiring that after a people's court has reviewed a case for which public prosecution has been initiated, where the indictment shows clear facts for a charged crime, it should decide to hold a trial. In essence, these

---

28 Chen Weidong (ed.), *Xingshi Susongfa Shishi Wenti Diaoyan Baogao* (Survey Report on Problems in Implementing the Criminal Procedure Law) (Beijing: Zhongguo Fangzheng Chubanshe, 2001), p. 131.

29 *Ibid.*, p. 132.

30 *Ibid.*, p. 130.

31 Xiong Qiuhong, 'Zhongguo Xingshi Sifa Zhidu Gaige Mubiao Zhi Fansi' (Reconsideration on the Reform Objectives of the Chinese Criminal Justice System), in Zhang Mingjie (ed.), *Gaige Sifa: Zhongguo Sifa Gaige De Huigu Yu Qianzhan* (Reforming the Judiciary: The Retrospect and Prospects of Judicial Reform in China) (Beijing: Shehui Kexue Wenxian Chubanshe, 2005), p. 173.

Articles require a procedure of dossier transfer before trial. However, what should be contained in the case dossier and evidence needs further elaboration. According to the Regulations on Criminal Procedure of People's Procuratorates (provisional implementation) issued by the SPP in 2012, people's procuratorates should transfer indictment, dossier and evidence to courts. Materials related to the withdrawal of confessions or witness statements, or in favour of suspects or defendants should also be transferred (Arts. 394 and 395). Article 47 states that the case dossier should include prosecution documents and evidence materials.[32] In the SPC's Interpretations on the Implementation of the Criminal Procedure Law, Article 180 lists nine detailed aspects for courts to examine after receiving dossiers transferred by the procuratorate, including the jurisdiction, defendants' identifications, criminal facts, evidence, victims, witnesses, and other participants, legal assistance, incidental civil litigation, formality materials during investigation and prosecution, and elements of non-prosecution.[33]

Summary Procedure and Its Expansion

The 1996 CrPL introduced a summary procedure for misdemeanours. Under Article 174 the summary procedure applies to: (1) cases of public prosecution with clear facts and sufficient evidence, which are punishable by less than three years' imprisonment, public surveillance or fines exclusively, and where the application of a summary procedure is conditional upon the agreement or suggestion of the procuratorate; (2) cases to be handled only upon complaint; (3) cases prosecuted by victims, when it is evident that they are minor criminal cases. In practice, summary procedure may only be used in cases of the first instance in the basic people's courts.

The summary procedure boasts various characteristics to improve the efficiency of the trial. The trial is conducted by a single judge instead of a collegiate panel of three judges, as is usually the case. While the procuratorate may or may not send a prosecutor to be present during the trial, the defendant still has the opportunity to present a statement in his defence. In cases where the procuratorate does send a prosecutor to the court, the defendant and his representative may, with the permission of the judge, debate with the public prosecutor. The court must then conclude the case within 20 days of receiving it.

It has been estimated that less than 50 per cent of total criminal cases are handled by summary procedure.[34] The restrictive application of summary procedure under the 1996 CrPL has resulted in local courts applying a so-called 'summarised procedure' (*Putong Chengxu Jianyishen*) in handling cases that should be tried by ordinary procedure. For instance, since 1999, the Basic People's Court and the Basic People's Procuratorate in the Haidian district in Beijing have initiated such an experiment. From August 2002, courts in Beijing started using summarised procedure to handle cases that should follow ordinary procedure according to the CrPL. Such cases must meet four conditions: (1) the defendant admits guilt; (2) the facts are clear, and the evidence provided by the procuratorate is sufficient; (3) the defendant is being prosecuted for a crime which carries a

32 *Renmin Jianchayuan Xingshi Susong Guize (Shixing)* (Regulations on the Criminal Procedure of People's Procuratorates [Provisional Implementation]), issued by the SPP on 22 November 2012. Available at http://news.jcrb.com/jxsw/201211/t20121123_993092.html. Last visited September 2013.

33 *Zuigao Renmin Fayuan Guanyu Shiyong Zhonghua Renmin Gongheguo Xingshi Susongfa De Jieshi* (Interpretations on the Implementation of the Criminal Procedure Law) issued by the SPC on 20 December 2012. *Fashi* No. 21 [2012]. Available at http://www.court.gov.cn/qwfb/sfjs/201212/t20121228_181551.htm. Last visited September 2013.

34 See Tan Shigui (ed.), *Zhongguo Sifa Gaige Yanjiu* (Research on Chinese Judicial Reform) (Beijing: Falu Chubanshe, 2000), p. 210.

sentence potentially no greater than three years' imprisonment; and (4) the defendant agrees to the use of the summarised procedure.[35]

In 2003 the SPC, SPP and the Ministry of Justice jointly issued a regulation to allow for the use of a summarised procedure in ordinary criminal cases where a defendant pleads guilty and raises no objection to the basic facts. Such cases are tried by a collegiate panel of three judges.[36] Though the regulations aim to tackle efficiency problems, the practice seems to bear a resemblance to plea-bargaining. Many Chinese commentators do not support transplanting plea-bargaining, a typical feature of the US criminal justice system, into China. They argue that plea-bargaining is contingent on a voluntary decision by the defendant who is conscious of the full consequences of his decision. Though this could be achieved through adequate advice with a defence lawyer, such access is extremely lacking in China. Moreover, judicial corruption remains widespread and a system of plea-bargaining may escalate this phenomenon. In addition, plea-bargaining in the USA is based on the conception of respecting a defendant's right to dispose of the case while receiving due process. Considering that Chinese traditional criminal theory does not recognise a defendant's right to dispose of a case, plea-bargaining lacks legitimacy.[37] The main arguments used by those who advocate the introduction of the plea-bargaining system into China are: such a system could increase judicial efficiency, and the judicial resources saved could then be used in handling serious criminal cases.[38]

In practice, the system of plea-bargaining has been cautiously experimented with in the Chinese criminal justice system. The first such plea-bargaining case was reported to have taken place in 2002 at Mudanjiang Railway Transportation Court in Heilongjiang province. The case concerned numerous people who were involved in a fight, one of whom was seriously injured. After 15 months, the police were unable to find those involved, with the exception of Mr Meng Guanghu who had started the fight. The prosecutor was uncertain whether they could find Mr Meng's accomplice and he was concerned that it would take too much time, thus he proposed to Mr Meng that they settle the case through plea-bargaining. Mr Meng agreed to plead guilty and bear civil liability for the injuries, while the procuratorate agreed to suggest to the court that they apply probation with a lenient punishment. The local court concluded the trial within 25 minutes, sentencing Mr Meng to three years' imprisonment with three years' probation.[39]

There are differing opinions on the expansion of summary procedure and the use of summarised procedure. Proponents of the approach have stressed that under certain circumstances, such as when the defendant voluntarily confesses, or a person is caught in the act, the judicial process should be simplified for the sake of efficiency. Opponents, however, argue that, in light of the common practice of torture and lack of protection for suspects who confess voluntarily, coupled

35 Xiong Qiuhong, '"Biansu Jiaoyi" Diyi'an' (The First Case of Plea Bargaining), in Xia Yong et al. (eds), *Zhongguo Fazhi Fazhan Baogao* (The Development Report of the Rule of Law in China), 2003 (1) (Beijing: Shehui Kexue Wenxian Chubanshe, 2004), pp. 268–269.

36 *Guanyu Shiyong Jianyi Chengxu Shenli Gongsu Anjian De Ruogan Yijian* (Several Opinions on Applying the Summary Procedure in Handling Cases Brought by Public Procuratorates), *Fafa* No. 6 [2003].

37 Pan Qingsong and Zhu Qing, 'Woguo Buyi Yinru Biansu Jiaoyi Zhidu' (China Should not Introduce the Plea Bargaining System), Jiangsu Fazhibao (Jiangsu Legal Daily), 7 June 2005.

38 Yi Yanyou, 'Lun Biansu Jiaoyi Yingdang Huanxing' (Discussion on Plea Bargaining Should Be Postponed), in Chen Xingliang et al. (eds), *supra* note 20, p. 569. The author himself takes the view that plea bargaining should not be introduced into the Chinese criminal justice system at the present time.

39 Xiong Qiuhong, *supra* note 35, pp. 263–264.

with a limited involvement of defence lawyers, the overemphasis of judicial efficiency may result in more violations of defendants' rights.[40]

The 2012 amendment has expanded the scope of applying the summary procedure, as well as imposing strict conditions on its use. The modified summary procedure makes it clear that only at the basic people's courts where the following types of cases are handled can a summary procedure apply: (1) the facts of a case are clear and sufficient evidence exists; (2) the defendant confesses to the crimes he committed and does not dispute the criminal facts charged; and (3) the defendant agrees to the use of a summary procedure (Art. 208). Meanwhile, Article 209 imposes restrictions on applications of summary procedure by excluding four circumstances: the defendant is blind, mute or deaf, or is a mentally ill person who has not completely lost his capacity to comprehend or control his behaviour. This has wide social ramifications. In addition, under Article 210, a single judge can only be used in cases where imprisonment of less than three years may be imposed. For other cases a collegiate panel should be formed, and prosecutors are no longer exempt from the obligation of attending the trial. Furthermore, Article 211 requires judges to confirm the defendant's agreement to follow a summary procedure. If a summary procedure is used then a court should conclude the case within 20 days of having accepted the case; in circumstances where a defendant may be sentenced to a fixed-term imprisonment of more than three years, the concluding period may be extended to one and a half months. With these amendments in place the summary procedure can be expected to be used in a vast majority of criminal cases in the years to come.

Witness Appearance in Court and the Protection of Witnesses

Article 48 of the 1996 CrPL provides that 'all those who have information about a case shall have the duty to testify. Physically or mentally handicapped persons or minors who cannot distinguish right from wrong or cannot properly express themselves shall not be qualified as witnesses.' While this Article conveys a citizen's general duty to testify, it does not, however, specify that he/she should testify in court. Article 157 states that public prosecutors and defenders should disclose witness testimony records and the conclusions of expert witnesses who are not present in court. This Article leaves a loophole for witnesses not to appear in the courtroom.

These legislative ambiguities have resulted in different judicial interpretations from the SPC and the SPP. According to the judicial interpretation of the SPC, the public prosecutor, victim, accused and defence lawyer can all request a witness or expert to appear before the court.[41] The SPP's interpretation states that the court should inform the witnesses and make arrangements for them to appear in court once a list of witnesses has been submitted before the hearing. Alternatively, the prosecutors will read out in court the written testimony of a witness who has been requested to appear but is not present.[42] Obviously, neither interpretation makes it clear whether it is the responsibility of the court or the procuratorate to call witnesses to appear in the courtroom. As a result, in practice, the court and procuratorate take differing positions on their responsibility in bringing witnesses to court. Public prosecutors hold the opinion that, if a list of witnesses has been given to the court before the hearing, it is the responsibility of the judge to call these witnesses to court. If a witness is not called to appear in court, the prosecutor can simply read out the testimony of that witness. Some judges consider that the public prosecutor is responsible, not only for proving

---

40 These opinions were expressed by judges and scholars I interviewed in Beijing in May 2010.

41 The 1998 SPC's Explanations concerning Several Issues in the Implementation of the Criminal Procedure Law, Articles 138–140.

42 Article 337 of the Rules on the Criminal Process for People's Procuratorates issued by the SPP on 18 January 1999.

that the accused is guilty, but also for calling witnesses to give evidence in court. Otherwise, judges have the right to decide that the written testimony of a witness is inadmissible.[43]

However, the common practice is that only witness statements, often not in full, are read out in the courtroom. The opportunity for the defence to examine the witness testimony is therefore limited. As a consequence, judges do not reach a verdict through testimony and cross-examination by both parties. Instead, they rely heavily on the material evidence and written documents provided by the prosecution. Inevitably, this aspect of the trial becomes something akin to a formality.[44]

A prominent Chinese criminal law scholar pointed out that, in most cases without giving any justification, judges refuse lawyers' applications to call witnesses and to have the victim appear in court to testify.[45] A Chinese lawyer wrote about the following case that he observed.[46] During the court's investigation of a case of fraud in an intermediate people's court in Henan province, the prosecutor read out a witness's written testimony obtained by the investigator at the pre-trial stage. The judge then asked the defence lawyer to examine the evidence. The lawyer argued that, 'since the witness should appear in the court but he did not, the defence lawyer cannot question and cross-examine the witness. We solemnly state: according to legal procedure, without cross-examination, the witness testimony cannot be used as evidence in determining the case according to the law.' To which the prosecutor replied, 'The questioning note was legally obtained by the investigator from the prosecution office, the witness signed it and gave a fingerprint on the note, thus the evidence is admissible.' In response, the defence lawyer argued that 'whether the investigation has followed legal procedure, the signature and fingerprint are real, and the questioning note reflects the true meaning of the questioned person, all need to be proved by the witness in court, the witness should accept the court's examination and cross-examination by the accused and his defence lawyer. This reflects the judicial power of the court, and the procedural rights of the accused and his defence lawyer, the former cannot be replaced, the latter cannot be deprived.' The prosecutor merely concluded that, 'What you said is the American-British system, this is China, not the USA.'

It is reported that witnesses appear before the court in approximately only 5 per cent of all criminal cases.[47] Another survey showed that, in the Intermediate People's Court in Shenzhen, the average rate was between 2–5 per cent. In the Intermediate People's Court in Yantai, the rate was lower than 1 per cent.[48]

Aside from the lack of an express principle of hearing direct oral statements in the 1996 CrPL, another prominent factor in explaining the dearth of witness appearances in the courtroom is the lack of protection for witnesses. Article 49 of the 1996 CrPL provides that courts, procuratorates and public security organs should ensure the safety of witnesses and their close relatives. Anyone who intimidates, humiliates, beats or retaliates against a witness or his close relatives, if his act constitutes a crime, should be made criminally responsible according to the law; if the case is not serious enough for criminal punishment, he should be punished for violation of public security in

43 Chen Ruihua, 'Anjuan Bilu Zhongxin Zhuyi: Dui Zhongguo Xingshi Shenpan Fangshi De Chongxin Kaocha' (Case File Centric: Reexamining China's Criminal Trial Model), 4 (2006) *Faxue Yanjiu* (CASS Journal of Law), p. 69.

44 Chen Weidong (ed.), *supra* note 28, pp. 127–128. Li Wenceng, 'Zhongguo Zhengren Chuting Zuozheng Zhidu De Wanshan' (Improvement in China's System of the Witness's Appearance in Court), available at http://article.chinalawinfo.com/Article_Detail.asp?ArticleID=46268. Last visited September 2011.

45 Chen Ruihua, *supra* note 43, p. 70.

46 *Ibid.*, p. 69.

47 Xiong Qiuhong, *supra* note 31, p. 173.

48 Chen Weidong (ed.), *supra* note 28, p. 126.

accordance with the law. However, there is no concrete legal provision for the physical protection of witnesses.

Many witnesses fear retaliation if they give evidence in court, and such concern is not without reason. In practice, witnesses are threatened, beaten and even murdered.[49] On 7 June 2007, the *Legal Daily* reported on the story of Mr Xiao Jingming, an individual who had witnessed two individuals from his hometown kill a man. The police asked Xiao for his cooperation in the matter, in return promising to keep his testimony confidential and attempting to reward him for his cooperation. Mr Xiao gave two names, Mr Long and Mr Qian, to the police. Though the police detained both suspects, the latter was released because he did not confess his involvement in the case and the public prosecutor had not approved his arrest. Upon his release, he immediately went to Mr Xiao's home and questioned what he had reported to the police. He told Mr Xiao that, when he was questioned at the police station, the police had revealed the identity of the informant to him. After that Mr Qian came to Mr Xiao's shop on numerous occasions, took goods, extorted money and threatened Mr Xiao and his family. Mr Xiao was therefore forced to sell his hairdressing business quickly at a low price and go into hiding in an isolated town with his wife and two young children. On 6 December 2006, the Intermediate People's Court in Ningbo convicted Mr Long of the crime of intentionally inflicting injury, and sentenced him to the death penalty with two years' reprieve. In the judgment, the names of Mr Xiao and his wife, as well as their testimony, were clearly referenced. The police had recommended that the court should not mention the real names of the witnesses. However, the court insisted that the key witness should not be anonymous or use a 'false name', as that would run the risk of violating a fair trial procedure. The people in Mr Xiao's hometown became aware of what he had done when the judgment was publicised. Mr Xiao, a man who had a decent income and quiet life, had to live in fear and borrow money from his family and friends to survive because of the information he had given to the police. He appealed a number of times to the police to whom he gave the testimony, but no help was forthcoming. According to the police, once a case is prosecuted, they can no longer control the identity of a witness. Even the prosecutor does not disclose the witness at the prosecution stage. However, in court, when cross-examination is conducted and the judgment is published, the witness's name and testimony all become public.[50]

Commenting on the aforementioned case, an anonymous prosecutor told a journalist that China is a rural society. Ordinary people have a deep clan mentality and are not bothered by things that are irrelevant to them. Under such circumstances, it is not unreasonable that witnesses do not appear in court. Instead, they prefer to give testimony. A functioning witness protection system could not even ensure that a witness will actively or truthfully give testimony. The prosecutor also made the blunt statement:

> I consider that at the present time we are unable, and it is also unnecessary, to set up a witness protection system. The reason being that it is difficult for a criminal suspect to locate an estranged witness in order to retaliate; when a witness belongs to a clan or a group with the same interests, they protect that person; an individual who does not have such clan affiliations knows that self-

---

49 Hu Yunteng, 'Zhengren Chuting Zuozhengnan Jiqi Jiejue Silu' (The Difficulty of Witnesses Appearing in Court and Ideas on Resolving This Problem), 5 (2006) *Huanqiu Falu Pinglun* (Global Law Review), pp. 557–561.

50 'Ningbo Xiongsha'an Zhengren Jujia Taowang Zheshe Falu Jiuji Zhique' (Witness to a Murder Case in Ningbo Has to Escape with His Family, which Reflects the Lack of Legal Protection for Witnesses), *Legal Daily*, 7 June 2007, available at http://news.sohu.com/20070607/n250437320_1.shtml. Last visited September 2013.

> protection can only be achieved by refusing to give the testimony or only passively giving it. As such, if somebody is willing to be a witness in a criminal proceeding, the onus is on them to weigh the advantages and disadvantages of doing so and understand that there is no formal judicial organ to offer protection.[51]

This pessimistic, even cynical, attitude may represent one strand of thought. Some Chinese legal experts have instead drawn up numerous ideas in order to improve this disappointing state of affairs. These include: strengthening legal provisions to oblige witnesses to appear in court to give testimony; creating a system of measures that courts could take following the refusal of a witness to appear in court without reasonable justification such as punishment, fines or even detention under certain circumstances; establishing systems for protecting the personal safety of witnesses and providing economic compensation to diminish people's fear and create conditions under which citizens will voluntarily appear in court; setting up an efficiency system that prioritises which types of cases witnesses are obligated to attend (for example certain types of case at the first instance must have witnesses, while trial at the second instance may not necessarily require witnesses appear in court); and enhancing the role of defence lawyers in trials in order to make witness appearances in court more meaningful.[52]

The 2012 amendment has both strengthened the rights and tightened the obligations of witnesses. For the obligation element, Article 187 provides that witnesses are obliged to appear before court to testify when the public prosecutor, the defendant or the lawyer raises any objection to a witness statement which has material influence on the determination of a conviction or sentence, and the court believes it to be necessary for the witness to testify in person. This also applies to police who witness a crime whilst on duty, and experts who provide their expert opinions. If an expert witness refuses the court's request for their appearance in court then their opinion cannot be utilised as a basis for that case decision. Article 188 stipulates that a witness who refuses to appear in court without sound justification, having already been summoned by the court, may be forced to attend. An exception is the spouse, parent or child of the defendant. A witness who refuses to appear before the court or refuses to testify without a justifiable reason should be given a warning; if the case is of a serious nature then the witness may be punished with detention of up to 10 days, upon the approval of the president of the court. The detainee can appeal to the relevant higher court for administrative review, but this would not affect the execution of the detention.

Meanwhile, the protection of witnesses is strengthened in two new provisions. Article 62 provides that in cases involving a crime endangering state security, crimes of terrorism, organised crime of an underworld or drug-related nature, and the like, when a witness, an expert or a victim testifies, and he or his relatives' personal safety is in danger, a court, a procuratorate and a public security organ is expected to use one or several protective measures. This may include not disclosing his or her true personal information, including name, residency and employer; not exposing his or her appearance or own voice when in court; prohibiting particular persons from contacting the witness, expert, victim and his relatives; providing special protection for his or her person and residence; other necessary protective measures. Article 63 guarantees compensation for witnesses' expenses resulting from transportation, accommodation and meal costs. The source of the testimonial compensation is to be included in the operating expenses of the judicial authorities and provided for by the financial department of the government at the same level. When a witness

51 *Ibid.*

52 Hu Yunteng, *supra* note 49, p. 560.

testifies, his or her employer may not directly or indirectly deduct salary, bonus, welfare or other remuneration. The implementation of these new provisions needs to be further observed.

The Exclusion of Evidence Obtained Illegally

Article 43 of the 1996 CrPL states:

> Judges, procurators and investigators must, in accordance with the legally prescribed procedure, collect evidence that can prove the criminal suspect's or defendant's guilt as well as innocence, and the gravity of his crime. It is strictly forbidden to extract confessions by torture and to collect evidence by threat, enticement, deceit or other unlawful means. Conditions must be guaranteed for all citizens who are involved in a case or who have information about the circumstances of a case to objectively and fully furnish evidence and, except in special circumstances, they may be brought in to help the investigation.

While this Article declares a prohibition on using torture and unlawful conduct to collect evidence, the 1996 CrPL does not outline the legal consequences of evidence that is obtained illegally. As a result, the 1996 CrPL does not technically establish a rule to exclude the introduction and use of such evidence in the courts.

This legislative loophole was to some extent filled by Article 61 of the 1998 SPC Explanations on Several Issues concerning the Implementation of the Criminal Procedure Law of the PRC, which provides that 'it is strictly forbidden to collect evidence by unlawful means. If it is proven that witness testimony, victim statements, or defendant statements were obtained by torture, threat, enticement, deceit or other unlawful means, they are inadmissible.'[53] Yet, judicial interpretation fails to go far enough in providing procedural rules once such an allegation of illegal evidence has been propounded, such as how such an investigation begins and who bears the burden of proof. Indeed, in judicial practice, there is hardly any precedent for the exclusion of such evidence by the courts. When defendants or their lawyers assert that the former were tortured, judges usually do not admit the claim.[54] In the high-profile trial of Liu Yong, even though the court of second instance stated that there was a possible occurrence of torture, it did not exclude the oral confession of the defendant; neither did it express whether there was any link between the claim of torture and a lenient sentence.[55]

Most of the torture takes place at the police investigation stage. For courts, the most pressing question is how judges should react when an accused states during the hearing that his confession was made under circumstances of torture, and whether they can exclude evidence that was obtained by illegal means. Based on Article 61 of the 1998 SPC Explanations on Several Issues concerning the Implementation of the Criminal Procedure Law of the PRC, the answer should be obvious. However, as stated, judges hardly ever declare evidence inadmissible simply because it is illegally obtained. Judges face a dilemma in excluding the illegally obtained evidence. If they confirm the existence of torture and make a judgment of innocence or hand down lenient punishment, the

53 Explanations on Several Issues concerning the Implementation of the Criminal Procedure Law of the PRC issued by the SPC on 2 September 1998.

54 Xiong Qiuhong, '"Liu Yong'an" Kaoyan Xingshi Sifa' (Liu Yong Case Tests Criminal Justice), in Xia Yong et al. (eds), *supra* note 21, p. 234.

55 *Ibid.*

accused could claim state compensation from the police or public procuratorate.[56] If judges do not confirm the use of torture, the accused may appeal to a higher court. If the original judgment is overturned by the appeal court, this may damage the record and reputation of the court of first instance. Within judicial practice, an undisclosed way around this has been developed by which courts usually request the procuratorate to investigate the torture claims within a fixed period of time; if it proves the existence of torture, the court will ask the procuratorate to withdraw the case.[57]

The insufficient legal guarantee to exclude illegally obtained evidence and the common problem of resorting to torture to obtain a confession have resulted in a growing demand within legal circles to introduce mandatory procedures effectively to prevent torture. In 2010 the SPC, the SPP, the Ministry of Public Security, the Ministry of State Security and the Ministry of Justice jointly issued two judicial interpretations on evidence: Several Issues concerning the Examination and Judgment of Evidence in Death Penalty Cases,[58] and Provisions on Several Issues concerning the Exclusion of Illegal Evidence in Criminal Cases.[59] Both the procedures and criteria for collecting and admitting evidence are detailed further, and their essence is adopted in the 2012 amended CrPL.

Article 50 (originally Article 43) bans the use of torture or extortion to obtain a confession, and the use of threat, inducement and deception and other illegal means to collect evidence. In addition, five new provisions are provided to effectuate the exclusion of illegally obtained evidence. Article 54 declares that 'confessions by a suspect or a defendant obtained through torture and other illegal means and witness testimonies and victim statements obtained through the use of violence, threats and other illegal means should be excluded'. Article 55 obliges a procuratorate to investigate any alleged illegal activities of investigators after receiving a report, accusation or a tip-off. In cases where it is confirmed that illegally-obtained evidence has been used, the procuratorate should provide some guidance and opinions on methods of correction; if any crime is committed then criminal liability should be investigated according to law. Article 56 further provides that during a trial, if judges have concerns about the possible use of illegal means to obtain evidence they should initiate a court enquiry on the legitimacy of evidence collection. An accused, his defender or defence lawyer would also have the right to request that the court exclude the evidence obtained illegally by providing relevant information or materials. Article 57 requests the procuratorate to prove during the court enquiry the legality of the collected evidence. If the legality cannot be established based on the existing evidence, a procuratorate may request that the court call the relevant investigators or others to give an explanation in court; the court may also take the initiative to do so. The relevant investigators or other persons may also file a request to appear in court. Those notified by the court to appear are obliged to do so. Article 58 concludes that after the court's enquiry, if the possible use of illegal means in collecting evidence as stipulated in Article 54 cannot be excluded, the court should rule the evidence inadmissible. In addition, as a

56 A suspect has the right to claim state compensation under the 1994 State Compensation Law. Article 15 provides that a victim has the right to claim compensation if an organ in charge of investigatory, procuratorial, judicial or prison administration work, or its functionaries, infringe upon his personal right in the exercise of its functions. Relevant situations include: wrongful detention of a person without incriminating facts or proof substantiating strong suspicion of the commission of a crime; wrongful arrest of a person without incriminating facts; a determination of innocence established upon re-trial held in accordance with the procedure of trial supervision, but after the original sentence has already been executed; extortion of a confession by torture or causing bodily injury or death to a citizen by using or instigating the use of violence; or causing bodily injury or death to a citizen by the unlawful use of weapons.

57 Liu Sida, *supra* note 5, p. 84.

58 *Fafa* No. 20 [2010], issued on 1 July 2010, became effective on 1 July 2010.

59 *Fafa* No. 20 [2010], issued on 13 June 2010, became effective on 1 July 2010.

supplementary guarantee, the 2012 revision requires that during a criminal suspect's interrogation, the investigator record the process by audio or visual means; and for crimes punishable by life imprisonment or death and other serious crimes, audio or video recording of the interrogation process is mandatory. The audio or video recording should cover the entire process of interrogation and should be complete (Art. 121).

It can be assumed that lawyers play a crucial role in delivering the enquiry system in courts. In the well-known *Beihai* case[60] in 2011, with the persistent and courageous efforts of lawyers the court was forced to investigate the legality of evidence in trial proceedings which resulted in the procuratorate withdrawing more than 10 pieces of evidence. As the court was unable to prove that any of it was illegally obtained, or that torture had been used, its withdrawal by the procuratorate is considered by some Chinese lawyers an exclusion of evidence. Lawyers in the case were also allowed to question the policemen in court. This case has thus made a pioneering contribution to criminal defence in China.[61]

The Roles of the Judge and the Prosecutor

Compared to earlier criminal trial procedure, the most salient changes relate to the role of the judge. Whereas before, judges were responsible for interrogating defendants, questioning witnesses and experts, reading out the written testimony of witnesses and experts in their absence, and presenting material evidence, these functions have since been shifted to the prosecutors and the defence. Thus, judges no longer play an active role in court investigation and debate. This creates a simplistic impression that the implementation of the 1996 CrPL has transformed the trial model from an inquisitorial to an adversarial one.

In reality, the 1996 CrPL creates a combination of the adversarial and inquisitorial models. On the one hand, it has adopted some features of the adversarial system. It replaced the 'dossier transfer' system with the 'transfer of copy' system which prevented judges from reaching conclusions prior to the trials. Furthermore, prosecutors and the defence have the right to question and cross-examine the defendant and witnesses. On the other hand, the 1996 CrPL retains some elements of the inquisitorial system. Even though the role of judges in the courtroom has been reduced in law, they maintain the right to investigate, question the defendant, and verify evidence if they deem it necessary. Moreover, judges have the right to interrupt the prosecutor, the accused or the defence lawyer if their remarks are 'irrelevant to the case' (Arts. 155 and 156 of the 1996 CrPL and Arts. 186 and 189 of the 2012 CrPL). What constitutes 'irrelevant' remarks is a subjective assessment made by the judge. It is not infrequent that, during a criminal trial, a judge stops an accused when he is defending himself, or a lawyer when he is presenting arguments that are favourable to the accused. On the other hand, it is rare for a judge to interrupt a prosecutor. Moreover,

> there is no intention to hide the close connection between the prosecutor and the trial personnel. Often before the trial, prosecutors will chat with either judges or secretaries in front of the defendant and the defence attorneys. It is well known that the *Gong*, *Jian* and *Fa* (police, procuracy, and court) are one big family, and the prosecutor has at least an equal, if not higher-ranking in comparison with the court.[62]

---

60 See *infra*, pp. 124–125.

61 Chen Youxi, 'Beihai'an Fazhi Fangmian de Bage Yiyi' (The Eight Significances of the Beihai Case on the Rule of Law), available at http://blog.sina.com.cn/s/blog_6b804b510101jkpn.html. Last visited September 2013.

62 Bin Liang, *The Changing Chinese Legal System, 1978–Present: Centralization of Power and Rationalization of the Legal System* (New York and London: Routledge, 2008), p. 152.

In judicial practice the work of Chinese scholars reveals a procedure which favours and centres upon the prosecution. Indications of this can be found in: the passive role of the judges during a trial, the prosecutor's possession of most of the evidence, and the reality that the accused only occasionally has a defence lawyer. Under Article 155 of the 1996 CrPL (Art. 186 of the 2012 CrPL), after the public prosecutor has read out the bill of prosecution in court, the defendant and the victim may present statements regarding the alleged crime, and the prosecutor may interrogate the defendant. The judges may also interrogate the defendant. However, the role of conducting the main interrogation of the defendant has shifted from the judge to the public prosecutor. In practice, before a prosecutor interrogates a defendant, he usually warns him 'to answer truthfully', or sometimes even a judge will give the same warning.[63]

In practice, it is the prosecution, rather than the judge, that has control and plays an active role in the hearing. To a large extent, judges only passively follow the prosecutors. As the well-known Chinese criminal law scholar Chen Ruihua wrote:

> Only after the end of the first instance trial … a defence lawyer has the opportunity to access the entire file of a case, and to examine how the court of first instance has admitted evidence. During the court investigation, the prosecutor, based on the advantage of holding the information and sources, controls the scope, order, and method of court investigation … As an arbitrator, a judge does not know all the information … Therefore, he only passively accepts and examines the written notes presented by the prosecutor in the courtroom. A defence lawyer also does not have an opportunity to check the file in its entirety, thus he can only conduct a passive defence, based on the evidence presented in the courtroom. An accused could disagree with the written notes, even overthrow his guilty plea, but he could not undermine the effect of the written note.[64]

Whether Article 172 of the 2012 amendment which provides the dossier transfer to courts will lead to some practical change concerning the role of judges will require further observation.

In April 2007 I observed the criminal trial of a traffic accident case at a basic people's court in Wuhan, Hubei province. The accused was a 57-year-old man who was driving his car without a licence and whilst intoxicated, subsequently causing a woman's death. During the trial, which lasted about two hours, he was not represented, remained handcuffed and stood for the entire time. The trial proceeded in the following manner:

1. One judge on the panel checked the name of the accused and asked him whether he had a criminal record. The reply was 'no'. Then the judge announced the names of the collegiate panel and the prosecutors and asked the accused whether he applied for withdrawal. The accused stated 'no'. The judge then asked the accused whether he had a lawyer and the accused answered 'no'.
2. To begin the court investigation, the prosecutor read the indictment to the courtroom. The presiding judge then asked the accused whether he had any disagreement with the indictment. The accused, continuing his succinct and simple responses, stated 'no'. The judge asked whether the prosecutor had any questions for the accused. The prosecutor posed a few questions and the accused replied briefly to the majority of the questions, by simply accepting everything stated.
3. During the court examination, the presiding judge asked the accused whether he knew that he should not drive whilst intoxicated, and furthermore why he did not try to help the injured woman. He

63 Sun Changyong, 'Xingshi Tingshen Fangshi Gaige Chuxian De Wenti Pingxi' (Analyses on Questions Relating to Criminal Justice Reforms), 3(2002) *Zhongguo Faxue* (China Legal Science), p. 146.

64 Chen Ruihua, *supra* note 43, p. 71.

replied that it was very dark that evening and that when he hit the tree on the street he did not see that a woman was there. After this response, the prosecutor submitted the following evidentiary material into the record: the police investigative record of the case; the written testimony of six witnesses from which the prosecutor selected a few paragraphs to read out loud, written notes and photos made by policemen at the scene of the crime; a formal statement by the police concerning the case; and the report of an expert on the deceased woman. The prosecutor took nearly an hour to present his evidence, during which time the courtroom was captivated solely by his voice. When he concluded, the presiding judge asked the accused whether he had anything to say in response to the evidence, to which the accused replied 'no'.

4. The court debate was again one-sided, with the prosecutor dominating. He quickly read a prepared statement, highlighting that the accused committed the crime of a violation of traffic regulations in accordance with Article 133 of the Criminal Law. He concluded by stating that the criminal facts were clear and the evidence was sufficient. The presiding judge then gave the accused an opportunity to respond to the charges set out by the prosecutor but he remained silent.
5. At the conclusion of the trial, the presiding judge announced that the collegiate panel would declare the judgment at a later date.

My impression of this trial was that the accused had not been afforded the opportunity to adequately defend himself. His defence consisted of uttering 'no' a number of times, which can hardly be considered adequate. Instead, the prosecutor systematically directed the proceedings, he was confident and nobody challenged anything he stated or presented. As the accused was not apprehended on the spot, all the witness testimony concerned the scene of the crime and not the accused. Moreover, he said he was driving a stolen car. Whilst sat in that courtroom it became increasingly apparent that the evidence was so ambiguous that in fact anybody could have been placed on trial for the crime in question. In reality, the possibility of the real perpetrator finding a replacement to take his place should not be disregarded.[65]

Similarly, in May 2007 at the Second Intermediate People's Court in Beijing, I observed a criminal trial concerning an intentional injury, which led to the victim's death. The accused was an unemployed 22 year-old-man from a city in the northeast of China. On the night in question, he had dinner with three young men at a restaurant in Beijing. After a few drinks, a quarrel erupted between the accused's group and some other young men at the next table. This led to a fight between all the men, involving the use of beer bottles and chairs. The altercation concluded with a patron from the next table sustaining an injury that caused bleeding to his head, which ultimately resulted in his death. The four men fled from the scene of the crime and the accused was not located until two years later, in June 2006, when he returned to his hometown to renew his ID card. He was then detained and brought to Beijing for trial.

During the trial, which lasted around two hours, the prosecutors read out a number of witness statements given by the men the accused had dined with as well as statements from people working at the restaurant on the night in question. None of the witnesses appeared in court. From the witness statements read by the prosecutor it was apparent that some had described the accused as a man wearing a white shirt, while others reported that he was wearing a blue shirt. There were additional discrepancies in the descriptions of how the victim was injured. Some witnesses said he hit the

65 For example, a recently reported case involved Mr Chen Wenhui, who, after becoming drunk, drove a car into a man, thus killing him. Mr Chen asked his brother-in-law to surrender himself to the police after the accident. The policemen found the brother-in-law's confession was contradictory to the police's findings at the accident site and eventually discovered that the brother-in-law was a replacement for Mr Chen. See *Anhui Shangbao*, 22 August 2007.

victim's head with a beer bottle and others said he used a chair. Furthermore, the witnesses were inconsistent in their description of the accused's height, which ranged from 1.6 to 1.75 metres. These inconsistencies suggested that the witness statements were full of contestable points.

From the evidence presented, it seemed certain that there was insufficient evidence to prove that the accused was the one who caused the fatal injury to the victim. Fortunately, the accused had two respectable and experienced lawyers. During the court examination, they raised a few questions to the prosecutor concerning the controversial witness statements. However, the prosecutor stubbornly replied directly that, 'this has been clarified in the testimony', then continued to read out another written statement. Although the trial seemed to follow the appropriate procedure, in that the prosecutor presented evidence and the accused and his lawyers were given the right to challenge the evidence, it lacked the requirement of the prosecutor being mandated to answer questions posed by the defence lawyer.

As the prosecutor presented further evidence, and the controversy surrounding it accumulated, his voice became weaker and he simply referred to the documents by number, without reading them out. The defence lawyers admitted that the accused was involved in the fight but argued that the evidence presented did not constitute a logical chain of evidence that could prove that the accused caused the man's death. The prosecutor's final statement relied on the fact that the other three men who were apprehended two years earlier all attested to it being the accused who had beaten the man to death. The panel of three judges were almost silent through the whole court session and at the end the presiding judge concluded the trial by saying that the collegiate panel would announce the judgment at a later date. It seemed apparent that the prosecutor was determined to declare the accused guilty of causing the man's death. However, from the evidence, his statements and even his body language, he did not appear entirely convinced himself. The case involved seven people in a fight, resulting in the death of one of them; the identity of the individual who actually caused the man's death was, naturally, highly uncertain.

In summary, trials of criminal cases in the courtroom continue to reveal serious problems: many defendants cannot exercise their rights without having access to a lawyer; prosecutor domination of the proceedings severely undermines the equality of arms; some basic procedural rules are either violated by prosecutors or judges or are impossible to pursue. For instance, cross-examination of witnesses by prosecutors and defence lawyers in most instances is simply not capable of being implemented due to the absence of witnesses in court. Despite the fact that the 1996 CrPL has strengthened defendants' rights, with the intention of guaranteeing fair trials, the reality of the past decades does not inspire optimism. A Chinese lawyer describes the hearings before and after the 1996 CrPL: 'before 1996 it was judges spoke, prosecutors slept; after 1996 it was prosecutors speak, and judges sleep'.[66]

The 2012 amended CrPL has strengthened the supervisory role of the procuratorate in the process of litigation by cementing Article 8 of the 1996 CrPL on how 'people's procuratorates exercise legal supervision over criminal proceedings according to law', with a new Article 47 which provides: a defender or lawyer who believes that a public security organ, a people's procuratorate, a people's court or any staff thereof has hindered his exercise of procedural rights, has the right to file a petition or accusation with the relevant level of the procuratorate. They should examine the petition or accusation promptly, and in cases in which such allegations are proven, the relevant organ should be informed in order to rectify it. How this Article will be implemented remains to be seen, granting such supervisory powers to procuratorates over courts certainly raises concern over interference in the courts' and judges' work by procuratorates.

66 Liu Sida, *supra* note 5, pp. 77–78.

The Rights of Suspects, the Accused, and Defence Lawyers

In light of the different stages of criminal proceedings, the 1996 CrPL created a distinction between a 'criminal suspect' and an 'accused'. 'Criminal suspect' refers to someone who is suspected by police of having committed a certain crime leading to a police investigation. Whereas 'accused' refers to someone who has been prosecuted in court by the public or private prosecution. Such a distinction remains in the 2012 amendments.

The 1996 Criminal Procedure Law gives the major rights of criminal suspects and defendants, and lawyers as: (1) The right to defend oneself. A suspect and a defendant have the right to defend themselves as well as to entrust one or more defenders, including lawyers to defend them. (2) At the investigation stage a criminal suspect may appoint a lawyer to provide him with legal advice and to file petitions or complaints on his behalf after he has been interrogated by an investigative organ for the first time, or from the day on which coercive measures are adopted against him. If a suspect is detained, the lawyer may apply for bail for his client. (3) Lawyers have the right to meet their clients in custody. (4) Lawyers have the right to access case materials from the date on which a procuratorate starts to examine a case for prosecution. (5) Lawyers have the right to collect materials pertinent to a case upon the approval of the witness or relevant work unit and individual, to request a procuratorate and a court to collect and obtain evidence, as well as to request a court to inform a witness to appear in court.

The lawyers' right to meet clients, to have access to case materials and to collect evidence are described as the three rights that enable lawyers to prepare their case in order to engage in a meaningful defence for the accused. However, these rights were generally provided in the 1996 CrPL with various restrictive and conditional clauses. Practice has proven that defence lawyers face various obstacles in exercising such rights. Consequently, their three rights (nos. 3–5 above) have been dubbed the 'three difficulties'.[67]

Over the past decade legal experts in China have appealed consistently and publicised various proposals to improve the provisions of the CrPL on the rights of suspects and defendants, and their lawyers. This resulted in key modifications in the 2012 amended CrPL; at the same time the amendments reflect the compromises of the various state powers involved. To a certain extent the amendments have failed to meet public demand for stronger protection of the procedural rights of criminal suspects and defendants. The key achievements and controversies reflect on four aspects.

(1) The time to engage a lawyer has been brought forward. Under Article 33 of the 1996 CrPL a criminal suspect could appoint a person as his defender from the date on which the case was transferred for examination before prosecution. A procuratorate was required, within three days from the date of receiving the file record of a case, to inform the criminal suspect that he has the right to entrust a person as his defender. Article 96 provided that after a criminal suspect was interrogated by an investigatory agency for the first time or from the day on which compulsory measures were imposed against them, they could appoint a lawyer to provide them with legal advice and to file petitions and complaints on their behalf. If the criminal suspect was arrested, the appointed lawyer could apply on his behalf to obtain a guarantor pending a trial. If a case involved state secrets, appointing a lawyer needed the approval of the investigatory organ. The appointed lawyer would have the right to find out about the suspected crime from the investigative organ, and

67 For critical observations on these difficulties, see Jerome A. Cohen, 'The Plight of China's Criminal Defence Lawyers', 33 (2003) *Hong Kong Law Journal*, pp. 231–248.

could meet with the suspect in custody to enquire about the case. The investigatory organ could be present at such meetings when deemed necessary.

In the 2012 amended CrPL, Article 96 was abolished. Article 33 has been modified as such that from the day a criminal suspect is interrogated by an investigatory organ for the first time or from the day when a compulsory measure is taken against him, he has the right to engage a defender; during the period of criminal investigation a criminal suspect may only appoint a lawyer as a defender. An investigative organ and a procuratorate should inform suspects of their rights.

(2) The notification of family in cases of detention and arrest. Under Article 64 of the 1996 CrPL, within 24 hours of a person being detained, his family or his work unit should be notified of the grounds of detention and the place of custody, except in circumstances where such notification would obstruct the investigation or there is no means by which they can be notified. This Article was modified as Article 83 of the 2012 amended CrPL which provides that after a person is detained, he should be immediately transferred to police custody within 24 hours. The family of a detainee should be notified within 24 hours following detention unless no means of notifying them is available or 'such notification may hinder criminal investigation in cases concerning threatening state security or terrorist activities'.

Different perceptions have emerged on whether Article 83 is a progressive or a regressive provision. According to the official interpretation, Article 83 certainly reflects improvement because the obstruction investigation clause under Article 64 could apply to any cases whereas under Article 83 it is strictly limited to cases involving a threat to state security and terrorism.[68] However, some legal professionals and netizens who have given comments on microblogs take the clause of there being no need to notify under the circumstances that 'it may hinder criminal investigation in cases concerning threatening state security or terrorist activities', as legalising 'secret detention' or as a 'disappearance clause'.[69]

Relevant to Article 83, another new article which has generated a great deal of public outcry is Article 73 of the 2012 amended CrPL. It provides that in cases involving crimes of endangering state security, terrorist activity, or extreme bribery, if carrying out residential surveillance[70] in the

68 See 'Quanguo Renda Changweihui Fagongwei Jiu "Xingshi Susongfa Xiugai" Da Jizhe Wen' (The Legal Committee of the NPCSC Replied to Questions Raised by Journalists), see http://www.xinhuanet.com/politics/2012lh/zhibo/20120308b/index.htm. Last visited September 2013.

69 Xiao Han, 'Guanyu Xingsufa Xiugai Jiqi Xiuzheng'an De Ruogan Xiangfa' (Several Thoughts on the Amendments of the CrPL). See http://czqlawyer.fyfz.cn/art/1047266.htm. Last visited January 2014.

70 Residential surveillance is house arrest. It is one of the three types of compulsory measures that can be imposed on suspects, the other two are enforced appearance (*juchuan*) and granting bail (*qubao houshen*). Enforced appearance refers to a suspect or defendant who can be called by an investigation authority, a procuratorate or a court to appear at a fixed time in a fixed place to answer questions. Granting bail means that an investigative authority, a procuratorate or a court may decide a suspect or a defendant who meets certain conditions need not stay in custody after providing a surety or paying a bond. A bailed person is requested to follow certain rules (Arts. 65 to 71). Compulsory measures restrict in various ways the liberty of suspects and defendants, but are alternatives to detention and arrest which deprive a person of their liberty.

The 2012 CrPL has reinforced residential surveillance by adding four new provisions, revising one and keeping another (Arts. 72 to 76). It applies to a suspect or defendant who meets the arrest conditions but falls into one of the following circumstances: suffering serious illness and cannot live on his own; a pregnant woman or a woman who is breastfeeding her own baby; a sole supporter of a person who cannot live by himself; considering the special circumstances of the case or as needed for handling the case, residential surveillance is more appropriate; the term of custody has expired but the case has not been closed, and residential surveillance is necessary. The period of residential surveillance cannot exceed six months.

residence of the suspect or defendant may obstruct the investigation, it may also be carried out in a 'designated abode' following approval by the procuratorate or public security agency at a higher level. A suspect's relative is to be notified of such residential surveillance within 24 hours, unless there is no means of doing so.

Some Chinese commentators have noted that imposing residential surveillance in 'a designated abode' in the 2012 revised CrPL amounts to the legalisation of secret arrest. Prior to this, the CrPL did not explicitly recognise secret arrest; thus such practice had no legitimacy even though it existed. It is now written into the Law; its evil impact would be huge under the legitimacy of the law. If a suspect meets the conditions of detention or arrest he will be detained in a jail where various regulations apply. But detaining a suspect in a 'designated abode' avoids the application of those rules. Such 'designated abodes' are just 'black jails' as they exist in China now. Detractors have warned that Article 73 legitimises the existence of 'black jails ', which leaves room for manoeuvre with regard to torture.[71] Similar views were also expressed by some deputies of the National People's Congress who advocated removing residential surveillance in 'designated abodes' in the amendment. They warned that placing a suspect in a designated location may create the right conditions for the practice of torture, which would compromise the efforts already made in prohibiting torture and excluding illegally obtained evidence.[72]

International commentators have also expressed serious concern over Article 73. Sophie Richardson, China Director at Human Rights Watch, stated:

> The draft criminal procedure law contains many positive provisions, but the government's stated goal of improving due process will be severely undermined by allowing incommunicado detention of people in undisclosed locations ... Such provisions represent a clear danger for government critics and human rights activists, and are in clear contravention of China's international obligations.[73]

Profound concern regarding residential surveillance in designated places is not without practical reason. Residential surveillance in law can be seen as house arrest, but the harsh reality is that without legal authority the police have caused the disappearance of criminal suspects and activists. The most recent cases, which took place in 2011, involved artist Ai Weiwei and some human

---

Article 57 of the 1996 CrPL became Article 75 of the 2012 CrPL which provides that a criminal suspect or defendant under residential surveillance should comply with the following provisions: (1) not to leave the residence where residential surveillance is in force without the approval of the executive agency; (2) not to meet or communicate with others without the approval of the execution organ; (3) to appear before court in time when summoned; (4) not to interfere by any means with the testimony of witnesses; (5) not to destroy or forge evidence or collude to give a false confession; (6) to submit passport, other documents of exit and entrance of the country, ID, driver's licence to the executive body for upholding. A new Article 76 provides that executive agencies may use electronic monitoring, random inspection and other surveillance means to examine whether a suspect or defendant has followed the residential surveillance rules; and during the investigation process, may monitor the communication of criminal suspects.

71 Xiao Han, *supra* note 69.

72 'Xingsufa Xiuzheng'an Tiaokuan Yin Zhengyi, Di 73 Tiao Bei Zhi Jiya Siquan' (The Draft Amendments of the Criminal Procedure Law Cause Debate, Article 73 Is Attacked as Extruding Private Rights), see http://news.qq.com/a/20120313/001149.htm. Last visited September 2012.

73 'China: Don't Legalize Incommunicado Detentions Proposed Legislation Would Violate International Standards', available at www.hrw.org/news/2012/03/12/china-don-t-legalize-incommunicado-detentions. Last visited September 2013.

rights lawyers.[74] Thus, Article 73 has also been named 'the Ai Weiwei Clause',[75] and 'the Jasmine Clause'.[76] Though all were eventually released, the effective legalisation of such disappearances aggravates distress.[77]

(3) Lawyers' rights to meet criminal suspects and defendants. Under Articles 36 and 96 of the 1996 CrPL, lawyers have the right to meet with criminal suspects in custody. However, it is also provided that, when lawyers meet with criminal suspects, the investigative organ may, in light of the seriousness of the crime and where it deems it necessary, send its people to be present at the meeting. If a case involves state secrets, lawyers need the approval of the investigative organ for any such meeting.

In reality, lawyers are often not permitted by the detaining authorities to meet their clients, sometimes without being given reasons. Some investigative organs arbitrarily expand the connotations and meaning of 'state secrets', using it as an excuse to refuse lawyers the opportunity to meet their clients.[78] Sometimes lawyers are required to present papers which are not readily available or accessible. Occasionally, they are even required to pay a fee in order to meet their clients. Such blatant infringement of the right to counsel has resulted in lawyers suing police agencies.[79]

---

74 Stanley Lubman, 'China's Criminal Procedure Law: Good, Bad and Ugly', available at http://blogs.wsj.com/chinarealtime/2012/03/21/chinas-criminal-procedure-law-good-bad-and-ugly/. Last visited September 2013.

75 Ai Weiwei, an outspoken artist, was taken by security agents from the Beijing airport before his departure for Hong Kong in April 2011. No indication of his whereabouts was given to his family. After days he was released and since then has been under residential surveillance.

76 In February 2011, when popular uprisings took place in the Middle East and North Africa, there were anonymous calls on the internet for 'jasmine rallies' in China. The government, concerned about possible organised events at that time, arrested, disappeared and placed 'soft detention' on hundreds of bloggers, lawyers and writers. See, 'Chinese Artist Ai Weiwei Arrested in Latest Government Crackdown', *Washington Post*, 3 April 2011, available at http://www.washingtonpost.com/world/chinese-artist-ai-wei-wei-arrested-in-latest-government-crackdown/2011/04/03/AFHB5PVC_story.html. Last visited September 2013.

77 Phelim Kine, 'No Valentine's Love for China's Illegitimate Leaders', *Washington Times*, 10 February 2012, available at http://www.hrw.org/news/2012/02/10/no-valentine-s-love-china-s-illegitimate-leaders. Last visited September 2013.

78 Jerome A. Cohen, *supra* note 67, p. 232. Ping Yu, 'Glittery Promise vs. Dismal Reality: The Role of a Criminal Lawyer in the People's Republic of China after the 1996 Revision of the Criminal Procedure Law', 35 (2002) *Vanderbilt Journal of Transnational Law*, pp. 836–837. See Nicola Macbean and Qinglan Li, 'The Death Penalty in China: A Baseline Document', in The European Initiative for Democracy and Human Rights, *Strengthening the Defence in Death Penalty Cases in the People's Republic of China* (London: The Rights Practice, 2003), p. 14. In the Six Ministries and Committee's Provisions (*supra* note 4), Art. 11 plainly states that investigative bodies cannot use the excuse that the offence concerns state secrets to refuse a lawyer access to a suspect in detention. However, state secrets are not defined and, in reality, investigative organs often still invoke this ground to refuse lawyers the right to meet their client in detention.

79 For example, in 1998, Chen Suyi, a lawyer in Hunan province sued the police bureau in Lianyuan City for refusing him access to his client who had been detained by the police, in violation of the CrPL. The Intermediate People's Court accepted the case. However, upon receiving a copy of the statement of claim, the police bureau acknowledged that the decision of the detention house had violated the law. Therefore, they decided to re-examine and abolish the illegal rules that restricted the rights of lawyers to meet with criminal suspects and defendants. The Bureau then sent its representatives to meet Chen and gave him a personal apology, offering to pay all of the costs he had incurred. They also committed to strengthen legal education for the police force, in order to enhance their capacity to carry out their functions according to the law. Mr Chen

The presence of investigative personnel at lawyer–client meetings is not exceptional. This certainly puts the suspect under psychological pressure, thereby limiting adequate communication with his lawyer. It has also been reported that some investigative agencies even record and videotape meetings between defence lawyer and suspects.[80] Chinese lawyers are of the opinion that, considering their right to meet with suspects and defendants is fully controlled and dictated by investigative authorities, who routinely impose restrictions on this right, even the limited guarantees provided by the law are difficult to implement in practice.[81]

In response to these practical problems the 2012 CrPL revised Article 36, and lawyers' rights to meet suspects and defendants have been both extended and restricted. On the one hand, Article 37 provides that a defence lawyer can request to meet with a detained criminal suspect or defendant by showing his practising license, a law firm certificate and a letter of attorney or an official legal aid letter (three certificates), following which police custody are required to arrange such a meeting promptly and no more than 48 hours later. At the meeting, the defence lawyer may enquire about the case and offer legal advice to the detained criminal suspect or defendant, and he may also verify the evidence with his client. The meeting between the lawyer and the suspect or the defendant is not to be monitored. Nevertheless, the same Article also stipulates that when a defence lawyer wishes to meet, during the course of the investigation, with a suspect of a crime of endangering state security, a crime of terrorism or a specifically significant crime of bribery, approval of the investigating authority must be sought. Consequently, Article 37 creates a guarantee of no barriers to lawyers meeting their clients if they provide the three documents requested; this is remarkable progress from Article 96 of the 1996 CrPL. However, the approval procedure *vis-à-vis* suspects of the three exempt crimes is regressive.

(4) Lawyers' rights to access case material and collect evidence. Under Article 36 of the 1996 CrPL defence lawyers may, from the date that a case is accepted by the court, consult, extract and duplicate the materials pertaining to the facts of the alleged crime. However, according to Article 150, when the procuratorate prosecutes a case, it only needs to submit to the court the bill of prosecution and a list of evidence, a list of witnesses, and copies or photos of the main evidence. This means that public prosecutors will not transfer a dossier with all the evidence to the court. As a result, lawyers do not have access to the actual evidence or witness testimony. Often, the list of evidence only contains inculpatory evidence and evidence to prove the gravity of the crime, not exculpatory evidence that provides mitigation for the defendant. The defence lawyer's information on the facts and evidence of the case is therefore limited, which prevents sufficient preparation and consequently weakens their defence in court. In addition, some lawyers have complained that, in some cases, the case documents were a few hundred pages, and lawyers were not allowed to make copies.[82]

The situation is to some extent improved in the 2012 CrPL by reforming the original Article 36. In the new revision, Article 38 allows defence lawyers and other defenders (with the permission of the court or procuratorate) to access, extract and copy case materials from the day the procuratorate

---

accepted the apology and a symbolic compensation of RMB 2 yuan. In return, he agreed to withdraw the case. See *Zhongguo Lushi Bao* (Lawyer's Newspaper), 10 June 1998.

80 Xu Jingcun and Sun Changyong, *supra* note 23, p. 305.

81 Wang Jiancheng and Yang Xiong, 'Chongsu Bianhu Lushi Yu Dangshiren Guanxi' (Rebuilding the Relationship between Defence Lawyers and Their Clients), 10 (2004) *Zhongguo Lushi* (Chinese Lawyers), pp. 73–74.

82 Chen Qiulan and Qian Lieyang, 'Zhongguo Lushi Zhiyenan' (Difficulties for Chinese Lawyers in Practising Law), 5 (2002) *Zhongguo Lushi* (Chinese Lawyers), pp. 53–54.

examines a case for prosecution. Article 39 states that a defender has the right to request the procuratorate or court to subpoena evidence proving the innocence of the suspect or defendant or the pettiness of a crime if the defender considers that during the investigation or prosecution such evidence has been collected but not submitted by the public security authority or the procuratorate.

With regard to the collection of evidence, Article 37 of the 1996 CrPL (Art. 41 of the 2012 amended CrPL) allows defence lawyers to collect relevant materials for a case from witnesses, entities and individuals with their approval. Lawyers may request that the procuratorate and court collect or obtain evidence, or request that the court notifies witnesses to appear in court. Lawyers may collect information from victims, their relatives, and witnesses provided by the victim. But this is conditional on their consent and the approval of the procuratorate or court. Thus, if they do not want to give information to the lawyers, it is difficult for the latter to procure evidence in favour of the accused.

In practice, when a lawyer collects evidence that is contrary to the evidence obtained by the investigative agencies or procuratorate, he runs the risk of being accused of falsifying evidence or preventing authorities from obtaining evidence. This accusation can lead to prosecution and conviction. In the face of these potential risks, most lawyers choose to do little work in pursuit of exculpatory evidence, which inevitably affects the quality of the defence.[83]

As demonstrated, the rights of defence lawyers are constrained by various conditions. These conditional clauses should be narrowly construed so that they only apply to 'exceptional' situations rather than 'ordinary' and mundane circumstances. However, in judicial practice, they have become routine practice rather than exceptional, which severely undermines a lawyer's ability to prepare any coherent defence. An even more pressing concern is the ignorance of the prosecutorial service and courts regarding or their unwillingness to facilitate the exercise of defence lawyers rights, rendering these legitimate rights unattainable. The objective of guaranteeing a fair trial is substantially weakened as a consequence.

Apart from obstacles imposed by police, procuratorates, and courts towards lawyers, it should be noted that the ruling Party's ideology towards criminals and lawyers is also a factor that contributes to the overall trend of neglecting the rights of lawyers. It has been pointed out that, 'for many CCP leaders, defending a criminal case is perceived with great cynicism: exploiting legal loopholes at best, speaking for bad people or colluding with, and covering up, criminals at worst'.[84] One can foresee that a substantive change in judicial attitude towards defence lawyers depends on whether or not the Party modifies its stance towards them.

Review of the Death Penalty

Currently, the number of people who have been sentenced to death and the number actually executed remain state secrets in China. Based on publicly available reports, Amnesty International has estimated that in 2005 at least 1,770 people were executed and that 3,900 people received the death sentence; the actual figures were believed to be much higher.[85] Since 2009 Amnesty International

83 Chen Weidong (ed.), *supra* note 28, p. 228.

84 Fu Hualing, 'When Lawyers Are Prosecuted … The Struggle of a Profession in Transition', 2 (2007) *Journal of Comparative Law*, p. 103.

85 Amnesty International Report 2006. Available at http://www.amnesty.org/en/library/info/POL10/001/2006. Last visited September 2013.

has ceased publishing its minimum estimate of such figures, and instead has challenged the Chinese authorities to make the figures public.[86] As yet no official information has been disclosed.

Under the 1979 Criminal Procedure Law, final approval of the death penalty rested with the Supreme People's Court. However, as a response to the increased workload resulting from the nation-wide 'strike hard' campaign on serious crimes,[87] in 1983 the National People's Congress Standing Committee amended the Organic Law of the People's Courts, authorising the SPC to delegate power of approval of the death sentence to the Higher People's Courts for crimes of 'homicide, rape, robbery, causing explosion and other crimes gravely endangering public security and disrupting social order' (Art. 13). Article 199 of the 1996 CrPL (Art. 235 of the 2012 revision) clearly provides that 'the death sentence should be subject to approval by the Supreme People's Court'. Article 200 (Art. 236 of the 2012 revision) states that 'a case of first instance where an intermediate people's court has imposed a death sentence, and the defendant does not appeal, shall be reviewed by a higher people's court and submitted to the SPC for approval. If the higher people's court does not agree with the death sentence, it may bring the case up for re-trial or remand the case for re-trial.' However, from 1980 to 1997 the SPC issued eight Notices delegating to some higher courts the right of final approval on death penalty cases.[88] Yet such approval by the HPCs has generated various deficiencies. Most serious is the inconsistent application of the law by the more than 30 HPCs, meaning that some courts have proven stricter than others in imposing the death sentence.[89] Consequently, the SPC has been unable to ensure a unified application of the death penalty. Furthermore, the HPCs approved simultaneously death sentences handed down by lower courts and acting as the court of second instance, rendering the possibility of an independent death sentence review procedure meaningless. Indeed, the increase in the number of cases reported concerning wrongly-sentenced or executed death sentences over the past few decades has shocked

---

86 The Amnesty International 2011 Report on Death Sentences and Executions, available at http://www.amnesty.org/en/library/asset/ACT50/001/2012/en/241a8301-05b4-41c0-bfd9-2fe72899cda4/act500012012en.pdf. Last visited September 2013.

87 The policy of 'Strike Hard' campaigns on serious crimes started at the beginning of the 1980s, resulting from the emergence of serious economic crimes precipitated by the Open Door Policy and economic reform. In 1982, the National People's Congress Standing Committee issued a Decision on Severe Punishment of Crimes Seriously Disrupting the Economy in which the crimes of smuggling and drug trafficking could be punishable by the death penalty. Given the increase of serious crimes, the NPCSC issued a Decision on Severe Punishment of Serious Crimes Disturbing Social Safety and Security in 1983, in which the crimes of hooliganism, causing intentional injury, human trafficking, the smuggling, sale and manufacture of illegal weapons and explosives, and the crime of facilitating or forcing women into prostitution could be punishable by the death penalty. Zhao Bingzhi and Xiao Zhonghua, 'Sixing De Xianzhi Yu Kuozhang Zhizheng' (Debate on the Restriction and Expansion of the Death Penalty), 10 (1998) *Faxue* (Law Jurisprudence), pp. 2–3.

88 See 'Zuigao Renmin Fayuan Guanyu Tongyi Xingshi Sixing Anjian Hezhunquan Youguan Wenti de Jueding' (The Decisions of the SPC on Relevant Issues concerning the Unified Application of Death Penalty), *Fashi* No. 12 [2006], available at http://www.mdshnx.com/law/sfjs/2006/sfjs06-12.htm. Last visited September 2013. The Decisions abolished the Eight Notices issued before.

89 One example of regional variations concerns sentencing for drug offences. While the Criminal Law (Art. 347) establishes a threshold of 50grams of heroin for drug offences which may result in the death penalty, in practice, this threshold varies between provinces; for instance, in Yunnan province, where drug trafficking is more prevalent, the threshold is considerably higher than in many other provinces. See 'The Rights Practice, the Death Penalty in China: A Baseline Document'. Paper prepared for the European Initiative for Democracy and Human Rights, 'Strengthening the Defence in Death Penalty Cases in the People's Republic of China, December 2003', p. 8. Available at http://www.ecba.org/extdocserv/DP_Baseline.pdf. Last visited September 2013.

the public. Meanwhile, some Chinese academics have been actively advocating for moderation in use of the death penalty, and even its abolition.[90]

Since 1997 there has been a conflict between the 1996 Criminal Procedure Law and Article 12 of the Organic Law of the People's Court. It was not until October 2006 that the NPCSC amended Article 12 of the Organic Law of the People's Court, returning the exclusive final approval of all death penalty verdicts to the SPC. This amendment came into effect on 1 January 2007. Given that 90 per cent of the death sentence review cases were previously handled by the HPCs,[91] this shift has led to a considerable increase in the SPC's caseload. Consequently, the SPC has established three new criminal chambers to cope. Around 300 judges from local courts have been redirected to the SPC in order to meet with such demand, alongside which, one or two new divisions have also been established within each HPC.[92]

Since 2007 the number of cases punishable by death and the actual execution figures have been gradually reduced. The reversion of the SPC's approval power sent a signal to local courts that they should be extremely cautious in their application of the death penalty. If under any circumstances the first and second instance courts can avoid using capital punishment then they should do so. It has been revealed that in the past when handling serious criminal cases some local courts automatically chose the death penalty. In contrast the courts will now first look for more lenient alternatives to try to avoid death penalty punishments. Sources from the procuratorates also show a dramatic decrease in the rate of appeals for an immediate execution in place of a two-year suspension, which shows a positive response by procuratorates to the new national criminal policy of reducing the use of the death penalty. It is estimated that since 2007 the number of executions has fallen by a half to two-thirds.[93] Susan Trevaskes points out that 'the return of the death sentence ratification process to the SPC would automatically bring about a situation whereby courts are "killing fewer, killing cautiously"'.[94]

Further confirmation of the change in approach to the death penalty is evident in the Criminal Law articles. Under the 1996 Criminal Law, 47 articles refer to the death penalty and 68 capital crimes are punishable by death, while in 2011 the eighth amended Criminal Law reduced 13 economically-related non-violent death penalty crimes. This is the first time that the number of crimes subject to the death penalty has been reduced since the Criminal Law was enacted in 1979.

---

90 Chen Xingliang, 'Zhongguo Sixing de Dangdai Mingyun' (The Current Fate of China's Death Penalty), 5 (2005) *Zhongwai Faxue* (Peking University Law Journal), pp. 513–533. Liu Renwen and Guo Li, 'Lun Sixing Fuhe Falu Jiandu De Wanshan' (On Improving Legal Supervision on the Death Penalty Review), 6 (2012) *Zhongguo Xingshifa Zazhi* (Criminal Justice), available at http://article.chinalawinfo.com/Article_Detail.asp?ArticleId=72976. Last visited September 2013. Qu Xinjiu, 'Tuidong Feichu Sixing: Xingfa Xuezhe de Zeren' (Promoting the Abolition of the Death Penalty: A Responsibility for Scholars in Criminal Law), 4 (2003) *Faxue* (Law Science), pp. 43–44.

91 'Returning Death Penalty Review to the Supreme People's Court: How Will the Court Staff the New Death Penalty Review Divisions?', available at www.chinareview.info/pages/legal.htm. Last visited September 2013.

92 Liu Renwen and Guo Li, *supra* note 90.

93 Liu Renwen, 'Zhongguo Sixing Gaige De Huigu Yu Zhanwang' (Retrospect and Prospect on the Reform of the Death Penalty in China), 2 (2012) *Henan Caijing Zhengfa Daxue Xuebao*, available at http://article.chinalawinfo.com/Article_Detail.asp?ArticleId=69742. See also Zhao Bingzhi, 'Shouhui Sixing Fuhequan Xianzhu Jianshao Sixing Shuliang' (Upon the Return of the Review Approval on Death Penalty to the SPC the Number of Death Penalty Sentences Has Notably Reduced), available at http://legal.people.com.cn/n/2012/0829/c188502-18859395.html. Both were last visited September 2013.

94 Susan Trevaskes, 'The Death Penalty in China Today: Kill Fewer, Kill Cautiously', 48(3) (May/June 2008) *Asian Survey*, p. 410.

However, despite the improvement in legislation and in the actual reduction of the number of executions based on official announcements and scholars' estimates, China at present remains the country with the highest rate of executions. Moreover, there is no official sign that the death penalty will be abolished in the criminal law regime. Roger Hood's observation that the transformation in attitude in Chinese legal circles since the end of the 1990s from vigorously defending the necessity of the death penalty towards a gradual acknowledgement of the irresistible trend towards its final abolition, and based on the statistics of recent public surveys, has led him to conclude that 'it is not so much the general public that needs to be influenced; rather it is the legal practitioners and political leaders who need to embrace the human rights objections to capital punishment'.[95]

Realising that abolition may take longer, legal scholars' advocacy has concentrated on reforming the SPC approval procedure to maximise the prevention of miscarriages of justice and to reduce the use of the death penalty. One suggestion is to introduce a third instance trial procedure for capital punishment which enables both defendants and prosecutors to present their arguments at a formal trial to be presided over by judges at the SPC.[96] However, such a proposal was not adopted in the 2012 amended CrPL, instead only a slightly improved procedure was introduced.

The death penalty review procedure in the 2012 amended CrPL comprises six articles. Apart from retaining the four articles of the 1996 CrPL – authorising the SPC as the sole court to approve the death penalty; requiring the submission of cases for approval by IPCs to HPCs, and then by HPCs to the SPC; requiring cases decided by IPCs on a death penalty with a two-year reprieve to be approved by HPCs; requiring the formulation by the SPC of a collegiate panel in review cases – two entirely new provisions were added. Article 239 provides that when reviewing a death penalty case the SPC should make a ruling to approve or disapprove of the death sentence.[97] In instances of disapproval the SPC may 'revert the case back for re-trial or render a new sentence'. Based on Article 350 of the SPC's Interpretations on the Implementation of the Criminal Procedure Law issued in November 2012,[98] there are four circumstances under which the SPC should send cases for re-trial to local courts when it disapproves a death penalty sentence: (1) the facts are unclear and evidence is insufficient; (2) during the review process new facts or evidence emerged which may affect the determination of the crime and the verdict; (3) the original verdict is correct in identifying the facts, but a death penalty should not be passed down according to law; (4) the original trial violated the legal procedure which may have affected the fairness of the trial. In practice, in most cases the SPC has sent cases back to local courts for re-trial.

The likelihood that the SPC will 'render a new sentence' is slim. Under Article 350(2), if an original judgment contains an error in ascertaining concrete facts or in application of the law it does not necessarily follow that it is inappropriate to sentence the defendant to death, in which case the SPC may correct the original judgment and make a new judgment or decide to approve the death penalty. Thus, under Article 350(2) 'render a new sentence' may result in the approval of

---

95 Roger Hood, 'Abolition of the Death Penalty: China in World Perspective', 1 (2009) *City University of Hong Kong Law Review*, p. 1.

96 Chen Weidong and Liu Jihua, 'Sixing Anjian Shixing Sanshen Zhongshenzhi Gaizao De Gouxiang' (Some Ideas on Reforming the System of the Third Instance as the Final in Capital Cases), 4 (2004) *Xiandai Faxue* (Modern Law Science), pp. 64–68.

97 When the SPC approves a death penalty verdict it will issue two documents to the enforcement court. One is the Death Penalty Criminal Judgment or Death Penalty Criminal Order. The other is the Death Penalty Execution Order signed by the president of the SPC. This information was obtained from the judge at the SPC in March 2013.

98 The SPC Interpretations on the Implementation of the Criminal Procedure Law, available at http://www.court.gov.cn/qwfb/sfjs/201212/t20121228_181551.htm. Last visited September 2013.

a death penalty. In addition, Article 351 provides that in the instance that one person was convicted of more than two crimes and sentenced to death, if upon review the SPC considers that some facts were unclear and evidence insufficient in respect of part of the crimes resulting in the death penalty, the SPC should dismiss the case as a whole, annul the judgment and send the case back for re-trial. Should the SPC consider that the facts have been ascertained correctly on part of the crimes in a death penalty judgment, but the person should not be given the death penalty according to law, the SPC may change the judgment, and make a decision to approve the death penalty on those crimes that should be punished by the death penalty. Consequently, under Article 351 the consequence of the SPC review is that the person will receive a death penalty.

Article 352 provides that if two or more defendants are sentenced to death in one case, if upon review the SPC considers that facts are not ascertained clearly and evidence insufficient with respect to some defendants, the SPC should disapprove the whole case, annul the judgment and send the case back for re-trial. Should the SPC be of the opinion that for some defendants the facts are ascertained correctly, but they should not be sentenced to death, the SPC may change the death sentence for them but still enforce it for the others for whom it is applicable. This creates the possibility that some defendants in a joint offence case may not have their death penalty approved by the SPC.

Finally, a breakthrough in improving the SPC review procedure is the introduction of the formal participation of the defendant, lawyer and the SPP in the review process. Article 240 of the 2012 amendment obliges the SPC to question the accused, and upon the request of the accused's lawyer the SPC is required hear the lawyer's opinion. In addition, the SPP may submit its opinion to the SPC. The SPC is then required to inform the SPP of the result of the review. From the wording of Article 240 it is mandatory rather than discretionary for SPC judges to question the accused, and to hear lawyers' opinions contingent upon request. The participation of the accused, defence lawyers and the SPP brings about a shift in the SPC review from an internal, closed procedure toward a more open proceeding which is conducive to the protection of defendants' rights. However, Article 240 does not provide the review procedure with a formal open trial, and involvement of the accused, their lawyers and the SPP is very limited.[99] According to an SPC source prior to the 2012 amendment becoming effective on 1 January 2013, SPC judges had questioned the accused during the review process in approximately 90 per cent of cases. When both facts and evidence are complicated the SPC is to engage in face-to-face questioning with the accused; however, in cases where facts are clear, there is sufficient and reliable evidence, the collegiate panel and the adjudicative committee of the first instance court, the second instance court as well as the collegiate panel of the SPC have the same opinion, and the defendant and his lawyers do not raise different opinions on facts and evidence, and circumstances cannot be considered for a lenient punishment, long-distance video questioning of the accused may be used.[100] According to Article 356 of the 2012 SPC's Interpretations on the Implementation of the Criminal Procedure Law, during the review procedure if a defence lawyer submits a request to give his opinion directly to the SPC, the collegiate panel should hear his opinions in the work place (*bangong changsuo*) and make notes. When written opinions are provided by the lawyer, they should be enclosed with the case file. Article 357 states that when the SPP gives its opinions, the SPC should review them and inform the SPP on whether the SPC agree with those opinions and the reasons for doing so. To make Article 240 truly functional requires vigorous defence lawyers, as well as a cooperative attitude on the part of the SPC.

---

99 Liu Renwen and Guo Li, *supra* note 90.

100 'Zuigaofa Xingsanting Fuzeren Jiedu Xin Xingsufa Sixing Fuhe Chengxu: Woguo Sixing Fuhe Anjian Tixunlv Da Jiucheng' (Head of the Third Criminal Chamber of the SPC Explains the Procedures of the Death Penalty Review of the New CrPL: The Rate of Questioning in Death Penalty Review Cases Reaches up to 90 per cent in China), *Legal Daily*, 23 March 2012.

Miscarriages of Justice: Case Studies

Notwithstanding the deficiencies of the 1996 CrPL in written form, if the law can be firmly adhered to by judicial organs and personnel, the criminal justice system in China will have a more commendable reputation than it does presently. The Chinese public have been repeatedly shocked by serious injustices that have been the result of judicial practice demonstrating the ignorance and violations of procedure by courts and judges.

The context of these miscarriages of justice is complex. The criminal justice system consists of a chain of three stages, first involving investigation by the police, then prosecution by prosecutors, and finally adjudication by judges. Problems at each stage may have ramifications for the next. However, as the last frontier to establish guilt or innocence, the courts and judges have a greater burden, and are expected to conduct trials with independence and impartiality. Their obligation is to safeguard the rights of a defendant as stipulated by law, to ensure that criminals are punished according to the law and to further prevent innocent individuals from becoming victims of injustice.

The following case studies of high-profile injustices[101] show that, despite the continuing efforts of the Chinese government and judicial organs to improve the criminal justice system, serious problems exist in modern day China, which contribute to social instability and incite fear in the lives of the public as a whole. This also gravely undermines judicial authority, which in turn hinders the construction of the rule of law in Chinese society.

Case 1: She Xianglin[102]

In April 1994, a female body was recovered from a village lake in Jingshan county of Hubei province. The local coroner established that the victim had sustained an initial blow to the head before drowning. It was consequently established that the victim had been murdered.

A village man named Mr Zhang reported to the local police that his sister had disappeared a few months previously, and that she had been having marital troubles with her husband, Mr She Xianglin. The local police quickly reached the conclusion that the dead body must be that of Mr She's wife, and he became the only suspect in the murder investigation. Under intense interrogation, the local police extracted a confession from Mr She, though his confession contained factual contradictions, such as the location where the body had been recovered.

---

101 For academic analysis on injustice cases in Chinese, see Gao Hongjun and Zhang Jianwei (eds), *supra* note 5. And Gao Hongjun and Zhang Jianwei (eds), 9 (2008) *Qinghua Fazhi Lunheng* (Tsinghua Forum of Rule of Law). The nine cases presented below have been widely exposed on the internet, a search in Google of the term '*yuan'an*' (injustice cases) in Chinese leads to plenty of articles. In October 2010 a Chinese scholar published online a list of 26 serious injustice cases revealed by the media, all concerned murders. The list was soon removed from the internet. See Tong Zhiwei, 'Xingsufa Xiugai Xianfa Shijiao Yanjiu' (Study on Modification of the Criminal Procedure Law from a Constitutional Perspective), available at http://blog.sina.com.cn/s/blog_6bf30a0c0100xwl2.html. Last visited September 2013.

102 For the case materials, see Zhang Jianwei, 'Collections of Criminal Injustice Case', in Gao Hongjun and Zhang Jianwei (eds), *supra* note 5, pp. 373–378. For a detailed collection of materials on this case, see Chen Chunlong, *Yuanjia Cuo'an yu Guojia Peichang: She Xianglin An De Fali Sikao* (Injustice Cases and State Compensation: Legal Thought on the She Xianglin Case) (Beijing: Zhongguo Jiancha Chubanshe, 2007). A similar case to She Xianglin is the case of Yui Tuyuan who was accused of murder in 2004. But, one year later, the supposedly dead person reappeared alive. To hide their wrongful handling of Yui's murder case, the local police continued Yui's detention on suspicion of swindling. Though the case was eventually withdrawn by the local procuratorate, Mr Yui was detained in police custody for more than a year. See Zhang Jiangwei, *ibid.*, pp. 365–368.

When the case was brought to the local procuratorate, prosecutors formed divergent views on the case. Some concluded that the facts of the case were unclear, and that there was insufficient evidence against Mr She. Furthermore, the case could not be prosecuted before a court based solely on the confession of the suspect. However, other prosecutors maintained that, given the grave nature of the crime, a speedy prosecution of the case was necessary in order to prevent public outcry. The local procuratorate therefore requested further evidence from the local police, but given that several months had passed since the discovery of the body, they were unable to recover any.

Irrespective of the evidence, the case was then brought by the procuratorate before the Jingzhou Intermediate People's Court (IPC). The indictment detailed Mr She's affair with another woman. Similarly, it described his poor relationship with his wife, to such an extent that it caused her psychological distress. It ultimately stated that Mr She intended to kill his wife, whom he believed to be mentally ill, so he would then be free to marry his mistress. It further asserted that, at 2 a.m. on 21 January 1994, Mr She brought his wife to the village lake, knocked her unconscious with a rock, and threw her into the water, where she subsequently drowned.

The defence argued that Mr She's guilt could not be established on two separate grounds. First, there was no causality between Mr She's affair and the alleged murder of his wife. Second, there was no positive evidence of guilt as Mr She's confession was both inadequate and factually incorrect. In the courtroom, Mr She repeatedly stated that he did not kill his wife. However, on 13 October 1994, the Jingzhou IPC issued the judgment that Mr She was guilty of murder. He was then sentenced to death.

Mr She's mother was convinced of his innocence as she believed that her daughter-in-law was in fact still alive. She petitioned the Hubei Higher People's Court with evidence that someone had recently seen her daughter-in-law. Deciding that the facts of the case were unclear and that the evidence was insufficient, in January 1995, the Hubei Higher People's Court requested a re-trial at a lower court. In addition, it requested that the investigation be re-opened by the local police who had carried out the initial investigation. Embarrassed at being forced to re-open the investigation twice, the local police did not search for new evidence. Given the lack of factual evidence, the procuratorate could not establish guilt or innocence for over a year following the re-opening of the case. Instead of looking for new evidence, the local police accused Mr She's mother of making false statements, and detained her.

In 1997, the case was brought before the Political and Legal Committee in the municipality of Jingman. The Committee consulted with the procuratorate and the court, who decided together that, given the unclear evidence, the sentence should be revised from the death penalty to a fixed-term imprisonment. According to these instructions, in June 1998, the Jingshan County Basic People's Court sentenced Mr She to 15 years in prison. Mr She's subsequent appeal was rejected by the Jinman Intermediate People's Court.

In March 2005, Mr She's wife surprisingly returned to the village. It transpired that rather than being murdered, she had left the village unannounced due to her mental instability. Her ghostly re-appearance, prompted the Jingman Intermediate People's Court to once again re-open the case and instructed the Jingshan County Basic People's Court to re-try the case. On 13 April 2005, the court ruled that the facts of the case were unclear, that the evidence was inadequate, and that the law had been wrongly applied. Accordingly, the judgment was overturned. After 11 years (3,995 days) in prison, Mr She was finally cleared of the murder of his 'live' wife.

In surveying this case, the clear abuse of police powers is both apparent and shocking; the extremes to which they had gone to avoid the case being reversed, appealed, petitioned or opened to inquiry is indeed unnerving. Some of these measures are unfathomable, including the detention of family members. After Mr She was imprisoned in April 1994, his older brother started to petition various authorities. In May 1995, he was detained by the police for 41 days. Mr She's mother was also placed in detention by the police for nine and a half months for posting her daughter-in-law's picture so that people could identify her and inform the family. Only after the family paid RMB 3,000 was she released, and in such a weak state that she died three months later, at the age of 54. When a village family stated that they had seen Mr She's wife alive, this was considered by the police an insult to their initial investigation of the crime, which had concluded that the body was that of Mr She's wife. The police punished the family: one family member was detained, and two others had to flee the village.[103] The police's practice of putting their pride and ego before justice and law enforcement is both destructive to lives and fundamentally jeopardises and calls into question the roles and powers assigned to them.

Case 2: Li Jiuming[104]

In July 2002, Mr Li Jiuming, a senior prison officer in Hebei province, was the suspect in a case of burglary in which the homeowners were severely assaulted. The police searched Mr Li's house and found a gun. Although, it was later proven that, as part of his duties as a senior prison officer, Mr Li was responsible for prison firearms, the gun recovered by the police had been given to him by a retired head of the prison. The police arrested Mr Li on a charge of the illegal possession of weapons. In police custody, Mr Li was severely tortured, which resulted in his confession to crimes of homicide and the illegal possession of weapons.

In November 2003, the IPC in Tangshan city convicted Mr Li and sentenced him to death, with a two-year reprieve. Mr Li appealed and told his lawyer that he had been severely tortured by the police. In an attempt to assist Mr Li, the lawyer went to several relevant organisations to discuss his case. In August 2004, the lawyer received an anonymous tip-off that the real murderer had been found in Wenzhou city in Zhejiang province, and that he had been sentenced to death for other crimes. The lawyer, a college friend of Mr Li, used all his possible contacts to bring this case to the attention of the central government. In November 2004, the Political and Legal Committee of Hebei province announced that Mr Li was a free man. However, Mr Li had already been deprived of his liberty for three years. In January 2005, seven policemen were tried for torturing Mr Li.

Case 3: Li Huawei[105]

In 1986, Mr Li Huawei returned home and discovered his wife dead on the floor. When he picked her up, her blood covered his clothing. During the initial investigation, the police conducted interviews with colleagues, neighbours and family. They concluded that Mr Li was the only suspect in the murder. Therefore, the prosecutor indicted Mr Li on the charge of intentionally murdering his wife, even though the evidence against him consisted solely of his blood-soaked clothing. In 1989, the IPC in Yingkou city sentenced Mr Li to the death penalty, with a two-year reprieve. Upon hearing the judgment, Mr Li cried, protesting his innocence. Though Mr Li never confessed to the crime, the judgment concluded that the court had clear facts about the crime, as well as adequate evidence that included the expert testimony of the police and prosecutors. The entire judgment contained a feeble 600 words.

103 Zhang Jianwei, *ibid.*, pp. 376–377.

104 For the case material, see *ibid.*, pp. 382–385.

105 *Ibid.*, pp. 385–388.

Mr Li's appeal to the HPC in Liaoning province was rejected. He continued to protest his innocence, and even whilst in prison he consistently refused to confess to the crime. His parents sold their house to raise the funds for a long journey to petition for their son's innocence. In order to get the attention of relevant government institutions and officials, they travelled to Beijing, and to Shenyang, the capital of Liaoning province. All of their attempts, however, failed.

Then in 2000, a man named Jiang Hai was apprehended by the police for a criminal offence. While in police custody, he confessed to the murder of Mr Li's wife, which he committed 14 years previously, when he was then only a 17-year-old neighbour of Mr Li. Mr Jiang described how, on the day of the murder, he had been drinking alcohol and watching pornographic films. He had then gone to Mr Li's house, drunkenly seeking to have sex with Mr Li's wife. When she refused, he took a knife from the kitchen and killed her.

Mr Jiang Hai had been interviewed during the initial police investigation. However, as he was considered too young to commit such a horrific crime, he was excluded from suspicion, and his alibi was never verified. The injustice suffered by Mr Li, that is, his mistaken imprisonment for 14 years for the murder of his own wife, shocked the country. Given the intense media focus on this case, Mr Li received several letters from numerous persons in Guizhou, Hebei and Heilungjiang provinces, detailing similar experiences. Many of those who wrote sought advice on how to address their cases. This phenomenon indicates that there are more hidden cases of injustice that cannot be exposed in a tightly-controlled media environment.

Case 4: Du Peiwu[106]

In April 1998, two police officers – one male, one female – were found shot dead in a car with their money and identification taken. Following an investigation, the local police identified the suspect as Mr Du Peiwu, the husband of the female victim, who was also a police officer. Mr Du refused to confess to the murders. He informed the prosecutor that he had been tortured during his interrogation, and furthermore, showed the cigarette burns that he had sustained on his hand. Regardless of his claim, he was arrested by the procuratorate and charged with homicide.

Mr Du's case was heard twice by the IPC in Kunming city – first in December 1998, and then in January 1999. In its judgment, the court found Mr Du guilty of homicide, and he was sentenced to death. He appealed to the Higher People's Court in Yunnan province, on the basis that he did not commit the murders, there were no clear facts in the case, there was inadequate evidence, and that he was tortured by police. The HPC took the view that there was sufficient evidence in the case, but that some of the evidence gave rise to doubt. Therefore, in November 1999, the HPC reduced the sentence to the death penalty with a two-year reprieve. Mr Du was imprisoned as a result. The judgment in this case reflects the courts' typical practice of 'doubt leads to lenient punishment' rather than a verdict of innocence.

Six months later, in June 2000, another serious case of car-jacking and murder was carried out by a group of people. A man named Yang Tianyong admitted that he and two others had killed the two police officers in 1998. A police search found a gun with ballistics matching the previous crime, as well as the items stolen from the officers. This evidence proved that Mr Du had clearly been wrongly convicted. In order to remedy this injustice, the Political and Legal Committee in Yunnan province intervened and Mr Du was released after 26 months in prison.

106 *Ibid.*, pp. 388–391.

Case 5: She Shuping[107]

In 2005, a man named Wang Shujin was detained by the police. Wang confessed to the rape and murder of four women in Hebei province. Based on the information he provided, the police were able to confirm that a woman had indeed been murdered in 1994 in the village he identified. However, a colleague of the murdered woman informed them that another man, She Shuping, had been convicted of the murder in 1994.

Although the court obstructed access to its files, further investigation by journalists revealed details of the case. At the time he was convicted of rape and murder and sentenced to death, Mr She was not yet 21 years of age. His mother told how her son's lawyer had claimed that his confession had been extracted under torture. As this was a rape and murder case, the trial was not open to the public. Furthermore, Mr She's mother was only given two minutes to meet with her son before the trial, during which they had no time to speak. His family did not know when he was sentenced to death, and had no knowledge of when he was executed. They requested a copy of the judgment of the death penalty from the HPC in Hebei province, but the court never complied. In April 1995, when Mr She's father visited the prison, he was informed that his son had been executed.

Under the pressure of media attention, the police, procuratorate and court in Hebei province issued a joint investigative report into the case. This report simply concluded that Mr She's case was not mishandled, and that Wang Shuping's confession was a fabrication. However, the evidentiary basis for the report was not disclosed. Furthermore, the investigative report was issued by the same police, procuratorate and court that had handled Mr She's case. Important questions arise as to the objectivity of the court in re-assessing the case.

Case 6: Chen Guoqing, Yang Shiliang, He Guoqiang, Zhu Yanqiang[108]

In July and August 1994, there were two instances in the city of Chengde, Hebei province of the murder and robbery of taxi drivers. The police investigation concluded that four men from a nearby village – Mr Chen and three farmers – were responsible for the crimes.

During the police interrogation, the four men confessed to the separate murders. However, when the case was brought before the Chengde IPC, all defendants retracted their confessions. They gave details to the court that their confessions had been obtained under torture, and showed evidence of wounds and scars on their bodies; however, the torture claims were simply ignored by the court. In August 1996, the Chengde IPC convicted them for the crime of robbery and sentenced them to death.

The convicted appealed to the Hebei Provincial HPC. As a result, in October 1996, the court found that the facts of the case were unclear, and requested that the IPC re-try the case. During the re-trial in August 1997, using the same facts and evidence as in the first trial, the Chengde IPC again issued a death sentence. However, the second judgment did not specifically mention that the facts of the case were clear, or that the evidence was adequate for the verdict. The omission of this standard judgment phrase led the Hebei Provincial HPC to once again send back the case, requesting a further re-trial by the IPC. The HPC's view was that the facts of the case were unclear and that this continued to remain the case, resulting in a third and fourth re-trial by the same process. However, at the conclusion of the fourth re-trial, the IPC sentenced only Chen Guoqing

107 *Ibid.*, pp. 378–381.

108 'Wugu Nanzi Wuci Beipan Sixing, Shinianhou Faxian Lingyou Zhenxiong' (Innocent Men Were Sentenced to Death Five Times, the Real Murderer Was Found 10 Years Later), available at http://news.sina.com.cn/s/2005-03-31/12416251935.shtml. Last visited September 2013.

and Yang Shiliang to death, He Guoqiang received a sentence of the death penalty with a two-year reprieve, and Zhu Yanqiang was sentenced to life imprisonment.

The failure of the IPC to clarify the facts on four occasions led the Hebei Provincial HPC to hold an open trial of the case in July 2003. During this trial, a collegiate panel with five judges allowed the four defendants to present details of how they were tortured, and approved their request to have their scars examined in the courtroom. However, the court did not give any opinion on whether torture had been inflicted. In March 2004, the HPC gave its final judgment, sentencing three of the defendants to death with a two-year reprieve, and the last to life imprisonment. In total, the case lasted over 10 years.

There were several doubts and questions concerning this case, including the fact that the defendants, who had no prior criminal records, claimed to be elsewhere at the time of the murders. Similarly, there was doubt about the motive to kill the drivers, who were unknown to them. They had all repudiated their confessions in the courtroom, and showed physical signs of torture. Importantly, the knife wounds inflicted on the victims did not match the type of knife that the police found at the homes of those convicted. Furthermore, the evidence collected by the lawyers, which was favourable to the defendants, was not admitted by the court. On the other hand, the fabricated evidence obtained by the police through the intimidation and threat of witnesses formed the basis of the case. As a result, the relatives of the defendants are not satisfied with the final judgment of the HPC and have appealed to the SPC, although, thus far this has been inconclusive. Since 2004, a group of eminent lawyers have organised a series of actions aiming to bring the case to re-trial and to achieve final justice, but, as of the date of writing, there has been no success.[109]

Case 7: Sun Wangang[110]

In January 1996, Ms Chen Xinghui was killed in a town in Yunnan province. The suspected murderer was Chen's boyfriend, 20-year-old Sun Wangang. However, under interrogation, Mr Sun made very contradictory statements. That August, the case was brought before the Zhaotong IPC and, in the following month, he was found guilty of murder and sentenced to death.

Mr Sun appealed to the Yunnan Provincial HPC, which decided that the IPC should re-try the case. However, in May 1998, the IPC upheld the death sentence. After a subsequent appeal, in November of that year, the Yunnan Provincial HPC gave the final judgment that Mr Sun would receive the death penalty, but given that the evidence against him was insufficient, he was granted a two-year reprieve on the sentence.

While Mr Sun was in jail, his family petitioned for his release. In 2003, their petition was brought to the Supreme People's Procuratorate. After uncovering numerous suspicious elements in the case, the Procuratorate requested a re-examination of the case by the Higher People's Procuratorate (HPP) of Yunnan province. The HPP indeed concluded that the facts in the case were unclear and that the evidence was inadequate. In September of that year, Mr Sun's case was re-tried by the HPC in Yunnan province. The original judgment was overturned and Mr Sun was declared innocent of the charges, albeit seven years after he had originally been convicted.

---

109 A search in Google of 'Yuanan Chen Guoqing' in Chinese will produce about 18,000 articles and comments on this case, see http://www.google.com/search?q=%E5%86%A4%E6%A1%88+%E9%99%88%E5%9B%BD%E6%B8%85&hl=en&start=90&sa=N. Last visited September 2013.

110 For the case material, see Zhang Jianwei, *supra* note 102, pp. 370–373.

Case 8: Zhao Zuohai[111]

In October 1997 in Zhaolou village in Zhecheng county of Shangqiu city, Henan province, Zhao Zuohai and Zhao Zhenshang had a fight. Four months later Zhao Zhenshang's nephew reported to the police that his uncle was missing.

On 8 May 1999, a headless, decomposed corpse was found in a well, and the police decided that the body belonged to Zhao Zhenshang. Zhao Zuohai was detained as a prime suspect.

During review of the prosecution, the procuratorate had previously declined three times to prosecute Zhao Zuohai as a murderer as there was no evidence to identify the body. According to the police, Zhao Zuohai had pleaded guilty nine times during the investigation, but every time he came to the procuratorate he denied it and claimed that he was tortured into confession by the police. In August 2002 the public security organ submitted the case to the Political and Legal Committee of Shangqiu city. The committee organised a collective meeting and decided that in Zhao's case the conditions for prosecution had been fulfilled, and the procuratorate finally decided to prosecute the case.[112]

On 5 November 2002, Zhao Zuohai was convicted by the Intermediate People's Court of Shangqiu city of murder, and sentenced to death with two years' reprieve. This sentence was later reviewed and approved by the Higher People's Court in Henan province with a judgment containing only 161 words.

On 30 April 2010, however, Zhao Zhenshang, the 59-year-old 'victim', returned to the village alive. He had fled for 13 years because he thought that he had murdered Zhao Zuohai during the fight. On 9 May 2012, the Higher People's Court in Henan province confirmed Zhao Zhenshang's identity and acquitted Zhao Zuohai. Until his acquittal, Zhao had been kept in prison for 11 years, and during this period his wife had left him, leaving his four children without education.

Case 9: Beihai Case[113]

Different to the aforementioned cases, in which the accused were victims of obvious violations of law by police, procuratorates and courts, as well as the lack of a strong, efficient and timely defence, the Beihai case represents a new beginning in the correction of injustice by defence lawyers acting before a murder verdict could be fabricated by the court. In November 2009 Huang Huanhai disappeared after his gang of youngsters had a fight with another group. Following the discovery of his dead body the local police bureau arrested Pei Jinde and another three suspects, who were forced by the police to confess that they killed Huang. When the case was first tried in September 2010 by the Beihai Intermediate People's Court, four local lawyers defended the accused by presenting evidence obtained through their own investigation, including eyewitness accounts, which indicated that their clients were not present when the murder took place. The police and the procuratorate were irritated by the witnesses' reversal in the courtroom, accused

111 For the case material, see Wang Jingqiong and Li Yuefeng, 'Murder Convict Set Free after "Victim" Turns up', available at http://www.chinadaily.com.cn/china/2010-05/10/content_9826537.htm. Elizabeth M. Lynch, 'When the Murder Victim Turns up Alive: Will Justice Be Served?', available at http://chinalawandpolicy.com/tag/zhao-zuohai/. Both last visited September 2013.

112 'Zhao Zuohai'an Shenli Neimu: Xianzhengfawei Huiyi Jiti Jueding Xiongshou' (The Inside Story of Zhao Zuohai: The Collective Determination of the Murder by the County Political and Legal Committee), available at http://news.sohu.com/20100511/n272039062.shtml. Last visited September 2013.

113 For case material, see http://policy.caing.com/2011/gxbhsls/. Last visited September 2013. *South China Morning Post*, 12 September, 2013.

the lawyers of encouraging the witnesses to provide false statements, and consequently arrested lawyer Yang Zaixin, and put the other three lawyers under residential surveillance. Local lawyers were warned not to get involved in the case. Yang's family contacted lawyer Yang Jinzhu in Hunan, who then contacted a few lawyers in Beijing to discuss how to help the four lawyers in trouble. Afraid of the possibility that persecuting defence lawyers might spread all over China after the notorious Li Zhuang case (lawyer Li Zhuang was jailed for one and a half years for the crime of enticing his client to give false evidence in 2011 – this case took place during the Bo Xilai movement of 'cracking down on underground society and singing red songs'), a dozen lawyers in Beijing and other places decided to form a *Beihai* Lawyers' Concern Group to support the four detained lawyers. Realising the four local lawyers would be cleared and free if the murder case could not be established by the court, they decided to take over the case by first defending the four accused. In July 2011, six lawyers from the group came to *Beihai* to provide legal assistance to the defendants. Following their arrival they were humiliated and beaten by unidentified men and women in the hotel where they stayed. Local police kept quiet about this. The court then changed the date of the trial sessions a few times to prevent the lawyers appearing in court. Despite all the barriers, the lawyers demonstrated a persistent determination in fighting the case to the end. During the trial they compelled the judges to examine all evidence and argued that the original confessions were obtained through torture and should not be admitted as evidence.

Meanwhile the lawyers had reported the case's progress on the internet. Within five days they successfully received online donations of RMB 750,000 to support them in representing the case. Thousands of people used internet space to comment on, chat about and express their support for the defence lawyers. Despite the absence of official newspaper reports, a few liberal journals, such as the *Southern People Weekly*, *21st Central Report* and *Democracy and the Legal System* reported the case, reflecting a positive response to the lawyers' defence from a broader circle.

After three years of deadlock, on 6 February 2013, the *Beihai* Intermediate People's Court finally decided to release the suspects and the so-called murder case was not proven by the court. At the same time, all four lawyers accused of instigating the defendants and witnesses were informed by the court that their cases had been withdrawn.

Reflecting on the *Beihai* case, a famous Chinese lawyer pointed out:

> we could imagine what would be the result of this case without the defence of the Lawyers Concern Group. Based on my previous working experience in a higher people's court, the principal offender would certainly be sentenced to the death penalty, at least two accessary offenders would be charged with life imprisonment … We must think seriously how many such cases take place, how few cases can be truly and efficiently defended by lawyers, how few cases could generate attention from lawyers all over China? … There are fewer than 10,000 specialised criminal defence lawyers in a country with more than 1.3 billion people. How can we safeguard our human rights? How can we prevent from being illegally persecuted?[114]

Lessons Learned from the Injustice Cases

In the aforementioned cases, She Xianglin was cleared after his 'murdered' wife reappeared alive; Zhao Zuohai was freed after the 'murdered' person reappeared alive; Li Jiuming, Li Huawei and Du Peiwu were freed after the actual murderers were found; She Shuping died in prison before

114 Chen Youxi, *supra* note 61.

the true murderer confessed years later; Chen Guoqing and others remained in prison over the period of several re-trials; and Sun Wangang was released from prison after seven years when the court finally determined during a re-trial that there was insufficient evidence to convict him in the first place.

Despite each case having its own negative features, as a whole they expose a number of common problems that exist in the Chinese criminal justice system. These cases demonstrate that serious studies on the causes of injustice are warranted. Furthermore, it needs to be determined how to reduce such cases as much as possible, and when they do occur, it needs to be understood what remedies can be used for redress. Discussion and calls for comprehensive reform are needed, ranging from a reassessment of the functions of criminal law and the criminal litigation system, to the reformation of technical rules, and the instigation of measures to ensure due process.

The Balance between the Punishment of Crimes and the Protection of Human Rights

The preceding examples of delays in and denials of justice have revealed some fundamental flaws in the Chinese criminal justice system. Aside from punishing and cracking down on crime, and the maintenance of public order and safety, another equally, or more, important function of the judiciary is the protection of the innocent and the protection of the human rights of the defendant in the judicial process. This is the dual function of the criminal justice system.

The criminal justice system involves three steps: investigation by the police, prosecution by the prosecutors, and trial by the judges. The core emphasis within the Chinese criminal justice system is placed on the police investigation, rather than on the trial. The traditional perception – which remains prevalent in the mind of many judicial officers – is that a case is solved once the police investigation has been finalised.[115] In their view, the trial process merely functions to prove the guilt of the defendant as already established by the police. The courts rarely give a verdict of 'not guilty' once a defendant is brought to trial. According to Chinese sources, approximately 99 per cent of all defendants brought to trial are found guilty.[116] The preceding cases illustrate that presumed guilt, regardless of doubt, is the prevailing mind-set and practice of the judiciary in China. Once an individual is suspected of committing a crime, public authorities focus their work on establishing the guilt of the suspect, rather than on establishing the facts of the case.

If the judicial system is to be used to protect the innocent, a choice needs to be made between whether to acquit the defendant, or to issue a more lenient sentence when there remains reasonable

115 This sort of mind-set has various impacts in practice. For instance, a recent media report found that the Zhengzhou City Bureau of Public Security in Henan province held a number of 'open arrests' of criminal suspects, most of whom were in their twenties. They were suspected of various offences, such as bribery, theft, intentional murder, drug-trafficking, rape and adultery. The police took the suspects from their detention centres and bound their feet with iron shackles. The policemen were each fully uniformed, including armoured helmets, and armed with large guns. The suspects were subsequently brought to schools and villages near the city, to conduct the ceremony of 'open arrest'. See 'Zhengzhou Juxing Gongbu Dahui Shimin He Cai Zhuanjia Zhiyi' (Open Arrest Was Held in Zhenzhou, Public Cheered, Experts Raised Doubts), available at http://news.sohu.com/20070910/n252052897.shtml. Last visited September 2013. This event was intended to have the effect of deterrence on the public at large. However, the Criminal Procedure Law only provides for 'open trial', not 'open arrest'. Based on the principle of presumption of innocence, before the judgment is handed down by the court, a suspect should not be considered or treated as guilty. As a consequence, the question could be raised as to whether publicly exposing these suspects not only humiliated them but also violated their right to be presumed innocent.

116 Fu Hualing, *supra* note 84, p. 119.

doubt as to their guilt. Article 162 of the 1996 CrPL provides that, if the evidence is insufficient and therefore the guilt of the defendant cannot be established, one cannot be found guilty. However, Chinese scholars have pointed out that the common practice is that, in cases of doubt, the accused will not be released, but will rather be punished with a more lenient sentence, for example a reduction from the death penalty to death penalty with a two-year reprieve, or a reduction to fixed-term imprisonment.[117]

This practice is explained by the fact that courts face various pressures that prevent them from declaring a defendant innocent in cases where there are doubts as to his guilt. Such pressure may come from relatives of victims who may threaten or attack judges, seek media coverage of the case, block traffic, go out on the street to demonstrate, or even take extreme measures for revenge. Furthermore, investigative organs and procuratorates may take a court's 'not guilty' decision as a negligent response to their hard work. In addition, pressure may also come from the Party and the government. For serious criminal cases the Political and Legal Committee of the Party usually calls the police, procuratorate and court together to discuss the case and compel the court to decide a case without sufficient evidence. Pressure could also come from improper media reports on a pending case, which strengthen victims' and Party officials' resistant attitudes towards a court's finding of innocence.[118]

Notwithstanding the foregoing, no matter what pressures may exist, it is a matter of principle for courts to strictly follow the law and prevent injustices from happening. In connection with this, a practical consequence of the court manipulating itself under external pressures to convict sees the innocent imprisoned while the real culprits remain free to commit new offences, thus resulting in more victims.

The judicial system is not only influenced by pressure from the police and the prosecutors, public opinion also has clout. Here, a relevant issue is how to balance public pressure with a strict adherence to legal procedure. The judiciary must be independent, and not be influenced by such pressure. Justice must be carried out by impartial and professional judges, not dictated by the desire of the public for retribution. The judiciary must carefully balance public scrutiny on the one hand, and on the other ensure that it can decide cases freely and independently, and when justice so requires, not succumb to the whims of public pressure.

Chinese traditional thinking stresses that the majority's interest (public at large) prevails over that of the minority (criminals). In practice, this has encouraged the increased punishment of criminals, rather than guaranteeing their rights. In recent years, a positive development has been that Chinese legal experts seemed to have reached a consensus on the balance that needs to be struck between combating crimes and the protection of human rights. Protection of human rights is understood in a broad sense to protect the legitimate rights of all citizens, which demands: punishing criminals to prevent infringement on other people's rights; guaranteeing that innocent people do not suffer from injustice; respecting and protecting the rights of suspects and accused in the criminal process; and imposing fair punishment on those convicted of crimes.[119] Whilst protecting the human rights of the public at large and protecting the rights of defendants may sometimes prove contradictory, Chinese judicial practice is apparently lacking in the realisation of

117 Xiong Qiuhong, 'Wuci Pan Sixing, Yuanyou Nai Xunwei' (Be Sentenced to Death Five Times, Reasons to Be Thought of), in Xia Yong et al. (eds), *supra* note 21, p. 244.

118 Jiang Guoan, 'Chulun Wuzui Tuiding Yuanze' (Discussion on the Principle of the Presumption of Innocence), available at http://www.chinacourt.org/public/detail.php?id=78218. Last visited September 2013.

119 Xiong Qiuhong, *supra* note 31, p. 166. Chen Ruihua, *supra* note 13, pp. 5–6.

defendant's rights. Some Chinese scholars have recognised this, thus propose placing human rights protection at the forefront of judicial reform.[120]

Strict Prohibition of Torture

Torture is a widespread problem affecting many police stations in China. Chinese officials have recognised that this is 'deeply entrenched', a 'stubborn illness', and a 'malignant tumour' that is difficult to eradicate.[121] The preceding cases demonstrate that the police were not under any constraints while trying to obtain the evidence they wanted. In recent years, there has been a growing willingness among officials and scholars to acknowledge China's torture problem. Academics and journalists have increasingly published detailed critiques on the practice of torture. According to a survey, 47.4 per cent of people interviewed indicated that they assume torture takes place commonly during police interrogation.[122]

Torture by the police has been widely condemned in China, but victims of torture are often afraid to report it, given the potential of further punishment. This is juxtaposed with the difficulties of the media in obtaining reliable information about torture. In the 2006 Report of the Special Rapporteur on Torture and Other Cruel, Inhumane or Degrading Treatment or Punishment, the methods of torture that were mentioned included:

> Beatings with sticks and batons; use of electric shock batons; cigarette burns; hooding/blindfolding; guard-instructed or permitted beatings by fellow prisoners; use of handcuffs or ankle fetters for extended periods (including in solitary confinement or secure holding areas); submersion in pits of water or sewage; exposure to conditions of extreme heat or cold; being forced to maintain uncomfortable positions, such as sitting, squatting, lying down, or standing for long periods of time, sometimes with objects held under arms; deprivation of sleep, food or water; prolonged solitary confinement; denial of medical treatment and medication; hard labor; and suspension from overhead fixtures with handcuffs. In several cases, the techniques employed have been given particular terminologies, such as the 'tiger bench', where one is forced to sit motionless on a tiny stool a few centimeters off the ground; 'reversing an airplane', where one is forced to bend over while holding legs straight, feet close together and arms lifted high; or 'exhausting an eagle', where one is forced to stand on a tall stool and subjected to beatings until exhaustion.[123]

After Mr She Xianglin regained his liberty, he informed a journalist that a few policemen interrogated him continuously for 10 days and nights; he was beaten, and deprived of sleep. After being subjected to this treatment, he was forced to sign a confession written by the police.[124] In the case of Li Jiuming, seven policemen were tried for torture following his release. Mr Li gave evidence to the court detailing how he was tortured. He testified that for seven days and eight

120 Xiong Qiuhong, *ibid.*, pp. 174–175.

121 See Report of the Special Rapporteur on Torture and Other Cruel, Inhuman or Degrading Treatment or Punishment, Mission to China, E/CN.4/2006/6/Add.6, para. 46.

122 Lin Lihong, 'Xingshi Zhencha Zhong Kuxing Gongzhong Yijian Diaocha Baogao' (Investigation Report of Public Opinions on Torture in Criminal Investigation), 4 (2006) *Faxue Pinglun*, p. 124.

123 Report of the Special Rapporteur on Torture and Other Cruel, Inhuman or Degrading Treatment or Punishment, Mission to China, E/CN.4/2006/6/Add.6, para. 45, *supra* note 121.

124 Comment: 'Xingyun Buzong Juangu Yuansizhe, You Duoshao Yuanyu Youdai Tuifan' (Luck Does Not Always Go with Those Who Died of Injustice, Many Injustice Cases Need to be Redressed), available at http://news.sina.com.cn/c/2005-04-06/10566304499.shtml. Last visited September 2013.

nights, the policemen tortured him whilst they were drunk. He was given electric shocks, and forced to drink water with hot peppers, and drink mustard oil. They beat his face, and smeared mustard into his eyes, nose and mouth. They also placed a bottle of water on his head; when the bottle fell, Mr Li was repeatedly forced to drink its contents. Mr Li said that under such conditions, he would have preferred death. There was no option but to follow the police inducements to make a confession that fitted the case they were fabricating.[125]

Chinese scholars' writing has exposed that courts seldom react to the claims of the accused that their confessions were given as a result of torture. In the alarming case of Chen Guoqing and others, during three rounds of trials the defendants claimed they were tortured by police investigators and requested that the Chengde Intermediate People's Court examine their wounds, but were refused. At the fourth instance, in order to prevent them from showing their wounds in the courtroom, they were handcuffed. Finally, at the trial by the Higher People's Court in Hebei province the defendants were allowed to show their physical injuries, and have experts examine them, but the court excluded the existence of torture solely based on the statement made by the police. The blatant ignorance towards the rule of exclusion of illegally-obtained evidence is outrageous.[126]

In the case of Liu Yong,[127] the court of appeal expressed doubt about torture in its ruling, which reflected progress in that at least the court paid attention to the allegation of torture. However, when the case was finally tried by the SPC, the SPC did not refer to the allegation of torture at all. Some Chinese scholars had hoped that, since the Liu Yong case had a high profile, it would mark a historical breakthrough if the SPC could address the torture issue raised by the accused and his lawyer. However, the reality was somewhat disappointing. Some legal experts were of the view that it was inappropriate to use the case of Liu Yong to advocate the prohibition of torture. Liu was a rich man and head of the mafia. Such a person is completely hated by the public, and a court's favourable judgment might lead the public to question whether Liu had bribed judges. On the other hand, one could argue that if in such a high-profile case, with strong defence lawyers and the support of pre-eminent legal scholars, the issue of torture could still be ignored by the court, how could one expect a poor, powerless defendant, such as those in the aforementioned injustice cases, to get the court to acknowledge and clarify the legal consequences of torture.

The problem of torture in China is aggravated by the fact that, apart from the lack of legal consciousness in judicial personnel regarding the protection of a criminal suspect's legitimate rights, there is a traditional practice of overemphasising the importance of confessions. This practice is standard in contemporary China and occurs at the expense of neglecting other evidence. However, a confession alone is not sufficient to convict. Article 46 of the 1996 CrPL (Art. 53 of the 2012 amendments) explicitly provides: 'A defendant cannot be found guilty and sentenced to a criminal punishment if there is only his statement without any other evidence; the defendant may be found guilty and sentenced to a criminal punishment if evidence is sufficient and reliable, even without his statement.' Therefore, investigators are obliged by law to provide evidence beyond the confession. But, this requirement is not sufficiently followed in practice.[128]

In examining torture in China, the UN Special Rapporteur on Torture has recommended:

125 'Tebie Guanzhu: Hebei Erji Jingdu Lijiuming Teda Yuan'an Shimo' (Special Attention: The Horrendous Injustice Case of Senior Prison Officer Li Jiuming), available at http://news.sina.com.cn/c/2005-02-28/09505221500s.shtml. Last visited September 2013.

126 Xiong Qiuhong, *supra* note 54, p. 246.

127 *Ibid.*

128 Alison W. Conner, 'True Confessions? Chinese Confessions Then and Now', in Karen G. Turner, James V. Feinerman and R. Kent Guy, *The Limits of the Rule of Law in China* (Seattle, WA and London: University of Washington Press, 2000), pp. 151–152.

> International practice has shown that the most effective way to fight torture is through self-generating and/or self-sustaining social and political institutions including: a free and investigatory press, citizen-based human rights monitoring organisations, independent, fair, and accessible courts and prosecutors, and the accountability that comes through regular elections. Judicial oversight is particularly important ... particularly in a context where police exercise wide discretion in matters of arrest and detention and are under great pressure to solve cases.[129]

Evidently, it requires all-inclusive efforts to change the widespread use of torture in criminal investigation. Given the fact that the Communist Party's criminal policy usually has a significant impact on how police function, particular emphasis should also be given to the Party's commitment to tackle the torture problem. If torture is actually tolerated by the Party leaders as an effective means of cracking down on crime to ensure social order, generous improvement against the use of torture in China can hardly be expected.

The introduction of the enquiry procedure under the 2012 amended CrPL should contribute to preventing torture in future. At the same time it should be stressed that more action is needed in the fight against torture, such as free media investigation and reporting, public campaigns organised by NGOs, and effective judicial oversight of the police.[130]

Ensuring Strict Adherence to the Criminal Procedure Law by Judicial Institutions and Personnel

In recent years, an increasing number of Chinese legal experts such as Bian Jianlin,[131] Tian Wenchang[132] and Chen Xingliang[133] have pointed out the need to rethink the purpose of criminal procedure law in China by emphasizing the necessity of abiding law by judicial institutions. Chen Ruihua indicates:

> Criminal procedure not only provides a forum for individuals to face the State powers represented by the prosecution and the judges, but also functions as a limit on the powers of judicial personnel involved in litigation. Even though the procedure creates obligations for the litigants, its primary task is to restrict the powers of judicial personnel. The purpose of requesting the police, prosecutors and judges to adhere to such rules is to prevent the infringement of individual freedoms and the arbitrary assignment of criminal liability. Also it is to avoid violations by judicial officers that would damage the rule of law and legal order. In order to build the rule of law, rather than use the law as an 'instrument of control', criminal procedure must not be used retributively. Criminal litigation should be considered as a rational contest between the state and the individual. Any acts

129 See Report of the Special Rapporteur on Torture and Other Cruel, Inhuman or Degrading Treatment or Punishment, Mission to China, E/CN.4/2006/6/Add.6, para. 58, *supra* note 121.

130 Such actions are advised by the UN Special Rapporteur, *Ibid.*

131 Bian Jianlin, Tan Xinze, 'Xingshi Susong Zhidu Kexue Goujian Lungang' (On Scientific Construction of China's Criminal Procedural System), 1 (2009) *Beifang Faxue* (Northern Legal Science), p. 59. Bian Jianlin, Guo Zhiyuan, 'Maixiang Lixing de Xingshi Susong Faxue' (Marching for Rational Criminal Procedure Law Research), 2(2007) *Zhongguo Faxue* (China Legal Science), p. 172.

132 Tian Wenchang, 'Xingshi Susongfa Zaixiugai Yu Renquan Baozhang' (The Revision of Criminal Procedure Law and the Protection of Human Rights), 3 (2006) *Zhongguo Falu* (China Law), p. 37.

133 Chen Xingliang, 'Wei Bianhuquan Bianhu: Xingshi Fazhi Shiyezhong De Bianhuquan' (Defence for the Right of Defence: Defence Right from a Perspective of Criminal Justice), 1 (2003) *Faxue* (Legal Science), p. 3.

> and decisions by the judicial organs must be derived from legitimacy, and not perceived as being politically motivated.[134]

Violation of the Criminal Procedure Law by judicial personnel, as in the case of Chen Guoqing and others, typically reflects upon various problems: investigators obtained evidence illegally and torture was used; the written testimonies of experts were easily modified and supplemented; material evidence was lost; police investigation reports were easily changed; the defendant's rights were violated (for example at the trial of Chen Guoqing and others at the IPC, the procuratorate only made two bills of prosecution, and at the last two trials, neither the accused nor their lawyers received the bill of prosecution); violation of law in composition of the collegiate panel (for example in the case of Chen Guoqing and others the presiding judge was the same at the first, second and third trials, while the Criminal Procedure Law provides that, in a re-trial, a new collegiate panel should be organised); expert opinions were not signed and sealed; all expert opinions were signed by one person who was viewed as representing all others; the second instance trial was combined with the death review procedure, thus two procedures were merged into one, and so on. Negligence of procedure resulted in destruction of the accountability of evidence and led to the failure of both substantial and procedural justice.[135]

Another flaw in the system is revealed by the fact that, although under the 1996 CrPL the prosecution must bring both exculpatory and inculpatory evidence to the courts, the reality is that both the police and prosecution are under social and moral pressure to resolve a case within a certain time limit, and therefore they often either deliberately or accidentally submit to the court only that evidence which helps prove a suspect is guilty and exclude presentation of evidence that would exonerate him regardless of how compelling it may be. This single-minded pursuit of a guilty judgment assaults the concept of justice and is anathematic to a system based on the rule of law.

In examining the difficulties of enforcing the 1996 CrPL, Randall Peerenboom has drawn particular attention to the problems of judicial organs:

> China's weak legal institutions have been unable to resist the combined pressure from an angry public demanding heavy punishments to deter criminals and a political regime seeking to shore up its legitimacy by pandering to the public's appetite for vengeance. Indeed, key institutions have not fully committed to reforms. Not surprisingly, perhaps given their law and order orientation, the police and procuracy in particular have resisted many of the changes. Even the judiciary has been, at best, lukewarm.[136]

Conclusion

The experience of the past decade has proven that the substantive improvements made in the 1996 CrPL, such as enhancing respect and protection for criminal suspects and defendants, strengthening the role of defence lawyers in the criminal process, and introducing adversarial elements in open hearings, have been largely neglected or even ignored by judicial organs and judicial personnel. A Chinese scholar describes China's criminal justice reality as follows:

134 Chen Ruihua, *supra* note 13, pp. 5–6.

135 Xiong Qiuhong, *supra* note 54, p. 245.

136 Randall Peerenboom, 'What Have We Learned about Law and Development? Describing, Predicting, and Assessing Legal Reforms in China', 27(3) (2006) *Michigan Journal of International Law*, p. 846.

> Once a criminal suspect is caught by police, he becomes an object to be moved by police. If the police assume the one is guilty, they can use various means to obtain confession. With the confession, the investigation is considered to achieve 50 per cent success. This is followed by the close cooperation of police, prosecutors and judges during which hardly anybody can say anything on the side of the suspect and the accused. Even if lawyers are involved, their role is extremely limited.[137]

It is not surprising that dissatisfaction with and incisive criticism of the criminal justice system is mounting in China. This has generated various attacks on the 1996 CrPL. Complaints about the CrPL come from different circles for different purposes. Some feel the Law is too 'Western' or too modern, while others feel it is not 'Western' or modern enough. Many lawyers and scholars complain about the limitations of the 1996 CrPL on defence lawyers, while policemen and public prosecutors deem that the 1996 CrPL has gone too far by allowing lawyers to be involved in a case at the investigation stage, which hinders normal investigation. Many judges feel the adversarial trial model cannot be realised due to the lack of various supplementary systems, such as witness appearances in court and disclosure of evidence prior to hearings. Public opinion is being changed by events. When the media reports on cases of injustice it catches public attention. People are angry and blame police brutality and the uselessness of the law and courts. When reports draw people's attention to serious violent cases, which threaten people's personal safety and property rights, they tend to support harsh crackdowns on crime without taking into account procedural rules provided in the CrPL.

Such an all-around criticism of the 1996 CrPL is not surprising since it reflects the phenomenal transition of the criminal justice system in China: the Law is working in some cases while neglected in others, and the effectiveness of the Law depends, for the most part, on the strengths and weaknesses of the various players involved. While neglecting the role of defence lawyers is by all means a common reality, one cannot deny that some courageous and skilful lawyers are rising stars, reshaping the traditional complete manipulation of the criminal process by judicial organs.

Currently, an important task is to improve the institutional capacity and professional quality of various actors involved in criminal justice proceedings. Intensified efforts need to be made to promote observance of the law by judicial organs and officers, in order to foster a culture of legality. Though police investigation and the subsequent prosecution are important as the first stages in the criminal justice system, we must emphasise that the courts are the last frontier for upholding justice, and thus deserve special attention. Handling criminal cases is more difficult than settling civil and commercial disputes as it requires courts and judges to be independent from public prosecutors and the police. The courts must ensure equality by treating prosecutors and defence lawyers alike. Only in this manner can the courts fairly balance state power and individual rights. The Chinese judiciary may need time, favourable policy changes, and legal guarantees in order to transform into a professional force capable of tackling the mission that it must complete. This goal may only be achieved through a long process of evolution.

137 Liu Sida, *supra* note 5, p. 74.

Chapter 5

The Civil Trial Process

Introduction

One of the most impressive developments in the judicial system of post-Mao China was the explosion of civil lawsuits in the 1980s and 1990s. In 1979, the total number of cases accepted by first instance courts was 389,943. By 1989, that number had increased to 2,511,017; in 1999, to 5,054,857; and in 2009 peaked at 5.797 million.[1] Thus, during the three decades from 1979 to 2009, the number of civil cases accepted by the first instance courts increased nearly 15 times.

Civil litigation cases in China include: civil disputes between individual litigants, known as 'natural persons', economic disputes between economic entities (companies) recognised as 'legal persons', and cases between natural and legal persons. Economic disputes form a large portion of all civil cases. In 1978, cases involving marriage, family and inheritance constituted 73.1 per cent of all civil cases. In 1988, this percentage gradually decreased to 39.2 per cent. This was the first time that this figure was lower than that for contract disputes, which accounted for 43.1 per cent of all civil cases. Since then, the percentage of contract disputes has remained the highest. In 2001, it reached 51.1 per cent. According to the statistics from 1978 to 2001, amongst civil cases, contract disputes have the highest average rate of increase at 38.8 per cent. More recent statistics illustrate that during the period 2008–2010, contract disputes amounted to 47.6 per cent of all civil cases received.[2]

Not only have the number of civil cases increased, they have also become more complex in nature and increasingly concern larger sums of capital. For instance, in 2008, Chinese courts concluded 1.14 million cases relating to: financial disputes, real estate disputes, company shareholding reforms, transfers of stock ownership, foreign-related disputes and maritime disputes. Additionally, the courts handled 286,221 labour dispute cases; 576,013 cases involving medical services, housing and the protection of consumer rights; 21,674 market disruption cases regarding fund accumulation fraud, illegal absorption of public deposits and the production and sale of substandard food and drugs; and 27,876 cases pertaining to the infringement of intellectual property rights.[3]

---

1 For the figures from 1979 to 2004, see Zhu Jingwen (ed.), *Zhongguo Falu Fazhan Baogao, Shujuku He Zhibiao Tixi* (Report on China Law Development, Database and Indicators) (Beijing: Zhongguo Renmin Daxue Chubanshe, 2007), p. 207. The figure from 2009 can be found in 2010 Work Report of SPC to the NPC. Available at http://www.court.gov.cn/qwfb/gzbg/201007/t20100716_7756.htm. Last visited September 2013.

2 Ran Jingfu, *Dangdai Zhongguo Minshi Susonglu Bianqian Yanjiu: Yige Bijiaofa Shehuixiu De Shijiao* (Researches on the Changes of Civil Litigation Rate in China, 1978–2002: From the Perspective of Comparative Sociology of Law) (Beijing: Zhongguo Renmindaxue Chubanshe, 2005), pp. 152–157. For the information from 2008 to 2010, see Xinhua Net, 'Zuigaofa: Quanguo Fayuan 3 Nian Shouli Minshi Anjian 1955 Wan Duo Jian' (SPC: Courts at All Levels Accepted More Than 19.55 Million Civil Cases within 3 Years), 24 June 2011. Available at http://www.gov.cn/jrzg/2011-06/24/content_1891589.htm. Last visited January 2014.

3 See 2009 SPC Work Report to the NPC, available at http://www.gov.cn/test/2009-03/17/content_1261386.htm. Last visited September 2013.

Civil cases account for approximately 80 per cent of the total number of cases handled by the courts of first instance.[4] The rapid expansion in number and the increase in new types of civil cases can be attributed to a number of factors. Economic reform has changed the centralised planned economy, under which there were fewer economic disputes arising in the first place and those that did occur were resolved by administrative authorities. New forms of economic entities, such as private businesses and foreign-invested companies have consequently emerged. State- and collectively-owned enterprises were reformed. Governmental intervention into the work of enterprises has been largely reduced. Disputes between enterprises have been gradually brought before the courts, though many are also increasingly settled through commercial arbitration.[5] In addition, a rise in the awareness and consciousness of citizens' legal rights has culminated in a greater number of civil disputes being brought before the courts.

The overwhelming growth of civil litigation coupled with the complexity of the cases in question has inevitably generated fresh challenges for the judiciary in both their capacity to handle cases in a timely fashion and also in gaining the trust of the relevant parties and the public at large. By the late 1980s, it became evident that the courts had to reform the civil trial procedure in order to manage the increased caseload. Such reforms have lasted more than two decades and still continue to this day. Some of the measures have proven successful and others have failed; importantly the effects of numerous reforms remain inconclusive.

The civil procedure law is a basic law that aims to protect parties to a civil dispute to ensure their litigation rights are exercised and also to provide guidance to the courts in the adjudication of civil disputes. This area of the law has also undergone significant transformation over the past 30 years. In 1982, the Civil Procedure Law (for Trial Implementation) was enacted by the National People's Congress Standing Committee. When the Law was created at the outset of the reform period, it reflected the typical inquisitorial system, which stressed state intervention in civil disputes. Judges were responsible for investigating and collating the evidence, parties took a passive position during the trial and mediation was specifically emphasised. Thus, Chinese critics viewed the 1982 CiPL as more politically than legally profound.[6]

In the mid-1980s, with the increasing number of civil law cases, local courts started to reform the civil trial procedure. Some of the reform experiments were incorporated into the 1991 Civil Procedure Law (CiPL), which contains 29 chapters and a total of 270 articles. The most notable

4 Lu Zhongmei, 'Juan Shouyu' (Foreword), in Wu Jiayou and Lu Zhongmei (eds), *Faguan Lun Minshanshi Shenpan* (Judges Writings on the Civil Litigation System) (Beijing: Falu Chubanshe, 2004), p. 3. According to another source civil cases constituted 85.41 per cent of total cases in 2004; 84.87 per cent in 2005; and 84.61 per cent in 2006. See Cheng Hu, 'Yifa Zhiguo Beijing Xia De Jiufen Jiejue Jizhi' (Research on Dispute Settlement Mechanisms against the Background of Ruling the Country According to Law), in Li Lin and Wang Jiafu (eds), *Yifa Zhiguo Shinian Huigu Yu Zhanwang* (Ruling the Country According to Law: One Decade in Retrospect and Prospect) (Beijing: Shehui Kexui Wenxian Chubanshe, 2007), p. 290.

5 The channels for the settlement of civil disputes mainly include litigation, arbitration and mediation by a people's mediation committee. Litigation is when only one party brings a case to court and the court then files the case. The outcome of litigation will be binding. Arbitration organs have jurisdiction over a dispute only under the condition that parties have a written agreement to accept arbitration. Mediation by the People's Mediation Committee is used to settle simple civil cases. The decision of arbitration or mediation agreement can only be mandatorily enforced by a court.

6 Xu Hui, 'Dalu Minshi Susong Zhidu De Guoqu, Xianzai Yu Weilai (The Past, Present and Future of Civil Procedure in Mainland China), in Dennis Tang et al. (eds), *Liang'an Sidi Falu Fazhan: Weixian Shencha Yu Xingzheng Susong* (Cross-Strait, Four Regions: Law Developments in Taiwan, China, Hong Kong and Macau: Constitutional Review and Administrative Litigation), vol. 2 (Taipei: Zhongyang Yanjiuyuan Faluxue Yanjiusuo, 2007), p. 213.

improvements brought about by the 1991 CiPL are often depicted as 'one highlight, three constraints and three changes'.[7] The first of these refers to the emphasis placed upon the primary function of civil procedure law as the protector, safeguarding the litigation rights of the parties; importantly, the courts' adjudication of these cases is secondary (Art. 2). The three constraints introduced by the CiPL include: restricting the scope of the investigation and collection of evidence by courts, with an emphasis on the responsibility of parties to collate and present evidence (Art. 64); a reduction in the scope of the courts' asset-preservation measures alongside an increased deference to the parties upon their requests (Art. 92); and partially limiting the scope of transferring the enforcement of judgments by courts, once again placing greater emphasis on the requests of the parties (Art. 216). Lastly, the three changes refer to: a shift from mediation on the basis of a court's decision to mediation pursued on a voluntary basis by the parties (Art. 9); allowing courts to carry out enforcement with a writ of referral, pursuant to an application from a party to the case (Art. 97); permitting the court of second instance to examine the disputed facts and the law in an appellate case rather than conducting a complete review of the facts and application of the law determined by the court of first instance (Art. 151). Thus, the 1991 CiPL has given the parties in a dispute a greater number of rights and a higher degree of influence in the civil procedure, which to a certain extent, alters the relationship between litigants and the courts.

However, many provisions of the 1991 CiPL retain a strongly inquisitorial character with both state intervention in civil affairs and courts taking an increasingly pro-active role.[8] Moreover, some of the new systems provided in the 1991 CiPL either are too general in their scope, as such, failing to offer sufficient guidance for judicial practice, or demand a change in judicial conduct with which the courts and judges are not familiar. Consequently, reforming the civil litigation system has continued since the promulgation of the 1991 CiPL. Within the courts, the reform reflects both a top-down approach through the Supreme People's Court (SPC) issuing numerous judicial interpretations to guide the local courts in their handling of civil cases, and a bottom-up approach whereby the local courts at various levels have initiated their own experiments in accordance with their respective situations. In addition, legal scholars have become more actively involved in the process of reform by critically examining the traditional litigation theories and the litigation culture, introducing Western civil litigation systems and advancing proposals for systematic and technical change. Procedural justice, the litigants' choice, and numerous principles associated with due process, have become the central focus of academic discussion and, to a certain extent, have affected the path of reform in civil trials.[9] In 2007 and 2012 the CiPL was amended, incorporating

7 Tian Pingan and Du Runzhe, 'Dangqian Minshi Shenpan Fangshi Gaige Fansi' (Rethinking the Current Reform of the Civil Trial System), in Jiang Ping and Chen Guiming (eds), *Minshi Shenpan Fangshi Gaige Yu Fazhang* (Civil Trial System Reform and Development) (Beijing: Zhongguo Fazhi Chubanshe, 1998), pp. 79–80.

8 Xu Hui, *supra* note 6, pp. 213–214.

9 Jiang Mingan et al. (eds), *Zhongguo Faxue Sanshinian* (Thirty Years of Jurisprudence in China (1978–2008)), (Beijing: Zhongguo Renmin Daxue Chubanshe, 2008), pp. 326–330. The influential works in the early years of reforming the civil trial system include: Zhang Weiping, 'Zhiquan Zhuyi Yu Dangshi Zguyi: Liangzhong Minshi Susong Jiben Moshi De Bijiao Yanjiu' (Litigant Centric and Inquisitorial: Comparative Study of the Basic Features of the Two Civil Litigation Models), 1 (1993) *Waiguo Faxue Yangjiu* (Foreign Laws Research); Zhang Weiping, 'Zhuanzhi Yu Yingbian: Lun Woguo Chuantong Minshi Susong Tizhi De Jiegouxing Biange' (Transition and Response: Discussion on the Structural Reform of China's Traditional Civil Litigation System), 4 (1994) *Xuexi Yu Tansuo* (Study and Exploration).

both new and revised provisions which make the various systems in the Law more responsive to practical demand.[10]

Generally speaking, over the past 30 years, civil litigation reform has responded in a timely fashion to changing economic and social circumstances. Furthermore, the settlement of millions of civil disputes in courts has contributed to the protection of individual rights and social stability. However, China is a vast country with more than 3,000 courts and a relatively infantile judiciary. Civil trial reform, as with other elements of judicial reform, has been carried out erratically, depending upon geographic location and the court in question. In economically-developed urban areas, especially in large cities such as Beijing and Shanghai where commercial disputes account for a large proportion of civil cases and where most of the judges have followed systematic legal studies, civil trial reform has been implemented with a more modern, adversarial procedure, reflected in a formalised system, where parties bear the burden of proof, cross-examination is utilised and so forth. Within the more remote regions, especially in rural or semi-urban areas, many of the local courts and tribunals continue to handle disputes in the traditional inquisitorial manner, which is mediatory rather than adjudicatory.[11]

This chapter focuses on an examination of the major changes which have been made in civil trial reform since the post-Mao period. Such reforms have been initiated by the local courts and supported by the SPC. The most visible reform measures have been codified into the 1991 Law (CiP). This Law has been further supplemented and consolidated by the judicial interpretations of the SPC, which were subsequently integrated into the 2007 and 2012 amendments of the CiPL. This chapter first explores the transition of civil trials from taking an inquisitorial stance to a combination of both the inquisitorial and adversarial models. In this process of reform, both the law and judicial practice have emphasised the importance of procedural justice, which provides the impetus behind the shift from traditional civil trials to a more modern procedure. However, the reform and implementation of the CiPL has not been carried out consistently everywhere, nor has it permeated every court. The judicial practice illustrates a mixture of the inquisitorial habit with certain modern adversarial traits. Secondly, mediation has proven to be a habitual strength in the settlement of civil disputes. The rise of mediation in the 1980s, its fall in the 1990s and then its partial revival in the 2000s, are analysed. The elements of political pressure with regard to the excessive use of judicial mediation cannot be underestimated; this has in turn ensured that

10 The 2007 amendments mainly enhanced a few provisions concerning the procedure on the enforcement of civil judgment and the procedures of trial supervision. The 2012 amendments initiated generally the new systems of public interest litigation, small claims lawsuits, and judicial recognition of mediation agreements, as well as improved the summary procedure, the trial supervision procedures and the evidence system.

11 It seems overly simplistic to generalise in one picture how the civil litigation system works in China. Some empirical studies have demonstrated that civil procedure at both pre-trial and trial stages has been implemented in various courts differently. See Margaret Y.K. Woo and Yaxin Wang, 'Civil Justice in China: An Empirical Study of Courts in Three Provinces', 53(4) (2005) *American Journal of Comparative Law*, pp. 911–940. Yu Zhong, *Xiangtu Zhongguo De Sifa Tujing* (Judicial Practice in Rural China) (Beijing: Zhongguo Fazhi Chubanshe, 2007). Yang Liu, 'Mohu De Falv Chanpin: Dui Liangqi Jiceng Fayuan Tiaojie Anjian De Kaocha' (Vague Legal Product: Studies on Two Cases Concluded by Mediation in the District Court), 1 (1999) *Beida Falu Pinglun* (Peking University Law Review), pp. 213–230; Wang Yaxin, *Shehui Biange Zhong De Minshi Susong* (Civil Litigation in Social Transformation) (Beijing: Zhongguo Fazhi Chubanshe, 2001); Zuo Weimin and Chen Gang, 'Zhijie Kaiting: Zhongguo Minsu Gaige De Yida Wuqu' (Direct Hearing: A Misleading Direction of the Reform of Civil Litigation in China), in Chen Guangzhong et al. (eds), *Susong Faxue Luncong: Zhongguo Faxuehui Susongfaxue Yanjiuhui 1995 Nian Nianhui Lunwenji* (Collected Works of Procedural Law: Symposium of the Annual Conference of the Procedural Law Research Institute of the China Law Society in 1995) (1995).

contemporary civil litigation reform is far more complicated than mere legal procedural reform. The final issue drawn upon in this chapter surrounds the discussion of the meagre record of the enforcement of civil judgments, which has generated public complaint and ultimately significantly undermined judicial authority during the course of the reform period. The 2007 amended CiPL contained several new provisions in an attempt to strengthen mandatory enforcement measures, the rights of parties in the enforcement process and the role of higher courts in securing efficient enforcement. Despite the latest empirical studies depicting notable improvement in a number of economically-developed regions, on the whole, the lack of enforcement of civil judgments remains a discouraging reality.

The Civil Procedure Law and Practice

Strengthening the Role of Party Responsibility in Collecting and Presenting Evidence

During the 1980s, courts developed a procedure commonly referred to as the 'four steps before a case would head into the courtroom' (*si bu dao ting*). The steps consisted of: interview, investigation, mediation and adjudication.[12] The judge would first meet the disputing parties to understand the issue at hand and then investigate and collect the relevant evidence based on the information provided by the parties. On the basis of that evidence, he would formulate his own opinions on the case. A popular expression commented that the 'parties opened their mouths and the judges ran tirelessly to find evidence' (dangshiren dongdong zui, faguan paoduan tui). During the third step, the judge would attempt to persuade the plaintiff and the accused to settle their differences through mediation. If the two parties agreed to mediate, the judge would preside over the procedure. Consequently, if the mediation succeeded, the case was closed. If the two parties did not accept mediation or the mediation failed, the fourth step would be to hold trial proceedings. Since the judge took the initiative to collect the evidence, which included any inquiries made with the relevant parties and witnesses, visiting the location where the dispute occurred, collecting evidence from the parties' workplace, and so on, during the trial the judge would present the evidence and raise questions to the parties directly. The trial would then come to a conclusion.

With the proliferation of cases in the mid-1980s the courts and judges could not solve all of the complaints on time. The delay in handling cases not only put pressure on the courts in question but also generated widespread public complaint. Some local courts began to shift the duty of collecting evidence from the judges to the parties themselves. This marked the beginning of the reform of the civil trial procedure. The immediate and direct outcome was a reduction in judges' workload and the active participation of litigants in the trial process.

The imposition of the 1991 CiPL correlated positively to the experiments of the local courts, by providing that parties should bear the responsibility of providing evidence in support of their claims, and that the court should only investigate and collect such evidence if for some objective reason it could not be obtained by the parties or their lawyers, or if the court considered it necessary in order to adjudicate the case (Art. 64). This fundamentally altered the provision in the 1982 CiPL which highlighted the duty of the courts to collect and examine evidence 'comprehensively and objectively' (Art. 56). The practical impact of Article 64 is profound. For the first time, it legally required that the burden of proof be manifested by the party making the claim. This has

12 Tan Shigui (ed.), *Zhongguo Sifa Gaige Yanjiu* (Research on Chinese Judicial Reform) (Beijing: Falu Chubanshe, 2000), pp. 212–215.

triggered a series of consequent reforms: expanding the use of open trials, improving the evidence system, strengthening the role of the collegiate panel and individual judges in their decision-making, elevating judges' level of professionalism, amongst others. All of these changes have gradually transformed the traditional inquisitorial civil trial procedure into a model consisting of an amalgamation of the inquisitorial and adversarial systems.

A logical consequence of shifting this duty to collect evidence from the judges to the parties is the necessity of establishing a detailed evidence system. The 1991 CiPL contained only 12 articles on evidence, which inevitably failed to offer sufficient legal guidance. Thus, the SPC has used its authoritative power to issue judicial interpretations in order to elaborate gradually on these rules concerning evidence. In 1992, the SPC's Opinions on Several Issues concerning the Implementation of the Civil Procedure Law consisted of nine articles on evidence. The SPC's Several Rules on the Reform of the Civil and Economic Trial System of 1998 contained more details on cross-examination, direct examination and the verification of evidence. Most importantly though, in 2001, the SPC issued Several Rules on Evidence in Civil Litigation (Evidence Rules),[13] which comprised 83 articles covering rules on the production of evidence by the relevant parties, the investigation and collection of evidence by courts, the time period for producing evidence, the exchange of evidence, cross-examination and the verification and affirmation of evidence. Moreover, in 2008, the SPC issued the Notice on Applying the Provisions on the Time Limit for Producing Evidence contained in the Several Rules on Evidence in Civil Litigation, which further elaborated on the time limitations for producing evidence.

In practice, the courts in different geographic locations employ varying approaches to the collection and presentation of evidence. Some courts indeed follow the principle that the party making the claim must bear the burden of proof. In other courts, parties collect most of the evidence and courts do not actively collect evidence unless it is for the purpose of clarifying facts that may affect the interests of the state, the interests of society, the legitimate interest of a third party or where the facts of the case affect procedure.[14] However, in various courts, judges have not fully altered their perceptions and often feel that they cannot rely on the evidence collated by the parties and so prefer to investigate and collect the evidence themselves.[15] Thus, judges 'were more apt to follow the traditional method of Chinese courts in conducting the investigation themselves and ascertaining the facts of a case prior to hearing'.[16] The individual who represents the court in collecting evidence can also vary between the different courts. Some distinguish the trial judge from the investigation judge, whilst other courts dispatch a law clerk, enforcement officer or even the judicial police to collect evidence.[17]

The collection of evidence has been separated from its examination as a result of the shift in the duty of investigation and collection of evidence from the judges to the litigants of a case. This has ensured the advancement of the procedural rights of litigants and enabled the courts to accept and subsequently adjudicate more civil cases. However, emerging criticism and concern has begun

13 *Fashi* No. 33 [2001], available at http://www.court.gov.cn/bsfw/sszn/xgft/201004/t20100426_4533.htm. Last visited September 2013.

14 Eu Jin Chua, 'Litigation and the People's Courts', in Michael J. Moser (ed.), *Managing Business Disputes in Today's China: Duelling with Dragons* (Alphen aan den Rijn: Kluwer Law International, 2007), pp. 148–149.

15 Jing Hanchao, *Pingheng Gongzheng Yu Xiaolu: Sifa Gaige Yanjianglu* (Balancing Fairness and Efficiency: Speeches on Judicial Reform) (Beijing: Zhongguo Qingnian Chubanshe, 2002), p. 135.

16 Margaret Y.K. Woo and Yaxin Wang, *supra* note 11, p. 927.

17 Jing Wei and Fu Yuling, 'Minshi Shenpan Zhidu Gaige Zhong Jidai Jiejue De Wenti' (Problems that Need to be Resolved in the Reform of the Civil Litigation System), 3 (1999) *Faxue Zazhi* (Law Journal), p.13.

to shed doubt on its effects in practice. One such concern is that the strengthening of the parties' responsibilities has not been complemented by the establishment of a procedure guaranteeing that the parties could collect the evidence. Consequently, the rights of parties and their lawyers to investigate and collate evidence is, to a large extent, an empty right.[18] The difficulties in collecting evidence in civil cases mainly come to light when evidence is in the hands of the opposing party, who may refuse to divulge it. Similarly, when a party requires a witness to give testimony in the courtroom, the witness can easily refuse to do so; some witnesses even turn down giving written testimony. When a party or his lawyer requires the investigation and collation of evidence from a third party, such as a bank, tax bureau, or an industrial or commercial bureau for the registration of companies, they could refuse on the grounds that their rules or internal documents do not allow them to disclose the information unless it is given to courts. Complaints surrounding the difficulties which parties realistically face in collecting documentary evidence, physical evidence, the testimony of witnesses, audio and visual materials and so on are commonplace.[19]

To address these difficulties surrounding the collection of evidence, the Higher People's Court in Shanghai first introduced the 'civil investigation order' system in 2000. As part of this system, when a party to a civil case encounters obstacles in meeting the burden of proof, they can apply to a court in order to obtain a court order. With this order, the party can request relevant bodies to provide evidence. Such bodies may include banks, industrial and commercial bureaus, tax bureaus, telephone companies, police offices, real estate agencies and so on. This system has been followed by numerous courts; however, it was not incorporated into the amended 2012 CiPL.[20]

The party's responsibility of bearing the burden of proof, the formalisation of the trial procedure and a shift from an inquisitorial to an adversarial hearing have also brought about an increasing demand by litigants for lawyers. Inevitably, lawyers play a significant role for their clients in civil litigation. However, representation by a lawyer in civil law proceedings is generally relatively low. In economically developed urban areas, the rate of legal representation is higher than in economically poorer areas. An empirical study of three IPCs demonstrated that in the two IPCs in Guangdong and Hubei, both of which are economically-prosperous provinces, the majority of all civil and economic cases of first instance had at least one party with an attorney present; while the IPC in Guizhou, a more poverty-stricken province, witnessed legal representation in less than 50 per cent of economic cases and 30 per cent of civil cases.[21] These statistics refer to IPCs, which are the first instance courts for civil cases involving large sums of money, and the second instance courts for cases appealed to by the parties. The worrying prospect in this regard is that representation by lawyers is limited even in the IPCs, which leaves little hope for legal representation in the basic courts. It has been rightly pointed out that, 'to the extent that court reforms are formalising

18 Li Hao, 'Minshi Zhengju Zhidu De Gaige Yu Wanshan' (Reform and Perfection of the Civil Evidence System), in Zhang Wusheng (ed.), *Sifa Xiandaihua Yu Minshi Susong Zhidu De Jiangou* (Modernisation of Administration of Justice and Perfection of the Civil Litigation System) (Beijing: Falu Chubanshe, 2003), p. 211.

19 Wang Xuemian, 'Diaocha Quzhenquan: Minshi Shenpan Fangshi Gaige Zhong Buneng Yiwang De Keti' (The Right to Investigate and Collect Evidence: An Unforgettable Issue in the Reform of the Civil Trial System), in Zhang Weiping (ed.), *Sifa Gaige Pinglun* (Judicial Reform Review), No. 2 (Beijing: Zhongguo Fazhi Chubanshe, 2002), pp. 318–326.

20 Wei Yang *et al.*, 'Dangshiren Diaocha Quzhengquan Zhi Chengxu Baozhang De Lujing Changshi' (Experiments in Ensuring Litigant's Rights to Investigate and Collect Evidence), in Wan Exiang (ed.), *Sifa Jiejue Jiufen De Duice Yu Jizhi* (Policy and Mechanism for the Settlement of Judicial Disputes) (Beijing: Renmin Fayuan Chubanshe, 2007), pp. 859–862.

21 Margaret Y.K. Woo and Yaxin Wang, *supra* note 11, p. 921.

procedure, one must consider the impact on legal representation for poor litigants. More formality in the absence of legal representation creates barriers to litigants and results in potential injustice.'[22]

In addition, while evidence is becoming more important in determining the success of a case,[23] understanding the relevant rules on the use of evidence is relatively unfamiliar to both the Chinese judiciary and litigants. A general complaint is that some judges mechanically apply evidentiary rules when handling cases, which can result in a party unnecessarily losing their case. At the same time, it is also reported that in rural areas, litigants can hardly understand the difference between a legal truth and an objective truth, and how they can use evidence to protect themselves. If there is an inadequate judgment, due to a litigant's inability to produce evidence, the party and public at large can hardly accept such a judgment.[24]

The issue of the appearance of witnesses in the courtroom is also relevant to the collection and presentation of evidence. The 1991 CiPL contains only one general article which requires all units and individuals who have information on the case to give testimony in court. In circumstances where it may be genuinely difficult for a witness to appear in court, he or she may submit written testimony with the prior consent of the court (Art. 70). Since it is difficult and costly to ask witnesses to present testimony in court, the parties and their lawyers usually only ask witnesses to produce a written statement, or interview the witness and submit a record of the conversation as oral evidence. Thus, the rate at which witness appearances in the courtroom to provide testimony is disconcertingly low. Courts overwhelmingly depend on documentary evidence provided by the witness as legal evidence. Oral testimony is, in fact, rare.[25] The absence of witnesses in the courtroom renders assessing the credibility of the testimony provided a gruelling task. On the other hand, according to a field survey, some Chinese judges considered 'oral evidence and witness testimony to be unreliable' since 'witnesses do not always speak the truth as they often have an interest in the disputes or are closely related to one interested party or the other'.[26]

In response to various problems in judicial practice the 2012 amended CiPL has strengthened the duty of the parties to provide evidence and the duty of witnesses to give testimony in court. A new provision (Article 65) requires parties to provide evidence in a timely manner in order to support their claims. A court is required to determine the evidence to be provided by the parties and the associated time limits according to the parties' claims and the trial proceedings. If a party has difficulty in providing the evidence within the stipulated time limit, it may request that the court extend the time limit and the court may, in accordance with this, decide the appropriate action to be taken. If a party fails to provide evidence in time, the court is required to request that the party provide a reasonable justification for this delay. If a party refuses to explain or the reasons cannot be established, a court can either deem the evidence inadmissible or allow its admittance but give the party a warning or impose a fine.

Article 72 states that a unit or individual who has relevant knowledge or information appertaining to the case in question is obliged to testify in court. This superseded Article 70 of the 1991 CiPL which stated generally that if a witness had difficulty appearing before the court he might submit written testimony upon the court's permission.

The new Article 73 specifies that upon the request of the court, a witness should give testimony in court; this is subject to mitigating factors which can rebut this obligation including non-appearance

22 *Ibid.*, p. 923.

23 Mo Zhang and Paul J. Zwier, 'Burden of Proof: Developments in Modern Chinese Evidence Rules', 10(2) (2003) *Tulsa Journal of Comparative and International Law*, pp. 419–471.

24 Interviews with judges in Wuhan in April 2007 and in Beijing in May 2008.

25 Li Hao, *supra* note 18, p. 211.

26 Margaret Y.K. Woo and Yaxin Wang, *supra* note 11, p. 935.

due to reasons of health, long distance and inconvenient traffic, natural disaster or other force majeure situations, and other justified reasons.

Article 74 further provides that the necessary expenses paid by a witness for the performance of their duty to testify in court, such as transportation costs, hotel accommodation and meals, and the loss of working hours shall be borne by the losing party to the case. In cases where a party applies for the witness testimony, the expenses should be paid in advance by the party; in circumstances where a court has notified the witness to appear in court, the court should provide the advanced payment.

Strengthening Procedural Justice

In traditional Chinese thinking, substantive justice was the ultimate objective for civil trials, while procedure was merely deemed the means through which that result could be achieved. If an outcome was justifiable then any shortcomings in procedure could be neglected; in order to seek substantive justice, some flexibility in procedure was acceptable. Thus, a fair trial was not measured on the basis of the extent to which the appropriate procedure was followed, but rather whether the judgment was rational and had the appropriate social effect.[27] In practice, substantive justice was excessively emphasised, which often led to the law surpassing justice or to a combination of both law and morality. The consequence was that procedural justice, and any system of rationality based on procedural justice, was overlooked. In the past two decades, a shift in the dominant traditional way of thinking has been noticeable, challenging notions of substantive justice and diversifying opinions. In general, there are three differing approaches: precedence of substantive justice, precedence of procedural justice and the equal importance of both. Some are of the view that, in light of the fact that procedural injustice is a more typical and commonplace problem in judicial practice, more emphasis and care should be afforded to promoting procedural justice.[28]

Some critics have observed that the most serious problems surrounding judicial unfairness are in regard to procedural injustice. Public complaints concerning the lack of judicial fairness are not limited to dissatisfaction with the judgments in concrete cases. Often there is dissatisfaction with the procedure that was followed. A nation-wide examination of law enforcement in all of the courts in China was conducted from January to October 1998, with the exploration of 4.41 million cases. Among them, 12,045 were found to have substantive errors, which accounted for 0.27 per cent of the total cases examined. 73,143 cases were found to contain procedural errors, accounting

27 Fan Yu, 'Chengxu Zhengyi Guannian Yu Zhongguo De Shehui Xianshi' (The Concept of Procedural Justice and China's Social Realities), available at http://article.chinalawinfo.com/Article_Detail.asp?ArticleID=420. Last visited September 2013. See also Zhong Jianhua and Yu Guanghua, 'Establishing the Truth on Facts: Has the Chinese Civil Process Achieved This Goal?', 13(2) 2004 *Journal of Transnational Law and Policy*, pp. 393–443.

28 Jing Hanchao, *supra* note 15, p. 229. Jiang Mingan *et al.* (eds), *supra* note 9, p. 336. It is observed that, in practice, litigants usually assess justice according to whether a judgment is the same as they expected. The public at large often judge the administration of justice according to whether a judgment reflects public values and opinions. Judges at the basic level prefer to prioritise substantive justice as they consider their main task to be settling cases. By settling cases they aim to prevent appeals to a higher court and stop litigants from applying to governmental authorities with further petitions. Judges who mainly deal with appellate cases are more concerned with procedural justice since their task is mainly associated with the correct application of procedural rules. See Research Office of the Supreme People's Court (ed.), *Shenpan Qianyan Wenti Yanjiu: Zuigao Renmin Fayuan Zhongdian Yanjiu Keti Baogao Ji* (Research on the Hot Topics on Adjudication: Collection of Key Research Topics of the Supreme People's Court), vol. 1 (Beijing: Renmin Fayuan Chubanshe, 2007), pp. 44–45.

for 85.86 per cent of all incorrectly-handled cases. Illustrations of such procedural errors included courts taking an excessively long time to conclude cases or making rulings which were outside their jurisdictional competence. Problems with other basic procedural systems, such as open hearings, withdrawal, neutrality of judges and independent adjudication, were also apparent.[29]

Since the 1990s, the reform of the civil litigation system has centred on amending the trial procedure. Courts have thus taken various measures to strengthen procedural justice. In particular, the shift of civil trials from closed to open reflects a considerable step in pursuing procedural justice. In the past, civil cases were often settled by judges who would interview the parties, collect evidence at the site and mediate between the parties separately. If mediation did not succeed, adjudication would take place informally, often in the judge's office or where the dispute had taken place. In the process, judges played a central role and often even prior to the case hearing, the judgment had already been ascertained – the hearing proving a mere formality. Article 120 of the 1991 CiPL provides that civil disputes should be heard publicly, except in cases relating to state secrets, personal privacy, divorce cases and cases concerning commercial secrets, when a party has so requested. The practice of open trial proceedings requires that judges are competent in controlling the court investigation, something which was an unfamiliar and challenging prospect to many judges upon this Law's promulgation. Some courts conducted a 'competition' to see who was able to most effectively handle cases in the courtroom. Judges who failed the test were moved to other positions. In some courts, a number of the old-fashioned judges who were more accustomed to the mediatory method were incapable of presiding over a public hearing and eventually had to resign from the civil trial chamber, while young judges with a university legal background were more easily able to adapt to the new requirements.[30]

Implementing the open trial procedure has, in reality, not been without its problems. For instance, Article 122 of the 1991 CiPL requires courts to notify the parties in a civil case three days prior to the opening of a court session. If a case is to be heard publicly, the names of the parties, the cause of action and the time and location of the court session should be announced publicly. However, some courts make the announcement immediately before the court session, change the courtroom location just before the hearing or restrict the public or journalists from attending the court session. In addition, administrative intervention and local protectionism concerning some commercial cases may result in the decision being made before the court hearing actually takes place. In such instances, the open trial is simply a formality.[31] Though most of the courts have made special efforts to conduct 'formal hearings', it has also been observed that 'judges do not always rely solely on the formal hearings to obtain the information they use to resolve cases. Despite the emphasis on "formal hearings", there were still many informal meetings.'[32] While recognising that some informal meetings may be inevitable in enabling judges to obtain the sufficient information concerning the case, these informal meetings should nonetheless follow certain minimum procedural requirements. Meeting one party ex parte without informing the other party, conducting such a meeting outside of the courtroom and failing to keep a record of the meeting all breach minimum procedural requirements.[33]

---

29 Jing Hanchao, *supra* note 15, p. 14.

30 *Ibid.*, pp. 190–191. Fu Hualing and Richard Cullen, 'From Mediatory to Adjudicatory Justice: The Limits of Civil Justice Reform in China', in Margaret Woo and Mary Gallagher (eds), *Chinese Justice: Civil Dispute Resolution in Contemporary China* (Cambridge: Cambridge University Press, 2011), p. 36.

31 Wang Liming, *Sifa Gaige Yanjiu* (Research on Judicial Reform) (Beijing: Falu Chubanshe, 2000), p. 323.

32 Margaret Y.K. Woo and Yaxin Wang, *supra* note 11, p. 929.

33 *Ibid.*, pp. 930–931.

It has been observed that after nearly two decades of civil litigation reforms, with emphasis placed on strengthening procedural justice, the disputing parties and their lawyers are taking procedural elements far more seriously now than ever before. If they consider that a judge has been neutral, impartial and followed the rules of procedure, even if they do not win the case and have differing opinions, they choose not to raise complaints against that judge. In contrast, even if substantive justice is achieved, if they doubt the judge's neutrality and impartiality and perceive that the judge has violated procedural rules, they may still consider a judgment unfair.[34]

Despite the degree of progress made in strengthening procedural justice, it should be noted that some experiments undertaken by local courts in the hope of further enhancing procedural justice were proven unsuccessful. For instance, in order to prevent judges reaching a 'conclusion' before the court hearing takes place, some local courts introduced the concept of 'one step to the courtroom' (*yi bu dao ting*). This meant that upon acceptance of a case by the court and before the opening of the hearing, judges did not have contact with the parties, had no access to evidence and might not even read the file materials. All claims and evidence were presented during the hearing, therefore judges could only learn about the case during the trial. This system may be suitable in settling simple civil cases, but obviously cannot be applied to complex cases in which the pre-trial study of the case materials is necessary.[35]

The strengthening of procedural justice is an ongoing, complicated process of reform which is still forced to confront various inherent barriers. In the first place, the neglect of procedural justice is rooted in the feudal tradition of 'official-centric' administration and the 'rule of men'. Some judges believe that adjudicatory power, rather than the rights of the litigants, is at the crux of civil procedural law. Following on from this reasoning, some judges assume that the rights of parties in the litigation process are not entrusted by the law, but rather, given by the judges.[36] Thus, the promotion of procedural justice modifies this judicial conception and balances between judicial power and the parties' rights. Some Chinese critics have also highlighted that the excessive powers afforded to judges have brought about judicial corruption. Thus, it is necessary 'to use rights to control power'.[37] Furthermore, some scholars have linked civil procedural rights to constitutional rights, and stressed that a party's right to participate, the right to be protected, the right to choose and procedural human rights, should all be guaranteed by civil procedure.[38] Procedural justice also faces interference from extra-judicial power. Procedural justice is contingent upon the courts and judges independently adjudicating cases, following only the law and the legally-prescribed procedure. Therefore, intervention by the Party, government, legislature, businesses or influential individuals all have the potential to impede upon the effective employment of procedural justice.

In addition, procedural justice may increase the overall cost of litigation. Shifting the burden of collecting and presenting the evidence from judges to the parties and formalising the trial procedure has brought about a feeling amongst litigants that hiring a lawyer is necessary. Alongside this runs

34 Jing Hanchao, *supra* note 15, p. 229.

35 Liu Guiming, 'Minshi Shenpan Fangshi Gaige: Rechao Zhongde Lengsikao Chen Guiming Jiaoshou Fangtanlu' (Reform of the Civil Trial System: Cautious Thinking in the Hot Wave – An Interview with Professor Chen Guiming), in Jiang Ping and Chen Guiming (eds), *Minshi Shenpan Fangshi Gaige Yu Fazhan* (Civil Trial System Reform and Development) (Beijing: Zhongguo Fazhi Chubanshe, 1998), p. 4.

36 Tian Pingan and Du Renzhe, 'Dangqian Minshi Shenpan Fangshi Gaige Fansi' (Rethinking the Current Reform of the Civil Trial System), in Jiang Ping and Chen Guiming (eds), *ibid.*, pp. 83–84.

37 Fu Yulin, 'Yi Quanli Zhiyue Quanli: Jianli Minshi Shenpan Zhiyue Jizhi De Jiben Silu' (Use Rights to Restrict Power: Basic Thoughts on Establishing a System of Limiting Civil Adjudication Power), available at http://article.chinalawinfo.com/Article_Detail.asp?ArticleID=27588. Last visited September 2013.

38 Jiang Mingan et al. (eds), *supra* note 9, p. 335.

the stark reality that lawyers' fees are becoming increasingly more expensive. Those who are unable to hire lawyers are in a disadvantaged position when preparing their defence, which may eventually result in injustice. Thus, it is contended: 'While formal procedures can increase consistency and predictability and serve as the cornerstones of rule of law, overly technical procedures can decrease rather than increase access to the courts, barring inexperienced litigants from ever reaching the merits of their cases.'[39]

The economic environment also has an effect on the materialisation of procedural justice. In economically disadvantaged areas, judges often compete for jurisdiction or handle cases outside their jurisdiction, which is an obvious violation of notions of procedural justice. This may be caused by judges' motivation to earn more litigation fees in order to trim down the court's budgetary difficulties. On the other hand, in wealthier areas, there is no reason for judges to compete for jurisdiction, thus judges' conceptions of procedural justice are far stronger. In the less-developed, poorer locations, it is also difficult to retain in office competent judges, while in economically richer areas there are a greater number of professionally qualified judges. The composition of the local judiciary leads to differences in their perceptions of procedural justice. In addition, the geographical location can have an impact on the effectiveness of procedural justice. In certain remote border areas of China's vast landscape, due to historical and political factors, there is a greater degree of instability than in the more centralised regions. Therefore, judges in remote regions, aside from their obvious considerations of judicial fairness, are arguably more concerned than other judges with maintaining social stability and ultimately any possible political impact ensuing from a case. In addition, in the large expanses of western China, a court's jurisdiction often covers a vast area. People live far from each other and some litigants live a few hundred kilometres from the court. This situation is further exacerbated through the underdevelopment of public transportation. As such, judges cannot handle cases according to the normal procedure, thus geographical factors also have an impact on a judge's perception of procedural justice.[40]

Despite these difficulties, turning toward strengthening procedural justice seems to be an inevitable choice for China. This decision is also linked with China's broader aims in modernising the judicial system. Such modernisation inevitably stimulates comparative thought as people look to systems in foreign countries which have achieved a developed and functioning system, something which to a large extent can now be viewed as having universal value. However, in order for a newly-introduced system to function as it eventually should requires not only time for it to materialise in full but also particular social conditions and a 'rule of law' environment. Unsurprisingly, at present, both modern and traditional characteristics are discernible in the civil trial procedure. While in cities with a developed market economy, trial procedures have been modified, largely resulting from the procedures laid down in the CiPL, in most people's tribunals where the population is dominated by rural people, judges still follow the traditional methods of handling civil cases. Empirical studies of people's tribunals have illustrated that the judges' primary concern is to resolve disputes in a practical manner wherein legal procedure does not have much of an impact. One such study has vividly described how a people's tribunal operates in reality.[41]

The Li Xin People's Tribunal is located in a remote mountainous area in the Fujian province and is equipped with a small three-storey building, a computer, printer, motorbike and a single courtroom.

39 Margaret Y.K. Woo and Yaxin Wang, *supra* note 11, p. 912.

40 Research Office of the Supreme People's Court (ed.), *supra* note 28, p. 43.

41 Yu Zhong *supra* note 11, pp. 22–54.

Three judges work at the tribunal, and none of them studied law at university. The example of how cases are handled by the judges in this setting is emblematic of the widespread informality.

1. For the convenience of the parties, the judges often met the parties at their homes.
2. As most residents in the Tribunal's jurisdiction are farmers, the judges have to accommodate their needs. For example, in order to help them write a bill of complaint and learn how to collect evidence, the Tribunal collected more than 30 different samples of documents such as bills of complaint, bills of defence, lists of evidence, and so on, and distributed them to the farmers. As a consequence, litigation costs were reduced. The judges also use language that can be understood by farmers, rather than the standard legal terms.
3. About 80 per cent of the cases are settled by mediation. At the forefront of mediation is the use of an informal procedure to convince the parties to make compromises and reach an agreement. In one case, concerning a contract executed between the plaintiff, who was a logger, and a village committee who breached their contract to follow a local policy, the judge began the mediation by ensuring that the parties were in two separate rooms. Determined to conclude an agreement, the judge ran between the two rooms several times with a calculator in his hand and even called the plaintiff's brother, an acquaintance, to help talk to the plaintiff. In the end, the parties could agree on the amount of compensation and the time schedule for payment. Interestingly, the judge did not use Contract Law or attribute blame to either of the parties, he only concentrated on the amount of compensation.
4. The separation of the two parties during mediation is common practice. For example, in a case involving a plaintiff who had not received payment for goods he had sold to a local company, the judge immediately called the defendant to the Tribunal and started the mediation. This led to the defendant agreeing to pay part of the money at that moment in time and the rest under a separate agreement that was reached. The case was settled within one day.
5. The Tribunal also exhibited a great deal of respect for local customs. For instance, one local custom requires that a divorced woman not return to the village where her former husband lives, as the villagers feel that the woman would bring bad luck. In one case, a woman had obtained a divorce judgment against her husband, but when she tried to enforce the judgment, the villagers blocked the road and prohibited her from proceeding. When this occurred, the judge went into the village and took the goods that were given to her in the settlement, while she waited outside the village.
6. The Tribunal furthermore takes flexible measures and promptly solves disputes. In locations where the farming trade is concentrated, the Tribunal tries to accept cases and send statements to the defendants on the same day, sometimes even conducting mediation on the same day if possible.

Increasing the Use of Summary Procedure

The 1991 CiPL contains brief provisions on the summary procedure. Summary procedure applies to simple cases where the facts are evident, the relationship between the rights and obligations is definite and the disputes are minor. Such procedures can only be used by basic courts and their tribunals. A plaintiff can bring a lawsuit in writing or make his complaint verbally. In addition, the trial is presided over by a single judge, following a simplified procedure which does not bind the court to its ordinary procedural obligations of investigation and court debate. A case handled through the summary procedure should be concluded within three months of the case being filed.[42] In the 1992 SPC's Opinions on Several Issues concerning the Implementation of the Civil Procedure Law, the requirement that the 'facts are evident' is interpreted as requiring that the parties to a case have consistent and correlating statements regarding the facts; therefore, they provide reliable evidence and the court does not need to investigate and collect evidence in order to ascertain the relevant facts and distinguish between the truth and mere fiction. The 'definite relationship between the rights and obligations' requires that there is a clear distinction between the person who bears the responsibility and the person to whom that responsibility is owed. The 'minor dispute' requirement ensures that there should not be any principal differences regarding the merits of the case, the responsibilities and the dispute over the object of an action.[43]

When the 1991 CiPL was drafted, the legislators believed that civil cases could be grouped into three categories: simple, ordinary and complex. Furthermore, they believed that most cases fell into the ordinary category, with few cases being classified as either simple or complex. Thus, the scope to which the summary procedure could be applied was intentionally formulated to be quite limited.[44] However, in judicial practice, basic courts have used the summary procedure beyond the scope prescribed in the law. It is estimated that approximately 80 per cent of the civil cases handled by basic courts across China have used the summary procedure. In some courts, 90 per cent or even 100 per cent of civil cases have been settled using this mechanism.[45] A survey conducted by the Higher People's Court in Beijing on the application of the summary procedure in 1999, illustrated that cases concluded by summary procedure in the basic people's courts in Beijing accounted for 88 per cent of the total cases. In the Haidian Basic People's Court Civil Chamber One, the percentage was 80.5 per cent and in Civil Chamber Two the figure stood at 98.2 per cent. In the Fengtai Basic People's Court Civil Chamber One it was 92.9 per cent, whilst in Civil Chamber Two it was 79.75 per cent.[46] These statistics demonstrate that the summary procedure is the main means through which basic courts tackle the civil cases brought to them.

The heavy caseload on judges is the justification for the courts' invocation of the summary procedure. Many courts only follow the procedure to the extent that a case is handled by a single judge. However, this single judge will still follow the ordinary procedures alongside both a court investigation and court debate during the hearing. Basic people's courts face a dilemma: if they strictly follow the procedural provisions as provided for in the CiPL and the SPC judicial interpretations, they can hardly manage all the cases brought before them. If they want to complete these cases, they are forced to exceed the legal scope and use the summary procedure. Most basic courts choose the latter option.[47] Thus, the summary procedure is widely used as a result of its ability to aid courts in completing their caseload. However, other legislative goals in using the summary procedure may to some extent be neglected. For instance, the CiPL provides that plaintiffs may file their complaints orally (Art. 143). This requires that courts arrange for such complaints to be accepted and recorded. However, in practice, courts hardly ever accept oral complaints. Some courts even refuse to file cases on the grounds that the bill of complaint does not meet the prescribed standard. In addition, the CiPL provides that a party or parties to a dispute may appear in court or a people's tribunal at the same time and the relevant court or tribunal can adjudicate

42 Arts. 142 to 146 of the CiPL.

43 Art. 168 of the Opinions on the CiPL.

44 Zhang Wusheng, 'Lun Minshi Jianyi Chengxu Zhi Chonggou' (Restructuring the Summary Procedure in Civil Litigation), available at http://www.civillaw.com.cn/Article/default.asp?id=23687. Last visited September 2013.

45 *Ibid.*

46 *Ibid.*

47 *Ibid.*

the case immediately or set a prospective date for the hearing (Art. 143). In practice, cases are filed by the case acceptance department and the file only reaches a responsible judge a few days later. These examples demonstrate that the purpose of using the summary procedure to help parties settle their disputes rapidly, as well as to aid the efficiency of the courts' work, has not necessarily fully materialised.[48]

It is largely recognised that the scope for applying the summary procedure, as provided in the CiPL, is too narrow. Those who support the extended use of the summary procedure argue that any litigation system has to achieve both fairness and efficiency. In practice, many cases are waiting to be handled by judges, many of which are debt or loan disputes that do not involve large sums of money, or instances where the amount is large but the allocation of responsibility in the case is clear. The costs involved for both the court and the litigants may exceed the disputed sum if the ordinary procedure is followed. In addition, due to the narrow scope of the summary procedure provided in the law, many basic courts and intermediate courts must form a collegiate panel as is also required by the ordinary procedure. However, this is a mere formality, the reality is that there is only one judge who has the knowledge of the case material and who writes the judgment, the other members of the panel just sign the 'collegiate opinions'. Some litigants have complained that, since they only meet one of the judges handling the case, how do the other two judges form their opinions on it? There have been numerous instances of trials beginning with three judges in attendance but as the hearing has progressed these members of the panel leave. Eventually, only the responsible judge remains. In some instances the responsible judge oversees the trial while the other two judges read other case files or write judgments for the other cases.[49]

Calls have come from legal scholars and judges to amend the CiPL by allowing the intermediate people's courts to apply the summary procedure. In economic cases, the amount of money involved in the dispute determines the court's jurisdiction. Thus, if a case concerns a large amount of money, it will be handled by an intermediate court or a higher court. However, it is argued that a large amount of money does not always mirror the complexity of a case. Furthermore, simple cases handled through the summary procedure in the basic courts have sometimes been brought to a court of second instance. Under the current law, courts of second instance are not permitted to use the summary procedure. Article 152 of the CiPL provides that when handling an appellate case, the court of second instance should form a collegiate panel to adjudicate the case. After verifying the relevant facts by consulting the files, making the necessary investigations and questioning the parties, if the collegiate panel believes that it is not necessary to hold an open trial, it may make a judgment or ruling without the need for a hearing. This actually provides for two differing approaches to the settlement of disputes at an appellate court. Making a judgment or ruling without holding a trial can be deemed a summary procedure. In addition, maritime cases are handled by special maritime courts in China and the court of first instance for handling maritime cases is at the intermediate level. In practice, many maritime cases are simple cases, but according to the law they are not capable of being handled by the summary procedure. Setting up a collegiate panel of three judges to deal with simple maritime cases obviously constitutes a waste of resources for the court.[50]

In order to expand the scope of the use of the summary procedure, some higher people's courts have issued their opinions on the implementation of Article 142 of the CiPL. For instance, in the 1997 Higher People's Court in Beijing's Reply to Several Questions concerning Applying the Summary Procedure in Trying Civil Cases, the summary procedure cannot be applied to 12 different

48 *Ibid.*

49 Jing Hanchao, *supra* note 15, p. 178.

50 Zhang Wusheng, *supra* note 44.

classifications of cases: circumstances where the parties have largely differing opinions on the facts and the legal relations are complicated; when the case is brought to court and the accused cannot be found; cases relating to disagreements over an arbitration decision rendered by a labour dispute arbitration committee; cases in which one of the parties has numerous litigants; cases in which one or both parties involved are not in China; cases relating to entities of a foreign country, Hong Kong, Taiwan or Macau; the infringement of name, reputation, picture and/or copyright laws; cases of real estate development and operation; cases sent back for re-trial or requested for re-trial; cases with broad social attention and impact; novel cases and other complex and problematic cases.[51]

Conversely, some experts have expressed concerns over the expansion of the use of the summary procedure. One argument is that the overall professional quality of judges is inadequate. They argue that if trials with collegiate panels using the ordinary procedure continue to have so many problems then the extended use of the summary procedure with a single judge could lead to even more complications. The current reality is such that many judges have not established a strong conception of procedural justice and overemphasis on the summary procedure may lead some of them to neglect the importance of a fair procedure in handling such cases.[52]

In response to the argument that civil procedure needs to be fair and efficient, and that the summary procedure could improve efficiency, which is why it is widely used in Western countries, some Chinese scholars argue that, in China, the summary procedure cannot guarantee fairness in practice and its efficiency fails to meet expectations. In their view, China is forced to confront different problems to those in Western countries. In China, the fundamental flaw is that fairness is not established, procedural justice is extremely weak and judicial legitimacy and efficiency are all challenged. The preference of Chinese courts for the widespread use of the summary procedure is due to a desire to solve as many disputes as possible, as quickly as possible. Whilst in Western countries a modern, standardised, carefully-designed judicial procedure and highly-professional judges can, for the most-part, guarantee judicial fairness, given the features of the summary procedure in China in providing a simple and vague way of settling disputes, it cannot meet the emerging demands for procedural justice and judicial professionalism. It has been stressed that, without adequate recognition of the role of parties as the central subjects of civil trials and an appropriate respect for procedural justice by the judiciary, an overemphasis on and the expansion of the use of the summary procedure can be contradictory to the ultimate goal of strengthening the rule of law.[53]

In 2003, the SPC issued Several Provisions concerning the Application of the Summary Procedure in the Trials of Civil Cases, which stressed that the purpose of the summary procedure is to guarantee and facilitate for parties the exercising of their litigation rights by ensuring that the courts hear civil cases in a just and timely manner. Article 1 provides that the summary procedure cannot be invoked in cases which have any of the following features: (1) the whereabouts of the defendant is unknown; (2) the case has been remanded for re-trial; (3) the case involves parties to a joint action or a large number of people as a single party; (4) the special procedures, procedures for trial supervision, procedures for supervising and urging the clearance of debt, procedures of public summons for exhortation, or procedures of bankruptcy and liquidation of a business corporation shall be applied as provided for by law; or (5) the court deems it inappropriate to apply the summary procedure in the trial.

51 Han Xiangqian, 'Jianyi Chengxu' (Summary Procedure), in Jiang Wei et al. (eds) *Minshi Susong Jizhi De Gaige* (Reform of the Civil Litigation System) (Beijing: Renmin Fayuan Chubanshe, 1998), pp. 454–455.

52 Jing Hanchao, *supra* note 15, p. 243.

53 Fu Yulin (ed.), *Minshi Sifa Zhidu De Gongneng Yu Jiegou* (The Functions and Structure of the Civil Justice System) (Beijing: Beijing Daxue Chubanshe, 2006) p. 192.

Article 2 states that where any basic court applies the ordinary procedure of first instance in the trial of a civil case, if the parties to that case choose to apply the summary procedure, such a procedure may be applied upon the examination and approval of the court. The court may not replace the ordinary procedure with the summary procedure in violation of the principle of free will of the parties. Obviously, the SPC's opinion reflects the trend that allows a greater degree of party autonomy in deciding whether to use the summary procedure or not.

The 2012 amended CiPL adopted Article 2 of the SPC's judicial interpretation by allowing parties to reach an agreement on the use of the summary procedure (Article 157). In addition, Article 162 introduces for the first time the small claims lawsuit system, by providing that for simple cases handled by the summary procedure, where the disputed amount of money is below the threshold of 30 per cent of the annual average employee salary of the relevant province, the judgment of first instance is final and binding. This arrangement allows small claims for debts or damages to be handled more efficiently. According to the National Bureau of Statistics, the average annual salary of urban Chinese workers in 2011 was RMB 41,799, and as such 30 per cent of this figure is around RMB 12,000, which is roughly equivalent to 1,887 USD.[54]

Given the fact that courts simply cannot manage the increasing number of cases, the 2012 CiPL expands the scope of cases wherein the summary procedure can be utilised, and grants the parties involved in a dispute the right to initiate the procedure. One can expect that the summary procedure will be used for most of the civil cases coming before the courts and the ordinary procedure will be used in solving the more complex and problematic cases. The small claims regime will ensure that many of the judgments decided at the first instance by basic courts are both binding and final. However, the finality of such judgments without taking into account any other circumstance has been challenged by some Chinese legal scholars.[55]

Mediation: Its Rise, Fall and Revival

China has a long-standing tradition of settling disputes through the means of mediation. The system can be traced back to Confucianism, which stressed that

> a social hierarchy existed, and people should conduct their lives in accordance with their respective social statuses. If people tried to destroy social differences and did not comport with reference to li (proper modes of behavior), conflicts would arise. Interpersonal conflicts would lead to social instability, which would disrupt cosmic harmony. Thus, when a dispute arose, the parties should try to resolve it promptly by yielding and compromising … By and large, codes were general guidelines for magistrates to perform their job, not for the illiterate populace to read. Since law had a mere deterrent effect, mediation accompanied by instruction and persuasion was the preferred means of resolving disputes.[56]

54 'China Amends Civil Procedure Law Following Third Reading', available at http://english.cri.cn/6909/2012/08/31/2561s719834.html. Last visited September 2013.

55 Shao Ming, 'Guanyu Minshi Susongfa Xiuzheng Yijian (San)' (Opinions on the Amendment of Civil Procedure Law (Part 3)). Full text is available at http://www.civillaw.com.cn/article/default.asp?id=54362. Last visited September 2013.

56 Vai Io Lo, 'Resolution of Civil Disputes in China', 18(2) (2000) *UCLA Pacific Basin Law Journal*, p. 123.

From the 1950s to the 1980s, the slogan of 'mediation as the core, adjudication as a supplement' had proven to be the guiding mantra. The 1982 CiPL provided that in handling civil cases, judges should 'accentuate mediation'. In practice, judicial mediation, which was hallmarked as being flexible, informal and somewhat coercive, had become the primary procedure for courts in settling individual disputes.

However, with the rapidly growing number of civil cases by the mid-1980s, the trial procedure, which featured pro-active judges who collated evidence and participated in time-consuming mediation, left the courts unable to deal with the accumulation of cases. The subsequent reform of the trial procedure resulted in placing the burden of proof on parties to the case, which strengthened adjudication and weakened mediation. Mandatory mediation has also become evidently contradictory to the peoples' increasing consciousness of their rights and the necessary procedures. In 1988, the SPC held the 14th National Judicial Work Conference, in which the relationship between mediation and adjudication was discussed and emphasis was placed on the proposition that, 'if a case is suited to mediation, it should be mediated. If a case is suited to adjudication, it should be adjudicated'. This actually served to weaken the dominating role played by mediation in the civil trial procedure.[57]

The 1991 CiPL stressed that mediation should be conducted on the basis of the 'the principle of party voluntariness and the principle of lawfulness'. If an agreement through mediation cannot be reached, courts should render judgments without delay (Art. 9). Thus, mediation was not especially 'stressed' in the 1991 CiPL. Moreover, the overall reform of the civil trial procedure in the 1990s significantly reduced the use of mediation in the settlement of civil disputes. In the 1980s, a large number of cases were concluded through mediation. For civil cases of the first instance, 70 per cent were concluded through mediation, thus, allowing for 30 per cent of cases to be concluded through judgments. In the 1990s, the cases concluded through mediation had declined to 30 per cent, while the percentage of cases concluded through adjudicative judgments had increased to 70 per cent. The number of cases of the second instance concluded by mediation has slowly diminished: 15.96 per cent in 1986, 11.05 per cent in 1996, and 8.54 per cent in 2005.[58]

However, a resurgence in mediation has taken place since the 2000s as a consequence of the Communist Party's interference in judicial matters. Before the turn of the twenty-first century, reform of the civil trial system was predominantly led by the SPC and resultantly the local courts responded with great enthusiasm by experimenting with various measures. The Communist Party was not substantively involved in this process. The general matrix changed in 2003, when petitions to central authorities in Beijing sharply escalated. According to statistics covering all the courts across China, they dealt with 3.65 million petition cases in 2002, 3.97 million cases in 2003, 4.22 million cases in 2004 and 3.99 million cases in 2005. In addition, the number of group petitions, wherein people with similar purposes and interests unite to petition in front of higher courts or government authorities, has increased. Some of them have even drawn upon more extreme methods of organising demonstrations by holding banners with words of protest, blocking streets, stopping buses and cars, storming government buildings, destroying public facilities, committing suicide, injuring judicial officers and other similar violent acts.[59]

Among these petitions a large proportion are court-related. This situation has been simplistically interpreted as having been caused by the failure of judicial reforms, especially the reform of the

57 Zhang Weiping, 'Susong Tiaojie: Shixia Shitai De Fenxi Yu Sikao' (Judicial Mediation: An Analysis of the Current Situation), 5 (2007) *Faxue* (Legal Science), available at http://article.chinalawinfo.com/Article_Detail.asp?ArticleID=39445. Last visited September 2013.

58 Cheng Hu, *supra* note 4, pp. 290–291.

59 Research Office of the Supreme People's Court (ed.), *supra* note 28, p. 60.

civil trial system, in which the formalisation and professionalisation of the procedure had resulted in the bureaucratic handling of cases by courts and the development of elitist attitudes amongst judges that merely distanced them from disputants. Instead of providing a forum in which to solve disputes, courts were blamed for becoming part of the problem. 'For the CCP, the courts have not only failed to end many disputes, the courts have actually aggravated the problem because of bureaucratic case handling, overcharged court fees, and real or perceived corruption.'[60]

In 2003, Luo Gan, the Secretary of the Central Political and Legal Committee of the CPC, launched a policy paper,[61] which called for a strengthening of the role of mediation in dispute settlement. He highlighted the need to set up a grand mediation scheme in which the Communist Party would play a leading role and in which people's mediation, administrative mediation and judicial mediation would reinforce each other. These three types of mediation should be interlinked in a mutually-supportive way to reduce confrontation between the parties in court. According to Luo Gan, mediation is a method of dispute resolution that allows legal, rational and moral factors to be taken into account with a view to promoting the peaceful settlement of disputes and thereby contributing to the creation of a harmonious society. Since 2004, mediation in the settlement of civil disputes has become not only an alternative to adjudication by courts, but also a political task of the judiciary in contributing to the creation of a more harmonious society.[62]

The SPC has responded to the Party's policy on prioritising mediation by issuing a number of judicial interpretations.[63] In March 2007 the SPC's Several Opinions on Further Displaying the Positive Roles of Litigant Mediation in Constructing Socialist Harmonious Society[64] emphasised that the courts should facilitate mediation in all cases where it would be appropriate and that mediation should particularly be promoted if coming within the remit of the following six situations:

1. cases involving broad public interests, in which a settlement requires the assistance of relevant government departments;
2. class action cases involving a large number of people with shared interests;
3. cases involving complex facts, where parties have entrenched positions, and neither side has an evidentiary advantage;
4. cases involving matters where the relevant laws are unclear, so the application of law is uncertain;
5. cases involving sensitive issues capable of generating significant social attention; and
6. cases where there is a request for re-trial.

60 Fu Hualing and Richard Cullen, *supra* note 30, p. 45.

61 Luo Gan, 'Zhengfa Jiguan Zai Goujian Hexie Shehui Zhong Fudan Zhongda Lishi Shiming He Zhengzhi Zeren' (The Significant Historical Missions and the Political Responsibility of Political and Legal Organisations in Constructing a Harmonious Society), 3 (2003) *Qiu Shi* (Seeking Truth).

62 Zhang Weiping, *supra* note 57. 'Harmonious society' is defined by the President of China Hu Jintao as 'a society characterised by democracy and the rule of law, fairness and justice, mutual trust and love, creativity and energy, stability and order, and the harmonious co-existence of man and nature'. See 'Hu Jintao Lun Hexie Shehui Liuda Tezheng' (Hu Jintao's Explanation of the Six Main Characteristics of Harmonious Society), available at http://www.ce.cn/xwzx/gnsz/gdxw/200508/15/t20050815_4430460.shtml. Last visited September 2013.

63 For instance, in August 2004, the SPC issued the Decisions on Several Issues concerning the Civil Mediation Work of the People's Courts (Zuigao Renmin Fayuan Guanyu Renmin Fayuan Minshi Tiaojie Gongzuo Ruogan Wenti De Guiding), *Fashi* No. 12 [2004]. Available at http://www.law-lib.com/law/law_view.asp?id=86820. Last visited September 2013.

64 *Fafa* No. 9 [2007]. Available at http://vip.chinalawinfo.com/newlaw2002/slc/slc.asp?db=chl&gid=89041. Last visited September 2013.

The Opinions have re-emphasised the need for mediation from the early stage of filing cases. Once a case is accepted, a court can conduct mediation with the mutual agreement of the parties. If the case involves complicated facts and the parties do not desire mediation, only then would the case be transferred to a trial chamber. Mediation at this stage should be concluded promptly and efficiently. For cases of the first instance, if the summary procedure is to be used, mediation at the pre-trial stage should in principle be concluded within 10 days from the case being accepted. In situations involving the use of the ordinary procedure, the mediation period cannot exceed 20 days. Furthermore, in principle, mediation is not offered when cases are accepted at the second instance. The Opinions also indicated that the courts may create or expand frameworks to involve external dispute resolution bodies, such as: peoples' mediation organisations at the grassroots level, trade unions and women's organisations. They could also invite members of the peoples' congresses, members of the peoples' political consultative congresses or lawyers to take part in proceedings. Some academics view the SPC's shift to judicial mediation, at least during President Xiao Yang's period (1998 to 2008), as reflecting 'a reluctant response to political demands to maintain social stability', and 'the government has … not taken drastic action to push the court onto a more "hard line" mediation track'.[65]

How this shift in judicial policy impacts on judicial practice is worthy of further examination. Whilst the courts in some urban areas may be influenced to a lesser extent,[66] courts in other places are experimenting with various measures, including imposing a rule that a certain percentage of cases must be mediated on a yearly basis and that this in turn should be linked to the evaluation of a judge's performance – the latter determines the size of bonus payments awarded to judges.[67] The operation of mediation in a basic court in Wuhan has been described in the following manner. When a case is filed, the plaintiff will be informed of the risks of litigation and asked whether he/she is willing to engage in such mediation. After the bill of complaint is sent, the 'quick-handling' chamber of the department for filing cases can call upon the parties to start the mediation. When a case reaches the civil trial chamber, the presiding judge promptly ascertains the opinion of the parties regarding whether they are willing to mediate or not. Mediation is subsequently invoked before the court session, in the evidence exchange stage, during the court hearing and the deliberation after the hearing. When a case enters the phase of enforcement, mediation is also conducted. If a case is re-tried according to the adjudication supervision procedure, mediation proceedings should ensure that the case is treated as though it was at the first instance stage, in order to involve the parties in mediation. Judges are encouraged to invite relevant people from companies, social organisations and experts with specific knowledge and experience to be involved in the mediation. If the parties agree, the court can delegate the mediation to a relevant person or organisation. Once an agreement has been reached, it is legally sanctioned by the court. If, during the process of litigation, the parties reach a mediation agreement by themselves, the court will confirm the agreement upon the parties' request.[68]

In the SPC Work Report to the NPC in 2009, it was stated that all courts hae highly emphasised the use of mediation in settling conflicts and disputes, as such, upholding the principle of 'prioritising

65 Fu Hualing and Richard Cullen, *supra* note 30, pp. 51–52.

66 *Ibid.*, p. 53.

67 Zhang Wusheng and Xiao Guoyu, 'Fayuan Tiaojie Yu Panjue De Guanxi' (The Relationship between Mediation and Judgment by Courts), 30(6) (2012) *Zhengfa Luntan* (Tribune of Political Science and Law), pp. 172–173.

68 Li Wei, 'Dali Jiaqiang Sifa Tiaojie Nuli Cujin Shehui Hexie' (Strengthening Judicial Mediation and Promoting Social Harmony), 14 (2007) *Tian Ping Yuandi* (The Journal of Wuhan Hong Shan District Basic People's Court), p. 7.

mediation by combining mediation and adjudication' and applying mediation in the process of filing cases, hearing cases and enforcing judgments. The courts have expanded the practice of mediation broadly in settling civil and commercial disputes, explored the use of mediation in minor criminal cases, strengthened mediation in solving criminal cases with civil compensation and fully utilised reconciliation in settling administrative cases. Courts have proven innovative in applying new methods of mediation and have strengthened the links between judicial mediation, people's mediation, administrative mediation and arbitration mediation. Courts have also appealed to trade associations, governmental departments and social organisations in judicial mediation. In 2008, it was stated that courts concluded 3.17 million civil cases through mediation, accounting for 58.86 per cent of the total number of civil cases.[69] Obviously, judicial mediation is returning to its position at the forefront of the settlement of civil disputes by courts.

Mediation has its inherent merits. It allows for the resolution of disputes in a way which is voluntarily accepted by all the parties involved; whereas a judgment is made based on judicial power being imposed on the parties and may consequently be resented by the parties. Mediation settlements may invoke easier enforcement. In addition, mediation is particularly suited to family disputes where parties might prefer to conduct the proceedings privately, in order to avoid further harm to the family relationship. As far as efficiency is concerned, since mediation can go beyond the facts of the case in order to understand the origins of the dispute, a successful agreement can lead to a complete resolution. As adjudication can only justify concrete litigation claims based on legally-acceptable facts, their scope is limited and may not be sufficiently thorough for parties whose dispute has built-up over a relatively long duration due to the accumulation of a diverse range of facts. Moreover, mediation cannot result in appealing that decision; the chances of appealing for re-trials and compulsory enforcement are also reduced; consequently mediation may be less costly than litigation.[70] For that reason, some Chinese scholars indicate that mediation is also preferred, in particular, by many judges because it is less precarious for them. An appeal and re-trial of a case could lead to changing the original judgment, which in China is often perceived to be a wrongly-handled case, which in turn, affects judges' bonus prospects, promotion opportunities and so forth. If a case is concluded through mediation, these risks can be avoided. However, the pitfall to litigants arises in situations where a party is more or less forced to accept mediation as the method for resolving the dispute and the case is concluded with a mediation agreement that may not be satisfactory to them; the lack of capacity to appeal this decision entails that the party cannot seek a further judicial remedy.[71]

Besides this, judicial mediation in civil litigation has other shortcomings. Firstly, the 1991 CiPL has a number of deficient provisions. Article 85 provides that mediation should be conducted in order to clarify the facts and distinguish what is right from wrong. Such an aim is not conducive to successful mediation in certain circumstances; clarifying facts and distinguishing right from wrong should be the objective of forming judgments. Mediation should respect the parties' willingness to resolve their disputes without necessarily attributing blame. Moreover, if the facts are already clear and the blame is evident, judges could simply form a decision quickly, rather than mediate. In addition, mediation can take place at the pre-trial stage, whereas a clarification of the facts and the attribution of responsibility can only be properly reached following court investigation and debate.[72] Article 91 of the 1991 CiPL further provides that if no mediation agreement is reached, or

69 The SPC Work Report to the NPC in 2009, available at http://www.gov.cn/test/2009-03/17/content_1261386.htm. Last visited September 2013.

70 Fu Yulin, *supra* note 53, p. 184.

71 Wang Liming, *supra* note 31, pp. 358–361.

72 Liu Guiming, *supra* note 35, p. 8. See also Jing Hanchao, *supra* note 15, pp. 144–145.

if one party retracts his reconciliation before the mediation agreement is served, the court should render a judgment without delay. This provision opened a loophole for parties to easily retract what they agreed upon in mediation proceedings and is also contrary to the principle of good faith. Many judges have complained about this provision and its ramifications. The 2004 SPC Decision on Several Issues concerning the Civil Mediation Work of the People's Court therefore provided, under Article 13, that if the parties concerned agreed that the mediation agreement should become effective upon the relevant formalities of being signed and sealed, the mediation agreement should be put into the written records or attached to the file after being examined and confirmed by the court, and should become effective upon being signed or sealed by the parties concerned, the judges and the court clerk.

Secondly, judicial mediation 'in general bears a relatively unusual and coercive form'.[73] It has been reported that in some basic courts the rate of mediation was extremely high – sometimes peaking at 90 per cent. The common practice was often to impose mediation upon parties and pressurise them to engage in mediation at every level. If a judge responsible for a case did not succeed with the mediation, the presiding judge of the case would continue. If the presiding judge failed, a deputy head of the civil trial division would continue. If the head of the division failed, responsibility for mediation would pass to the vice-president of the court and finally the president of the court. If a party did not agree with the mediation then the court would not conclude the case.[74] Judges may use various tactics to induce parties to accept mediation, such as saying to the parties 'you should realise a judgment may not be in your favour, but once it is made you have to accept it. If you accept mediation, you may at least get something you want.' In cases concerning a breach of contract, a judge may say to a plaintiff: 'mediation could ensure you get some compensation. If the accused does not want to enforce the court's judgment, we can do nothing.'[75] A party may not want to sign the mediation agreement, but could be concerned that a judgment would result in a direr situation, so reluctantly signs.

Thirdly, the judge mediating a case is often the same judge who would adjudicate the case. Thus, the power to decide the outcome of the case is always in the hands of that same judge. This too often reinforces a party's impression that if one does not accept mediation and challenges the decision, the ramifications of such a protestation would result in a more severe and dire judgment being invoked. This inevitably places a greater degree of pressure on parties to accept mediation. In economic disputes, mediation is often abused by a debtor as a tactic to delay paying the debt. A case may take a long time, even after reaching a mediation agreement. If the debtor does not enforce the agreement voluntarily, the creditor/plaintiff has to apply to the court for enforcement. During the process of enforcement, the debtor may escape, hide and/or transfer away their assets. This provides the basis upon which creditors tend to avoid mediation.[76]

Fourthly, a court's insistence on mediation often puts the plaintiff in a disadvantaged position. Jing Hanchao, Vice-President of the SPC has vividly described how a judge might handle a debt

73 Michael Palmer, 'Controlling the State: Mediation in Administrative Litigation in the People's Republic of China', 16 (2006) *Transnational Law and Contemporary Problems*, p. 184. See also Zhang Weiping, *supra* note 57; Shao Ming, *supra* note 55; and Xu Xin, '"Tiaojie Youxian"de Sifa Zhengce Yingdang Tiaozheng' (The Judicial Policy of Prioritising Mediation Should Be Adjusted), *Zhongguo Shehui Kexue Bao* (Newspaper of Social Science in China), 25 March 2010.

74 Jing Hanchao, *supra* note 15, p. 142. See also Zhang Wusheng and Xiao Guoyu, *supra* note 67, pp. 170–171.

75 The author heard statements to this effect whilst observing court sessions in Wuhan in April 2007 and in Beijing in May 2008.

76 Jing Hanchao, *supra* note 15, pp. 142–143.

case. The judge first met with the plaintiff and told him to be grateful if the defendant was capable of repaying the RMB 1 million which he was owed and that he should forget the extra RMB 50,000 in interest that he had requested. The judge then met the defendant and told him that he owed RMB 2.3 million for the original sum, along with the interest payments and a fine for violating his contract. The defendant then agreed to pay half of the interest. Thus, the judge obtained a favourable compromise between the parties and eventually decided that the defendant only had to pay the plaintiff the 1 million. Such a result satisfied both parties. However, this process was to a large extent fully controlled by the judge and the judge also decided the outcome. In most cases involving debt, creditors have to make a compromise to debtors in order to reach a mediation agreement – debtors are rarely asked to pay their debt in full. This is another reflection of the fact that the principle of fairness is undermined in mediation.[77]

Fifthly, experts have observed that there were hardly any rules or procedures for guidance during the course of mediation proceedings, or at least judges did not feel they were guided by any rules. A survey in Shenzhen has showed that 62 per cent of the judges expressed that there was little or no guidance when it came to mediation and 38 per cent indicated only indirect rules and constraints.[78]

Given the pros and cons of judicial mediation, unsurprisingly, the current surge in re-emphasising judicial mediation has been critically challenged by legal scholars both from within China and on the global stage.[79] Some point out that 'the return of mediation is primarily guided by the Party-state policy as a tool for political purpose'.[80] Some view the revival as a simple, insensitive, excessive judicial reaction to a political requirement. The overwhelming accentuation of mediation is undermining the basic legal principle of the need for party autonomy as a prerequisite upon which mediation can ensue. Such a trend may even cause the exacerbation of legal nihilism. As a result of seeking and setting a high rate of mediation-settled disputes, and linking it to an evaluation of a judge's work performance, judges are pressing parties to settle disputes by mediation using various means. A common consequence is that, those to whom an obligation is owed have to make a compromise, which equally entails that those who are under the obligation are not under the requirement to, or do not adequately, carry out their duties. In light of the fact that a strict following of the law by citizens, companies and courts has always proven problematic, the current, obviously politicised, judicial mediation has the potential to further weaken the authority of law and the rule of law principle, which is importantly at a highly-sensitive embryonic stage of development.[81]

The 2012 CiPL codifies the policy of 'prioritising mediation' with a new Article 122, providing that when appropriate, mediation should be used unless the parties refuse. In addition, two new articles are provided concerning the recognition of a mediation agreement reached according to the 2010 Law on People's Mediation. Article 194 states that an application for the judicial confirmation of a mediation agreement should be jointly submitted by both parties within 30 days

77 *Ibid.*, p. 142.

78 Fu Hualing and Richard Cullen, *supra* note 30, p. 30.

79 Benjamin Liebman, 'China's Courts: Restricted Reform', 21 (2007) *Columbia Journal of Asian Law*, pp. 1–44; Zhang Xianchu, 'Civil Justice Reform with Political Agendas', in Yu Guanghua (eds), *The Development of the Chinese Legal System: Change and Challenges* (London and New York: Routledge, 2011), pp. 259–262. Fu Yulin, '"Suqian Tiaojie" Yu Fayuan De Jiaose' (Pre-trial Mediation and the Role of Courts), 4 (2009) *Falu Shiyong* (Journal of Law Application). Zhao Gang, 'Nengdong Sifa Zhi Zhengque Lijie Yu Kexue Jianxing: Yi Minshi Sifa Wei Shijiao De Jiexi' (Correct Understanding and Scientific Practice of Judicial Activism: Analysis from the Perspective of Civil Justice), 2 (2011) *Faxue Pinglun* (Law Review).

80 Zhang Xianchu, *supra* note 79, p. 260.

81 Zhang Weiping, *supra* note 57.

of the date that the agreement became effective, to the basic people's court where the mediation organisation is located. The court, according to Article 195, should review the application and decide the validity of the agreement. If one party refuses to perform or only partially performs, the other party may apply to the court for enforcement. If a court decides that an application for the confirmation of the agreement is not in compliance with the law, the court should reject the application. Parties may, however, change the agreement through mediation or reach a new mediation agreement; as previously stated, they maintain the theoretical right to bring the case to court.

Some Chinese legal scholars do not endorse the notion of incorporating the policy of 'prioritising mediation' into the CiPL. In their view, the overwhelming emphasis on mediation in resolving an array of civil disputes is a misleading political incursion into the ambit of the judiciary. 'Prioritising mediation' as such is taken to mean actual compulsory mediation. It may lead to many cases not being accepted by courts in time, which amplifies the already grave problem of having a case filed by the court (li' an nan).[82]

The Enforcement of Civil Judgments

In China, civil judgments are enforced by the courts. Prior to the 1980s, there was no clear separation of the adjudicative and enforcement functions of the judiciary. The judges who handed down the judgments were also the ones to enforce them. In the 1980s, in parallel with the increasing number of civil and commercial cases, the workload in enforcing civil judgments increased. Article 163 of the 1982 CiPL provided that ordinary enforcement work should be carried out by the enforcement officers and law clerks, whilst the judicial police should only participate in matters involving significant enforcement issues. Since 1983, some local courts have started to establish an enforcement division, which separates enforcement from the adjudicative sectior of the judiciary. Article 209 of the 1991 CiPL provided that, when necessary, basic people's courts and intermediate people's courts may set up an enforcement organ, whose functions should be defined by the SPC. This provides the legal basis for courts to set up a new division in order to carry out the enforcement of judgments. At the end of the 1980s, the SPC set up the Enforcement Group of the Economic Adjudication Chamber, and in 1995 it set up the Enforcement Work Office. In April 1996, nearly 94 per cent of the basic and intermediate courts and 30 higher courts had set up such enforcement divisions, specialising in the execution of civil judgments.[83]

The separation of the adjudicative and enforcement functions reflects judicial efforts to strengthen the enforcement of civil judgments, which is necessitated by the persistent difficulty in enforcing civil judgments in local courts. In the 1990s, it was reported that the rate of mandatory enforcement was high and, moreover, approximately 50 per cent of all civil judgments were unenforceable.[84] From 1992 to 1998, the number of enforcement cases, both accepted and resolved,

82 Xu Hui, 'Xianxing Tiaojie De Guifan Yu Shiyong' (Provision and Application of Mediation Prior to Trial), *Renmin Fayuan Bao* (People's Court Daily), 17 October 2012. Full text is available at http://www.law-lib.com/lw/lw_view.asp?no=22341. Last visited September 2013.

83 Tong Zhaohong et al. (eds), *Minshi Zhixing Diaocha Yu Fenxi* (Investigation and Analysis of Civil Judgment Enforcement) (Beijing: Renmin Fayuan Chubanshe, 2005), pp. 138–140.

84 It is impossible to provide an accurate percentage of unenforced judgments. In the 1998 report to the National People's Congress, President Zheng Tianxiang of the SPC indicated that 20 per cent of judgments in economic cases went unenforced in 1985 and 1986, and 30 per cent in 1987. Some authors put the number at over 50 per cent. See Donald C. Clarke, 'Power and Politics in the Chinese Court System: The Enforcement

increased each year. Due to the fact that the number of settled cases was lower than the number of cases accepted, the unsettled cases accumulated, reaching 536,338 in 1998. In order to tackle these enforcement problems actively, 1999 was deemed by the SPC to be 'the year of enforcement'. As a result, the number of settled cases exceeded the number of cases accepted that year, which gradually modified the passive situation.[85] But the difficulties surrounding enforcement have not been substantively improved over time. According to a SPC source, in 2006, around 50 per cent of enforcement cases could still not be carried out.[86] In March 2009, the SPC published detailed information on 6.17 million cases that required enforcement.[87]

The SPC has identified the enforcement problem as the courts' most serious deficiency. In 1987, at the National Conference on Courts' Work, the issue of the difficulties arising in enforcing judgments was specifically discussed. In the Work Report of the SPC to the NPC in 1988, the expression 'difficulty of enforcement' was mentioned for the first time. Since then, issues of enforceability have consistently been addressed in the SPC's report which is submitted annually to the NPC.[88] In 1998, the SPC issued the Regulations on Several Issues concerning Enforcement Work of People's Courts (for Trial Implementation).[89] The first Five-Year Reform Programme of People's Courts set a target of having at least 15 per cent of the total staff members of each court working at the enforcement division. The HPCs at the provincial levels were entrusted with managing and coordinating the enforcement work within their jurisdictions on a unified basis. In January 2000, on the basis of court experience, the SPC issued the Regulations concerning Several Issues Related to the Centralised Administration of Enforcement Work by Higher People's Courts.[90] The HPCs are responsible for supervising, coordinating and organising the enforcement work of the lower courts under their jurisdiction. Aggrieved parties may apply to the HPC directly for a review of any illegal or erroneous enforcement rulings by the lower courts.

The inadequate enforcement of civil judgments is due to both extrinsic and intrinsic factors. With regard to the external factors, some companies are simply shell companies with few assets.

of Civil Judgements', 10(1) (1996) *Columbia Journal of Asian Law*, p. 28. In 1999, some Chinese scholars pointed out that according to media estimates, about 90 per cent of civil and economic judgments could not be enforced or fully enforced. See Xin Chunying, 'Preface', in Xin Chunying and Li Lin (eds), *Yifa Zhiguo Yu Sifa Gaige* (Ruling the Country by Law and Judicial Reform) (Beijing: Zhongguo Fazhi Chubanshe, 1999), p. 2.

85 Tong Zhaohong et al. (eds), *supra* note 83, p. 2.

86 Ye Doudou, 'Minsu Xiufa Qiujie Liang Nan' (Amendment of the Civil Procedure Law Seeks to Solve "Two Difficulties"), 198 (2007) *Caijing Zazhi* (Finance and Economy), available at http://magazine.caijing.com.cn/2007-07-08/110064035.html. Last visited September 2013.

87 'Quanguo Fayuan Beizhixingren Xinxi Chaxun Pingtai Kaitong, Liubai Yishi Qiwan Bei Zhixingren Xinxi Kechaxung' (The National Enquiry Platform on Information about Persons against whom a Judgment Is Executed Is Opened; Information about 6.17 Million Persons against whom a Judgment Is Executed Is Now Available on the Website), available at http://www.legaldaily.com.cn/0801/2009-03/31/content_1062496.htm. Last visited September 2013.

88 Tong Zhaohong et al. (eds), *supra* note 83, p. 2. The difficulty in enforcement has also roused the attention of the central government. In July 1999, the Central Committee of the Communist Party issued the Document No. 11, which transmitted the Report of the Party Committee of the Supreme People's Court on 'Difficulties in Enforcement'. In November 2002, the Report of the 16th Session of the Communist Party committed itself to effectively solve the problem of enforcement difficulties.

89 The Regulations in Chinese are contained in *Zhonghua Renmin Gongheguo Zuigao Renmin Fayuan Gongbao* (1998) (Gazette of the Supreme People's Court (1998)), pp. 91–98.

90 Fafa 3 (2000), available at http://www.court.gov.cn/spyw/zxgz/201004/t20100414_4104.htm. Last visited January 2014.

When their businesses fall into trouble, they often flee in order to avoid bearing any liability.[91] In rural areas, some farmers have little property against which an order can be enforced. Moreover, patriarchal clan forces have also led to the use of violent means to resist enforcement. The number of enforcement cases relating to torts, such as compensation concerning traffic accidents or personal injury, has increased. In such cases, those applying for enforcement and the parties who are the subject of the enforcement order, all belong to socially-disadvantaged groups. Enforcement of such cases is therefore inevitably problematic.[92] When state-owned enterprises (SOE's) are the judgment debtor, the enforcement of a judgment may be 'halted if such SOE is financially unable to satisfy the judgment or the enforcement would threaten the survival of the SOE. A SOE may not sell or be forced to sell its assets to satisfy a court judgment.'[93]

Similarly, it is also difficult when the parties against whom enforcement is sought are governmental institutions. Such cases often relate to the delay of payment for projects and services such as: the building of new schools, offices or public facilities; car repairs, or entertainment costs. Courts cannot impose mandatory enforcement when public institutions are involved. In practice, courts would inquire as to whether the public institutions could remove some money from their regular budgets, or urge the institutions to reduce some of their normal expenses, or factor the debt into the upcoming annual budget.[94] Jaing Bixin, Vice-President of the SPC, stated in 2009, that among the 6.17 million persons (natural and legal) involved in cases where the enforcement of the judgment was yet to materialise, approximately 2 million were legal persons or governmental agencies; as such, courts could hardly impose mandatory enforcement on them.[95]

Furthermore, local protectionism is an enormous obstacle to enforcing commercial judgments. When local enterprises are executees, the local government usually imposes barriers to make a court's enforcement action difficult or next to impossible.[96] It was reported that the Legal Committee of the National People's Political Consultative Conference once conducted an investigation into the courts in Hilongjiang province and found that 67 local enterprises were involved in lawsuits and enforcement issues. However, local governments instructed the courts not to let the enterprises lose their cases. If they did lose, the executable judgments would not be enforced. In some places, there was also a 'unit established jointly by the courts and enterprises', which was used by the enterprises as a way to obtain local judicial protection.[97] Local protectionism is driven by a desire

---

91 He Xin, 'The Enforcement of Commercial Judgments in China', p. 5. Available at http://www.fljs.org/sites/www.fljs.org/files/publications/Xin%2520He%25231%2523.pdf. Last visited September 2013.

92 Tong Zhaohong et al. (eds), *supra* note 83, p. 101.

93 Mo Zhang, 'International Civil Litigation in China: A Practical Analysis of the Chinese Judicial System', 25(59) (2002) *Boston College International and Comparative Law Review*, p. 92.

94 See 'Jianshe Fazhi Zhengfu, Bojie Zhengfu Caichan "Zhixingnan"' (Constructing a Government Under the Rule of Law and Overcoming Difficulties in the Enforcement of a Judgment Involving Government Property). Available at http://www.cnr.cn/allnews/201004/t20100421_506317475.html. Last visited September 2013.

95 'Liubai Yishi Qiwan Bei Zhixingren Xinxi Kechaxun' (Information on the 6.17 Million Persons against Whom Enforcement Is Sought by People's Courts available on the Website). Available at http://www.gmw.cn/content/2009-03/31/content_903606.htm. Last visited September 2013.

96 Ramon E. Reyes, 'The Enforcement of Foreign Court Judgements in the People's Republic of China: What the American Lawyer Needs to Know', 23(1) (1997) *Brooklyn Journal of International Law*, pp. 241–270. Jerome Cohen, 'China's Civil Procedure: Judging the Courts', 45 (1997) *The American Journal of Comparative Law*, pp. 799–800.

97 Zhao Donghui and Liu Hongcan, 'Diaocha Biaoming: Difang "Fazhi Geju" Yanzhong' (Investigation Shows That Local Judicial Protection Is Serious', February (2003) *Falu Yu Shenghuo* (Law and Life). Full text is available at http://www.people.com.cn/GB/shehui/47/20030219/926168.html. Last visited September 2013.

to protect the local economy. Some officials view the court's role as merely a servant to economic development. Thus, when economic interests are at stake, a court's ruling is ignored.

As to internal factors, some judicial officers are incompetent and, to a lesser degree, the poor record of judgment enforcement can be partially attributed to a lack of standardisation in the enforcement procedure itself. There have been instances where enforcement could not be carried out smoothly due to delays, or even as a result of the enforcement judges lacking certain professional skills. Their methods are often too simple, they can be rude or even shout abuse, and sometimes they detain people instead of pursuing the enforcement of judgments. Such behaviour has often instigated resistance in the parties towards the courts.[98]

In addition, some enforcement cases concern a large amount of property, such as the public auction of a building. In such cases, the enforcement bureau of a court plays a significant role in the process of auctioning property. In recent years, the abuse of power by the heads of enforcement bureaus has resulted in some serious judicial corruption cases at both the local courts and the SPC. In 2010, Huang Songyou, who was the former Head of the Enforcement Division, Vice-President of Guangdong Higher People's Court, as well as the Vice-President of the SPC, was accused of manipulating the law in the adjudication and enforcement of judgments in several cases, so as to benefit Chen Zuolun and five other lawyers from a law firm in Guangdong province. In return for these favours, he received a total of RMB 3.9 million in bribes from these lawyers. Moreover, in 1997, while in the position of the president of the Intermediate People's Court of Zhanjiang city, Guangdong province, Huang Songyou colluded with numerous other individuals in defrauding RMB 3.08 million from his own work unit, of which he received 1.2 million. In 2010, he was sentenced to life imprisonment, deprivation of political rights for life and confiscation of all his personal property.[99]

At the local level, in November 2005, Deng Ning, who was the former Deputy Head of the Second Division of the Enforcement Bureau of Qingdao Intermediate People's Court, was accused of the crimes of abusing power, accepting bribes and using public money for private gain.[100] In June 2008, five judges at the Enforcement Bureau of Zhangzhou Xiangcheng District Court in Fujiang province were prosecuted for violating the parties' interests, abusing their power and accepting bribes. The former deputy head of the enforcement bureau was sentenced to 12 years' imprisonment, one judge received seven years' imprisonment and the three other judges were also punished.[101] In January 2008, the former vice-president of Shenzhen Intermediate People's Court was sentenced to life imprisonment for accepting bribes and providing no justifiable source for

98 *People's Courts Daily*, 7 December 1999. President Wang Shengjun of the SPC, in his report to the 1st session of the 11th NPC Standing Committee in 2009, indicated that 'The enforcement of court orders of civil cases are challenged by corruption, government red tape and low efficiency … Some civil case enforcement officers could not discipline themselves to reject dinner invitations or briberies, and handled cases unfairly for nepotism or personal benefits.' See 'Enforcement of Court Rulings Challenged by Corruption, Red Tape: Top Judge', available at http://en.chinacourt.org/public/detail.php?id=4581. Last visited September 2013.

99 'Zuigao Renmin Fayuan Yuan Fuyuanzhang Huang Songyou Yishen Beiban Wuqituxing' (Huang Songyou, the former Vice-President of the Supreme People's Court, Was Sentenced to Life Imprisonment in the Trial of the First Instance), available at http://news.sohu.com/20100119/n269681967.shtml. Last visited September 2013.

100 'Zhixingnan Beihou De Sifa Fubai' (Corruption Behind Enforcement Difficulties), available at http://news.xinhuanet.com/legal/2006-01/11/content_4037320.htm. Last visited September 2013.

101 'Fujian Zhangzhou Xiangchengqu Fayuan Zhixingju Bufen Faguan Fubai'an Jingshi' (The Corruption Case of Judges at the Enforcement Bureau of Zhangzhou Xiancheng District Court in Fujian Province), available at http://fuxing.bbs.cctv.com/viewthread.php?tid=11831308. Last visited September 2013.

large amounts of money in his possession. His criminal record was linked with four judges at the Enforcement Bureau who were accused of accepting large amounts of money in bankruptcy cases.[102]

The enforcement bureaus of higher courts have a certain centralised role in overseeing the enforcement of judgments – the more powerful the court, the higher the risk of corruption. In 2006, Wu Zhenhan, the former President of the Higher People's Court in Hunan province, was charged with the crime of accepting bribes and sentenced to death with a two-year reprieve. His illegal profits stemmed from his abuse of power in enforcing a commercial judgment involving placing a commercial building up for auction to pay off the debt.[103] In March 2007, Luo Shuping, the former head of the Enforcement Bureau of the Higher People's Court, along with the former head of the Enforcement Bureau of Chengdu City Intermediate People's Court in Sichuang province, were subject to a suspension investigation for seeking private gain while making enforcement decisions.[104] Yang Xiancai, the former head of the Enforcement Bureau of the Higher People's Court in Guangdong province, who was named 'China's No. 1 Head of the Bureau of Enforcement' because of his leading role in maintaining a good record in the enforcement of civil judgments in all courts in Guangdong province, was sentenced to life imprisonment on charges of bribery and the crime of retaining a vast amount of property from unidentified sources.[105] It was reported that in this specific higher court, some of the enforcement judges had asked parties to provide them with a 'red bag' containing money, if a judgment was successfully enforced. Such judges felt that they had helped parties greatly by enforcing the judgments; therefore they thought the parties would not mind paying a sum for the service. Large enforcement cases of corruption also often occurred, involving the evaluation and auction of assets.[106] In July 2009, Wu Xiaoqing, the head of the Enforcement Bureau of the Higher People's Court in Chungqing, was accused of abusing his power for private gain in enforcement cases involving the auction of property. He committed suicide in custody.[107]

In 2007, the first amended CiPL mainly addressed both the difficulties in enforcing civil judgments and the re-trial procedure. With regard to the enforcement of civil judgments, three major improvements can be noted. Firstly, the amendments have strengthened the compulsory enforcement measures. Article 216 introduces an 'expedite compulsory execution' system, to be applied in situations involving a judgment debtor who fails to fulfil his obligations specified in the related legal documentation and attempts instead to transfer or conceal his assets. Article 217 establishes a 'compulsory property report system' which requests that a judgment debtor who fails to fulfil his obligations, as instructed by the informant notice, should report his property situation. If he refuses to do so or issues a false report, the court may, based on concrete circumstances, impose a fine or detain that individual, his legal representative, the principal leading personnel of the unit or

102 'Yang Xiancai Luoma Keneng Yinzhi Guangdong Fayuan Gengduo Wo'an' (The Case of Yang Xiangcai May Lead to the Exposure of More Corrupt Judges at the Enforcement Bureau of Courts in Guangdong), available at http://www.singtaonet.com/china/200807/t20080721_816769.html. Last visited September 2013.

103 'Dafaguan Wu Zhenhan De Fubai Tongmeng' (Chief Judge Wu Zhenghan and His Corruption Alliance), available at http://qkzz.net/article/cfa7e3ee-f3ec-48e5-9eac-fb2c7bcc3be9.htm. Last visited September 2013. 'Hunanshen Gaoji Fayuan Yuan Yuanzhan Wu Zhenhan Yishen Beipan Sihuan' (Former President of the Higher Peoples' Court in Hunan Province Was Sentenced to Death Penalty with Reprieve), *Procuratorate Daily*, 10 November 2006.

104 *Procuratorate Daily*, *ibid.*

105 'Former Chief Judge Yang Xiancai Key Person in Bribery Case', available at http://english.caijing.com.cn/2010-07-05/110473179.html. Last visited September 2013.

106 *Ibid.*

107 'Wu Xiaoqing, Ex-Judge Facing China Bribery Charges, Commits Suicide', available at http://www.huffingtonpost.com/2009/11/30/wu-xiaoqing-ex-judge-faci_n_373698.html. Last visited September 2013.

the person directly responsible. Under Article 104, a fine on individuals can consist of any amount up to RMB 10,000 and a fine on a unit can range from RMB 10,000 to 300,000. This amount is 10 times more than those specified in the 1992 CiPL. Moreover, Article 231 provides that if a person fails to fulfil his enforcement obligations specified in the related legal documentation, the court has the power to adopt or advise a unit concerned to assist in adopting the measure of restricting the person's departure from China, making records on the credit system, making public details regarding non-performance of the person's duty through public media, and other lawful measures.

Secondly, parties involved are granted more rights. Article 202 confirms the right of a party to bring a written objection to the court if they consider the enforcement judgment to be in violation of legal provisions. The court is required to review the objection within 15 days of its receipt. In cases where the objection is tenable, the court should rule to cancel or correct the enforcement. However, in situations where the objection is untenable, the court should rule to reject the objection. If a party is not satisfied with the ruling, they may apply for a review by the relevant higher-level court within 10 days of the ruling being served. Article 203 entrusts the individual who has applied for the enforcement with the right to apply to a court at the next level for enforcement, in instances where the original court fails to bring about enforcement within six months upon receiving the application for enforcement. The relevant higher court may order the original court to guarantee enforcement within a specified period of time, or may decide to take the enforcement matter into its own hands or direct any other court to conduct enforcement. To protect third parties whose property may be mistakenly enforced, Article 204 provides that during the course of enforcement, if an individual who is not involved in the case raises a written objection to the subject matter of enforcement, the court should review the objection within 15 days of receiving it. In case the objection is admitted, the court should rule to cancel the enforcement on the subject matter; in case the objection is not permitted, the court should reject it. If that individual is dissatisfied with the ruling, they can bring a lawsuit to the court within 15 days upon the ruling being served.

Thirdly, there is a greater degree of protection for debtors. Aside from maintaining the provision that the court of first instance is the court to carry out enforcement matters, Article 201 contains a new stipulation that the same level court where the property is located can also be the court of enforcement. This enables the debtor to choose the court of enforcement, subject to concrete need. In addition, the new Article 215 extends the time period for the submission of an application for enforcement to two years, while Article 219 of the 1991 CiPL had a capped period of six months for individuals and one year for corporations. The longer period of time given to the parties involved increases the possibility of reaching agreement.

The 2012 amended CiPL made the 'expedite compulsory enforcement' more straightforward by providing in Article 240 that the enforcement officer should, upon receiving the application for enforcement or the writ of referral directing enforcement, send an enforcement notice to the person subjected to the enforcement, and may carry out this compulsory enforcement immediately. Article 247 states that if an individual fails to fulfil his obligations upon expiration of the period, a court 'should' sell the sealed-up or detained property by publicising its availability, while in Article 223 of the 2007 CiPL a weaker formulation provided that the court 'may' proceed with sale of the assets.

The latest empirical studies on numerous local courts show some improvements in the enforcement of civil judgments.[108] However, research in general has demonstrated the 'continuing

108 Xin He, 'Enforcing Commercial Judgments in the Pearl River Delta of China', 57 (2009) *The American Journal of Comparative Law*, pp. 419–457. This empirical study was conducted in 2005 by studying how 66 commercial cases were enforced at a basic people's court in Guangdong province. The author drew the conclusion that 'the enforcement outcomes are reasonable, the enforcement process is relatively efficient,

problem' of civil judgment enforcement.[109] Official documents from the SPC and the Central Political and Legal Committee also confirm that the enforcement of civil judgments continues to be problematic in many Chinese courts.[110] In October 2009 the President of the SPC, in a report to the National People's Congress Standing Committee, pointed out that the enforcement of court orders of civil cases was fundamentally undermined by corruption, government red tape and low levels of efficiency, despite notable achievements. He blamed the fact that, 'some civil case enforcement officers could not discipline themselves to reject dinner invitations or bribes, and handled cases unfairly for nepotistic or personal benefits'.[111]

The enforcement aspect in commercial disputes in China is certainly an issue of concern for foreign business entities who either have investments in China or engage in trade with Chinese companies. Foreign lawyers advise foreign companies to choose courts in major cities for their enforcement applications because they believe the enforcement judges in city courts are better trained and have more enforcement experience than judges in rural areas. Courts in Beijing and Shanghai 'are also better resourced to carry out more sophisticated investigations associated with locating the whereabouts of a respondent's bank accounts and assets. Delays are also said to be less likely in major city courts.'[112] It is obvious that improvements in the enforcement of court judgments can only be achieved if all of the parties involved change their attitude.

---

the problem of local protectionism is not serious, and the plaintiffs' impressions of the courts are also quite positive'. In another study in which he studied 60 debt collection cases at a basic court in a less-developed region in 2008 in China, Xin He also reached less critical results than most existing publications. See Xin He, 'Debt Collection in the Less Developed Regions of China: An Empirical Study from a Basic-level Court in Shaanxi Province', 206 (2011) *The China Quarterly*, pp. 253–275. Such encouraging results certainly show positive improvement in local courts, however, it is uncertain to what extent it represents a wider reality of enforcement of civil judgments in China. Another field study on courts in Shanghai illustrated that court enforcement is relatively efficient: about 80 per cent of the winning plaintiffs who requested court enforcement had their judgments enforced within one year. However, the actual result of enforcement is not very optimistic: 21 per cent replied that the courts' mandatory enforcement resulted in the full collection; 13 per cent reported that they received two-thirds or more of their judgments; 19 per cent received less than one-third; 19 per cent received nothing. Based on such data the authors concluded that approximately 50 per cent of court judgments could be characterised as unsuccessfully enforced. See Minxin Pei, Zhang Guoyan, Pei Fei and Chen Lixin, 'A Survey of Commercial Litigation in Shanghai Courts', in Randall Peerenboom (ed.), *Judicial Independence in China: Lessons for Global Rule of Law Promotion* (Cambridge: Cambridge University Press, 2010) p. 227.

109 Benjamin L. Liebman, supra note 79, pp. 23–25.

110 See *supra* note 95, 'Liubai Yishi Qiwan Bei Zhixingren Xinxi Kechaxung' (Information on the 6.17 Million Persons against Whom Enforcement Is Sought by People's Courts available on the Website).

111 See *supra* note 98, 'Enforcement of Court Rulings Challenged by Corruption, Red Tape: Top Judge'.

112 Friven Yeoh, 'Enforcement and Dispute Outcomes', in Michael J. Moser (ed.), *supra* note 14, p. 290. There are various forms of settlement of commercial disputes between Chinese and foreign companies, such as: negotiation, mediation, arbitration and litigation. Most commercial disputes are resolved by arbitration. 'In general, arbitration will be the most attractive option in most China-related disputes.' Litigation may not be advised as an attractive option for foreign companies that are involved in commercial disputes in China. This is mainly due to the underdeveloped nature of the Chinese civil litigation system as discussed above. Apart from the fact that litigation is both time-consuming and expensive, major disadvantages for foreign companies exist such as the fact that local people's courts are funded by the local government, which results in evident judicial partiality and local protectionism. In addition, litigation makes a case public, which could lead to the politicisation of the case, making a final settlement difficult. See Richard Chalk and John Choong, 'Dispute Settlement Options: An Overview', in Michael Moser (ed.), *supra* note 14, pp. 18, 14–15.

In March 2009, the SPC launched the website Quanguo Fayuan Beizhixingren Xinxi Chaxan Pingtai (National Platform for the Enquiry of Information about Parties against Whom Enforcement Is Sought by People's Courts).[113] The public can access this website to find detailed information concerning 6.17 million cases in which the enforcement of judgments is yet to materialise. By providing the information in such a transparent way, the SPC hoped it would prove to be a deterrent for debtors and pressure them into carrying out the enforcements voluntarily.[114]

Conclusion

Civil litigation in China since the 1980s has been evaluated by a Chinese commentator as encompassing elements of 'expansion, new, difficult, and big', meaning that the number of civil litigation cases has increased rapidly; new types of cases have constantly emerged; the acceptance of cases, the adjudication of cases and the enforcement of civil judgments have proven difficult; and the quantity of money involved in the cases has increasingly grown.[115] In response to these fresh challenges, Chinese courts have initiated numerous reform measures: shifting the responsibility for the collection and presentation of evidence from judges to the litigant parties; strengthening the role of open and formal hearings; enhancing judges' powers to make judgments by restricting judicial and non-judicial interference; expanding the use of the summary procedures in order to accelerate the handling of the majority of cases; and improving the enforcement of judgments by establishing new institutions and implementing various programmes.

At present, the civil trial system remains in a state of continuous experimentation and different modifications have been instigated according to the location and court in question. In the reality of settling civil and economic disputes, two distinctive pictures appear. One is the emphasis on the modern conceptions of the rule of law, due process, litigation efficiency, the system of withdrawal, burden of proof and evidentiary rules. The other is that of judges continuously applying the mediatory method of handling civil disputes, pro-actively getting involved in both the pre-trial and trial stages. They also take the initiative to visit villagers and enterprises to help them solve any possible legal disputes on the spot.

Generally speaking, Chinese courts and judges have played a unique role in strengthening the judicial settlement of disputes and ultimately contributing to social stability and economic prosperity by solving a large number of civil and commercial cases. Consequently, public access to judicial remedies has improved. However, the process of reforming civil litigation, as a component part of overall judicial reform, has been limited by both external restraints and internal incapability. Reform has mainly touched upon some procedural issues, whilst issues which are intricately connected to politics, which affect civil justice, remain largely unaffected. For instance, judicial independence from the governmental institutions remains to a large extent unattainable. As a result, the enforcement of civil judgments cannot be improved substantively, cases involving

113 *Quanguo Fayuan Beizhixingren Xinxi Chaxun Pingtai* (National Platform for the Enquiry of Information about Parties against Whom Enforcement Is Sought by People's Courts). Available at http://zhixing.court.gov.cn/search/. Last visited September 2013.

114 See *supra* note 95, 'Liubai Yishi Qiwan Bei Zhixingren Xinxi Kechaxun' (Information on the 6.17 Million Persons against Whom Enforcement Is Sought by People's Courts available on the Website). See also 'Quanguo Fayuan Beizhixingren Xinxi Chaxun Shiyong Shengming' (Instruction on the Use of the National Platform for the Enquiry of Information about Parties against Whom Enforcement Is Sought by People's Courts), available at http://zhixing.court.gov.cn/search/. Last visited September 2013.

115 Han Xiangqian, *supra* note 51, p. 452.

state-owned enterprises cannot be decided strictly according to the law, and courts have to collude with various non-judicial bodies in settling politically or socially sensitive cases. In addition, the political intervention that resulted in the resurgence of mediation in recent years has also set back attempts for civil trial reform, as it has reinforced the traditional model of mediatory justice. This change of judicial policy and practice demonstrates that judicial reform has not really changed the unbalanced relationship between judicial and political powers. Courts are in a vulnerable position in the unrelenting spotlight of political power and influence.

Within the judiciary itself, the reform started with, and has mostly emphasised, the need for efficiency in the handling of civil disputes by courts. Some courts publicised this opinion, stating explicitly that, 'the purpose of reforming the (civil) trial process is to maximise trial efficiency and accelerate the speed of trials'.[116] Some Chinese scholars have pointed out that this approach to reforming civil trials was erroneous from the very outset. It was not aimed at establishing a highly efficient, democratic and fair trial system, but rather to reduce the burdensome workload of the judges. Thus, courts mistakenly thought the reform was merely an attempt to expedite the conclusion of cases.[117] Measures of reform such as open trials, placing the burden of proof on the parties and emphasising trial procedures, are all thought to create conditions which reduce the overall burden placed on judges.[118] Judicial fairness was initially neglected. As judicial reform has deepened, judicial fairness and efficiency have been highlighted by the SPC as the objective of judicial work in the twenty-first century, though there is still a lack of concrete measures which are needed in order to achieve this goal. Furthermore, to comply with the state's prioritisation of economic development, judicial policy has disproportionately stressed that civil litigation should serve economic activities. This has resulted in the eagerness of courts to handle economic cases and proactively provide legal services, while cases involving socially vulnerable groups are often neglected.

116 Research Office of the Supreme People's Court (ed.), *Zouxiang Fating* (Going to the Court) (Beijing: Falu Chubanshe, 1997), p. 87.

117 Tian Pingan and Du Renzhe, *supra* note 36, pp. 77–79.

118 *Ibid.*, p. 78.

Chapter 6
The Administrative Trial Process

Introduction

In China, a citizen bringing a lawsuit against the decision of a governmental organ and its personnel is popularly referred to as 'common people against officials' (*min gao guan*). The court may: annul the governmental decision if it believes it to be illegal, order the defendant to perform its duty, or correct an administrative penalty that the court considers unfair.[1] Under the current legal framework, companies and other organisations (such as NGOs or State-run NGOs) have the same legal right as individuals to initiate lawsuits challenging the administrative actions of government.[2]

Compared to criminal and civil trial systems, the formal administrative litigation system in the PRC emerged only in the late 1980s.[3] In 1980, the Income Tax Law on the Sino-Foreign Joint Venture provided that if a joint venture was not satisfied with an act of the tax bureau, it could bring the dispute to court (Art. 15). The promulgation of this law reflects the interests of business entities in challenging unfavourable administrative decisions. In 1982, the Civil Procedure Law (for Trial Implementation) prescribed, for the first time, the procedure for trying administrative cases in courts. In 1986, the Regulations on Security Administration Punishment stipulated that people might bring an administrative suit before a court if they were not satisfied with the decision made by the public security organ on their appeal against security administration punishment (Art. 39). As a result, an increased number of security administrative cases were handled by the courts, which consequently launched the establishment and development of administrative trials in courts.[4]

Legislation on administrative litigation law started in 1986 when the Legal Affairs Committee of the National People's Congress Standing Committee (NPCSC) formed a research group consisting of scholars and representatives of the relevant governmental departments. The initial idea was to draft a substantive administrative law and a procedural law as in the fields of civil

1 Article 54 of the Administrative Litigation Law, promulgated by the National People's Congress on 4 April 1989 and entered into force on 1 October 1990. For publications in English on the ALL, see Kevin J. O'Brien and Lianjiang Li, 'Suing the Local State: Administrative Litigation in Rural China', 51 (January 2004) *The China Journal*, p. 75. Susan Finder, 'Like Throwing an Egg against a Stone? Administrative Litigation in the People's Republic of China', 3 (1989) *Journal of Chinese Law*, pp. 1–29. Pei Minxin. 'Citizens v. Mandarins: Administrative Litigation in China', 152 (1997) *The China Quarterly*, pp. 832–862.

2 A large proportion of plaintiffs are individual citizens; legal persons are very limited, and social organisations are even more limited. There is no nation-wide information on the composition of plaintiffs in administrative cases. A limited survey in Hubei province showed that individuals accounted for about 80 per cent of plaintiffs, 17 per cent were legal persons and 3 per cent were other social organisations. See Lin Lihong, Shen Xiaoping and Huang Qihui, 'Hubei Xingzheng Shenpan Xianzhuang Diaocha Baogao' (An Investigation Report on the Status Quo of Administrative Trial in Hubei Province), 10 (2009) *Hubei Shehui Kexue* (Hubei Social Science), p. 168.

3 For a short overview of the development of judicial review in China, see Lin Feng, *Administrative Law Procedures and Remedies in China* (Hong Kong and London: Sweet & Maxwell, 1996), pp. 114–115.

4 Fan Fu, 'Wouguo Xingzheng Shenpan De Lishi Huigu Yu Zhanwang' (Historical Recall and Future Prospect of China's Administrative Litigation System), 10 (2004) *Xingzheng Zhifa Yu Xingzheng Shenpan*, p. 177.

and criminal law. However, it soon proved too difficult to draft a substantive administrative law. Professor Jiang Ping, one of the members of the research group, proposed drafting legislation which aimed to primarily meet the increased need of judicial practice in the administrative law arena. This was accepted by the Legal Affairs Committee of the NPCSC. Thus, in February 1987, the group commenced drafting the statute.[5] This legislative initiative was supported by the Central Communist Party. In 1987 the Report of the 13th Communist Party Congress proposed 'to enact legislation on administrative litigation in order to strengthen oversight of administrative work and administrative personnel, and to punish ignorance of duty and other conduct violating law and disciplines'.[6] In November 1988, the *People Daily* published the Draft Administrative Litigation Law to solicit public opinions. In April 1989, the Administrative Litigation Law (ALL) was promulgated by the National People's Congress, and entered into effect in October 1990.[7] The enactment of ALL is considered a milestone in the unification and standardisation of administrative litigation in China.

It is important to note that the ALL contains only 75 Articles, most of which are too general to provide a strong and sufficiently clear basis for the regular handling of cases by the courts. Subsequently, the SPC has issued a number of judicial opinions to provide detailed explanations and guidelines to courts. These include: the 1991 Explanations on Several Issues concerning the Implementation of Administrative Litigation Law (for trial implementation),[8] which was modified in 2000; the 1997 Rule on Several Issues concerning Adjudication of Administrative Compensation Cases;[9] the 2002 Rules on Several Issues concerning Administrative Litigation Evidence;[10] the 2008 Rules on Several Issues concerning Jurisdiction over Administrative Cases;[11] the 2008 Rules on Several Issues concerning Withdrawal of Administrative Litigation;[12] the 2009 Rules on Several Issues concerning Trial of Administrative License Cases;[13] and the 2011 Rules on Several Issues concerning Trial of Administrative Cases about Disclosure of Government Information.[14] In response

5 *Ibid.*, p. 178.

6 Liang Fengyun, 'Guanyu Wanshan Xingzheng Shenpan Tizhi Dewenti' (Issues on Perfecting the Administrative Trial System), in Jiang Bixin et al. (eds), *Zhongguo Xingzheng Susong Zhidu De Wanshan: Xingzheng Susongfa Xiugai Wenti Shiwu Yanjiu* (Improvement of the Administrative Litigation System in China) (Beijing: Falu Chubanshe, 2005), p. 7.

7 For the legislative background, see Susan Finder, *supra* note 1, pp. 1–29. Chinese legal scholars have contributed significantly to drafting the ALL. In the 1980s, Professors Wang Mingyang, Gong Xiangre, Luo Haocai and Ying Songnian translated or edited foreign books and articles concerning foreign administrative law and administrative litigation law. Though China did not transplant a foreign administrative litigation law, study of foreign law was used as a reference in developing the Chinese system. See Fan Fu, *supra* note 4, pp. 176–177.

8 *Fa (xing) fa* No. 19 [1991]. Available at http://www.law-lib.com/law/law_view.asp?id=7697. Last visited September 2013.

9 *Fashi* No. 10 [1997]. Available at http://www.lawyee.net/Act/Act_Display.asp?ChannelID=1010100&ItemID=541026&RID=25252#541026. Last visited September 2013.

10 *Fashi* No. 21 [2002]. Available at http://www.law-lib.com/law/law_view.asp?id=40817. Last visited September 2013.

11 *Fashi* No. 1 [2008]. Available at http://www.law-lib.com/law/law_view.asp?id=243717. Last visited September 2013.

12 *Fashi* No. 2 [2008]. Available at http://www.law-lib.com/law/law_view.asp?id=243716. Last visited September 2013.

13 *Fashi* No. 20 [2009]. Available at http://www.law-lib.com/law/law_view.asp?id=305821. Last visited September 2013.

14 *Fashi* No. 17 [2011]. Available at http://www.law-lib.com/law/law_view.asp?id=358265. Last visited September 2013.

to China's entry into the WTO, the SPC issued a number of opinions to meet the need of judicial review, such as: the 2002 Rules on Several Issues concerning Adjudication of Administrative Cases of International Trade; the 2002 Rules on Several Issues concerning Administrative Cases of Anti-dumping; and the 2002 Rules on Several Issues concerning Administrative Cases of Anti-subsidy.[15]

In addition, following the promulgation of the ALL, a number of important pieces of administrative legislation were promulgated by the NPCSC.[16] The 1994 State Compensation Law provides citizens the right to request compensation for illegal government acts alongside an administrative litigation action, or present them directly to the relevant government bureau. The 1996 Administrative Penalty Law stipulates that the imposition of fines and other punitive measures by governmental organs should be based on laws and administrative regulations, and that the implementation of administrative penalties should follow legal procedures. The 1999 Administrative Reconsideration Law allows citizens to submit an application to competent departments for the administrative reconsideration of government actions that violate their legal rights and interests. The 2004 Administrative Licensing Law provides courts with jurisdiction in handling disputes relating to administrative licensing. These administrative laws, coupled with the ALL, not only constitute the major sources of law that courts use to handle administrative cases but also set limits on the arbitrary acts of government.[17]

Originally, administrative cases were tried by judges in courts' civil chambers, but from 1986, local courts began establishing administrative chambers. On 6 October 1986, the Intermediate People's Court in Wuhan city of Hubei province became the first intermediate court to set up an administrative chamber in China. On the same date, the Basic People's Court in Miluo city of Hunan province established the first administrative chamber among all the basic people's courts in

15 The WTO-related judicial interpretations have been viewed as significant to the development of the judicial review system in China. In joining the WTO, China committed to comply with the WTO principles of transparency and judicial review, which means administrative decision-making in various trade-related areas are subject to judicial review. See Chris X. Lin, 'A Quiet Revolution: An Overview of China's Justice Reform', 4(2) 2003 *Asian-Pacific Law and Policy Journal*, pp. 291–292.

16 For English version of these Laws, see the website of the Congressional Executive Committee on China, http://www.cecc.gov/pages/selectLaws/administrativeLaw/administrativeLaw.php Last visited September 2013. Traditionally, China did not have a set of administrative and administrative litigation laws to offer private parties legal remedies against governmental institutions. Why then since the 1990s has the central government allowed the development of administrative law and the administrative litigation system? According to He Xin, 'China's legal system has not evolved in a vacuum; it is a part of politics. More specifically, China's administrative law is not simply an application of modern legal principles such as "administrative fairness", "due process", "balancing" or "power control". It is also a mechanism for the State to restrain the power of lower-level governments and to discipline their relevant behaviour, ultimately achieving the goal of *political* control. Since it is a kind of control that is exercised through laws and legal institutions, it might be called "judicial control".' He Xin, 'Administrative Law as a Mechanism for Political Control in Contemporary China', in Stephanie Balme and Michael W. Dowdle (eds), *Building Constitutionalism in China* (New York: Palgrave Macmillan, 2009), pp. 144–145.

17 After 30 years of legal construction it is evident that requiring government organs and officials to follow the law is essential to foster a culture of legal authority. Peerenboom has pointed out: 'China's administrative officials are themselves one of the major obstacles to rule of law. They regularly abuse their authority, ignore central laws and pass inconsistent administrative regulations that promote their own institutional interests. Accordingly, one of the biggest challenges facing administrative law reformers has been to overcome the traditional attitude of governmental officials and create a culture of legality.' Randall Peerenboom, 'A Government of Laws: Democracy, Rule of Law and Administrative Law Reform in the PRC', 12(34) 2003 *Journal of Contemporary China*, p. 54.

China.[18] The Supreme People's Court set up the administrative division in 1988. By 1990, all of the higher people's courts, 99 per cent of the intermediate people's courts and 91 per cent of the basic people's courts had an administrative chamber.[19]

Despite the institutional advancement, the gap between the objectives of the ALL and its actual implementation by courts cannot be underestimated. This gap can be assessed from two contrasting perspectives that consequently outline a positive and a negative aspect. Regarding the negative, there are 'three difficulties' in implementing the ALL, namely: the difficulty in having cases accepted by courts; the difficulty in having cases handled fairly by the court; and the difficulty in enforcing the court's judgment. The positive aspect has evolved from changes that have taken place since the ALL was drafted in 1989, when courts had sporadic experience in handling administrative cases and the types of administrative cases were also incredibly limited, meaning the ALL contains some fundamental restrictions on the courts' ability to file and adjudicate cases. However, over the past two decades, consciousness accorded to citizen's rights has increased, coupled with a rise in the number and variety of administrative cases; this has forced the courts to take a more extensive approach in interpreting the ALL. As a result courts have been handling some administrative cases which could be considered to be beyond the scope of the ALL.

This chapter first examines the limits of the ALL with respect to the scope of acceptance and handling of cases by courts, and the process whereby judicial practice has progressively developed ahead of the law. Second, it discusses the shortcomings of the jurisdiction of the courts in handling administrative cases and the subsequent appeal for establishing special administrative courts. Third, the main differences between the adjudication of civil and administrative cases are reviewed. Fourth, data is used to illustrate that the number of administrative cases is relatively small as a result of various factors, and that the comparatively high rate of cases won by plaintiffs is largely due to voluntary or reluctant withdrawal. The withdrawal of claims can be generally viewed as a win for the plaintiff because it usually means the defendant has favourably adjusted their original action or an out of court agreement has been reached. The final section will demonstrate the positive impact of the ALL upon the courts' handling of administrative cases and the challenges that the Chinese judiciary face in improving the currently infantile administrative litigation system.

The Administrative Litigation Law and Practice

The Scope of Case Acceptance and Handling

Concrete versus abstract administrative actions The 1989 ALL combines both enumerative and exclusive approaches in setting out the scope of the courts' jurisdiction to accept administrative cases. Article 11 provides that the courts should accept actions initiated by citizens, legal persons or other organisations against 'concrete administrative actions' of administrative organs. These 'concrete administrative actions' are spelled out in Art. 11 as:

1. administrative penalties such as detention, fines, revocation of a business license or permit, order of suspension of production or business activities, or confiscation of property;

---

18 Liang Fengyun, *supra* note 6, p. 6.

19 Xing Chungying, 'Ershiyi Shiji: Zhongguo Xuyao Shenmeyangde Sifaquanli?' (Twenty-first Century: What Kind of Judicial Power Does China Need?), in Xing Chungying (ed.), *Gong Fa* (Public Law) (Beijing: Falu Chubanshe, 2002), p. 8.

2. compulsory administrative measures such as restriction of freedom of the person or the sealing up, seizure or freezing of property;
3. infringement by an administrative organ of the managerial autonomy of a business as stipulated by law;
4. refusal to issue or refusal to reply to an application for a permit or license conforming to the provisions of law;
5. refusal to perform a duty required by law regarding the protection of one's personal and property rights;
6. failing to distribute a pension according to law;
7. demanding administrative organs to perform their duties according to law;
8. infringement of other personal and property rights.

In order not to be completely limited by the eight types of acts, Article 11 concludes with the general provision that the courts should also accept other administrative cases, which may be initiated in accordance with the provisions of relevant laws and regulations.

Article 12 excludes the courts' jurisdiction to review the following four categories of cases:

1. state acts relating to defence and foreign affairs;
2. administrative rules and regulations, or decisions and orders with general binding force issued by administrative organs – these are generally referred to as abstract administrative actions;
3. decisions made by an administrative organ concerning rewards, punishments, appointments, and dismissal of administrative agency personnel[20] – these are considered internal personnel acts;
4. final decisions made by some administrative organs with the authority to issue final decisions.[21]

20 Excluding such internal decisions from judicial review was justified on the basis that at the establishment of the administrative litigation system, priority was given to administrative acts that affect external entities. Moreover, at that time, the civil servant system was not fully established and hence it would have been too difficult for courts to examine internal decisions. However, this exclusion has generated widespread criticism. Some experts suggest that when the ALL is revised, administrative acts concerning fundamental rights of the personnel of administrative organs should be included in the scope of judicial review. It is argued that decisions regarding appointment, demotion, removal and mandatory retirement ages affect the professional career, salary and welfare of civil servants. Thus, such decisions should be viewed as affecting their fundamental rights and should not be excluded from judicial review. Cai Xiaoxue, 'Guanyu Xingzheng Susong Shou'an Fanweide Jige Wenti' (A Few Issues on the Scope of Accepting Administrative Cases), in Jiang Bixin, *supra* note 6, p. 78.

21 According to the laws in China, the circumstances within which administrative organs have the authority to issue final decisions include: (1) The decisions made after administrative review by the governments at provincial level confirming the right of ownership in or the right to the use of natural resources such as land, mineral resources, waters, forests, mountains or hills, grassland, wasteland, tidal flats and sea areas, on the basis of the decisions made by the State Council or the governments at provincial level regarding the survey, delimitation or readjustment of administrative division or regarding land requisition, are final (Article 30(2) of Administrative Reconsideration Law). (2) If an applicant refuses to accept a specific administrative act taken by a department under the State Council or by the government at provincial level, he or she could apply to the department or the government stated above for administrative review. If he or she still refuses to accept a decision made after administrative review, he or she could bring an administrative lawsuit to the court or apply to the State Council for arbitration, which should give a final ruling (Article 14 of Administrative Reconsideration Law). (3) If a foreigner who is fined or detained by a public security organ refuses to accept the penalty, he may, within 15 days of receiving notification, appeal to the public security organ at the next

The most controversial issue in the scope of acceptance of administrative cases revolves around the debate between 'concrete administrative actions' versus 'abstract administrative actions'. Concrete administrative actions are defined as acts which concern the rights and duties of citizens, legal persons and other organisations and are carried out by governmental agencies and their officers, organisations receiving delegated powers via laws or regulations, or organisations or individuals entrusted by administrative organisations with the power to carry out administrative functions.[22] Abstract administrative actions refer to the rules and decisions issued by various administrative organs with a general legally binding nature. They can be administrative regulations of the State Council, rules of ministries or rules and normative documents from all levels of local governments.

The issue as to whether the scope of acceptance of administrative cases should be limited only to concrete administrative actions has been long debated. Those who choose not to include abstract acts within the scope of the ALL argue that if such acts violate laws, they can be corrected by the supervisory system provided for in the Constitution and the Legislative Law. For instance, the National People's Congress has the power to abolish administrative regulations and decisions of the State Council if they are contrary to the Constitution and law; the Local People's Congress Standing Committee has the power to withdraw inappropriate decisions and orders of the corresponding government level; the State Council has the power to change or withdraw inappropriate orders, instructions, rules and decisions of ministries and local governments. Additionally, the local government at the county level and above has the power to change or withdraw inappropriate orders and decisions made by lower-level governments. Thus, for the proponents of concrete actions, the operation of the existing supervisory system is sufficient to remedy those situations where abstract administrative actions violate the law. It is further argued that because abstract administrative actions have general binding force, if any person could potentially bring a lawsuit against an abstract act to court, the courts could become overwhelmed. Moreover, detractors suggest that if an abstract administrative action satisfies the interest of the majority, the minority who wish to challenge the abstract action should respect the public interest represented by the majority. If an abstract administrative action should violate the majority's interest, it would be more effective to utilise the legislative organ or higher-level administrative organs to correct the action rather than to entrust responsibility to individual citizens to rectify the situation by initiating a lawsuit.[23]

Notably, most administrative law experts support the inclusion of abstract administrative actions within the scope of acceptance by courts.[24] In their opinions, the existing supervision system lacks procedural clarity and its practical operation has proven that it is significantly difficult to rectify

---

higher level, which will make the final decision; he may also directly file a suit to the court (Article 29 of Law on Control of Entry and Exit of Foreigners). (4) If a citizen who is fined or detained by a public security organ refuses to accept the penalty, he may, within 15 days of receiving notification, appeal to the public security organ at the next higher level, which will make the final decision; he may also directly file a suit to the court (Article 15 of Law on the Control of the Exit and Entry of Citizens).

22 See the SPC's 1991 Explanations on Several Issues in Implementing Administrative Litigation Law (for trial implementation), Art. 1(1).

23 Discussed in Jiang Mingan (ed.), 'Xingzhengfa Yu Xingzheng Susongfa' (Administrative Law and Administrative Litigation Law) (Beijing: Beijing Daxue Chubanshe, 1999), p. 318.

24 See Jiang Bixin, 'Xingzheng Susongfa Yu Chouxiang Xingzheng Xingwei' (Administrative Litigation Law and Abstract Administrative Actions), 3 (2009) *Xingzheng Faxue Yanjiu* (Administrative Law Review), p. 13. Ma Huaide, 'Xiugai Xingzheng Susongfa Xu Zhongdian Jiejue De Jige Wenti' (Several Key Problems to Be Solved in Revising the Administrative Litigation Law), 26 (2005) *Jiangsu Shehui Kexue* (Journal of Jiangsu Social Science), p. 111. Hu Jinguang, 'Lun Woguo Chouxiang Xingzheng Xingwei De Sifa Shencha' (Research on the Judicial Review of Abstract Administrative Actions in China), 5 (2005) Zhongguo Renmin Daxue Xuebao (Journal of Renmin University of China), p. 9.

problems of unlawful abstract administrative actions efficiently. The difficulty arises because although the State Council and local people's congress have the power to amend administrative rules, decisions or orders (under the recording system provided by the Legislative Law), in practice they have not effectively exercised that power. Consequently, this has allowed serious violations of citizens' interests, such as the illegal collection of fees, to be committed and remain unchallenged.

They also point out that many abstract administrative actions are issued as 'red stamp documents' (*hongtou wenjian*), which lack the nature of 'law' but in reality have the function of law. It is not uncommon that such documents contain provisions in violation of law and regulation, and directly infringe citizens' legitimate rights. Consequently, as abstract administrative actions affect citizens on a larger scale, if the actions violate the law the adverse impacts have the potential to be wider and more destructive than unlawful concrete administrative actions. Since an abstract administrative action is often the root of a concrete administrative action, correction should be made at the origin. Furthermore, over the last decade judges have accumulated experience in reviewing abstract administrative actions in order to decide the legality of concrete administrative actions.[25]

In practice, not only may it prove difficult to determine whether an action is abstract or concrete, but when reviewing the legality of a concrete action judges often have to examine an abstract action. It was reported that after the ALL became effective, about 30 per cent of requests from higher people's courts to the Supreme People's Court concerned issues regarding the scope of acceptance of cases.[26] Taking this controversy into account, the 2000 SPC Explanations on Several Issues concerning the Implementation of Administrative Litigation Law (Explanations) did not use the term 'concrete administrative actions'. Article 1 of the Explanations states that it is within the jurisdiction of the people's courts to hear cases brought pursuant to the law by citizens, legal persons or other organisations who are unsatisfied with the administrative actions decided by competent state administrative organs and their personnel. Article 1 can therefore be interpreted as an extension of Article 11 of the ALL, but at the same time cannot be said to have amended Article 11. This is because judicial opinions of the Supreme People's Court cannot change promulgations by the highest legislature, such as the ALL. Thus, Article 1 explicitly mentions that administrative actions (including abstract administrative actions) listed in Article 12 of the ALL are excluded from the scope of acceptance of cases. Despite the remaining ambiguity, the Explanations changed the approach employed to define the parameters of the scope from a combination of enumerative and exclusive methods to a combination of general confirmative and exclusive methods – a desirable transformation. One might expect a future amendment of the ALL to replace the term 'concrete administrative actions' with simply 'administrative actions'. Several reform-minded Chinese legal experts suggest that under the current legal framework, judges should not interpret concrete administrative actions narrowly. These experts further argue that a revised ALL should provide generally that citizens, legal persons and social organisations who are not satisfied with the administrative actions or absence of acts of administrative organs or non-administrative organs exercising public power may bring lawsuits to courts in accordance with the law.[27]

Personal and property rights, and other rights Article 2 of the ALL stipulates that citizens, legal persons or social organisations should have the right to bring lawsuits to courts if they believe their 'legitimate rights and interests' are infringed by a concrete administrative action of an administrative organ and its personnel. At the same time, Article 11 of the ALL explicitly specifies

25 Cai Xiaoxue, *supra* note 20, pp. 46–52.

26 *Ibid.*, p. 94.

27 *Ibid.*, p. 94.

that courts should accept citizens' actions against concrete administrative actions that are deemed to have infringed 'personal and property rights'. It remains uncertain whether courts are competent in reviewing administrative actions which allegedly violate other rights that are not clearly 'personal and property rights' such as the freedom of association, freedom of assembly, freedom of religion and other political rights.[28]

The reason for limiting the definition of 'legitimate rights and interests' to 'personal and property rights' can be explained by the fact that when the ALL was drafted, there were inadequate substantive laws upon which courts could handle cases beyond those involving personal and property rights.[29] However, since the ALL became effective, a number of laws concerning other rights have been promulgated by the National People's Congress Standing Committee, including the 1989 Law on Assembly and Demonstration, the 1994 Labour Law and the 1995 Law on Education. The State Council has also issued administrative regulations, such as the 1989 Regulations on Registration and Administration of Social Organisations and the 1997 Regulations on Publishing Administration. Thus, sufficient substantive laws on citizens' rights other than personal and property rights appear to be available to provide a legal basis for courts to review the legality of administrative actions with regard to these rights.

It is debatable, however, that Article 11 does not actually exclude other rights. This is because its last clause provides that courts should also accept other administrative cases, which may be initiated in accordance with the provisions of relevant laws and regulations. This general description can be interpreted to suggest that administrative litigation cases are not merely limited to those involving personal and property rights, but also include other legitimate rights, such as the right to work, the right to education, political rights and other social rights. Although this interpretation may not have been the intention of the legislature, it can be utilised to prevent a narrow interpretation of Article 11. To go further, China has ratified the International Covenant on Economic, Social and Cultural Rights, and signed the International Covenant on Civil and Political Rights. Both these Covenants request that states parties protect their citizens' right to life, right to move, right to work, right to education and other personal freedoms. Therefore, a revised ALL should provide a judicial remedy to reflect the protection of these rights in order to make Chinese law comply with international human rights law.

Some recently promulgated laws have used the general term 'legitimate rights and interests'. For instance, Articles 60 and 61 of the 2006 amended Law on Protection of Minors and Article 52 of the 2005 amended Law on Protection of Women's Rights and Interests clearly provide that an individual can bring a suit against concrete administrative actions infringing his or her legitimate rights and interests.[30] Consequently, when the ALL is revised, other legitimate rights ought expressly to be included in its scope.

In judicial practice, the narrow approach of limiting the scope of judicial review to personal and property rights cannot continue considering the pressure on courts to resolve an increasing number

28 Jianfu Chen, *Chinese Law: Context and Transformation* (Leiden and Boston, MA: Martinus Nijhoff, 2008), p. 249. Fu Yulin and Randall Peerenboom, 'A New Analytic Framework for Understanding and Promoting Judicial Independence in China', in Randall Peerenboom (ed.), *Judicial Independence in China: Lessons for Global Rule of Law Promotion* (Cambridge: Cambridge University Press, 2010), p. 131.

29 Cai Xiaoxue, *supra* note 20, pp. 53–54.

30 The Law on the Protection of Minors was promulgated in 1991 and amended in 2006. The Law on Protection of Women's Rights and Interests was promulgated in 1992 and amended in 2005. Art. 15 provides that the state will guarantee women cultural and educational rights equal to those enjoyed by men. Art. 52 provides that when a woman's legitimate rights are violated, she has the right to require the relevant administrative organ to resolve the situation, or to bring a lawsuit to court in accordance with law.

of types of administrative disputes. Over the past two decades, Chinese courts have gradually increased the acceptance of administrative cases beyond personal and property rights. This can be demonstrated, for example, in *Dong Jian v. Ministry of Health*. In 2004, Dong Jian and a few eye experts submitted an application to the Ministry of Health to establish an 'association of love eyes' (the intention was to set up an association with the purpose of helping people to take good care of their eyes). Under the Chinese legal framework, the formulation of an association first requires the approval of a relevant administrative organ as a sponsor, followed by approval from the civil affairs bureau of the government. Despite making contact several times with the Ministry, Mr Dong did not receive any written reaction from the Ministry. In February 2005, Mr Dong brought the case to the No. 1 Intermediate People's Court in Beijing, claiming that the absence of formal reaction by the Ministry constituted an 'absence of administrative action'.[31] Interestingly, this case touches upon the politically sensitive issue of freedom of association in China.[32] Although Mr Dong did not win the case, the fact that the Court actually heard the case was a testament to the extension of judicial recognition – that is, if a citizen's initiative to establish an association is ignored by a governmental organ, the former has legal standing to sue the latter in court.

While the *Dong* case only incidentally illustrates how the court has tried to expand the scope of the ALL, the courts' handling of cases relating to the right to education represents a systematic breakthrough with a wider social impact. Article 46 of the Constitution and Article 9 of the 2006 amended Law on Education all provide for a citizen's right to education. Article 30 of the 1998 Law on Higher Education provides that all higher education institutions and universities enjoy the status of being a legal person from the day of establishment, and concomitantly enjoy civil rights and bear civil liability. According to Article 28 of the 2006 amended Law on Education, schools (including universities) and other educational institutions enjoy wide administrative powers relating to educational management, such as control over admissions, rewarding and punishing students, and the issuance of certificates of graduation, diplomas, degrees. There are some additional administrative regulations which entrust universities with a variety of administrative powers. In reality, a university plays a dual function – having the status of both civil subject and administrative subject.

However, it remains debatable whether students can challenge an action of a university by initiating an administrative case against it. A narrow interpretation of Article 11 of the ALL would exclude such a dispute since it would fall beyond a citizen's personal and property rights. In judicial practice, many cases of students litigating against universities were declared by the courts to be inadmissible.[33] For example, one reported case was that of a female student in a university in southwest China who went travelling with her boyfriend in the summer of 2002. After their trip,

31 Li Gang, 'Dong Jian Su Weishengbu Budafu Choubei Shetuan Shenqing Xingzheng Susong'an: Baiyu Yixue Zhuanjia Changyi Sheli "Aiyan Xiehui" 5 nian Weiguo, Faqiren Qisu Qingqiu Baohu Jieshe Ziyou' (The Administrative Case of *Dong Jian v. Ministry of Health* against the Latter's Absence of Action Concerning Application for Setting Up an Association: Hundreds of Doctors Took the Initiative for the Establishment of the 'Association of Love Eyes' for Five Years without Result, the Initiators Sued to Appeal for Protection of Freedom of Association), available at http://www.china-review.com/lafi.asp?id=17559. Last visited September 2013.

32 For the current legal and practical situation on freedom of association in China, see Yuwen Li (ed.), *Freedom of Association in China and Europe: Comparative Perspective in Law and Practice* (Leiden and Boston, MA: Martinus Nijhoff, 2005).

33 Courts often refuse such claims on the grounds that such dispute belongs to the internal management of the university. See He Bing, 'Lihai De Fenpei: Women Shenbian De Falu' (Distribution of Interests: Law around Us), (Shanghai: Sanlian Shudian, 2005), pp. 180, 192–193.

she tested pregnant at the university hospital. The student induced an abortion in a hospital outside the university. However, the university hospital informed the relevant department of the university about her pregnancy. When the teacher in charge of her class requested the university to investigate what happened to her, she admitted the fact that she was pregnant, but refused requests to 'provide details of sexual intercourse' and to 'confess that she is degenerate'. Her rejection resulted in her and her boyfriend's dismissal from the university. The girl's family supported her in bringing the case to court with the hope that the university would withdraw its 'administrative punishment decision'. The court tried to mediate between the two parties, but failed. The court then rejected the complaint on the excuse that 'the university's decision is an issue of internal administrative management conduct, which is beyond the court's jurisdiction'. The student appealed to a higher court and was rejected under the same rationale.[34]

Nevertheless, the growing number of disputes between students and universities that are brought to court make it impossible to ignore students' claims. The main argument used to support the courts' acceptance of cases relating to education is that the right to education is enshrined in the Constitution. Judicial remedies should therefore be provided when such a right is deemed to have been violated.

In 1998, the case *Tian Yong v. Beijing Science and Technology University* opened to judicial review the administrative management and degree management of universities. Tian Yong began his study at Beijing Science and Technology University in 1994. In February 1996, he was found carrying a note containing an electromagnetic formula while taking an examination. Though he did not look at the formula, he was judged to be a cheat by the inspecting teacher and, in March 1996, the university ordered Tian Yong to quit the university according to the university's rules. However, the university did not carry out the proper procedure in discontinuing his university study. Tian Yong completed his four years' study with good results and met all the requirements for obtaining a certificate of graduation. However, in 1998, the university refused to issue the certificate on the grounds that he had lost his qualification to study at the university in 1996.

The Basic People's Court in Haidian district in Beijing handled the case, by supporting most of Tian Yong's claims. The court stated that, under the current situation, although some public units (*shiye danwei*) and other organisations did not have the status of administrative organs, the law had entrusted them with certain functions of administrative management. The ALL specifies that administrative organs are the defendants in administrative litigation cases, in order to protect the rights of the people who are under the authority of such administrative functions and to supervise public units and social organisations in carrying out their functions according to law. Based on this, the court decided it had the jurisdiction to handle Tian Yong's case. The court took the view that the punishment of ordering Tian Yong to quit the university exceeded the relevant rules of the Ministry of Education. Thus, it ordered the university to issue the certificate of graduation to Tian Yong. Tian Yong also claimed RMB 3,000 in economic compensation. However, the court considered this claim was beyond the scope of administrative compensation provided in Arts 3

34 This case highlights some important procedural issues. The court of the first instance started mediation between the parties, which illustrates its actual acceptance of the case. But, instead of trying the case and delivering a judgment, the court simply decided to reject the case on the pretext that it was beyond its jurisdiction. He Bing observed that it was impossible to obtain the true reasons about why the court refused to handle the case. Nonetheless, an important consideration of the court may well have been its reluctance to challenge the authority of the higher education institutions. Universities control educational resources that are extremely valuable for citizens. Such resources may be used as weight and leverage by universities in the power-dealing market. This weight, coupled with the complex network of personal relationships, led to the loss of judicial balance in the court. He Bing, *ibid.*, pp. 161–162.

and 4 of the State Compensation Law, which covered only actual damage to personal and property rights. Furthermore, in response to Tian Yong's claim that the university should issue him a public apology in order to restore his reputation, the court held that although the decision to order him to quit the university could not be sustained, the university's actions had not impaired his reputation.[35]

Another landmark case is *Liu Yanwen v. Peking University*. In this case Liu Yanwen, a PhD student at the Faculty of Radio at Peking University, completed all the courses and defended his PhD thesis. The thesis was approved by the Committee of Thesis Defence and the Committee on Grades of the Department of Radio. According to the procedure, the thesis was submitted to the Degree Review Committee of Peking University, where Liu's thesis was rejected. Liu tried various channels to discover why his thesis had been rejected, but the only answer he received was that there were 'not many votes in his favour'. After he failed to resolve the issue with the university, Liu brought his case to the Basic People's Court in Haidian district in Beijing in 1999, where he won the case but only to a limited degree.[36] The judgment requested Peking University to issue a certificate of graduation to Liu since he completed all the courses required. As to the diploma, the court ordered the Degree Review Committee of Peking University to re-evaluate the thesis. It did not, however, ask the university to issue the diploma of PhD degree since the Committee did not give a positive review.[37] Ultimately though, the court did not engage in a penetrating investigation and as a consequence the real reasons behind the Committee's refusal of Liu's thesis remained unanswered. One informal theory is that the disapproval of Liu's thesis was actually a retaliatory strike at Liu's promoter who once disapproved the thesis of another PhD candidate. The theory holds that the disgruntled promoter of the student who Liu's promoter had rejected sat on Liu's Review Committee and took the opportunity to seek revenge by disapproving Liu's thesis.[38] Whatever happened, the court missed the opportunity to find the truth of the case and consequently the chance to grant full-fledged protection to the student.

The case of Liu Yanwen has generated heated debate among legal scholars in Beijing. Some distinguished law scholars in China have expressed that the court should not accept such cases at all. Their reasoning is based on the fact that when the court handled the academic dispute it interfered with academic freedom. Professor Su Li, at the Law School of Peking University argued that the court's dealing with Liu's case was laughable because the court infringed academic freedom.[39] Professor Wang Liming, at the Law School of Renmin University, indicated:

> The Court was doing a thing that it was incapable of doing. The judiciary had better not get involved in academic decisions. Academic decisions are to be made autonomously by universities. A court's judgment that intends to change such academic decisions, not only hinders the autonomy of the university, but also shows disrespect to academic freedom.[40]

35 The judgment was published in 4 (1999) *Gazette of the SPC*, pp. 139–142.

36 The judgment can be found at http://www.publiclaw.cn/Comment/Details.asp?NewsId=631&ClassId=&ClassName=典型案例. Last visited September 2013.

37 It is worth noting that, in this case, the court took the Degree Review Committee of Peking University as the defendant. In other cases relating to obtaining a university diploma, *Wu Yaxue v. Jinan University*, *He Je v. Huanan Normal University*, *Yang Qing v. Zhongshan University*, different courts had treated the universities as defendants rather than the relevant committees. See Dou Jiaying, 'Guangzhoushi Liangji Fayuan Shenli Gaoxiao Xingzheng Anjian De Tansuo' (Experiments of Two Level Courts in Guangzhou in Handling University Administrative Cases), 18 (2006) *Xingzheng Zhifa Yu Xingzheng Shenpan*, pp. 134–135.

38 He Bing, *supra* note 33, p. 193.

39 *Ibid.*, p. 179.

40 *Ibid.*, p. 179. He cited *Zhongguo Qingnianbao* (China Youth Daily), 9 January 2000.

He Bing, as Liu's lawyer, commented on the irony of these particular professors' positions. He noted that they often call for judicial justice, and desire that the radiance of the judiciary will illuminate every corner of the land. However, when the dispute touches their own field, academia, they hold up the flag of academic freedom to shield themselves. He incisively pointed out:

> Let us imagine, if freedom itself can be used to refuse the judiciary, like if the freedom to conclude contracts which is provided in the contract law, or the freedom of speech guaranteed in the Constitution, could all be used as shields to keep the court away, then what could a court do?[41]

In He Bing's view, the bringing of disputes raised in academic management to court does not necessarily result in academia losing its freedom. A court cannot resolve academic disputes, but this does not mean that the court cannot resolve disputes of academic management and certification. These are two different kinds of disputes.[42]

The cases of *Liu Yanwen v. Peking University* and *Tian Yong v. Beijing Science and Technology University* have been referred to by other courts in handling similar cases.[43] Importantly, from the two cases the status of the university as a subject of administrative litigation is confirmed in judicial practice.[44] Hence, case law has played a significant role in the courts' acceptance of cases relating to the right to education. A narrow interpretation of Article 11 of the ALL could exclude courts from hearing such cases. This has not occurred due to the above-mentioned two cases, which have been widely reported and supported by the SPC. As a result, judicial practice reveals that though the scope of the courts' acceptance of cases is based on the general provision in law, for certain ambiguous cases, case law has been used as a supplement to widen the ambit of areas subject to judicial review.

Significantly, the fact that courts have been allowing the judicial review of cases relating to certificates of graduation and diplomas reflects the courts' progressively growing liberal attitude in interpreting and applying the ALL. Following the precedent cases, numerous similar cases have been dealt with by courts all over China. Given the autonomy of university education, freedom of academics and the capacity of judicial review, some courts ceased to accept such cases temporarily, but resumed hearing them later on.[45] According to a report made by the Administrative Chamber of the Higher People's Court in Shanghai, from 2003 to April 2005, courts in Shanghai handled and concluded a total of 31 such cases. The outcome was: three judgments were in favour of the administrative actions of the universities; one judgment nullified the university's administrative action; 13 judgments refuted student litigation claims; three decisions retorted student appeals; in 10 cases students withdrew themselves; and one case was moved to another organisation to handle it. Most universities responded in a timely fashion to the courts. When they realised there

41 *Ibid.*, p. 193.

42 *Ibid.*

43 According to an interview I conducted with a judge who has worked for more than 10 years in the administrative chamber of Hongshan Basic People's Court in Wuhan, she handled a number of cases where students sued universities by relying on the two cases mentioned as a reference. Hongshan Court is located in the university area of Wuhan; therefore the number of administrative cases related to students suing universities is relatively high.

44 Shanghai Gaoji Renmin Fayuan Xingzheng Shenpanting (Administrative Adjudication Chamber of the Higher People's Court in Shanghai), 'Guanyu Shanghaishi Gaoxiao Jiaoyu Xingzheng Anjian De Diaocha Yangjiu' (Investigation Research on University Education Administrative Cases in Shanghai), 17 (2006) *Xingzheng Zhifa Yu Xingzheng Shenpan*, p. 105.

45 *Ibid.*

were some shortcomings in the exercise of their functions, they usually took initiatives to reconcile and resolve these cases outside court. Of the 10 cases in which students withdrew from the courts, seven withdrawals took place under such circumstances. Thus, for the universities the rate of losing such cases is low.[46] This trend is very similar to other investigative reports, which state that the trend of high success rates for universities is largely due to the administrative organs making some compromises after they recognise that they have made some form of error. However, the report also pointed out that some universities tried all kinds of ways to interfere with judicial independence, such as taking advantage of the local Communist Party Committee or government, or asking higher-level governmental organs to intervene. Although sometimes they gained something from this intervention, the harm caused to the image of universities in society is sizeable in comparison to the trifling gains achieved.[47]

Most of the cases involve students who violate university rules and are punished by the university's refusing to issue them with certificates of graduation and/or diplomas. Many of these cases focus on whether the university punishment is proportionate, while others challenge the legitimacy and rationality of the rules. In judicial practice, the courts have stopped refusing to accept all of these types of cases, and have begun to deal selectively with some of them. This process reflects the growing trend of courts to be innovative in exercising their jurisdiction, and illustrates how judicial practice has responded to newly emerging social needs.

In April 2008 the SPC issued the Announcement on Fully Realising the Role of Administrative Litigation in Providing Forceful Judicial Guarantee for People's Livelihoods.[48] It particularly clarifies the scope of acceptance of administrative cases to include cases concerning citizens' right to education, right to work, distribution of income, medical care and other areas relevant to people's livelihoods.

The principle of legality Article 5 of the ALL states that when handling administrative cases, courts should examine the situation to determine the legality of the concrete administrative action. The legality of an administrative action is examined according to certain standards: sufficiency of evidence, accuracy in the application of legislation, proper observance of legal procedure, acting within power, proper use of power, failure or delay in the performance of statutory duty, and obvious unfairness in imposing administrative punishment (Article 54).

Article 5 is often cited to support the conclusion that the ALL recognises only the principle of legality; namely, that courts can only determine the legality of the special administrative actions, not the appropriateness.[49] The rationale supporting this conclusion is the separation of administrative and judicial power. The concept of administration means not only that administrative organs are bound to follow laws in performing their functions, but also that they enjoy certain discretionary powers in implementing laws. The latter involves a certain appropriateness, with which courts should not interfere. In addition, administration touches various professional fields, which require rich administrative experience and professional knowledge. Judges lack such knowledge, and are consequently incapable of reviewing the appropriateness of administrative actions. Moreover, if

46 *Ibid.*, p. 104.

47 *Ibid.*

48 *Fa* No. 125 [2008]. Available at http://vip.chinalawinfo.com/newlaw2002/slc/slc.asp?db=chl&gid=105575. Last visited September 2013.

49 Tang Jun, 'Lun Xingzheng Susong Bohui Susong Qingqiu Panjue Yu Hefaxing Shencha Yuanzi Zhi Yiban Guanxi' (The Relationship between the Judgment of Rejecting a Litigation Claim and the Principle of Legality in Administrative Litigation), 11 (2004) *Xingzheng Zhifa Yu Xingzheng Shenpan*, p. 84.

courts examine the appropriateness of administrative actions, they may take the risk of interfering with the ability of administrative organs to perform their functions effectively.[50]

However, limiting judicial review to the principle of legality has been challenged by both Chinese legal scholars and judges. Some take the view that though the principle of legality is the basic principle of administrative litigation, this should not prevent the consideration of the principle of appropriateness in some cases. For instance, if an administrative action reflects an abuse of power, the court should nullify it. Likewise, if an administrative punishment is obviously unfair, the court should have the power to request the administrative agency change it. Thus, the principle of legality does not exclude any consideration by courts on appropriateness. It is unwise to make legality and appropriateness contradictory to each other.[51]

In judicial practice, the overwhelming majority of cases are determined by courts according to the principle of legality. However, in recent years some courts have cautiously experimented with a new approach. For instance, in the case of *Lu Miaoshou v. the House and Land Administrative Bureau* of Songjiang district in Shanghai, the first and the second instance court both upheld the decision of the defendant on the basis of the principle of legality. However, the Higher People's Court in Shanghai rejected the orders of the lower courts, and supported the plaintiff on the basis of the principle of appropriateness.[52] Many cases concerning house relocation are said to be disputed on the fact that administrative action is legal but inappropriate. For quite some years the courts have recognised the problems of the inappropriateness of administrative actions, but, due to the restrictions caused by the principle of legality, they could not cancel or change such administrative actions. Instead, courts could only suggest that administrative organs consider the issue of appropriateness. Whether such suggestions were in turn accepted by the administrative organs remained beyond the control of the courts.[53]

It is a challenge for courts to apply the principle of appropriateness since this involves using judicial discretionary power to judge administrative discretionary power. Under the current legal framework the ALL lacks provisions on the principle of appropriateness. Therefore, judges can only rely on their high professional skills, their deep understanding of modern administrative law, their sympathy for plaintiffs who suffered unfair treatment by administrative organs, and their courage for helping citizens. Unsurprisingly, not all judges can reach such a level. It is also unrealistic to require most judges to do so by taking legal as well as political risks.

Furthermore, over the past three decades the sources of law have become complex. The inconsistency between laws and regulations, and national regulations and local rules has led to a complicated application of the legality principle in administrative cases. This can be seen in the review of cases concerning re-education through labour (RTL). RTL is a unique system in China. It is a form of administrative punishment imposed on those who have violated laws or regulations in a non-serious manner so as to absolve the offender from criminal liability. However, with the recommendation of the police authority, one can be sent to a labour camp for up to three or four years by the decision of a RTL Committee affiliated to the police office at the county or district level. What is alarming is that there is no valid law creating or administering the system; the valid 'legal basis' is the Decision on Re-education through Labour issued by the State Council in 1957,

50 Jiang Bixin and Liang Fengyun, 'Xingzheng Susong Jiben Yuanze Lunyao' (Discussion of the Basic Principles of Administrative Litigation), 18 (2006) *Xingzheng Zhifa Yu Xingzheng Shenpan*, p. 4.

51 *Ibid.*, pp. 6–7.

52 For details of the case, see Wu Kailin, 'Xingzheng Susong Helixing Yuanze Shiyong Zhi Shizheng Panjie' (Analysis of Cases that Applied the Principle of Appropriateness in Administrative Litigation), 10 (2004) *Xingzheng Zhifa Yu Xingzheng Shenpan*, pp. 60–63.

53 *Ibid.*, p. 62.

and the 1982 State Council Notice on Re-Issuing the Ministry of Public Security's Trial Methods for Implementation of Re-education through Labour. However, in 2000, the Law on Legislation was issued by the National People's Congress, which provides that the deprivation of the political rights of a citizen, or compulsory measures and penalties involving restriction of personal freedom can only be made by national law (Art. 8). The 1996 Administrative Punishment Law also provides that administrative penalties in the form of restriction of freedom of person should only be created by law (Art. 9). In the past decades the RTL has been consistently criticised by Chinese and foreign commentators as contravening rights set forth in the Universal Declaration of Human Rights and the International Covenant on Civil and Political Rights as well as China's own laws. Some Chinese scholars and legal experts have appealed to the government to abolish the RTL. In November 2007, lawyers, legal scholars and public intellectuals submitted a proposal to the National People's Congress Standing Committee requesting it conduct a constitutional review of the RTL system. In July 2008, more than 15,000 Chinese citizens, led by numerous legal scholars and lawyers, signed a petition to abolish RTL and circulated a draft proposal for a 'Law on the Correction of Unlawful Acts' (*weifa xingwei jiaozhi fa*) to supplant RTL.[54] Under pressure from academia and the media, the central government finally made a move forward. In January 2013, at the National Conference of Political and Legal Affairs, the Secretary of the Central Political and Legal Committee, Meng Jianzhu, announced that the use of RTL would be suspended in 2013 following approval from the NPCSC.[55] Up to March 2013, three provinces, Guangdong, Yunnan and Hunan, have suspended the approval of RTL.[56]

The controversy between the RTL regulations and the law is obvious. The inconsistency of legal sources places the courts in a difficult position; they cannot annul the regulations, neither can they ignore the argument that deprivation of personal freedom can only be based on national law. Some courts have taken the approach not to base cases on the 1957 and the 1982 regulations. For instance, in 2003, in the case of *Chai Xiaorui v. Re-education through Labour Committee* in Luoyang city in Henan province, the court decided the Committee's decision was based on an incorrect application of law, and thus cancelled the decision.[57] The case of Chai Xiaorui gained nation-wide attention.[58]

---

54 Congressional-Executive Commission on China, *Annual Report 2008*, p. 37. Available at http://frwebgate.access.gpo.gov/cgi-bin/getdoc.cgi?dbname=110_house_hearings&docid=f:45233.pdf. Last visited September 2013. For studies of the RTL system, in English, see Zou Keyuan, 'The "Re-education through Labour" System in China's Legal Reform', 12 (2001) *Criminal Law Forum*, pp. 459–485. Sarah Biddulph, *Legal Reform and Administrative Detention Powers in China* (Cambridge: Cambridge University Press, 2007). Exceptionally, Randall Peerenboom has argued that China should not abolish the RTL system since that could leave many minor offenders to the even worse criminal justice system. See Randall Peerenboom, 'Out of the Pan and into the Fire: Well-Intentioned but Misguided Recommendations to Eliminate All Forms of Administrative Detention in China', 98(3)2004, *Northwestern University Law Review*, pp. 991–1104.

55 See 'Meng Jianzhu: Jinnian Jiang Tingzhi Shiyong Laojian Zhidu' (Meng Jianzhu: The Use of RTL Will Be Suspended This Year), available at http://news.ifeng.com/mainland/detail_2013_01/07/20909473_0.shtml. Last visited September 2013.

56 See 'Ji Guangdong, Yunnan Hou, Hunan Tingzhi Shiyong "Laojiao" Zhidu' (Hunan Suspends the Use of RTL Following Guangdong and Yunnan), available at http://www.afinance.cn/new/shxw/201303/546495.html. Last visited September 2013.

57 'Guoshi Fagui Ying Shishi Siwang' (Outdated Regulations Should Be Formally Abolished). Available at http://www.chinaqking.com/fl/2008/16204.html. Last visited September 2013.

58 'Laojiao Kunjing Yinfa "Yuhui" Zhihui' (Re-education through Labour Generates 'Indirect' Wisdom), 3 (2008) *Zhongguo Xinwen Zhoukan*, available at http://www.gotoread.com/s/e/?vo=6627&p=38. Last visited September 2013.

In other cases, the courts supported the plaintiff's claim by deciding inappropriate application of the regulations by the RTL committee. For instance, a young man, Cui Jiancun, stole RMB 3,000 while helping his classmate move house. Cui was detained by the police, who submitted the case to the local procuratorate, which decided on non-prosecution because it was a minor crime. The police submitted the case to the local RTL committee. Accusing Cui of the crime of theft, the committee decided to send Cui for one year to the re-education through labour camp. Cui challenged the committee's decision in the Intermediate People's Court in Bingzhou city in Shangdong province. The Court cancelled the Committee's decision on the basis of an incorrect application of law. The Committee appealed the case to the Higher People's Court in Shandong province, which in turn reached two different opinions, and thus submitted the case to the Supreme People's Court for instruction. The Supreme People's Court reviewed the case, and concluded that based on the facts that Cui had stolen once and was without a previous criminal record, the case did not meet the criteria for re-education through labour. Thus, the SPC did not support the Committee's decision.[59]

Court Jurisdiction and Special Court

About 90 per cent of all administrative cases at first instance are handled by basic people's courts.[60] This reveals that the overwhelming majority of cases are against governmental agencies at a lower level. Thus, it has been observed that the ALL is used

> to harness the energy of private litigants to help police the behaviour of lower-level state actors. In establishing this mechanism, China's leadership consciously opened the doors to the use of law and the courts to check state action and to create a society in which the legality of state action will increasingly be a measure of its legitimacy.[61]

However, basic courts often face local governmental intervention that restricts them from handling cases independently. Some Chinese judges have proposed the elevation of the court of first instance from the level of the basic people's court to the intermediate people's courts. They argue that the administrative chamber of basic courts often review administrative actions of county-level government. Since Chinese judges follow the official ranking of administrative personnel, when judges with a lower ranking title adjudicate cases in which the defendants have a higher administrative ranking, judges often face inevitable pressure and extra-judicial intervention that makes the independent and fair handling of cases unfeasible. At some BPCs. the rate of appeal was as high as 70 per cent, reflecting low confidence in the decisions of these courts. Abolishing the administrative chamber at the basic people's court and concentrating administrative cases of first instance at the intermediate people's court could avoid this lower-ranked judge vs. higher-ranked official dilemma. Furthermore, the number of administrative cases seen at the BPCs accounted for only a small proportion (5 per cent in 2002) of the total number of cases handled at this level. Such low numbers has resulted in judges at the administrative chamber of the basic people's courts often being called to temporarily do other work in the courts. To have judges specialised in

59 Zhou Honggeng and Wang Zhenyu, 'Guanyu Dui Zhiyou Yici Daoqiexingwei De Gongmin Yingfou Shishi Laodong Jiaoyang de Wenti' (Issues concerning Whether Re-education through Labour Should Be Imposed on Citizens Who Steal Once – How to Understand and Apply the No. 8 Reply (2005) of the Supreme People's Court), 17 (2006) *Xingzheng Zhifa Yu Xingzheng Shenpan*, pp. 85–87.

60 Fan Fu, *supra* note 4, p. 182.

61 John Ohnesorge, 'Chinese Administrative Law in the Northeast Asian Mirror', 16 (2007) *Transnational Law and Contemporary Problems*, p. 142.

handling administrative cases would enable them to accumulate experience and be more effective in tackling such cases.[62] This practical proposal to abolish the administrative chamber at the basic people's courts has so far not been accepted. However, the SPC has issued judicial opinions on strengthening and expanding the scope of the intermediate people's courts' jurisdiction in handling administrative cases.

Article 14 of the ALL lists three types of cases that are tried in the first instance by intermediate people's courts: (1) cases confirming patent rights of invention and cases handled by the customs authorities; (2) actions initiated against concrete administrative actions taken by departments of the State Council or by the governments at provincial level; and (3) important and complicated cases in areas under their jurisdiction. The 2000 SPC Explanations on Several Issues concerning the Implementation of ALL further elaborates (3) to include: cases wherein the defendant is the government above the county level and therefore it is inappropriate to try the case in the basic people's courts; cases of joint actions and class actions with significant social impact; cases of a foreign-related nature or involving Hong Kong, Macao or Taiwan; or other important and complicated cases (Art. 8).

In January 2008, the SPC issued a judicial opinion on Rules concerning Jurisdiction of Administrative Cases (the Rules), which further expanded the jurisdiction of the intermediate people's courts.[63] The Rules provide that if a plaintiff considers the case to be significant and complicated, and the case is not suitable to be handled by the basic people's court (which would otherwise have jurisdiction), the plaintiff may bring the suit directly to the intermediate people's court. The intermediate court should then decide, within seven days, whether to designate the case to a basic people's court under its jurisdiction, or to handle the case itself, or to instruct the plaintiff in written form to bring the claim to the basic people's court having jurisdiction over the matter. In addition, the rules provide that if a plaintiff files a suit at a basic people's court with jurisdiction, but the court fails to accept or deny the complaint within seven days, the plaintiff may bring the case to the intermediate people's court. Thus, more options are given to plaintiffs.

The Rules also provide that where a case otherwise falls under the basic people's court's jurisdiction, if an intermediate people's court considers it necessary, it can decide to remove the case from the basic people's court and handle it at the intermediate people's court instead, or alternatively, assign the case to another basic people's court. The last option is mainly to avoid situations where judges at basic courts face too much pressure and interference from the local government. Accordingly, this judicial option can be viewed as a reformative measure reflecting on the one hand, respect for plaintiffs' interests, and on the other hand an attempt to minimise administrative intervention in the basic people's courts.

The courts' jurisdiction in administrative cases is linked to overall court reform in China. In view of the special nature of administrative cases, some reform-minded judges and scholars have proposed to establish administrative courts separate from ordinary courts. One proposal is to establish administrative courts under the direct leadership of the Supreme People's Court, which would fulfil the functions that are currently performed by the administrative chambers of all courts. They advocate that such administrative courts should have independent finance and personnel, which would liberate them from local government intervention. Moreover, such courts would be conducive to adjudicative efficiency, since they could prevent judges from being habitually called on to serve on other posts. Furthermore, it would enable judges to accumulate valuable

62 Liang Fengyun, *supra* note 6, pp. 8–11.

63 *Fashi* No. 1 [2008]. Available at http://news.xinhuanet.com/legal/2008-01/16/content_7432428.htm. Last visited September 2013.

adjudication experience in administrative law. Such development of administrative expertise could make it possible for some cases to be decided by a single judge.[64]

To support this proposal it is pointed out that judges at administrative chambers are too often marginalised. Compared to civil and criminal chambers, the number of cases handled by the administrative chamber is small. Moreover, such cases are often politically sensitive and difficult for the court to handle. Many judges prefer not to work in the administrative chamber. It is reported that some intermediate people's courts do not even have the minimum requirement of three judges in the administrative chamber to compose a collegiate panel; and some basic people's courts have only one or two judges in their administrative chamber. Some courts assign judges to work at the administrative chamber on a rotation basis. This adverse effect of this is many judges are rotated out of the administrative chamber at the point when they have just become familiar with administrative trial processes; while the judges rotated in have to learn the procedure all over again. In some instances, judges serving in administrative chambers and adjudicating cases strictly in accordance with laws, have been put under high pressure by local government, were forced to leave their posts, or were delayed for promotion. Further, some court leaders do not take the administrative chamber seriously enough, and treat it as a 'waiting' chamber from where judges, whenever needed, will be sent for. Some courts have even integrated the administrative chamber into other chambers, thus leaving the existence of the administrative chamber only in name.[65]

Another proposal is to establish administrative courts separately from the current court structure. This proposal ventures to establish a Supreme Administrative Court, Appellate Administrative Courts, and Local Administrative Courts to handle all administrative cases and inspect local governments. Under this system, judges at the administrative courts would be appointed by and responsible to the National People's Congress, so they are independent from local government, thus preventing them from becoming 'local judges'. They would be sent from the central level to a local administrative court for a fixed term, and then move to another local administrative court. This would also prevent one judge becoming too entrenched in one locality, which undoubtedly would result in various contacts with local government being made that affect the judge's independence.[66]

At present, the summit of the political leadership is not ready to accept proposals for specific administrative courts as this would significantly alter the structure of the courts and bring forth institutional change on a large scale. .However, in the long run, special independent administrative courts can be expected to balance executive and judicial powers, and provide effective oversight in ensuring that governmental organs follow the law.

Adjudication

Similar to the court's handling of civil cases, when an administrative case is brought to court, the case filing department will first examine the admissibility of the case. If a case is initiated, it will be given to the administrative chamber. When the chamber decides to hear a case, a collegiate panel must be formed consisting of three or more judges, or a combination of judges and people's assessors (Art. 46 of the ALL). Under this Article, a common understanding is that summary procedures, which are handled by a single judge, cannot be utilised in administrative cases. However in 2010, SPC issued the Notice on Pilot Implementation of Summary Procedure for Administrative Cases in

64 Liang Fengyun, *supra* note 6, p. 24, 28.

65 *Ibid.*, pp. 8–9.

66 He Bing, 'Gaizao Xingzheng Shenpan, Baohu Guotu Ziyuan' (Reform of the Administrative Litigation System, Protection of National Land Resources), available at www.gmw.cn/content/2007-07/28/content_644260.htm. Last visited September 2013.

which summary procedures for administrative cases are partially approved of within given courts and given types of cases.[67] Other mechanisms, such as withdrawal, open trial procedures and a binding second trial are all procedures provided for in the ALL.

Generally speaking, the trial procedure for administrative cases is similar to the trial of civil cases. However, there are two distinct differences. The first is that the ALL makes it clear that the defendant administrative agency not only bears the burden of proof for the concrete administrative action it has taken, but should also provide the court with evidence and regulatory documents upon which its decision was based (Art. 32). Moreover, during the course of proceedings the defendant is not allowed to collect evidence from the plaintiff or witnesses on its own authority (Art. 33). Such authority lies only with the courts (Art. 34). In reality, academic work has pointed out that 'governments have used extra-legal means to force courts to adopt more flexible ways in implementing burden of proof provisions … governments have been hiding behind the concept of "confidentiality" and hence have refused to disclose various kinds of documents relating to their decisions.'[68]

Although the burden of proof rests with the defendant, this does not mean that the plaintiff need not provide evidence. According to Article 27 of the Explanations on Several Issues concerning the Implementation of the ALL issued by the SPC in 2000,[69] the plaintiff of the administrative litigation should bear the burden: (1) to prove that the litigation meets the statutory requirements except when the defendant thinks that the litigation brought by the plaintiff has exceeded the time limit; (2) to prove the facts in a case in which the plaintiff sues the defendant for its inactions; (3) to prove the fact that the plaintiff has suffered losses due to the harm caused by administrative action in the administrative compensation case which is brought together with the administrative litigation; and (4) to prove other issues that the plaintiff raises.

Another attribute of the ALL is that Article 50 explicitly provides that a people's court should not apply mediation in trying administrative cases. This has been regarded as one of the principles of administrative litigation law. Its origins can be traced back to the Announcement concerning People's Courts' Non-Use of Mediation in Handling Economic and Administrative Cases issued by the SPC in 1985.[70] The prohibition of mediation in administrative litigation was based on the oversimplified theory that administrative power belongs to the state, and therefore it is a power

---

67 *Fa* No. 446 [2010]. Article 1 of the Notice indicates that the summary procedure could be applied in handling first instance cases in which basic facts are clear, the legal relationship is simple, and rights and duties are clear. Such cases may include: (1) cases involving a smaller amount of property value, or cases wherein administrative organs make the following decisions on the spot: administrative expropriation, administrative penalties, administrative supply of benefits, administrative licensing, administrative enforcement and so on; (2) cases of administrative inactions; and (3) cases to which summary procedure may apply as voluntarily chosen by all parties concerned and upon examination and approval by people's courts. The summary procedure can be presided over by a single judge. After receiving the court summons, if a plaintiff does not appear in the court without justified reason, the case will be deemed a withdrawal; if a defendant does not appear in the court without justified reason the court can continue the trial in the absence of the defendant. A case handled by summary procedure should be concluded within 45 days of the case being accepted by the court. The Notice is available at http://www.court.gov.cn/spyw/xzspgjpc/201012/t20101210_12042.htm. Last visited September 2013.

68 Jianfu Chen, *Chinese Law, Towards an Understanding of Chinese Law, its Nature and Development* (The Hague, London and Boston, MA: Kluwer Law International, 1999), p. 162.

69 *Fashi* No. 8 (2000). Available at http://vip.chinalawinfo.com/newlaw2002/slc/slc.asp?db=chl&gid=26982. Last visited September 2013.

70 The text is available at http://vip.chinalawinfo.com/NewLaw2002/Slc/slc.asp?db=chl&gid=2595. Last visited September 2013.

that could not be discharged. The initial idea was to prevent administrative organs from arbitrarily discharging their administrative powers without competence. However, it neglected the reality that administrative agencies have considerable discretionary power, and their actions do not always represent the public interest.[71] Many administrative litigation cases concern the civil rights of the parties involved. Examples of these can be a dispute over compensation for injury caused by a policeman while carrying out his duty; a dispute over removal and compensation relating to a construction project.

Mediation has had a long-standing role in civil litigation and administrative litigation was born from civil litigation. For that reason, it is an unsurprisingly 'open secret' that many BPCs have not only used, but continually encourage parties to engage in mediation to resolve disputes. Mediation may be invoked when a judge handling an administrative case deems it difficult to deliver a fair judgment according to the existing laws because of deficiencies in those laws, or when there is a risk that the judgment could be misunderstood or impossible to enforce. The court might make a proposal to the defendant to modify its concrete administrative action in order to give the plaintiff the opportunity to withdraw the lawsuit, thus terminating the litigation. To avoid conflict with the ALL, courts call this *xietiao* (reconciliation) rather than *tiaojie* (mediation). However, there is no substantive distinction between *xietiao* and *tiaojie* – reconciliation is *de facto* mediation.

Mediation in administrative litigation has both light and dark sides. The objective of mediation is to resolve disputes by reaching compromise on a voluntary basis. If mediation can be fairly conducted by neutral judges, it can lead to satisfaction for the plaintiff, the defendant and the court. This is why mediation is so prevalent. Some Chinese scholars take the view that mediation is conducive to certain types of administrative cases, such as civil disputes involving administrative decisions, administrative contracts, administrative compensation, or the failure of an administrative organ to perform its duty.[72]

However, the major criticism of mediation in practice is that it is not abnormal for courts and defendants to put pressure on or even force plaintiffs to mediate. Michael Palmer has observed that 'the present system of judicial mediation in administrative cases is one in which the plaintiff may well experience significant coercion and find mediation to be a mandatory, rather than a consensual, process'.[73] Some Chinese scholars have been extremely disparaging of widespread mediation because of the resulting large number of withdrawals of administrative cases, which showcased a negative practice contrary to the spirit of the administrative litigation system.[74] Despite the *de jure* equal status of the plaintiff and the defendant in administrative litigation, in reality, the positions are not equal. Plaintiffs are private persons who are a vulnerable group compared to defendants who are backed by state power. In mediating between these two uneven parties, the neutrality of judges, or even a bias towards the weaker party, is necessary. However, on many occasions, the opposite may be true.

---

71 See Wang Weiyun and Wang Jianbing, 'Guanyu Jianli Xingzheng Susong Tiaojie Zhidu De Tantao' (An Inquiry on the Establishment of the Mediation System in Administrative Litigation). Available at www.chinacourt.org/public/detail.php?id=180843. Last visited September 2013.

72 Wang Yan, 'Tiaojie Yu Xingzheng Susong Zhidu Chuangxin' (Mediation and Innovation in the Administrative Litigation System), 10 (2004) *Xingzheng Zhifa Yu Xingzheng Shenpan*, pp. 52–56.

73 Michael Palmer, 'Controlling the State: Mediation in Administrative Litigation in the People's Republic of China', 16 (Fall 2006) *Transnational Law and Contemporary Problems*, p. 185.

74 Wang Yan, *supra note* 72, p. 49.

Since 2003 as a response to the grand mediation movement launched by the Central Political and Legal Committee, mediation has regained an important role within the courts.[75] In January 2007, the SPC issued the Several Opinions on Providing Judicial Guarantee for Construction of Socialist Harmonious Society which addressed the issue of the proper use of reconciliation in administrative litigation.[76] In March 2007, the SPC issued the Several Opinions on Further Displaying the Positive Roles of Litigant Mediation in Constructing Socialist Harmonious Society.[77] The Opinions specified that depending on the circumstances of the case at hand, courts should promote reconciliation between parties by referring to principles and procedures of civil mediation.

At the local level, the higher people's courts in Shanghai, Guangdong, Chongqing and Shandong provinces and some intermediate people's courts have issued opinions on administrative coordination and reconciliation.[78] For instance, in August 2007, the Shanghai Higher People's Court issued the Opinions on Strengthening Conciliation in Administrative Cases,[79] which provides guiding rules for courts in Shanghai to use conciliation in the handling of different types of administrative cases. These include cases wherein:

1. the concrete administrative action challenged by the plaintiff is unlawful, but rescinding the act would cause serious damage to state interests, public interests and others' legitimate rights and interests;
2. the administrative action challenged is lawful, but its reasonableness and appropriateness are questionable;
3. legal provisions are unclear or inconsistent with the relevant policy;
4. decisions made by the administrative organ concern the civil disputes of parties with equal legal status, or administrative actions affecting a person's life and the right to life;
5. the dispute relates to land acquisition in rural areas, household relocations in urban cities, labour and social security, changes of enterprise ownership, threats to natural resources and the environment, state interests, public interests and social stability, or there exists a potential that the dispute may generate massive conflict;
6. a government official/agency has omitted to execute a duty;
7. the plaintiff's claim cannot easily be supported by the court because of practical difficulties, yet, the problem must be addressed; and
8. other circumstances that can be reconciled according to law.

The Opinions of the Shanghai Higher People's Court also calls on courts to apply reconciliation creatively, by communicating and cooperating between the administrative chamber and the 'letter and visit' department of the court, and if necessary, invite relevant units and influential people

75 Luo Gan, 'Zhengfa Jiguan Zai Goujian Hexie Shehui Zhong Fudan Zhongda Lishi Shiming He Zhengzhi Zeren' (The Significant Historical Missions and the Political Responsibility of Political and Legal Organisations in Constructing a Harmonious Society), 3 (2003) *Qiu Shi* (Seeking Truth).

76 *Fafa* No. 2 [2007]. Available at http://rmfyb.chinacourt.org/public/detail.php?id=105458. Last visited September 2013.

77 *Fafa* No. 9 [2007]. Available at http://vip.chinalawinfo.com/newlaw2002/slc/slc.asp?db=chl&gid=89041. Last visited September 2013.

78 Zhang Lijuan, 'Guanyu Yunyong Xietiao Fangshi Chuli Xingzheng Jiufen Anjian De Diaoyan' (Research on Handling Administrative Cases by Way of Coordination and Reconciliation), 22 (2009) *Fazhi Yu Shehui* (Legal System and Society), p. 200.

79 *Hugaofa* No. 93 (2007). Available at http://gov.eastday.com/renda/gonggao/node2524/node8854/node8855/node8859/u1a1362349.html. Last visited September 2013. The document is with the author.

to support and participate in the conciliation with the purpose of truly settling the dispute. The presiding judge could inform the head of the administrative chamber, the president, and vice-presidents of the court, and ask them to participate in the conciliation if necessary.

The Opinions state that reconciliation can be conducted at the pre-trial as well as the trial stage before a court ruling is issued. Reconciliation can be organised with all parties together or separately, and can be either open or closed. The contents of an agreement reached through reconciliation are not limited to the plaintiff's claims. However, any agreement reached cannot violate the prohibitive provisions of laws and regulations, harm state interests, public interests or other's legitimate rights and interests, and cannot go against the will of the parties. Thus, the Opinions provide guidelines so the courts can efficiently manage reconciliation in terms of both procedure and outcome.

Given the fact that mediation is effective under certain circumstances and that it is widely used in administrative cases, a feasible option for China would be to legalise mediation by the courts in administrative litigation while the ALL is amended, and at the same time stress the voluntary principle and standardise mediation procedures to prevent coercion and other misuses of mediation.

Analysis of the Number of Cases and the Success Rate of Plaintiffs

Confined by the context in China, finding accurate data on the number of administrative cases accepted or concluded by all courts each year is always problematic. Both the SPC Work Report to the NPC and the *China Law Yearbook* have provided most, though not complete, data in this regard. However, due to inconformity in the methodology and an insufficiency in the recording system, an inconsistency is observed between the two. For the purpose of conducting an analysis in this chapter, data from the *China Law Yearbook* is used.

Table 6.1 The number of administrative cases concluded in the first instance by all courts (1988–2011)

Year	Number	Year	Number
1988	8,029	2000	86,614
1989	9,742	2001	95,984
1990	12,040	2002	84,943
1991	25,202	2003	88,050
1992	27,116	2004	92,192
1993	27,958	2005	95,707
1994	34,567	2006	95,052
1995	51,370	2007	100,683
1996	79,537	2008	109,085
1997	88,542	2009	120,530
1998	98,390	2010	129,806
1999	98,759	2011	136,361

Source: *China Law Yearbook* (1989–2012).

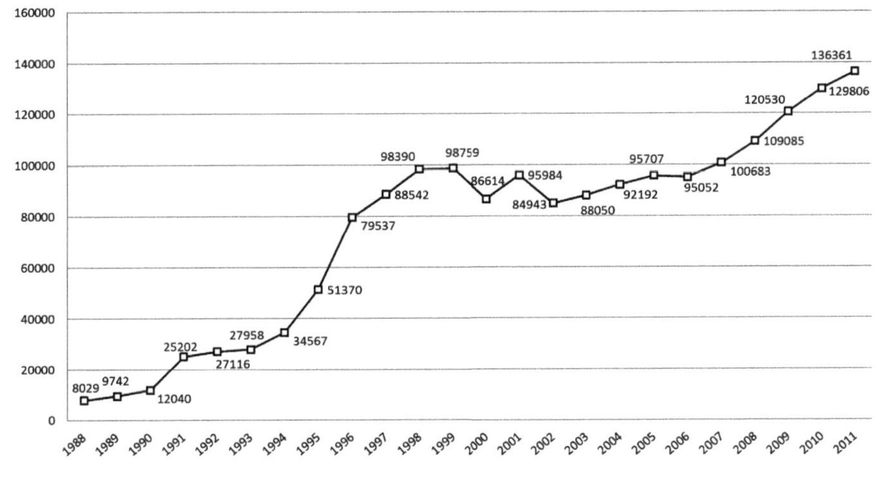

Figure 6.1 The trend in the increasing number of administrative cases concluded in the first instance by all courts from 1988 to 2011

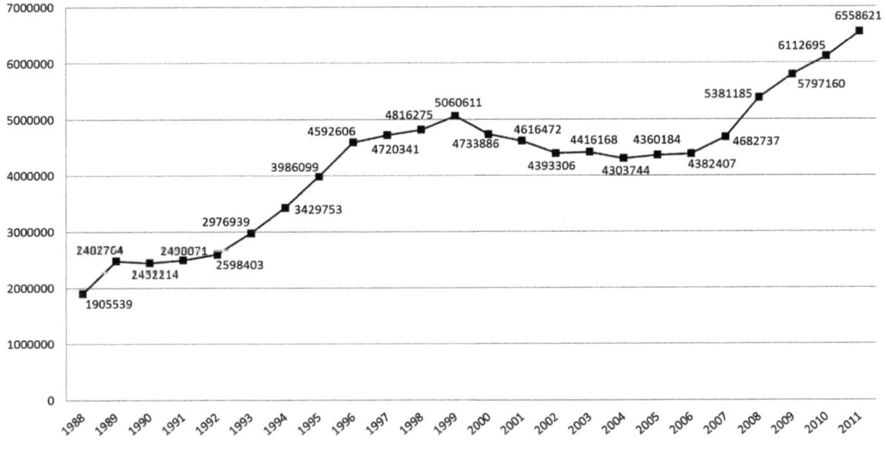

Figure 6.2 The trend in the increasing number of civil cases concluded in the first instance by all courts from 1988 to 2011

Source: *China Law Yearbook* (1989–2012).

As Table 6.1 illustrates, the number of administrative cases has increased radically since the establishment of the administrative litigation system. In 1989 when the ALL was issued, the total number of administrative cases concluded by courts at first instance was 9,742. After the ALL became effective in October 1990, the number increased to 25,202 in 1991, more than twice the number in 1989. In 1995, the number jumped sharply to 51,370. After a continual increase during the mid-1990s to mid-2000s, the number first exceeded 100,000 in 2007 and reached a peak in 2011 with 136,361 cases. As Figure 6.1 shows, in recent years however, the increase in number of administrative cases was not as dramatic as it was the 1990s. This is mainly due to a shift in policy towards constructing a harmonious judiciary in which mediation is employed more than

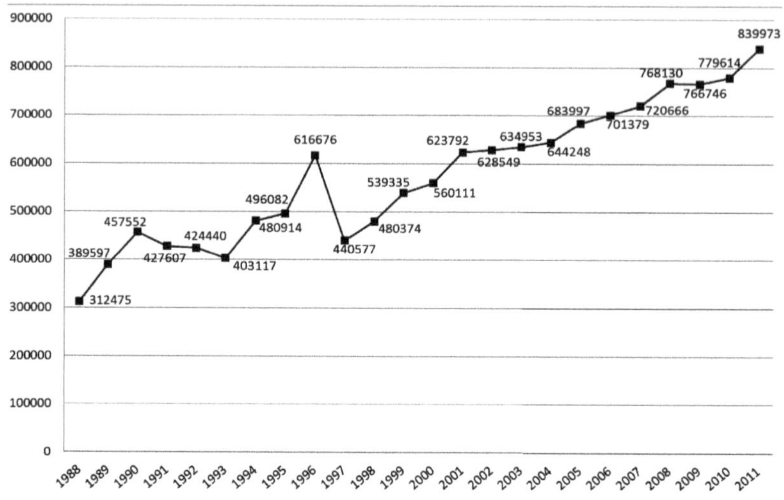

Figure 6.3 The trend in the increasing number of criminal cases concluded in the first instance by all courts from 1988 to 2011

Source: *China Law Yearbook* (1989–2012).

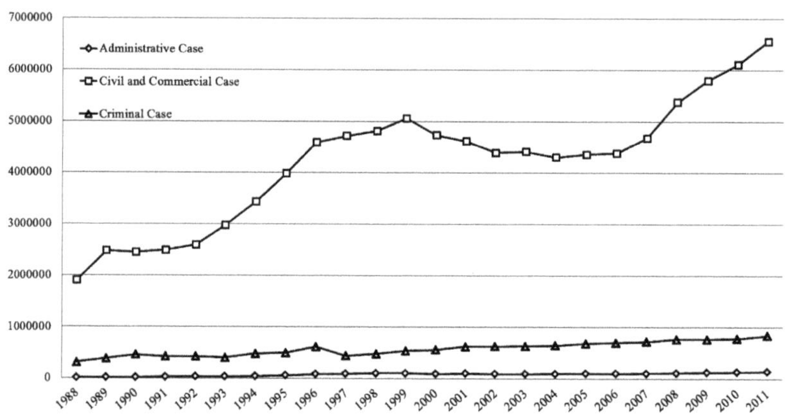

Figure 6.4 Comparison of the number of administrative, civil and criminal cases concluded in the first instance by all courts from 1988 to 2011

ever, which has resulted in many administrative disputes being dispelled at the pre-litigation stage. The number of administrative litigation cases has also diminished due to petitions, complaints and other alternative forms of dispute resolution.

In a country with a population of 1.3 billion, with 'the extensive nature and powers of bureaucracy and the growing rights-consciousness of the Chinese citizenry, it is surprising that the rate of increase in administrative suits has remained low – especially in comparison with the figures for civil litigation',[80] which can be observed in Figure 6.4. The number of administrative cases handled by different courts can vary. According to one empirical study, at a basic people's

80 Michael Palm, *supra* note 73, p. 179.

court in Hebei province, administrative cases were extremely scarce: the highest number was four in 1994, with zero in 1993 and 1996.[81]

Several reasons explain the low number of administrative litigation cases. First, the narrow scope of case acceptance provided for in the ALL excludes many cases from court. Moreover, such cases are not truly welcomed by the courts. When a case is brought to a court, the case filing department decides whether the case can be accepted by the court and which chamber will handle it. Such departments often refuse to file cases; thus, a public complaint that is commonly heard is 'difficulty in having a case filed by the court' (*li'an nan*).[82] This simply reflects the repulsive reality of 'officials always protecting each other' (*guanguan xianghu*).

In contrast to the difficulty of having a case accepted, courts seem to have demonstrated an active handling of cases regarding the compulsory execution of administrative actions. Under Article 66 of the ALL, if a citizen, a legal person or any other organisation does not, during the period prescribed by law, initiate a litigation or carry out the concrete administrative action, the administrative organ may apply to a court for compulsory execution or proceed with compulsory execution according to law. This allows courts to assist administrative organs in enforcing administrative decisions. It was reported that, from 1989 to 2004, the courts reviewed 3,056,927 cases of non-litigious execution of administrative cases, which amounts to 3.4 times the total administrative cases of first instance.[83] According to another survey, conducted by Arthur Chening, in 1990 the number of first instance administrative cases was 13,006, while the applications for enforcement of administrative decisions was 18,052; in 1991, the former increased to 25,667 while the latter grew to 40,863. The tendency of the number of applications for enforcement to grow each year became more and

81 Sida Liu, 'Beyond Global Convergence: Conflicts of Legitimacy in a Chinese Lower Court', 3 (2006) *Law & Social Inquiry*, p. 89.

82 *Li'an nan* is the toughest problem faced by people, in terms of abuse of power by basic-level officials, in cases such as: illegal collection of fees, land confiscation, home demolition, and selling off village land. The courts' refusal of such cases or its weak position in settling such disputes has forced grievant villagers to seek non-judicial address, such as via the 'letter and visit' channel to petition higher-level government or the pursuit of journalists to expose the case in order to seek government attention. See Kevin J. O'Brien and Lianjiang Li, supra note 1, pp. 75–95. If courts' refuse cases, lawyers sometimes advise their clients to submit the case as a civil case in order to ensure the case entering the court procedure. When the case is heard, lawyers can then prove the root of the dispute derived from a wrong decision made by the local government. In reality this could cause long and painstaking suffering without necessarily providing a positive outcome for victims. For instance, in May 2008 a lawyer in Beijing told me once about a case he was handling concerning taxi drivers in Qingdao. A few taxi drivers launched in 2003 a complaint regarding the local traffic department in Qingdao who illegally collected fees from taxi drivers. The local court simply refused to accept the case. After three years of continuing complaints, the key organisers and a few taxi drivers lost their jobs, their houses were searched by local police, and they were labelled 'trouble makers' by local authorities. Due to the internal rectification, the local traffic department had to stop collecting fees from taxi drivers. However, the traffic department reached a 'gentleman's agreement' with taxi companies to allow the latter to collect the fees, which were then transferred to the traffic department. Consequently, taxi drivers still have to pay the fees. Having agreed to represent the taxi drivers in this case, a lawyer in Beijing has advised the group to submit a civil dispute against the taxi companies. It was a long process to settle the case. According to the judgment of the Basic People's Court in Beiqu in Qingdao Municipality of Shandong province, issued on 20 August 2009 (No. 535, 2009 of Civil Chamber of the People's Court in Beiqu), the taxi drivers lost the case. I once met one of the taxi drivers who played a leading role in organising the drivers; he came to meet a lawyer in Beijing and I was totally astonished by his appearance – due to years of humiliation and living in fear he was ill with diabetes.

83 Fan Fu, *supra* note 4, p. 186.

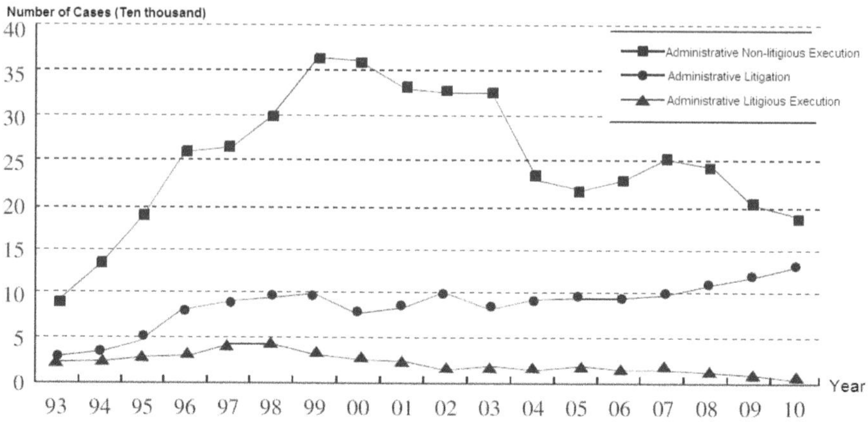

Figure 6.5 Comparison of the numbers of administrative litigation cases, administrative litigious executions and administrative non-litigious executions

more apparent after 1993. For example, in 2001, the number of first hearing administrative cases was 100,921 and the number of applications for enforcement was 334,217.[84]

Figure 6.5[85] demonstrates the contrast between the number of administrative litigation cases and the number of enforcements of administrative decisions. It has become a major function of the administrative trial chamber at basic people's courts to assist administrative organs in executing the latter's decisions. As a consequence, some Chinese have argued that the courts have become an arm of the governmental organs, and that the joining of administrative and judicial powers against administrative counterparts undermines the foundation of the administrative litigation system.[86]

In cases where citizens sue government agencies and expose certain serious social problems, the courts sometimes prefer to avoid or feel incapable of handling them. For instance, in 2006, Mr Jiang Shilin, a farmer who was the head of the village committee, sued the Bureau of Finance of Changning city in Hunan province. The farmer claimed the defendant abused its tax income by buying luxury cars that exceeded the allowed budget. The court refused to accept the case.[87] This 'simple' case represents a common problem in China today whereby governmental agencies violate financial laws and rules. Although Chinese citizens are aware of the violations, they rarely dare to criticise. In Mr Jiang's case, if the court had decided to accept his lawsuit the right of tax payers to supervise governmental agencies through administrative litigation would be confirmed, which could bring forth similar cases in the future. At the same time a danger exists in that if the court did accept the case and decided in favour of the defendant, the court would be accused of

84 See Arthur Chening, 'China's Administrative Litigation Law', Autumn (2005) *Public Law*, pp. 566–567.

85 Figure 6.5 is cited from He Haibo, 'Kundun De Xingzheng Susong' (Administrative Litigation in Dilemma), 2 (2012) *Huadong Zhengfa Daxue Xuebao*, p. 95.

86 See Shen Kaiju and Wang Hongjian, 'Lun Xingzheng Qiangzhi Zhixingquan De Xingzhi: Jianlun Fayuan Zai Zhixing Zhong De Zuoyong' (Analysis on the Nature of Compulsory Execution Power: Study of the Function of Court in the Execution) (2006). Full text available at http://article.chinalawinfo.com/Article_Detail.asp?ArticleID=42020#m13. Last visited September 2013.

87 Huang Yuanjian, 'Gongyi Susong Yu Caizheng Jiandu – Jiang Shilin su Hunan Sheng Changning Shi Caizhengju An' (Jiang Shilin v. Financial Bureau in Changning City of Hunan Province' (Public Interest Litigation and Financial Supervision), in Wu Ge (ed.), *Zhonguo Yingxiangxing Susong* (The Impact of Litigation in China) (Beijing: Zhongguo Jiancha Chubanshe, 2007), pp. 67–69.

endorsing the unlawful acts of governmental agencies, which would decrease the already low public opinion of the courts. Thus, even such a small case may reflect large-scale, complicated, political and social problems. Chinese courts are neither strong nor independent enough to make a right or wrong judgment on such issues.

Currently a major type of administrative case that courts do not want to accept but sometimes are forced to deal with are cases concerning *chaiqian* disputes (having one's house pulled down and being evicted). According to the Annual Report of Work of the People's Courts (2011),[88] about 18.26 per cent of administrative cases relate to such cases. Usually they involve problems associated with corruption or local economy handed down by previous governments, which often make them too sensitive to handle. Yet, as such cases have become a growing social and political problem courts are compelled to handle them.[89]

A survey by the Chinese Academy of Social Sciences in 2004 revealed that, among the 632 petitioners who took their cases to the central authority in Beijing, nearly two-thirds of them had at the outset brought their cases to local courts; and 43 per cent reported that the courts did not want to accept their cases, which impelled them to petition in Beijing.[90] To further compound the problem, courts assign cases that should be handled by the administrative chamber to the civil chamber, or alternatively, after the acceptance of such cases, often persuade individuals to withdraw their case. Furthermore, even after the court has already accepted a case, it may, for fear of offending the governmental organisation, willingly delay the handling of the case by repeated reconciliation, or in some cases even withhold judgment on the legality of the administrative conduct in question.[91]

Significantly, many Chinese citizens, companies and organisations are reluctant to initiate cases against government bodies. Many people are still influenced by the traditional thinking that an individual confronting a government organ and its officials equates to 'throwing an egg against a stone' – the result is a broken egg. A common attitude taken is maximum tolerance even with the knowledge that their legal rights have been infringed. A popular saying has it that 'you may win one case, but lose in the rest of life'. This describes how people who win their cases subsequently suffer from isolation and retaliation. Such situations influence others to doubt the worthiness of suing government agencies. Additionally, there exists some difficulties with regards to the enforcement of judgments.[92]

Some governmental organisations react antagonistically toward administrative litigation. In the minds of many officials, administrative power is superior and the official position is the root of everything (*guanbenwei*). Officials are supposed to be the parents of lay people and to decide

88 *Annual Report of Work of People's Courts* (2011) (Beijing: Renmin Fayuan Chubanshe, 2012), p. 38.

89 See generally Matthew Erie, 'Property Rights, Legal Consciousness and the New Media in China: The Hard Case of the "Toughest Nail-house in History"', 26(1) (2012) *China Information*, pp. 35–59; and Helen Yu, 'Just Compensation: Ideal or Compromise – A Comparison of the Implementation of the Just Compensation Clause and Forced Urban Evictions in China and South Korea', 16 (2006–2007) *Transnational Law and Contemporary Problems*, pp. 189–220. The Chinese lawyer Wang Cailiang, a well-known expert in this field, has published the *Annual Reports of Eviction in China* since 2010. The latest version of the annual report is available at http://www.21ccom.net/articles/zgyj/gqmq/article_2013012275577.html. Last visited September 2013.

90 Congressional Executive Commission on China, *Annual Report, 2007*, p. 151. Full text is available at http://www.gpo.gov/fdsys/pkg/CHRG-110hhrg38026/pdf/CHRG-110hhrg38026.pdf. Last visited September 2013.

91 Wang Liming, *Sifa Gaige Yanjiu* (Research on Judicial Reform) (Beijing: Falu Chubanshe, 2000), p. 285.

92 Stanley B. Lubman, *Bird in a Cage: Legal Reform in China after Mao* (Stanford, CA: Stanford University Press, 1999), p. 210.

things for them. Some officials even still consider that 'officials are noble and ordinary people are low-down' (*guangui minjian*), and that a 'citizen's rights are bestowed by officials' (*enci*). Thus, some local officials view the court's acceptance of administrative cases as intentionally causing trouble with the local government. When the court decides a case against the government, it is perceived as opposing the government and as a disturbance of the government's work.[93] A senior judge once pointed out that some local governments have issued policy documents that instruct courts not to accept certain types of cases and warn courts that they will have to bear the political and social ramifications if they act otherwise. Some local governments have used the decision of the Communist Party to collect fees to avoid possible administrative cases (since Party organs are not administrative organs, they are not subject to the ALL). Some local officials have insisted that courts can only accept cases with the signature of the local Party leader. While other local officials have used the opportunity of courts reporting their adjudicative work to impose their own opinions on the courts, still others have used the notion of 'serving the broad interests of society' to request that courts suspend illegal administrative actions. Some administrative organs have abused their power to threaten, retaliate and force the plaintiff to withdraw. All these methods of governmental interference have resulted in many courts becoming reluctant to accept administrative cases.[94]

Despite all the difficulties and hindrances, the number of administrative cases are growing and the proportion of cases won by plaintiffs deserves some attention. At the outset it should be noted that the rate of successful outcomes in administrative cases is difficult to establish. Generally speaking, the rate of success for plaintiffs can be viewed from two angles: the rate of decisions to cancel administrative actions, and the rate of withdrawal by plaintiffs after defendants change the administrative actions in question. The number of failed cases can be estimated by the rate of administrative actions holding and the rate of willing withdrawals by plaintiffs.

A general estimation is that in the first 10 years of implementation of the ALL (1990 to 2000), the average rate of success in administrative litigation cases was about 40 per cent for cases concluded by the first instance courts.[95] Randall Peerenboom compared this rate with that of the

93 'According to one survey, almost half of the officials surveyed thought at the time of the implementation of the Administrative Litigation Law that it would decrease administrative efficiency. Many feared that it would decrease the authority of government officials. The idea of officials being hauled into courts to account for their actions was both threatening and demeaning.' See Randall Peerenboom, *supra* note 17, p. 55.

94 Lu Zhongmei, *Fayan Guanting – Chuanxing Yu Jiaoshou He Faguan Zhijian*' (Using Legal Eyes to Observe the Courtroom) (Beijing: Beijing Daxue Chubanshe, 2006), p. 131. Courts will not accept any case that challenges a decision of a Party organ. A well-known case is Guo Luoji, a former professor of philosophy of Peking University. In 1979 he criticised mistreating people as criminal simply because they expressed different political thoughts. He was moved to Nanjing University where in 1991 he was informed that according to the decision of the Party Committee of Nanjing University he could not retain his professorship due to his problematic political background. He complained to the Jiangsu Provincial Party Committee but received no reply. He then sued the Party Committee at the Jiangsu Higher People's Court, but the Court did not accept the case giving as its main reason, the Party Committee 'does not meet the requirement to be a respondent according to the ALL'. See Song Bing, 'Assessing China's System of Judicial Review of Administrative Actions', 1–2 (1994) *China Law Reporter*, pp. 11–12.

95 Li Guoguang, 'Li Guoguang Fuyuanzhang Zai Jinian Zhonghua Renmin Gongheguo Xingzheng Susongfa Shishi Shi Zhounian Zuotan Huishang De Jianghua' (Li Guoguang Vice-President of the SPC's Speech at the Seminar on Celebrating the Ten-Year-Anniversary of the ALL), 1 (2000) *Xingzheng Zhifa Yu Xingzheng Shenpan Cankao*, p. 6.

USA and Taiwan, where the average rate of success for administrative claims is only 12 per cent.[96] However, one cannot be too optimistic about this rate of success.

The high rate is largely due to the striking feature of the high rate of withdrawal. Two types of withdrawal can be identified: one whereby the plaintiff voluntarily withdraws their claims, and the other whereby the defendant modifies their administrative action, and as a result, the plaintiff agrees to withdraw. In the latter, the defendant has made a compromise, which can be considered success for the plaintiff. A general survey illustrates that during the period 1987 to 1997 the average withdrawal rate was relative high, reaching 57.3 per cent in 1997; from 1997 to 2002 it decreased to 30.67 per cent; and from 2002 to 2004 it was around 31 per cent.[97] A local survey of administrative cases of first instance in Jiangsu province revealed that the relatively low rate of cases lost by plaintiffs was largely due to plaintiff withdrawal. From 2002 to 2005, the average rate of plaintiffs withdrawing was 39.70 per cent. Among those cases withdrawn, 895 followed after the relevant administrative organs changed their original decisions. In a further 6,214 of those cases, the withdrawals occurred even though the administrative organs did not clearly change their decisions, yet the interests of the plaintiff had nonetheless been admitted and respected.[98]

Voluntary withdrawal by a plaintiff is difficult to distinguish. While in some cases withdrawal occurs on a voluntary basis without external pressure, many others involve non-voluntary withdrawal, in which the plaintiffs and the defendants reach an agreement 'out of court'. The case of *Xu Jiangguo v. The Local Police Bureau* illustrates how voluntary withdrawal may not actually be 'entirely voluntary'. This case is generally cited as the first in which local police were sued for making an illegal body search. On 23 May 2006, lawyer Xu Jiangguo exited a train station and was stopped by three policemen who forcefully asked him to show his ID card. Xu asked the police to follow strictly the Law on Resident's Identification Card. This law requires that the police explain their reason for examining the ID card and show a law enforcement card while examining the ID card. However, the police refused Xu's request that the procedures be followed and in turn forced Xu to go to the police station for further questioning. Prof. Ling Lihong, a legal aid lawyer at the Centre for Protection of the Rights of Disadvantaged Citizens of Wuhan University, represented Mr Xu and brought the case to the basic court.

After the court filed the case, the defendants visited the plaintiff a few times to apologise and expressed their willingness to pay compensation and litigation fees. The plaintiff refused to withdraw. However, after the case was reported in newspapers and the internet, the head of the defendant police bureau sought to contact the officials of the local political and legal committee, who were the superiors of the plaintiff, to advise the plaintiff to withdraw. Finally the plaintiff could bear no further pressure and agreed to withdraw on the condition that the defendant offered an apology and paid litigation fees and other actual costs.[99]

---

96 Randall Peerenboom, *China's Long March towards Rule of Law* (Cambridge: Cambridge University Press, 2002), p. 400. Peerenboom stated that this would not mean Chinese courts do a better job than US Courts. 'It could be that in the United States, administrative agencies generally comply with the law and thus should be expected to prevail more often, whereas in China administrative agencies actually comply with the law even less than the 40% plaintiff victory rate could suggest' (p. 400).

97 Zhu Jingwen (ed.), *Zhongguo Falu Fazhan Baogao Shujuku He Zhibiao Tixi* (Report on China Law Development: Database and Indicators) (Beijing: Zhongguo Renmin Daxue Chubanshe, 2007), p. 228.

98 Higher People's Court in Jiangsu Province, 'Jiangsusheng Xingzheng Zhifa Xianzhuang, Fazhan Qushi Ji Duice De Diaocha Yanjiu' (An Investigation Report on Trial of Administrative Litigation Cases by Various Levels of Courts in Jiangsu Province), 18 (2006) *Xingzheng Zhifa Yu Xingzheng Shenpan*, p. 121.

99 'Quanguo Shouli Zhuanggao Gong'an Jiguan Feifa Chayan Shenfenzheng An' (The First Case of Illegal Check ID Card in China), available at http://www.ccwhu.com/html/xueshuziyuan/gong

In a 1995 case, 44 villagers sued the township government for infringing the villagers' right to manage collectively a lake in Hubei province. Due to interference by the city government, the court did not accept the case within the period requested by the law, nor did it make a decision not to accept the case. The legal aid lawyer invited a television journalist to interview the villagers, but the news was not sent out because of further intervention by the city's government. The accused party used provincial officials to put pressure on the legal aid lawyer to advise the plaintiffs to withdraw. However, the lawyer convinced the officials that the case had genuine merit, and the latter decided not to intervene. The lawyer sent a formal letter to urge the court to file the case. The court reported to the city government with the hope that the latter would resolve the matter soon. The city government set up a committee which consisted of one deputy Party secretary, one deputy mayor, one deputy director of the judicial bureau, one deputy president of the court and others. This resulted in the city government's recognition of the legal effectiveness of the agreement, which was signed by the 44 villagers and the village committee, and agreed, in large part, with the plaintiffs' compensation claim. The plaintiffs sent a withdrawal statement to the court. The lawyer never received a letter of filing or a statement of approval from the court.[100]

Even in cases in which an administrative action is evidently wrong, it is very difficult for plaintiffs to win administrative cases and lawyers have to use all possible wisdom to win. This is illustrated by one simple case. On 7 August 2008, one day before the opening of the Olympic Games in Beijing, the Publishing Press of China University of Finance and Economics posted on the homepage of its official website the words 'Cheer Up for Olympic Games, Cheer Up for China' to express their best wishes for and pride in the Olympic Games taking place in Beijing. On 27 September 2008, the Publishing Press received an order from the Industrial and Commercial Bureau of Haidian District in Beijing (hereafter the Bureau), indicating that the use of 'Olympic Games' on the website had potential commercial purposes and infringed the copyright of the Olympic Games, and that the Publishing Press must immediately stop the tortious act and pay a fine of RMB 10,000. The Publishing Press challenged this administrative punishment decision by bringing the case to the Basic People's Court in Haidian district in Beijing and requesting that the court order the defendant to rescind the administrative punishment decision. The court supported the decision of the Bureau and the plaintiff lost the case.

The plaintiff then appealed to the No. 1 Intermediate People's Court in Beijing. The plaintiff's lawyer felt that some public support would be needed to win the case. He thus organised a seminar to discuss the case and the judgment of the first instance court. Eminent professors in administrative law and lawyers in Beijing discussed the arguments of the plaintiff and the defendant, and the possible application of law to the case – ultimately, all agreed that the fine should not be sustained. The experts' opinions were published in the *Legal Daily* and the lawyer of the Publishing Press sent copies to relevant judges in both the first and the second instance courts. Media coverage of the case seemed to have had an impact on judges at the court of appeal. The case was soon heard, and the lawyer had the impression that the judge in charge would issue a favourable judgment. However, after two months passed, the lawyer did not receive any news from the court. Worried that the 'media pressure' on the judges might fade away as time passed, the lawyer organised experts to publish their opinions on the case in *China Youth Daily* and sent the newspapers to the judges too. Soon after this, the Court of Appeal issued a decision stating that the defendant had rescinded its administrative punishment decision and agreed to pay RMB 25 litigation fee to the

fapanli/20090228/147.html. Last visited September 2013.

100 Lin Lihong, *Zhongguo Xingzheng Jiuji Lilun Yu Shiwu* (China Administrative Remedies Theory and Practice) (Wuhan: Wuhan Daxue Chubanshe, 2000), pp. 279–281.

court. The plaintiff won the case as it wanted.[101] The lawyer in this case was Li Xuan, a reputable scholar at the Law School of China University of Finance and Economics. Owing to his reputation, he was able to publish in newspapers the opinion of experts supporting his case. It is questionable, though, how many lawyers could succeed in doing the same, and moreover, what decision could be expected from the court.

Stanley Lubman has pointed out that the relatively high rate of success in administrative cases in China reflects that '[b]ureaucratic arbitrariness is endemic in Chinese society'.[102] A Chinese expert has grouped the reasons why government agencies lose their cases into the 'four sicknesses': 'swell-up sickness' – the excessive expansion of power by the arbitrary collection of fees and imposition of fines; 'fatuous sickness' – the muddy issuance of documents and affixation of seals; 'foolish sickness' – the granting of approvals without prior study of the details; and 'indolent sickness' – the absence of action in accordance with duty.[103]

Of course, to a certain extent cases won by plaintiffs also illustrate the growing competence of courts in adjudicating administrative cases. Although it is an undeniable fact that in general, administrative power prevails over judicial power in China, courts in handling some concrete cases have displayed increasing authority by placing checks on arbitrary and illegal government actions. This is precisely the role courts are supposed to be playing. In addition, some Chinese studies have ascertained that at the basic level, administrative litigation has been a stimulus to administrative agencies and functionaries to adhere to the law in carrying out their administrative powers (*yifa xingzheng*).[104] A reported example of this comes from Baokang county in Hubei province.[105] This is a relatively isolated, mountainous county where mountaineers follow the tradition of the Confucian proverb, 'it is better to die of starvation than to become a thief; it is better to be vexed to death than to bring a lawsuit'. This area saw hardly any administrative litigation case. Indeed, at one time the county had only three cases annually. Some administrative officers had therefore become accustomed to their casual way of enforcing administrative penalties. With the promulgation of the Administrative Penalty Law, the number of administrative litigation cases increased. However, some administrative officers remained steadfast in their customary manner of imposing administrative penalties. In 1996, the court in Baokan county concluded 44 administrative cases, with 43 being lost by the administrative agencies. In 1997, the court handled 81 cases, all of which the government defendants lost. The situation caught the attention of the county Party department, the county People's Congress and the county's government, and they jointly took measures to provide legal training to administrative officers and requested that the heads of the administrative agencies appear in the courtroom when their offices were the defendants. The county court, on the one hand, continually adjudicated cases according to the laws, yet, on the other hand provided legal knowledge to local administrative agencies to improve their understanding of the trial of administrative litigation cases. The administrative agencies also strengthened their internal supervision and began disciplining and punishing enforcement officers who had acted illegally. Following this all-channels effort, in 2002, the court delivered judgments on 34 administrative litigation cases, of which the defendant local administrative agencies won 28 (82 per cent), a sharply different outcome to the period before 1998, in which the local administrative agencies lost nearly all the lawsuits.

101 Discussion on the case can be found in *Legal Daily* (weekend issue), 23 April 2009. More details on the case can be found at http://law.cufe.edu.cn/article/default.asp?id=1994. Last visited September 2013.

102 Stanley B. Lubman, *supra* note 92, p. 211.

103 Lu Zhongmei, *supra* note 94, pp. 117–121.

104 He Xin, supra note 16, pp. 144–145.

105 Lu Zhongmei, *supra* note 94, pp. 133–135.

Conclusion

The creation of a judicial review system to control the conduct of governmental organs and functionaries represents a completely new facet of the legal system in post-Mao China. The most significant impact of the ALL is that, by allowing ordinary people to sue the government, it has changed the conception of the relationship between citizens and governmental officials. The changes 'have more explicitly set limits on state power and established procedures for citizens to defend themselves against intrusion or infringement by the state and its agents'.[106]

Despite the modest number of administrative litigation cases and major problems in implementing the ALL, Chinese courts have handled a wide array of cases involving citizens against governmental organs ranging from ministries at the top, to township government organs at the bottom. Various powerful governmental agencies, such as the public security bureaus, industrial and commercial departments, city construction departments, tax bureaus, traffic departments, county and township governments, and universities have been put on the defendants' side of the courtroom. The courts' handling of administrative cases has not only protected the legitimate rights of many citizens, but has also made some positive impacts on administrative agencies' adherence to the law in performing their functions. Given the limited and somewhat unclear power the ALL has entrusted to the courts, and the unbalanced power between strong administrative organs and relatively weak courts, in the past two decades the Chinese judiciary has demonstrated a certain pragmatic approach in settling administrative disputes, which signifies an increasing judicial competency in adjudicating administrative cases.

However, the administrative litigation system retains some fundamental problems in terms of both the ALL and its implementation. The ALL – with its 75 articles, compared to 284 articles in the 2012 revised CiPL and 290 articles in the 2012 revised CrPL – is obviously too simple and general. The restrictions set up in the ALL concerning the scope of acceptance of cases have largely limited judicial control over administrative actions. Further, some provisions, such as the prohibition of mediation and the limitation of judicial review to the principle of legality, have been proven by judicial practice to be unworkable. Thus, modification of the ALL is inevitable. Indeed, some Chinese administrative law experts have already published scholars' proposed drafts of a new ALL.[107] After years of postponement the NPCSC started to deliberate on the first version of an amended ALL in December 2013.[108]

As to judicial practice, a common public complaint is the courts' refusal to file cases. This is particularly problematic in cases concerning a large group of citizens, or where the relevant government policy is ambiguous, or where a conflict of interest between citizens and local government is at stake, or in cases involving rural land use, urban relocation, abuse of administrative power and corruption and so forth. The courts' refusal has not only forced many victims to seek

106 Pei Minxin, *supra* note 1, p. 862.

107 For instance, 'Xingzheng Susongfa Xiugai Jianyigao (Beida Ban)' (Scholars' Draft on Administrative Litigation Law (Peking University)), it contains 93 articles. The text is available at http://www.publiclaw.cn/article/Details.asp?NewsId=3688&classid=-9&classname=%B9%AB%C3%F1%B2%CE%D3%EB%C1%A2%B7%A8. Last visited September 2013. Ma Huaide (ed.), 'Sifa Gaige Yu Xingzheng Susong Zhidu De Wanshan – Xingzheng Susongfa Xiugai Jianyigao Ji Liyou Shuomingshu' (Judicial reform and Perfecting of the Administrative Litigation System – Proposed Draft on Administrative Litigation Law and Explanations), (Beijing, *Zhongguo Zhengfa Daxue Chubanshe*, 2004).

108 'Amendment to Administrative Procedure Law Hailed in China', available at http://news.xinhuanet.com/english/china/2013-12/24/c_132993358.htm. Last visited January 2014.

non-judicial remedies, such as petitioning local and central government organs, but also resulted in aggravating social problems.

In recent years, courts and judges have been rigorously using mediation in settling administrative cases as a response to the central government's call to the judiciary to serve in the building of a harmonious society and its reminder to judges to keep in mind the political, legal and social consequences in dealing with cases. Even though mediation can resolve some individual disputes, mediating practice often has a compulsory nature and the neutrality of judges is not guaranteed.

Another daunting barrier to implementing the administrative adjudication system is the issue of judicial independence. A Western system of separation of powers does not exist in China. The Chinese system requests that the three powers – executive, legislative and judicial – cooperate with and facilitate each other. However, when dealing with a case involving a governmental body and an individual citizen, a court or judge will be biased if they take a cooperative attitude towards the governmental body. The trial of administrative cases tests both the relationship between individuals and officials, and the relationship between judicial power and administrative power. Since administrative power in general prevails over judicial power, courts cannot effectively do away with local governmental intervention. Some courts even report to the governmental organs concerned to seek their opinions before deciding whether to deal with the case. Consequently, improvement of the administrative adjudication system is largely dependent on changing the relationship between judicial and administrative powers. Endowing judicial independence is a precondition for a trustful and efficient judicial system. To achieve this, China needs to reform its fundamental political system – this requires political courage, wisdom and proper timing.

In summary, China's administrative litigation system remains an infant system. It is premature, but it also shows great potential for innovation and systematic enhancement. Since approximately 80 per cent of laws and administrative regulations are enforced by administrative organs,[109] administration in accordance with law not only affects the rights and interests of a large population, but is also essential for building a rule of law society in China. The Chinese experience in implementing the ALL has demonstrated that, 'Getting entrenched bureaucrats to abide by the law when in the past they were the law has not been easy'.[110] However, judicial review is playing an increasingly special role in ensuring that governmental organs and officials follow the law strictly and appropriately.[111] To develop a fair and efficient administrative litigation system takes a long time and will require a wide range of efforts by the CPC, the government, the court, citizens, lawyers and the public media.

109 Fan Fu, *supra* note 4, p. 181.

110 Randall Peerenboom, *supra* note 17, p. 56.

111 Judicial review under the ALL is only one of the few types of supervision on administrative decisions. Other methods of government oversight include: legislative supervision by the People's Congresses; administrative reconsideration (*xingzheng fuyi*), and the letters and petitions (*xinfang*) process, which handles complaints lodged by citizens against administrative organs.

Chapter 7
The Role of the Legal Profession in the Judicial System

Introduction

In the aftermath of the lawless period of the Cultural Revolution toward the end of the 1970s, the Chinese legal profession was revived as part of an overhaul of the legal system. This revival was first alluded to by permitting the defence of the accused in criminal cases, which was quickly extended to encompass the representation of clients in civil and commercial cases. Chinese lawyers now play a greater role than ever in the sphere of litigation. Meanwhile, economic reform has brought alongside it ample opportunities for lawyers to engage in non-litigious services. Lawyers have indeed proven their worth as key players involved in domestic business transactions, foreign trade and investment. In the 1990s the legal profession was once a 'flourishing industry', an overwhelmingly popular choice of profession, promising both a respectable income and the enjoyment of a higher social status.

Despite the undeniable progress attained by China in just 30 years with regard to the growing number of lawyers and law firms, the expanding scale of legal practice, the role of lawyers in facilitating economic development and their position as an indispensable arm of the judicial system, the commonly-held notion that law in China is an ideal profession is far from true.[1] This is attributable to the widespread and deeply-rooted resentment of lawyers held in Chinese tradition; the nascent legal profession has been forced to develop in the thorny conditions of an institutional framework of socialist ideology and an authoritarian regime.[2] While the continuity of China's economic, legal and political reforms offers lawyers unprecedented and wide-ranging prospects in their practice, the transitional nature of the systems and society in its entirety throws up unique challenges and quandaries for the legal profession. Just as the judicial system is undergoing a transformation, the legal profession is similarly experiencing a process of change.

This chapter provides an in-depth assessment of the development of the legal profession over the past three decades. It begins with an analysis of the traditional disregard for lawyers and the rapid change since the 1980s. It then examines the key provisions of the 1996 Lawyers Law and its amendments in 2007 and 2012,[3] with particular focus on the rights and duties of lawyers in practising law. The relative successes of lawyers in providing legal services cannot veil the

---

1 'Legal practice for many Chinese lawyers is fraught with difficulties and dangers. The challenges they routinely face include various forms of obstruction, harassment, intimidation, and even physical abuse, often at the hands of personnel in the public security administration (the police system), the procuracy (the public prosecutor's office), and courts – lumped together in common parlance as the *gongjianfa*.' Ethan Michelson, 'Lawyers, Political Embeddedness, and Institutional Continuity in China's Transition from Socialism', 113(2) (2007) *AJS*, p. 352. Available at www.indiana.edu/~emsoc/Publications/Michelson_lawyers.pdf. Last visited September 2013. This research provides comprehensive information on the legal profession in China from 1979 to 2006.

2 For the institutional foundation of the legal profession in China, see Carlos Wing-Hung Lo and Ed Snape, 'Lawyers in the People's Republic of China: A Study of Commitment and Professionalization', 53 (2005) *American Journal of Comparative Law*, pp. 433–455.

3 Since the Lawyers Law was promulgated in 1996, it has been amended in 2001, 2007 and 2012. The 2001 amendment concerned only Article 6 on the qualification of lawyers. 2007 amendments contain

disheartening reality that defence lawyers are incessantly faced with grave risks. Witnessed in abundance are cases involving the mistreatment, wrongful detention and prosecution of lawyers – such phenomena will be discussed in order to illustrate the dire reality of the seriousness of the violation of lawyers' rights in the judicial process. Aside from the shortcomings in the law, such as Article 306 of the Criminal Law which is widely criticised by Chinese and Western legal scholars alike, in creating a trap for defence lawyers, this chapter also endeavours to examine the tension and hostility between defence lawyers and law enforcement officers in the context of both economic and social change.

The Traditional Disregard for Lawyers and Recent Developments

Lawyers in the Pre-PRC Period

According to scholars of Chinese legal history, ancient China developed numerous rules to regulate litigation. For instance, compliance papers had to be written in accordance with a certain format, otherwise the plaintiff would be punished. Since ordinary citizens had insufficient knowledge of litigation, they were forced to seek expert assistance. Thus, some 'intellectuals' – often referred to as 'litigation tricksters' (*songgun*) – became specialised in assisting people in formulating their complaints, becoming notorious in society during the Ming and Qing dynasties.[4] Yet, this field of expertise failed to translate into the emergence of a legal profession in imperial China. Moreover, these 'litigation tricksters' were widely condemned and in the most severe of instances were punished by the authorities for their involvement.[5] 'The legal annals of the Qing dynasty contain a number of reports of cases in which legal draughtsmen received three years of penal servitude or worse for their efforts.'[6]

The appearance of lawyers in China in the modern era can be traced back to the role played by foreign influences. After the Opium War in 1840, when several European countries acquired extra-territorial consular jurisdiction and established consular courts, foreign lawyers began their work in China. Lawyers were initially employed to work in foreign concessions, but later their sphere of influence was extended to encompass roles as legal counsel or as representatives in the Chinese courts. Such a development in the scope of lawyers' influence can be conveyed through the fact that these professionals were acting on behalf of foreigners and Chinese citizens alike. Out of concern for the situation in which some Chinese citizens relied on foreign legal representation to defend them in disputes with foreigners, the Minister for Law Reform of the late Qing Dynasty, Shen Jiaben, wrote to the Emperor suggesting that foreign lawyers would not help the Chinese people where this would have led to disadvantaging their fellow countrymen. Thus, he suggested the establishment of a system that would produce Chinese lawyers. Consequently, the criminal and civil procedural codes – drafted in 1910 – imitated the Western system; these codes provided

---

some substantive improvements. The 2012 amendments modified six provisions, mainly to make the Law consistent with the 2012 revised Criminal Procedure Law.

4 Xiao Shengxi et al. (eds), *Lushi Xue* (Lawyers' Studies) (Beijing: Jiaoyu Chubanshe, 1996), p. 21.

5 Henry R. Zheng, 'The Evolving Role of Lawyers and Legal Practice in China', 36 (1988) *American Journal of Comparative Law*, p. 474. See also William P. Alford, 'Tasselled Loafers for Barefoot Lawyers: Transformation and Tension in the World of Chinese Legal Workers', in Stanley Lubman (ed.), *China's Legal Reforms* (Oxford: Oxford University Press, 1996), p. 26.

6 Timothy A. Gelatt, 'Lawyers in China: The Past Decade and Beyond', 23 (1991) *International Law and Politics*, p. 751. See also Xiao Shengxi et al. (eds), *supra* note 4, p. 26.

provisions for the qualification of lawyers, registration requirements, responsibilities, appropriate punishment procedures and the like. However, these draft codes were never legitimised and brought into binding force.[7]

In 1911, Sun Yat-sen led the Xinhai revolution, which overthrew the Qing dynasty and established the Republic of China. Of notable importance is the fact that Sun Yat-sen endorsed the drafting of a law on lawyers, but his government did not survive long enough – a mere three months. In 1912, Yuan Shikai founded the Peking government and inherited the legal system created at the end of the Qing dynasty. This government issued the Provisional Regulations on Lawyers, the Provisional Regulations on the Registration of Lawyers and other detailed rules – ultimately codifying and legitimising the basic rules for lawyers. This included the following prerequisites and requirements: lawyers had to be above the age of 20, graduates from universities of politics and law, and expected to have passed the lawyer's examination. At this time, women were not permitted to enter the legal profession. To practise law, a lawyer had to be a member of a lawyers' association.[8] The Provisional Regulations also laid down the lawyers' functions in court. Lawyers were authorised to appear in both ordinary and special courts and were appointed either through a client or by a court order. These pivotal Regulations were symbolic as the first codified endorsement of lawyers and their appearance in Chinese courts. When the Provisional Regulations were later revised in 1917, other legal functions associated with the role of lawyers received formal recognition, including the drafting of contracts and wills and the drawing up of contracts and other legal documents on a client's behalf.[9]

From 1927 to 1944, the Chiang Kai-shek Government continued to apply the previous legal system, while both revising old laws and enacting new ones. Importantly, women were subsequently allowed to become lawyers. The minimum permitted age for a lawyer was raised to 21. The functions of the lawyers' associations were expanded to include producing proposals to the Minister of Justice on the subject of law reform. A special procedure for handling the punishment of lawyers was established. These laws formed the constituent framework of the legal system during the Kuo Mindang period and formed the basis upon which the legal system of present-day Taiwan is built.[10]

From the late Qing Dynasty to the creation of the Republic of China, each authority ensured that they paid ample attention to the legal system. Consequently, the legal profession gradually became established and bar associations emerged in large cities. The Shanghai Bar Association was the most dynamic and well-known. Of particular significance was how this noteworthy association had acted against foreign legal privileges and championed judicial independence.[11] However, due to the disruption caused by continuous wars, the frequent changes in government and the underlying discontent within traditional values of using lawyers in Chinese society, the legal system was prevented from blossoming in full. In 1913, there were only around 1,700 lawyers registered with the Ministry of Justice. By 1935, this figure had risen to 10,249, while by 1943, it had fallen slightly to 9,245. By the early 1940s, the population of China stood at around 450 million. Despite

7 See Xiao Shengxi et al. (eds), *supra* note 4, p. 26.

8 Tao Mao et al. (eds.), *Lushi Shiyong Daquan* (Applied Encyclopaedia for Lawyers) (Shijiazhuang: Hebei Renmin Chubanshe, 1993), pp. 20–21.

9 A.W. Conner, 'Lawyers and the Legal Profession During the Republican Period', in Kathryn Bernhardt and Philip C.C. Huang (eds), *Civil Law in Qing and Republican China* (Stanford, CA: Stanford University Press, 1994), pp. 216–217.

10 See Tao Mao et al., *supra* note 8, p. 21.

11 See Conner, *supra* note 9, p. 240, and Henry R. Zheng, *supra* note 5, p. 27.

China technically having around 10,000 lawyers at this time, the overall ratio of lawyers in the population was exceedingly low, standing at one per 45,000.[12]

Lawyers in the PRC

The establishment and development of the Chinese legal system since the founding of the PRC has proven far from steady; its formulation can generally be divided into three distinct stages.

The first period is the reconstruction of the legal profession from 1950 to 1957. Upon the PRC's establishment on 1 October 1949, the government issued the Common Programme[13] (a provisional constitution) and announced the abolition of the Kuo Mindang legal system. The judicial system in itself, along with the affiliated legal profession was considered no exception. The Circular concerning the Abolition of Underground Lawyers and Litigation Tricksters issued by the Ministry of Justice in December 1950, clearly stated the abrogation of the legal system, the dissolution of lawyers' organisations and the cessation of lawyers' activities carried out under the previous regime.[14] Furthermore, lawyers cultivated from this vanquished regime were denounced as representatives of an exploitative class. This downtrodden collection of lawyers was subject to further insult through government proclamations that 'only a few lawyers were upright and fair-minded and dared to speak for the people'.[15]

Having abolished the previous regime, the government sought to develop a brand new system through the enactment of new laws. The General Principles of the People's Courts issued by the central government in 1950, alongside the 1954 Constitution and the Organic Law of the People's Courts provided the right for an accused individual to be entitled to a defence and thus established a system of defence lawyers.[16]

In July 1954, the Ministry of Justice authorised Beijing, Shanghai and a couple of other large cities to create 'legal advisory offices' to engage in legal work.[17] In January 1956, the Ministry of Justice submitted to the central government a Report concerning Establishing Our Country's Lawyers' Work, which suggested setting up a system for lawyers by enacting rules at a national level. Following this, the Provisional Regulations on Lawyers were drafted in 1957. In the period leading up to June 1957, 19 lawyers' associations and 817 legal advisory offices were established. There were around 2,500 full-time lawyers and 300 adjunct lawyers working in 33 cities in China at that time. Lawyers were treated as civil servants and private law firms were not permitted to exist. The professional work of a lawyer during this period included matters of criminal defence,

12 See Conner, *supra* note 9, pp. 229–230.

13 Its English translation is contained in Albert P. Blaustein (ed.), *Fundamental Legal Documents of Communist China* (New Jersey: Fred B. Rothmanse Co., 1962), pp. 34–53.

14 Zhang Geng et al. (eds), *Zhonghua Renmin Gongheguo Lushifa Quanshu* (Encyclopaedia of the Law of the People's Republic of China on Lawyers) (Beijing: Lan Tian Chubanshe, 1996), p. 38.

15 *Ibid.*, p. 474.

16 Zhang Zhiming, 'Dangdai Zhongguo De Lushiye: Yi Minquan Weijiben Chidu' (Lawyers in Contemporary China: A Civil Rights Perspective), in Xia Yong et al. (eds), *Zouxiang Quanli De Shidai: Zhongguo Gongmin Quanli Fazhan Yanjiu* (Toward a Time of Rights: A Perspective of Civil Rights Development in China) (Beijing: Zhongguo Zhengfa Daxue Chubanshe, 1995), p. 144. See also Gelatt, *supra* note 6, pp. 752–754; and see Zhang Geng et al. (eds), *supra* note 14, pp. 38–39.

17 See Zhang Geng et al. (eds), *supra* note 14, p. 39; and Xiao Shengxi et al., *supra* note 4, p. 24.

acting as a legal adviser and representative in civil law cases, drafting legal documentation and responding to legal inquiries.[18]

The second period is the destruction of the legal profession from 1957 to 1977. The most profound feature of this period was the absence of practising lawyers in China. By the middle of 1957, the growth of the Anti-Rightist Movement resulted in many lawyers being treated as 'rightists'; resultantly, they were exiled to the countryside. The legal profession was criticised and ultimately defamed as a capitalist relic of a bygone era. In 1959, the situation had worsened further with the removal of the Ministry of Justice and the dismantling of lawyers' organisations.[19]

The third period is the resumption and formalization of the legal profession from 1978 to the present day. As part of the nationwide reconstruction of the country's legal system, the government soon decided to take steps to accommodate and reincorporate the legal profession into the legal sphere. The 1978 Constitution re-established the system of advocacy. The 1979 Criminal Law, the Criminal Procedure Law and the Organic Law of the People's Courts provided for the right of the accused to be defended at the trial stage of legal proceedings, as well as enunciating the basic principles of criminal defence by lawyers. In 1979, a greater degree of experimentation with regard to professional legal work was instigated: in the Hulan county of Heilongjiang province, criminal defence through lawyers was permitted on a probationary basis; in Guangzhou city, a legal advisory office was established in order to handle foreign-related maritime cases; and in Shanghai, a lawyer's organisation was established.[20]

In September 1979, the Ministry of Justice returned. Amongst numerous other functions, it was attributed the power to assume responsibility over the administration of the legal profession. In August 1980, the Provisional Regulations of the People's Republic of China on Lawyers were promulgated by the National People's Congress Standing Committee.[21] Provisions were crafted with regard to the responsibilities, rights, qualifications and business organisations of lawyers. Lawyers were defined as 'legal workers of the state', with the task of providing legal assistance to the government, businesses and citizens. 'Legal advisory offices' were considered to be the business organisations in which lawyers practised. Lawyers could serve as legal advisers, act as representatives in civil litigation, mediation, arbitration and as defence counsel in criminal cases, give legal assistance in non-litigious matters, provide consultative advice and draft various legal documents. In order to be formally accepted as a lawyer, irrespective of qualifications, one had to cherish the PRC, support the socialist system, and have the right to vote and stand for election. Moreover, lawyers were subject to the examination and approval of the local bureau of justice, affiliated to the provincial government.

Although the Regulations contained a mere 21 general provisions they importantly legitimised, for the first time, the legal profession in the PRC. Since this time, the ranks of the legal profession have grown extensively. In 1981, there were around 8,571 lawyers; since 2012 this number has risen to around 230,000.[22] This is an increase of 27 times over the past 30 years.

---

18 See Zhang Zhiming, *supra* note 16, p. 144. During this period, lawyers' involvement in economic activities was rather limited due to the underdeveloped economy, and especially underdeveloped industry and commerce.

19 See Zhang Geng et al. (eds), *supra* note 14, p. 40; and Tao Mao et al., *supra* note 8, p. 23.

20 See Zhang Geng et al. (eds), *supra* note 14, p. 40.

21 The official English translation of the text can be found in *The Laws of the People's Republic of China (1979–1982)*, compiled by the Legislative Affairs Commission of the National People's Congress Standing Committee of the People's Republic of China (Beijing: Foreign Languages Press, 1987), pp. 177–181.

22 The 1981 figure is from Zhu Jingwen (ed.), *Zhongguo Falu Fazhan Baogao Shujuku He Zhibiao Tixi* (Report on China Law Development: Database and Indicators) (Beijing: Zhongguo Renmin Daxue

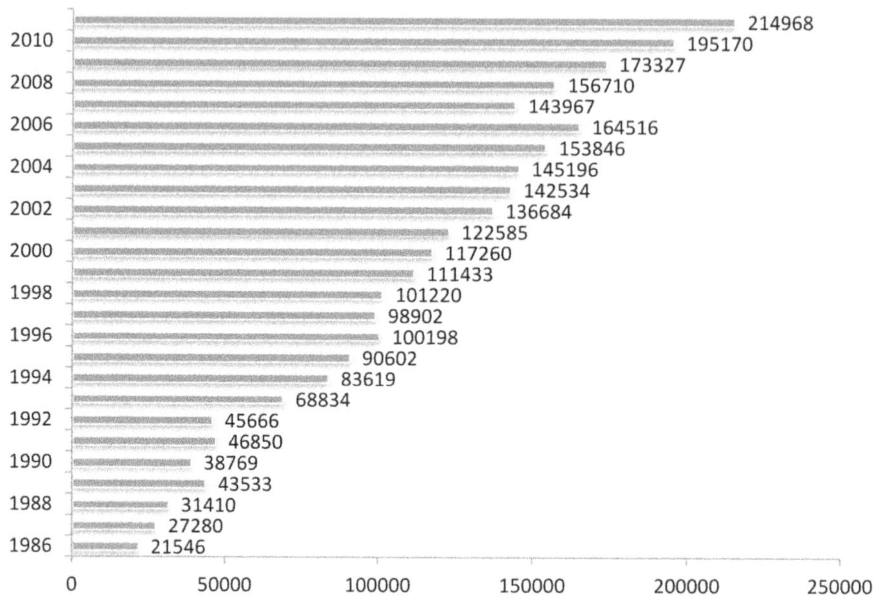

Figure 7.1 Changes in the number of lawyers in China (1987–2011)

Source: China Law Yearbook.

Along with the overall growth in the number of lawyers, a system for lawyers has gradually taken shape. In 1986, a National Bar Examination (NBE) was for the first time administered by the Ministry of Justice, initially on a twice-yearly basis, and since 1993 reduced to annually. In 1986, 11,024 candidates sat the examination, of which 3,307 passed. Ten years on, the number of candidates undertaking the examination had increased to 127,000. In November 1998, an overwhelming 180,000 candidates took the NBE. Partaking candidates ranged in age from young graduates to older retired judges and prosecutors.[23] In 2002, the NBE was replaced by the National Unified Judicial Examination (NUJE). Potential lawyers, judges and prosecutors are all required to have first passed this examination in order to further pursue a legal career.

Business organisations in which lawyers practise have also undergone considerable change. Until 1988, state-owned law firms were the only organisations in which lawyers could practise. The first co-operative law firm then appeared in Baoding city in Hebei province. Subsequently, similar law firms began to appear in other large cities.[24] In May 1988, the Ministry of Justice issued the Trial Scheme for Co-operative Law Firms, which formally legalised these firms. In 1993, the Ministry of Justice issued the Proposals on Deepening Lawyer's Reform, which legitimised the existence of partnership law firms.[25] In 2007, the amended Lawyers Law formally recognised individual law firms.

Chubanshe, 2007), p. 340. The 2012 figure is from Marco Marazzi and Chen Youxi, 'A Tale of Two Cities: The Legal Profession in China', a work paper at International Bar Association's Human Rights Institute (Ibahri), available at http://www.chenyouxi.com/cnweb/html/youxizhuzuo/201301272415.html. Last visited September 2013.

23 Lawyers Committee for Human Rights, *Lawyers in China: Obstacles to Independence and the Defense of Rights* (New York: Lawyers Committee for Human Rights, March 1998), p. 39.

24 See Xiao Shengxi et al. (eds), *supra* note 4, p. 25.

25 The document is contained in Zhang Geng et al. (eds), *supra* note 14, pp. 665–671.

The scope of legal practice has also expanded from traditional civil representation and criminal defence, to participating in contract negotiations, acting as agent *ad litem* in trademark, patent and copyright lawsuits, and in dealing with matters in other emerging and more technical fields of law. In the larger cities, lawyers are deeply involved in foreign investment, trade, BOT (build, operate and transfer) and other highly-profitable commercial spheres.

The growth of the legal profession is also mirrored in lawyers' financial strength. At present, some private lawyers are considered the highest earners. Of course, a great disparity of income exists between lawyers in different regions and interestingly also among lawyers in the same region. 'While the national average income is approximately 80,000 RMB, the average income for a lawyer in Beijing and many other coastal cities has reached 300,000 RMB or more. Within cities with a profitable legal profession, the top 20 per cent of the lawyers generate 80 per cent of the income. There is thus a great concentration of wealth among the legal profession among a selected few firms'.[26]

The Lawyers Law and Legal Practice

The expansion in both the number of lawyers and the quantity of work has increased public expectations of professionalism. In 1989, the Ministry of Justice began drafting a law which aimed to govern the legal profession. Seven years later the Lawyers Law of the People's Republic of China was finally promulgated by the National People's Congress Standing Committee on 15 May 1996.[27] It came into force on 1 January 1997, containing 53 articles regulating the qualification of lawyers, the management of law firms, the rights and duties of lawyers, legal liability and legal aid. This Law has played a positive role in standardising legal practices and fortifying the legal system as a whole. However, the rapid development of the legal profession also brought with it an increasing need for modification, in order to meet emerging challenges and problems. To date the Lawyers Law has been amended three times: in 2001, 2007 and 2012. Some substantive elements of progress are reflected in the 2007 and 2012 amendments.[28]

Qualifications to Become a Licensed Lawyer

Article 2 of the 1996 Lawyers Law defined lawyers as 'legal practitioners', holding a certificate which entitles them to practise law and 'provide legal services to society'. The term 'legal practitioners' replaced 'state legal workers' in the 1980 Provisional Regulations of the People's Republic of China on Lawyers, and confirms the status of lawyers as independent professionals, in lieu of other judicial workers who hold the status of civil servant. The 2007 amended Lawyers

26 Fu Hualing, 'When Lawyers are Prosecuted … The Struggle of a Profession in Transition', 2 (2007) *Journal of Comparative Law*, p. 113. It was observed that the 'financial success of lawyers in China's top corporate law firms working on international commercial transactions belies the grim reality that most Chinese lawyers are struggling for survival'. See also Ethan Michelson, 'The Practice of Law as an Obstacle to Justice: Chinese Lawyers at Work', 40 (2006) *Law and Society Review*, p. 10.

27 The English translation of the Law is available at http://www.lawinfochina.com/display.aspx?lib=law&id=1155&CGid. Last visited September 2013. The Law applies only to licensed attorneys.

28 For the text of the 2007 amended Law on Lawyers, see http://www.csclawyers.org/letters/Lawyers%20Law%202007.pdf. Last visited September 2013. For the text of the 2012 amended Law on Lawyers, see http://law.law-star.com/showtxt?multiSearch=&dbsType=chl/lar/iel/scs/hnt/eag/cas&dbsText=&isopen=1&keywords=&dbn=chl&fn=chl390s527.txt&file=&upd=9. Last visited September 2013.

Law further requires lawyers to 'provide legal services for clients'. Such a notion could be conveyed as a change in the conception of relationships in the legal field, with the emergence of the nature of the lawyer–client relationship, as opposed to the previous lawyer–society relationship.

An individual may become a qualified lawyer through one of two routes. The former involves passing the National Unified Judicial Examination, followed by working as a trainee for one year at a law firm, and then applying for a certificate to practise law from the local judicial bureau. The latter route grants the title of 'lawyer' upon an assessment and subsequent approval (*kaohe*) by the judicial administrative department of the State Council. Eligible candidates include those who: have attained a Bachelor or higher-level degree from a university, work and specialise in a field which lacks the necessary legal service staff, possess a minimum of 15 years of professional experience, and retain a senior professional title or have attained an equivalent level of professional skill.[29]

At present, the first route – passing the NUJE – is the most common channel taken to obtain legal qualification. The *kaohe* system is intended merely to supplement the NUJE. During the renewal of the legal profession, which saw its reinvigoration between 1979 and 1986, the *kaohe* system provided the only means through which one could become a qualified lawyer.[30] The importance of *kaohe* was confirmed in the drafting of the 1996 Lawyers Law, as the Minister of Justice explained how certain candidates 'are of a higher cultural level and have engaged in legal professional work for a longer period of time and are of a higher level of legal proficiency. Qualifying them as lawyers through *kaohe* was suitable to the reality.'[31] Although the *kaohe* system is scarcely used in practice, the 2007 amended Lawyers Law retained it. The primary reason behind the retention of this method lay in the flexibility it allows for, in opening the legal profession to those with expertise in international trade rules, finance, securities, intellectual property, as well as the ability to use English as a working language.[32]

The NUJE is considered to be an arduous examination for potential lawyers, judges and prosecutors. After it was first introduced in 2002, through to 2007 a mere 135,000 of the approximately 1,120,000 individuals who sat the exam passed with the required grade. Consequently, the average pass rate stands at around 10 per cent.[33] Yet this number continues to rise; during the last 10 sittings of the NUJE, from 2002 to 2012, approximately 500,000 applicants gained the legal professional qualification.[34]

---

29 Article 8 of the 2007 amended Lawyers Law.

30 The *Kaohe* system was further confirmed in the 'Proposal for Deepening the Reform of Lawyers' Work' issued by the Ministry of Justice in 1993. The text can be found in Zhang Geng et al. (eds), *supra* note 14, pp. 665–671. It stated that the judicial organs should grant a lawyer's title to one who works in a law firm and meets one of the following conditions: holds a senior title from a law school of a university or law research institute; holds a senior title and has worked in the legal field in governmental institutions; holds a senior title, and is engaged in economic or scientific work, and is familiar with legal issues in a particular field, and has participated in a legal training course for more than six months; obtained a law degree or above at Master's level abroad, has worked in a law firm for more than a year upon returning to China; has obtained a law degree at or above Master's level in China and has worked more than one year in a law firm.

31 This speech is contained in Zhang Geng et al. (eds), *supra* note 14, pp. 14–15.

32 'Sifabu Fuzeren Jiu Xiudinghou De Lushifa Da Xinhuashe Jizhewen' (Replies of the Official of the Ministry of Justice on the Newly Amended Lawyers Law), available at http://news.xinhuanet.com/legal/2007-10/30/content_6975949.htm. Last visited September 2013.

33 'Guojia Sifa Kaoshi Wunian Zhutui Yifa Zhiguo' (Five Years Unified Judicial Examination Contributes to Ruling the Country According to Law), available at www.legalinfo.gov.cn/moj/sfkss/2007-09/17/content_703272.htm. Last visited September 2013.

34 'Gaige Wanshan Sifa Kaoshi Zhidu Qude Xinjinzhan, 10 Ci Sifa Kaoshi 50 Wan Ren Huode Falu Zhiye Zige' (New Improvements Have Been Achieved in Reforming UJE, and 500,000 People Obtained

A lawyer's licence is renewed annually by the local judicial bureau. When this occurs, lawyers must submit an application, a summary of their work over the last year and a certificate of the completion of their training.[35] Lawyers are unable to pass the annual assessment if any of the following issues are applicable to their circumstances: breached disciplinary rules, engaged in unethical conduct and, in some extreme cases, involved in politically sensitive cases.

Some restrictions disallow certain individuals from practising law. According to Article 7 of the 2007 amended Lawyers Law, persons who cannot be granted certificates to practise law include: those who have no capacity or a limited capacity for civil conduct;[36] those who have been subject to a criminal penalty with the exception of instances of negligence; or those who have been dismissed from public employment or whose certificate to practise as a lawyer has been revoked. The revocation of a lawyer's certificate is the severest punishment of all, as once revoked, one can no longer practise. Although, under the Administrative Litigation Law, a lawyer is capable of bringing a lawsuit against the revocation decision of the relevant judicial bureau, in practice, such challenges rarely occur. There have been instances in which a lawyer, whose license had been revoked in one area, relocated to an area where there was no record of the revocation, and having not been tracked to that area, continued practising.[37]

In facing the problem that some government officials moonlight as lawyers, the Lawyers Law prohibits employees in government institutions from acting concurrently as practising lawyers.[38] In addition, lawyers who formerly acted as judges or procurators must not serve as agents *ad litem* or defence counsel within two years of leaving their post in the courts or procuratorate.[39] In the 1980s and 1990s, many practising lawyers had a background of having worked in either a court or procuratorate. Nowadays, this percentage is decreasing. There are both positive and negative ramifications in lawyers with a judicial background going on to work in the legal profession. The positive aspects of such centre on the extensive knowledge they hold of the inner workings of the judicial system, and their ability to use their experience, or even 'personal relationships' with prosecutors or judges to have their cases dealt with fairly. This is especially important under the current judicial system where judicial independence is deficient, and judges and prosecutors frequently neglect lawyers' rights and opinions, resulting in unfair or even wrongfully-handled cases. However, the negative impact draws upon how a lawyer's links with judicial personnel may further exacerbate the practice of relationships playing an improper role in the judicial process, consequently harming normal legal practice and endorsing judicial corruption.

Legal Professional Qualifications during the Last 10 Exams), available at http://www.moj.gov.cn/sfkss/content/2012-02/13/content_3347463.htm?node=299. Last visited September 2013.

35 The Ministry of Justice has issued an internal circular calling on all lawyers to take 40 hours of training each year. The training courses must be approved by the Ministry of Justice and administered by the same Ministry or local judicial departments, bar associations or other authorised entities. Such courses focus mainly on introducing new laws and professional responsibility. Lawyers Committee for Human Rights, *supra* note 23, p. 63.

36 This sets the age limit at over 18, because under Articles 11, 12 and 13 of the General Principles of the Civil Law of the PRC (referred to as the Civil Code by Chinese scholars), a citizen aged 18 or over is an adult, and has full capacity for civil acts. A minor aged 10 or over is a person with limited capacity for civil acts; a minor under the age of 10 and a mentally ill person, who is unable fully to account for his own conduct, is a person having no capacity for civil acts.

37 Interviews with Chinese lawyers, Beijing, August 2009.

38 Article 11 of the 2007 amended Lawyers Law.

39 Article 41 of the 2007 amended Lawyers Law.

Due to the sharp increase in market demand for lawyers in the 1980s and 1990s, not everyone who claimed that they held the title of 'lawyer' could realistically be considered to be a qualified, licensed lawyer. In fact, the misuse of the title to practise law was not at all uncommon. At that time it was a commonly-held belief that in order to be a successful law firm, the firm needed to hire three different kinds of personnel: those who had adequate knowledge of substantive law, those who knew how to conduct litigation, and those who had a 'wide network of relations' in order to acquire business for the firm. For their own convenience, some law firms acquired personnel who were ill-qualified to act as lawyers. In recent years, the situation has gradually changed. With increasing numbers of qualified lawyers on the market, law firms prefer to hire lawyers with legal knowledge. Law graduates from well-known and renowned universities also hold an advantage over those who have graduated from less-accomplished institutions.

Furthermore, an emerging pattern has begun to take shape in which law graduates are less inclined to pursue a career as a lawyer, or prefer to choose another profession after a few years of practising law. An investigation uncovered that around 10 per cent of young lawyers could not endure the first three years of practising law, for three main reasons.[40] Firstly, their income was considered too low. Among those investigated, aged between 25 and 35, around 60 per cent earned less than RMB 50,000 annually. Secondly, their capacity to generate cases was deficient. Some complained that in order to get cases, they were forced to use various methods, for instance, distributing business cards to the public in order to increase business; some even resorted to waiting outside the courts to provide legal services. Thirdly, they lacked guidance from senior lawyers. The reality is that, after years of tough studying at law school, and having passed the extremely competitive National Unified Judicial Examination, graduates then enter a profession with a low income and that is rife with risks.

Many young lawyers are forced to choose other occupations or return to university to complete advanced studies. Many young graduates are indeed afraid of becoming lawyers. A survey reported that roughly 75 per cent of students desired a job in the legal profession when they began law school; prior to their graduation that rate had fallen to a mere 10 per cent.[41] In the late 1980s and 1990s, it was considered admirable for judges and public prosecutors to resign their positions and become lawyers. Yet, nowadays, seeking a job in the court or procuratorate is far more popular than taking the route of becoming a lawyer. This reflects the increasingly competitive nature of a career as a lawyer. One has to generate one's own income in order to survive and be successful when becoming a partner of a law firm. Otherwise, one has to work as an assistant to a lawyer, which is both low-paid and lacks job security. In comparison, a job in a court or procuratorate provides security. Normally, after a number of years, promotion to the position of judge or public prosecutor is probable. The salary entitlements have also increased over time, which guarantees that judges and prosecutors in cities can afford a good quality of life. And with a certain amount of both will and luck, promotion to a higher judicial position, with a higher income and social status, as well as other privileges, may also beckon.

---

40 Chen Hongwei, 'Guanzhu Qingnian Lushi: Buyao Rang Qingnian Lushi De Lu Yuezou Yuezhai' (Care About Young Lawyers: Don't Let Them Go Towards a Narrow Road), available at http://news.xinhuanet.com/legal/2007-09/10/content_6695267.htm. Last visited September 2013.

41 *Ibid.*

Law Firms

A law firm is an organisation in which lawyers practise. Importantly, lawyers cannot accept cases in their own name; instead, law firms accept cases in a uniform manner and conclude contracts with their clients on a collective basis, instead of through individual lawyers.[42] The requirements for establishing a law firm are relatively straightforward: a name, an address, articles of association, qualified lawyer(s), founder(s) with certain professional experience and without a record of punishment or licence suspension within three years; and with a certain minimum of assets.[43] With regard to the last of these requisites, the amount currently stands at RMB 100,000. There were originally three types of law firms in China: state-funded, co-operative and partnership. However, the 2007 amended Lawyers Law repealed the classification of the co-operative law firm,[44] and replaced it with the individual law firm.

Most of the law firms in China currently take the form of a partnership. In June 1988, the Ministry of Justice decided formally to allow the creation of a few such partnership firms as an experiment. These were the first privately-owned firms after the founding of the PRC. Under the previous law, a firm's property was provided by the partners and belonged to the firm as an entity. Partners bore unlimited joint liability for the debts of said firm. This in turn meant that if one partner had an issue, the other partners had to bear joint liability. The 2007 amended Lawyers Law consequently allows for a greater degree of flexibility, either to form ordinary partnerships or special-ordinary partnerships. A special-ordinary partnership is similar to a limited partnership. The official explanation given in allowing such partnerships was based on the consideration of developing large-scale law firms, with the idea of strengthening China's position internationally in a competitive market.[45] Ultimately, partners bear liability for the debt of the law firm according to the form of the partnership which they have predetermined (Art. 15). The total income of such a firm, after the deduction of costs, taxes and reserved funds, is divided between the partners according to the arrangements made between them. In turn, the lawyers hired to work for such firms receive a beneficial salary. The details of any remuneration are stipulated in the agreement between the partners and the hired lawyers.

Because of controversial opinions expressed during the drafting process of the Lawyers Law, the 1996 Law avoided the recognition of individual law firms, although, in reality, some such firms existed, particularly in the Special Economic Zones. For instance, in June 1996, the Standing Committee of the People's Congress in Hainan province passed the Regulations of the Hainan Special Economic Zone on Practising Lawyers. The Regulations provided the first example of local law legitimising individual law firms. In 1997, there were 34 state-funded, 38 partnership and 14 individual law firms in Hainan province.[46] At the state level, the 2007 amended Lawyers Law formally recognises individual law firms. To establish such a firm, the founder must have at least five years of experience practising law and be capable of and willing to bear unlimited liability for the debts of the firm. Individual law firms have the advantages of low operating costs

42 Article 25 of the 2007 amended Lawyers Law.

43 Article 14 of the 2007 amended Lawyers Law.

44 The co-operative law firm was originally operated by lawyers who resigned from state-funded law firms and who felt confident that they would have a sufficient number of cases to generate a reasonable income. Over time, most of such firms transformed into partnership law firms.

45 'Sifabu Fuzeren Jiu Xiudinghou De Lushifa Da Xinhuashe Jizhewen', *supra* note 32.

46 Li Jingzhong, 'Tantu Jiuzai Jiaoxia: Hainan Jiansheng Shinian Lushi Gongzuo Gaige Huimou' (The Road Is Under One's Feet: Retrospective on Reform on Lawyers' Work over the Last Ten Years in Hainan Province), 1 (1998) *Zhongguo Lushi* (Chinese Lawyer), p. 9.

and a clear hierarchy and distribution of responsibility, and are especially suitable for lawyers providing legal services at the grass-roots level.[47]

State-funded law firms are those established by judicial administrative organs with state funds, which carry out legal business operations independently, and assume liability for the debts of the firm with their whole assets.[48] A lawyer's salary is based on a flexible system, which takes into account the total number of years spent at the firm, experience, and the quality and quantity of cases handled by the individual. State-funded law firms were the first organisations through which Chinese lawyers were able to practise law after the revival of the legal system with lawyer-involvement in 1979. Initially, lawyers enjoyed civil servant status and received a fixed salary from the state. From 1983, reforms were framed to make them increasingly financially self-sufficient. By June 1995, of the 5,500 state-funded law firms, accounting for 76.4 per cent of the total number of law firms, 2,674 (48.6 per cent) no longer relied upon the government for financial support.[49]

By the end of 1997, there were approximately 5,519 state-funded law firms, 1,014 co-operative, and 1,851 partnership law firms, accounting for about 70 per cent, 10 per cent and 20 per cent, respectively, of total law firms in the PRC.[50] At that time, state-funded law firms dominated. However, by 2007, of the 13,096 law firms in China, only 1,470 were state-funded law firms, constituting 11 per cent of the total figure. State-funded law firms are now extinct in Beijing, Shanghai and some provinces.[51] This marked shift reflects the development of the Chinese legal profession from the state-owned, public sector to the privately-owned, service-providing sector. The remaining state-funded law firms continue to function in the north-west of China, in the less economically-developed regions, where it has been reported that lawyers were absent in 206 counties. Such firms can realistically only survive with government funding. Despite a degree of support being afforded to the idea of abolishing state-funded law firms, the Ministry of Justice insists that they are necessary in the poor areas, in order to provide the bare minimum legal services to local people.[52]

The number of law firms has blossomed from 3,291 in 1987 to 19,361 in 2012.[53] Most law firms, though, remain small in stature. For instance, according to a 2005 survey in Beijing, where the legal profession is the most developed in China, most law firms operate on a small scale with the number of partners ranging from three to 10. Nearly 50 per cent of law firms have fewer than 10 licensed lawyers.[54] However, in recent years, a number of partnership law firms have quickly

47 'Sifabu Fuzeren Jiu Xiudinghou De Lushifa Da Xinhuashe Jizhewen', *supra* note 32.

48 Article 20 of the 2007 amended Lawyers Law.

49 See Zhang Geng et al. (eds), *supra* note 14, p. 95.

50 See Qian Guzhou, interview with Duan Zhenkun, head of the department of lawyers in the Ministry of Justice, 1 (1998) *Zhongguo Lushi* (Chinese Lawyer), p. 7.

51 Ni Xiao, 'Lushi Fa Xiuding Cao'an Youwang Shiyue Chutai, "Guozisuo" Reng Baoliu' (Amended Lawyer's Law Is Expected to Be Issued in October, 'State-owned Law Firms' Continue to Exist), available at http://news.xinhuanet.com/legal/2007-08/09/content_6501134.htm. Last visited September 2013. Sun Jian, 'Beijing Lushiye Zhuangkuang De Shuzi Guancha' (Statistical Observation of Beijing's Legal Profession), 12 (2004) *Zhongguo Sifa* (Chinese Justice), p. 31.

52 Ni Xiao, *ibid.*

53 For the 1987 figure, see China Law Yearbook 1988; the 2012 figure can be found in the 2012 report of the All China Lawyers Association. Available at http://politics.gmw.cn/2013-08/26/content_8708878.htm. Last visited September 2013.

54 'A Current Survey on Management of Law Firms in Beijing', conducted by Beijing Lawyers Association. The report of the survey is available at http://www.china-lawyering.com/main/list.asp?Unid=872. Last visited September 2013. According to the Shenzhenshi Lushi Shiwusuo Guanli Xianzhuang Diaocha Baogao Ji Lushi Zhiye Yu Shengcun Xianzhuang Diaocha Baogao (Survey of Management of Law Firms and

expanded with notably impressive results. Indeed, the difference between small and large law firms is vast. Most of the large law firms are located in Beijing, Shanghai, Guangzhou and Shenzhen. A number of them, most notably, King & Wood, Jun He, Fangda, Dacheng and Zhonglun, are gaining increasing international recognition and playing a larger role on the world stage. Similar to larger law firms in Western countries, the large Chinese firms are fully adept at handling the business market, providing a wide range of legal services, especially with regard to foreign-related banking, investment, trade, general corporate matters, securities and M&A (mergers and acquisitions), dispute resolution, intellectual property protection, bankruptcy, real estate. It has been observed that, even though the Chinese legal profession as a whole 'is still in its formative stage, a small sector of elite corporate lawyers has already emerged and controls much of the most profitable and prestigious legal work'.[55]

The Management System for Lawyers and Law Firms

Lawyers and law firms come under the dual leadership and control of the Ministry of Justice and its local bureau of justice, and the All China Lawyers Association and its local branches.

Since 1980, the Ministry of Justice and its affiliated bureaus of justice at the local level have continued to exercise organisational leadership over (*zuzhi lingdao*), and professional supervision of (*yewu jiandu*) law firms. The Ministry of Justice is the highest government institution with authority over the affairs of lawyers as a whole. In recent years, the Ministry of Justice has strengthened the Communist Party's role with regard to law firms by requesting that they establish Party branches. In March 2008, the Ministry of Organisation of the Central Communist Party and the Ministry of Justice jointly issued the Announcement on Further Strengthening and Improving the Party's Work in the Lawyer Profession, which called on law firms to do just this. In response, around 90 per cent of law firms had set up such branches by 2009. In May 2009, 200 lawyers, who were also Party branch secretaries of law firms, attended a political training programme organised by the Ministry of Justice. This was the first such political training for Party secretaries in law firms.[56] In practice, if a law firm consists of three or more Party members, three of them can be selected to form a Party branch, with one secretary at the forefront. If a law firm has less than three Party members, it can select a 'political assistant officer' (*zhengzhi xieliyuan*) from amongst Party members. If a law firm has no Party members, it can hire one adjunct lawyer to fill this gap, such as a university lecturer.[57]

Local bureaus of justice have considerable power in controlling lawyers and law firms. Under the 2007 amended Lawyers Law, the bureau of justice at a provincial level awards certificates to practise law (Article 6), examines and verifies the establishment of law firms (Article 18), and has the capacity to revoke a lawyer's certificate to practise where said lawyer has been convicted of an

---

the Survey of Lawyers' Professional Work and Life in Shenzhen) published by the Shenzhen Bar Association in 2008, in Shenzhen the law firms with three to 10 partners account for 90.72 per cent of all law firms; the law firms with more than 10 partners account for 8.25 per cent. Compare this to Beijing and Shanghai, the law firms with three to 10 partners account for 91.37 per cent in Beijing, and 65.52 per cent in Shanghai. These figures are available at http://book.dajianet.com/996709/859319/?validated=true. Last visited September 2013.

55 Sida Liu, 'Client Influence and the Contingency of Professionalism: The Work of Elite Corporate Lawyers in China', 40 (2006) *Law & Society Review*, p. 751.

56 '"Teshu Baolei" De Tebie Peixun, Lushi Shiwusuo Dangzhishu Naru Peixun Tixi' (Special Training for the 'Special Force', the Party Branch Secretary of Law Firms are Trained). Available at http://www.infzm.com/content/29527. Last visited September 2013.

57 Interview with lawyers, Beijing, August 2009.

intentional crime with penal punishment (Article 49). The bureaus of justice at a district level are empowered to issue warnings, fines, confiscate illegal gains and suspend a lawyer's practice for three months to one year as punishment (Articles 48 and 49).

Lawyers' associations acting as self-regulating social organisations of lawyers were first created at a provincial level and in municipalities at the end of the 1970s and in the early 1980s. In July 1986, the All China Lawyers Association (ACLA) was established. Chinese lawyers must be members of the local lawyers' association in their area of residence. Simultaneously, they become a member of the ACLA.

Although lawyers' associations are indeed self-regulating social organisations of lawyers, Chinese lawyers' associations do not take the same form as they often do in Western countries, with less emphasis upon the institutions as independent and professional organisations. Lawyers' associations in China are led by the Ministry of Justice and its affiliated local bureaus. The ACLA is registered as a social organisation sponsored by the Ministry of Justice; local lawyers' associations are registered with the sponsorship of the corresponding local judicial bureaus. Such affiliation with the governmental judicial department is a strength as well as a weakness for the lawyers' associations. For the ACLA, the close links with the Ministry reinforces its formal authority, but, at the same time, forces it to serve the interests of the Ministry, which on some occasions may put the ACLA in a controversial position of having to protect lawyers' professional interests against complying with the policy of the government. A similar situation likewise applies to local lawyers' associations and local judicial bureaus.

The functions of lawyers' associations, as provided for in the 2007 amended Lawyers Law, include: (1) ensuring that lawyers practise law according to the law and that the law safeguards lawyers' legitimate rights; (2) summarising and exchanging the work experience of lawyers; (3) issuing professional standards and punishment rules; (4) organising professional training to educate, examine and supervise lawyers in professional ethics and legal practice disciplines; (5) organising and managing internships for prospective lawyers; (6) giving rewards and imposing punishments on lawyers and law firms; (7) handling petitions against lawyers, to mediate in disputes arising during the course of legal practice, and in handling lawyers' complaints; and, (8) carrying out any other functions provided by the law, administrative regulations and rules, and charters of lawyers' associations. It is interesting to note that the 2007 amendment deleted the requirement 'to organise exchanges between the Chinese and foreign lawyers', which was provided in the 1996 Lawyers Law as one function of lawyers' associations.

As the most vital function listed in the Lawyer's Law, the primary task of associations is to protect the legal rights of lawyers. This has been carried out by both local lawyers' associations and the ACLA in turn. In July 1998, the ACLA set up a Committee for the Protection of Lawyers' Legitimate Rights and Interests, consisting of 60 lawyers recommended by lawyers' associations at the provincial level.[58] Similar committees also exist in various localities. These are the functional bodies led by these associations, with practising lawyers participating, in the mission of advocating rights for lawyers. They investigate cases of violations of lawyers' rights, propose opinions for handling cases, provide legal aid to lawyers, and put aside funds for the advocacy of lawyers' rights.[59] Local lawyers' associations usually report cases of serious violations of lawyers' rights to

58 Qi Xiangchu, 'Baohu Lushi Renzhong Daoyuan: Quanguo Zhaokai Weihu Lushi Zhiye Quanyi Zuotan Hui' ('A Long Way to Go in the Protection of Lawyers: Seminar on the Protection on Lawyers' Rights by All China Lawyers Association'), 9 (1998) *Zhongguo Lushi* (Chinese Lawyer), pp. 4–7.

59 'Quanguo Luxie Weiquan Gongzuo Baogao' (Report of the Work on Right Advocacy by the ACLA) (2002), see http://www.acla.org.cn/program/article.jsp?CID=998977585&ID=1808. Last visited June 2012.

the ACLA, which then sends an investigative team to help resolve the problem.[60] For cases with a national impact, the ACLA sometimes organises meetings consisting of experts in order to seek solutions. It has also sent the highest-qualified lawyers to defend or represent those lawyers who were prosecuted simply for doing their job. Furthermore, the ACLA is active in reporting cases to the relevant central governmental organisations, and in utilising the public media to help solve some difficult cases of the violation of lawyers' rights.

However, the ACLA has also recognised the lack of formal channels through which individual lawyers who have been treated unfairly by the courts or procuratorates can seek recompense. This led to lawyers raising concerns about both the ACLA itself and local lawyers' associations; consequently weakening the sense of belonging that lawyers have to the ACLA or local associations.[61] On the official website of the ACLA a lawyer wrote:

> Lawyer associations should be strong in protecting lawyers' practising rights, but this is not the reality. When lawyers are accused of the crime of perjury or assisting perjury, lawyers associations often use such cases as 'a bad example' to educate lawyers. If complaints by the court or procuratorate are sent to the associations, the latter too often punish lawyers without a careful examination of the real situation. As a professional organisation, the major role of the association should be on fostering, helping, managing, supervising and punishing. But if it only focuses on administration, supervision, punishment and collecting fees, the individuals of such associations have to take good care of themselves.[62]

It is often reported that it is common for lawyers to help each other when a crisis occurs, but organised, public action is much more infrequent. The strongest instance of a lawyers' association taking action in protecting a lawyer occurred in December 1997, when the Lawyers' Association in Yueyang city of Hunan province came to the aid of lawyer Liu Zhengqing. The Association issued a document informing lawyers in Yueyang city:

> Lawyer Liu Zhengqing in acting as a defence lawyer, was illegally arrested for more than 28 days by the procuratorate on suspicion of the crime of falsifying evidence … (the Association) has petitioned the relevant departments several times for Liu's release, without success. In order to uphold the dignity of law, personal rights, the right of lawyers to practise law, and to guarantee that lawyers' rights are not infringed, the Association … decides that: due to our city not providing the basic conditions for lawyers to handle criminal cases and the fact that lawyers' personal rights cannot be guaranteed, from today onwards all lawyers in our city should suspend working on any criminal cases. … The above announcement must be followed by each law firm.[63]

---

60 However, the ACLA complained that some local associations have not paid adequate attention to complaints by lawyers, which resulted in some lawyers appealing to the ACLA directly. The procedure should be that a local association first investigates, attempting to resolve the problem and only submitting the case to the ACLA if it fails to find a solution. The ACLA often requests that local associations provide their opinions on individual cases, but too often the ACLA receives no reply. *Ibid.*, p. 5.

61 Carlos Wing-Hung Lo and Ed Snape, *supra* note 2, pp. 451–452.

62 Chen Wei, 'Lushi Yao Xiaoxin Bozishang De Lijian' (Lawyers Should Be Careful about the Sword at Their Neck), available at http://www.yz148.com/rjwx_detail.php?id=71. Last visited September 2013.

63 Cited from Zhang Sizhi, 'Zhang Sizhi Lushi Zhi Beijing Luxie Zhuxi De Yifeng Gongkaixin' (An Open Letter from Lawyer Zhang Sizhi to the Chairman of the Beijing Lawyers Association), 1 (2006) *Lushi Yu Fazhi*, published by the Bureau of Judicial Affairs of Zhejing Province.

Such an act and public display of disapproval from the local lawyers' association is unprecedented. When Liu's case was on trial, the local Association organised more than 100 lawyers to attend the hearing, leading to both verbal and physical conflict with the judges in the courtroom. Two lawyers were taken out of the courtroom, beaten and handcuffed by the judicial police of the court. Only with the intervention of the higher court were the two lawyers later released. Lawyer Liu was declared innocent by the court and the procuratorate provided him with RMB 11,000 in compensation.[64] Another instance of collective action was observed when lawyer Ma Guanjun in Inner Mongolia was tried for the crime of perjury. The local lawyers' association appointed two eminent lawyers to defend him; and hundreds of lawyers were present at the court hearing.[65]

There have also been cases in which lawyers fall into trouble because of their defence of other lawyers. One well-known catastrophic case is that of Mr Guo Guoting, a successful lawyer in maritime law in Shanghai. When his fellow lawyer, Zheng Enchong, was arrested for the crime of disclosing state secrets, Guo Guoting courageously acted as Zheng's defence lawyer. This experience shifted his career from a successful commercial lawyer to a human rights lawyer in 2003, and afterwards he encountered immense problems, and was eventually forced to leave China with his family.[66]

One special feature of the management of Chinese lawyers and law firms is the capacity for direct interference of judicial bureaus and lawyers' associations in the lawyers' handling of individual cases. This has developed, in practice, into a 'reporting and approval system'. Local judicial bureaus have issued documents requiring lawyers and firms to report 'major or difficult' cases (*zhongda yinan anjian*) to the local justice department either for filing or approval purposes. It was reported that in 1999, the Beijing Judicial Bureau formally set up a 'leading group' to deal with such reports. This group consisted predominantly of chief officials from the Bureau, and had the power of scrutinising cases relating to state security and those involving high-ranking officials and influential celebrities. 'Lawyers handling such cases must report to and abide by decisions, which may concern the substantive outcome of a case, made by the leading group.'[67] In April 2006, the Judicial Bureau of Shenyang city in Liaoning province issued Several Opinions on Reporting and Approval by Shenyang Lawyers in Handling Significant and Difficult Cases. Under the Opinions, the significant and difficult cases included criminal cases which contained different opinions on the classification of crimes; cases where lawyers intended to present a 'not guilty' defence; cases exposed by the media involving ambiguous facts; cases of mergers and bankruptcy of state-owned enterprises; cases of compensation for land appropriated in rural areas or relating to farmers' interests; cases with complex legal issues on housing revocations in cities; and cases of the illegal gathering of funds, which generate social attention and have an impact on social stability and the public interest. The Opinions

64 Liu Zhengqing, 'Zhongguo Diyili Lushi Babian De Taiqian Muhou' (The Background to China's First Strike by Lawyers), 11 (1999) *Zhongguo Lushi* (Chinese Lawyer), pp. 40–41.

65 Terence C. Halliday and Sida Liu, 'Birth of a Liberal Moment? Looking Through a One-Way Mirror at Lawyers' Defence of Criminal Defendants in China', in Terence C. Halliday, Lucien Karpik and Malcolm M. Feeley (eds), *Fighting for Political Freedom: Comparative Studies of the Legal Complex and Political Liberalism* (Oxford: Hart Publishing, 2007), p. 93.

66 For his experience and thought in Chinese, see 'My Twenty Years Legal Practice', available at http://blog.boxun.com/hero/guoguoting/2_1.shtml. Last visited September 2013. For information about the Guo Guoting case in English, see Al Young, 'The Continuing Lack of Independence of Chinese Lawyers', 18 (2005) *Georgetown Journal of Legal Ethics*, pp. 1134–1150.

67 Ping Yu, 'Glittery Promise vs. Dismal Reality: The Role of a Criminal Lawyer in the People's Republic of China after the 1996 Revision of the Criminal Procedure Law', 35 (2002) *Vanderbilt Journal of Transnational Law*, pp. 833–834.

requested lawyers to quickly report to the local judicial bureau and the lawyers' association with information regarding the trustees, content of the trust, the governmental departments involved, the basic facts and relevant legal issues of the case, the legal and defence opinions of lawyers and their firms, and other requested information. It stressed that lawyers and law firms should not, in handling the aforementioned cases, give interviews to journalists or openly express opinions or publish articles without the approval of the judicial bureau.[68]

In recent years, conflicts caused by rural land appropriation, urban forced evictions, the privatisation of state-owned enterprises and environmental pollution, have led to some so-called 'mass cases' in which several individuals or a group of people bring a lawsuit against local government agencies. With an increasing consciousness of citizens regarding rights and with liberal media coverage, some lawyers have courageously borne the responsibility to represent weak groups in lawsuits against local governments. In March 2006, the ACLA published the ACLA Guiding Opinions concerning Lawyers' Handling of Mass Cases.[69] A 'mass case' is defined as a suit involving 10 or more plaintiffs suing organs of the government. The Opinions request that law firms rapidly report to the local association if they have been asked to represent a 'mass case'. The decision of whether or not to accept a case is to be decided by at least three partners of the relevant firm. The director of the law firm is to take responsibility for lawyers when they handle cases and quickly take control if they make a mistake. Lawyers should co-operate with the relevant governmental institutions, advise clients to strictly follow the law and advise them against petitioning to higher-tier authorities or organising themselves as a group. After handling such a case, law firms are required to report to the local association. If it is an influential 'mass case', the lawyers' association is required to report to the judicial bureau at the corresponding level. If the lawyer or law firm does not follow the Opinions, causing harmful consequences, lawyers' associations have the authority to punish the lawyer according to the relevant professional rules or request that the judicial bureau impose a punishment. The Opinions require local lawyers' associations to aid, guide and supervise lawyers in handling such cases and also caution law firms to be wary of briefing the media.[70]

According to lawyer Wang Cailiang, who first suggested that the ACLA should draft a document to guide lawyers in handling 'mass cases', he had two reasons for taking the initiative. First, most of the victims of 'mass cases' belong to weaker factions of society who need lawyers' assistance. However, some local rules forbid judges to accept such cases.[71] Such a practice has resulted in the

---

68 For discussion on the Opinions, see Human Rights Watch, *A Great Danger for Lawyers: New Regulatory Curbs on Lawyers Representing Protesters* (Human Rights Watch, 2006), p. 39. Available at http://www.hrw.org/reports/2006/china1206/7.htm. Last visited September 2013.

69 'Zhonghua Quanguo Lushi Xiehui Guanyu Lushi Banli Quntixing Anjian Zhidao Yijian' (20 March 2006), available at http://www.lawyers.com.cn/info/11bbfabc2ecafed984ec364d6e6b8877. Last visited September 2013. The document is with the author.

70 Actually the Opinions are contradictory to the Development Outline of the Chinese Legal Profession (2002–2006) issued by the Ministry of Justice, in which it pointed out that one of the main tasks of the legal profession in the coming five years was to 'lead and push forward lawyers to participate in the settlement of various disputes, especially significant massive disputes, providing services to reduce the burden of farmers, reemployment of laid-off workers, to facilitate solving social conflicts, to contribute to social stability ....' . See Ministry of Justice, Zhongguo Lushi Wunian (2002-2006 nian) Fazhan Gangyao (Development Outline of the Chinese Legal Profession (2002–2006)), Sifa No. 6[2002], 9 (2002) *Zhongguo Lushi* (Chinese Lawyer), p. 15.

71 For instance, in 2003 the Higher People's Court in Guangxi Zhuangzu Autonomous Region issued No. 180 document (*Guigaofa*, 180 [2003]), which listed 13 types of cases courts would not accept, such as disputes over fund-gathering and real estate disputes caused by decisions of local government. Refusal to

weaker groups becoming even more vulnerable and has also escalated social conflict. Second, the particularities of 'mass cases' mean that lawyers bear higher risks. However, in order to uphold social justice, they are forced to accept such cases. Due to a lack of experience, some lawyers encourage clients to take excessive measures, which have caused governmental officials to blame lawyers. Lawyer Wang has worked with a few lawyers in producing a draft proposal on guiding lawyers in handling 'mass cases'.[72] However, the draft was revised by the ACLA, with the resulting document containing more restrictions that have been heavily criticised by lawyers. Some view the issuance of the Opinions as a demonstration that lawyers have lost their ability to practise law independently and that the Opinions will lead more lawyers to refuse accepting 'mass cases'. Thus, some expressed that the Opinions have resulted in placing further restrictions on lawyers representing 'mass cases' rather than providing mechanisms which encourage and protect such positive action by lawyers.[73]

In practice, it is not uncommon for local judicial bureaus to prohibit lawyers from acting in certain cases. For instance, in 2004, the serious Tuojiang water pollution accident in Sichuan province gravely affected the water supplies in five cities, causing the economic loss of about RMB 300 million.[74] Facing such a disaster, the local Judicial Bureau in Yanjiang district of Ziyang city unexpectedly issued an official document requesting all law firms and legal service offices within its jurisdiction not to act as lawyers for parties claiming compensation from the disaster.[75] In 2008, when the tainted milk powder scandal was exposed, the local judicial bureau issued a notice to ask local lawyers to report to the bureau if they were asked to represent the parents of victims. For Chinese lawyers, this was a clear warning, instructing them to steer clear of any involvement in these cases.

The Personal Rights of Lawyers

Article 32 of the 1996 Lawyers Law provides that the personal rights of lawyers are inviolable during the course of their legal practice. Article 37 of the 2007 amended Lawyers Law retained this provision and added that opinions and remarks made by defence lawyers in the courtroom cannot lead to prosecution, unless they threaten national security, maliciously slander others or seriously disturb the order of court proceedings. This enhanced provision reflects a lawyer's right to civil and penal immunity, namely that lawyers should not bear civil and criminal liability for any statements which they may choose to propound in the courtroom. This principle is enshrined

---

accept such cases has a simple reason – they involve local governmental institutions. Some judges expressed that even if such cases are handled by the courts, the outcome may not be really in the favour of the weaker group since the judgment may just be a piece of paper ignored by the local government.

72 Wang Cailiang, 'Qicaoren Wang Cailiang Tan Lushi Banli Quntixing Anjian Zhidao Yijian' (The Drafter Wang Cailiang Discusses the Guiding Opinion in Dealing with Mass Cases), available at http://www.china-lawyering.com/main/list.asp?unid=434. Last visited September 2013.

73 Interviews with five Chinese lawyers, Beijing, August 2008.

74 'Tuojiang Teda Wuran Shigu An Yishen Panjue Liuren Bei Panxing' (The Serious Pollution Case in Tuojiang, Six People Were Convicted of Crimes by the First Instance Court), available at http://env.people.com.cn/GB/1072/3684760.html. Last visited September 2013.

75 'Sichuan Ziyang Sifaju Buzhun Lushi Jie Tuojiang Wuran Guansi' (The Judicial Bureau of Ziyang in Sichuan Province Does Not Allow Lawyers to Represent Victims of Tuojiang Pollution Case), available at http://info.water.hc360.com/html/001/001/37903.htm. Last visited September 2013.

within the United Nations Basic Principles on the Role of Lawyers.[76] However, the newly-attached exceptional clause, with the vague and ambiguous terms of preventing any threats to national security, slandering others or disturbing court order, has left extensive discretion for judicial officers to interpret and apply it as they see fit. Coupled with the lack of judicial independence and a weak tradition of respecting lawyers, the effectiveness of this provision in relation to the protection of lawyers could be called into question. Preventing abuse of the exceptional clause by arbitrary judicial decisions may become a new frontier for conflict between lawyers and judicial authorities.

In addition, Article 37(3) provides that if a lawyer is detained or arrested on suspicion of any involvement in a crime related to a case during court proceedings, the detaining and arresting organ should inform the lawyer's family, their law firm and the local lawyers' association within 24 hours. Clearly this provision was added due to the continual issue of lawyers being detained or arrested simply for doing their job, and their 'disappearance' often remaining unknown to their families for days or weeks.[77] However, the 2012 amendments now require that the investigating organ is required to promptly inform the law firm to which the lawyer belongs or the local lawyers' association, and inform the lawyer's family according to the relevant provisions of the Criminal Procedure Law.

The barring of any infringements to the personal rights of citizens is a constitutional principle. However, the fact that the Lawyers Law specifically draws upon this has practical significance. Since the resumption of the system of lawyers, the number of publicised cases of serious infringements of lawyers' personal rights remains alarmingly high. Some lawyers have been kidnapped, humiliated or slandered according to media reports. The homes of a number of lawyers have been searched and their property confiscated; some lawyers have even been beaten-up.[78] In 1995, the exposure of a dozen grave cases led to the question being posed publicly: 'who protects Chinese lawyers?'[79] On 22 March 1995 in Hunan province, when lawyer Peng Jie met the accused in detention, the accused escaped after colluding with the custody officials. Peng was charged with the crime of dereliction of his duties and was sentenced to three years' imprisonment by the local court. His conviction was quashed on appeal. On 30 March 1995, lawyer Ren Shangfei from Hebei province was commissioned by his client to travel to Hunan province to handle a dispute. He was subsequently kidnapped and taken hostage by the other party to the dispute. He was beaten up, denied food and subjected to other inhumane treatment, and was rescued only in July 1995, with the help of the ACLA. In 1995, lawyer Ma Haiwang in Shanxi province accepted the commission to act as agent *ad litem* in a divorce case. He was attacked by the other party, which caused him to lose sight in his right eye and suffer other serious injuries.[80] On 11 July 1995, lawyer Zhou Chengxi was handcuffed by three judges in an intermediate people's court and beaten over a

76 Principle 20 provides that 'Lawyers shall enjoy civil and penal immunity for relevant statements made in good faith in written or oral pleadings or in their professional appearances before a court, tribunal or other legal or administrative authority'. For the full text see http://www.unhcr.org/refworld/docid/3ddb9f034.html. Last visited September 2013.

77 For cases of serious violation of lawyers personal rights, see Jerome A. Cohen, 'The Plight of China's Criminal Defence Lawyers', (33) 2003 *Hong Kong Law Journal*, pp. 231–248.

78 A Ji, 'Zhongguo Lushiye De Xianzhuang He Weilai' (The Present Status and Future Perspective of the Chinese Lawyer Profession), 8 (1996) *Zhengfu Fazhi*, p. 5.

79 *Ibid.*

80 Ji Xiangde, 'Zhongguo Xingshi Bianhu Zhidu Fazhan De Mingyun' (The Developmental Fate of the Chinese Criminal Defence System), available at http://journal.chinalawinfo.com/Article_Info.asp?Id=129847. Last visited September 2013.

period of 75 minutes as a result of his insistence in voicing his opinion in a civil case. He suffered serious mental and physical injuries.[81]

Although these cases occurred prior to the promulgation of the 1996 Lawyers Law, the situation after the enactment remains similarly vexing. In May 1998 in Henan province, lawyer Jia Yaojin was beaten in the courtroom by the opposing party who then accused the lawyer of having beaten him. The court took no action against the opposing party until the local government ordered it to do so. Local lawyers also organised a demonstration to support lawyer Jia.[82] In 2002, the ACLA reported that the number of cases involving the violation of a lawyer's personal rights, property rights or other legitimate rights in the practice of law had escalated. From 1999 to 2001 there were around 42 visible cases in which lawyers were kidnapped, beaten up or illegally detained, which accounted for approximately 53 per cent of all cases involving the violation of a lawyer's rights.[83]

A recently-exposed case of a judge beating a lawyer once again demonstrates how dire the situation can become. In March 2006, lawyer Wang Ling from Beijing went to Nankai District Court in Tianjing municipality to file an administrative litigation case on behalf of 11 clients, who were being forced to move away from their houses because of the local government's construction plan. In court, the head of the department for filing cases told the lawyer he could not decide whether the case could be accepted and that he had to ask the head of the division of administrative litigation, Judge Wang Xuelin. Judge Wang met the lawyer and his clients, and told them that because it was a joint suit the court would not accept it. When the lawyer explained he could divide the suit into individual cases, Judge Wang said that he would still not accept this because the case was not against a concrete administrative act of the local governmental institution. The lawyer asked Judge Wang to provide a written note to prove that he did not want to accept the case, Wang refused to do so. The lawyer then asked whether Judge Wang could represent the court in making such a decision. Judge Wang replied: 'I am the court and the court is me, if I say we don't accept the case, we don't file the case.' The lawyer replied that if Judge Wang refused the case, and would not give a written note as evidence of the refusal, he would complain and take the matter to the higher court. The judge then became angry, crossed his desk and hit the lawyer. One of the clients took a photo of this, which caused a dozen judicial police to run to the client and a fight ensued. Judge Wang was outraged with lawyer Wang. Only with the clients' help was lawyer Wang freed, and some of the clients were taken to the hospital.[84]

As the above-mentioned cases reveal, violations of lawyers' personal rights are capable of being committed by either law enforcement officers or non-state actors.[85] In some cases, the perpetrators cannot even be definitively identified. Such a case was recently reported, and has brought a chill to

81 See Xiao Shengxi et al. (eds), *supra* note 4, p. 88.

82 Zeng Cun et al., 'Henan Linzhou: Lushi Dangting Beida Shijian Shimo' (Henan Linzhou: The Experience of a Lawyer Who Was Beaten Up in a Court Room), 9 (1998) *Zhongguo Lushi* (Chinese Lawyer), pp. 12–13.

83 Report on the Work on Rights Advocacy by the ACLA (2002), available at http://202.196.33.227/kns50/detailcyfd.aspx?filename=N2006041237000295&dbname=CYFD. Last visited September 2013.

84 Zhu Tao, 'Beijing Lushi Zishu zai Tianjin Fayuan Zao Faguan Qia Bozi Ouda'(A Beijing lawyer recounted that he was strangled and beaten by a judge in a Tianjin court), Huaxia Shibao (China Times), 11 April 2006. Available at http://news.sina.com.cn/c/p/2006-04-11/10209587608.shtml. Last visited June 2014.

85 In my interviews with lawyers I was told that violations of lawyers' personal rights are committed more by individuals who irrationally blame lawyers for their loss of cases, than by law enforcement officers. However, lawyers hardly publicise their suffering at the hands of individuals except extremely serious physical damage. In discussing the civil violation of lawyers' rights, Fu Hualing observed that in China: 'Law is not a solemn institution and does not command the respect of the general public as it does in a mature legal system, and the standard of judging rights should be set within this particular social context. Unlawful detention, for example, is commonly perpetrated by the government, businesses and individuals, with the abuse in each sphere tending to reinforce that in the others. Frustrated litigants not only verbally and physically abuse lawyers for their and the other side, they

Chinese legal circles. In the late afternoon of 29 September 2007, lawyer Li Heping was abducted in the car park of his law firm in Beijing. His head was hooded and he was driven to an unknown location in the suburbs of Beijing, where he was beaten with bottles and attacked with electrified batons by a few unidentified men who told him to leave Beijing. After hours of physical torture, lawyer Li was dumped in the woods on the morning of the second day.[86] Lawyer Li reported this to the local police but there was no success in identifying the perpetrators' identities. Li Heping is a lawyer who is well known for his commitment to defending claimants in sensitive cases involving religious groups, independent writers and human rights activists. Inevitably, the defence of such people is a highly uncertain and perilous business for a lawyer. While the hidden background of the perpetrators is worrisome, it also demonstrates the complex reality and escalating risks for lawyers.[87] A similarly grave situation occurred when lawyer Zhou Jian in Jiangsu province was kidnapped, handcuffed and beaten by a dozen unidentified people after he defended an accused in a criminal case. It later transpired that the kidnappers were policemen working for the local public security department.[88]

One can only hope that such disheartening episodes are capable of rousing the necessary action from the government to both investigate the criminal act and punish the offenders. It would demonstrate the willingness and commitment of the government to the pursuit of the rule of law if such events led to a nationwide campaign for the protection of lawyers' rights. To date, the reality is somewhat demoralising and in turn generating a worrisomely uncertain future for the rights of lawyers. In today's China, launching a more provocative approach to the safeguarding of lawyers' rights requires the concomitant political courage. At the same time, if the violations of lawyers' personal rights are not effectively addressed, the risk to the personal safety of lawyers will become increasingly serious. Lawyers will not be able to fulfil the role expected of them in fighting legal cases if their personal rights cannot be fully respected and subsequently protected. Ultimately, if this is allowed to continue, this will undermine on-going efforts in improving judicial fairness and pursuing the rule of law in China.

Rights during the Course of Litigation

Judicial neglect of the role of lawyers in the trial process is evidently common. Lawyers often complain of biased treatment, where judges prevent them from presenting their arguments at critical moments, or even order lawyers to leave the courtroom. A recently reported case taking place in a Beijing court illustrates the seriousness of the challenges faced. In September 2007, the Haidian District Court in Beijing handled a criminal case, involving 16 people. The clients hired

---

also attack judges, often in the court rooms immediately after a decision is given.' See Fu Hualing, *supra* note 26, pp. 102–103.

86 'Document – China: Fear for safety: Li Heping', available at http://www.amnesty.org/en/library/asset/ASA17/046/2007/en/f66d4783-d364-11dd-a329-2f46302a8cc6/asa170462007en.html. Last visited September 2013.

87 In 2007, Li Heping, Teng Biao and four other lawyers gave a not guilty plea in defending Falun Gong practitioner Wang Bo at the Shijiazhuang Municipal Intermediate People's Court in Hebei Province. After the court hearing, the judges were furious at the lawyers, ordered a bailiff to grab the defence documents from Lawyer Li Heping and ordered bailiffs to beat Lawyer Teng Biao. 'Eleven Lawyers and 127 Family Members Co-Sign Letter to Protest against Shijiazhuang Municipal Intermediate Court', available at http://www.clearharmony.net/articles/200905/48928.html. Last visited September 2013.

88 'Quanguo Luxie Weiquan Gongzuo Baogao' (All China Lawyers Association's Report of Work on the Protection of Lawyers Rights), available at http://www.acal.org.cn/program/article.jsp?CID=998977585&ID=1808. Last visited June 2012. The document is with the author.

more than 10 defence lawyers. The trial lasted more than two hours, and the judge became very impatient as a result. When one lawyer read his defence statement, the judge told him to cut down his statement as the court was short of time. According to the judge, the lawyer needed only to inform the court whether he wanted to make an innocent or guilty plea. When the lawyer continued to read his defence statement, the judge halted proceedings and told him to simply declare whether the client was guilty or innocent. The lawyer instead insisted on completing his defence opinions. The judge then ordered the judicial police to take the lawyer out of the courtroom.[89] It is somewhat surprising to learn that such an event happened in the Haidian District Court, which is one of the most prestigious courts, with highly-qualified professional judges, located in the capital, Beijing. It is understandable that often judges wish to expedite proceedings, but it should not be at the expense of vindictively depriving the right of a defence lawyer to defend his client.

Judges' abuse of power and their intolerance towards lawyers has also brought about some bizarre cases. For instance, in 1992, lawyer He Xin in Jiangxi province was representing a litigation case stating that the Lianhua County People's Court had violated the law in the trial of the case. This enraged the president of the court, Li Chunting, who then ordered the court to exclude He from participating in any further litigation in that court. Lawyer He felt that this deprived him of his right to practise law, and in 1995 he wrote a letter of complaint to the Party Disciplinary Committee of Jiangxi province, in which he pointed out the prejudice of Li Chunting in instructing the court staff not to accept any case in which he was the representative. At a similar time, an anonymous letter was also sent to the governmental organ. All of these letters were passed to Li Chunting. Li ordered the court to start an investigation of He's hand-writing in the documents of the court archive, and then presented an expert opinion detailing the parallels between the hand-writing in the court documents and the anonymous letter to the procuratorate and requested the indictment of He for writing the anonymous letter. The procuratorate examined the case materials, and was of the opinion that He's act was not incriminating, and thus made a decision not to prosecute. In April 1996, Li launched his own prosecution regardless, accusing He of the crime of slander. It took a year for the court to hold an open trial of the case. At the same time He brought a lawsuit against Li Chunting (*fan su*) for spreading false rumours alleging 'He Xin does not have a qualified certificate to practise law and the procuratorate is investigating him', and depriving him of the ability to appear in court for four years. This went on for about two years, with the courts of both first and second instance supporting Li Chunting, and convicting He Xin of the crime of slander with the consequent punishment of one year in prison. On 7 December 1999, He Xin was released upon completion of his sentence.[90]

A lawyer's role in facilitating the proper enforcement of the law seems far from being accepted by the Chinese judiciary. The reality is summed up in the popular saying: 'you (lawyer) defend as you will, I (judge) decide what I will'. This stark reality often results in some lawyers having to employ their own underhand countermeasures, such as setting up private relationships with judges, or even bribing judges. It seems that improving respect for the rights of lawyers during the course of litigation will help judges to apply the law with a greater degree of accuracy, which is absolutely necessary as both legislation and cases are becoming more complex than ever.

89 'Beijing Yi Bianhu Lushi He Faguan Zhengchao Bei Zhuchu Fating' (Beijing Defence Lawyer Had a Quarrel with a Judge and Was Forced to Leave the Courtroom), available at http://news.163.com/07/0925/02/3P721TAL00011229.html. Last visited September 2013.

90 'Lushi Jubao Fayuan Yuanzhang, Fayuan Yuanzhang Zhuanggao Lushi' (A Lawyer Complained about a President of a Court, the President Sued the Lawyer), available at http://www.gmw.cn/01wzb/2000-05/04/GB/2000%5E1743%5E0%5EWZ3–0421.HTM. Last visited September 2013.

Recognising these serious flaws in the system, the 2007 amended Lawyers Law made some advancements in providing adequate protection for the rights of lawyers. Article 33 states that a lawyer has the right to meet criminal suspects, and to procure information about the case after such a person has been interrogated for the first time by an investigative organ or on the day coercive measures are imposed on them. Furthermore, Article 33 adds that in meeting a client, a lawyer is only required to show his/her certificate as a qualified lawyer, the letter of the law firm and the letter of attorney, or the letter of legal aid. Such meetings should not be monitored. These provisions were adopted in the 2012 amended Criminal Procedure Law, consequently, the 2012 amended Lawyers Law referred to the amendments. Moreover, Article 47 of the 2012 amended Criminal Procedure Law provides that if a defender or his representative considers that a public security organ, a procuratorate, a court or any staff member thereof has impeded his ability to exercise his procedural rights, he has the right to file a petition or accusation with the procuratorate at the same or next higher level. The procuratorate should review the petition or accusation on time, and if it is true, notify the organ involved to make a correction. This important new provision can be expected to be used by lawyers to protect their rights effectively.

Duties and Legal Liability

The 2007 amended Lawyers Law expresses the general duty of lawyers to preserve the principle of confidentiality of state secrets, business secrets and the privacy of the parties concerned (Article 38). This Article requires that lawyers maintain confidentiality in the information that they receive through their practice, including the non-disclosure of information relating to clients. However, a lawyer's duty of confidentiality does not extend to criminal facts and information concerning state security, public safety and serious infringements to the safety of persons or property, which have already been committed or remain in the preparatory stage. These added exceptions are viewed as necessary to balance a lawyer's duty to, on the one hand, maintain the confidentiality of information which they obtain from clients and, on the other, hold state and public interests above all else, which is consistent with the legal obligation of citizens in other laws.[91] Furthermore, a lawyer is not allowed to represent both parties in the same case (Art. 39).[92] In response to many of the challenges in practice, the Lawyers Law further prohibits lawyers from taking illicit gains in cash and by any other means (Article 40).[93] Bribery of judicial officers by lawyers remains a part of the corruption which is rife in the Chinese judicial system. As a result, the Lawyers Law requires that lawyers must not meet judges, procurators or arbitrators in breach of the regulations, nor must they entertain them, send gifts to them or bribe them (Article 40). In addition, the 2007 amendment forbids lawyers from enticing or instigating parties to use measures aimed at disturbing public order, threatening public safety or using any other illegal measures to settle disputes (Article 40).

91 'Sifabu Fuzeren Jiu Xiuding Hou De Lushifa Da Xinhuashe Jizhe Wen', *supra* note 32.

92 Article 39 should be understood as meaning that a lawyer cannot represent parties whose interests are in conflict. For instance, a criminal case may involve a number of accused parties: some are principal offenders, others are accessories. There is a difference between the serious and minor crimes that may have been committed. A lawyer may not represent all the accused because this may lead to a contradictory defence. See Zhang Geng et al. (eds), *supra* note 14, pp. 142–143.

93 In practice some lawyers have accepted an excessive amount of money from relatives of the accused, and then have tried by various means to free the accused. There is even a saying that it is possible if enough money is offered, even a person who has been investigated with an offence that could warrant the death penalty could be released. See A Ji, *supra* note 78, p. 5.

In practice, the most common forms of misconduct performed by lawyers include: failing to act as the defence counsel or representative after accepting a commission without a proper reason; failing to appear in court at the appointed time to participate in litigation or arbitration without reasonable justification for doing so; revealing commercial secrets or infringing the privacy of the parties concerned; making illicit profits from the disputed rights and interests in the case by using the advantage gained by being the lawyer in the case; losing or damaging important client evidence; delaying the case without good reason, causing litigation to become time-barred; making significant errors regarding the nature of a case and inducing a client to sign or agree to a contract or an agreement that is obviously to the client's detriment.[94]

Resulting from a breach in their legal duties, a lawyer may be punished with a warning, a fine, the suspension of his/her licence to practise, and the confiscation of any illicit gains. If a lawyer's act constitutes a crime, he or she must bear criminal liability.[95] Although there is a lack of official statistics on the punishment of lawyers, some limited information gives an impression of the general situation. From 1985 to 1991, the Ministry of Justice approved the revocation of 63 lawyers' licences: of these, 24 were revoked for bribery, larceny and the like; 21 were revoked because the lawyer in question had frequented brothels or had conducted an improper relationship with relatives of the parties, or due to 'hooliganism'; 18 were revoked for breaches of professional ethics. In 2005 the Ministry of Justice announced that, during their year-long campaign for the intensified education and rectification of lawyers, a total of 719 lawyers and 213 law firms had been punished in various forms. The figures show that 261 lawyers received administrative penalties, of which 47 had their licences revoked, 109 were ordered to stop practising, 23 had their illicit gains confiscated and 82 received warnings. Seventy-two law firms received administrative penalties, of which 14 lost their licenses, 21 were ordered to suspend operation for rectification, 13 had their illicit gains confiscated and 24 received warnings. Furthermore, 458 lawyers received disciplinary punishment, of which 47 had their membership revoked, 73 were publicly denounced, 210 were criticised in a circulation and 128 received admonition. Disciplinary punishment was also meted out to 141 law firms, 14 of which had their membership revoked, 20 were publicly denounced, 82 were criticised in a circulation and 25 received admonition. The main illegal activity conducted by lawyers included illegitimate communication between lawyers and judges, especially bribing judges; the unauthorised handling of cases and arbitrary charging of clients; failure in delivering stipulated legal services to clients; unfair competition, including defaming other lawyers, payment of referral fees, false advertising; and disruption of the order of legal practices.[96]

The Opportunities and Risks for Defence Lawyers

The criminal defence component of the criminal justice system has been weak throughout China's history. After the founding of the People's Republic of China, criminals were treated as 'enemies' of the state, and consequently their rights in the criminal process were either refused or minimally protected. In 1977, in the trial of the highly politically-sensitive case of the 'Gang of Four', the central government appointed politically reliable legal workers (some worked at the judicial office

94 Yan Gaoshang, 'Shilun Lushi Shiwusuo De Peichang Zeren' (Discussion of the Compensation Liability of Law Firms), 4(5) (1996) *Anhui Lushi* (Anhui Lawyer), p. 34.

95 Articles 47, 48, 49 of the 2007 amended Lawyers Law make lawyer's legal liability more stringent.

96 Liang Jie, '719 Ming Lushi 213 Jia Lusuo Shou Chufa' (719 Lawyers and 213 Law Firms are Punished) *Guangming Ribao* (Guangming Daily), 19 January 2005. Available at http://www.gmw.cn/01gmrb/2005-01/19/content_167861.htm. Last visited September 2013.

of the government, others were law professors) to the defendants. At that time, some of them were reluctant to act as the defendant's lawyers, either feeling ashamed or nervous. However, they were forced to accept the case as a political task rather than to actually defend the accused. The defence was therefore described as meagre or rather non-existent.[97]

In the early years of the 1980s, a lawyer's role in defending criminals was limited. Lawyers were not allowed to involve themselves with the pre-trial stage and had only seven days before the trial to prepare the defence. Although lawyers could in theory create an innocent plea for their client, in reality, this hardly occurred since a defendant's guilt was largely considered established at the investigative stage.[98]

However, in the late 1980s and early 1990s, the trial of the Tian'anmen dissidents marked a fundamental change in criminal defence. The trial provided the first example of a serious and energetic defence, with some courageous lawyers risking their careers to defend the dissidents, and presenting an effective defence. Although many suffered as a result of doing so, it sparked a long-term change in the criminal defence process in the post-Mao reform period.[99]

Since the 1990s, rapid economic reform has advanced China's development towards a market economy, and at the same time, the number of economic crimes and corruption cases has also increased. This has raised market demand for defence lawyers and led them from initially defending ordinary crimes, such as theft, murder and rape, to engaging in defending new crimes such as corruption, economic crimes, organised crime and the like. This has marked a new phase in criminal defence in China in which some lawyers have showed unprecedented courage and independence, which has, of course, coupled with corresponding economic rewards.

Another reason that explains why lawyers are able to provide such strong defences can be attributed to the various loopholes in the law. For instance, in 2001, Ma Kedong successfully defended the so-called 'Number one mafia case in Guangzhou'. This was a case handled by the Intermediate People's Court in Guangzhou. The case involved 24 people accused of the crime of organising the mafia. Based on the judicial interpretation of the Supreme People's Court Explanation of Concrete Application of Law in Dealing with Crimes of the Mafia, issued on 5 December 2000, the mafia had four features. One was to have a governmental institution behind it as a protective umbrella. Ma Kedong succeeded in proving that these 24 people did not have such an umbrella. This case was later reported to the National People's Congress. As a result, in April 2002, the National People's Congress Standing Committee passed a legislative interpretation of Article 294 of the Criminal Law, which redefined the mafia by deleting the requirement of umbrella protection.[100]

Since the 1990s, lawyers' independence has been, and continues to be, strengthened. Some criminal lawyers believe their mission is to protect the legitimate rights of their clients according to the law so as to reach the ultimate goal of upholding justice. In a criminal defence trial, a lawyer's task is to defend the accused to gain more lenient treatment or a declaration of innocence.[101] This change of mindset has resulted in an improved, client-driven independence of lawyers. A group of

97 David Bonavia, *Verdict in Peking: The Trial of the Gang of Four* (London: Burnett Books, 1984), p. 202.

98 Timothy A. Gelatt, *supra* note 6, p. 781.

99 Fu Hualing, *supra* note 26, p. 108; Timothy A. Gelatt, *supra* note 6, p. 796.

100 'Ma Kedong Shexian Zhapian An Jingdong Quanguo Lushi Jie' (The Case of Ma Kedong's Alleged Crime of Fraud Shocked the Legal Profession), available at http://news.sina.com.cn/c/l/2007-10-07/092214031821.shtml. Last visited September 2013. The document is with the author.

101 Xiong Qiuhong, '"Liu Yong An" Kaoyan Xingshi Sifa' (The Case of Liu Yong Tests Criminal Justice), in Xia Yong et al. (eds), *Zhongguo Fazhi Fazhan Baogao 2 (2004)* (The Development Report of Rule of Law in China: 2 (2004)) (Beijing: Shehui Kexue Wenxian Chubanshe, 2005), p. 231.

well-known criminal defence lawyers, dedicating legal services to the cause of justice, are gaining increasing attention both in legal circles and in society, inside and outside China.

Moreover, even specialised law firms have emerged. In September 2006, Shangquan Law Firm, the first Chinese law firm dedicated to criminal cases, was established in Beijing. The name 'Shangquan', means 'advocating for rights'. The firm announced its mission to uphold the spirit of law and the superiority of rights, to protect the legitimate rights of suspects and defendants, and to push forward the reform of the criminal defence system.[102]

The quality of criminal defence has generally improved, with some lawyers showcasing their excellent qualities. For example, lawyer Zhang Sizhi made a successful defence of an innocence plea for lawyer Zheng Enchong,[103] who was accused of the crime of 'leaking state secrets'. Zhang's defence statement was extraordinarily admirable. It criticised some of the contents in the bill of prosecution as being contrary to the law, challenged the main evidence, pointed out that local regulations were incompatible with the law and even questioned whether the judicial interpretation of the Supreme People's Court was beyond the court's mandate and contrary to the law promulgated by the National People's Congress. In his concluding defence statement, Zhang Sizhi stated:

> In examining the occurrence and the developmental process of the case of Zheng, and how the Court has adjudicated the case, we are deeply impressed by the objective and efficient working style of the judges. And, we also truly realise the pressure of external intervention on the case, which illustrates the case's complex social background, and the obscurity for the collegiate panel in upholding judicial independence. As a lawyer, I am worrisome. I do not want to give further opinion and comment on the qualification of Zheng as a lawyer which is evidently obvious. But I want to stress that Zheng, during his years-long legal practice in assisting large groups of evicted residents in lawsuits against the local government and the real estate developer, has demonstrated diligence, fairness, hard-work, virtuousness, more merit and less fault, and consistence for years. Due to all of this, he has gained true respect from many people. Pityingly, he is an 'inflexible man' and 'lacks consciousness of self-protection', which led to some people using various means to find mistakes he might have made. The police showed arbitrary behaviour during the investigation. The prosecutors indicted him with false accusations. I beg the court to take into account his current attitude and his long, good practice of law. And consider that his conduct has not caused any social harm and that he does not pose any danger to society. The reality is that there is no guilt on him at all. Clear his name and allow him to serve the interests of ordinary people in our society.[104]

Improvement of the quality of defence also reflects fully on the use of procedural rights by lawyers. In defending Chen Dehui, defence lawyers at the courts of appeal consistently insisted that the court follow procedural rules. On 6 September 2001, when the Intermediate People's Court in Dalian held an open trial of Chen's case, his two lawyers defended him as innocent. However,

102 The Law Firm's website is: http://www.sqxb.com/index.html. The website contains numerous articles by the lawyer Zhang Qingsong, the founder of the Shangquan Law Firm. Lawyer Zhang's blog sheds light on the development of the minds of the leading Chinese criminal defence lawyers. Last visited September 2013.

103 For the case of human rights lawyer Zheng Enchong, see 'Zheng Enchong Detained and Beaten Again', available at http://www.hrichina.org/content/64. Last visited September 2013.

104 'Zhang Sizhi Lushi Guanyu Zheng Enchong Anjian De Bianhuci' (Defence Statement by Lawyer Zhang Sizhi in the Case of Zheng Enchong), available at http://blog.sina.com.cn/u/48e43808010006v5. Last visited September 2013. See a collection of his excellent work, Zhang Sizhi, *Wode Bianci Yu Mengxiang* (My Defence Statements and Dreams) (Shanghai: Xuelin Chubanshe, 2001).

the court presented an expert's conclusion provided by the Tax Bureau of Dalian city in which Chen was proven to have committed tax evasion. Chen's lawyers immediately protested that this important new evidence had not been shown to the defence, and stated that the court had violated the procedural law. The collegiate panel were consequently forced to adjourn. However, when the trial was restarted, the panel did not adopt the defence's opinion. When the lawyer obtained permission to express his opinion, he read out Article 55 of the 1998 SPC judicial interpretation on Explanations Concerning Several Issues in the Implementation of the Criminal Procedure Law, in which it clearly stipulated: 'When a people's court investigates or examines evidence in a publicly prosecuted case, if it finds new evidence which is significant to decide the facts of the case, the court should inform the public prosecutor and defence lawyer.' The presiding judge was forced to adjourn once more. On 13 September 2001, the trial was again held openly, with the lawyers challenging the validity of the expert opinion given by the Tax Bureau in Dalian, on the basis that the tax bureau had a conflict of interest in this case, and therefore claiming that it should withdraw. The trial was adjourned for nearly an hour, but when it resumed, the presiding judge declared that he had received an instruction from the president of the court that there was no need for the tax bureau to withdraw. On 27 December 2001, the court opened the trial of the case for the third time and presented another expert opinion, this time from the tax bureau of Liaoning province. Once again, this opinion was challenged by the lawyers. They argued that, as this bureau was the superior tax bureau in Dalian, the hierarchical relationship called into question its objectivity. The trial was subsequently brought to an end without a judgment. More than one year later, on 24 January 2003, the court finally made its judgment acquitting Chen of the crime of tax evasion and released him immediately.[105]

While the quality of defence lawyers is notably improving, a disappointing reality is that a strong defence may not necessarily lead to a favourable result for the defendants. It has been observed that

> in a system like the Chinese where judicial independence and legal professionalism have not been fully established, and the rule of law and the principle of presumed innocence have not been fully integrated, the overemphasis on the right to legal representation may not be to the advantage of the accused. It might become a liability, rather than an asset for the defendant as the stronger the defence the more severe the punishment is likely to result.[106]

An empirical study on Chinese courts illustrated that whether or not a defendant was represented by a lawyer made no significant impact on judicial decisions.[107]

However, the emergence of strong defence lawyers demonstrates the progress of the Chinese legal system in general, and of the legal profession in particular. Predictably, this new development encounters various impediments. While a defence lawyer's role is expanding, political pressure, misunderstanding by the public, harassment, intimidation, prosecution or even conviction by the judiciary also place defence lawyers at higher risk than ever before. This reflects the current process of development of criminal defence proceedings in China: opportunities for defence lawyers have broadened, while the risks have increased in parallel.

---

105 'Chilai De Panjue, Nande De Panli: Yi Lushi Shexian Toushuian Shenpan Zhuizong (Judgment in Delay: Following the Case of a Lawyer's Alleged Tax Invasion), available at http://news.xinhuanet.com/newscenter/2003-01/25/content_707136.htm. Last visited September 2013.

106 Hong Lu and Terance D. Miethe, 'Legal Representation and Criminal Processing in China', 42(2) (2002) *British Journal of Criminology*, p. 271.

107 *Ibid.*

The most serious professional risks originate from law enforcement organs and officers, in the form of professional revenge. According to lawyers,

> the most humiliating and brutal treatment they face can be explained by the lack of political support or institutional protection for the profession. Lawyers are silenced in court, thrown out of court by judges; handcuffed immediately after making their closing argument, tortured by police and prosecutors; or tied up and paraded in the street while prosecutors cheer.[108]

Due to the lack of reliable statistics in this regard, no accurate figures can be given on how many lawyers have suffered from violations of their rights whilst undertaking their professional duties. An estimation of such, is that around 100 lawyers per year have been punished for merely doing their work.[109] Violations of lawyers' rights take various forms, ranging from less severe cases, when judicial organs impede lawyers from investigating and collecting evidence or deprive and restrict lawyers from defending their clients or even compel lawyers to leave the court room, to more serious cases of limiting lawyers' liberty, such as beating them or placing them in jail.

Due to the high risks associated with this field, many lawyers prefer to avoid representing criminal cases. A 2002 report by the Beijing Lawyers Association indicated that the number of lawyers in Beijing defending criminal cases stood at less than one lawyer per case. In 2000, Beijing had 5,495 lawyers and they handled a total of 4,300 criminal cases.[110] Even when lawyers do accept such cases, most lawyers choose to engage in light defence, though under Article 35 of the 1996 Criminal Procedure Law (also the same provision in the 2012 revision of the CrPL), lawyers could make innocent pleas if they so desired. Lawyers usually concentrate on calling for a more lenient punishment on the basis of mitigating factors such as: their client's lack of capacity during the committal of the crime (for example being a minor or mentally-challenged), offering the offender's confession, a good attitude and/or no prior criminal record. Thus, it was observed that

> when attorneys provide a defence that legitimises the system (e.g. 'the defence of capacity' or 'the defence of character') the defence is more likely affirmed by the court, and results in more favourable sentencing outcomes for the defendant. However, when the defence challenges the system by arguing about the truthfulness of the facts presented in the court (e.g. 'defence of fact'), the court is typically unlikely to accept such a defence.[111]

In present-day China, any success brought about in such a case may bring with it catastrophic effects for lawyers, where selective and flexible implementation of the law is unpredictable. The case of Ma Kedong reflects such a reality. Ma Kedong was a well-known lawyer from southern China's Guangdong province.[112] In 2007, he was arrested and prosecuted on suspicion of having committed the crime of fraud for charging a client RMB 1 million in 2001. On 10 September 2007, Ma was put on trial by a basic court in Liaoning province, in the north-east of China. Ma's defence

---

108 Fu Hualing, *supra* note 26, p. 112.

109 *Ibid.*, p. 97.

110 Hu Xiying and Duanmu Zhengyang, 'Bugan Ti "Xingshi Fanzui Xianyiren" Bianhu De Zhongguo Lushi' (Chinese Lawyers Who Don't Dare to Defend 'Suspects'), 7 (2002) *Zhongguo Lushi* (Chinese Lawyer), p. 27.

111 Hong Lu and Terance D. Miethe, *supra* note 106, p. 277.

112 'Ma Kedong Shexian Zhapian An Jingdong Quanguo Lushi Jie' (The Case of Ma Kedong's Alleged Crime of Fraud Shocked the Legal Profession), available at http://news.sina.com.cn/c/l/2007-10-07/092214031821.shtml. Last visited September 2013.

lawyer put forward a not-guilty defence by arguing that the 1 million RMB was the lawyer's fee, which had been previously agreed by the parties. Moreover, they challenged the court's jurisdiction on the basis that as the suspect lived in Guangzhou, and the alleged crime took place in Guangzhou, according to the Criminal Procedure Law, the court's jurisdiction in a criminal case should be based on either where the criminal offence occurred or where the accused resides. The trial judge replied to the jurisdiction challenge by stating that the Supreme People's Court had appointed the district court in Laoning to hear the case. As to the 1 million RMB lawyer's fee, the public prosecutor presented to the court the statement made by Ma Kedong when he was first interrogated by the police, in which he admitted receiving RMB 1 million as the lawyer's fee. The public prosecutor accused Ma of telling his client that he knew the head of the criminal division of the court handling the case and could find the relevant people in the court to help free the client. According to the public prosecutor, he lied about this. Ma Kedong defended himself by saying: 'relationships play an important role in society. In the current legal environment defending the client according to law is the primary goal, and forming relationships is supplementary to this. Nearly all clients, when they hire lawyers, ask lawyers whether they have good relations with the court and judges'. The court investigation proved that Ma took RMB 1 million from the client as his lawyer's fee. However, Ma never put this amount in the bank account of his firm. Ma's defence lawyer argued this was misconduct, which could not amount to a charge of incrimination for swindling. A local judge commented on this point, saying that because the RMB 1 million was not deposited into the law firm's account, this implied Ma was illegally avoiding tax. Consequently, Ma could be charged with the crime of tax evasion.[113]

Ma Kedong was charged with the crime of fraud and was sentenced to 11 years' imprisonment by the court of first instance.[114] He immediately appealed, but for such a controversial case, the court of appeal did not hold an open hearing – it merely examined the written papers and then decided to sustain the judgment of the first instance court. Ma's lawyer was denied the opportunity to meet his client. Additionally, the court did not give Ma's lawyer any chance to present her opinions, and the lawyer did not receive the judgment until a few days after it was made.[115] During the court's handling of Ma's case, the ACLA, the Guangdong Provincial Lawyers Association and the Guangzhou Municipal Lawyers Association organised expert seminars to discuss the case with the intention of preventing Ma Kedong from receiving unfair and disproportionately severe punishment. After the first instance court charged Ma Kedong with the crime of fraud, 253 lawyers from Guangzhou and Shenzhen signed a letter of appeal to the National People's Congress and the Ministry of Justice calling on them to pay attention to the case for the sake of the protection of personal safety and the dignity of defence lawyers.[116] All of these efforts were made in vain.

---

113 Jerome Cohen once pointed out: 'Tax evasion has proved a readily available pretext for prosecution in a country where tax law and administration are in need of serious reform, non-compliance is rife and prosecution is selective.' See Jerome A. Cohen, *supra* note 77, p. 244.

114 'Ma Kedong Zhapiang'an Yinzhen Lushiye' (Ma Kedong Swindling Case Generated a Shock in Lawyer's Circle), available at http://news.sohu.com/20080603/n257257023.shtml. Last visited September 2013.

115 'Lushi Zhapian Heilaoda Ma Kedong An Ershen Mimi Xuanpan' (The Case of Ma Kedong, a Lawyer Charged of Defrauding the Gangster Leader: Secret Judgment of the Trial at Second Instance). Available at http://news.sina.com.cn/c/2008-10-15/021214574086s.shtml. Last visited September 2013.

116 'Guangdong 253 Ming Lushi Guanzhu Ma Kedong An Shangshu Sifabu' (253 Lawyers in Guangdong Province Paid Attention to Ma Kedong's Case and Sent an Appeal Letter to the Ministry of Justice). Available at http://news.sina.com.cn/c/2008-07-27/110016007963.shtml. Last visited September 2013.

There may be some complexities behind Ma Kedong's case. He was a well-known criminal defence lawyer in Guangzhou, and successfully defended the so-called 'Number one mafia case in Guangzhou' in 2001.[117] He was blamed by some officials of using loopholes in the law to prevent serious criminals from being punished on time, which resulted in a continuation of mafia activities including the involvement of a group of policemen and high-ranking police officers in corrupt activities.[118]

To update the current status of criminal defence lawyers, one cannot conclude without remarks on the newly emerged *Sike* lawyers. *Sike* is a term emanating from a local dialect in north-east China, denoting to fight against someone or something vigorously. Normally, it refers to a situation where a person never gives up or compromises. Since 2012 the term has been used to describe a dozen criminal defence lawyers who have been determined to defend their clients to the end, withstanding pressures and humiliations deriving from the police, procuratorate and courts. Such lawyers achieved their success after nearly three years of persistent efforts in the Beihai case,[119] won a hard case in Xiaohe Court in Guizhou province in 2012,[120] and are continuing their representation in a number of controversial cases.

The surfacing of *Sike* lawyers is exhilarating in contemporary China where one can finally witness cases that were eventually decided by the courts in favour of the opinions of a small group of criminal defence lawyers after fiery debate in the courtroom. This can also be pondered as a gradual progress of the judicial system with strict adherence to the Criminal Procedure Law. However, the long-term survival of such lawyers remains inconclusive. One of the unique traits of *Sike* lawyers, demonstrated in the Beihai case, is their unity: coming from different parts of the country, they aim to work for the same purpose of realising justice through fair trial. Nevertheless, after the triumph of the Xiaohe case, the differentials among the few leading lawyers on how to incessantly strengthen their influence in reshaping criminal defence in China have gradually been exposed; and the response of the central authorities, including the Supreme People's Court, the Ministry of Justice, the ACLA, on the *Sike* lawyers, is currently indistinct.

---

117 He was also the defence lawyer for Chen Kejie, Deputy Chairman of the National People's Congress, who was convicted for serious corruption and who received the death penalty.

118 'Guangzhou Zhuming Lushi Shexian Zhapian Duxiao Yibaiwan Jinri Shoushen (Guangzhou Famous Lawyer Was Suspected of Defrauding Mafia 1 Million, the Case Opened Today). Available at http://society.people.com.cn/GB/6240862.html. Last visited September 2013.

119 See Chapter 4, pp. 124–125.

120 In 2012 Xiaohe Court handled a case in which about 50 defendants were accused of organised crime. Lawyer Zhou Ze from Beijing was first involved in the case and called for lawyers from other places to participate. Eventually 88 lawyers represented the defendants, and the trial lasted more than 40 days. During some of the trial sessions lawyers submitted withdrawal requests, which were refused by the judges; the latter also refused to investigate evidence which was questioned by lawyers as illegally obtained by investigation organs. The tension and conflict between lawyers and judges resulted in the judges asking the court policemen to pull a few lawyers out of the courtroom. In one trial session, the judge asked court police to take lawyer Chi Susheng (a famous female lawyer from north-east China; she is also a deputy of the National People's Congress) out of the courtroom; Chi was emotionally shocked by the judge's conduct, fell to the ground and was immediately taken to hospital. Lawyer Chi's courage and tireless fight in court illustrates a stirring aspect of *Sike* lawyers. Ye Zhusheng, 'Sikepai Lushi' (Sike Lawyers), *Nanfeng Chuang*, 18 September 2013, available at http://zhangyansheng.blog.caixin.com/archives/60832. Last visited September 2013.

Article 306 of the Criminal Law: A Trap for Defence Lawyers

Article 306 of the Criminal Law provides that if a lawyer destroys or forges evidence, helps any of the parties to destroy or forge evidence, or intimidates a witness or entices him into changing his testimony in defiance of the facts or give false testimony, he/she could be sentenced to a fixed-term imprisonment of no more than three years or be placed in criminal detention. If the circumstances are serious, the lawyer could be sentenced to a fixed-term imprisonment of no less than three but no more than seven years. Within Chinese legal circles, Article 306 is referred to as the 'crime of falsification of evidence by lawyers'. The flaw in Article 306 is that there is no yardstick for judging the terms 'intimidate' and 'entice'. In questioning witnesses, lawyers may employ certain methods to persuade witnesses to give evidence, which could be unfairly interpreted as 'enticing' witnesses. The absence, and indeed the impossibility, in defining 'intimidate' and 'entice' places lawyers in a vulnerable position, since prosecutors could easily use them for their own purposes. Thus, Article 306 is often referred to as the 'sword of Damocles' hanging over the head of criminal defence lawyers, ready to fall on them at any time.

Many Chinese scholars and lawyers view Article 306 as a fundamental defect in the law, which ultimately harms lawyers. It could be argued that, from a legislative point of view, Article 306 reflects professional discrimination against lawyers. During the criminal process, destroying or forging evidence, assisting parties to destroy or forge evidence, or intimidating the witness or enticing them into changing their testimony in defiance of the facts or give false testimony, can be committed by lawyers, police, public prosecutors or even judges. According to Article 306, if a lawyer commits the crime of destroying or fabricating evidence, he or she could be punished with the crime of falsification of evidence. On the other hand, Article 307 of the Criminal Law on the crime of falsification of evidence by judicial personnel provides that a crime can be established only if the judicial personnel utilises violence, threat, bribery or other means.

In practice, despite the fact that lawyers are indicted for various criminal offences, falsification of evidence under Article 306 has the highest percentage of prosecutions. It is alleged that around 80 per cent of the cases involving violations of lawyers' rights relate to Article 306 offences.[121] This Article is often invoked against lawyers in situations where a witness has given testimony to the police and prosecutor, but in the courtroom the witness reverses the original testimony. Public prosecutors are usually surprised by this and request an adjournment by the judges. The handling of the case would be temporarily terminated, and attention then turns to the fabrication of evidence by the witness. In a number of publicised cases, no matter whether a witness has committed the crime of fabrication, as soon as the witness changed his testimony the lawyers were detained and arrested for investigation and subsequent prosecution.[122] This also applies to defendants who retract their confession in the courtroom. Most of the cases have shown that it takes a few months, or even one or two years, to investigate and prosecute lawyers for the alleged crime of fabricating evidence, during which time the lawyers are detained in custody. Eventually, in most cases lawyers are found not guilty and released. 'Anecdotal evidence suggests that up to 80 per cent of all the lawyers who were detained, arrested or prosecuted for violating Article 306 or other provisions have been subsequently cleared of wrongdoing.'[123] A more specific account is that, amongst the 23 criminal charges against lawyers under Article 306 that the ACLA received and handled, in 11 cases lawyers

121 Fu Hualing, *supra* note 26, p. 98.

122 Chen Ruihua, 'Lushi Weizhengzui – Cun yu Fei' (Retaining or Repealing the Crime of Falsification of Evidence by a Lawyer), available at http://article.chinalawinfo.com/Article_Detail.asp?ArticleId=914. Last visited September 2013.

123 Fu Hualing, *supra* note 26, pp. 118–119.

were found not guilty or the cases were withdrawn, six were found guilty, one was made exempt from criminal punishment, and five cases were pending.[124] This is 'an astonishingly high rate of not guilty verdicts in a country with 99 per cent record of guilty verdicts'.[125]

For most of the lawyers, even though they were eventually cleared of the charges made against them, the suffering they experienced during the course of the allegations fills one's heart with sadness. In July 2001, the well-known lawyer Wang Wanxiong from Wuhan was detained for inducing witnesses to give false statements in a serious murder trial. In January 2002, he was declared not guilty by the Basic People's Court in Qianjiang City. But the People's Procuratorate in Qianjiang appealed to the higher court, with the argument that the judgment of the first instance court was based on incorrect facts, resulting in an improper application of the law. Wang was detained again, and two days later he received a final judgment from the Intermediate People's Court in Hanjiang in which he was accused of committing the crime of assisting a witness in falsifying evidence, and received a sentence of one year's imprisonment. In prison, Wang wrote long complaint letters, and the Lawyers Association in Hubei province also attempted to help him. It took nearly four years, when finally, in 2004, the Higher People's Court in Hubei province declared his innocence. The only consolation one can draw from this tragic case is that, after he was cleared, Wang was able to resume his legal practice, and nowadays is a well-respected defence lawyer.[126] Another publicly-known case is that of lawyer Ma Guangjun, a 50-year-old lawyer from Ningcheng county in Inner Mongolia. In 2003, while defending a rape case, he was accused by the prosecutor of advising witnesses to commit perjury. Having been detained for 210 days, he was finally declared innocent by the appellate court thanks to the intervention of the Inner Mongolian Lawyers Association and the ACLA. After his release he gave an interview on China Central Television expressing his heart-breaking experience of being transformed from a defence lawyer to a defendant.[127]

---

124 'Zaoyu Sifa Fubai, Kunming Liang Lushi Fenran Dunru Kongmen' (After Suffering Judicial Corruption, Two Lawyers from Kunming Became Monks), available at http://news.eastday.com/epublish/gb/paper148/20010615/class014800018/hwz412089.htm. Last visited September 2013. This is similar to the figures given by Fu Hualing.

125 Fu Hualing, *supra* note 26, p. 119.

126 'Bianhu Chenggong Er Mengqu Zai Shangsheng, "Lushi Weizheng Zui" Youwang Quxiao' (Successful Defence Results in Lawyers in Trouble; 'Lawyer Perjury' Is Expected to Be Cancelled). Available at http://www.chinanews.com/n/2004-04-27/26/430350.html. Last visited September 2013. On his blog, Wang Wanxiong recently shared his opinion on five ethical principles for lawyers defending death penalty cases: (1) Lawyers should have the spirit of upholding truth. In facing death penalty cases, a lawyer cannot give up easily. This is the essential professional ethic of a death penalty defence lawyer. (2) Lawyers cannot use improper methods to achieve a goal. If improper methods are used in dealing with a death penalty case, such as discussing the case privately with a witness, it will not only harm the lawyer, but also the accused. This is the professional bottom line of a defence lawyer. (3) A lawyer should defend his clients with full enthusiasm. To defend an accused facing a possible death penalty is to defend a life. A lawyer without passion cannot undertake a vigorous defence for life. (4) China is transitioning towards the rule of law in society. If judicial practice cannot guarantee procedural justice, and if legal means cannot resolve a case, a lawyer should carefully consider using other legitimate force in order to achieve substantive justice. (5) Experienced and excellent lawyers have the duty to guide young lawyers. They should use their experience to stimulate young lawyers to increase their professional responsibility, while mentoring young lawyers to avoid conducting excessively passionate, results-orientated, negative defences, as such an approach is like treating the accused's life as an experiment. Available at http://wg1958wg.blog.sohu.com/rss. Last visited September 2013.

127 Terence C. Halliday and Sida Liu, *supra* note 65, pp. 81–83.

Another chilling case concerns lawyer Wang Yibing. In November 1998, he was prosecuted by Mile County Procuratorate for the suspected crime of the falsification of evidence in a case involving the alleged crime of causing explosions. In this case, the accused's fiancée, a 22-year-old farmer, reversed her testimony in the courtroom, and the prosecutor blindly believed that she was influenced to do so by lawyer Wang. The court of first instance decided that Wang had violated the code of conduct of lawyers by not immediately correcting the accused's fiancée and by failing to tell her to repudiate her testimony. However, considering that Wang's misconduct was minor, the court declared him not guilty. However, the procuratorate could not accept the fact that after more than one year of busy work to indict lawyer Wang, he was proclaimed innocent. Thus, it launched protests to the higher court. Wang could also not accept the court's judgment, which declared him innocent, but had claimed that he had committed the crime of falsification of evidence, and so he too appealed. In December 1999, the court of second instance declared Wang innocent on the basis that the accused fiancée decided to reverse her testimony before she decided to hire the lawyer. During the two years that his liberty was deprived, Wang suffered mistreatment by the police and prosecutors. The law firm he had established was forced to close and his family spent all their savings protesting his innocence. After he was freed, he and his wife had to survive by selling newspapers on the street. This incident made him leave the legal profession to become a monk and devote his life to a temple. With the care and persuasion of the local government, however, he finally returned to practising as a lawyer after more than a year of temple life.[128]

Lawyer Wang Zhonglin from Henan province is an experienced lawyer with more than 20 years of practice. In defending a client accused of murder with intent, he found out that the defendant was tortured, with visible wounds on his body. Wang collected some evidence and submitted it to the court. In the court, he argued that the evidence presented by the prosecutor was not sufficient to charge the defendant. On 23 December 1999, after the court session, he was immediately questioned and detained by the police. Due to the disapproval of the local procuratorate over his arrest, he was allowed bail. The local police modified bail to house surveillance. In Henan province, house surveillance could be considered a deprivation of personal liberty, not merely a limitation, as it required that an individual under house surveillance must stay at either an administrative detention house or an assigned hotel where security guards surround the premises and the family are forced to pay the costs. The individual under surveillance would not be permitted contact with other people, nor allowed to meet with family members. On 3 April 2001, the procuratorate agreed to formally arrest Wang on the basis that the court did not adopt his defence opinion. The defendant was charged with intentional murder. After Wang was arrested for two months, one witness (a relative of the defendant) provided testimony that the defendant had lied to lawyer Wang and Wang had known of this lie. This led to Wang being charged with the crime of assisting a witness to falsify evidence, which carried with it a sentence of seven months' imprisonment. Due to the fact that Wang had already been detained for seven months, he was released immediately after the judgment.[129]

The most recent case which triggered national debate on the flaws of the criminal justice system was the case of lawyer Li Zhuang. In 2009 during the extremely controversial campaign against organised crime in Chongqing, Li accepted the defence of an organised crime suspect, Gong Gangmo. Lawyer Li met Gong in police custody once. Mysteriously Gong reported to the police that lawyer Li pressured him to testify deceitfully. Lawyer Li was immediately arrested, in 18 days

128 'Zaoyu Sifa Fubai, Liang Lushi Fenran Dunru Kongmen' (Two Lawyers in Kunming Became Monks Due to Judicial Corruption), available at http://news.eastday.com/epublish/gb/paper148/20010615/class014800018/hwz412089.htm. Last visited September 2013.

129 Chen Qiulan and Qiang Lieyang, 'Zhongguo Lushi Zhiyenan' (Difficulties of Practising Law for Chinese Lawyers), 5 (2002) *Zhongguo Lushi* (Chinese Lawyer), p. 52.

the court tried him, and sentenced him to 30 months in prison for inciting the client to testify falsely. The trial was organised in such a rapid manner that it was concluded even before Gong's trial was opened. During the trial, the testimonies of eight witnesses were read out, however not one witness was present in the courtroom.[130] On 11 June 2011, Li Zhuang completed his imprisonment and was released as a free man.[131]

Chinese scholarly assessments have indicated that in numerous cases where lawyers were accused of the crime of falsifying evidence, those lawyers actually had participated in some form of misconduct to a greater or lesser degree – such as violating professional ethics or not defending their client seriously or fairly enough. The same assessment concludes that perhaps only a few lawyers were 'absolutely clean' when charged. Nonetheless, assigning criminal liability to lawyers accused of minor misconduct or shortcomings in professional ethics is an extremely harsh punishment.[132] It continues to be a running debate in China as to where the line should be drawn between unethical professional conduct and criminal liability under Article 306. It is not surprising, therefore, that many Chinese lawyers, scholars and even prosecutors have proposed the abolition of Article 306.[133] International human rights organisations and legal experts have also appealed to the Chinese government to eradicate this provision.[134]

The Tensions between Lawyers and Law Enforcement Officers

In order to represent their clients defence lawyers have to confront judicial organs. In China, judicial organs mainly refers to the courts and procuratorates. Public security organs (the police) belong to the administrative organs. Yet, when they carry out criminal investigative activities, they are considered to be semi-judicial organs. The criminal process involves investigation by public security organs, indictment by public prosecutors (they also have the function of investigating crimes committed by civil servants), and adjudication by the courts. Despite the formal division of labour, public security organs, procuratorates and courts co-operate in working towards the common goal of controlling and punishing crimes severely, strictly and promptly. The police, public prosecutor and judge represent state power, while defence lawyers represent private parties. Consequently, conflicts of interest between the two are unavoidable. Due to the lack of recognition of the different roles of law enforcement officers and defence lawyers in enabling a fair judicial system, specifically the irreplaceable position of lawyers, a criminal defence lawyer is in an extremely weak position compared to judges, prosecutors and the police.

---

130 'Chongqing Dahei Lushi Li Zhuang Shexian Weizheng'an Jinri Shangwu Yishen Xuanpan' (Judgment on Li Zhunag's Falsifying Evidence Crime during the Combat against Mafia-like Organisations was Issued Today), available at http://news.sohu.com/20100108/n269443599.shtml. Last visited September 2013. 'Chongqing Sheheian Bianhu Lushi Quzheng Jiannan Tingshen Zhizheng Yin Zhengyi' (Difficulties for Lawyers Defending Mafia-Like Crimes in Chongqing, Arguments Raised During the Trial), available at http://news.sina.com.cn/c/sd/2010-01-27/111519557722.shtml. Last visited September 2013. 'The Case of Li Zhuang', available at http://english.caing.com/2010/lizhuang/. Last visited September 2013.

131 'Li Zhuang Zhuli Ma Xiaojun Su Chongqing Gong'anju' (Li Zhuang's Assistant Ma Xiaojun Proceeds against Public Security Bureau), available at http://www.wanghuiyong.com/article/?type=detail&id=549. Last visited September 2013.

132 Chen Ruihua, *supra* note 122.

133 Hu Xiying and Duanmu Zhengyang, supra note 110, p. 26.

134 See Report of the Special Rapporteur on Torture and Other Cruel, Inhuman or Degrading Treatment or Punishment, para. 82(I), E.CN.4/2006/6/Add.6.

Clearly tensions between law enforcement officers and defence lawyers exist in any society. However, the serious degree of hostility and its adverse repercussions on lawyers in today's China deserves special attention. A survey of the reasons underlying the hardship placed on defence lawyers sheds some light on the situation. When 100 law students at the Law School of Peking University were asked to give their views on this issue, it was revealed that 81 students blamed law enforcement organs and personnel; 16 thought it was due to deficiencies in the legislation; and three thought it was the lack of competence on the part of lawyers.[135]

The grave confrontation between law enforcement officers and defence lawyers must be examined in the context in which it occurs – a context in which the laws and rules are not sufficiently clear to ensure adequate certainty for law enforcement. Furthermore, in a civil law system, legislation is always limited by its general character when being applied to specific, concrete and complex cases. Moreover, some contradictory judicial interpretations and internal instructions issued by the Supreme People's Procuratorate in favour of departmental interests have further complicated, rather than smoothed out, the law enforcement process.

If law enforcement organs and their personnel had the willingness and competence to implement the Criminal Procedure Law and the Criminal Law in good faith, they would be expected to co-operate constructively to enable lawyers to exercise their rights to a sufficient degree. Lawyers could then provide checks and balances in the criminal process by ensuring fair trials and guaranteeing that the innocent are protected, and the guilty punished – all in accordance with the law. This result would add credit to judicial fairness and authority. However, the reality in China is abysmal. The Report concerning the Implementation of the Lawyers Law, issued by the National People's Congress Standing Committee states: 'Some law enforcement and judicial officials have a biased view of lawyers and do not trust lawyers, holding the view that lawyers' participation in the adjudication process will affect the proper handling of cases.'[136]

The imposition of various barriers by police and prosecutors intended to disable lawyers from exercising their rights is mainly a result of judicial discrimination against defence lawyers. There is an overarching clash of ideas on the role of lawyers in the criminal justice system. The old ideology and perceptions remain deeply-rooted in the minds of many investigative officers and prosecutors. Detainees are thought of as the evil and guilty party. Subsequently, lawyers paid by these criminals will side with them, and absolve the accused from guilt. Thus, psychologically, they repel lawyers. In addition, some are afraid that lawyers may give harmful advice that would affect the process of truth-finding in the criminal process; some are afraid that their evidence is thin, and if lawyers get involved, they may not overcome the defence arguments; some are suspicious of lawyers, fearing that they may induce suspects to organise their statements so as to confuse the criminal facts.[137]

It is also a growing phenomenon that the style of defence lawyers is changing from being completely passive, by simply stating the case, to being more aggressive and effective, even to the extent of entering a plea of not guilty. Some prosecutors are not used to, or cannot tolerate, this

135 Ji Xiangde, *supra* note 80, p. 95

136 Gu Xiulian, 'Quanguo Renda Changweihui Zhifa Jianchazu Guanyu Jiancha Zhonghua Renmin Gongheguo Lushifa Shishi Qingkuang De Baogao' (Report of the Law Enforcement Examination Unit of the National People's Congress Standing Committee on the Situation of the Implementation of the Lawyers' Law of the People's Republic of China), 6 (2005) *Zhonghua Renmin Gongheguo Quanguo Renmin Daibiao Dahui Changwu Weiyuanhui Gongbao* (Communique of the National People's Congress Standing Committee), p. 524.

137 Sun Yequn, 'Zuo Yige Xingbian Lushi Jiujing You Duonan: Lushi Canyu Xingshi Susong Huodong Youguan Wenti Sikao' (How Difficult It Is to Be a Defence Lawyer: Some Thoughts on Problems Concerning the Role of Lawyers in Criminal Procedure), 4 (2003) *Zhongguo Lushi* (Chinese Lawyer), p. 67.

new style of vigorous and aggressive defence by lawyers. For the sake of not losing their cases, some prosecutors use all means available to retaliate against defence lawyers. They may request an adjournment of proceedings, detain witnesses to obtain a change in their statements or openly criticise the defence lawyer.

A rational understanding of a lawyer's involvement in criminal defence is needed to guarantee a fair trial and to prevent injustice. However, it seems that such a line of thinking is not akin to that of many Chinese judicial personnel. Moreover, the strong self-belief of judicial personnel that they represent 'officials' makes them feel distinctly more privileged than defence lawyers, who represent ordinary people. China steadfastly remains a society centred upon officials.

The different backgrounds of judicial officials and lawyers may also cause a psychological gap between the two. Many judges, prosecutors and police are former military officers, while most lawyers are law graduates from universities. The two groups have no common language, and lack formal channels with which to communicate or interact, leading to a stubborn state of mind.[138] Some lawyers do not want to offend judges and create an awkward position. Nor do they want to act condescendingly, which would cause a loss of dignity. Lawyers tend to keep a neutral, distant relationship with judges during the course of litigation. The consequence of this is that lawyers too often have unexpected troubles in court.[139]

Another reality is that the income of some lawyers has increased dramatically as a result of the privatisation of the legal profession. Some judicial officers are jealous of lawyers, which inevitably brings about attempts to make life more difficult for lawyers. Some prosecutors and judges intentionally humiliate lawyers to show that their 'power' is above lawyers' 'money'. As judges have the final power to decide cases, and other deeply-rooted judicial problems can be coupled with this, lawyers can hardly win cases based on their ability and knowledge. For many lawyers, developing 'personal connections' with judges is a pragmatic choice which could prove advantageous. It has been assessed that 'many lawyers would much prefer to rely on legal arguments than personal relationships to serve their clients. However, given the present realities, they have no choice but to rely on connections, and fear that, if they do not, their client will be disadvantaged.'[140]

Conclusion

The rapid growth of the legal profession in a legal system that is going through systematic change entails quandaries that have simultaneously arisen in the Chinese legal profession. First, there is

138 The expansion of legal education after 1977 resulted in the gradual improvement of the educational background of many judges and prosecutors. According to statistics, in 1995, the percentage of judges with college degrees was 6.9 per cent, and this increased to 51.6 per cent in 2005. For public prosecutors, 41.3 per cent had college degrees in 2003. See Sida Liu and Terence C. Halliday, 'Dancing Handcuffed in the Minefield: Survival Strategies of Defense Lawyers in China's Criminal Justice System', Center on Law and Globalization, Research Paper, no. 08-04, p. 9, available at http://papers.ssrn.com/sol3/papers.cfm?abstract_id=1269536. Last visited September 2013. The developmental trend is that judges, public prosecutors and lawyers will have similar law degrees from universities, thus enabling them to have a shared understanding of law. But, reaching this point may take years.

139 Li Xuan, 'Zhidu Quesun Yu Guannian Diwu: Dangdai Zhongguo Lushiye De Liangda Nanti' (Institutional Deficiencies and Conceptual Backwardness: Two Big Difficulties Facing the Chinese Legal Profession), p. 6, available at http://www.lawbook.com.cn/lw/lw_view.asp?no=677&page=7. Last visited September 2013.

140 See Lawyers Committee for Human Rights, *supra* note 23, p. 67.

a lack of competence and professional responsibility. Inadequate experience, along with tradition and a high demand for lawyers within a relatively short period of time, has meant that Chinese lawyers seem to have had little or no time or opportunity to become fully-trained before they take on the responsibility of practising law. One consequence is that the profession is seen to be excessively profit-seeking. The public image of Chinese lawyers has changed from over-political (*zhengzhihua*) to over-commercial (*shangyehua*). Most lawyers and law firms focus on enlarging their market in profitable fields. Malpractice is a common price to pay to achieve this. Some lawyers even bribe judges in order to win cases.

Another consequence is a lack of interest in criminal defence. Despite the fact that the 1996 Criminal Procedure Law has strengthened the role of lawyers in criminal procedure, lawyers continue to face various obstacles in acting as defence counsel. Discrimination against lawyers by police, public prosecutors and judges has resulted in many instances of lawyers being humiliated, arrested, prosecuted or even convicted simply because they did what a lawyer is supposed to do. Mistreatment by non-state actors is also alarming. Some lawyers have been kidnapped, beaten or threatened by relatives of the victims of criminal offences. Under such a reality, the overwhelming majority of Chinese lawyers inevitably prefer to avoid criminal cases.

Moreover, there is a lack of adequate government support for the legal profession. This can be showcased through various factors. There are few lawyers in the national or local people's congresses. Thus, only a small degree of pressure from lawyers can be placed on the legislature. The authority in charge of lawyers' work is the Ministry of Justice. However, this ministry and its local branches are weak in protecting the interests and rights of lawyers, when the latter are in trouble with the court, procuratorate, police or other governmental institution.

Furthermore, judicial discrimination against lawyers remains widespread. Judges, public prosecutors and investigative police all represent state power that belongs to the civil servant class in China. In contrast, lawyers are individuals who practise law independently and without official status. In today's China, where formal official titles enjoy disproportionate privileges, lawyers are discriminated against by governmental officials.

Despite all these problems, the role of lawyers in the legal system is increasing and is becoming stronger and more diversified. The ambit within which lawyers are able to represent clients in litigation is expanding. Nowadays, Chinese lawyers represent clients in a large number of cases involving civil and commercial matters, criminal defence, administrative litigation and foreign-related work. For civil and commercial cases, a lawyer's role is the most obvious and appreciated by both clients and courts. The growing complexity of cases makes it impossible for parties to a dispute to follow court hearings without a lawyer's representation. At the same time, a lawyer's involvement makes judges' work easier because lawyers know both the laws and court procedures. In administrative cases, lawyers represent plaintiffs who usually suffer under the administrative decisions of local governments. Because of the courage of many lawyers and the increasing rights consciousness of the citizens, more and more people dare to bring lawsuits against the government. In criminal cases, though the number of lawyers specialising in criminal defence is rather limited, the quality of defence lawyers has increased. Some defence lawyers have gained an eminent reputation both inside and outside China. It is likely that Chinese lawyers will be a major force in pushing forward further judicial reform in China.

Chapter 8
Conclusions

Progress and Limitations: A Judicial System with Chinese Characteristics

There is little doubt that, since the end of the 1970s, judicial reconstruction and reform in China have achieved impressive progress. As the caseloads have grown from 1,168,715 in 1980, to 3,211,758 in 1990, 5,918,411 in 2000, and 11,712,349 in 2010,[1] courts in China have managed to deal with this 'litigation explosion' in a relatively functional manner. However, it is also indisputable that the existing judicial system is fraught with various challenges and problems. In accordance with notable transitions in Chinese society, the judicial system is also in a state of fluctuation. Some typical Chinese characteristics of the current judicial system can be drawn upon in order to facilitate a better understanding of how the system has transformed and what the challenges to further enhancement are that lay ahead.

A System of Multi-layered Supervision over the Judicial Work

Supervision of the courts' work can be seen in many different forms in the Chinese legal system. It may be internal, external, law-provided, or provided without a legal basis through the implementation of convention. Internal supervision refers to the hierarchy within a court: as far as handling cases is concerned, an individual judge and collegiate panel are supervised by the heads of the civil, criminal or administrative chambers; the heads are supervised by deputy presidents; and deputy presidents are supervised by the president of the court. When a collegiate panel is uncertain about a case, it will refer the case to be decided by the head of the chamber; if the head remains uncertain, he will pass the decision-making power to the adjudication committee of the court. The adjudication committee in each court functions as the highest body to decide significant and important cases. Such committees consist of the president, vice-presidents, heads of trial chambers and some senior judges. The relationship among judges within a court reflects the administrative way in which judges are managed – in essence, it is a reflection of the administration of adjudicative power.

The court's work is also supervised by extra-judicial bodies, including Communist Party organs, people's congresses, government and the public procuratorate. To a certain extent such supervision constitutes a kind of external interference in adjudicative power, a power which ought to be exercised exclusively by courts subject to formal legal norms and proceedings. The Party's oversight of judicial work is performed by the Central Political and Legal Committee and its local branches. Apart from implementing Party ideology and policy, these committees play the role of coordinating the public security department, procuratorate and court in handling grand cases (*da an*) and major cases (*yao an*). Consequently, a judgment is not solely made by a court; instead,

1 The figures for 1980, 1990 and 2000 are from Zhu Jingwen (ed.), *Zhongguo Falu Fazhan Baogao Shujuku He Zhibiao Tixi* (Report on China Law Development: Database and Indicators) (Beijing: Zhongguo Renmin Daxue Chubanshe, 2007), pp. 202–203. The 2010 figure is from the 2011 work report of the SPC to the NPC. The text is available at http://www.court.gov.cn/qwfb/gzbg/201112/t20111220_168518.htm. Last visited January 2014.

it is a 'collective' decision made by all of the actors involved, and in which the political and legal committee plays a leading role. As a popular Chinese saying goes: small, ordinary cases can be decided according to law; middle-level important cases are decided depending on their impact on society, economy and politics; significant cases are decided by politics rather than by courts (*xiao'an jiang falu, zhong'an jiang yingxiang, da'an jiang zhengzhi*).

The supervision of judicial work provided by people's congresses is a constitutional arrangement. Under Article 3 of the Constitution, 'All administrative, judicial and procuratorial organs of the State are created by the people's congresses to which they are responsible and by which they are supervised.' The NPCSC supervises the work of the SPC (Art. 67) and people's congress standing committee at local levels supervise the work of local courts at the corresponding levels (Art. 104). Concrete formal supervision includes: review and approval of the annual work report of the court at the corresponding level; appointment and dismissal of a court's president, vice-presidents and judges; following the legal procedure to make an inquiry to a court; handling public complaints and petitions on particular issues relating to a court.[2] In judicial practice, the most controversial issue is the phenomenon of people's congresses providing supervision on individual cases handled by courts. This can happen to pending cases as well as cases in which effective judgments have been delivered by courts. Despite the fact that the Supervision Law promulgated in 2006[3] has formally abandoned such conventional practice, supervision on individual cases by people's congresses still takes place in some localities.

Similar to other countries, the main function of the procuratorate is to bring public prosecution to courts. Apart from this, the Chinese procuratorates have an important power of legal supervision. A trial supervision procedure on courts' adjudication is provided in the CrPL, the CiPL and the ALL, respectively. This procedure enables a procuratorate to lodge a protest to a court if it finds violations of legal provisions and regulations in a legally effective judgment or order of the court, in criminal, civil or administrative cases. Despite criticism of the procuratorates' role in supervising civil judgment, the 2012 amended CiPL has strengthened rather than weakened such supervision, which displays the might of the procuratorate in China.

In terms of legally provided supervision by higher courts over lower courts, the system of remand for re-trial (*fahui chongshen*) and the system to re-open a trial (*zaishen*) are quite unique. *Fahui chongshen* refers to when a court of appeal remands a case to the first instance court for re-trial if the facts in the original judgment are unclear or the evidence is insufficient, or if the original court has violated procedural rules. *Zaishen* means that if a definite error in a legally effective judgment is found by a higher-level court, it can request the lower-level court which made the judgment to re-try the case. Both systems are provided for in the procedures for trial supervision in the CrPL, the CiPL and the ALL.

Forms of supervision that exist as customary judicial practice, without explicit statute provision, include the system of request for instruction, whereby a lower-level court asks a higher-level court to give opinions on difficult cases and, in turn, the opinions are used in the judgment of the lower-level court. Another example is the so-called system of correction of wrongly decided cases (*cuo'an zhuijiu zhi*), which requires judges to take responsibility for 'misjudged cases'. The system was introduced by local courts as a measure to aid judicial supervision in ensuring that judges entrusted with greater adjudicative power provide better deliverance of justice. However, it is difficult to define what a misjudged case is. In judicial practice, some courts have regarded cases remanded

2 See Arts. 8, 26, 27, 28 and 44 of the Organic Law of People's Congress and People's Governments at Various Levels.

3 The Law on the Supervision of the Standing Committees of People's Congresses at Various Levels, adopted at the 23rd Meeting of the Standing Committee of the Tenth NPC of China on 27 August 2006.

for re-trial or re-opened for trial by a higher court order as cases that have been misjudged at the first instance. Some courts even consider cases reversed by the appellate court as misjudged cases. The occurrence of such cases can affect the work record of the judges concerned and, sometimes, the judges' bonus can be reduced. This system was extended in the 1990s, and although it has been renounced, it has not totally disappeared.

The Overriding Emphasis on Mediation

Mediation has a long history in the settlement of civil disputes in China. From the 1950s to the early 1980s, this tradition was developed into a guiding principle for courts of 'mediation as the core, adjudication as a supplement'. Judicial mediation was employed as the main means of settling civil disputes, which manifestly had a coercive nature. To address this problem, the 1991 revised CiPL emphasised that mediation should be used on the basis of the principles of party voluntariness and lawfulness; and if no mediation agreement could be reached, courts should deliver judgments without delay. With the growing complexity of commercial disputes, as well as the reform of the civil trial system which heightened the significance of procedural justice, judicial mediation was diminished in the 1990s.

However, in the early 2000s, judicial mediation resurged as a consequence of the Party's tightened control over judicial work. In 2003, the Central Political and Legal Committee issued a policy paper calling for a grand mediation scheme whereby people's mediation, administrative mediation and judicial mediation would support each other to promote the peaceful settlement of disputes and make a contribution to building up a harmonious society.[4] In responding to the Party's policy, the SPC has issued a number of judicial opinions to prioritise judicial mediation.

Following a meticulous examination of the SPC's shift to revive judicial mediation, a distinction can be made with regards to the approach taken. Under President Xiao Yang (1998–2008), mediation was promoted as an alternative to address the problem posed by disgruntled parties bringing petitions to higher government authorities, which caused the top politicians to see courts as trouble-makers instead of trouble-solvers. However, under President Wang Shengjun (2008–2013), judicial mediation has been upgraded to a political task of the courts. In judicial practice, mediation is imposed from the case filing stage, to trial and to the final stage of enforcing a judgment. The mandatory nature of such mediation has become publicly advocated by the courts. Chinese scholars, on the other hand, describe this distorted mediation referral practice as a mechanism

> to promote the mediation by coercion (*yi ya cu tiao*); to compel the mediation by indicating that the result of the judgment will be the same as, or even worse than, mediation, regardless of whether mediation is accepted or not (*yi pan ya tiao*); to compel the mediation by delaying the delivery of a judgment (*yi tuo ya tiao*); and to compel the mediation by temptation (*yi you ya tiao*).[5]

This applies to both civil and administrative cases, and for criminal cases a purported criminal reconciliation system has also been gradually developed. Moreover, many local courts have set up annual mediation ratio targets, and have invented a financial incentive system by linking the

4 Luo Gan, 'Zhengfa Jiguan Zai Goujian Hexie Shehui Zhong Fudan Zhongda Lishi Shiming He Zhengzhi Zeren' (The Significant Historical Missions and the Political Responsibility of Political and Legal Organisations in Constructing a Harmonious Society), 3 (2003) *Qiu Shi* (Seeking Truth).

5 Wang Jun, 'Dui Fayuan Xingzheng Susong Anjian Xietiao Wenti De Yanjiu' (Research on the Reconciliation of Administrative Cases Used by Courts) (2013). Available at http://article.chinalawinfo.com/article_print.asp?articleid=76033. Last visited January 2014.

number of cases successfully mediated by judges with the judges' bonus, rewards and prospects of career promotion. Involving judges' own interests in mediation inevitably engenders problematic judicial behaviour, which consequently undermines public trust in the judicial authority.

Judicial mediation is now under attack from many Chinese legal scholars and is the subject of resistance on the part of judges. The dismay may not be directed at mediation as an alternative dispute resolution, but rather it may be a rejection of the way in which mediation is being politicised and compelled in the name of maintaining social stability. For many, the Party's real motivation for imposing judicial mediation is to prevent people petitioning the central authorities. The former Secretary of the Central Political and Legal Committee once urged officials at village and town levels to guarantee that 'small problems do not leave the village, large problems do not leave the township, and conflicts are not passed up to higher authorities'.[6] Courts and judges, especially those at lower levels, bear the daunting task of preventing disputants from petitioning higher government authorities. At the present time, whether judicial mediation has contributed effectively to achieving such a goal remains unprovable.

Public Participation in the Judicial Process

The people's assessor system is the most obvious reflection of public participation in the judicial process. This system was originally introduced at the end of the Qing dynasty, continually used during the Republic period, and popularly used by the Communist Party in the Communist-controlled revolutionary base in the north-west of China in the 1930s and 1940s. While the people's assessor system was provided in both the 1954 and 1978 Constitutions, the 1982 Constitution did not mention it. Moreover, the 1983 amended Organic Law of People's Courts made the use of people's assessors optional for the courts of first instance in formulating collegiate panels. This voluntary feature was then reflected in the 1989 ALL, the 1991 CiPL and the 1996 CrPL.

The people's assessor system is mainly used by basic people's courts in handling cases by ordinary procedure whereby a collegiate panel with three adjudicators is required, of which one or two can be people's assessors. Despite the fact that laws entrust people's assessors with the same power as judges in determining both facts and the application of law, in reality, too often people' assessors cannot perform their functions effectively. A common public image of the people's assessor is their role of accompanying judges by sitting in a courtroom without actually participating in adjudication (*pei er bu shen*). However, since the early 2000s, the people's assessor system has been incrementally strengthened through its promotion by the SPC. Moreover, in 2004 the NPCSC, for the first time, issued the Decisions on the Perfection of the People's Assessor System, which outlines the required qualifications and remuneration for assessors. The Decisions also oblige the courts of first instance to form collegiate panels with assessors in order to handle cases with substantial social impact, or cases whereby parties involved request the participation of people's assessors.

In connection with the new judicial policy of democratisation of the judiciary, pushed forward by the SPC in its third Five-Year Reform Programme of People's Courts (2009–2013), the people's assessor system has been further strengthened as a major measure to promote judicial populism.[7]

---

6 Zhou Yongkang, 'Shenru Tuijin Shehui Maodun Huajie' (Deeply Pushing Forward the Resolution of Social Conflict), *Qiushi*, 16 February 2010, available at http://www.qstheory.cn/zxdk/2010/201004/201002/t20100209_20841.htm. Last visited January 2014.

7 Judicial populism refers to the phenomenon that judgments and activities of courts are driven by the expectations of mass society, or certain groups of people and their subjective perception of 'justice'. The opponent of judicial populism is judicial professionalism. One of the most firm advocators of judicial professionalism is

In commenting on the Programme, a vice-president of the SPC pointed out that courts should take initiatives to organise ordinary citizens to join judges in adjudication activities, and that public opinions should be used as the ultimate standard in assessing the success and failure of the judicial work.[8]

Under such guidance, since 2009, some local courts have initiated a so-called people's jury experiment. Jurors are selected from citizens without a legal background, but who are enthusiastic about the courts' work. A jury usually consists of a dozen jurors. They attend court hearings, can question defendants with the permission of the presiding judge, and eventually give their opinions on the case to be used by judges as reference. Until now the jury experiment has been used by only a few courts. Despite the positive impact in attracting ordinary people to participate in court hearings, the nascent system needs to be further tested prior to it obtaining statutory recognition. At this moment its political consideration seems greater than its legal consequences.

In addition, the internet and new communication technology have also had a spontaneous effect on public participation in judicial work.[9] At least three aspects of this can be identified. Firstly, for the public at large, the internet, which is now a major source of disseminating information, has enabled people to have broader exposure to judicial information. In the past, courts' handling of cases was virtually a state secret and miscarriages of justice happened without public notice. Nowadays, the internet and social media have changed the situation. Too often, sensitive pending cases, high-profile cases, and injustice cases are exposed by local newspapers, immediately reposted on various websites, become the subject of discussion on certain online fora. In some instances this has generated the attention of the SPC and other higher-level government organs.

Secondly, the internet has become a forum on which people express and exchange opinions. People not only receive the information, but can also post their comments on the reported cases. The collective reactions form a kind of social force which, via the internet, transmits public opinions to courts and judges. Taking one of the most frequently used communication tools – Sina Weibo – for example, keyword searches of 'pubic opinions' (*yulun*) and 'judiciary' (*sifa*) show more than 1.2 million posts up to January 2014. Courts and judges cannot ignore these opinions completely, either in making decisions or in correcting decisions already made.

Thirdly, the internet is also a useful tool broadly used in judicial work. Live trials are transmitted via television and the internet. This new form was even adopted by the SPC in the recent case of *360 v. QQ*.[10] In 2012, the HPC in Zhejiang province cooperated with Taobao.com to conduct a

---

He Weifang, who has pointed out that law is a field with specific requirements on the knowledge, rationality and ethics of its practitioners. Thus, he strongly opposes that demobilised soldiers are qualified to become judges. The debate between the two approaches was mainly of an academic nature. However, in 2009 when Shen Deyong, Vice-President of the SPC, stated that the relationship between judicial professionalism and judicial populism had dialectical unity, it was revealed that the SPC was beginning to recognise judicial populism. See People.com.cn, 'Zuigao Renmin Fayuan Changwu Fuyuanzhang Shen Deyong Zuoke Qiangguo Luntan Tan Zhuoli Jiaqiang Fayuan Zishen Jianshe' (The Executive Vice-President of the SPC – Shen Deyong – Participated in the Qiangguo Forum and Expressed His Opinions on Enhancing the Development of Courts Themselves), 2 March 2009. Available at http://live.people.com.cn/bbs/note.php?id=57090225105627_ctdzb_062. Last visited January 2014.

8 *Ibid.*

9 For an updated analysis on media, the internet and judicial work in China, see Benjamin Liebman and Tim Wu, 'China's Network Justice', 8 (2007–2008) *Chicago Journal of International Law*, pp. 257–322; and Benjamin Liebman, 'The Media and the Courts: Towards Competitive Supervision?', 208 (2011) *The China Quarterly*, pp. 833–850.

10 For more information, see Sina, 'Zhongguo Hulianwang Fan Longduan Di Yi An '(The Top 1 Anti-monopoly Case in the Field of Internet in China). Available at http://tech.sina.com.cn/z/360qq2013/. Last visited January 2014.

judicial auction online. Although this innovation incurred criticism and challenges regarding its legality, the act of instigating such online judicial auctions has spread to other courts, such as the Zhongshan city court in Guangdong province.[11] The internet has also expedited judicial procedures through mechanisms such as the online reception of cases and online delivery of judicial documents.[12] Most courts have opened official accounts on Weibo and other communication applications in order to communicate with citizens and facilitate their judicial work. Judges also use the internet to gain access to legal scholars' Weibo posts, to obtain information on cases handled by other courts, to write their own legal blogs and so on.[13]

However, due to the characteristics and the nature of the way that information is produced and transmitted on the internet, caution is needed regarding the public's interaction with the judiciary via the medium. Firstly, there is an explosion of information on the internet which makes it extremely difficult to distinguish between fact and fiction. Secondly, information is often fragmented and piecemeal. Meticulous elaboration and analysis are no longer popular and welcomed by readers; instead, short posts with a maximum of 140 words, as Sina Weibo requires, have become the prevalent form used to express and exchange opinions. Thirdly, the way that information is produced and transmitted has been transformed from a traditional era in which official media creates, selects and disseminates information, to an era which is dubbed the 'We-media age' (*zi mei ti shi dai*). All of these characteristics have strongly shaped how the internet and media can affect the dynamics between the public and judiciary, in terms of both the direction and the degree of influence.

The role of public authorities in selecting, verifying and disseminating judicial information in a top-down manner has been gradually dissolved, or at least diluted by this internet-based bottom-up approach. However, it should also be noted that, due to the paramount influence of political forces in China over judicial work, the actual effect of internet-based public influence on courts is yet to be ascertained. The changing fate of the courts' decisions on high-profile cases, as previously discussed, is not merely due to public pressure. The defining factor is that public reaction has been known to attract the attention of top political officials, and the latter's intervention has compelled courts to decide cases according to the official's instruction. Thus, the role of the public in discussing pending cases is inflammatory, stimulating change, rather than determining the change. Furthermore, increasingly intensive censorship of internet-based discussion casts a gloom over the actual effects of internet-based public influences on the judiciary. A glimpse of the internet's influence can be found in the recent judicial interpretation on handling cases of libel that take advantage of internet technology, which prescribes that any libel information that has been forwarded more than 500 times on the internet will incriminate the poster of such information.[14]

11 See 'Zhejiang Sheng Gaoyuan Huiying Wangluo Sifa Paimai Zhiyi: Wanquan Hefa' (HPC in Zhejiang Province Responded to Criticism of Online Judicial Auction: Totally Legal), *Fazhi Ribao* (Legal Daily), 10 August 2012, available at http://news.xinhuanet.com/yuqing/2012-08/10/c_123562145.htm; 'Zhongshan Shuaixian Quansheng Shishui Wangluo Sifa Paimai Zuo Zai Taobao Shangxian' (Zhongshan Adopts Online Judicial Auction for the First Time Yesterday at Taobao.com), in *Nanfang Ribao* (Southern Daily), 24 December 2013, available at http://zs.nfdaily.cn/news_list/content/2013-12/24/content_88133374.htm. Both were last visited January 2014.

12 See 'Beijing Fayuan Sifa 1Yue 1 Ri Qi Zai Wangshang Tigong Susong Fuwu' (An Online Litigation Service Is to Be Provided by Beijing Courts from January 1), *Fazhi Wanbao* (Legal Evening News), 31 December 2013, available at http://www.isc.org.cn/zxzx/jsyy/listinfo-28586.html. Last visited January 2014.

13 See Benjamin Liebman and Tim Wu, *supra* note 9, p. 260.

14 See Article 2 of the Interpretations of the SPC and the SPP on Several Issues of the Application of Law on Handling Libel Cases by Using Informational Internet Networks and Other Criminal Cases, *Fashi*

Nevertheless, one can observe the growing use of the internet by the public as a means of asserting influence over the judiciary, and the influence that was once created unintentionally, is now being exercised in an intentional manner. In short,

> the rationalisation progress of adjudication in China has encountered an institutional and cultural bottleneck. The lack of judicial independence from government power and the painful fact of judicial corruption cause people to turn to so-called public opinion supervision. Especially for the disadvantaged, mobilizing media support becomes a useful weapon in seeking justice against the powerful.[15]

The Limited Role of Lawyers in Judicial Proceedings

Over the past three decades, the legal profession has undergone dramatic transformation: from being almost non-existent in the 1970s, to experiencing growth in the 1980s, and then rapid expansion in the 1990s. In the past 10 years, concurrent with the continuing enlargement of the legal profession, some Chinese lawyers, especially those specialised in criminal defence and human rights protection, have faced increasing political pressure and biased judicial treatment. Generally speaking, whereas some commercial lawyers who mainly provide non-litigation legal services enjoy social admiration and financial security, most litigation lawyers, especially those specialising in criminal and administrative cases, face formidable difficulties.

Three of the most striking features of the legal profession in China are outlined here. First, the legal profession is managed by a dual system: the Ministry of Justice and its local judicial bureaus take on the responsibilities of 'organisational leadership and professional supervision' over lawyers. The All China Lawyers Association and its local branches are professionally responsible units of lawyers. Although these associations are deemed self-regulating social organisations of lawyers, in reality, they barely have autonomy due to their close affiliation with the governmental judicial departments. The dual leadership system inevitably affects the independence of the legal profession in China, and reduces the protection provided to the legal profession by the lawyers' associations.

Second, lawyers are considered 'extra-institutional persons' (*tizhiwai de ren*). The 1980 Provisional Regulations on Lawyers defined lawyers as 'state legal workers', which illustrated that there was no distinction between lawyers and the judicial workers who mainly provided legal aid and received a salary from the government budget. The 1996 Lawyers Law redefined lawyers as 'legal practitioners' with a qualified certificate to practise law and 'provide legal services to society'. The 2007 amended Lawyers Law further redefined the lawyers' function to 'provide legal services for clients'. The modifications in the definition manifest the progressive recognition of the legal profession as independent and clarify the lawyer–client relationship. However, as Chinese society remains official-centric (*guan benwei*), the losing of official status has both advantages and disadvantages. One of the remarkable disadvantages is that lawyers are unfairly rejected by judges, prosecutors and government officials alike. On the other hand, some lawyers are gaining growing economic strength and social credibility; they are more concerned about their legal practice than treatment by official bureaucrats.

Third, on the whole, the position of criminal defence lawyers is vulnerable. Traditionally, their position in the justice system was always frail, and it remains weak in general, despite the fact that

No. 21 [2013]. Full text is available at http://legal.people.com.cn/n/2013/0909/c42510–22859612.html. Last visited January 2014.

15 Ji Weidong, 'The Judicial Reform in China: The Status Quo and Future Directions', 20(1) (2013) *Indiana Journal of Global Legal Studies*, p. 207.

the CrPL and the Lawyers Law have stipulated better protection of a lawyer's rights to meet clients, to have access to case materials and to defend clients. A popular saying in China has it that judges depend on power, prosecutors depend on privilege and lawyers have to make do with knowledge.[16] In general, lawyers play a limited role in defending their clients. Some lawyers, with the courage to exercise their legal rights in presenting vigorous defence, have been mistreated, even jailed. Some have been compelled to leave the legal profession. Alongside this apparent hopelessness, however, an emerging change in the face of defence lawyers can be observed. In the recent landmark cases of *Beihai* and *Xiaohe*,[17] a group of lawyers came together and supported one another in pursuing resilient, 'not guilty' defences, and they won the cases. Even if such successes are exceptional and may not adequately represent the overall reality of criminal defence lawyers, at least they signal a surfacing transformation of the defence lawyer.

Serious Judicial Corruption

In parallel with the growing significance of the courts in Chinese society as a consequence of the rapid economic and social transition over the past three decades, judicial corruption has also expanded and intensified. From the late 1980s, the acceptance of dinner invitations and cash by judges gradually spread and became a 'hidden rule' for parties who expected to obtain a favourable judgment. This individual misconduct snowballed, and nowadays there seems to be an alarming degree of systemic and organised corruption within courts, as examined in Chapter 3.

The SPC work report in 2012 revealed that 519 court personnel were punished for violations of law and discipline and, among them, 77 were subjected to criminal investigation. The high-profile judicial corruption cases that have recently been exposed are a disgrace to the Chinese judiciary. The corrupt judges ranged from top-ranking judges such as the vice-president of the SPC, to several presidents of the BPCs. Some of them received the severe punishment of life imprisonment for receiving huge bribes and embezzling funds. As the division of judgment enforcement within each court has become economically significant in the sense that such cases involve huge amounts of property, the heads of the enforcement divisions have become high-risk targets for judicial corruption. Another distinctive feature of the judicial corruption is the 'collective case' (*wo an*). This refers to a group of judges within one court who collaborate to commit economic crimes. In some cases, more than a dozen judges within a court were found guilty of crimes at the same time. The disclosure of such cases has shocked the public at large and has seriously undermined judicial credibility.[18] In connection with this, a relatively new revelation is that courts (as well as police and procuratorates) have been illegally spending the cash, or selling the goods, that they have seized;

16 Li Xuan, 'Zhidu Quesun Yu Guannian Diwu: Dangdai Zhongguo Lushiye De Liangda Nanti' (Institutional Deficiencies and Conceptual Backwardness: Two Big Difficulties Facing the Chinese Legal Profession), p. 21, available at http://www.lawbook.com.cn/lw/lw_view.asp?no=677&page=7. Last visited January 2014.

17 For *Beihai* see Chapter 4. For *Xiaohe* see Chapter 7.

18 As early as 1988 a distinguished Chinese legal scholar warned that nothing causes more harm to the rule of law in society than judicial corruption. The public perceives judges not only as arbitrators of disputes but also as those who uphold legal rules. Judicial corruption, even if it only relates to some judges, pollutes the origin of justice, weakens public confidence in the judicial system and inevitably causes people to seek other options to settle disputes rather than through courts. He Weifang, *Sifa De Linian Yu Zhidu* (Judicial Conceptions and Systems) (Beijing: Zhongguo Zhengfa Daxue Chubanshe, 1988), p. 9.

thus, when a case is found to have been wrongly handled, it cannot easily be corrected because the seized property has already gone.[19]

Judicial corruption in China has numerous root causes. Apart from the subjective element, namely, the low professional ethics of judges, external causes constitute deep-seated sources of judicial corruption. For instance, the lack of judicial independence results in much interference in judicial judging, leaving room for judicial corruption. Moreover, judicial corruption cannot be isolated from administrative and political corruption. With the abuse of public power by public officials for private gain being extensive within the bureaucratic spectrum, judges find it hard to remain clean as they observe other bureaucrats accumulating wealth for their families, relatives and friends. As a consequence the SPC has issued various rules providing lists of prohibitive acts to guide judges' judicial and extra-judicial behaviour. The SPC has also periodically launched anticorruption campaigns to intensively punish corrupt judges. These *ad hoc* measures may have some instant short-term effects, but judicial corruption has become more widespread and intensified over time.[20]

Judicial Reform: An Unfolding Process of Modernisation rather than Westernisation

The path taken by judicial reform over the past three decades has purposefully been designed not to replicate a Western model; rather, it has been a pragmatic, piecemeal approach to modernisation of the judicial system, which is concomitant with the economic modernisation and social transformation in China. This is clearly exhibited by the inauguration of the altered civil trial process which was initiated by local courts out of a practical need. Originally, Chinese judges collected evidence by themselves when handling civil disputes. Nonetheless, in the mid-1980s, when increasing numbers of cases were brought to courts, it became impossible for judges to tackle them within the period prescribed by law. Therefore, courts started to introduce a system whereby the burden of proof was placed upon the party who made the claim. While judges were confident about the reliability of evidence that they collected themselves, they were uncertain about the soundness of the evidence collected and presented by parties. Consequently, this made court investigation and court debate a necessity. This again stimulated the active participation of lawyers in hearings, and the increased sophistication of rules pertaining to evidence. Judges were also pressured to improve their skills in handling court hearings. From 1988 to 1997, judicial reform was mainly reflected in the improvement of the civil trial procedure, which featured innovative experiments by local courts. Since then, reform has gradually been expanded to the whole civil justice system, and has included the innovations of separating case filing from adjudication, strengthening parties' autonomy and boosting the enforcement of civil judgment.

The introduction of a modern administrative litigation system was also largely an internal initiative. It started with allowing economic entities to bring lawsuits to the courts against decisions

19 The information was provided by a famous Chinese lawyer Tian Wenchang at a public seminar held at the China University of Political Science and Law in Beijing in November 2013. See Sina Comments, 'Xin Xingshi Xia Sifa Gaige Yu Zhongguo Fazhi Yuanjing' (Perspectives of the Judicial Reform and the Rule of Law in China under the New Circumstances), available at http://news.sina.com.cn/pl/2013-11-24/083928795385.shtml. Last visited January 2014.

20 This phenomenon corresponds with the observation in general that 'corruption in China has increased to epidemic or even endemic levels since the advent of reform in the late 1970s'. See Andrew Wedeman, 'The Intensification of Corruption in China', 180 (2004) *The China Quarterly*, p. 895.

of administrative authorities.[21] However, the distinction made in the ALL concerning concrete and abstract administrative actions, and the narrow scope of judicial review applicable only to infringement of personal and property rights, reflects the limits of law-makers at the end of the 1980s. In judicial practice, the wide use of judicial reconciliation and compelled withdrawal by plaintiffs, the negligence in administrative litigation and the strong administrative interference by administrative agencies demonstrate the particular hindrances and challenges China is experiencing. At the same time, the judiciary has reacted cautiously to newly-emerged social needs by accepting and handling certain types of cases which are not – in a strict application of the law – within the scope of the courts' jurisdiction. This includes the handling of cases concerning the right to education, the right to be not discriminated against in the labour market, the right to information and so on. The growth in citizens' consciousness on rights and some lawyers' passionate, active commitment in administrative litigation are the main driving forces that have pushed forward and modernised this particular litigation system in China.

With regard to reform of the criminal trial system, China is modernising its system, despite confrontation with a variety of hurdles, stemming from inside and outside courts. The promulgation of the 1996 CrPL marked a new phase in which some modern principles and systems were generally introduced to facilitate fair trials. These included: strengthening the rights of accused and defence lawyers, more sophisticated evidence rules, the principle of presumption of innocence, the principle of prohibition of torture and the exclusion of illegally obtained evidence by courts. The SPC and the SPP have also, respectively or jointly, issued a large array of judicial interpretations with more detailed implementing rules to guide courts in handling criminal cases. However, in judicial practice, the implementation of the CrPL has proved more problematic than might have been expected. One of the major problems is the disregard of defence lawyers' rights in judicial proceedings. If lawyers' rights cannot be meaningfully realised, the rights of the accused become empty, and subsequently a fair trial cannot be achieved. It should be noted that in China a fair trial of criminal cases is, in some circumstances, not solely determined by courts and judges. Political intervention on sensitive cases makes a fair trial difficult or in some cases even unattainable. Such cases may concern politically sensitive issues, such as high-ranking official corruption, economic crimes with political complication, religious activities, as well as murder relating to ordinary citizens.

Judicial reform from the mid-1980s to the present can be categorised into four distinct periods. The first is from the 1980s to 1997, in which reform was an experiment conducted mainly by local courts as they sought to find practical solutions to solve the major challenges in handling the growing number of cases. The second is from 1998 to 2008 when Xiao Yang was the President of the SPC. During this 10-year period, two Five-Year Reform Programmes of People's Courts were issued by the SPC, which covered a wide range of reform measures concerning the trial systems, professionalisation of the judiciary, redefining jurisdictions among courts at different levels, court management and more. This period of reform is often referred to by Chinese legal experts as the 'golden period of reform', in which modern conceptions of the judicial system were advocated and indeed influenced the judiciary. The third period is from 2008 to 2013, during which Wang Shengjun was the President of the SPC. In contrast to that of his predecessor, the reform under

21 For instance, the Income Tax Law on Chinese-Foreign Equity Joint Ventures of 1980 provided that 'in case of a dispute with the tax authorities over tax payment, a joint venture must pay tax according to the relevant regulations before applying to higher tax authorities for administrative reconsideration. If it does not accept the decision made after the reconsideration, it may bring a lawsuit to the local people's court' (Article 15). See also the Maritime Environmental Protection Law of 1982 (Articles 41 and 42) and the Law on Administration of Entry and Exit of Foreigners of 1986 (Article 29).

his presidency has been labelled a 'retreat'. The third Five-Year Reform Programme of People's Courts obviously reflected the SPC's response to the Party's calling on the judiciary to serve the Party's central tasks; mediation was raised to a political task for courts and judges in order to maintain social stability. The change in presidency of the SPC, to Zhou Qiang in 2013, marked the start of the fourth period in which it is as yet unclear how judicial reform will proceed in the coming five or 10 years; however, it seems clear that the SPC cannot continue in the direction set up by its previous President, Wang Shengjun. A publication that is currently a cause for concern is the new decisions issued by the CPC in late 2013 – Decisions on Several Major Issues concerning Comprehensively Deepening Reforms of the Central Committee of the China Communist Party (the Decisions) – which were adopted at the Third Plenary Session of the 18th CPC Central Committee in November 2013.[22] Both systematic and concrete judicial reforms are mentioned in the Decisions. Though yet to be implemented in practice, based on the crucial importance of the CPC's decisions in guiding the direction of the development of the whole nation, the Decisions could be deemed a markable overture to a new round of judicial reform.

Mapping the Path towards Further Judicial Reform

The Inevitability of Further Judicial Reform

When looking ahead, the fundamental question is whether further judicial reform is needed. The answer is definitely yes. Reasons for this are three-fold. Firstly, economic reform and the open-door policy of the last 30 years in China have brought profound economic and social transformation to the country. In such a transforming era, the judicial system has played a unique role in solving disputes, safeguarding economic development, protecting citizens' and companies' legal rights and so on. Chinese courts have never been so important in the nation's history. Moreover, the role of courts in society can only become even more significant as China proceeds further with deepening economic reform and modernisation. Secondly, there has been a surge in demand from citizens for greater justice, fairness and equality and, at the same time, for various reasons, the judiciary has yet to meet the public's expectations. This has created an imbalance between social demand and judicial supply. Judicial unfairness and corruption have become the main sources of popular resentment and social instability. This not only impairs public trust in the judiciary, but also challenges the legitimacy of the Party's ruling of the country. Thirdly, as administrative power has reached the social and economic spheres to an unprecedented degree and scale, review of administrative actions by the judiciary is of crucial necessity in order to guarantee that administrative power is not exercised in an arbitrary and capricious way. Taking these factors into concern, further judicial reform is inevitable.

A following question concerns who will be the leader of the new round of judicial reform. Previous experiences with either SPC-led or CPLC-led reform have displayed both advantages and disadvantages. The advantage of SPC-led reform was that the leadership knew the real problems of the judicial work and adopted pragmatic approaches to address them. However, its main limitation was that the reform measures mostly served to fulfil the functions of the courts, without sufficiently considering social demands. The advantage of the CPLC-led judicial reform was that it was

22 Full text in Chinese is available at http://news.xinhuanet.com/politics/2013-11/15/c_118164235.htm; for an English translation, see http://chinacopyrightandmedia.wordpress.com/2013/11/15/ccp-central-committee-resolution-concerning-some-major-issues-in-comprehensively-deepening-reform/. Both were last visited in January 2014.

efficient, though limited, to coordinate various powerful state branches in resolving some issues which the SPC could not have tackled alone, such as being able to get funding from the central authority for courts in economically poor regions. However, the disadvantage was also obvious: placing too much emphasis on the judicial reform serving the central task of the Party, rather than basing the reform on the nature of the judicial system.

To weigh up the pros and cons of the institutions, the eminent Chinese legal scholar, He Weifang, suggests establishing a judicial reform committee under the NPC in which more than half the members would be legal scholars, lawyers and representatives of NGOs.[23] The establishment of a special judicial reform commission is highly desirable, given the immense significance of the courts in China's economic and social transition. Realistically speaking, deciding which institution should lead future judicial reform is a matter of political choice. Despite this, the idea of drawing constituents from legal scholars, lawyers and NGOs deserves recognition. In this context, it should be acknowledged that, over the past years, some legal scholars and lawyers have actively and courageously pushed forward the judicial reform. Scholars are more neutral and can be expected to represent the public interests and social justice better. Lawyers, as the watchdogs of courts' compliance with substantive and procedural standards set in law, could also contribute to further judicial reforms by bringing in ideas from their professional perspectives and by ensuring that the reformers abide by their commitment. Furthermore, there is a need to foster a civil society and an independent media that may better represent interests and claims from different groups, and provide channels and forums for expressing and exchanging ideas.

It seems that the central authority should seize the opportunity to take full advantage of this social positive energy (*zheng neng liang*) to moderate internal pressure from the Party and central authority. The neglect, marginalisation, isolation and even suppression of social elites and intellectuals will ultimately disappoint, frustrate, chill, silence and hinder them from making further constructive contributions to the nation. Without the intellectual support of scholars, lawyers and other social elites, it is predictable that judicial reform will be partial, piecemeal and unstable. Regression and retreat may occur without supervisors and supporters who are enthusiastic to enforce and implement such reforms.

Based on the current situation of tightened control over the judiciary by political power, further judicial reform can be expected to continually follow a slow but incremental pattern of addressing both pragmatic and fundamental issues in order to develop a fair and efficient judicial system. No matter how slow it proceeds, and how frustrating it may be when progress is barely seen or when minor regressions occasionally occur, judicial reform is inevitable simply because no power in China can stop the trend of recognition and use of the courts to solve social disputes, to protect citizens' legal rights and to achieve social harmony and political stability.

Pulling Out of the Retreat and Carving a New Path

The next question then concerns where the new round of judicial reform should be directed. At present, the first step should be to correct the wrong judicial policies and working methods promoted by the SPC since 2008. The most salient feature of the post-2008 reform is the politicisation of judicial work. This is reflected in several aspects, for example, through adherence to the Party's leadership in judicial reform, the assistant role of courts in maintaining social stability via the

23 See Cheng Li, 'Introduction: Fighting for a Constitutional China: Public Enlightenment and Legal Professionalism', in He Weifang, *In the Name of Justice: Striving for the Rule of Law in China* (Washington, DC: Brookings Institution Press, 2012), p. xviii. Available at http://www.brookings.edu/~/media/press/books/2012/inthenameofjustice/inthenameofjustice_intro.pdf. Last visited January 2014.

excessive use of mediation and so on. The political feature of judicial work is epitomised in the so-called 'Three Supremacies': the supremacy of the course of the CPC, the supremacy of the interests of the people and the supremacy of the Constitution and the laws. Making the 'Three Supremacies' the guiding principle for adjudication is inappropriate. Judges have to consider, each time they are about to deliver a verdict, what kind of judgment will not impair the Party's course, will accord with peoples' interests and will accord with the Constitution and the laws; however, their understanding of the Party's course and peoples' interests may differ tremendously. Therefore such a guiding principle will impair the integrity and stability of the judicial system.

Moreover, the post-2008 reforms also contain a characteristic of de-professionalisation, which stands in sharp opposition to the judicial professionalism promoted in Xiao Yang's time. The Third Five-Year Reform Programme of People's Courts reinvigorates the so-called 'mass line' in political-legal affairs, which was for a long time the creed of the CPC. As part of this reform, the adjudication committee's role is further intensified, as is the system of request for instruction by lower courts. This reflects the tendency of the administration to impose significant influence over adjudication powers. To summarise, in the sense of correcting the wrongs, the most imminent concern would be the de-politicisation and re-professionalisation of the judiciary.

Besides pulling out of the so-called 'retreat era', the goal of judicial reform should be reinstated and strengthened to avoid potential setbacks and regression. The direction of judicial reform should be based on the nature and functions of the judicial system, instead of contemporary political needs and volatile civilian appeals. The ultimate goal of the judicial system is to guarantee judicial fairness, supplemented by judicial effectiveness and judicial authority. This requires professional, neutral judges, open trial proceedings, independent courts and judges and the unified enforcement of the law. The judicial reform should be centred on establishing impartial, neutral and independent courts, to enable judges to adjudicate cases according to law without fear of any sort of internal or external interference.

To accomplish this goal fully, both political reform and judicial reform are necessary. From a practical perspective, the question arises as to whether judicial reform can be successful while the Party hesitates or resists promoting political reforms. Judicial reform needs political support. Without adequate political backup, the judicial reform led by the SPC is likely to draw a pie in the sky (*hua bing chong ji*), and will not be able to achieve substantive progress in reshaping the judicial system. With regard to structural issues of political reform, the key task is the redistribution of judicial, legislative, executive and political power (the relationship with the CPC). Until now, there has been no fundamental or substantive changes made regarding the relations of these organs; however, some recent developments and changes can be noticed. The unique role of courts in society has increased their social legitimacy, which can be used in strengthening their relations with political powers. Moreover, political wisdom is called upon: the Party should consider judicial reform from the perspective of the national interest rather than the Party's power.

It can be expected that the new round of judicial reform will be more arduous than the one led by the SPC between 1998 and 2008; this is because steps taken then were deemed innovative and progressive, and thus gained wide academic and practical support. However, following the post-2008 regression period, the values and goals that were once cherished in the previous reform are now deemed to be hazardous for the Party's leadership and social stability. Thus, greater restrictions are being set on academic discussion and judicial practices concerning judicial reform. Advocates of judicial reform are also becoming more cautious in making relevant proposals.

Nonetheless, the driving forces of future judicial reform can be identified. To approach the goal of reform, the driving forces may be court-centric, with enthusiastic support from legal scholars who are a knowledgeable source. Apart from a united force between the judicial elite (especially judges at the SPC) and leading legal scholars in driving change, as demonstrated in the previous round of reform, the active participation of lawyers as well as broad public involvement via the internet and social media are to be expected. Public enthusiasm regarding judicial work in general may be conveyed via the internet; however, it is the commentary on individual cases that reveals the monumental possibilities of the public's involvement. Public participation is conducive to gaining broader social support in strengthening judicial efforts; thus, courts should cautiously involve them rather than rebuff them.

Interdependent Approach

In essence, judicial reform needs to address three aspects simultaneously. First, measures to improve the competence and ethics of the judiciary must be considered. The development of courts has formerly been stunted by economic factors, especially in the western areas of China. However, along with economic development and payment transfer, the competence of judges has now become the decisive factor of judicial development. Judges are those who deliver the final justice and accordingly, they must be professionally qualified with legal knowledge, practical experience and high standards of judicial ethics. Judicial reform and the improvement of judges' competence are interdependent, with one supplementing the other. Judges may have the opportunity to improve their abilities as a result of judicial reform, while they also function decisively for the success of judicial reform. Currently in China, quite a number of judges, and leaders of courts who manage judges, still have a limited legal education and little background knowledge on legal practices. There are also batches of graduates who work on adjudication immediately after their graduation. Obviously, these students lack social experiences that are crucially needed in adjudicative work and they cannot easily translate what they learn from books into practice. The selection and promotion of judges can be reformed to further implement the policy of recruiting judges at higher courts from lower courts, as well as recruiting judges from experienced lawyers.

Strengthening judicial ethics was once a central reform issue. In 2001, the SPC issued the Code of Conduct for Judges which contains 50 articles describing the principles of judicial impartiality, judicial efficiency, integrity of judges, judicial decorum, self-improvement of judges and restriction of extra-judicial activities. The Code even outlined what ideal and professional judges should be like. Judicial ethics is part of judicial professionalism. However, stressing judicial professionalism should not create an impression of detaching judges from common people. Chinese culture is not in favour of creating any class above common people. This is evident in the current public resistance to 'the second generation of *nouveau riches*' (*fu er dai*) and 'the second generation of families with high official ranking' (*guan er dai*). A judge's detachment from common people carries the risk of being used by those with political power, against judicial power, if needed. Thus, the Chinese judiciary has to strike a balance between being highly professional and at the same time knowing that they come from the people and should serve the people. A bureaucratic and non-committal judiciary undermines its social support.

Secondly, internal court reform must take place in order to improve the trial system and the relevant systems relating to it. This could be conducted in the following ways. Firstly, by normalising the way that adjudicative power is exercised and separating it from the administration of the court; secondly, by increasing judicial transparency and openness in judicial conduct; and thirdly, by promoting procedural justice. To be clear, the collegiate panel system should be strengthened to ensure that those handling the cases have the full power to decide the outcome of the cases, as well as bear the responsibility if the case is obviously wrongly decided. Relevant to this, it may also be deemed important to restrict the role of the adjudication committee in handling individual cases;

abolish the case report system in which a lower court reports cases to a higher court for its opinion; further clarify and standardise the jurisdiction between lower and higher courts; further reform the people's assessor system for its effective use at the basic level; abolish the ranking system among judges by making judges equal, with seniority differences only on the basis of age and experience; promote and improve the case guidance system; and increase the accessibility and openness of judgments and other judicial documents. It should be noted that some proposals on concrete reforms of the judicial system have been made in the 2013 CPC Decisions. In Item 33, reform on the system of adjudication committees in particular is mentioned. It also states that 'the responsibility system of presiding judges and collegial panels should be improved; judges should adjudicate the case and adjudicators should be responsible for their decisions'. This proclamation largely weakens the role of adjudication committees and strengthens the independence and responsibility of judges. Judicial transparency is also emphasised in Item 33 by requiring that 'trial documents should be fully recorded and filed; elaborate reasoning should be strengthened in legal documents; and open access to valid judgments should be promoted'. With regards to popular participation in the judicial process, the Decisions also emphasise the role of people's assessors and people's supervisors. It proposes that channels that facilitate popular participation in adjudication in an organised manner should be broadened.

Thirdly, future judicial reform should aim to strengthen judicial independence in China. The notion of judicial independence should be understood from an internationally recognised perspective, which embraces the ideas that judges should be independent from each other when deciding a case; courts at different levels should be independent from each other in exercising adjudicative power; and judges and courts should be independent from any extra-judicial interference in their handling of cases. The task of judicial reform in this regard is to solve the two highlighted problems of judicial localisation (*sifa difanghua*) and administration of the judiciary (*sifa xingzhenghua*). The former problem refers to the phenomenon that the personnel, budget and property of courts come under the control of local governments. Courts are even deemed to be a functioning department of local governments, and have to deliver judgments that are catered to local governments' needs. The latter problem refers to the administrative manner in which judiciaries are managed. The institutional relationship between courts at lower levels and higher levels indicates a strong administrative feature, which is reflected in particular in the system of 'request for instructions'. Furthermore, the management of judges is quite administrative as it seems to be based on a quasi-civil-servant managerial system. The relationship between presidents, heads of each chamber within courts and judges is deemed to be superior–subordinate. These two problems are also specifically dealt with in the CPC Decisions. In Item 32 of the Decisions, it is asserted that

> the independence and fairness of the judicial and procuratorial power should be ensured. Unified management of staff members, budget and properties of local courts and procuratorates below the provincial level will be promoted. The establishment of a judicial jurisdictional system which is separated from the administrative jurisdictional system will be explored. The integrated and correct implementation of national laws should be guaranteed.

Though the reform of unified management is limited to below the provincial level, both measures – unified management and separate judicial jurisdiction – will still have a decisive influence on solving the problem of local judicial protectionism, and abating inappropriate interference with the courts by local governments, people's congress and so on. However, it should be noted that the Decisions did not touch upon the sensitive issue of the Party's leadership over the judicial work. Without solving this problem, judicial independence will remain limited.

From the institutions and social forces involved, we can reach a positive prediction on the trend: more judicial independence will be achieved in the years to come. In the first place, the SPC and local courts are firm supporters of expanded judicial independence. Secondly, the public at large – especially represented by liberal intellectuals, reformist officials, legal scholars and journalists – is in favour of such reform. Lawyers will certainly play a more important role in promoting judicial independence by fighting for, and exercising, their legal rights. Although China cannot be expected to achieve fully-fledged judicial independence within a short period of time, efforts must be made step by step. Reaching the goal of a reasonable standard of judicial independence is an accumulative process rather than a one-step pursuit. This also implies that to build a largely new, fundamentally improved judicial system will incur a long and somewhat laborious process. However, the reward is an undoubtedly auspicious one: justice will be improved.

Appendix 1

Contents of the Judges Law (2001)

Chapter	**Title**	**Total No. of Articles**	**Amendments 2001**
Chapter One	General Provisions (Articles 1–4)	4	Article 1
Chapter Two	Functions and Responsibilities (Articles 5–6)	2	
Chapter Three	Duties and Rights (Articles 7–8)	2	Articles 7, 9
Chapter Four	Qualifications for a Judge (Articles 9–10)	2	
Chapter Five	Appointment and Removal (Articles 11–15)	5	Articles 12, 13, 14
Chapter Six	Posts to Be Avoided (Articles 16–17)	2	Article 17
Chapter Seven	Grades of Judges (Articles 18–20)	3	
Chapter Eight	Appraisal (Articles 21–25)	5	Article 24
Chapter Nine	Training (Articles 26–28)	3	
Chapter Ten	Awards (Articles 29–31)	3	
Chapter Eleven	Punishment (Articles 32–35)	4	Article 32
Chapter Twelve	Salary, Insurance and Welfare (Articles 36–38)	3	
Chapter Thirteen	Resignation and Dismissal (Articles 39–41)	3	Article 40
Chapter Fourteen	Retirement (Articles 42–43)	2	
Chapter Fifteen	Petition and Complaint (Articles 44–47)	4	Articles 44, 46, 47
Chapter Sixteen	Commission for Examination and Assessment of Judges (Articles 48–49)	2	
Chapter Seventeen	Supplementary Provisions (Articles 50–53)	4	Articles 50, 51
Total No. of Articles		53	

Appendix 2

Contents of the Criminal Procedure Law (2012)

Chapter	Title	Total No. of Articles	Amendments 2012
Part One	General Provisions	106	
Chapter One	Objectives and Basic Principles (Articles 1–17)	17	Articles 2, 14, 20, 31, 33–40, 42, 46, 47, 49, 50, 52–59, 62, 63, 65, 68, 69–71, 72–74, 75, 76, 79, 83, 84, 86, 91, 93, 95, 96, 97, 99, 101, 103
Chapter Two	Jurisdiction (Articles 18–27)	10	
Chapter Three	Withdrawal (Articles 28–31)	4	
Chapter Four	Defence and Representation (Articles 32–47)	16	
Chapter Five	Evidence (Articles 48–63)	16	
Chapter Six	Compulsory Measures (Articles 64–98)	35	
Chapter Seven	Incidental Civil Actions (Articles 99–102)	4	
Chapter Eight	Time Periods and Service (Articles 103–105)	3	
Chapter Nine	Other Provisions (Articles 106)	1	
Part Two	Filing a Case, Investigation, and Initiation of Public Prosecution	71	
Chapter One	Filing a Case (Articles 107–112)	6	Articles 115, 116–118, 121, 122, 130, 133, 135, 139, 140, 142, 143, 145, 157, 158–160 Section Eight of Chapter Two, 164, 165, 170–173
Chapter Two	Investigation (Articles 113–166)	54	
Section One	General Provisions (Articles 113–115)	3	
Section Two	Interrogation of the Criminal Suspect (Articles 116–121)	6	
Section Three	Questioning of the Witnesses (Articles 122–125)	4	
Section Four	Inquest and Examination (Articles 126–133)	8	
Section Five	Search (Articles 134–138)	5	
Section Six	Seizure and Impoundment of Physical Evidence and Documentary Evidence (Articles 139–143)	5	
Section Seven	Forensic Identification and Evaluation (Articles 144–147)	4	
Section Eight	Technical Investigation Measures (Articles 148–152)	5	
Section Nine	Wanted Orders (Article 153)	1	
Section Ten	Conclusion of Investigation (Articles 154–161)	8	
Section Eleven	Investigation of Cases Directly Accepted by the People's Procuratorates (Articles 162–166)	5	
Chapter Three	Initiation of Public Prosecution (Articles 167–177)	11	

Chapter	Title	Total No. of Articles	Amendments 2012
PART THREE	TRIAL	70	
Chapter One	Trial Organisation (Articles 178–180)	3	Articles 181–184, 187, 188, 192, 193, 196–198, 200, 202, 206, 208–214, 223–226, 232, 234, 240, 242, 246
Chapter Two	Procedure of First Instance (Articles 181–215)	35	
Section One	Cases of Public Prosecution (Articles 181–203)	23	
Section Two	Cases of Private Prosecution (Articles 204–207)	4	
Section Three	Summary Procedure (Articles 208–215)	8	
Chapter Three	Procedure of Second Instance (Articles 216–234)	19	
Chapter Four	Procedure for Review of Death Sentences (Articles 235–240)	6	
Chapter Five	Procedure for Trial Supervision (Articles 241–247)	7	
PART FOUR	EXECUTION (ARTICLES 248–265)	18	Articles 253, 259, 262
PART FIVE	SPECIAL PROCEDURES	24	Part Five
Chapter One	Procedures for Juvenile Criminal Cases (Articles 266–276)	11	
Chapter Two	Procedures for Public Prosecution Cases Where Parties Have Reached Settlement (Articles 277–279)	3	
Chapter Three	Confiscation Procedures for Illegal Income in Cases Where a Criminal Suspect or Defendant Escapes or Dies (Articles 280–283)	4	
Chapter Four	Procedures for Involuntary Medical Treatment of Mental Patients Legally Exempted from Criminal Liability Supplementary Provisions (Articles 284–289)	6	
Supplementary Provisions		1	
Total No. of Articles		290	

Appendix 3

Contents of the Civil Procedure Law (2012)

Chapter	Title	Total No. of Articles	Amendments
PART ONE	GENERAL PROVISIONS	118	
Chapter 1	Purposes, Scope of Application and Basic Principles (Articles 1–16)	16	(2007) Articles 103,104
Chapter 2	Jurisdiction (Articles 17–38)	22	(2012) Articles 13, 14, 16, 25, 26, 36, 38, 39, 44, 45, 55, 56, 58, 63, 67, 69, 70, 72, 74, 79, 87, 82, 92–95, 103, 104, 110–113
Section 1	Jurisdiction by Levels of Courts (Articles 17–20)	4	
Section 2	Territorial Jurisdiction (Articles 21–35)	15	
Section 3	Jurisdiction by Transfer and Jurisdiction by Designation (Articles 36–38)	3	
Chapter 3	Trial Organisation (Articles 39–43)	5	
Chapter 4	Recusal of Adjudicating Personnel (Articles 44–47)	4	
Chapter 5	Litigation Participants (Articles 48–62)	15	
Section 1	Parties (Articles 48–56)	9	
Section 2	Litigation Represents (Articles 57–62)	6	
Chapter 6	Evidence (Articles 63–81)	19	
Chapter 7	Time Periods and Service (Articles 82–92)	11	
Section 1	Time Periods (Articles 82–83)	2	
Section 2	Service (Articles 84–92)	9	
Chapter 8	Mediation (Articles 93–99)	7	
Chapter 9	Property Preservation and Advance Enforcement (Articles 100–108)	9	
Chapter 10	Compulsory Measures Against Obstruction of Civil Actions (Articles 109–117)	9	
Chapter 11	Litigation Fees (Article 118)	1	
PART TWO	TRIAL PROCEDURE	105	
Chapter 12	Ordinary Procedure of First Instance (Articles 119–156)	38	(2007) Articles 178–181, 184, 187, 188
Section 1	Filing and Accepting Lawsuits (Articles 119–124)	6	
Section 2	Pretrial Preparation (Articles 125–133)	9	(2012) Articles 122–124, 127, 133, 138, 140, 156, 157, 159, 162, 163, 169, 170, 171, 177, 194–197,
Section 3	Courtroom Trial (Articles 134–149)	16	
Section 4	Lawsuit Suspension and Conclusion (Articles 150–151)	2	
Section 5	Judgment and Rulings (Articles 152–156)	5	

Chapter	Title	Total No. of Articles	Amendments
Chapter 13	Summary Procedure (Articles 157–163)	7	198–202, 206, 209–212, 217
Chapter 14	Procedure of Second Instance (Articles 164–176)	13	
Chapter 15	Special Procedures (Articles 177–197)	21	
Section 1	General Stipulations (Articles 177–180)	4	
Section 2	Cases Concerning the Credentials of Voters (Articles 181–182)	2	
Section 3	Cases Concerning the Declaration of Missing or Dead Persons (Articles 183–186)	4	
Section 4	Cases Concerning the Determination of Citizens' Capacities in Civil Conducts (Articles 187–190)	4	
Section 5	Cases Concerning the Determination of Ownerless Property (Articles 191–193)	3	
Section 6	Cases of Confirming Mediation Agreement (Articles 194–195)	2	
Section 7	Cases of Realising Real Rights for Security (Articles 196–197)	2	
Chapter 16	Procedure of Adjudication Supervision (Articles 198–213)	16	
Chapter 17	Procedure for Hastening Debt Recovery (Articles 214–217)	4	
Chapter 18	Procedure of Public Summon (Articles 218–223)	6	
PART THREE	PROCEDURE OF ENFORCEMENT	35	
Chapter 19	General Stipulations (Articles 224–235)	12	(2007) Articles 201–205, 215–217, 231 (2012) Articles 230, 237, 240, 242, 243
Chapter 20	Application and Referral of Enforcement (Articles 236–240)	5	
Chapter 21	Enforcement Measures (Articles 241–255)	15	
Chapter 22	Suspension and Termination of Enforcement (Articles 256–258)	3	
PART FOUR	SPECIAL PROVISIONS OF THE CIVIL PROCEDURES INVOLVING FOREIGN ELEMENTS	26	
Chapter 23	General Principles (Articles 259–264)	6	(2012) Article 267
Chapter 24	Jurisdiction (Articles 265–266)	3	
Chapter 25	Service and Time Periods (Articles 267–270)	3	
Chapter 26	Arbitration (Articles 271–275)	5	
Chapter 27	Judicial Assistance (Articles 276–284)	9	
Total No. of Articles		284	

Appendix 4

Contents of the Administrative Litigation Law (1989)

Chapter	Title	Total No. of Articles
Chapter One	General Provisions	10
Chapter Two	Scope of Accepting Cases	2
Chapter Three	Jurisdiction	11
Chapter Four	Participants in Proceedings	7
Chapter Five	Evidence	6
Chapter Six	Bringing Suit and Accepting a Case	6
Chapter Seven	Trial and Judgment	22
Chapter Eight	Execution	2
Chapter Nine	Liability for Compensation for Infringement of Rights	3
Chapter Ten	Administrative Procedure Involving Foreign Interests	4
Chapter Eleven	Supplementary Provisions	2
Total No. of Articles		75

Appendix 5

Contents of the Lawyers Law (2012)

Chapter	Title	Total No. of Articles	Amendments
Chapter One	General Provisions (Articles 1–4)	4	(2007) Articles 1–4
Chapter Two	Licence for Legal Practise by Lawyers (Articles 5–13)	9	(2001) Article 6 (2007) Articles 5–13
Chapter Three	Law Firms (Articles 14–27)	14	(2007) Articles 14–24, 26–27
Chapter Four	Business, Rights and Obligations of Lawyers (Articles 28–42)	15	(2007) Articles 28–40, 42 (2012) Articles 28, 31, 33, 34, 37, 38
Chapter Five	Lawyers Associations (Articles 43–46)	4	(2007) Articles 44–46
Chapter Six	Legal Liability (Articles 47–56)	10	(2007) Articles 47–56
Chapter Seven	Supplementary Provisions (Articles 57–60)	4	(2007) Article 60
Total No. of Articles		60	

Select Bibliography

Academic Works in Chinese

Cai Dingjian (ed.). 2005. *Jiandu Yu Sifa Gongzheng: Yanjiu Yu Anli Baogao* (Supervision and Judicial Fairness: Research and Case Report). Beijing: Falu Chubanshe.

——. 2003. *Heibai Fangyuan* (Collection of Papers on Rule of Law, Democracy, Rights and Justice). Beijing: Falu Chubanshe.

——. 1999. *Lishi Yu Bian'ge: Xin Zhongguo Fazhi Jianshe De Licheng* (History and Reform: Development of the Legal System in New China). Beijing: Zhongguo Zhengfa Daxue Chubanshe.

Chen Chunlong. 2007. *Yuanjia Cuo'an Yu Guojia Peichang: She Xianglin An De Fali Sikao* (Injustice Cases and State Compensation: Legal Thought on the She Xianglin Case). Beijing: Zhongguo Jiancha Chubanshe.

——. 2006. *Zhonghua Renmin Gongheguo Xingshi Susong Fa Zai Xiugai Zhuanjia Jianyigao Yu Lunzheng* (Scholar's Draft on the Criminal Procedure Law of the People's Republic of China and Its Deliberation). Beijing: Zhongguo Fazhi Chubanshe.

Chen Guangzhong. 2002. 'Principle and Basic Theory of Chinese Non-Prosecution System', in *Non-Prosecution Policies: A Sino-German Comparison*, edited by Hans-Jörg Albrecht and Chen Guangzhong, pp. 99–110. Freiburg i. Br.: Iuscrim.

Chen Guangzhong and Daniel Prefontaine. 1998. *Lianheguo Xingshi Sifa Zhunze Yu Zhongguo Xingshi Fazhi* (The United Nations Standards and China's Legal System of Criminal Justice). Beijing: Falu Chubanshe.

Chen Hui. 2003. 'Guanyu Woguo Fayuan Tiaojie Zhidu Gaige De Sikao' (Thinking on Reforms of Judicial Mediation in China's Courts), in *Faguan Lun Susong* (Judge's Views on Litigation), edited by Wu Jiayou et al., vol. 2, pp. 242–250. Beijing: Falu Chubanshe.

Chen Qiulan and Qian Lieyang. 2002. 'Zhongguo Lushi Zhiye Nan: Quanguo Luxie Zuotanhui Ceji' (Difficulties Faced by the Chinese Legal Profession: Report on a Seminar Organised by the All China Lawyers Association), *Zhongguo Lushi* (Chinese Lawyer) 5:52.

Chen Ruihua. 2006. 'Anjuan Bilu Zhongxin Zhuyi: Dui Zhongguo Xingshi Shenpan Fangshi De Chongxin Kaocha' (Case File Centric: Re-examining China's Criminal Trial Model), *Faxue Yanjiu* (CASS Journal of Law) 4:63.

——. 2003. *Wenti Yu Zhuyi Zhijian: Xingshi Susong Jiben Wenti Yanjiu* (Between Problems and Doctrines: Research on the Basic Issues of the Criminal Justice System). Beijing: Zhongguo Renmin Daxue Chubanshe.

——. 1999. *Xingshi Susong De Qianyan Wenti* (Frontier Issues on Criminal Procedure). Beijing: Zhongguo Renmin Daxue Chubanshe.

Chen Sixi. 2005. 'Tanxun Ge'an Jiandu Yu Sifa Gongzheng De Qihe: Yi Renda Ge'an Jiandu Shizheng Diaocha Anli Fenxi' (Discussion on the Supervision of Individual Cases and Judicial Fairness: Analysis on the Empirical Study on the Supervision of Individual Cases in NPC), in *Jiandu Yu Sifa Gongzheng: Yanjiu Yu Anli Baogao* (Supervision and Judicial Fairness: Research and Case Report), edited by Cai Dingjian, pp. 72–99. Beijing: Falu Chubanshe.

Chen Weidong (ed.). 2001. *Xingshi Susongfa Shishi Wenti Diaoyan Baogao* (Survey Report on Problems in Implementing the Criminal Procedure Law). Beijing: Zhongguo Fangzheng Chubanshe.

Chen Weidong et al. (eds). 2000. *Xingshi Susong Faxue Xinjie* (New Analysis on Criminal Procedure Law). Beijing: Hualing Chubanshe.

Chen Weidong and Hao Yinzhong. 1999. 'Zhen Jian Yitihua Moshi Yanjiu: Jianlun Woguo Xingshi Sifa Tizhi Gaige De Biyaoxing' (Research on Investigation and Prosecution Models: Necessity of Reform of the Criminal Justice System in China), *Faxue Yanjiu* (CASS Journal of Law) 1:57.

Chen Xingliang et al. (eds). 2005. *Runwu Wusheng: Xingshi Yitihua Yu Xingshi Zhengce* (Criminal Law and Criminal Policy). Beijing: Falu Chubanshe.

Chen Xingliang (ed.). 2004. *Zhongguo Xingshi Zhengce Jiantao: Yi Yanda Xingshi Zhengce Wei Shijiao* (Examination of China's Criminal Policy: From the Perspective of 'Strike Hard'). Beijing: Zhongguo Jiancha Chubanshe.

Chen Zexian (ed.). 2005. *Sixing: Zhongwai Guanzhu De Jiaodian* (Death Penalty: The Global Focus). Beijing: Zhongguo Renmin Gong'an Daxue Chubanshe.

Cheng Rongbin. 2004. 'Renmin Fayuan Duli Shenpan De Huigu He Zhanwang' (Retrospect and Prospect of Judicial Independence), *Faxue Jia* (Jurists Review) 4:3.

Chongqingshi Gaoji Renmin Fayuan Ketizu (Research Team of the Higher People's Court in Chongqing). 2007. 'Guanyu Wanshan Faguan Baozhang Zhidu de Diaoyan Baogao' (Investigation Report on Improving Judges' Rights and the Insurance System), in *Shenpan Qianyan Wenti Yanjiu: Zuigao Renmin Fayuan Zhongdian Yanjiu Keti Baogao Ji* (Research on Cutting Edge Issues in Judicial Practice: Collection of Key Research Topics of the Supreme People's Court), edited by Zuigao Renmin Fayuan Yanjiushi (Research Office of the Supreme People's Court), vol. 2, pp. 1079–1114. Beijing: Renmin Fayuan Chubanshe.

Cui Sixing. 2003. 'Peishen Zhidu De Cunfei Wenti Yanjiu' (Research on Keeping or Abolishing the People's Accesser System), in *Faguan Lun Susong* (Judge's Views on Litigation), edited by Wu Jiayou et al., vol. 2, pp. 100–110. Beijing: Falu Chubanshe.

Dangdai Zhongguo Congshu Bianji Weiyuanhui (Editorial Committee on Series Books of Modern China). 1995. *Dangdai Zhongguo De Sifa Xingzheng Gongzuo* (Judicial Administration Work in Modern China). Beijing: Dangdai Zhongguo Chubanshe.

Dong Hao et al. (eds). 2009. *Sifa Yixian Baogao* (Report Coming from the Judicial Frontier). Beijing: Renmin Fayuan Chubanshe.

Du Gangjian and Li Xuan. 1997. *Zhongguo Lushi de Dangdai Mingyun* (The Fate of Chinese Lawyers). Beijing: Gaige Chubanshe.

Fan Chongyi and Chen Yongsheng. 2005. 'Jiaocha Xunwen Zhidu Zai Woguo De Queli Yu Wanshan' (Establishment and Improvement of Cross-Examination in China), *Zhongguo Lushi* (Chinese Lawyer) 12:49.

Fan Fu. 2004. 'Woguo Xingzheng Shenpan De Lishi Huigu Yu Zhanwang' (Retrospect and Prospect on China's Administrative Litigation System), in *Xingzheng Zhifa Yu Xingzheng Shenpan* (Administrative Regulation and Judicial Review), edited by Jiang Bixin et al., pp. 175–188. Beijing: Falu Chubanshe.

Fan Yu. 2000. *Fei Susong Jiufen Jiejue Jizhi Yanjiu* (Research on the Settlement System on Non-litigation Conflicts). Beijing: Zhongguo Renmin Daxue Chubanshe.

Fan Zhiming. 2005. *Sifa Gongzheng Yu Susong Chengxu* (Judicial Justice and Litigation Procedure). Beijing: Renmin Fayuan Chubanshe.

Fan Zhongxin. 1999. 'Sifa Fubai De Leixing Yu Zhidu Zhuyin Fenxi' (Types of Judicial Corruption and an Analysis of the System Element), in *Yifa Zhiguo Yu Sifa Gaige* (Ruling the Country

According to Law and Judicial Reform), edited by Xin Chunying and Li Lin, pp. 105–127. Beijing: Zhongguo Fazhi Chubanshe.

Feng Qunhui. 2003. 'Chengxu Gongzheng De Lixing Renshi Yu Zhuiqiu' (Thinking on Procedure Justice), in *Faguan Lun Susong* (Judge's Views on Litigation), edited by Wu Jiayou et al., vol. 2, pp. 161–168. Beijing: Falu Chubanshe.

Fu Yulin. 2006. *Minshi Sifa Zhidu De Gongneng Yu Jiegou* (The Function and Structure of the Civil Judicial System). Beijing: Beijing Daxue Chubanshe.

——. 2005. 'Zhuanxing Zhong De Zhongguo Minshi Susong Zhidu' (Chinese Civil Procedure in the Transition Period), in *Qinghua Fazhi Lunheng: Fazhi Yu Faxue Hechu Qu* (Tsinghua Forum of the Rule of Law: Direction of the Rule of Law and Jurisprudence), edited by Gao Hongjun, vol. 6, pp. 67–95. Beijing: Qinghua Daxue Chubanshe.

Gao Hongjun and Zhang Jianwei (eds). 2008. *Qinghua Fazhi Lunheng: Yuan'an Shi Zenyang Zaocheng De* (Tsinghua Forum of the Rule of Law: How Injustice Cases Were Made), vol. 10. Beijing: Qinghua Daxue Chubanshe.

——. 2008. *Qinghua Fazhi Lunheng: Yuan'an Shi Zenyang Zaocheng De* (Tsinghua Forum of the Rule of Law: How Injustice Cases Were Made), vol. 9. Beijing: Qinghua Daxue Chubanshe.

Gao Qicai et al. 2009. *Jiceng Sifa: Shehui Zhuanxing Shiqi De Sanshi Ge Xianjin Renmin Fating Shizheng Yanjiu* (Judicial System at the Basic Level: An Empirical Study of the Thirty People's Tribunals at the Period of Social Transition). Beijing: Falu Chubanshe.

Gong Benxin (ed.). 2005. *Faxuejia Chazuo* (Teahouse for Jurists), vols 1–4. Shandong: Shandong Remin Chubanshe.

Gong Pixiang. 1999. *Fazhi Xiandaihua De Lilun Luoji* (Theories on the Modern Legal System). Beijing: Zhongguo Zhengfa Daxue Chubanshe.

Guo Zaiyu. 2003. 'Chengxu Zhengyi Youweilun' (Procedure Justice), in *Faguan Lun Susong* (Judge's Views on Litigation), edited by Wu Jiayou et al., vol. 2, pp. 29–40. Beijing: Falu Chubanshe.

Gu Peidong. 2003. *Cong Jingji Gaige Dao Sifa Gaige* (From Economic Reform to Judicial Reform). Beijing: Falu Chubanshe.

Han Xiutao (ed.). 2003. *Sifa Duli Yu Jindai Zhongguo* (Judicial Independence and Modern China). Beijing: Qinghua Daxue Chubanshe.

He Bing. 2005. *Lihai De Fenpei: Women Shenbian De Falu* (Distribution of Interests: The Law around Us). Shanghai: Sanlian Shudian.

He Lanjie et al. (eds). 1993. *Dangdai Zhongguo De Shenpan Gongzuo* (Judicial Work on Modern China). Beijing: Dangdai Zhongguo Chubanshe.

He Weifang. 2003. *Fabian Yumo* (Collection of Short Legal Articles), 2nd edition. Beijing: Falu Chubanshe.

——. 2001. 'Lushi De Zhengzhi Canyu' (Lawyers' Political Participation), *Zhongguo Lushi* (Chinese Lawyers) 1:46.

——. 1998. *Sifa De Linian Yu Zhidu* (Judicial Theory and System). Beijing: Zhongguo Zhengfa Daxue Chubanshe.

——. 1997. 'Zhongguo Sifa Guanli Zhidu de Liangge Wenti' (Two Problems of the Administration of Justice in China), *Zhongguo Shehui Kexue* (Social Science in China) 6:116.

He Weifang and Wei Fuhua. 2002. 'Gaizao Quanli: Falu Zhiye Jieceng Zai Zhongguo De Xingqi' (Changing Power: The Rise of the Law Profession in China), *Fazhi Yu Shehui Fazhan* (Legal System and Social Development) 6:24.

He Yongjun. 2004. 'Zuigao Fayuan Faguan: Yige Chubu de Lishi Kaocha' (Supreme Court Judges: A Fundamental Historical Analysis), in *Zuigao Fayuan Yanjiu* (Research on Supreme Courts), edited by Zuo Weimin et al., pp. 211–244. Beijing: Falu Chubanshe.

Hou Meng. 2007. *Zhongguo Zuigao Renmin Fayuan Yanjiu: Yi Sifa De Yingxiangli Qieru* (Research on the Supreme People's Court of the People's Republic of China: Starting from the Judicial Impact). Beijing: Falu Chubanshe.

Hu Yunteng. 1995. *Sixing Tonglun* (General Study of the Death Penalty). Beijing: Zhongguo Zhengfa Daxue Chubanshe.

Hu Yuteng and Zhou Zhenjie. 2007. 'Yan'ge Xianzhi Sixing Yu Yanli Chengfa Sizui: Dangdai Sixing Zhidu De Jiben Tedian Yu Weilai Zouxiang' (Strictly Limit Capital Penalty and Severely Punishing Crimes with the Death Penalty: Basic Characters and Development Trend in the Contemporary Death Penalty System), *Zhongguo Faxue* (China Law) 2:17.

Huai Xiaofeng. 1998. *Chutan Mingqing Fazhi* (Study on the Legal System in the Ming and Qing Dynasties). Beijing: Falu Chubanshe.

Huo Xiandan. 2007. *Zhongguo Faxue Jiaoyu Fansi* (Rethinking Legal Education in China). Beijing: Zhongguo Renmin Daxue Chubanshe.

Huzhou Zhongji Renmin Fayuan Xinghzeng Shenpan Ting (Administrative Chamber of the Huzhou Intermediate People's Court). 2006. 'Guanyu Xingzheng Jiguan Fuzeren Chuting Yingsu Zhidu De Diaocha Baogao' (Research Report on Administrative Organs' Appearance in Court), in *Xingzheng Zhifa Yu Xingzheng Shenpan* (Administrative Regulation and Judicial Review), edited by Xi Xiaoming et al., vol. 17, pp. 143–151. Beijing: Falu Chubanshe.

Ji Weidong. 1999. *Fazhi Zhixu De Jiangou* (Construction of the Rule of Law). Beijing: Zhongguo Zhengfa Daxue Chubanshe.

——. 1993. 'Falu Chengxu De Yiyi: Dui Zhongguo Fazhi Jianshe De Lingyi Zhong Si Kao' (The Significance of Legal Procedure: Further Reflection on China's Construction of a Legal System), *Zhongguo Shehui Kexue* (Social Science in China) 9:83.

Jia Weijie and Xia Lihua. 2003. 'Peishen Zhidu Gaige Wenti Yanjiu' (Research on the People's Accessor System), in *Faguan Lun Susong* (Judge's Views on Litigation), edited by Wu Jiayou et al., vol. 2, pp. 78–88. Beijing: Falu Chubanshe.

Jiancha Lilun Yanjiusuo (Research Institute on Procuratory Theory). 2000. *Fubai He Qizha Fanzui De Chengzhi Yu Fangfan* (The Punishment and Prevention of Corruption and Fraud Crimes). Beijing: Zhongguo Jiancha Chubanshe.

Jiang Bixin. 2005a. 'Lun Tingshen Zhidu De Gaige' (Research on the Reform on Court Trial), in *Xingzheng Zhifa Yu Xingzheng Shenpan* (Administrative Regulation and Judicial Review), edited by Xi Xiaoming et al., vol. 14, pp. 1–8. Beijing: Falu Chubanshe.

Jiang Bixin et al. (eds). 2005b. *Zhongguo Xingzheng Susong Zhidu De Wanshan: Xingzheng Susongfa Xiugai Wenti Shiwu Yanjiu* (Improvement of the Administrative Litigation System in China). Beijing: Falu Chubanshe.

Jiang Huiling. 2001. 'Tigao Sifa Xiaolu De Yiwu' (The Obligation to Enhance Judicial Efficiency), *Falu Shiyong* (Journal of Law Application) 6:4.

Jiang Ming'an et al. (eds). 2008. *Zhongguo Faxue Sanshi Nian (1978–2008)* (Thirty Years of Legal Development in China 1978–2008). Beijing: Zhongguo Renmin Daxue Chubanshe.

Jiang Ping and Chen Guiming (eds). 1998. *Minshi Shenpan Fangshi Gaige Yu Fazhan* (Civil Trail System Reform and Development). Beijing: Zhongguo Fazhi Chubanshe.

Jiang Qibo and Sun Bangqing. 2008. *Susong Guanxia* (Jurisdiction of Litigation). Beijing: Renmin Fayuan Chubanshe.

Jiang Wei and Yang Rongxin (eds). 1998. *Minshi Susong Jizhi De Bian'ge* (Reform of the Civil Procedure System). Beijing: Renmin Fayuan Chubanshe.

Jiangsusheng Gaoji Renmin Fayuan Ketizu (Research Team of the Higher People's Court in Jiangsu Province). 2007. 'Jiufen De Youxiao Jiejue: Renmen Fayuan Sifa Nengli Jianshe De Diaoyan Baogao' (Effective Settlement of Dispute: Investigation Report of Building up the People's Court Judicial Capacity), in *Shenpan Qinayan Wenti Yanjiu: Zuigao Renmin Fayuan Zhongdian Yanjiu Keti Baogao Ji* (Research on Judicial Cutting Edge Issues: Collection of Key Research Topics of the Supreme People's Court), edited by Zuigao Renmin Fayuan Yanjiushi (Research Office of the Supreme People's Court), vol. 1, pp. 33–179. Beijing: Renmin Fayuan Chubanshe.

Jiangxisheng Gaoji Renmin Fayuan Ketizu (Research Team of the Higher People's Court in Jiangxi Province). 2007. 'Minshi Zaishen Zhidu Gaige Shizheng Yanjiu' (Applied Research on the Retrial System of Civil Cases), in *Shenpan Qinayan Wenti Yanjiu: Zuigao Renmin Fayuan Zhongdian Yanjiu Keti Baogao Ji* (Research on the Hot Topics on Adjudication: Collection of Key Research Topics of the Supreme People's Court), edited by Zuigao Renmin Fayuan Yanjiushi (Research Office of the Supreme People's Court), vol. 1, pp. 182–214. Beijing: Renmin Fayuan Chubanshe.

Jilinsheng Gaoji Renmin Fayuan (Jilin Province Higher People's Court). 1997. *Shenpan Gongzuo Guifanhua Xize* (Detailed Rules on Trial Work). Changchun: Jilin Renmin Chubanshe.

Jin Qi and Tian Bingchuan (eds). 1999. *Dianxing Shewai Jingji Anli Pingxi* (Analysis of Typical Foreign Related Economic Cases). Beijing: Falu Chubanshe.

Jing Hanchao. 2002. *Gongzheng Yu Xiaolu Pingheng: Sifa Gaige Yanjianglu* (Balance Fairness and Efficiency: Speeches on Judicial Reform). Beijing: Zhongguo Qingnian Chubanshe.

Jing Hanchao and Lu Zijuan. 1997. *Shenpan Fangshi Gaige Shilun* (Discussion on the Reform of the Trail System). Beijing: Renmin Fayuan Chubanshe.

Kang Junxin. 2004. *Fayuan Gaige Yanjiu: Yi Yige Jiceng Fayuan De Tansuo Wei Shidian* (Research on Court Reform: From the Perspective of a Basic Court). Beijng: Zhongguo Zhengfa Daxue Chubanshe.

Lan Rongjie. 2008. 'Susong Guize Difanghua Shizheng Yanjiu' (Empirical Research on the Localisation of Litigation Rules), *Zhengzhi yu Shehui Fazhan* (Law and Social Development) 14:13.

Li Buyun. 2006. *Xianzheng Yu Zhongguo* (Constitutionalism and China). Beijing: Falu Chubanshe.

Li Chun and Wang Shangxin. 1998. *Zhongguo Xingfa Xiuding De Beijing Yu Shiyong* (Background on the Revision of Chinese Criminal Law and Its Implementation). Beijing: Falu Chubanshe.

Li Guoguang. 2000. 'Li Guoguang Fu Yuanzhang Zai Jinian Zhonghuarenmingongheguo Xingzheng Susong Fa Shishi Shi Zhounian Zuotanhui Shang de Jianghua' (Speech by Deputy President Li Guoguang at the Seminar on Celebrating the Tenth Anniversary of Administrative Litigation Law), in *Xingzheng Zhifa Yu Xingzheng Shenpan Cankao* (Reference to Administrative Regulation and Judicial Review), edited by Li Guoguang et al., vol. 1, pp. 1–3. Beijing: Falu Chubanshe.

Li Haibin and Li Yingjuan (eds). 1996. *Gong'an Xingzheng Zhifa Zhinan* (Guideline on the Enforcement of Law by Police). Changchun: Jilin Renmin Chubanshe.

Li Hao. 1998. 'Minshi Shenpan Zhong De Tiaoshen Fenli' (The Separation of Mediation and Adjudication in Civil Trial), in *Minshi Shenpan Fangshi Gaige Yu Fazhan* (Reform and Development of the Civil Trial Method), edited by Jiang Ping and Chen Guiming, pp. 203–224. Beijing: Zhongguo Fazhi Chubanshe.

Li Lin and Wang Jiafu. 2007. *Yifa Zhiguo: Shinian Huigu yu Zhanwang* (Ruling the Country in Accordance with Law: A Decade of Retrospect and Prospect). Beijing: Zhongguo Fazhi Chubanshe.

Liang Baojian (ed.). 1999. *Renming Fayuan Gaige Lilun Yu Shijian* (Theory and Practice of People's Court Reform). Beijing: Renmin Fayuan Chubanshe.

Liang Shuying. 1997. *Waiguoren Zaihua Daiyu* (The Treatment of Foreigners in China). Beijing: Zhongguo Zhengfa Daxue Chubanshe.

Liu Genju et al. (eds). 2006. *Xingshi Sifa Chuangxinlun* (New Study on the Criminal Justice System). Beijing: Beijing Daxue Chubanshe.

Liu Hainian et al. (eds). 1999. *Renquan Yu Sifa: Zhongguo–Danmai Sifa Zhong De Renquan Baozhang Xueshu Yantaohui Wenji* (Human Rights and the Administration of Justice: Collected Papers from the Chinese–Danish Symposium on the Protection of Human Rights in Judicial Work). Beijing: Zhongguo Fazhi Chubanshe.

——. 1999. *Renquan Yu Xianzheng: Zhongguo–Ruishi Xianfa Guoji Yantaohui Wenji* (Human Rights and Constitutionalism: Collected Papers from the Chinese–Swiss Symposium on Constitutional Law). Beijing: Zhongguo Fazhi Chubanshe.

——. 1996. *Yifa Zhiguo Jianshe Shehuizhuyi Fazhi Guojia* (Ruling the Country According to Law and Building a Socialist Rule of Law Country). Beijing: Zhongguo Fazhi Chubanshe.

Liu Renwen. 1999. 'Sifa Tizhi Gaige de Fanwei, Mubiao Yu Yuanze' (The Scope, Goals and Principles of the Judicial Reform), in *Yifa Zhiguo Yu Sifa Gaige* (Ruling the Country According to Law and Judicial Reform), edited by Xin Chunying and Li Lin, pp. 31–38. Beijing: Zhongguo Fazhi Chubanshe.

Long Zongzhi. 2002. 'Lun Woguo Xingshi Shenpan Zhongde Jiaocha Xunwen Zhidu' (Discussion on Cross-Examination in the Criminal Justice System in China), *Zhongguo Faxue* (Chinese Legal Science) 4:81.

Lu Zhongmei. 2006. *Fayan Guanting: Chuanxing Yu Jiaoshou He Faguan Zhijian* (Using Legal Eyes to Observe the Court Session: Experience as a Professor and a Judge). Beijing: Beijing Daxue Chubanshe.

Luo Haocai (ed.). 1996. *Zhongguo Sifa Shencha Zhidu* (China's Judicial Review System). Beijing: Beijing Daxue Chubanshe.

Pan Weiqun. 2005. 'Fuyin Chulai De Weizheng Zui: Anhui Lushi Wang Hongzhu Shexian Weizao Zhengju Yi'an Jishi' (Crime of the Fabrication of Evidence: Record on the Case of Anhui Lawyer Wang Hongzhu's Alledged Fabrication of Evidence), *Zhongguo Lushi* (Chinese Lawyers) 8:73.

Qiao Xianzhi (ed.). 2000. *1999 Shanghai Fayuan Anli Jingxuan* (Collection of Cases in Shanghai Courts in 1999). Shanghai: Remin Chubanshe.

Ran Jingfu. 2007. 'Jiaqiang He Gaishan Dang Dui Sifa Gongzuo De Lingdao Fangshi' (Strengthening and Improving the Leadership of the Party on Judicial Work), in *Yifa Zhiguo: Shinian Huigu yu Zhanwang* (Ruling the Country in Accordance with Law: A Decade of Retrospect and Prospect), edited by Li Lin and Wang Jiafu, pp. 351–361. Beijing: Zhongguo Fazhi Chubanshe.

——. 2005. *Dangdai Zhongguo Minshi Susong Lu Bianqian Yanjiu: Yige Bijiaofa Shehuixue De Shijiao* (Researches on the Changes of Civil Litigation Rate in China 1978–2002: By the Approach of Comparative Sociology of Law). Beijing: Zhongguo Renmin Daxue Chubanshe.

Research Office of the Supreme People's Court (ed.). 2007. *Shenpan Qianyan Wenti Yanjiu: Zuigao Renmin Fayuan Zhongdian Yanjiu Keti Baogao Ji* (Research on the Hot Topics on Adjudication: Collection of Key Research Topics of the Supreme People's Court), vols 1 and 2. Beijing: Renmin Fayuan Chubanshe.

—— (ed.). 1997. *Zouxiang Fating* (Going to the Court). Beijing: Falu Chubanshe.

Shanghai Gaoji Renmin Fayuan Xingzheng Shenpan Ting (Administrative Chamber of the Shanghai Higher People's Court). 2006. 'Guanyu Shanghai Shi Gaoxiao Jiaoyu Xingzheng Anjian De Diaocha Yanjiu' (Research Report on Administrative Cases Relating to Education in Shanghai

Universities), in *Xingzheng Zhifa Yu Xingzheng Shenpan* (Administrative Regulation and Judicial Review), edited by Xi Xiaoming et al., vol. 17, pp.103–116. Beijing: Falu Chubanshe.

Sichuansheng Gaoji Renmin Fayuan Ketizu (Research Team of the Higher People's Court in Sichuan Province). 2007. 'Guanyu Sifa Gongxinli Jianshe De Diaoyan Baogao' (Investigation Report on Public Confidence in the Judiciary), in *Shenpan Qianyan Wenti Yanjiu: Zuigao Renmin Fayuan Zhongdian Yanjiu Keti Baogao Ji* (Research on the Hot Topics on Adjudication: Collection of Key Research Topics of the Supreme People's Court), edited by Zuigao Renmin Fayuan Yanjiushi (Research Office of the Supreme People's Court), vol. 1, pp. 476–559. Beijing: Renmin Fayuan Chubanshe.

Sifabu Sifa Xiezhuju (Department of Judicial Assistance of the Ministry of Justice). 1996. *Sifa Xiezhu Yanjiu* (Research on Judicial Assistance). Beijing: Falu Chubanshe.

Song Zhenjiang. 2006. 'Wei Hebei She Xianglin Shaqi An Bianhu' (The Defence of She Xianglin Who Was Accused of 'Murdering his Wife' in Heibei), *Lushi Yu Fazhi* (Lawyers and the Legal System) 3:6.

Su Li. 2004a. *Daolu Tongxiang Chengshi: Zhuanxing Zhongguo De Fazhi* (Pathway towards the Metropolis: Rule of Law in Transition of China). Beijing: Falu Chubanshe.

——. 2004b. *Yexu Zhengzai Fasheng: Zhuanxing Zhongguo De Faxue* (It May Be Happening: Jurisprudence in Transitional China). Beijing: Falu Chubanshe.

——. 2000. *Songfa Xia Xiang: Zhongguo Jiceng Sifa Zhidu Yanjiu* (Bring Law to the Countryside: Research on the Chinese Legal System at the Basic Level). Beijing: Zhongguo Zhengfa Daxue Chubanshe.

——. 1998. *Fazhi Ji Qi Bentu Ziyuan* (Rule of Law and Indigenous Resources). Beijing: Zhongguo Zhengfa Daxue Chubanshe.

Sun Changyong. 2002. 'Xingshi Tingshen Fangshi Gaige Chuxian De Wenti Pingxi' (Analyses on Questions Relating to Criminal Justice Reforms), *Zhongguo Faxue* (China Legal Science) 3:143.

Tan Shigui (ed.). 2000. *Zhongguo Sifa Gaige Yanjiu* (Research on Chinese Judicial Reform). Beijing: Falu Chubanshe.

Tang, Dennis T.C. et al. (eds). 2007. *Liang'an Sidi Falu Fazhan: Weixian Shencha Yu Xingzheng Susong* (The Cross-Strait Four Regions: Law Developments in Taiwan, China, Hong Kong and Macau: Constitutional Review and Administrative Litigation), vols 1 and 2. Taipei: Zhongyang Yanjiuyuan Faluxue Yanjiusuo.

Tian Pingan and Du Runzhe. 1998. 'Dangqian Minshi Shenpan Fangshi Gaige Fansi' (Rethinking the Current Reform of the Civil Trial System), in *Minshi Shenpan Fangshi Gaige Yu Fazhan* (Civil Trail System Reform and Development), edited by Jiang Ping and Chen Guiming, pp. 73–89. Beijing: Zhongguo Fazhi Chubanshe.

Tian Shumei and Su Yingxu (eds). 1997. *Shewai Anjian Shenpan Shiwu* (Practical Book on Trails of Foreign Related Cases). Changchun: Jilin Renmin Chubanshe.

Tong Zhaohong (ed.). 2005. *Minshi Zhixing Diaocha Yu Fenxi* (Investigation and Analysis on the Enforcement of Civil Judgment). Beijing: Renmin Fayuan Chubanshe.

Wan Exiang (ed.). 2007. *Sifa Jiejue Jiufen De Duice Yu Jizhi* (Policy and System on the Judicial Settlement of Disputes). Beijing: Renmin Fayuan Chubanshe.

Wan Zuofu (ed.). 1997. *Zhongguo Xingfa De Xiugai Yu Buchong* (Revision and Supplement on Criminal Law). Beijing: Zhongguo Jiancha Chubanshe.

Wang Chenguang and Zhang Huning. 2005. 'Renda Jiandu Yu Sifa Duli He Sifa Gongzheng' (Supervision by the People's Congress and Judicial Independence and Judicial Fairness), in *Jiandu Yu Sifa Gongzheng: Yanjiu Yu Anli Baogao* (Supervision and Judicial Fairness: Research and Case Report), edited by Cai Dingjian, pp. 104–125. Beijing: Falu Chubanshe.

Wang Fuhua et al. 2007. 'Minshi Susong Fahui Chongshen Zhidu Zhi Jiantao' (Examining the Retrial System of Civil Cases), *Faxue Yanjiu* (CASS Journal of Law) 1:3.

Wang Jiancheng and Wang Minyuan. 2001. 'Xingshi Susong Faxue Yanjiu Shuping' (Overview of Research on Criminal Procedure Law), *Faxue Yanjiu* 1:140.

Wang Liming. 2000. *Sifa Gaige Yanjiu* (Research on Judicial Reform). Beijing: Falu Chubanshe.

Wang Minyuan (ed.). 2006. *Xingshi Zhengjufa Zhong De Quanli Baohu* (The Protection of Rights in Criminal Evidence Law). Beijing: Zhongguo Renmin Daxue Chubanshe.

Wang Yan. 2004. 'Tiaojie Yu Xingzheng Susong Zhidu Chuangxin' (Mediation and the Administrative Litigation System), in *Xingzheng Zhifa Yu Xingzheng Shenpan* (Administrative Law Enforcement and Administrative Litigation), 10:48.

Wang Yaxin. 2001. *Shehui Bian'ge Zhongde Minshi Susong* (Civil Litigation in Social Transition). Beijing: Fazhi Chubanshe.

Wang Yimin and Pan Ruwen. 2003. 'Qiantan Quxiao Peishen Zhidu Zhi Wojian' (My Ideas on the Abolishment of the People's Accessor System), in *Faguan Lun Susong* (Judge's Views on Litigation), edited by Wu Jiayou et al., vol. 2, pp. 111–118. Beijing: Falu Chubanshe.

Wang Zhenmin. 2004. *Zhongguo Weixian Shencha Zhidu* (Judicial Review on Violations of the Constitution in China). Beijing: Zhongguo Zhengfa Daxue Chubanshe.

Wu Jiayou et al. (eds). 2006. *Faguan Lun Sifa Nengli* (Judge's Views on Judicial Capacity). Beijing: Falu Chubanshe.

Xia Yong (ed.). 2000. *Zouxiang Quanli De Shidai* (Toward an Age of Rights). Beijing: Zhongguo Zhengfa Daxue Chubanshe.

Xiao Jianguo. 2000. *Minshi Susong Chengxu Jiazhi Lun* (Values on Civil Litigation Procedures). Beijing: Zhongguo Renmin Daxue Chubanshe.

Xiao Jianguo et al. (eds). 2007. 'Guanyu Wanshan Faguan Baozhang Zhidu De Diaoyan Baogao' (Investigation Report on Improving the Judges' Rights Protection System), in *Shenpan Qinayan Wenti Yanjiu: Zuigao Renmin Fayuan Zhongdian Diaoyan Keti Baogao Ji* (Research on Cutting Edge Issues in Judicial Practice: Collection of Key Research Topics of the Supreme People's Court), edited by Zuigao Renmin Fayuan Yanjiushi (Research Office of the Supreme People's Court), vol. 2, pp. 1115–1193. Beijing: Renmin Fayuan Chubanshe.

Xiao Shengxi (ed.). 1996. *Lushi Xue* (Lawyers). Beijing: Gaodeng Jiaoyu Chubanshe.

Xie Hongfei. 2004. 'Zongli Wei Nongfu Zhuitao Gongqian: Fazhi Jiaodu de Fansi' (Premier Got the Wages back for a Female Farmer: A Reflection from the Perspective of the Rule of Law), in *Zhongguo Fazhi Fazhan Baogao* (Development Report on the Rule of Law in China), edited by Xia Yong et al., pp. 195–202. Beijing: Shehui Kexue Wenxian Chubanshe.

Xin Chunying (ed.). 2001. *Gongfa* (Public Law), vol. 3. Beijing: Falu Chubanshe.

Xin Chunying and Li Lin (eds). 1999. *Yifa Zhiguo Yu Sifa Gaige* (Ruling the Country According to Law and Judicial Reform). Beijing: Zhongguo Fazhi Chubanshe.

Xiong Daguo and Huang Xiangwu. 2003. 'Lun Woguo Xingsufa Yu Chenmoquan De Heli Chongtu Ji Lifa Jiejian' (Discussion on Conflict between the Criminal Procedure Law and the Right to Be Silent and Suggestions on the Legislation), in *Faguan Lun Susong* (Judge's Views on Litigation), edited by Wu Jiayou et al., vol. 2, pp. 352–357. Beijing: Falu Chubanshe.

Xiong Qiuhong. 2005a. 'Xingshi Susong Faxue Yanjiu Redian' (Hot Topics in the Science of Criminal Procedure Law), in *Zhongguo Fazhi Fazhan Baogao* (Development Report on the Rule of Law in China), no. 2 (2004), edited by Xia Yong et al., pp. 365–382. Beijing: Shehui Kexue Wenxian Chubanshe.

——. 2005b. 'Liu Yong An Kaoyan Xingshi Sifa' (The Liu Yong Case Questions Criminal Justice), in *Zhongguo Fazhi Fazhan Baogao* (Development Report on the Rule of Law in China), no. 2 (2004), edited by Xia Yong et al., pp. 226–237. Beijing: Shehui Kexue Wenxian Chubanshe.

——. 2004. 'Biansu Jiaoyi Diyian' (The First Case of 'Plea Bargaining'), in *Zhongguo Fazhi Fazhan Baogao* (Development Report of the Rule of Law in China), no. 1 (2003), edited by Xia Yong et al., pp. 263–274. Beijing: Shehui Kexue Wenxian Chubanshe.

Xiong Xianjue. 1999. *Zhongguo Sifa Zhidu Xinlun* (New Views on the Chinese Judicial System). Beijing: Zhongguo FaZhi Chubanshe.

Xiong Xianjue and Pi Chunxie (eds). 1993. *Zhongguo Zuzhi Faxue* (Chinese Organic Law). Taiyuan: Shanxi Jiaoyu Chubanshe.

Xu Cui. 2003. 'Ye Lun Woguo Fayuan Tiaojie Zhidu De Buzu Yu Wanshan' (Discussion on the Shortcomings and Improvements of the Judicial Mediation System), in *Faguan Lun Susong* (Judge's Views on Litigation), edited by Wu Jiayou et al., vol. 2, pp. 274–283. Beijing: Falu Chubanshe.

Xu Hui. 2007. 'Dalu Minshi Susong Zhidu De Guoqu, Xiangzai Yu Weilai' (The Past, Present and Future of Civil Procedure in Mainland China), in *Liang'an Sidi Falu Fazhan: Weixian Shencha Yu Xingzheng Susong* (The Cross-Strait Four Regions: Law Developments in Taiwan, China, Hong Kong and Macau: Constitutional Review and Administrative Litigation), edited by Dennis T.C. Tang et al., vol. 2, pp. 201–229. Taipei: Zhongyang Yanjiuyuan Faluxue Yanjiusuo.

——. 2001. *Shewai Minshangshi Susong Guanxiaquan Chongtu Yanjiu* (Research on Jurisdiction Conflicts on Foreign Related Civil and Commercial Litigation). Beijing: Zhongguo Zhengfa Daxue Chubanshen.

Xu Xianming and Qi Yanping. 2008. 'Lun Sifa Fubai De Zhiduxing Fangzhi' (Systemic Prevention of Judicial Corruption), in *Yifa Zhiguo Yu Lianzheng Jianshe* (Using Law to Rule the Country and the Building of an Incorruptible Government), edited by Liu Hainian et al., pp. 318–333. Beijing: Shehui Kexue Wenxian Chubanshe.

Xu Xin et al. 2010. *Zhongguo Sifa Gaige Niandu Baogao 2010* (Annual Report on China's Judicial Reform 2010). Available at http://www.caijing.com.cn/upload/zzz.pdf. Last visited December 2013.

——. 2009. *Zhongguo Sifa Gaige Niandu Baogao 2009* (Annual Report on China's Judicial Reform 2009). Available at http://www.caijing.com.cn/2011–01–21/110625360.html. Last visited December 2013.

Yang Kai. 2003. 'Fayuan Tiaojie Zhidu Gaige De Lilun Toushi Yu Lifa Sikao: Yi Chengxu Gongzheng Yu Susong Xiaolu Wei Zhongxin De Fenxi' (Research and Legislative Suggestions on Judicial Mediation: Analyses on Procedural Justice and Litigation Rules), in *Faguan Lun Susong* (Judge's Views on Litigation), edited by Wu Jiayou et al., vol. 2, pp. 171–195. Beijing: Falu Chubanshe.

Yang Liu. 1999. 'Mohu De Falu Chanpin: Dui Liangqi Jiceng Fayuan Tiaojie Anjian De Kaocha' (Vague Legal Product: Studies on Two Cases Concluded by Mediation in the District Court), *Beida Falu Pinglun* (Peking University Law Review) 1:213.

Yu Zhong. 2007. *Xiangtu Zhongguo De Sifa Tujing* (Judicial Practice in Rural China). Beijing: Zhongguo Fazhi Chubanshe.

Yunnansheng Gaoji Renmin Fayuan Ketizu (Research Team of the Higher People's Court in Yunnan Province). 2007. 'Guanyu Wanshan Faguan Baozhang Zhidu De Diaoyan Baogao' (Investigation Report on Improving Judges' Rights and the Insurance System), in *Shenpan Qinayan Wenti Yanjiu: Zuigao Renmin Fayuan Zhongdian Yanjiu Keti Baogao Ji* (Research on the Hot Topics on Adjudication: Collection of Key Research Topics of the Supreme People's Court), edited by *Zuigao Renmin Fayuan Yanjiushi* (Research Office of the Supreme People's Court), vol. 2, pp. 1052–1078. Beijing: Renmin Fayuan Chubanshe.

Zhang Bofeng (ed.). 2000. *Zhongguo De Sifa Zhidu* (The Judicial System in China). Beijing: Falu Chubanshe.

Zhang Min and Jiang Huiling. 1998. *Fayuan Duli Shenpan Wenti Yanjiu* (Research on Judicial Independence in Trial). Beijing: Renmin Fayuan Chubanshe.

Zhang Mingjie (ed.). 2005. *Gaige Sifa: Zhongguo Sifa Gaige De Huigu Yu Qianzhan* (Reforming the Judiciary: The Retrospect and Prospects of Judicial Reform in China). Beijing: Shehui Kexue Wenxian Chubanshe.

Zhang Sizhi. 2002. 'Bushi De Lushi Weizheng: Ling Xiaosong Lushi Weizheng Jishi De Bianxi' (Wrong Prosecution on a Lawyer's Fabrication of Evidence: Analysis of the Report on Lawyer Ling Xiaosong's Alleged Fabrication of Evidence), *Zhongguo Lushi* (Chinese Lawyers) 6:61.

——. 2001. *Wo De Bianci Yu Mengxiang* (My Defence Statements and Dreams). Shanghai: Xuelin Chubanshe.

Zhang Weiping. 2007. 'Susong Tiaojie: Shixia Shitai De Fenxi Yu Sikao' (Mediation in Litigation: Analysis and Thoughts on Contemporary Circumstances), *Faxue* (Legal Science Monthly) 5:18.

——. 2001. *Sifa Gaige Pinglun No. 1* (Review on Judicial Reform). Beijing: Zhongguo Fazhi Chubanshe.

Zhang Wusheng. 2002. *Minshi Jianyi Chengxu Yangjou* (Research on Summary Procedure in Civil Litigation). Beijing: Renmin Daxue Chubanshe.

Zhang Wusheng and Yang Yanyan. 2007. 'Woguo Qunti Susong De Lifa Yu Sifa Shijian' (The Legislation and Judicial Practice of China's Group Action), *Faxue Yanjiu* (CASS Journal of Law) 2:112.

Zhang Zhongbin and Li Hongyi. 2003. 'Peishen Zhidu Cunfei Wenti Yanjiu' (Research on Keeping or Abolishing the People's Accessor System), in *Faguan Lun Susong* (Judge's Views on Litigation), edited by Wu Jiayou et al., vol. 2, pp. 128–141. Beijing: Falu Chubanshe.

Zhao Bingzhi. 2004. *Xingshi Fazhi Fazhan Yanjiu Baogao* (Research Report on the Development of the Criminal Justice System). Beijing: Zhongguo Renmin Gong'an Daxue Chubanshe.

Zhao Gang. 2011. 'Nengdong Sifa Zhi Zhengque Lijie Yu Kexue Jianxing: Yi Minshi Sifa Wei Shijiao De Jiexi' (The Correct Understanding and Scientific Practice of Judicial Activism: Analysis from the Perspective of Civil Justice), *Faxue Pinglun* (Law Review) 2:3.

Zhejiangsheng Gaoji Renmin Fayuan Ketizu (Research Team of the Higher People's Court in Zhejiang Province). 2007. 'Guanyu Xingzheng Anjian Guanxia Wenti De Diaoyan Baogao' (Investigation Report on the Jurisdiction of Administrative Litigation), in *Shenpan Qinayan Wenti Yanjiu: Zuigao Renmin Fayuan Zhongdian Yanjiu Keti Baogao Ji* (Research on the Hot Topics on Adjudication: Collection of Key Research Topics of the Supreme People's Court), edited by *Zuigao Renmin Fayuan Yanjiushi* (Research Office of the Supreme People's Court), vol. 2, pp. 1336–1366. Beijing: Renmin Fayuan Chubanshe.

Zhonghua Renmin Gongheguo Sifabu Sifa Yanjiusuo, Zhonghua Renmin Gongheguo Sifabu Sifa Xiezhu Waishisi and Yingguo Zhuhua Dashiguan Wenhua Jiaoyuchu (Institute of Judicial Research of the Ministry of Justice of the PRC, Foreign Affairs Section of Judicial Assistance of the Ministry of Justice of the PRC, and Cultural and Education Section of the British Embassy in China) (eds). 2000. *Zhong Ying Xingshi Susong Yantaohui Lunwen Ji* (A Collection of Papers from the Chinese-Britain Symposium on Criminal Proceedings). Beijing: Falu Chubanshe.

Zhou Hanhua. 1999. 'Lun Jianli Duli, Kaifang Yu Nengdong De Sifa Zhidu' (Discussion on Establishing an Independent, Open and Dynamic Judicial System), *Faxue Yanjiu* (CASS Journal of Law) 5:1.

Zhu Jingwen (ed.). 2007. *Zhongguo Falu Fazhan Baogao Shujuku He Zhibiao Tixi* (Report on China Law Development: Database and Indicators). Beijing: Zhongguo Renmin Daxue Chubanshe.

Zhu Liyu. 1999. *Peng Zhen Minzhu Fazhi Sixiang Yanjiu* (Research on Democracy and Legal Thoughts). Beijing: Zhongguo Renmin Daxue Chubanshe.

Zuigao Renmin Fayuan Yanjiushi (Research Office of the Supreme People's Court) (ed.). 2007. *Shenpan Qianyan Wenti Yanjiu: Zuigao Renmin Fayuan Zhongdian Yanjiu Keti Baogao Ji* (Research on Cutting Edge Issues in Judicial Practice: Collection of Key Research Topics of the Supreme People's Court), vols 1 and 2. Beijing: Renmin Fayuan Chubanshe.

—— (ed.). 1997. *Zou Xiang Fa Ting: Minshi Jingji Shenpan Fangshi Gaige Shifan* (Towards the Court: Trial Model on Civil and Economic Cases). Beijing: Falu Chubanshe.

Zuo Weimin et al. (eds). 2004. *Zuigao Fayuan Yanjiu* (Research on Supreme Courts). Beijing: Falu Chubanshe.

——. 2002. *Zhongguo Sifa Zhidu* (Chinese Judicial System). Beijing: Zhongguo Zhengfa Daxue Chubanshe.

Academic Works in English

Alford, William. 2003. 'Of Lawyers Lost and Found: Searching for Legal Professionalism in the People's Republic of China', pp. 182–204, in *East Asian Law: Universal Norms and Local Cultures*, edited by Arthur Rosett, Lucie Cheng and Margaret Woo. London: Routledge.

——. 1995. 'Tasselled Loafers for Barefoot Lawyers: Transformation and Tension in the World of Chinese Legal Workers', *The China Quarterly* 141:22.

Balme, Stéphanie. 2010. 'Local Courts in Western China: The Quest for Independence and Dignity', in *Judicial Independence in China: Lessons for Global Rule of Law Promotion*, edited by Randall Peerenboom, pp. 154–179. Cambridge: Cambridge University Press.

——. 2009. 'Ordinary Justice and Popular Constitutionalism in China', in *Building Constitutionalism in China*, edited by Stéphanie Balme and Michael Dowdle, pp. 179–198. New York: Palgrave Macmillan.

——. 2005. 'The Judicialisation of Politics and the Politicisation of the Judiciary in China (1978–2005)', *Global Jurist Frontiers* 5:1.

Balme, Stéphanie and Dowdle, Machel (eds). 2009. *Building Constitutionalism in China*. New York: Palgrave Macmillan.

Biddulph, Sarah. 2007. *Legal Reform and Administrative Detention Powers in China*. Cambridge: Cambridge University Press.

Blackstone, William. 1809. *Commentaries on the Laws of England*. London: Cadell and Davies.

Bo, Yin and Duff, Peter. 2010. 'Criminal Procedure in Contemporary China: Socialist, Civilian or Traditional?', *International and Comparative Law Quarterly* 59:1099.

Bonavia, David. 1984. *Verdict in Peking: The Trial of the Gang of Four*. London: Burnett Books.

Brants-Langeraar, C.H. 2007. 'Consensual Criminal Procedures: Plea and Confession Bargaining and Abbreviated Procedure to Simplify Criminal Procedure', *Electronic Journal of Comparative Law* 11:19.

Cabestan, Jean-Pierre. 2005. 'The Political and Practical Obstacles to the Reform of the Judiciary and the Establishment of a Rule of Law in China', *Journal of Chinese Political Science* 10:43.

Cai, Dingjian. 1999. 'Development of the Chinese Legal System since 1979 and Its Current Crisis and Transformation', *Cultural Dynamics* 11:135.

Cai, Dingjian and Wang, Chenguang (eds). 2010. *China's Journey toward the Rule of Law: Legal Reform, 1978–2008*. Leiden: Brill.

Chase, Carol. A. 1995–1996. 'Hearing the "Sounds of Silence" in Criminal Trials: A Look at Recent British Law Reforms with an Eye Toward Reforming the American Criminal Justice System', *University of Kansas Law Review* 44:929.

Chen, Albert. 2011. *An Introduction to the Legal System of the People's Republic of China*, 4th edition. Hong Kong: LexisNexis/Butterworths.

——. 2000. 'Toward a Legal Enlightenment: Discussions in Contemporary China on the Rule of Law', *UCLA Pacific Basin Law Journal* 17:125.

Chen, Jianfu. 2008. *Chinese Law: Context and Transformation*. Leiden: Martinus Nijhoff.

——. 2002. 'A Criminal Justice System for a New Millennium?', in *China's Legal Reforms and Their Political Limits*, edited by Eduard B. Vermeer and Ingrid d'Hooghe, pp. 77–122. Hamburg: Curzon Press.

Chiu, Hungdah. 1992. 'China's Criminal Justice System and the Trial of Pro-Democracy Dissidents', *International Law and Politics* 24:1181.

Clarke, Donald (ed.). 2008. *China's Legal System: New Developments, New Challenges*. Cambridge: Cambridge University Press.

——. 2007. 'China: Creating a Legal System for a Market Economy'. The George Washington University Law School Public Law and Legal Theory Research Paper Series No. 396. Available at http://ssrn.com/abstract=1097587. Last visited February 2014.

——. 2003a. 'Empirical Research into the Chinese Judicial System', in *Beyond Common Knowledge: Empirical Approaches to the Rule of Law*, edited by Erik Jensen and Thomas Heller, pp. 164–192. Stanford, CA: Stanford University Press.

——. 2003b. 'Puzzling Observations in Chinese Law: When Is a Riddle Just a Mistake', in *Understanding China's Legal System: Essays in Honor of Jerome A. Cohen*, edited by C. Stephen Hsu, pp. 93–121. New York: New York University Press.

——. 1996. 'Power and Politics in the Chinese Court System: The Enforcement of Civil Judgments', *Columbia Journal of Asian Law* 10:1.

——. 1991. 'Dispute Resolution in China', *Journal of Chinese Law* 5:245.

Cohen, Jerome. 2005. 'Law in Political Transitions: Lessons from East Asia and the Road Ahead for China', *N.Y.U. Journal of International Law and Politics* 37:423.

——. 2003. 'The Plight of China's Criminal Defense Lawyers', *Hong Kong Law Journal* 33:231.

——. 1997. 'Reforming China's Civil Procedure: Judging the Courts', *The American Journal of Comparative Law* 45:793.

——. 1969. 'The Chinese Communist Party and "Judicial Independence": 1949–1959', *Harvard Law Review* 82:967.

——. 1968. *The Criminal Process in the People's Republic of China, 1949–1963: An Introduction*. Cambridge, MA: Harvard University Press.

——. 1966. 'Chinese Mediation on the Eve of Modernization', *California Law Review* 54:1201.

Cohen, Jerome and Randle, Edwards R. (eds). 1980. *Essays on China's Legal Tradition*. Princeton, NJ: Princeton University Press.

Conner, Alison. 2000. 'True Confessions? Chinese Confessions Then and Now', in *The Limits of the Rule of Law in China*, edited by Karen G. Turner, James V. Feinerman and R. Kent Guy, pp. 132–162. Seattle, WA and London: University of Washington Press.

——. 1994. 'Lawyers and the Legal Profession during the Republican Period', in *Civil Law in Qing and Republican China*, edited by Kathryn Bernhardt and Philip Huang, pp. 215–248. Stanford, CA: Stanford University Press.

Cumaraswamy, Param. 1999. *Report of the Special Rapporteur on the Independence of Judges and Lawyers*. E/CN.4/1999/60.

Diamant, Neil Jeffrey, Lubman, Stanley and O'Brien, Kevin J. (eds). 2005. *Engaging the Law in China: State, Society, and Possibilities for Justice*. Stanford, CA: Stanford University Press.

Dowdle, Michael. 2009. 'Beyond "Judicial Power": Courts and Constitutionalism in Modern China', in *Building Constitutionalism in China*, edited by Stéphanie Balme and Michael Dowdle, pp. 199–218. New York: Palgrave Macmillan.

Feinerman, James. 2000. 'The Rule of Law Imposed from Outside: China's Foreign-Oriented Legal Regime since 1978', in *The Limits of the Rule of Law in China*, edited by Karen G. Turner, James V. Feinerman and R. Kent Guy, pp. 304–324. Seattle, WA: University of Washington Press.

Finder, Susan. 1996. 'Inside the People's Courts: China's Litigation System and the Resolution of Commercial Disputes', *China Law & Practice* 10:16.

——. 1993. 'The Supreme People's Court of the People's Republic of China', *Journal of Chinese Law* 7:145.

——. 1989. 'Like Throwing an Egg against a Stone? Administrative Litigation in the People's Republic of China', *Journal of Chinese Law* 3:1.

Fu, Hualing. 2011. 'Institutionalizing Criminal Process in China', in *The Development of the Chinese Legal System: Change and Challenges*, edited by Yu Guanghua, pp. 26–48. London and New York: Routledge.

——. 2009. 'Access to Justice and Constitutionalism in China', in *Building Constitutionalism in China*, edited by Stéphanie Balme and Michael Dowdle, pp. 163–178. New York: Palgrave Macmillan.

——. 2007. 'When Lawyers are Prosecuted ... The Struggle of a Profession in Transition', *Journal of Comparative Law* 2:95.

——. 2005. 'Putting China's Judiciary into Perspective: Is it Independent, Competent, and Fair?', in *Beyond Common Knowledge: Empirical Approaches to the Rule of Law*, edited by Eric Jensen and Thomas Heller, pp. 193–219. Stanford, CA: Stanford University Press.

——. 1998. 'Criminal Defence in China: The Possible Impact of the 1996 Criminal Procedural Law Reform', *The China Quarterly* 153:31.

——. 1997. 'Criminal Procedure Law', in *Introduction to Chinese Law*, edited by Wang Chenguang and Zhang Xianchu, pp. 129–168. Hong Kong-Singapore: Sweet & Maxwell Asia.

Fu, Hualing and Cullen, Richard. 2011. 'From Mediatory to Adjudicatory Justice: The Limits of Civil Justice Reform in China', in *Chinese Justice: Civil Dispute Resolution in Contemporary China*, edited by Margaret Woo and Mary Gallagher, pp. 25–57. Cambridge: Cambridge University Press.

——. 2008. 'Weiquan (Rights Protection) Lawyering in an Authoritarian State: Building a Culture of Public-interest Lawyering', *The China Journal* 59:111.

Fu, Yulin and Peerenboom, Randall. 2010. 'A New Analytic Framework for Understanding and Promoting Judicial Independence in China', in *Judicial Independence in China: Lessons for Global Rule of Law Promotion*, edited by Randall Peerenboom, pp. 95–133. Cambridge: Cambridge University Press.

Gechlik, Mei Ying. 2005. 'Judicial Reform in China: Lessons from Shanghai', *The Columbia Journal of Asian Law* 19:97.

Gelatt, Timothy. 1993. *Lawyers Committee for Human Rights: Criminal Justice with Chinese Characteristics*. New York: Lawyers Committee for Human Rights.

——. 1991. 'Lawyers in China: The Past Decade and Beyond', *International Law and Politics* 23:751.

——. 1982. 'The People's Republic of China and the Presumption of Innocence', *The Journal of Criminal Law and Criminology* 73:259.

Ginsburg, Tom. 2010. 'Judicial Independence in East Asia: Lessons from China', in *Judicial Independence in China: Lessons for Global Rule of Law Promotion*, edited by Randall Peerenboom, pp. 247–259. Cambridge: Cambridge University Press.

Ginsburg, Tom and Chen, Albert (eds). 2008. *Administrative Law and Governance in Asia: Comparative Perspectives*. New York: Routledge.

Gold, Thomas, Guthrie, Doug and Wank, David (eds). 2004. *Social Connections in China: Institutions, Culture, and the Changing Nature of Guanxi*. Cambridge: Cambridge University Press.

Guo, Yong. 2008. 'Corruption in Transitional China: An Empirical Analysis', *The China Quarterly* 194:349.

Haese, David. 1985. 'International Bar Association Project on Minimum Standards of Judicial Independence', in *Judicial Independence: The Contemporary Debate*, edited by S. Shetreet and J. Deschênes, pp. 382–392. Dordrecht: Martinus Nijhoff.

Halegua, Aaron. 2005. 'Reforming the People's Mediation System in Urban China', *Hong Kong Law Journal* 35:715.

Halliday, Terence and Liu, Sida. 2007. 'Birth of a Liberal Moment? Looking Through a One-Way Mirror at Lawyers' Defence of Criminal Defendants in China', in *Fighting for Political Freedom: Comparative Studies of the Legal Complex and Political Liberalism*, edited by T. Halliday, L. Karpik and M. Feeley, pp. 65–108. Oxford: Hart Publishing.

Hand, Keith. 2009. 'Citizens Engage the Constitution: The Sun Zhigang Incident and Constitutional Review Proposals in the People's Republic of China', in *Building Constitutionalism in China*, edited by Stéphanie Balme and Michael Dowdle, pp. 221–242. New York: Palgrave Macmillan.

He, Weifang. 2012. *In the Name of Justice: Striving for the Rule of Law in China*. Washington, DC: Brookings Institution Press.

He, Xin. 2011. 'Debt Collection in the Less Developed Regions of China: An Empirical Study from a Basic-level Court in Shaanxi Province', *The China Quarterly* 206:253.

——. 2010. 'The Judiciary Pushes Back: Law, Power, and Politics in Chinese Courts', in *Judicial Independence in China: Lessons for Global Rule of Law Promotion*, edited by Randall Peerenboom, pp. 180–195. Cambridge: Cambridge University Press.

——. 2009a. 'Administrative Law as a Mechanism for Political Control in Contemporary China', in *Building Constitutionalism in China*, edited by Stéphanie Balme and Michael Dowdle, pp. 143–162. New York: Palgrave Macmillan.

——. 2009b. 'Enforcing Commercial Judgments in the Pearl River Delta of China', *The American Journal of Comparative Law* 57:419.

——. 2007. 'The Recent Decline in Economic Caseloads in Chinese Courts: Exploration of a Surprising Puzzle', *The China Quarterly* 190:352.

Henderson, Keith. 2010. 'Halfway Home and a Long Way to Go: China's Rule of Law Evolution and the Global Road to Judicial Independence, Judicial Impartiality, and Judicial Integrity', in *Judicial Independence in China: Lessons for Global Rule of Law Promotion*, edited by Randall Peerenboom, pp. 23–36. Cambridge: Cambridge University Press.

——. 2007. 'The Rule of Law and Judicial Corruption in China: Half-way Over the Great Wall', in *Global Corruption Report 2007: Corruption in Judicial Systems*, edited by Transparency International, pp. 151–158. New York: Cambridge University Press.

Howson, Nicolas Calcina. 2010. 'Judicial Independence and the Company Law in the Shanghai Courts', in *Judicial Independence in China: Lessons for Global Rule of Law Promotion*, edited by Randall Peerenboom, pp. 134–153. Cambridge: Cambridge University Press.

Hsu, C. Stephen. 2003. *Understanding China's Legal System: Essays in Honor of Jerome A. Cohen*. New York: New York University Press.

Huang, Daphne. 1998. 'The Right to a Fair Trial in China', *Pacific Rim Law and Policy Journal* 7:171.

Huang, Philip. 2010. *Chinese Civil Justice, Past and Present*. Lanham. MD: Rowman & Littlefield.

——. 2006. 'Court Mediation in China, Past and Present', *Modern China* 32:275.
——. 2001. *Code, Custom, and Legal Practice in China: The Qing and the Republic Compared.* Stanford, CA: Stanford University Press.
——. 1996. *Civil Justice in China: Representation and Practice in the Qing.* Stanford, CA: Stanford University Press.
——. 1993. 'Between Informal Mediation and Formal Adjudication: The Third Realm of Qing Civil Justice', *Modern China* 19:251.
Ji, Weidong. 2013. 'The Judicial Reform in China: The Status Quo and Future Directions', *Indiana Journal of Global Legal Studies* 20:185.
——. 2009. '"To Take the Law as the Public": The Diversification of Society and Legal Discourse in Contemporary China', in *Building Constitutionalism in China*, edited by Stéphanie Balme and Michael Dowdle, pp. 125–140. New York: Palgrave Macmillan.
Jones, William. 2003. 'Trying to Understanding the Current Chinese Legal System', in *Understanding China's Legal System: Essays in Honor of Jerome A. Cohen*, edited by C. Stephen Hsu, pp. 7–45. New York: New York University Press.
——. 1976. 'A Possible Model for the Criminal Trial in the People's Republic of China', *The American Journal of Comparative Law* 24:229.
Josephs, Hilary. 2000. 'The Upright and the Low-Down: An Examination of Official Corruption in the United States and the People's Republic of China', *Syracuse Journal of International Law and Commerce* 27:269.
Keith, Ronald C. 1994. *China's Struggle for the Rule of Law*. Houndmills: St. Martin's Press.
Keith, Ronald C. and Lin, Zhiqiu. 2006. *New Crime in China: Public Order and Human Rights.* London and New York: Routledge.
——. 2001. *Law and Justice in China's New Marketplace*. New York: Palgrave.
Kellogg, Thomas. 2011. 'The Constitution in the Courtroom: Constitutional Development and Civil Litigation in China', in *Chinese Justice: Civil Dispute Resolution in Contemporary China*, edited by Margaret Woo and Mary Gallagher, pp. 340–379. Cambridge: Cambridge University Press.
——. 2007. '"Courageous Explorers"? Education Litigation and Judicial Innovation in China', *Harvard Human Rights Journal* 20:141.
Kim, Marie Seong-Hak. 1996. 'A Distant Premise: Judicial Independence in the People's Republic of China', *Korean Journal of Comparative Law* 24:17.
King, Leonard. 1985. 'The IBA Standards on Judicial Independence: An Australian Perspective', in *Judicial Independence: The Contemporary Debate*, edited by S. Shetreet and J. Deschênes, pp. 403–413. Dordrecht: Martinus Nijhoff.
Koguchi, Hikota. 1987. 'Some Observations about "Judicial Independence" in Post-Mao China', *Boston College Third World Law Journal* 2:195.
Komaiko, Richard and Que, Beibei. 2009. *Lawyers in Modern China*. Amherst, NY: Cambria Press.
Lawyers Committee for Human Rights. 1993. *Criminal Justice with Chinese Characteristics*. New York: Lawyers Committee for Human Rights.
Leheny, David and Liu, Sida. 2010. 'The Politics of Crime, Punishment, and Social Order in East Asia', *Annual Review of Law and Social Science* 6:239.
Leng, Shao-chuan and Chiu, Hungdah. 1985. *Criminal Justice in Post-Mao China: Analysis and Documents*. Albany, NY: State University of New York Press.
Lester, Joseph. 2005. 'Presumed Innocent, Feared Dangerous: The Eighth Amendment's Right to Bail', *Northern Kentucky Law Review* 32:8.

Li, Ling. 2010. 'Corruption in China's Courts', in *Judicial Independence in China: Lessons for Global Rule of Law Promotion*, edited by Randall Peerenboom, pp. 196–220. Cambridge: Cambridge University Press.

Li, Victor. 1978. *Law without Lawyers: A Comparative View of Law in China and the United States*. Boulder, CO: Westview Press.

——. 1970. 'The Role of Law in Communist China', *The China Quarterly* 44:66.

Li, Yuwen. 2003. 'Professional Ethics of Chinese Judges: A Rising Issue in the Landscape of Judicial Practice', *China Perspectives* 47:28.

——. 2002. 'Court Reform in China: Problems, Progress and Prospects', in *Implementation of Law in the People's Republic of China*, edited by Jianfu Chen et al., pp. 55–84. The Hague: Kluwer Law International.

——. 2001. 'Judicial Independence: Applying International Minimum Standards to Chinese Law and Practice', *China Information* 15:67.

——. 2000. 'Lawyers in China: A "Flourishing" Profession in Rapidly Changing Society', *China Perspectives* 27:30.

Liang, Bin. 2008. *The Changing Chinese Legal System, 1978–Present Centralization of Power and Rationalization of the Legal System*. New York and London: Routledge.

——. 2005. 'Severe Strike Campaign in Transitional China', *Journal of Criminal Justice* 33:387.

Liao, Kuangsheng. 1983. 'Independent Administration of Justice and the PRC Legal System', *Chinese Law and Government* 16:123.

Liebman, Benjamin. 2011a. 'The Media and the Courts: Towards Competitive Supervision?', *The China Quarterly* 208:833.

——. 2011b. 'A Populist Threat to China's Courts?', in *Chinese Justice: Civil Dispute Resolution in Contemporary China*, edited by Margaret Y.K. Woo and Mary E. Gallagher, pp. 269–313. Cambridge: Cambridge University Press.

——. 2009. 'Assessing China's Legal Reforms', *Columbia Journal of Asian Law* 23:17.

——. 2007. 'China's Courts: Restricted Reform', *Columbia Journal of Asian Law* 21:16.

——. 2005. 'Watchdog or Demagogue? The Media in the Chinese Legal System', *Columbia Law Review* 105:1.

Liebman, Benjamin and Wu, Tim. 2007–2008. 'China's Network Justice', *Chicago Journal of International Law* 8:257.

Lin, Chris. 2003. 'A Quiet Revolution: An Overview of China's Judicial Reform', *Asian-Pacific Law & Policy Journal* 4:255.

Lin, Feng. 1996. *Administrative Law Procedures and Remedies in China*. Hong Kong: Sweet and Maxwell.

Liu, Nanping. 2008–2009. 'Trick or Treat: Legal Reasoning in the Shadow of Corruption in the People's Republic of China', *North Carolina Journal of International Law and Commercial Regulation* 34:179.

——. 1997. *Opinions of the Supreme People's Court Judicial Interpretation in China*. Hong Kong: Sweet & Maxwell Asia.

——. 1991. '"Legal Precedents" with Chinese Characteristics: Published Cases in the Gazette of the Supreme People's Court', *Journal of Chinese Law* 5:107.

Liu, Sida. 2006a. 'Beyond Global Convergence: Conflicts of Legitimacy in a Chinese Lower Court', *Law & Social Inquiry* 31:75.

——. 2006b. 'Client Influence and the Contingency of Professionalism: The Work of Elite Corporate Lawyers in China', *Justice Quarterly* 40:751.

Liu, Sida and Halliday, Terence. 2009. 'Recursivity in Legal Change: Lawyers and Reforms of China's Criminal Procedure Law', *Law & Social Inquiry* 34(4):911.

Lo, Vai Io. 2000. 'Resolution of Civil Disputes in China', *UCLA Pacific Basin Law Journal* 18:117.

Lo, Carlos Wing-Hung. 1995. *China's Legal Awakening, Legal Theory and Criminal Justice in Deng's Era*. Hong Kong: Hong Kong University Press.

Lo, Carlos Wing-Hung and Snape, Ed. 2005, 'Lawyers in the People's Republic of China: A Study of Commitment and Professionalization', *American Journal of Comparative Law* 53:433.

Lu, Hong and Miethe, Terance D. 2002. 'Legal Representation and Criminal Processing in China', *British Journal of Criminology* 42:267.

Lu, Hong and Zhang, Lening. 2005. 'Death Penalty in China: The Law and the Practice', *Journal of Criminal Justice* 33:367.

Lubman, Stanley. 2006. 'Looking for Law in China', *Columbia Journal of Asian Law* 20:1.

——. 1999. *Bird in a Cage Legal Reform in China after Mao*. Stanford, CA: Stanford University Press.

Luo, Wei. 2000. *The Amended Criminal Procedure Law and the Criminal Court Rules of the People's Republic of China: with English Translation, Introduction, and Annotation*. New York: William S. Hein & Co.

McConville, Mike. 2011. *Criminal Justice in China: An Empirical Enquiry*. Cheltenham: Edward Elgar.

Michelson, Ethan. 2007. 'Lawyers, Political Embeddedness, and Institutional Continuity in China's Transition from Socialism', *American Journal of Sociology* 113:352.

——. 2006. 'The Practice of Law as an Obstacle to Justice: Chinese Lawyers at Work', *Law and Society Review* 40:1.

——. 1998a. 'Tradition in the Shadow of Modern Legal Practice: Continuing and Change in the Delivery of Justice in China (I)', *Chinese Law and Government* 31(5):39.

——. 1998b. 'Tradition in the Shadow of Modern Legal Practice: Continuing and Change in the Delivery of Justice in China (II)', *Chinese Law and Government* 31(6):3.

Minzner, Carl. 2011. 'China's Turn Against Law', *The American Journal of Comparative Law* 59:935.

Nowak, Manfred. 2006. *Report of the Special Rapporteur on Torture and Other Cruel, Inhuman or Degrading Treatment or Punishment (Mission to China)*. E/CN.4/2006/6/Add.6.

O'Brien, Kevin. 2009. 'Local People's Congresses and Governing China', *The China Journal* 61:131.

Ohnesorge, John. 2006. 'Chinese Administrative Law in the Northeast Asian Mirror', *Transnational Law & Contemporary Problems* 16:103.

Palm, Michael. 2006. 'Controlling the State: Mediation in Administrative Litigation in the People's Republic of China', *Transnational Law and Contemporary Problems* 16:165.

Peerenboom, Randall. 2011a. 'Economic Development and the Development of the Legal Profession in China', in *Chinese Justice: Civil Dispute Resolution in Contemporary China*, edited by Margaret Woo and Mary Gallagher, pp. 114–138. Cambridge: Cambridge University Press.

——. 2011b. 'Economic and Social Rights: The Role of Courts in China', *San Diego International Law Journal* 12:303.

——. 2010a. 'China Stands Up: 100 Years of Humiliation, Sovereignty Concerns, and Resistance to Foreign Pressure on PRC Courts', *Emory International Law Review* 24:653.

—— (ed.). 2010b. *Judicial Independence in China*. Cambridge: Cambridge University Press.

——. 2006. 'Judicial Independence and Judicial Accountability: An Empirical Study of Individual Case Supervision', *The China Journal* 55:67.

——. 2002. *China's Long March toward Rule of Law*. Cambridge: Cambridge University Press.

——. 2001. 'Globalization, Path Dependency and the Limits of Law: Administrative Law Reform and the Rule of Law in the People's Republic of China', *Berkeley Journal of International Law* 19:161.

——. 1999. 'Ruling the Country in Accordance with Law: Reflections on the Rule and Role of Law in Contemporary China', *Cultural Dynamics* 11:315.

Pei, Minxin. 1997. 'Citizens v. Mandarins: Administrative Litigation in China', *The China Quarterly* 152:832.

Pei, Minxin, Zhang, Guoyan, Pei, Fei and Chen, Lixin. 2010. 'A Survey of Commercial Litigation in Shanghai Courts', in *Judicial Independence in China: Lessons for Global Rule of Law Promotion*, edited by Randall Peerenboom, pp. 221–234. Cambridge: Cambridge University Press.

Pfenning, Werner. 1984. 'Political Aspects of Modernization and Judicial Reform in the PRC', *Journal of Chinese Studies* 1:79.

Pils, Eva. 2009. 'Rights Activism in China: The Case of Lawyer Gao Zhisheng', in *Building Constitutionalism in China*, edited by Stéphanie Balme and Michael Dowdle, pp. 243–260. New York: Palgrave Macmillan.

Potter, Pitman. 2011. 'Court in Xinjiang: Institutional Capacity in China's Periphery', in *New Courts in Asia*, edited by Andrew Harding and Penelope Nicholson, pp. 350–366. London and New York: Routledge.

——. 2004. 'Legal Reform in China: Institutions, Culture, and Selective Adaptation', *Law & Social Inquiry* 29:465.

——. 2001. *The Chinese Legal System: Globalization and Local Legal Culture*. London and New York: Routledge.

——. 1994. 'The Administrative Litigation Law of the PRC: Judicial Review and Bureaucratic Reform', in *Domestic Law Reforms in Post-Mao China*, edited by Pitman Potter, pp. 270–304. New York: M.E. Sharpe.

——. (ed.). 1991. *The Administrative Litigation Law of the PRC: Changing the Relationship Between the Courts and Administrative Agencies in China*, a special issue of *Chinese Law and Government*, no. 3.

Reyes, Ramon. 1997. 'The Enforcement of Foreign Court Judgements in the People's Republic of China: What the American Lawyer Needs to Know', *Brooklyn Journal of International Law* 23:241.

Shetreet, Shimon. 1985. 'The Emerging Transnational Jurisprudence on Judicial Independence: The IBA Standards and Montreal Declaration', in *Judicial Independence: The Contemporary Debate*, edited by S. Shetreet and J. Deschênes, pp. 393–402. Boston, MA: Martinus Nijhoff.

Simonsen, Craig. 1991. 'Development and Organisation of the Governmental and Legal Systems of the People's Republic of China', *China Law Reporter* 6:239.

Tanner, Harold. 1999. *Strike Hard! Anti-crime Campaigns and Chinese Criminal Justice, 1979–1989*. Ithaca, NY: East Asia Program, Cornell University.

Transparency International. 2007. *Global Corruption Report 2007: Corruption in Judicial Systems*. New York: Cambridge University Press.

Trevaskes, Susan. 2011. 'Political Ideology, the Party, and Politicking: Justice System Reform in China', *Modern China* 37:315.

——. 2010a. *Policing Serious Crime in China*. London and New York: Routledge.

——. 2010b. 'The Shifting Sands of Punishment in China in the Era of "Harmonious Society"', *Law & Policy* 32(3):332.

——. 2007. *Courts and Criminal Justice in Contemporary China*. Lanham, MD: Lexington Books.

Turner, Karen, Feinerman, James V. and Guy, R. Kent (eds). 2000. *The Limits of the Rule of Law in China*. Seattle, WA and London: University of Washington Press.

Upham, Frank. 2005. 'Who Will Find the Defendant If He Stays with His Sheep? Justice in Rural China', *Yale Law Journal* 114:1675.

Wallace, Clifford. 1998. 'Resolving Judicial Corruption While Preserving Judicial Independence: Comparative Perspectives', *California Western International Law Journal* 28:345.

Wedeman, Andrew. 2004. 'The Intensification of Corruption in China', *The China Quarterly* 180:895.

Woo, Margaret. 2000. 'Law and Discretion in Contemporary Chinese Courts', in *The Limits of the Rule of Law in China*, edited by Karen G. Turner, James V. Feinerman and R. Kent Guy, pp. 163–195. Seattle, WA: University of Washington Press.

——. 1991. 'Adjudication Supervision and Judicial Independence in the P.R.C.', *American Journal of Comparative Law* 39:95.

——. 1989. 'The Right to a Criminal Appeal in the People's Republic of China', *The Yale Journal of International Law* 14:146.

Woo, Margaret and Gallagher, Mary (eds). 2011. *Chinese Justice: Civil Dispute Resolution in Contemporary China*. Cambridge: Cambridge University Press.

Woo, Margaret and Wang, Yaxin. 2005. 'Civil Justice in China: An Empirical Study of Courts in Three Provinces', *American Journal of Comparative Law* 53:911.

Xin, Chunying. 2004. *Chinese Courts: History and Transition*. Beijing: Law Press.

——. 2003. 'What Kind of Judiciary Power Does China Need?', *International Journal of Constitutional Law* 1:58.

Xin, Ren. *Tradition of the Law and Law of the Tradition: Law, State, and Social Control in China*. Westport, CT and London: Greenwood Press.

Yu, Guanghua. 2011. *The Development of the Chinese Legal System: Change and Challenges*. London and New York: Routledge.

Zemans, Frances Kahn. 1999. 'The Accountable Judge: Guardian of Judicial Independence', *Southern California Law Review* 72:654.

Zhang, Mo. 2010. 'The Socialist Legal System with Chinese Characteristics: China's Discourse for the Rule of Law and a Bitter Experience', *Temple International and Comparative Law Journal* 24:1.

——. 2002. 'International Civil Litigation in China: A Practical Analysis of the Chinese Judicial System', *Boston College International and Comparative Law Review* 25:59.

Zhang, Mo and Zwier, Paul. 2003. 'Burden of Proof: Developments in Modern Chinese Evidence Rules', *Tulsa Journal of Comparative and International Law* 10:419.

Zhang, Qianfan. 2003. 'The People's Court in Transition: The Prospects of the Chinese Judicial Reform', *Journal of Contemporary China* 12(34):69.

Zhang, Xianchu. 2011. 'Civil Justice Reform with Political Agendas', in *The Development of the Chinese Legal System: Change and Challenges*, edited by Yu Guanghua, pp. 253–271. London and New York: Routledge.

Zheng, Henry. 1988. 'The Evolving Role of Lawyers and Legal Practice in China', *American Journal of Comparative Law* 36:474.

Zhong, Hua, Hu, Ming and Liang, Bin. 2011. 'Public Opinions on Criminal Trials in China: A Comparative Study of Chinese College Students in the PRC and Hong Kong', *Asian Criminology* 6:191.

Zhu, Suli. 2010. 'The Party and the Courts', in *Judicial Independence in China: Lessons for Global Rule of Law Promotion*, edited by Randall Peerenboom, pp. 52–68. Cambridge: Cambridge University Press.

——. 2009. '"Judicial Politics" as State-Building', in *Building Constitutionalism in China*, edited by Stéphanie Balme and Michael Dowdle, pp. 23–36. New York: Palgrave Macmillan.

Zou, Keyuan. 2006. *China's Legal Reform Towards the Rule of Law*. Leiden: Martinus Nijhoff.

——. 2000. 'Judicial Reform versus Judicial Corruption: Recent Developments in China', *Criminal Law Forum* 11:323.

Index

For Product Safety Concerns and Information please contact our EU
representative GPSR@taylorandfrancis.com
Taylor & Francis Verlag GmbH, Kaufingerstraße 24, 80331 München, Germany

www.ingramcontent.com/pod-product-compliance
Ingram Content Group UK Ltd.
Pitfield, Milton Keynes, MK11 3LW, UK
UKHW050753180926
475701UK00007B/1020

* 9 7 8 1 1 3 8 6 3 7 6 2 7 *